CASES AND MATERIALS ON
Family Law

"*The daring publisher, Universal Law Publishing Company, among the foremost in the law publishing field and progressive in venturing to bring out rare legal literature of* avant garde *character has rightly enriched the* corpus juris *of India*"

Justice V R Krishna Iyer
Random Reflections, page 14

CASES AND MATERIALS ON Family Law

Third Edition

Kusum
MA., LL.M.
Former Research Professor
Indian Law Institute

Law Publishing Co. Pvt. Ltd.
NEW DELHI - INDIA

First Edition : 2007
Second Edition : 2010
Third Edition : **2013**

ISBN: 978-93-5035-244-1

© Publishers

No part of this publication can be reproduced or transmitted in any form or by any means, without prior permission of the Publishers.

Published by
UNIVERSAL LAW PUBLISHING CO. PVT. LTD.
C-FF-1A, Dilkhush Industrial Estate,
(Near Azadpur Metro Station) G.T. Karnal Road,
Delhi-110 033
Tel.: 011-47082254, 27438103, 27215334
Fax : 011-27458529
E-mail *(For sales inquiries)* : unilaw@vsnl.com
E-mail *(For editorial inquiries)* : edit@unilawbooks.com
Website : www.unilawbooks.com

Recommended citation: Kusum, *Cases and Materials on Family Law,* 3rd Edn. (New Delhi: Universal Law Publishing Co. Pvt. Ltd., 2013).

This publication is being sold on the condition and understanding that the information, comments, and views it contains are merely for guidance and reference and must not be taken as having the authority of, or being binding in any way on, the author, editors, publishers, and sellers, who do not owe any responsibility whatsoever for any loss, damage, or distress to any person, whether or not a purchaser of this publication, on account of any action taken or not taken on the basis of this publication. Despite all the care taken, errors or omissions may have crept inadvertently into this publication. The publishers shall be obliged if any such error or omission is brought to their notice for possible correction in a future edition. In the case of binding defect, misprint, missing pages, etc., the publishers' liability is limited to replacement of the defective copy within one month of its purchase by a copy of the same edition or reprint.
All disputes are subject to the jurisdiction of competent courts in Delhi.

Computer Typeset at Aesthetic and *Printed* at Mudrak, Delhi.

PREFACE

The book 'Cases and Materials on Family Law' is a collection of cases decided by the High Courts and the Supreme Court of India on various issues connected with family law. For the convenience of readers, the cases have been classified subject-wise; also the issues involved in the cases, facts, and orders along with brief comment, have been analysed in each case. While there is always a scope for improvement, it is hoped that this publication will be useful to students of law, lawyers and academicians as also others who are interested in the subject.

Kusum
Former Research Professor
Indian Law Institute

CONTENTS

- *Preface* v
- *Table of Cases* xxxv
- **Marriage** 1
  - HIV Status of Person: Right to Marry whether Absolute 1
    * *Mr. X v. Hospital Z*, AIR 1999 SC 495: 1998 AIR SCW 3662: (1998) 8 SCC 296 1
    * *Mr. X v. Hospital Z*, AIR 2003 SC 664: 2002 AIR SCW 5335: (2003) 1 SCC 500 2
  - Registration of Marriage 3
    * *Seema v. Ashwani Kumar*, AIR 2006 SC 1158: 2006 AIR SCW 858: (2006) 2 SCC 578 3
  - Jurisdiction of Registrar: Whether Residence of Parents Compulsory 4
    * *Vikram Aditya Singh v. Union of India*, II (2006) DMC 689 (Del DB): AIR 2007 Del 101: 2006 (133) DLT 369 4
  - Whether Presence of Parties is Mandatory 4
    * *Chiranjit Kaur Nagi v. Government of NCT, Delhi*, I (2008) DMC 45 (Del) 4
  - Marriage of Woman Already Married is Void 5
    * *Sushma Chourie v. Hetendra Kumar Borkar*, AIR 2010 Chh 30: 2010 (2) Cg LJ 37 5
- **Both Parties should be Hindu** 7
  - Pre-marriage Convert to Hinduism is Hindu: Marriage not Void 7
    * *Madhavi Ramesh Dudani v. Ramesh K. Dudani*, AIR 2006 Bom 94: 2006 (40) All Ind Cas 446: I (2006) DMC 386 7
  - Marriage between Christian and Hindu not Valid under Hindu Marriage Act 8
    * *Gullipilli Sowria Rai v. Bhandaru Pavani*, AIR 2009 SC 1085: 2009 AIR SCW 244: (2009) 1 SCC 714 8
  - Marriage between Hindu and Christian not Valid under Act even if Registered 9
    * *Nilesh Narin Rajesh Lal v. Kashmira Bhupenderbhai Banker*, AIR 2010 Guj 3: 2010 (2) CCC 757: 2010 (1) Guj LH 499 9
  - Wife, a Born Hindu, Converted to Islam and then Reconverted to Hinduism: Marriage with Hindu valid 11
    * *Flg Officer Rajiv Gakhar v. Bhavna @ Sahar Wasif*, AIR 2011 SC 2053 (P&H) 11
- **Marriage below the legal age** 12
  - Marriage not Void 12
    * *Pinninti Venkataramana v. State*, AIR 1977 AP 43 (FB): 1977 Cr LJ 368: ILR (1976) AP 837 12

> * *V. Mallikarjunaiah* v. *H.C. Gowramma*, AIR 1997 Kant 77:
> ILR 1997 Kant 964: 1997 (1) Kant LJ 570   14
> * *Ravi Kumar* v. *State* and *Shikha Sharma* v. *State*, 2005 (1) DLT 124   15

- **Matrimonial Reliefs and Grounds**   17
- **Adultery**   18
  - Wife Continuing to Live in Adultery Despite Promise that Would not Repeat: Marriage Dissolved   18
    > * *K.J.* v. *Smti K. w/o K.J.*, AIR 1952 Nag 395: ILR (1952) Nag 570   18
  - Adultery-Finding in Maintenance Proceedings Under Section 125, Cr. P.C., Can Be Used In Subsequent Divorce Proceedings   19
    > * *Narayan Rath* v. *Kuntala Kumari Rath*, AIR 2005 Ori 49: 2004 (2) CLR 748: 2005 Mat LR 263   19
- **Cruelty**   21
  - Intention to be Cruel Immaterial   21
    > * *P.L. Sayal* v. *Sarla Rani*, AIR 1961 Punj 125: 63 Punj LR 377   21
  - Husband's Debility and Sexual Weakness – Cruelty on Wife – Decree of Separation Sought by her Granted   22
    > * *Rita Nijhawan* v. *Balkishan Nijhawan*, AIR 1973 Del 200: (1973) 75 Punj LR (D) 168   22
  - Spouse Ceasing to be Hindu – *Locus* to File Petition under Hindu Marriage Act   23
    > * *Vilayat Raj* v. *Sunila*, AIR 1983 Del 351: (1983) 23 DLT 434: II (1983) DMC 164   23
  - Dowry Demand – *Per se* is Cruelty   24
    > * *Shobha Rani* v. *Madhukar Reddy*, AIR 1988 SC 121: (1988) 1 SCC 105: JT 1987 (5) SC 433   24
  - Cruelty based on Allegations made in Written Statement   26
    > * *V. Bhagat* v. *D. Bhagat*, AIR 1994 SC 710: 1994 AIR SCW 45: (1994) 1 SCC 337   26
  - Acts Alleged to Constitute Cruelty – Not Serious Enough – No Cruelty   28
    > * *S. Hanumantha Rao* v. *S. Ramani*, AIR 1999 SC 1318: 1999 AIR SCW 1012: (1999) 3 SCC 620   28
  - Wife Unable to Conceive – Ill-treated – Husband Married Again – Held Cruelty by Husband   29
    > * *Suneer Sharma* v. *Madhurlata Sharma*, AIR 2000 MP 26: 1999 (2) MP LJ 603: 2000 (1) CCC 315   29
  - Mental Cruelty to be Assessed having Regard to Various Factors Like Status, Education etc., of Parties   30
    > * *G.V.N. Kameswara Rao* v. *G. Jabilli*, AIR 2002 SC 576: 2002 AIR SCW 162: (2002) 2 SCC 296   30
  - Non-consummation of Marriage and Rude & Abusive Behaviour is Cruelty   31

- * *Praveen Mehta* v. *Inderjit Mehta*, AIR 2002 SC 2582:
  2002 AIR SCW 2886: (2002) 5 SCC 706 — 31
- Not Any or Every Abnormal Act Would Constitute Mental Cruelty — 32
  - * *B.N. Panduranga Shet* v. *S.N. Vijay Laxmi*, AIR 2003 Kant 357:
    ILR (2003) 3 Kant 1852: 2003 (3) Kant LJ 247 — 32
- Mental Cruelty – Retraction of Charges Once Levelled – Damage Already Done – Does not Absolve Party of Mental Cruelty — 32
  - * *Vijaykumar Ramchandra Bhate* v. *Neela Vijaykumar Bhate*, AIR 2003 SC 2462: 2003 AIR SCW 2530: (2003) 6 SCC 334 — 32
- Wife Gang Raped: No Cruelty on Husband — 34
  - * *Rajesh Kumar Singh* v. *Rekha Singh*, AIR 2005 All 16: 2005 All LJ 102: 2004 (23) All Ind Cas 365 — 34
- Mere Bald Statements, Routine Wear and Tear Vague Allegations: No Cruelty — 35
  - * *Asha Gupta* v. *Rajiv Kumar Gupta*, AIR 2005 P&H 134: 2005 (2) CCC 106: 2005 (2) Punj LR 45 — 35
- Cruelty by Wife's Parents – Whether Cruelty by Wife — 36
  - * *Kamlesh Kumar Agarwal* v. *Mamta Devi*, AIR 2005 Jhar 10: II (2004) DMC 706: 2004 (4) Civ LJ 535 — 36
- Refusal to have Sex and Long Separation etc., is Cruelty — 37
  - * *Usharani Lenka* v. *Panigrahi Subhash Chandra Dash*, AIR 2005 Ori 3: 2004 (23) All Ind Cas 583: 2005 (1) Marri LJ 476 — 37
- Filing of criminal cases/complaints *per se* is not cruelty — 39
  - * *Kamleshwari Bai* v. *Peeluram Sahi*, AIR 2010 Chh 16 — 39
- Filing False Criminal Cases and Resiling From Agreement to Withdraw Criminal Cases after taking Substantial Amounts under the Agreement is Cruelty — 40
  - * *Pinki Jain* v. *Sanjay Jain*, AIR 2005 Del 273: 2005 (2) CCC 795: I (2005) DMC 241 — 40
- Cruelty Based on Allegations Made in Written Statement — 41
  - * *Manisha Sandeep Gade* v. *Sandeep Vinayak Gade*, AIR 2005 Bom 180: 2005 (1) All MR 564: 2005 (1) Bom CR 554 — 41
- Mental Cruelty Alleged: Decree Granted on Humanitarian Ground as Marriage was Practically Dead — 44
  - * *Vinita Saxena* v. *Pankaj Saxena*, AIR 2006 SC 1662: 2006 AIR SCW 1585: (2006) 3 SCC 778 — 44
- Wife's Allegations of Bigamy and Dowry Demand and Against Husband's Potency in Reply to his Allegations Against her – Held Does not Amount to Cruelty — 45
  - * *P. Malleswaramma* v. *P. Prathap Reddy*, AIR 2006 AP 4: 2006 (38) All Ind Cas 840: 2005 (5) Andh LT 319 — 45
- Absence of Formal Complaints to Police etc., no Reason to Dislodge Allegations of Cruelty — 46

- *Varsha Pravin Patil v. Pravin Madhukar Patil*, AIR 2009 Bom 60: I (2009) DMC 649: 2009 (2) Hindu LR 121 — 46
- *Hemwanti Tripathi v. Harish Narain*, AIR 2012 Del 1 — 47
- Cruelty Alleged: Middle Path Adopted — 48
  - *Manisha Tyagi v. Deepak Kumar*, AIR 2010 SC 1042: 2010 AIR SCW 1306: (2010) 4 SCC 339 — 48
- Wife Undergoing Abortion without Consent/Knowledge of Husband is Cruelty — 51
  - *Anjali Bhan v. Ajay Kumar Bhan*, AIR 2011 J&K 54 — 51

Cruelty and Condonation — 53
- No Decree, if Cruelty is Condoned — 53
  - *N.G. Dastane v. S. Dastane*, AIR 1975 SC 1534: (1975) 2 SCC 326: (1975) 3 SCR 967 — 53
- Wife Enduring Cruelty is not Condonation of Cruelty — 55
  - *K. Preetha v. N. Bhaskaran*, AIR 2011 Ker 27 — 55

Desertion — 57
  - *Bipinchandra Jaisinghbai Shah v. Prabhavati*, AIR 1957 SC 176: 1957 SCR 838: 1957 SCC 48 — 57
- Wife's Refusal to give up Job & Join Husband – Whether Amounts to Desertion — 59
  - *Kailash Wati v. Avodhia Parkash*, (1977) 79 Punj LR 216: 1977 Hindu LR 175 — 59
- Locale of Matrimonial Home when Both Spouses Working at Different Places – Wife's Withdrawal not Unreasonable — 61
  - *Swaraj Garg v. K.M. Garg*, AIR 1978 Del 296: 1978 Hindu LR 332: 1978 Raj LR 525 — 61
- There can be no Desertion without Cohabitation — 64
  - *Savitri Pandey v. Prem Chandra Pandey*, AIR 2002 SC 591: 2002 AIR SCW 182: (2002) 2 SCC 73 — 64
- Wife Refusing to Stay with Husband's Parents: No Desertion — 66
  - *Vikas Sharma v. Anita Sharma*, AIR 2011 Utr 43 — 66

Fraud — 67
- Misrepresentation about Boys' Particulars Made by Father to Girl's, Mother – Held Fraud on Girl – Annulment Decreed — 67
  - *Babui Panmato v. Ram Agya Singh*, AIR 1968 Pat 190 — 67
- Misrepresentation as to Age — 68
  - *Vidyut Kumar Verma v. Manju*, AIR 2011 Pat 110 — 68
- Fraudulent Divorce Petition through Impostor — 69
  - *Sanjay Singh v. Garima Singh*, (1998) 8 SCC 375 — 69
- Concealment of Vasectomy by Husband is Fraud — 70
  - *Best Morning v. Nirmalendu*, AIR 1987 Gau 63: II (1987) DMC 214: (1987) 2 Gau LR 324 — 70

* *Sushil Kumar* v. *Minto Kumari*, AIR 2012 Raj 1	71

- **Impotency**
  - Impotency *Per se* does not Render Marriage a Nullity — 72
    * *Ram Devi* v. *Raja Ram*, AIR 1963 All 564: 1963 All LJ 658 — 72
  - Person could be Impotent event if Structurally Normal — 73
    * *Shantabai Alias Gourabai* v. *Tarachand*, AIR 1966 MP 8: 1965 MP LJ 615: 1965 Jab LJ 770 — 73
  - Impotency – Need not be Incurable to get Relief — 74
    * *Samar Roy Chowdhury* v. *Snigdha Roy Chowdhury*, AIR 1977 Cal 213: (1976) 2 Cal LJ 322: ILR (1977) 1 Cal 44 — 74
  - Vasectomy is not Impotency but Concealment of Same is Fraud Entitling Wife to Decree of Annulment — 75
    * *Best Morning* v. *Nirmalendu*, AIR 1987 Gau 63: II (1987) DMC 214: (1987) 2 Gau LR 324 — 75
  - Wife's Virginity is no Proof of Husband's Impotency — 76
    * *Bhaswati Sarkar* v. *Angshuman Sarkar*, AIR 2000 Cal 210: 2000 (2) Cal LJ 219: II (2001) DMC 237 — 76

- **Irretrievable Breakdown of Marriage** — 78
  - Broken Marriage – Divorce Decreed — 78
    * *Chanderkala Trivedi* v. *Dr. S.P. Trivedi*, (1993) 3 SCALE 541: (1993) 4 SCC 232: JT (1993) 4 SC 644 — 78
  - Irretrievable Breakdown – Divorce Granted — 79
    * *Kanchan Devi* v. *Promod Kumar Mittal*, AIR 1996 SC 3192: 1996 AIR SCW 1933: (1996) 8 SCC 90 — 79
  - Lengthy Litigation *Per Se* – No Ground for Considering Marriage as Broken — 80
    * *Neeta Kirit Desai* v. *Bino Samuel George*, AIR 2003 Bom 7: 2003 (1) Bom LR 310: I (2003) DMC 151 — 80
  - Divorce Granted Despite Petitioner Husband's own Fault Simply Because Relationship Broken Beyond Repair — 81
    * *Poonam Gupta* v. *Ghanshayam Gupta*, AIR 2003 All 51 — 81
  - Marriage Broken – Divorce Granted with View to do "Complete Justice" — 82
    * *A. Jayachandra* v. *Aneel Kaur*, AIR 2005 SC 534: 2005 AIR SCW 163: (2005) 2 SCC 22 — 82
  - Where no Alleged Ground Proved – Relief cannot be Granted on Ground of Irretrievable Breakdown of Marriage — 84
    * *Ajay Sayajirao Desai* v. *Rajashree Ajay Desai*, AIR 2005 Bom 278: 2005 (3) All MR 577: 2005 Bom CR Sup 793 — 84
  - Alleged Ground not Proved but Marriage Broken – Relief Granted — 86
    * *Dinesh Kumar Mandal* v. *Mina Devi*, AIR 2005 Jhar 77: 2005 (27) All Ind Cas 752: 2005 (3) Civ LJ 339 — 86

- Broken Marriage – Divorce Granted – Support of "Cruelty" Taken by Court   87
  * *Naveen Kohli* v. *Neelu Kohli*, AIR 2006 SC 1675: 2006 AIR SCW 1550: (2006) 4 SCC 558   87
- Ground Statutorily not Provided so no Relief though Hard Case   89
  * *Visnu Dutt Sharma* v. *Manju Sharma*, AIR 2009 SC 2254: 2009 AIR SCW 2984: (2009) 6 SCC 379   89
- Both Parties at Fault – Marriage Broken but Relief Based on 'Cruelty'   90
  * *N. Shaṇkar* v. *S. Saraswathi*, (2010) 1 MLJ 959 (Mad)   90

♦ **Leprosy**   92
- Decree Granted   92
  * *Swarajya Lakshmi* v. *G.G. Padma Rao*, AIR 1974 SC 165: (1974) 1 SCC 58: (1974) 2 SCR 97   92

♦ **Mental Disorder**   94
- Non-cohabitation for a Month – No Inference of Mental Disorder   94
  * *R. Lakshmi Narayan* v. *Santhi*, AIR 2001 SC 2110: 2001 AIR SCW 1820: (2001) 4 SCC 688   94
- Psychological Depression is not Mental Disorder   95
  * *Hema Reddy* v. *Rakesh Reddy*, AIR 2002 AP 228   95
- Minor Aberrations – No Mental Disorder   95
  * *Devi Sharma* v. *Chandra Mohan Sharma*, AIR 2003 P&H 327: 2003 (2) Hindu LR 259: 2004 (1) Marri LJ 385   95
- Alleged Conduct need not be Abnormally Excessive   96
  * *Vandana* v. *Suresh Charan*, AIR 2005 Raj 193: 2005 (2) CCC 142: 2005 (2) Hindu LR 628   96

♦ **Mutual Consent**   99
- Can Consent, Once given, be Unilaterally Revoked   99
  * *Sureshta Devi* v. *Om Prakash*, AIR 1992 SC 1904: 1991 AIR SCW 373: (1991) 2 SCC 25   99
- Consent Decree even after Consent Withdrawn by One of the Parties   101
  * *Ashok Hurra* v. *Rupa Bipin Zaveri*, AIR 1997 SC 1266: 1997 AIR SCW 1314: (1997) 4 SCC 226   101
- Unilateral Silence at Time of Second Motion is not Withdrawal of Consent: Divorce Granted   103
  * *Suman* v. *Surendra Kumar*, AIR 2003 Raj 155: 2003 Mat LR 428: 2003 (1) CCC 393   103
- *Mala fide* Retraction   104
  * *Satinder Pal Singh* v. *Daman Preet*, I (2009) DMC 196 (Del)   104
- Extra-ordinary Powers of Apex Court to Dispense with Consent   105
  * *Anil Kumar Jain* v. *Maya Jain*, AIR 2010 SC 229 (MP): 2009 AIR SCW 5899: (2009) 10 SCC 415   105

- Withdrawal of Consent: Apex Court Refuses Decree — 107
  * *Hitesh Bhatnagar* v. *Deepa Bhatnagar,* AIR 2011 SC 1637 — 107
- Withdrawal of Consent without Substantial Ground: Divorce Granted — 108
  * *Prakash Alumal Kalandari* v. *Jahanvi,* AIR 2011 Bom 119 — 108
- Waiver of Six Months Waiting Period when Divorce Petition Already Pending — 109
  * *Dineshkumar Shukla* v. *Neeta,* AIR 2005 MP 106: 2005 (2) Civ LJ 709: 2005 (2) CCC 161 — 109
- Waiver of Waiting Period Sought: Not Granted — 110
  * *Poonam* v. *Sumit Tanwar,* AIR 2010 SC 1384: 2010 AIR SCW 2084: (2010) 4 SCC 460 — 110
- Waiver of Statutory Period of One Year Sought: Refused as High Court has no such Power — 111
  * *Urvashi Sibal* v. *Government of NCT of Delhi,* AIR 2010 Del 157 — 111
- No Waiver of Statutory Period in Circumstances of the Case — 112
  * *Manish Goel* v. *Rohini Goel,* (2010) 4 SCC 393: AIR 2010 SC 1099: 2010 AIR SCW 1277 — 112
- Annulment Decree in Appeal Converting to Consent Divorce — 115
  * *Radha* v. *Mohinder Kumar,* (1998) 8 SCC 530 — 115
- Exemption from Personal Appearance on Medical Grounds — 115
  * *Roopa* v. *Santosh Kumar,* AIR 2005 All 172: 2005 (25) All Ind Cas 672: 2005 (2) CCC 798 — 115

♦ **Non-resumption of cohabitation after a decree of judicial separation or restitution** — **117**
- Separation Decree – Mere Absence of Efforts to Resume Cohabitation is no Wrong so as to Disentitle Relief — 117
  * *Madhukar Bhaskar Sheorey* v. *Saral Madhukar Sheorey,* AIR 1973 Bom 55: 1972 Mah LJ 762: ILR (1973) Bom 113 — 117
- Decree of Restitution – Mere Non-compliance or Non-inclination to Join not a Wrong so as to Deny Divorce — 118
  * *Dharmendra Kumar* v. *Usha Kumar,* AIR 1977 SC 2218: 1977 (2) SCJ 471: (1978) 1 SCR 315 — 118
- Long Separation – No Divorce but Judicial Separation Granted — 120
  * *Angrez Kaur* v. *Baldev Singh,* AIR 1980 P&H 171: 1979 Hindu LR 561: 1980 Marri LJ 54 — 120
- Restitution Decree – Non-Compliance of – Spouse Thwarting Attempts to Comply – Cannot take Advantage — 121
  * *Sunita Rajendra Nikalje* v. *Rajendra Eknath Nikalje,* AIR 1996 Bom 85: 1996 (1) All MR 446: 1996 (2) Bom CJ 47 — 121
- No Vested Right to Divorce on this Ground — 121
  * *Hirachand Srinivas Managaonkar* v. *Sunanda,* AIR 2001 SC 1285: 2001 AIR SCW 1196: (2001) 4 SCC 125 — 121
- Consent Separation Decree: Non-cohabitation thereafter – Ground for Divorce — 122

- * *M. Aruna Kumari* v. *A.V. Janardhan Rao,* 2003 (5) SCALE 290 — 122
- • Consent Restitution Decree not *per se* Collusive — 123
  - * *Saroj Rani* v. *Sudarshan Kumar Chadha,* AIR 1984 SC 1562: (1984) 4 SCC 90: 1984 Marri LJ 499 — 123
- • Non-cohabitation after Restitution or Seperation Decree — 125
  - * *Bijaya Lakshmi Kundingi* v. *Kamala Lochana Kundingi,* AIR 2005 Ori 120: 2005 (33) All Ind Cas 580: 2005 (2) Ori LR 23 — 125
- • Husband Continuing to Live with Another Woman: Not Entitled to Relief — 127
  - * *Kanchan Sanjay Gujar* v. *Sanjay Gujar,* AIR 2009 Bom 151: 2009 (4) CCC 509: II (2009) DMC 566 — 127

♦ **Repudiation of Marriage** — 129
- • Court to be 'Satisfied' that Wrong-doer does not take Advantage — 129
  - * *M. Ajith Kumar* v. *K. Jeeja @ Sanila,* AIR 2009 Ker 100: 2009 (78) All Ind Cas 372: 2009 (1) Ker LT 634 — 129
- • Constitutional Validity of the Provision — 131
  - * *Roop Narayan Verma* v. *Union of India,* AIR 2007 Chh 64: 2007 Mat LR 538: 2007 (3) ALJ (NOC) 526 — 131
- • Minor Girl Filing Petition for Repudiation Through Brother even while Father Alive — 132
  - * *Ramesh Kumar* v. *Sunita Devi,* AIR 2005 P&H 55: II (2005) DMC 575: 2005 (1) Hindu LR 360 — 132

♦ **Restitution of Conjugal Rights** — 133
- • Constitutional *Vires* of Restitution Provision — 133
  - * *T. Sareetha* v. *T. Venkata Subbaiah,* AIR 1983 AP 356: II (1983) DMC 172: (1983) 2 Civ LJ 158 — 133
  - * *Harvinder Kaur* v. *Harmander Singh Choudhry,* AIR 1984 Del 66: ILR (1984) 1 Del 546: 1984 Raj LR 187 — 135

♦ **Reasonable Cause for Withdrawal** — 137
- • Husband's Blindness: Reasonable Cause for Wife's Withdrawal — 137
  - * *Mohinder Singh* v. *Preet Kaur,* 1981 HLR 321 (P&H): AIR 1981 JK 25: 1981 Marri LJ 118 — 137
- • Wife's Employment — 137
  - * *Geeta Jagdish Mangtani* v. *Jagdish Mangtani,* AIR 2005 SC 3508: 2005 AIR SCW 4755: (2005) 8 SCC 177 — 137
- • Wife Subjected to Mental/Physical Torture: Reasonable Ground for Withdrawal — 139
  - * *Kuldeep Kumar Dogra* v. *Monika Sharma,* AIR 2010 HP 58 — 139
  - * *Santana Banerjee* v. *Susanta Kumar Banerjee,* AIR 2012 Cal 16 — 140
- • Alternate Relief in Petition for Restitution — 141
  - * *Vijay Lakshmi Devi* v. *Gautam Krishna Mishra,* AIR 2010 Pat 56: 2010 (3) Civ LJ 231 — 141

Contents   xv

- **Reconciliation Efforts**   **143**
  - No Divorce Decree on Basis of Conciliator's Recommendations   143
    - *Raj Kumar Bansal v. Anjana Kumari,* AIR 1995 P&H 18:
      1994 (1) Hindu LR 417: 1995 (21) Marri LJ 302   143
  - Failure to Appear in Reconciliation Proceedings – Court cannot Strike Down Defence   144
    - *Love Kumar v. Sunita Puri,* AIR 1997 P&H 189: ILR (1997) 2 P&H 79:
      II (1998) DMC 711   144
  - Wife Allegedly Duped: *Ex Parte* Divorce – Appeal Rejected – Court Ought to have Tried Reconciliation and Allowed Appeal   145
    - *Balwinder Kaur v. Hardeep Singh,* AIR 1998 SC 764:
      1998 AIR SCW 474: (1997) 11 SCC 701   145
  - Issuance of Non-bailable Warrants to Try Reconciliation   146
    - *Jagraj Singh v. Birpal Kaur,* AIR 2007 SC 2083:
      2007 AIR SCW 3201: (2007) 2 SCC 564   146
  - Reconciliation Efforts even when Ground for Relief is Conversion   147
    - *Bini v. Sundaran K.V.,* AIR 2008 Ker 84: ILR (2008) 1 Ker 203:
      2008 (1) Ker LJ 162   147

- **Division of Matrimonial Assets**   **148**
  - Section 27, Hindu Marriage Act *vis-a-vis* Wife's Right to a Flat when She is Co-owner on Record   148
    - *Sunita Shankar Salvi v. Shankar Laxman Salvi,* AIR 2003 Bom 431:
      2003 (1) All MR 267: 2003 (3) Bom LR 424   148
  - Matrimonial Court's Jurisdiction to Dispose of Even Such Properties which are not Joint of the Spouses   149
    - *Hemant Kumar Agrahari v. Lakshmi Devi,* AIR 2004 All 126:
      2004 All LJ 972: 2004 (2) CCC 50   149
  - Jurisdiction of Family Courts under Section 7(1)(c), Family Courts Act *vis-à-vis* section 27 of Hindu Marriage Act   150
    - *Sangeeta B. Kadam v. Balkrishna Ramchandra Kadam,*
      AIR 2005 Bom 262: 2005 (2) Bom CR 515: I (2006) DMC 296   150

- **Re-marriage**   **153**
  - Re-marriage Pending Appeal of Divorce Decree   153
    - *Tejinder Kaur v. Gurmit Singh,* AIR 1988 SC 839: JT 1988 (1) SC 395   153
  - Re-marriage after Annulment Decree   154
    - *Lata Kamat v. Vilas,* AIR 1989 SC 1477: (1989) 2 SCC 613:
      JT 1989 (3) SC 48   154

- **Bigamy**   **157**
  - Constitutional Validity of Anti-bigamy Provisions in Hindu Marriage Act   157
    - *Ram Prasad v. State of Uttar Pradesh,* AIR 1961 All 334:
      1961 All LJ 383: 1961 All WR (HC) 252   157

- Bigamous Marriage – Second Marriage should be Legally Valid for Conviction ... 158
  - *Bhaurao Shankar Lokhande v. State of Maharashtra*, AIR 1965 SC 1564: 1966 (1) SCJ 298: (1965) 2 SCR 837 ... 158
- Bigamous Marriage not Legal even if Spouse Consents ... 159
  - *Santosh Kumari v. Surjit Singh*, AIR 1990 HP 77: 1990 Cr LJ 1012: (1989) 2 Hindu LR 111 ... 159
- When First Marriage Void, Subsequent Marriage not 'Plural Marriage' but Reprehensible Conduct ... 160
  - *M.M. Malhotra v. Union of India*, AIR 2006 SC 80: 2005 AIR SCW 5497: (2005) 8 SCC 351 ... 160
- Wife Leaving House: No Justification for Husband to take Second Wife "for the sake of his family" ... 161
  - *Saygo Bai v. Cheeru Bajrangi*, AIR 2011 SC 1557 ... 161
- Court Acquiesing in Husband's Bigamous Marriage ... 162
  - *Kiran Devi v. Batul Kumar Verma*, AIR 2011 Pat 16 ... 162

♦ **Conversion and Bigamy** ... 165
- Hindu Husband Embracing Islam, Solemnizing a Second Marriage during Subsistence of First Marriage – Second Marriage is Void ... 165
  - *Sarla Mudgal v. Union of India*, AIR 1995 SC 1531: 1995 AIR SCW 2326: 1995 Cr LJ 2926 ... 165
- Hindu Husband Converting to Islam and Marrying during Subsistence of First Marriage – Guilty of Bigamy ... 166
  - *Lily Thomas v. Union of India*, AIR 2000 SC 1650: 2000 AIR SCW 1760: 2000 Cr LJ 2433 ... 166

♦ **Matrimonial Home/Properties/Right of Residence** ... 170
- Does a Husband have a Legal Right to Stay in Accommodation Allotted to his Wife? ... 170
  - *B.R. Mehta v. Atma Devi*, AIR 1987 SC 2220: (1987) 4 SCC 183: JT 1987 (4) SC 474 ... 170
- Divorced Wife's Right to be Impleaded as Respondent in Eviction Proceedings Filed by Landlord against her Husband ... 171
  - *Ruma Chakraborty v. Sudha Rani Banerjee*, JT 2005 (12) SC 134: AIR 2005 SC 3557: 2005 AIR SCW 4938 ... 171
- Deserted Wife's Right to Contest Eviction Proceedings Filed by Landlord against her Husband ... 174
  - *B.P. Achala Anand v. S. Appi Reddy*, (2005) 2 SCALE 105: AIR 2005 SC 986: 2005 AIR SCW 934 ... 174
- Property Belonging to In-laws: Estranged Wife cannot Re-enter as Matter of Right ... 177
  - *S.R. Batra v. Taruna Batra*, AIR 2007 SC 1118 (Del): 2007 AIR SCW 1088: (2007) 3 SCC 169 ... 177

Contents xvii

- Estranged Wife's Right of Residence in the Matrimonial House 180
  * *Komalam Amma* v. *Kumar Pillai Raghavan*, AIR 2009 SC 636:
    (2008) 14 SCC 345: 2008 AIR SCW 7799 180
- Damages to Wife 181
  * *Mukund Martand Chitnis* v. *Madhuri Mukund Chitnis*,
    AIR 1992 SC 1804: 1992 AIR SCW 2025: 1993 (1) Bom CR 401 181
- Damages to Deserted Wife by NRI Husband 183
  * *Neeraja Saraph* v. *Jayant Saraph*, (1994) 6 SCC 461 183
- Paternity/DNA Tests 184
  * *Gautam Kundu* v. *State of West Bengal*, AIR 1993 SC 2295:
    1993 AIR SCW 2325: 1993 Cr LJ 3233 184
- DNA Test on Discharged Foetus to Establish Paternity 185
  * *X* v. *Z*, AIR 2002 Del 217: 2002 (96) DLT 354: I (2002) DMC 448 185
- Child's Application for DNA Test to Establish Parentage 186
  * *Master X* v. *Y*, AIR 2003 Del 195: 2003 (69) DRJ 21: 2003 Mat LR 561 186
- Court's Power to Order DNA Test – Discretionary 187
  * *S. Thangavelu* v. *S. Kannammal*, AIR 2005 Mad 106:
    2005 (25) All Ind Cas 496: 2004 (4) Mad LJ 508 187
- DNA/paternity Test to Establish Adultery 187
  * *Sunil Trambake* v. *Leelavati Trambake*, AIR 2006 Bom 140:
    2006 (42) All Ind Cas 527: II (2006) DMC 461 187

- **Injunctions** **189**
  - Injunction Against Second Marriage: Not Allowed 189
    * *Umashankar Prasad Singh* v. *Radha Devi*, AIR 1967 Pat 220 189
  - Injunction Against Second Marriage: Allowed 190
    * *Kirti Sharma* v. *Civil Judge, Senior Division, Etah*, AIR 2005 All 197:
      2005 (59) All LR 53: 2005 (2) All WC 1741 190
  - Injunction Against Forced Entry into Matrimonial Home 191
    * *Pratiksha* v. *Pravin Tapaswi*, 2002 (2) HLR 551 (MP) 191
  - Injunction Against Using Husband's Surname after Divorce 192
    * *Neelam Dadasaheb Shewale* v. *Dadasaheb Bandu Shewale*,
      I (2010) DMC 344 (Bom) 192

- **Live-in Relationships** **194**
  - Right to Maintenance in a Live-in Relation 194
    * *Chanmuniya* v. *Virendra Kumar*, (2010) 10 SCALE 602:
      2010 AIR SCW 6497 194
  - Property Rights of Children of Live-ins 195
    * *Bharatha Matha* v. *R. Vijaya Renganathan*, AIR 2010 SC 2685:
      2010 AIR SCW 3503: (2010) 6 SCALE 53 195
  - Maintenance Rights in Live-in Relationship 196
    * *D. Velusamy* v. *D. Patchaiammal*, AIR 2011 SC 479 196

xviii   *Cases and Materials on Family Law*

- **Maintenance**   **199**
- **Maintenance for Wives and Allied Issues**   **200**
  - Order of Dismissal of Main Decree not "any decree" under Section 25   200
    - * *Chand Dhawan* v. *Jawaharlal Dhawan,* (1993) 3 SCC 406: 1993 AIR SCW 2548: 1993 Cr LJ 2930   200
  - Petition for Nullity of Marriage – Whether Maintenance *pendente lite* can be Claimed   201
    - * *Sushila Viresh Chhawda* v. *Viresh Nagshi Chhawda,* AIR 1996 Bom 94: 1996 (2) Bom CR 531: 1996 (1) CCC 700   201
  - Whether Proceedings under Limitation Act are "Proceedings" for Purpose of Section 24   202
    - * *Ghari Lal* v. *Surjit Kaur,* AIR 1997 J&K 72: 1997 Marri LJ 434   202
  - Maintenance under Section 25, when Appeal against Divorce Pending   203
    - * *Surendra Kumar Bhansali* v. *Judge, Family Court,* AIR 2004 Raj 257: 2004 (19) All Ind Cas 685: 2004 (3) CCC 194   203
  - Marriage Void: No Maintenance   204
    - * *Yamunabai Anantrao Adhav* v. *Anantrao Shivaram Adhav,* AIR 1988 SC 644: JT 1988 (1) SC 193: 1988 Cr LJ 793   204
  - Marriage Void: No Maintenance but Damages Granted   205
    - * *Ranjit Kumar Bhattacharyya* v. *Sabita Bhattacharyya,* AIR 1996 Cal 301: 1996 (1) Cal LJ 465: 1996 (1) Hindu LR 520   205
  - Compliance of All Essential Ceremonies to Establish Legal Marriage not Essential under Section 125 Cr. P.C   205
    - * *Dwarika Prasad Satpathy* v. *Bidyut Prava Dixit,* 2000 Cr LJ 1 (SC): AIR 1999 SC 3348: 1999 AIR SCW 3844   205
  - Woman Living with a Man cannot be Equated as Wife   207
    - * *Malti* v. *State of Uttar Pradesh,* 2000 Cr LJ 4170 (All): 2000 All LJ 2116: 2001 (1) Hindu LR 403   207
  - If Marriage Void – Wife not Entitled to Maintenance   208
    - * *Bhau Saheb* v. *Leelabai,* AIR 2004 Bom 283 (FB): 2004 (13) All Ind Cas 948: 2004 (1) Hindu LR 615   208
  - No Maintenance to Wife where Marriage Void   210
    - * *Savitaben Somabhai Bhatiya* v. *State of Gujarat,* AIR 2005 SC 1809: 2005 Cr LJ 2141: 2005 AIR SCW 1601   210
  - Marriage Void: Inherent Powers under CPC cannot be Invoked   212
    - * *Mangala Bhivaji Lad* v. *Dhondiba Rambhau Aher,* AIR 2010 Bom 122: 2010 (4) All MR 716: 2010 (4) Mah LJ 486   212
  - Marriage Complete Nullity: No Maintenance under Section 125 Cr. P.C.   215
    - * *Ratneshwar Saikia* v. *Kalpana Saikia,* Crl Rev No. 88/2006 Gau 20-5-11   215
- **Income of Claimant**   **217**
  - Claimants Income not to be Ignored   217
    - * *Bhagwan Dutt* v. *Kanta Devi,* AIR 1975 SC 83: 1975 Cr LJ 40: (1975) 2 SCC 386   217

Contents   xix

- Young Educated Lady – Whether Expected to be Capable of Own Maintenance   217
  * *Chandana Guha Roy* v. *Gautam Guha Roy*, AIR 2004 Cal 36: 2004 (17) All Ind Cas 790: I (2005) DMC 607   217
- Husband cannot seek Production of Documents of Family Assets to Establish Wife's Means   218
  * *Pushkar Navnitlal Shah* v. *Rakhi Pushkar Shah*, AIR 2007 Guj 5: 2007 (55) All Ind Cas 505: 2007 (1) Guj LR 859   218

♦ **Income/Capacity of Non-applicant**   **221**
- Relevance of Non-applicant's Income and Capacity   221
  * *K.M.P. Kovilamma* v. *Moopil Eradi*, (1973) Cr LJ 1878: 1973 Ker LT 757: 1972 Ker LJ 893   221
- Capacity to Maintain – Presumption   222
  * *Dasarathi Ghosh* v. *Anuradha Ghosh*, 1988 Cr LJ 64 (Cal): II (1986) DMC 120: 1986 (2) Hindu LR 165   222
- Husband Becoming *Sadhu* not Absolved of Liability to Maintain Wife   223
  * *Hardev Singh* v. *State of Uttar Pradesh*, 1995 Cr LJ 1652 (All): II (1995) DMC 624: 1995 All LJ 446   223
- Maintenance claim by Wife – Status of Husband and not her Parents to be Considered   224
  * *Meenu Chopra* v. *Deepak Chopra*, AIR 2002 Del 131: 2002 (1) CCC 239: II (2001) DMC 264   224
- Can Wife claim Maintenance for Husband's Mother also   225
  * *Amit Kumar Sharma* v. *VIth Addl. District and Sessions Judge, Bijnor*, AIR 1999 All 4: 1999 All LJ 25: 1999 (1) CCC 272   225
- Assessing the Income – What is the Crucial Time   226
  * *S.S. Bindra* v. *Tarvinder Kaur*, AIR 2004 Del 442: 2004 (23) All Ind Cas 189: II (2004) DMC 297   226
- Whether Medical Expenses to be Included   227
  * *R. Suresh* v. *Chandra*, AIR 2003 Kant 183: ILR (2003) 3 Kant 1638: 2003 (2) Kant LJ 67   227
- Maintenance – Whether Includes Right to Reside in Tenanted Premises   228
  * *Ajit Bhagwandas Udeshi* v *Kumud Ajit Udeshi*, AIR 2003 Bom 120: 2003 (3) Bom CR 224: I (2003) DMC 602   228
- Right of Residence as Part of Maintenance – A Personal Right; is not Heritable   229
  * *Sheela Rani* v. *Jagdish Chander Sharma*, AIR 2004 Del 158: 2003 (107) DLT 309: 2003 (71) DRJ 122   229

♦ ***Mala fide* Transfers**   **230**
- *Mala fide* Transfer of Property cannot Defeat Wife's Claim for Maintenance   230
  * *Hari Lal* v. *Balvantia*, AIR 1998 All 211: 1998 All LJ 1371: 1998 (3) CCC 275   230

- **Maintenance – Protection Against *Mala Fide* Transfers** — 231
  - *Kangal v. Atwariya Devi,* AIR 2002 All 77: 2002 All LJ 603: 2002 (2) CCC 210 — 231
- **Bars to Maintenance claim** — 232
  - Decree of Restitution against Wife – No Absolute Bar to her Maintenance Claim — 232
    - *Pandit Dattaraya Kulkarni v. Laxmi Pandit Kulkarni,* (2001) 1 Femi-Juris CC 47 (Bom) — 232
- **When Free Legal Aid** — 233
  - Litigation Expenses when Free Legal Aid Available — 233
    - *Ramesh Babu v. Usha,* AIR 2003 Mad 281: II (2003) DMC 272: 2003 (1) Mad LJ 576 — 233
- **Limitation** — 234
  - Bar of Limitation – When Applicable — 234
    - *Shantha v. B.G. Shivananjappa,* AIR 2005 SC 2410: 2005 Cr LJ 2615: 2005 AIR SCW 2613 — 234
- **Settlement/Consent whether Bar to Subsequent Claim** — 236
  - Surrender of Right to Claim Maintenance *vide* Settlement Deed – No Bar to Subsequent Claim — 236
    - *Bai Laxmiben v. Bharatbhai Vechatbhai Patel,* 1986 Cr LJ 1418 (Guj): I (1986) DMC 129: 1986 (27) Guj LR 272 — 236
- **Earlier Compromise** — 238
  - Earlier Compromised Agreement – No Bar to Subsequent Claim for Enhancement — 238
    - *Joydel Kumar Biswas v. Madhuri Biswas,* 1994 Cr LJ 3342 (Cal): I (1996) DMC 12: 1996 (2) Hindu LR 290 — 238
- **Wife Consenting to give up Claim** — 239
  - Wife Agreeing to give up Claim under Consent Divorce Decree – No Bar to Claiming Maintenance in Future — 239
    - *Geeta Satish Gokarna v. Satish Gokarna,* AIR 2004 Bom 345: 2004 (20) All Ind Cas 839: 2004 (3) Mah LJ 159 — 239
  - Parents cannot Barter Away Children's Right — 240
    - *Mohinder Singh v. Ravneet Kaur,* 2008 MLR 68 (P&H) — 240
- **Date of Award** — 242
  - Maintenance *pendente lite* – Date from which to be Awarded — 242
    - *Popri Bai v. Teerath Singh,* AIR 2004 Raj 128: 2004 (3) Civ LJ 107: 2004 (2) CCC 262 — 242
- **Conduct of Parties** — 244
  - Husband Allowing Dismissal of his Main Petition – Liable to Pay Arrears of Maintenance — 244
    - *Lataben Y. Goswami v. Yogendra Kumar Shankargir Goswami,* AIR 1996 Guj 103: 1996 (1) CCC 188: 1996 (1) Hindu LR 712 — 244

- Husband's Remarrying Sufficient Cause for First Wife's Withdrawal
  & Claiming Maintenance 245
  * *Ashabi B. Takke* v. *Bashasab Takke*, AIR 2003 Kant 172:
    ILR 2003 (1) Kant 737: 2003 (2) Kant LJ 420 245
- Wife Taking Advantage of own Wrong 246
  * *Sudha Suhas Nandanvankar* v. *Suhas Ramrao Nandanvankar*,
    AIR 2005 Bom 62: 2005 (26) All Ind Cas 801: 2005 (1) Hindu LR 130 246
- **Quantum** 248
  - Quantum of Maintenance 248
    * *Captain Ramesh Chander Kaushal* v. *Veena Kaushal*, AIR 1978 SC 1807:
      (1978) 4 SCC 70: 1978 Cr LJ 3 248
- **Interim Maintenance** 250
  - Interim Maintenance Order 250
    * *Savitri* v. *Govind Singh*, 1986 Cr LJ 41 (SC): AIR 1986 SC 984:
      (1985) 4 SCC 337 250
- **Execution of Maintenance Decree** 251
  - Maintenance Already Due: Widow can Proceed Against Assets
    of Deceased Husband 251
    * *Aruna Basu Mullick* v. *Dorothea Mitra*, AIR 1983 SC 916:
      (1983) 3 SCC 522: II (1983) DMC 289 251
- **Arrears Till Life of Husband** 252
  - Only Arrears Till Husband's Life can be Recovered 252
    * *Prithviraj Singh* v. *Pavanvir Singh*, 1986 Cr LJ 1432 (P&H):
      ILR (1986) 2 P&H 205 252
  - Wife's Claim for Maintenance does not Stand Satisfied after Defaulting
    Husband's Imprisonment for Non-payment 252
    * *Kuldip Kaur* v. *Surinder Singh*, 1989 Cr LJ 794 (SC): AIR 1989 SC 232:
      (1989) 1 SCC 405 252
- **Orders by Gram Panchayat** 254
  - Execution of Maintenance Orders Made by *Gram Panchayat* 254
    * *Padmo* v. *Surat Ram*, 2003 Cr LJ 237 (HP): I (2003) DMC 483:
      2003 (1) Hindu LR 523 254
- **Non-Compliance of Order to Pay Litigation Expenses** 256
  - Defence can be Struck Down 256
    * *Bani* v. *Parkash Singh*, AIR 1996 P&H 175: I (1997) DMC 5:
      ILR (1997) 1 P&H 118 256
  - Order under Section 24, Non-compliance by Husband: No *ex parte*
    Divorce in his favour Because of Wife's Non-filing Written Statement 256
    * *Dinesh Kumar* v. *Santosh Devi*, AIR 2007 All 30: 2007 (1) ALJ 138:
      2006 (65) All LR 889 256
  - Mode of Divorce Immaterial to Claim for Maintenance by Wife 257
    * *Kongini Balan* v. *M. Visalakshy*, (1986) Cr LJ 697 (Ker) 257

- **Simultaneous Remedies** — 259
  - Army Officer's Wife may Claim Maintenance under Army Act as well — 259
    - *Capt. Suneel v. Union of India*, AIR 2004 Del 95: 2003 (12) All Ind Cas 915: 2003 (107) DLT 224 — 259
- **Jurisdiction** — 261
  - Maintenance Claim by Wife – Jurisdiction of Court — 261
    - *Sucheta Singh Ghate v. Dilip Shanta, Ram Ghate*, AIR 2003 Bom 390 — 261
- **Rights and Duties of Parents** — 262
  - Father not Unable to Maintain Himself – Not Entitled — 262
    - *Attar Singh Jain v. Amit Singh Jain*, (1982) Cr LJ 211 (Del) — 262
  - Mother's Liability to Maintain Children — 262
    - *T.P.S.H. Selva Saroja v. T.P.S.H. Sasinathan*, (1989) Cr LJ 2032 (Mad) — 262
  - Mother does not Include Step-Mother — 263
    - *Kirtikant D. Vadodaria v. State of Gujarat*, (1996) 4 SCALE 44: (1996) 4 SCC 479: JT 1996 (6) SC 244 — 263
  - Mother's Right to 'stay' in 'sons' House — 264
    - *Anandi D Jadhav v. Nirmala Ramchandra Kore*, AIR 2000 SC 1386: 2000 AIR SCW 1161: (2000) 3 SCC 703 — 264
  - Parent may Claim Maintenance from any one of their Children — 265
    - *Mahendra Kumar Gaikwad v. Gulabbhai*, 2001 Cr LJ 2111 (Bom): 2000 (2) CCC 692: 2000 (2) Mah LJ 378 — 265
  - Court of Jurisdiction where Claimant is a Parent — 266
    - *Ananth Gopal v. Gopal Narayan*, 1985 Cr LJ 152 (Kant): 1985 (1) Hindu LR 222: ILR 1985 Kant 2607 — 266
    - *Ganga Sharan Varshney v. Shakuntala Devi*, 1990 Cr LJ 128 (All): 1990 All LJ 34: I (1990) DMC 71 — 266
    - *N.B. Bhikshu v. State of Andhra Pradesh*, 1993 Cr LJ 3280 (AP): I (1994) DMC 396: 1993 (2) Hindu LR 697
    - *Vijay Kumar Prasad v. State of Bihar*, AIR 2004 SC 2123: 2004 Cr LJ 2047: 2004 AIR SCW 2276 — 266
- **Rights and Duties of Daughters** — 269
  - Married Minor Daughter's Right to Claim Maintenance — 269
    - *Ramchoddas Narottamdas v. Emperor*, AIR 1949 Bom 36: 49 Cr LJ 630 — 269
  - Adult Unmarried Daughter's Right to Maintenance (under HAMA) — 270
    - *Viswambharan v. Dhanya*, AIR 2005 Ker 91: ILR 2005 (1) Ker 374: 2005 (1) Ker LJ 330 — 270
  - Adult Unmarried Daughter to Prove Physical or Mental Abnormality — 271
    - *T.P.S.H. Selva Saroja v. T.P.S.H. Sasinathan*, (1989) Cr LJ 2032 (Mad) — 271
    - *Pathumma v. Cholamarakkar*, I (2009) DMC 466 (DB Ker) — 271
  - Maintenance of Adult Unmarried Daughter – Provisions of Cr. P.C. vis-a-vis Hindu Adoption and Maintenance Act
    - *Raj Kumari Awasthi v. State of Uttar Pradesh*, (2008) 3 ALJ 100 — 273

- **Duties of Daughters** — 276
  - Married Daughter's Liability to Maintain Parents — 276
    - *Vijaya Manohar Arbat* v. *Kashirao Rajaram Sawai*, AIR 1987 SC 1100: 1987 Cr LJ 977: (1987) 2 SCC 278 — 276
- **Widowed Daughter-in-law** — 278
  - Widowed Daughter-in-law's Right to Maintenance — 278
    - *Balbir Kaur* v. *Harinder Kaur*, AIR 2003 P&H 174: 2003 (2) CCC 80: 2003 (2) Marri LJ 499 — 278
  - No Enforcement of Maintenance Against Property of Mother-in-law — 279
    - *Vimalben Ajitbhai Patel* v. *Vatslaben Ashokbhai Patel*, (2008) 4 SCC 649: AIR 2008 SC 2675: 2008 AIR SCW 4475 — 279
- **Husband's Right to Maintenance** — 282
  - Husband Incapable of Earning Entitled to Maintenance under Hindu Law and Parsi Law — 282
    - *Lalit Mohan* v. *Tripta Devi*, AIR 1990 J&K 7: 1989 Kash LJ 96: II (1989) DMC 23 — 282
    - *Monika Rana* v. *Yogeshwar Singh Sapehia*, AIR 2011 HP 54 — 283
- **Christian Parties** — 284
  - Maintenance under CPC Provisions — 284
    - *K. Kumar* v. *Leena*, (2010) II DMC 519 (Ker): AIR 2010 Kant 75: ILR 2010 Kant 1221 — 284
- **Custody and Guardianship** — 285
  - Custody to Parent Living Outside Court's Jurisdiction — 285
    - *Margaret* v. *Chacko*, AIR 1971 Ker 1 — 285
  - Fact that Mother is Working – Not to Affect her Right to Child's Custody (Case under Parsi Law) — 285
    - *Thrity Hoshie Dolikuka* v. *Hoshiam Shavaksha Dolikuka*, AIR 1982 SC 1276: (1982) 2 SCC 544: II (1982) DMC 288 — 285
  - Constitutional Validity of Some Sections under Hindu Minority and Guardianship Act and Guardians and Wards Act — 286
    - *Githa Hariharan* v. *Reserve Bank of India* and *Vandana Shiva* v. *J. Bandhopadhyaya*, AIR 1999 SC 1149: 1999 AIR SCW 811: (1999) 2 SCC 228 — 286
  - Mother Flouting Court Custody Order – Yet Custody Awarded in View of Welfare of Children — 288
    - *Sarita Sharma* v. *Sushil Sharma*, JT 2000 (2) SC 258: AIR 2000 SC 1019: 2000 Cr LJ 1459 — 288
  - Guardianship given to Paternal Grandfather Despite Adoption by Maternal Grandfather — 289
    - *Jai Prakash Khadria* v. *Shyam Sunder Agarwalla*, AIR 2000 SC 2172: 2000 AIR SCW 2341: (2000) 6 SCC 598 — 289

- Legal Right of Party is Immaterial   290
  * *Rajesh K. Gupta v. Ram Gopal Agarwala*, AIR 2005 SC 2426:
    2005 Cr LJ 2581: 2005 AIR SCW 2418   290
- Superior Financial Position of any Party – *Per se* no Consideration   291
  * *Surabhai Ravi Kumar Minawala v. State of Gujarat*, AIR 2005 Guj 149:
    2005 (31) All Ind Cas 472: 2005 (2) Civ LJ 554   291
- Mothers' Re-marriage does not Defeat her Right to Custody   292
  * *Lekha v. Anil Kumar*, (2006) 12 SCALE 163   292
- "Positive Test" as to what is in Child's Interest   294
  * *Nil Ratan Kundu v. Abhijit Kundu*, (2008) 7 MLJ 248 (SC):
    AIR 2009 SC (Supp) 732   294
- Plea of Continuity   297
  * *Gaurav Nagpal v. Sumedha Nagpal*, AIR 2009 SC 557 (Del):
    2008 AIR SCW 7687: (2009) 1 SCC 42   297
- Variation of Custody Orders   298
  * *Vikram Vir Vohra v. Shalini Bhalla*, AIR 2010 SC 1675 (Del):
    2010 AIR SCW 2261: (2010) 4 SCC 409   298
- Jurisdiction in Child Custody Suit   299
  * *Sarabjit v. Piara Lal*, AIR 2005 P&H 237: 2005 (35) All Ind Cas 236:
    2005 (3) CCC 179   299
- Jurisdiction   300
  * *Amal Saha v. Basana Saha*, AIR 1988 Gau 22: (1987) 2 Gua LR 84:
    (1987) 2 Civ LJ 238   300
- No Third Party Intervention in Custody Dispute when both
  Parents Alive   301
  * *Akash v. State of Andhra Pradesh*, AIR 2000 AP 261: II (2000) DMC 490:
    2000 (2) Hindu LR 603   301
- Hindu Minority and Guardianship Act: Alienation of Minor's Property   302
  * *Vishwambar v. Laxminarayana*, AIR 2001 SC 2607:
    2001 AIR SCW 2616: (2001) 6 SCC 163   302
- Alienation of Minor's Property   303
  * *P.V. Madhavi v. P.V. Balakrishnan*, AIR 2010 Ker 111   303

- **Adoption**   **305**
  - Applicability of Hindu Adoptions and Maintenance Act   306
  - Act not Applicable to Pre-Act Adoptions   306
    * *Nagireddi Lakshmi v. Nagireddi Nagaraju*, AIR 2005 AP 17   306
- **Age of Adoptee**   **308**
  - Adoptee over 15 when Adopted: Custom Proved   308
    * *Atluri Brahmanandan (dead) through L.R's v. Anne Sai Bapuji*,
      AIR 2011 SC 545   308
  - Adoptee over 15 when Adopted: Custom not Proved   309

- * *Amit Chandubhai Chauhan* v. *Ahmedabad Municipal Corporation*, AIR 2011 Guj 145 — 309
- • Adoption of Muslim Child by Hindu — 311
  - * *Kumar Sursen* v. *State of Bihar*, AIR 2008 Pat 24: 2008 (2) AIR JharR 6: 2008 (4) CCC 569 — 311
- ♦ **Adoption by Female** — 312
  - • Adoption by Married Female — 312
    - * *Brajendra Singh* v. *State of Madhya Pradesh*, AIR 2008 SC 1056: 2008 AIR SCW 652: (2008) 1 SCALE 372 — 312
  - • Adoption by Divorced Female before Re-marriage and Proxy Adoption — 313
    - * *Narinderjit Kaur* v. *Union of India*, AIR 1997 P&H 280: 1997 (1) Hindu LR 442: 1997 Marri LJ 331 — 313
- ♦ **Consent of Wife/Wives** — 315
  - • Wife's Consent Necessary for Adoption — 315
    - * *Siddaramappa* v. *Gouravva*, AIR 2004 Kant 230: 2004 (2) Hindu LR 438: ILR (2004) 3 Kant 3611 — 315
  - • Wife's Consent to be Explicit — 316
    - * *Ghisalal* v. *Dhapubai*, AIR 2011 SC 644 (MP) — 316
- ♦ **Adoption by Widow** — 319
  - • Adoption by Widow under Act: Would the Child be Deemed to be Child of Deceased Husband — 319
    - * *Sawan Ram* v. *Kalawanti*, AIR 1967 SC 1761: (1967) 3 SCR 687: 1968 (2) SCJ 316 — 319
  - • Widowed Mother-in-law's Right to Adopt in Presence of Widowed Daughter-in-law — 320
    - * *Ashabai Kate* v. *Vithal Bhika Nade*, AIR 1990 SC 670 (Bom): JT 1989 (4) SC 163: 1989 Mat LR 449 — 320
  - • Adoption by Widow when Widowed Daughter-in-law Alive — 322
    - * *Ningappa* v. *Shivappa*, 1994 AIHC 2068 (Kant) — 322
  - • Co-widow's Consent not Required — 323
    - * *Vijayalakshmamma* v. *B.T. Shankar*, AIR 2001 SC 1424: 2001 AIR SCW 1347: (2001) 4 SCC 558 — 323
  - • Merely Bringing up Step-child – No Proof of Adoption — 324
    - * *Ram Das* v. *Gandiabai*, AIR 1997 SC 1563: 1997 AIR SCW 317: (1997) 1 SCC 74 — 324
  - • Mere Fact of Living in Same House is No Proof of Adoption — 325
    - * *Prafulla Bala Mukherjee* v. *Satish Chandra Mukherjee*, AIR 1998 Cal 86 — 325
  - • Holding of Joint Accounts – No Presumption of Adoption — 325
    - * *Nilima Mukherjee* v. *Kanta Bhusan Ghosh*, AIR 2001 SC 2725: 2001 AIR SCW 3062: (2001) 6 SCC 660 — 325

- **Presumption in Case of Registered Adoption Deed** — 327
  - Presumption not Irrebutable — 327
    - *Jai Singh v. Shakuntala,* AIR 2002 SC 1428: 2002 AIR SCW 1280: (2002) 3 SCC 634 — 327
  - Registered Adoption Deed: Minor Discrepancies Immaterial — 328
    - *Ranjit Singh Dhillon v. Punjab School Education Board,* AIR 2004 P&H 382: 2004 (24) All Ind Cas 920: 2005 (1) Marri LJ 314 — 328
  - Change of Caste after Adoption — 329
    - *Khazan Singh v. Union of India,* AIR 1980 Del 60 — 329
  - Multiple Adoption not Permissible — 330
    - *Sandhya v. Union of India,* AIR 1998 Bom 228: I (1999) DMC 143: 1998 (1) Hindu LR 653 — 330
  - No Divesting on Adoption — 332
    - *Kisan Baburao Memane v. Suresh Sadu Memane,* AIR 1996 Bom 50: 1996 (1) Civ LJ 794: 1996 (1) ICC 625 — 332
  - Validity of Pre-adoption Agreements — 332
    - *Jupudi Venkata Vijaya Bhartiar v. Jupudi Kesava Rao,* AIR 2003 SC 3314: 2003 AIR SCW 4706: (2003) 8 SCC 282 — 332
  - Adopted Child cannot take away Right of Parents to Dispose of Property — 333
    - *Ugre Gowda v. Nagegowda,* AIR 2004 SC 3974: 2004 AIR SCW 4308: (2004) 12 SCC 48 — 333
  - Son Adopted 45 Years after Death of Freedom-Fighter: No Right to his Pension — 334
    - *Abhishek Sharma v. State of Uttar Pradesh,* AIR 2009 All 77: 2009 (2) ALJ 435: 2009 AIHC 1745 — 334
  - Compassionate Appointment of Child of Unmarried Male — 335
    - *State Bank of India v. Shweta Sahu,* (2010) 3 SCALE 44 — 335
  - Adoption *vis-à-vis* Juvenile Justice Act — 335
    - *In the matter of adoption of Payal @ Sharinee Vinay Pathak* — 335
  - Right to Adopt: Component of Right to Life — 337
    - *Philips Alfred Malsvin v. V.J. Gonsalves,* AIR 1999 Ker 187: ILR (1999) 2 Ker 43: 1999 (1) Ker LJ 247 — 337
  - Guidelines for Foreign Adoptions — 338
    - *Lakshmi Kant Pandey v. Union of India,* AIR 1984 SC 469: (1984) 2 SCC 244: (1984) 2 SCR 795: 1984 Marriage LJ 249 — 338
  - Guidelines do not Apply when Child given in Adoption to Foreign Couple by Biological Parent — 341
    - *Anokha v. State of Rajasthan,* AIR 2004 SC 2820: 2004 AIR SCW 1363: (2004) 1 SCC 382 — 341
- **Hindu Succession Act** — 343

Contents   xxvii

- ♦ **Applicability of the Act**   344
  - Act not Applicable to Scheduled Tribes   344
    - * *Kailash Singh* v. *Mewalal Singh Gond,* AIR 2002 MP 112: 2002 (1) MPHT 526: 2002 (2) MPLJ 163   344
  - Enlargement of Widow's Pre-Existing Limited Right   345
    - * *C. Masilmani Muddaliar* v. *Idol of Swaminathaswami,* AIR 1996 SC 1697: 1996 AIR SCW 1780: (1996) 8 SCC 525   345
  - Widow's Pre-existing Right but Acknowledgement that it was Limited   346
    - * *Vankamamidi Venkata Subba Rao* v. *Chatlapalli Seetharamaratna Ranganayakamma,* AIR 1997 SC 3082: 1997 AIR SCW 3122: (1997) 5 SCC 460   346
  - Widow's Pre-Exsisting Right not Effected by any Subsequent Document etc.   347
    - * *Raghubar Singh* v. *Gulab Singh,* AIR 1998 SC 2401: 1998 AIR SCW 2393: (1998) 6 SCC 314   347
  - Widow's Pre-Act Void Marriage – Affect on her Right   348
    - * *Velamuri Venkata Sivaprasad* v. *Kothuri Venkateswarlu,* AIR 2000 SC 434: 1999 AIR SCW 4583: (2000) 2 SCC 139   348
  - Widow's Right – Entire Ancestral Property cannot be given   350
    - * *Gulabrao Balwant Rao Shinde* v. *Chhabubai Balwant Rao Shinde,* AIR 2003 SC 16   350

- ♦ **Dwelling House and Female Heirs**   351
  - Riders on Female Heirs (Pre – 2005 Amendment)   351
    - * *Narashimaha Murthy* v. *Susheelabai,* AIR 1996 SC 1826: 1996 AIR SCW 2120: (1996) 3 SCC 644   351
  - Female Heirs Right to Dwelling House Partly Rented out   352
    - * *Kamal Basu Mazumdar* v. *Usha Bhadra Chowdhury,* AIR 2004 Cal 185: 2004 (2) Cal HN 383: 2005 (1) Hindu LR 294   352
  - Pending Cases under Section 23 *vis-à-vis* 2005 Amendment   354
    - * *M. Revathi* v. *R. Alamelu,* AIR 2009 Mad 86: 2009 (77) All Ind Cas 812: 2009 (5) Mad LJ 376   354

- ♦ **Widowed Daughter-in-law**   356
  - Widowed Daughter-in-law's Right only in Coparcenary Property of Husband   356
    - * *Daljit Singh* v. *Dara Singh,* AIR 2000 Del 292: 2000 (85) DLT 794: II (2000) DMC 134   356
  - Widowed Daughter-in-law: Properties of Deceesed Husband in Possession of Father-in-law   357
    - * *V. Muthusami* v. *Angammal,* AIR 2002 SC 1279: 2002 AIR SCW 1083: (2002) 3 SCC 316   357

- **Rights of Step Children** — 358
  - Step-Son's Right — 358
    - *Rattan Prakash v. Bela Sihare*, AIR 1996 Del 356: 1997 (1) Hindu LR 204: 1997 Marri LJ 46 — 358
    - *Bhagwan Dass v. Prabhati Ram*, AIR 2004 Del 137: 2004 (14) All Ind Cas 807: 2003 (108) DLT 25 — 359
    - *Debabrata Mondal v. State of West Bengal*, AIR 2008 Cal 13: 2008 (2) AIR BomR 222: 2007 (60) All Ind Cas 523 — 360
  - Step-Daughter's Right — 361
    - *Raj Rani v. Bimla Rani*, AIR 2011 Del 170 — 361
  - Devolution of Property of Female — 362
    - *Bhagat Ram v. Teja Singh*, AIR 2002 SC 1: 2001 AIR SCW 4507: (2002) 1 SCC 210 — 362
    - *Om Prakash v. Radhacharan*, (2009) 7 SCALE 51 — 363
  - Time for Ascertaining Heirship — 364
    - *Seethalakshmi Ammal v. Muthuvenkatarama Iyengar*, AIR 1998 SC 1692: 1998 AIR SCW 1462: (1998) 5 SCC 368 — 364
  - Wife of Murderer Son is Disqualified — 365
    - *Vallikannu v. R. Singaperumal*, AIR 2005 SC 2587: 2005 AIR SCW 2820: (2005) 6 SCC 622 — 365
  - No Disinheritance of Statutory heir — 367
    - *Raman Khanna v. Sham Kishore Khanna*, AIR 2009 HP 42 — 367
  - Right of Pre-emption — 368
    - *Ganeshappa v. Krishnamma*, AIR 2005 Kant 160: ILR 2005 Kant 358: 2005 (2) Kant LJ 262 — 368
  - Karnataka Amendment and Married Daughter's Right — 368
    - *Nanjamma v. State of Karnataka*, 1999 AlHC 3003 (Kant): ILR 1999 Kant 1094 — 368
  - Married Daughter's Right to Claim Compensation in Case of Parent's Death — 370
    - *Naraini Bai v. State of Haryana*, AIR 2004 P&H 206: 2004 (17) All Ind Cas 367: 2004 (1) Hindu LR 478 — 370
  - Married Daughter's Parents Right to Claim Compensation in Case of Daughter's Death — 371
    - *Ganny Kaur v. State*, AIR 2007 Del 273: 2008 (1) AKant (NOC) 44: 2007 (142) DLT 35 — 371
- **Indian Succession Act** — 373
  - Repeal of Travancore Christian Succession Act — 373
    - *Mary Roy v. State of Kerala*, AIR 1986 SC 1011: 1986 2 SCC 209: 1986 (2) Supreme 296 — 373
  - Testamentary Dispositions – Discriminatory Provisions are *ultra vires* Constitution — 374

* *John Vallamattom* v. *Union of India,* AIR 2003 SC 2902:
  2003 AIR SCW 3536: (2003) 6 SCC 611 374
♦ **Suspicious Circumstance** 377
  • Unequal Distribution in a Will *per se* is not Suspicious Circumstance ... 377
    * *Sridevi* v. *Jayaraja Shetty,* AIR 2005 SC 780: 2005 AIR SCW 605:
      (2005) 2 SCC 784 377
♦ **Customary Law** 378
  • Marriage under Customary Law: No Religious Rites Required 378
    * *Sumitra Devi* v. *Bhikan Choudhary,* AIR 1985 SC 765: 1985 Cr LJ 528:
      (1985) 1 SCC 637 378
  • Children of Marriage which is Valid under Customary Law are
    Legitimate 379
    * *M. Govindaraju* v. *K. Munisami Gounder,* AIR 1997 SC 10:
      1996 AIR SCW 4157: (1996) 5 SCC 467 379
  • Tribal Parties, no Custom Established to Prove Second Marriage as Void:
    Husband not Liable to be Prosecuted for Bigamy 380
    * *Dr. Surajmani Stella Kujur* v. *Durga Charan Hansdah,* (2001) I Femi –
      Juris CC 96 (SC): AIR 2001 SC 938: 2001 AIR SCW 711 380
  • Absence of Material on Record: Case Remanded to Ascertain
    Prevalence of Custom 381
    * *Yamanaji H. Jadhav* v. *Nirmala,* AIR 2002 SC 971: 2002 AIR SCW 674:
      (2002) 2 SCC 637 381
  • "Arrangement to Live Separately" is not Divorce Unless such Custom
    Pleaded or Established 382
    * *Bauramma* v. *Siddappa Jeevappa Patarad,* AIR 2003 Kant 342:
      ILR 2003 (1) Kant 579: 2003 (1) Kant LJ 581 382
  • Divorce under Custom – No need to go to Court when Custom Proved ... 383
    * *Jasbir Singh* v. *Inderjit Kaur,* AIR 2003 P&H 317: 2003 (2) Hindu LR 654:
      2004 (1) Marri LJ 175 383
  • Mizo Customary Law 384
    * *Germanthangi* v. *F. Rokunga,* AIR 2004 Gau 42: 2005 (1) Gau LR 338:
      2004 (2) Marri LJ 145 (Aizawl Bench) 384
  • Alleged Divorce by Registered Document *"chhor chithi"* – Custom not
    Proved 385
    * *Ramesh Chandra Ram Pratap Daga* v. *Rameshwari Ramesh Chandra Daga,*
      (2005) 2 SCC 33: AIR 2005 SC 422: 2004 AIR SCW 6990 385
  • Alleged Divorce by Customary Dissolution deed: Custom not Proved ... 388
    * *Subramani* v. *M. Chandralekha,* AIR 2005 SC 485: 2004 AIR SCW 7099:
      (2005) 9 SCC 407 388
  • Married Woman Remarrying without Establishing Customary Divorce:
    Second Marriage Void – Husband has no Right to Compassionate
    Appointment after Wife's Death 389

- * *Vishnu Kumar* v. *State of Uttar Pradesh*, 2006 (65) ALR 888 (All): AIR 2007 All 31: 2007 (1) ALJ 152 — 389
- • Document Purporting to be Dissolution deed under Custom not Proved: First Marriage held Subsisting — 390
  - * *Mohan Lal Sharma* v. *Parveen*, AIR 2010 P&H 65: 2010 (1) CCC 418: 2010 (1) ICC 212 — 390
- • Customary Divorce: No Ground for Decree under Hindu Marriage Act — 391
  - * *Mahendra Nath Yadav* v. *Sheela Devi*, II (2010) DMC 487 (SC) — 391
- • Marriage Dissolved by *"fahrkhati nama"*: Wife not Entitled to Restitution — 392
  - * *Kewal Kumar* v. *Pawna Devi*, AIR 2011 HP 58 — 392

♦ **Select Cases under Muslim Law** — 394
- • Validity of Marriage — 394
  - * *Ghulam Kubra Bibi* v. *Md. Shafi Mohammad Din*, AIR 1940 Peshawar 2 — 394
- • Legal Status of Marriage with a Pregnant Woman — 395
  - * *Amina* v. *Hassan Koya*, AIR 2004 SC 1227: 2003 Cr LJ 2540: 2003 AIR SCW 2496 — 395
- • Marriage – "Assurance" is not "Acceptance" to Marry — 396
  - * *Rashida Khatun* v. *SK. Islam*, AIR 2005 Ori 56: 2005 (1) CLR 162: 2005 Mat LR 296 — 396

♦ **Divorce** — 398
- • Impotency — 398
  - * *Mt. Altafan* v. *Ibrahim*, AIR 1924 All 116: 21 All LJ 811: 75 Ind Cas 502 — 398
- • Wife cannot be Compelled to Submit to Husband to Prove that he Ceased to be Impotent — 399
  - * *Abdul Azeem* v. *Fahimunnisa*, AIR 1969 Mys 226: (1967) 1 Mys LJ 675: 10 Law Rep 412 — 399
- • Husband's Failure to Maintain – Wife's Ground for Divorce — 400
  - * *A. Yousuf Rawther* v. *Sowramma*, AIR 1971 Ker 261: 1970 Ker LJ 544: ILR (1971) 1 Ker 154 — 400
- • Dissolution of Marriage in Terms of a Compromise — 402
  - * *Md. Abdul Zalil Ahmed* v. *Marina Begum*, AIR 1999 Gau 28: 1999 (2) Gau LR 369: 1999 (2) Hindu LR 576 — 402
- • Dissolution of Muslim Marriages Act *vis-a-vis* Theory of Break-down of Marriage — 403
  - * *Amma Khatoon* v. *Kashim Ansari*, AIR 2001 Jhar 28: 2001 AIR Jhar HCR 1: 2001 (2) BLJR 1228 — 403
- • *'Talaq'* to be Effective, has to be Explicitly 'Pronounced' — 404
  - * *Shamim Ara* v. *State of Uttar Pradesh*, (2002) 7 SCALE 183 — 404
- • Husband's Second Marriage: Ground for Divorce — 406
  - * *Abdurahiman* v. *Khairunneesa*, I (2010) DMC 707 (Ker DB) — 406

Contents xxxi

    * *Parakkattil Abu* v. *Pachiyath Beekkutty,* AIR 2011 Ker 88 407
- Option of Puberty 408
      * *Ghulam Sakina* v. *Falak Sher Allah Baksh,* AIR 1950 Lah 45:
  Pak Cas 1949 Lah 104 408

♦ **Restitution of Conjugal Rights** 410
- First Wife may Refuse Restitution where Husband Marries Another Woman 410
      * *Itwari* v. *Asghari,* AIR 1960 All 684: 1960 All LJ 523:
  1960 All WR (HC) 397 410

♦ **Maintenance** 413
- Muslim Husband's Liability under Section 125 413
      * *Mohd. Ahmad Khan* v. *Shah Bano Begum,* AIR 1985 SC 945:
  1985 Cr LJ 875: (1985) 2 SCC 556 413
- Muslim Women (Protection of Rights on Divorce) Act does not Affect Right of Minor Children of Divorced Muslim Parents to Claim Maintenance under the Code 414
      * *Noor Saba Khatoon* v. *Mohd Quasim,* AIR 1997 SC 3280:
  1997 Cr LJ 3972: 1997 AIR SCW 3343 414
- Constitutional Validity of Muslim Women (Protection of Rights on Divorce) Act 416
      * *Danial Latifi* v. *Union of India,* (2001) 6 SCALE 537: AIR 2001 SC 3958:
  2001 Cr LJ 4660 416
- Maintenance – Earlier under Section 125, Cr. P.C. – Later under Section 3 of Muslim Women Act, 1986 – Held Abuse of the Process of Court 420
      * *Sayeed Khan Faujdar Khan* v. *Zaheba Begum,* AIR 2006 Bom 39:
  II (2006) DMC 294: 2006 Mat LR 261 420
- Maintenance under Section 125 even after Iddat 420
      * *Shabana Bano* v. *Imran Khan,* AIR 2010 SC 305 (MP):
  2009 AIR SCW 7490: 2010 Cr LJ 521 420
      * *Kunhimohammed* v. *Ayishakutty,* AIR 2010 (NOC) 992 (Ker) 422
- Payment of Customary Amounts 423
      * *Thilothama* v. *Kunjappan,* 1983 Cr LJ 273 (Ker): I (1983) DMC 241:
  1983 Ker LT 90 423
- Can Payment under Customary Law Absolve Husband of his Liability under the Code of Criminal Procedure 424
      * *Bai Tahira* v. *Ali Hussain Fissalli Chothia,* AIR 1979 SC 362:
  1979 Cr LJ 151: (1979) 2 SCC 316 424

♦ **Guardianship and Custody** 426
- Welfare of Child and not Legal Right of the Parties to be Considered 426
      * *Farjanabai* v. *S.K. Ayub Dadamiya,* AIR 1989 Bom 357:
  1989 Mah LJ 373: (1989) 1 Hindu LR 717 426

- Welfare of Child to have Precedence over Personal Law — 427
  * *Irfan Ahmad Shaikh* v. *Mumtaz*, AIR 1999 Bom 25:
    1998 (2) Hindu LR 485: 1998 (3) Mah LJ 583 — 427
- Mother not Earning is Immaterial — 428
  * *Wazid Ali* v. *Rehana Anjum*, AIR 2005 MP 141: 2005 (2) Hindu LR 562:
    2005 (3) MPLJ 319 — 428
- Welfare of Child and not Personal Law nor Re-marriage to Determine Custody — 429
  * *Poolakkal Ayisakutty* v. *Parat Abdul Samad*, AIR 2005 Ker 68:
    ILR (2005) 1 Ker 14: 2005 (1) Ker LJ 7 — 429

♦ **Select cases under Christian Law** — 431
- Incompatibility or Absence of Prospects of Happy Life: No decree on ground of Mental Illness/Abnormality — 431
  * *C. Solomon* v. *Josephine*, AIR 1959 Mad 151: (1959) 1 Mad LJ 171:
    ILR (1959) Mad 278 — 431
- No Mutual Consent Divorce (Pre-2001 Amendment) — 432
  * *Reynold Rajamani* v. *Union of India*, AIR 1982 SC 1261:
    (1982) 2 SCC 474: II (1982) DMC 268 — 432
- Strong Plea for Uniform Marriage Laws — 433
  * *Jorden Diengdeh* v. *S.S. Chopra*, AIR 1985 SC 935: (1985) 3 SCC 62:
    II (1985) DMC 42 — 433
- Annulment of Marriage: Concealment of Vasectomy before Marriage is Fraud — 434
  * *Best Morning* v. *Nirmalendu*, AIR 1987 Gau 63: II (1987) DMC 214:
    (1987) 2 Gau LR 324 — 434
- Constitutional Vires of Pre-amendment Act (Divorce Law) — 434
  * *Ammini E.J.* v. *Union of India*, AIR 1995 Ker 252: 1995 (1) Ker LJ 624 — 434
- Jurisdiction of Ecclesiastical Courts — 436
  * *George Sebastian* v. *Molly Joseph*, I (2000) DMC 716 (Ker) — 436
- Amendment of Divorce Act – Operation to be Prospective — 437
  * *Deepa Raj Kumar Singh* v. *Deepak Kumar*, AIR 2005 Pat 71 (FB):
    II (2005) DMC 352: 2005 (2) Hindu LR 193 — 437
- Waiting Period of Two Years for Petition for Mutual Consent Divorce Arbitrary: Reduced to One Year — 438
  * *Saumya Ann Thomas* v. *Union of India*, II (2010) DMC 526 (Ker) — 438
- Child Custody and Visitation: Father Flouting Court Order — 440
  * *Elizabeth Denshaw* v. *Arvind M. Denshaw*, AIR 1987 SC 3:
    (1987) 1 SCC 42: 1986 (4) Supreme 487 — 440

♦ **Family Courts** — 441
- Constitutional Validity of Family Courts Act, 1984 — 441
  * *Lata Pimple* v. *Union of India*, AIR 1993 Bom 255:
    1994 (1) Bom CR 668: 1993 (2) Civ LJ 208 — 441

- Plea for Providing Legal Assistance 442
  * *Leela Mahadeo Joshi* v. *Mahadeo Sitaram Joshi,* AIR 1991 Bom 105:
    II (1991) DMC 125: 1991 (1) Hindu LR 313 442
- Legal Representation not Allowed 443
  * *Kailash Bhansali* v. *Surender Kumar,* AIR 2000 Raj 390:
    2001 (1) Marri LJ 601: 2000 (2) Raj LR 697 443
- Appearance of Recognised Agent not Barred 444
  * *Cyprian D'Souza* v. *Rene D'Souza,* AIR 2003 Kant 64:
    ILR (2002) 4 Kant 5145: 2003 (1) Kant LJ 401 444
  * *Pavithra* v. *Rahul Raj,* AIR 2003 Mad 138: 2003 (4) All Ind Cas 283:
    2003 (2) Hindu LR 680 445
- Jurisdiction 446
  * *K.A. Abdul Jaleel* v. *T.A. Shahida,* AIR 2003 SC 2525:
    2003 AIR SCW 2710: (2003) 4 SCC 166 446
  * *Leby Issac* v. *Leena M. Ninan,* AIR 2005 Ker 285: ILR 2005 (3) Ker 597:
    2005 (2) Ker LJ 652 447
  * *K.B. Anil Kumar* v. *N.S. Sheela,* AIR 2012 Ker 1 448

♦ **Foreign Divorce Decree** 450
- Forum Hunting to Invoke Jurisdiction 450
  * *Satya* v. *Teja Singh,* AIR 1975 SC 105: 1975 Cr LJ 52: (1975) 1 SCC 120 450
- Divorce Decree Passed by a Foreign Court, Having Neither Jurisdiction nor Ground—Such Decree cannot be Recognised in India 451
  * *Narasimha Rao* v. *Y. Venkatalakshmi,* (1991) 2 SCALE 1:
    (1991) 3 SCC 451 451
- Non Contest of Petition does not Imply Submission to Jurisdiction 453
  * *Veena Kalia* v. *Jatinder Nath Kalia,* AIR 1996 Del 54: 1995 (59) DLT 635:
    1996 Marri LJ 423 453

♦ **Miscellanceous** 455
- Parsi Law – Presence of Delegates in Matrimonial Trials 455
  * *Pistonji Kekobund Bharucha* v. *Aloo,* AIR 1984 Bom 75:
    I (1983) DMC 468: (1983) 2 Bom CR 312 455
- *Stridhana* & Criminal Breach of Trust and Misappropriation 456
  * *Pratibha Rani* v. *Suraj Kumar,* AIR 1985 SC 628: 1985 Cr LJ 817:
    (1985) 2 SCC 370 456
- Accident Claims Compensation to Wife Living Separately 457
  * *Sachdeva Rice Mills* v. *Raj Anand,* AIR 1988 P&H 136:
    (1986) 90 Punj LR 576: 1987 ACJ 821 457
- *Ex-parte* Decree – Whether Abates on Death of Decree-holder 458
  * *Yallawwa* v. *Shantavva,* AIR 1997 SC 35: 1996 AIR SCW 4185:
    1997 (11) SCC 159 458
- Right of Children of Void Marriage 460

- * *Rameshwari Devi* v. *State of Bihar,* AIR 2000 SC 735:
  2000 AIR SCW 273: (2000) 2 SCC 431 — 460
- Husband's Property Forfeited under SAFEMA: Wife no Right to Appeal — 461
  - * *Shobha Suresh Jumani* v. *Appellate Tribunal, Forfeited Property,*
    AIR 2001 SC 2288: 2001 Cr LJ 2583: 2001 AIR SCW 2051 — 461
- Settlement deed *per se* does not Confer Absolute Right in Properties — 462
  - * *Kokilambal* v. *N. Raman,* AIR 2005 SC 2468: 2005 AIR SCW 2435:
    (2005) 11 SCC 234 — 462
- Petition for Annulment: Death of Mother whether Child can
  Continue Litigation — 463
  - * *Balwinder Kaur* v. *Gurmukh Singh,* AIR 2007 P&H 74:
    2007 (56) All Ind Cas 466: 2007 (2) CCC 587 — 463
- Court's Inherent Powers to Quash Proceedings under
  Section 498A etc., IPC — 465
  - * *B.S. Joshi* v. *State of Haryana,* (2003) 4 SCC 675: AIR 2003 SC 1386:
    2003 Cr LJ 2028 — 465
- Wife of void Marriage: Whether 'relative' under Section 498A, IPC — 466
  - * *Ranjana Gopalrao Thorat* v. *State of Maharashtra,* 2007 Cr LJ 3866 (Bom):
    2007 (5) AIR BomR 271: 2007 All MR (Cri) 2298 — 466
- Allegations of Dowry Harassment where Marriage not Valid — 467
  - * *Reema Aggarwal* v. *Anupam,* AIR 2004 SC 1418: 2004 Cr LJ 892:
    2004 AIR SCW 344 — 467

TABLE OF CASES

A

A. Ahathinamiligai v. Arumughnam, 1988 Cr LJ 6 (Mad): 1987 Mad LW (Cri) 278	265
A. Jayachandra v. Aneel Kaur, AIR 2005 SC 534: 2005 AIR SCW 163: (2005) 2 SCC 22	82
A. Yousuf Rawther v. Sowramma, AIR 1971 Ker 261: 1970 Ker LJ 544: ILR (1971) 1 Ker 154	400
A.K. Rathod v. B.A. Rathod, I (2001) DMC 87 (Guj)	233
A.V. Janardhan Rao v. M. Aruna Kumari, AIR 2000 AP 127: 2000 (1) CCC 690: II (2000) DMC 118	123
Abbayolla M. Subba Reddy v. Padmamma, AIR 1999 AP 19: 1998 (3) CCC 426: I (2000) DMC 266	214, 387
Abdul Azeem v. Fahimunnisa, AIR 1969 Mys 226: (1967) 1 Mys LJ 675: 10 Law Rep 412	399
Abdul Jaleel v. Shahida, AIR 2003 SC 2525	449
Abdurahiman v. Khairunneesa, I (2010) DMC 707 (Ker DB): 2010 (1) KLT 891	406, 407, 408
Abhishek Sharma v. State of Uttar Pradesh, AIR 2009 All 77: 2009 (2) ALJ 435: 2009 AIHC 1745	334
Ajay Sayajirao Desai v. Rajashree Ajay Desai, AIR 2005 Bom 278: 2005 (3) All MR 577: 2005 Bom CR Sup 793	84
Ajit Bhagwandas Udeshi v Kumud Ajit Udeshi, AIR 2003 Bom 120: 2003 (3) Bom CR 224: I (2003) DMC 602	228
Ajith Kumar v. Shaima, AIR 2010 (NOC) 229 (Ker)	253
Akash v. State of Andhra Pradesh, AIR 2000 AP 261: II (2000) DMC 490: 2000 (2) Hindu LR 603	301
Altafan v. Ibrahim, AIR 1924 All 116	399
Amal Saha v. Basana Saha, AIR 1988 Gau 22: (1987) 2 Gua LR 84: (1987) 2 Civ LJ 238	300
Amarendra Mansingh v. Sanatan Singh, AIR 1933 PC 155: ILR 12 Pat 642: 60 Ind App 242	322
Amina v. Hassan Koya, AIR 2004 SC 1227: 2003 Cr LJ 2540: 2003 AIR SCW 2496	395
Amit Chandubhai Chauhan v. Ahmedabad Municipal Corporation, AIR 2011 Guj 145	309
Amit Kumar Sharma v. VIth Addl. District and Sessions Judge, Bijnor, AIR 1999 All 4: 1999 All LJ 25: 1999 (1) CCC 272	225
Amma Khatoon v. Kashim Ansari, AIR 2001 Jhar 28: 2001 AIR Jhar HCR 1: 2001 (2) BLJR 1228	403
Ammini E.J. v. Union of India, AIR 1995 Ker 252: 1995 (1) Ker LJ 624	434, 439
Anandi D Jadhav v. Nirmala Ramchandra Kore, AIR 2000 SC 1386: 2000 AIR SCW 1161: (2000) 3 SCC 703	264
Ananth Gopal v. Gopal Narayan, 1985 Cr LJ 152 (Kant): 1985 (1) Hindu LR 222: ILR 1985 Kant 2607	266
Angrez Kaur v. Baldev Singh, AIR 1980 P&H 171: 1979 Hindu LR 561: 1980 Marri LJ 54	120
Anil Kumar Jain v. Maya Jain, AIR 2010 SC 229 (MP): 2009 AIR SCW 5899: (2009) 10 SCC 415	105, 107, 111, 112
Anita Jain v. Rajendra Jain, AIR 2010 Raj 56	439
Anita Karmokar v. Birendra Chandra Karmokar, AIR 1962 Cal 88: 65 Cal WN 786: ILR (1962) 2 Cal 23	192
Anita Sabharwal v. Anil Sabharwal, (1997) 11 SCC 490	106, 114
Anjali Bhan v. Ajay Kumar Bhan, AIR 2011 J&K 54	51
Annie Besant v. G. Narayaniah, AIR 1914 PC 41: 12 All LJ 1155	295
Anokha v. State of Rajasthan, AIR 2004 SC 2820: 2004 AIR SCW 1363: (2004) 1 SCC 382	341
Anu Seth v. Rohit Narain Seth, (2000) 87 DLT 486: 2001 (3) Civil LJ 308	179
Anupama v. Ashwani Kumar, I (2002) DMC 665 (P&H)	256
Aruna Basu Mullick v. Dorothea Mitra, AIR 1983 SC 916: (1983) 3 SCC 522: II (1983) DMC 289	251

Asha Gupta v. Rajiv Kumar Gupta, AIR 2005 P&H 134: 2005 (2) CCC 106:
2005 (2) Punj LR 45   35
Ashabai Kate v. Vithal Bhika Nade, AIR 1990 SC 670 (Bom): JT 1989 (4) SC 163:
1989 Mat LR 449   320, 323
Ashabi B. Takke v. Bashasab Takke, AIR 2003 Kant 172: ILR 2003 (1) Kant 737:
2003 (2) Kant LJ 420   245
Ashok Hurra v. Rupa Bipin Zaveri, AIR 1997 SC 1266: 1997 AIR SCW 1314:
(1997) 4 SCC 226   101, 106, 114
Atluri Brahmanandan (dead) through L.R's v. Anne Sai Bapuji, AIR 2011 SC 545   308
Attar Singh Jain v. Amit Singh Jain, (1982) Cr LJ 211 (Del)   262

B

B. Sivanandy v. P. Bhagavathyamma, AIR 1962 Mad 400: 75 Mad LW 161   12
B.N. Panduranga Shet v. S.N. Vijay Laxmi, AIR 2003 Kant 357: ILR (2003) 3 Kant 1852:
2003 (3) Kant LJ 247   32
B.P. Achala Anand v. S. Appi Reddy, (2005) 2 SCALE 105: AIR 2005 SC 986:
2005 AIR SCW 934   173, 174, 181
B.R. Mehta v. Atma Devi, AIR 1987 SC 2220: 1987 4 SCC 183: JT 1987 (4) SC 474   170, 178, 179
B.S. Joshi v. State of Haryana, (2003) 4 SCC 675: AIR 2003 SC 1386: 2003 Cr LJ 2028   465
Babui Panmato v. Ram Agya Singh, AIR 1968 Pat 190   67
Baby Sarojam v. S. Vijayakrishnan Nair, AIR 1992 Ker 277: ILR (1992) 2 Ker 449:
1992 (2) Ker LJ 257   430
Bai Laxmiben v. Bharatbhai Vechatbhai Patel, 1986 Cr LJ 1418 (Guj): I (1986) DMC 129:
1986 (27) Guj LR 272   236
Bai Tahira v. Ali Hussain Fissalli Chothia, AIR 1979 SC 362: 1979 Cr LJ 151:
(1979) 2 SCC 316   424
Bajrang Rai v. Ismail Mian, AIR 1978 Pat 339: 1978 BLJR 497: 1978 Pat LJR 519   192
Bakulbai v. Gangaram, 1988 (1) SCALE 188   204, 350
Balbir Kaur v. Harinder Kaur, AIR 2003 P&H 174: 2003 (2) CCC 80:
2003 (2) Marri LJ 499   278, 356
Baldev Raj v. Bimla Sharma, AIR 2006 HP 33   142
Balkrishna Kadam v. Sangeeta Kadam, AIR 1997 SC 3562: 1997 AIR SCW 3667:
(1997) 7 SCC 500   151
Balwinder Kaur v. Gurmukh Singh, AIR 2007 P&H 74: 2007 (56) All Ind Cas 466:
2007 (2) CCC 587   463
Balwinder Kaur v. Hardeep Singh, AIR 1998 SC 764: 1998 AIR SCW 474: (1997) 11 SCC 701   145
Balwinder Singh v. Gurpal Kaur, AIR 1985 Del 14: I (1985) DMC 35: (1985) 1 Hindu LR 369   384
Bani v. Parkash Singh, AIR 1996 P&H 175: I (1997) DMC 5: ILR (1997) 1 P&H 118   256
Bauramma v. Siddappa Jeevappa Patarad, AIR 2003 Kant 342: ILR 2003 (1) Kant 579:
2003 (1) Kant LJ 581   382
Benjamin Cardoza v. Gladys Benjamin Cardoza, AIR 1997 Bom 175P: II (1997) DMC 460:
1997 (2) Hindu LR 677   434
Best Morning v. Nirmalendu, AIR 1987 Gau 63: II (1987) DMC 214:
(1987) 2 Gau LR 324   70, 75, 434
Bhagat Ram v. Teja Singh, AIR 2002 SC 1: 2001 AIR SCW 4507: (2002) 1 SCC 210   362
Bhagat Singh v. Emperor, (1910) 11 Cr LJ 427 (Punj): (1910) 6 Ind Cas 960   273
Bhagat Singh v. Teja Singh, AIR 1999 SC 1944: 1999 AIR SCW 1626: (1999) 4 SCC 86   362
Bhagwan Dass v. Prabhati Ram, AIR 2004 Del 137: 2004 (14) All Ind Cas 807:
2003 (108) DLT 25   359
Bhagwan Dutt v. Kanta Devi, AIR 1975 SC 83: 1975 Cr LJ 40: (1975) 2 SCC 386   217
Bharat Heavy Plates and Vessels Ltd. (in re:), AIR 1985 AP 207: (1985) 2 Andh LT 127:
(1985) 3 Com LJ 1   175
Bharat Kumar v. Selma Mini, II (2007) DMC 538: AIR 2007 Ker 197: ILR (2007) 1 Ker 696   448

Bharatha Matha v. R. Vijaya Renganathan, AIR 2010 SC 2685: 2010 AIR SCW 3503:
(2010) 6 Scale 53   195
Bhartiraj v. Sumesh Sachdeo, AIR 1986 All 259   184
Bhaswati Sarkar v. Angshuman Sarkar, AIR 2000 Cal 210: 2000 (2) Cal LJ 219:
II (2001) DMC 237   76
Bhau Saheb v. Leelabai, AIR 2004 Bom 283 (FB): 2004 (13) All Ind Cas 948:
2004 (1) Hindu LR 615   208
Bhaurao Shankar Lokhande v. State of Maharashtra, AIR 1965 SC 1564: 1966 (1) SCJ 298:
(1965) 2 SCR 837   158, 349
Bhavna Adwani v. Manohar Adwani, AIR 1992 MP 105: I (1992) DMC 286:
1992 (1) Hindu LR 549   142
Bhoolaram v. Ramlal, AIR 1989 MP 198   316
Bhupinder Kaur v. Vijaya Singh, 2003 AlHC 4033 (P&H)   283
Bijaya Lakshmi Kundingi v. Kamala Lochana Kundingi, AIR 2005 Ori 120:
2005 (33) All Ind Cas 580: 2005 (2) Ori LR 23   125
Bimla Devi v. Subhash Chandra Yadav, AIR 1992 Pat 76: 1991 (1) Civ LJ 471:
II (1991) DMC 587   295
Bini v. Sundaran K.V., AIR 2008 Ker 84: ILR (2008) 1 Ker 203: 2008 (1) Ker LJ 162   147
Bipinchandra Jaisinghbai Shah v. Prabhavati, AIR 1957 SC 176: 1957 SCR 838: 1957 SCC 48   57
Braj Kishore Sinha v. Rekha Sinha, I (1992) DMC 331: AIR 1992 Pat 173: 1991 (2) BLJR 990   192
Brajendra Singh v. State of Madhya Pradesh, AIR 2008 SC 1056: 2008 AIR SCW 652:
(2008) 1 SCALE 372   312, 317
Brijendra Singh v. State of Madhya Pradesh, (2008) 1 MLJ 1083   318
Buddhi Sahu v. Lohusani Sahuni, ILR 1970 Cut 1215   12

C

C. Masilmani Muddaliar v. Idol of Swaminathaswami, AIR 1996 SC 1697:
1996 AIR SCW 1780: (1996) 8 SCC 525   345
C. Solomon v. Josephine, AIR 1959 Mad 151: (1959) 1 Mad LJ 171: ILR (1959) Mad 278   431
C.M. Arumugam v. S. Rajgopal, AIR 1976 SC 939: (1976) 1 SCC 863: (1976) 3 SCR 82   329
C.P. Saji v. Union of India, AIR 2012 Ker 23   444
Capt. Ramesh Chander Kaushal v. Veena Kaushal, AIR 1978 SC 1807: (1978) 4 SCC 70:
1978 Cr LJ 3   224, 248
Capt. Suneel v. Union of India, AIR 2004 Del 95: 2003 (12) All Ind Cas 915:
2003 (107) DLT 224   259
Chain Singh Verma v. Kavita, (2006) 3 Shimla LC 206   393
Chakki v. Ayyappan, 1988 (1) KLT 556   430
Chand Dhawan v. Jawaharlal Dhawan, (1993) 3 SCC 406: 1993 AIR SCW 2548:
1993 Cr LJ 2930   200, 204, 387
Chandana Guha Roy v. Gautam Guha Roy, AIR 2004 Cal 36: 2004 (17) All Ind Cas 790:
I (2005) DMC 607   217
Chander Kanta v. Hans Kumar, AIR 1989 Del 73: I (1988) DMC 509: (1988) 14 DRJ 337   100
Chander Prakash v. Sita Rani, AIR 1968 Del 174: 1968 Cr LJ 1153: 71 Punj LR (D) 167   222
Chanderkala Trivedi v. Dr. S.P. Trivedi, (1993) 3 SCALE 541: (1993) 4 SCC 232:
JT (1993) 4 SC 644   42, 78, 90
Chandra Mohini Srivastava v. Avinash Prasad Srivastava, AIR 1967 SC 581:
(1967) 1 SCR 864: 1967 (1) SCJ 42   153
Chandrakala Menon v. Vipin Menon, (1993) 2 SCC 6: 1993 All CriC 144   295
Chanmuniya v. Virendra Kumar, (2010) 10 SCALE 602: 2010 AIR SCW 6497   194, 207
Chantan v. C. Mathu, AIR 1917 Mad 276: ILR 39 Mad 957: 17 Cr LJ 16   269
Chetan Dass v. Kamla Devi, AIR 2001 SC 1709: 2001 AIR SCW 1660: (2001) 4 SCC 250   114
Chiranjilal Srilal Goenka v. Jasjit Singh, AIR 2001 SC 266: 2000 AIR SCW 4323:
(2001) 1 SCC 486   334

Chiranjit Kaur Nagi v. Government of NCT, Delhi, I (2008) DMC 45 (Del) 4
Chitra Sengupta v. Dhruba Jyoti Sengupta, AIR 1988 Cal 98: II (1987) DMC 162:
    1987 Mat LR 306 192
Cyprian D'Souza v. Rene D'Souza, AIR 2003 Kant 64: ILR (2002) 4 Kant 5145:
    2003 (1) Kant LJ 401 444

D

D. Velusamy v. D. Patchaiammal, AIR 2011 SC 479 195, 196, 207
Daggupati Jayalakshmi v. State, 1993 Cr LJ 3162 (AP): 1993 (3) Crimes 1117:
    II (1993) DMC 581 466
Daljit Singh v. Dara Singh, AIR 2000 Del 292: 2000 (85) DLT 794: II (2000) DMC 134 356
Danial Latifi v. Union of India, (2001) 6 SCALE 537: AIR 2001 SC 3958:
    2001 Cr LJ 4660 416, 421
Dasarathi Ghosh v. Anuradha Ghosh, 1988 Cr LJ 64 (Cal): II (1986) DMC 120:
    1986 (2) Hindu LR 165 222
Debabrata Mondal v. State of West Bengal, AIR 2008 Cal 13: 2008 (2) AIR BomR 222:
    2007 (60) All Ind Cas 523 360
Deen Dayal v. Sanjeev Kumar, AIR 2009 Raj 122 316
Deepa Raj Kumar Singh v. Deepak Kumar, AIR 2005 Pat 71 (FB): II (2005) DMC 352:
    2005 (2) Hindu LR 193 437
Deeplakshmi Zingade v. S.R. Zingade, AIR 2012 Bom 16 39
Devaki v. Narayan, 2006 (3) HLR 505 (Ker) 448
Devaney v. L'Esperance, 195 NJ 247 (2008) 198
Devi Sharma v. Chandra Mohan Sharma, AIR 2003 P&H 327: 2003 (2) Hindu LR 259:
    2004 (1) Marri LJ 385 95
Dhani Ram v. Ram Devi, 1954 All LJ 626 224
Dharmendra Kumar v. Usha Kumar, AIR 1977 SC 2218: 1977 (2) SCJ 471:
    (1978) 1 SCR 315 118, 121, 124, 126, 128, 130
Dikhtar Jahan v. Md. Farooq, AIR 1987 SC 1049: 1987 Cr LJ 849: (1987) 1 SCC 624 184
Dinesh Kumar Mandal v. Mina Devi, AIR 2005 Jhar 77: 2005 (27) All Ind Cas 752:
    2005 (3) Civ LJ 339 86
Dinesh Kumar v. Santosh Devi, AIR 2007 All 30: 2007 (1) ALJ 138: 2006 (65) All LR 889 256
Dinesh Nagda v. Shantibai, AIR 2012 MP 40 40
Dineshkumar Shukla v. Neeta, AIR 2005 MP 106: 2005 (2) Civ LJ 709: 2005 (2) CCC 161 109
Dr. Abdur Rahim Undre v. Padma Abdur Rahim under, AIR 1982 Bom 341:
    I (1982) DMC 204 175
Dr. Surajmani Stella Kujur v. Durga Charan Hansdah, (2001) I Femi - Juris CC 96 (SC):
    AIR 2001 SC 938: 2001 AIR SCW 711 380
Durga Prasanna Tripathy v. Arundhati Tripathy, AIR 2005 SC 3297: 2005 AIR SCW 4045:
    (2005) 7 SCC 353 114
Durgaprasada Rao v. Sudarsanaswamy, AIR 1940 Mad 513: ILR 1940 Mad 653 63, 329
Dwarika Prasad Satpathy v. Bidyut Prava Dixit, 2000 Cr LJ 1 (SC): AIR 1999 SC 3348:
    1999 AIR SCW 3844 205

E

Elizabeth Denshaw v. Arvind M. Denshaw, AIR 1987 SC 3: (1987) 1 SCC 42:
    1986 (4) Supreme 487 295, 440

F

Farjanabai v. S.K. Ayub Dadamiya, AIR 1989 Bom 357: 1989 Mah LJ 373:
    (1989) 1 Hindu LR 717 426
Flg Officer Rajiv Gakhar v. Bhavna @ Sahar Wasif, AIR 2011 SC 2053 (P&H) 11
Fuzlunbi v. K. Khader Vali, AIR 1980 SC 1730: 1980 Cr LJ 1249: (1980) 4 SCC 125 425

G

G.V.N. Kameswara Rao v. G. Jabilli, AIR 2002 SC 576: 2002 AIR SCW 162: (2002) 2 SCC 296   30
Gajara Naran Bhura v. Kanbi Kunverbai Parbat, AIR 1997 Guj 185: 1998 (1) MarriLJ 198:
    1998 Mat LR 306   15
Gajna Devi v. Purshotam Giri, ILR (1977) 1 Del 725: AIR 1977 Del 178: 1978 Hindu LR 116   119
Ganeshappa v. Krishnamma, AIR 2005 Kant 160: ILR 2005 Kant 358: 2005 (2) Kant LJ 262   368
Ganga Sharan Varshney v. Shakuntala Devi, 1990 Cr LJ 128 (All): 1990 All LJ 34:
    I (1990) DMC 71   266
Ganny Kaur v. State, AIR 2007 Del 273: 2008 (1) AKant (NOC) 44: 2007 (142) DLT 35   371
Gaurav Nagpal v. Sumedha Nagpal, AIR 2009 SC 557 (Del): 2008 AIR SCW 7687:
    (2009) 1 SCC 42   297
Gautam Kundu v. State of West Bengal, AIR 1993 SC 2295: 1993 AIR SCW 2325:
    1993 Cr LJ 3233   184, 188
Geeta Jagdish Mangtani v. Jagdish Mangtani, AIR 2005 SC 3508: 2005 AIR SCW 4755:
    (2005) 8 SCC 177   137
Geeta Satish Gokarna v. Satish Gokarna, AIR 2004 Bom 345: 2004 (20) All Ind Cas 839:
    2004 (3) Mah LJ 159   239
George Sebastian v. Molly Joseph, I (2000) DMC 716 (Ker)   436
Germanthangi v. F. Rokunga, AIR 2004 Gau 42: 2005 (1) Gau LR 338:
    2004 (2) Marri LJ 145 (Aizawl Bench)   384
Ghari Lal v. Surjit Kaur, AIR 1997 J&K 72: 1997 Marri LJ 434   202
Ghisalal v. Dhapubai, AIR 2011 SC 644 (MP)   316
Ghulam Kubra Bibi v. Md. Shafi Mohammad Din, AIR 1940 Peshawar 2   394
Ghulam Sakina v. Falak Sher Allah Baksh, AIR 1950 Lah 45: Pak Cas 1949 Lah 104   408
Gindan v. Barelal, AIR 1976 MP 83: 1976 MPLJ 102: 1976 Hindu LR 270   13
Githa Hariharan v. Reserve Bank of India and Vandana Shiva v. J. Bandhopadhyaya,
    AIR 1999 SC 1149: 1999 AIR SCW 811: (1999) 2 SCC 228   286
Goka Kameswari v. Goka Venkataramaiah, AIR 2012 AP 23   39
Gollins v. Gollins, 1964 AC 644: (1963) 3 WLR 176: (1963) 2 All ER 966   44
Gopal Chandra Pal v. Kadambini Dasi, AIR 1924 Cal 364: 73 Ind Cas 235   278
Gourab Datta v. Arundhati Majumdar, AIR 2011 Gau 183   29
Goverdhan Lal v. Gajendra Kumar, AIR 2002 Raj 148: 2001 (3) Raj LR 638:
    2002 (1) WLC 419   295
Govind Singh v. Vidya, AIR 1999 Raj 304: 1999 (3) CCC 219: II (2000) DMC 693   283
Govindrao Ranoji Musale v. Sou. Anandibai, AIR 1976 Bom 433: 1977 Hindu LR 465:
    (1977) 79 Bom LR 73   208
Gulabrao Balwant Rao Shinde v. Chhabubai, Balwant Rao Shinde, AIR 2003 SC 16   350
Gullipilli Sowria Rai v. Bhandaru Pavani, AIR 2009 SC 1085: 2009 AIR SCW 244:
    (2009) 1 SCC 714   8, 10, 11
Gumpha v. Jaibai, (1994) 2 SCC 511   345
Gurbachan Kaur v. Sardar Swaran Singh, AIR 1978 All 255: 1978 All LJ 284:
    1978 All WC 371   43
Gurdit Singh v. Angrez Kaur, AIR 1968 SC 142: (1967) 2 SCR 789   384, 392
Gurpinder Kaur Sahsi v. Ravinder Singh Sahsi, AIR 2005 P&H 187: 2005 (2) Hindu LR 118:
    2005 (3) CCC 66   110
Gursharan Kaur v. State of Rajasthan, 1993 Cr LJ 2076 (Raj): 1993 Cr LR Raj 96:
    1993 (1) Raj LW 103   466
Gurunath v. Kamalabai, (1955) 1 SCR 1135: AIR 1955 SC 206: 1955 SCJ 178   321, 322

H

H (infants) (in re:), (1966) 1 All ER 886: (1966) 1 WLR 381   440
Hamid Khan v. Jammi Bai, ILR 1978 MP 595   424

Hanmant Laxman Salunke v. Shrirang Narayan Kanse, AIR 2006 Bom 123:
   2006 (42) All Ind Cas 158: 2006 (2) Hindu LR 331 — 310
Harcharan Kaur v. Nachhattar Singh, AIR 1988 P&H 27: (1987) 2 Hindu LR 184:
   II (1987) DMC 305 — 100
Hardev Singh v. State of Uttar Pradesh, 1995 Cr LJ 1652 (All): II (1995) DMC 624:
   1995 All LJ 446 — 223
Hari Lal v. Balvantia, AIR 1998 All 211: 1998 All LJ 1371: 1998 (3) CCC 275 — 230
Harvinder Kaur v. Harmander Singh Choudhry, AIR 1984 Del 66: ILR (1984) 1 Del 546:
   1984 Raj LR 187 — 135
Hema Reddy v. Rakesh Reddy, AIR 2002 AP 228 — 95
Hema v. Parthasarthy, 2003 (1) HLR 8 — 256
Hemant Kumar Agrahari v. Lakshmi Devi, AIR 2004 All 126: 2004 All LJ 972:
   2004 (2) CCC 50 — 149
Hemwanti Tripathi v. Harish Narain, AIR 2012 Del 1 — 47
Hirabai Bharucha v. Pirojshah Bharucha, AIR 1945 Bom 537: 47 Bom LR 514 — 239
Hirachand Srinivas Managaonkar v. Sunanda, AIR 2001 SC 1285: 2001 AIR SCW 1196:
   (2001) 4 SCC 125 — 121, 126
Hitesh Bhatnagar v. Deepa Bhatnagar, AIR 2011 SC 1637 — 107
Horton v. Horton, 1940 (3) All ER 380: 163 LT 314: 109 LJP 108 — 44
Hoshie Shavaksha Dholikuka v. Thrity Hoshie Dholikuka, AIR 1982 SC 1457:
   1982 Cr LJ 1937: (1982) 2 SCC 577 — 286
Howarth v. Northcott, 152 Conn 460 — 295

I

Irfan Ahmad Shaikh v. Mumtaz, AIR 1999 Bom 25: 1998 (2) Hindu LR 485:
   1998 (3) Mah LJ 583 — 427
Itwari v. Asghari, AIR 1960 All 684: 1960 All LJ 523: 1960 All WR (HC) 397 — 410

J

Jagalur Madhukeshwar v. B.G. Kamalakshi, AIR 2012 Karn 22 — 36
Jagdish Jugtawat v. Manju Lata, (2002) 11 UP Cr R 313 (Sup Cr): (2002) 5 SCC 422:
   2002 (6) Bom CR 189 — 273
Jagdish Mangtani v. Geeta Jagdish Mangtani, XLIV(i) 2003 Guj LR 309 — 138
Jagir Kaur v. Jaswant Singh, AIR 1963 SC 1521: (1963) 2 Cr LJ 413: (1964) 2 SCR 73 — 267, 273
Jagraj Singh v. Birpal Kaur, AIR 2007 SC 2083: 2007 AIR SCW 3201: (2007) 2 SCC 564 — 146
Jai Prakash Khadria v. Shyam Sunder Agarwalla, AIR 2000 SC 2172:
   2000 AIR SCW 2341: (2000) 6 SCC 598 — 289, 430
Jai Singh v. Shakuntala, AIR 2002 SC 1428: 2002 AIR SCW 1280: (2002) 3 SCC 634 — 327
Jaishree Mohan Otavnekar v. Mohan Govind Otavnekar, AIR 1987 Bom 220:
   1987 Mah LJ 160: 1987 Mah LR 617 — 42
Jamieson v. Jamieson, 1952 AC 525: (1952) 1 All ER 875: (1952) 1 TLR 833 — 21
Jasbir Singh v. Inderjit Kaur, AIR 2003 P&H 317: 2003 (2) Hindu LR 654:
   2004 (1) Marri LJ 175 — 383, 392
Jatina Samir Shah v. Samir Mohit Shah, AIR 2009 (NOC) 2149 (Bom) — 382
Jayashree Ramesh Londhe v. Ramesh Bhikaji Londhe, AIR 1984 Bom 302:
   (1984) 1 Bom CR 586: 1984 Mah LJ 308 — 100
Jinia Keotin v. Kumar Sitaram Manjhi, (2003) 1 SCC 730 — 196
John Vallamattom v. Union of India, AIR 2003 SC 2902: 2003 AIR SCW 3536:
   (2003) 6 SCC 611 — 374
Jordan Diengdeh v. S.S. Chopra, AIR 1985 SC 935: (1985) 3 SCC 62: II (1985) DMC 42 — 166, 433
Joydel Kumar Biswas v. Madhuri Biswas, 1994 Cr LJ 3342 (Cal): I (1996) DMC 12:
   1996 (2) Hindu LR 290 — 238
Jupudi Venkata Vijaya Bhartiar v. Jupudi Kesava Rao, AIR 2003 SC 3314:
   2003 AIR SCW 4706: (2003) 8 SCC 282 — 332

K

K. Kumar v. Leena, II (2010) DMC 519 (Ker): AIR 2010 Kant 75: ILR 2010 Kant 1221	284, 431
K. Preetha v. N. Bhaskaran, AIR 2011 Ker 27	55
K. Venkat Reddy v. Chinnapareddy Viswanadha Reddy, AIR 2009 AP 1: 2009 (73) All Ind Cas 523: 2008 (6) Andh LT 360	293
K. Vimla v. K. Veeraswamy, JT 1991 (2) SC 182: 1991 AIR SCW 754: (1991) 2 SCC 375	387
K.A. Abdul Jaleel v. T.A. Shahida, AIR 2003 SC 2525: 2003 AIR SCW 2710: (2003) 4 SCC 166	446
K.B. Anil Kumar v. N.S. Sheela, AIR 2012 Ker 1	448
K.I. Mohanan v. Jeejabai, AIR 1988 Ker 28: 1986 Ker LJ 833: (1986) 2 Hindu LR 467	100
K.J. v. Smti K. w/o K.J., AIR 1952 Nag 395: ILR (1952) Nag 570	18
K.M.P. Kovilamma v. Moopil Eradi, (1973) Cr LJ 1878: 1973 Ker LT 757: 1972 Ker LJ 893	221
Kailash Bhansali v. Surender Kumar, AIR 2000 Raj 390: 2001 (1) Marri LJ 601: 2000 (2) Raj LR 697	443
Kailash Singh v. Mewalal Singh Gond, AIR 2002 MP 112: 2002 (1) MPHT 526: 2002 (2) MPLJ 163	344
Kailash Wati v. Avodhia Parkash, (1977) 79 Punj LR 216: 1977 Hindu LR 175	59, 63
Kalaben Kalabhai Desai v. Alabhai Karamshibhai Desai, AIR 2000 Guj 232: I (2001) DMC 295: 2001 (1) Hindu LR 493	233
Kalawati v. Devi Ram, AIR 1961 HP 1	12
Kamal Basu Mazumdar v. Usha Bhadra Chowdhury, AIR 2004 Cal 185: 2004 (2) Cal HN 383: 2005 (1) Hindu LR 294	352
Kamla Devi v. State of Himachal Pradesh, AIR 1987 HP 34: (1986) 3 Crimes 151	295
Kamlakar v. T.K. Sambhus, AIR 2004 Bom 479	149
Kamlesh Kumar Agarwal v. Mamta Devi, AIR 2005 Jhar 10: II (2004) DMC 706: 2004 (4) Civ LJ 535	36
Kamleshwari Bai v. Peeluram Sahi, AIR 2010 Chh 16	39
Kanchan Devi v. Promod Kumar Mittal, AIR 1996 SC 3192: 1996 AIR SCW 1933: (1996) 8 SCC 90	79, 113
Kanchan Sanjay Gujar v. Sanjay Gujar, AIR 2009 Bom 151: 2009 (4) CCC 509: II (2009) DMC 566	127
Kangal v. Atwariya Devi, AIR 2002 All 77: 2002 All LJ 603: 2002 (2) CCC 210	231
Kanna alias Mahalakshmi Ammal v. Krishnaswami Achari, AIR 1972 Mad 247: 84 Mad LW 755	140
Karnot (in re:), (1964) 2 All ER 339	285
Kashibai v. Parwatibai, 1995 AIR SCW 4631: (1995) 6 SCC 213: JT 1995 (7) SC 48	316, 317
Kaslefsky v. Kaslefsky, 1950 (2) All ER 398: 66 TLR (Pt. 2) 616	21, 54
Kenchaya Kom Sanyallappa Hosmani v. Girimalappa Channappa Samasagar, AIR 1924 PC 209: 51 Ind App 368: 48 Bom 569	366
Keshav Ganpatrao Hedau v. Damodhar Udaramji Kandrikar, AIR 2005 Bom 118: 2005 (2) Civ LJ 279: 2005 (1) Hindu LR 140	293
Kewal Kumar v. Pawna Devi, AIR 2011 HP 58	392
Khagembam Sadhu v. Khangembam Ibohal Singh, AIR 2001 Gau 95	310
Khatijan v. Abdulla, AIR 1943 Sind 65: ILR 1942 Kant 535	401
Khazan Singh v. Union of India, AIR 1980 Del 60	329
King v. King, 1952 (2) All ER 584: 1953 AC 124: (1952) 2 TLR 429	44
Kiran Devi v. Batul Kumar Verma, AIR 2011 Pat 16	162
Kiran v. Sharad Dutt, (2000) 10 SCC 243	106, 114
Kirti Sharma v. Civil Judge, Senior Division, Etah, AIR 2005 All 197: 2005 (59) All LR 53: 2005 (2) All WC 1741	190
Kirtikant D. Vadodaria v. State of Gujarat, (1996) 4 Scale 44: (1996) 4 SCC 479: JT 1996 (6) SC 244	263

Kirtikumar Maheshankar Joshi v. Pradipkumar Karunashanker Joshi, AIR 1992 SC 1447:
   1992 AIR SCW 1528: (1992) 3 SCC 573   295
Kisan Baburao Memane v. Suresh Sadu Memane, AIR 1996 Bom 50: 1996 (1) Civ LJ 794:
   1996 (1) ICC 625   332
Kokilambal v. N. Raman, AIR 2005 SC 2468: 2005 AIR SCW 2435: (2005) 11 SCC 234   462
Komal S. Padukone v. Principal Judge, AIR 1999 Kant 427: ILR 1999 Kant 1866:
   1999 (5) Kant LJ 667   445
Komalam Amma v. Kumar Pillai Raghavan, AIR 2009 SC 636: (2008) 14 SCC 345:
   2008 AIR SCW 7799   180
Kongini Balan v. M. Visalakshy, 1986 Cr LJ 697 (Ker)   257
Krishnakant Mulashankar Vyas v. Reena Krishna Vyas, AIR 1999 Bom 127:
   1999 (1) CCC 423: II (1999) DMC 221   208
Krishnakant v. Reena, 1999 (1) Mah LJ 388: AIR 1999 Bom 127: 1999 (2) Hindu LR 479   386
Krishnaswami Ayer v. Chandravadana, (1918) 25 MLJ 349: AIR 1914 Mad 594:
   ILR 37 Mad 565   273
Krishni Devi v. Tulsan Devi, AIR 1972 P&H 305: 1972 Cur LJ 434: 74 Punj LR 561   12
Kuldeep Kumar Dogra v. Monika Sharma, AIR 2010 HP 58   139
Kuldip Kaur v. Surinder Singh, 1989 Cr LJ 794 (SC): AIR 1989 SC 232: (1989) 1 SCC 405   252
Kulsumbai Kom Abdul Kadir v. Abdul Kadir Walad Saikh Ahmad,
   ILR 1921 Vol. XLV Bom 157   396
Kumar Sursen v. State of Bihar, AIR 2008 Pat 24: 2008 (2) AIR JharR 6: 2008 (4) CCC 569   311
Kunhi Moyin v. Pathumma, 1976 KLT 87   424
Kunhimohammed v. Ayishakutty, AIR 2010 (NOC) 992 (Ker)   422

L

L.J. Formosa v. Formosa, (1962) 3 All ER 419   451
Lachman Singh v. Kirpa Singh, AIR 1987 SC 1616: 1987 2 SCC 547:
   JT 1987 (3) SC 175   358, 360, 361
Lakshmi Kant Pandey v. Union of India, 2010 (6) SCALE 23   305, 340
Lakshmi Kant Pandey v. Union of India, AIR 1984 SC 469: (1984) 2 SCC 244:
   (1984) 2 SCR 795: 1984 Marri LJ 249   305, 338, 341
Lakshmikant Pandey v. Union of India, (2001) 9 SCC 379: (2003) 10 SCALE 536   341
Lakshmikant Pandey v. Union of India, AIR 1992 SC 118: 1991 AIR SCW 2806:
   (1991) 4 SCC 33   341
Lalit Mohan v. Tripta Devi, AIR 1990 J&K 7: 1989 Kash LJ 96: II (1989) DMC 23   282
Lana v. Lana, 1955 AC 402: (1954) 3 All ER 571: (1954) 3 WLR 762   58
Larley v. John alias Johny, AIR 2004 Pat 53: 2004 (2) Hindu LR 339:
   2005 (30) All Ind Cas 770 (FB)   438
Lata Kamat v. Vilas, AIR 1989 SC 1477: (1989) 2 SCC 613: JT 1989 (3) SC 48   154
Lata Pimple v. Union of India, AIR 1993 Bom 255: 1994 (1) Bom CR 668:
   1993 (2) Civ LJ 208   441
Lata v. Vikas, AIR 1987 Bom 231: I (1987) DMC 484: (1987) 1 Hindu LR 440   155
Lataben Y. Goswami v. Yogendra Kumar Shankargir Goswami, AIR 1996 Guj 103:
   1996 (1) CCC 188: 1996 (1) Hindu LR 712   244
Lawsen v. Lawsen, 1955 (1) All ER 341: (1955) 1 WLR 200   58
Le Mesurier v. Le Mesurier [1895] AC 517   450
Leby Issac v. Leena M. Ninan, AIR 2005 Ker 285: ILR 2005 (3) Ker 597:
   2005 (2) Ker LJ 652   447, 449
Leela Mahadeo Joshi v. Mahadeo Sitaram Joshi, AIR 1991 Bom 105: II (1991) DMC 125:
   1991 (1) Hindu LR 313   442
Lekha v. Anil Kumar, (2006) 12 SCALE 163   292
Lila Gupta v. Laxmi Narian, AIR 1978 SC 1351: (1978) 3 SCC 258: 1978 (2) SCJ 428   153
Lily Thomas v. Union of India, AIR 2000 SC 1650: 2000 AIR SCW 1760: 2000 Cr LJ 2433   166

Lissack v. Lissack, 1950 (2) All ER 233: 1951-P 1   21
Love Kumar v. Sunita Puri, AIR 1997 P&H 189: ILR (1997) 2 P&H 79: II (1998) DMC 711   144

M

M. Ajith Kumar v. K. Jeeja @ Sanila, AIR 2009 Ker 100: 2009 (78) All Ind Cas 372:
   2009 (1) Ker LT 634   129
M. Areefa Beevi v. K.M. Sahib, 1983 Cr LJ 412 (Ker): ILR (1982) 2 Ker 49: 1982 Ker LJ 186   277
M. Aruna Kumari v. A.V. Janardhan Rao, 2003 (5) SCALE 290   122
M. Govindaraju v. K. Munisami Gounder, AIR 1997 SC 10: 1996 AIR SCW 4157:
   (1996) 5 SCC 467   379
M. Revathi v. R. Alamelu, AIR 2009 Mad 86: 2009 (77) All Ind Cas 812:
   2009 (5) Mad LJ 376   354
M.D. Krishnan v. M.C. Padma, AIR 1968 Mys 226: (1967) 2 Mys LJ 432: 12 Law Rep 209   149
M.K. Hari Govindan v. A.R. Rajaram, AIR 2003 Mad 315: 2003 (3) Ind LD 856   295
M.M. Malhotra v. Union of India, AIR 2006 SC 80: 2005 AIR SCW 5497:
   (2005) 8 SCC 351   11, 160
M.V. Elizabeth v. Harwan Investment and Trading Pvt. Ltd., AIR 1993 SC 1014:
   1993 AIR SCW 177: (1992) 1 SCR 1003   284
Ma Hari v. Director of Consolidation, 1969 All LJ 623: 1969 All WR (HC) 303   12
Madhavi Ramesh Dudani v. Ramesh K. Dudani, AIR 2006 Bom 94:
   2006 (40) All Ind Cas 446: I (2006) DMC 386   7
Madhu Limaye v. State of Maharashtra, (1977) 4 SCC 551: AIR 1978 SC 47:
   1978 Cr LJ 165   465
Madhubala v. Pushpa Devi, AIR 2010 (NOC) 980 (Utr)   448
Madhukar Bhaskar Sheorey v. Saral Madhukar Sheorey, AIR 1973 Bom 55:
   1972 Mah LJ 762: ILR (1973) Bom 113   117
Madhuri Mukund Chitnis v. Mukund Martand, 1992 Cr LJ 111: 1991 (1) Bom CR 683:
   1991 Bom LR 157   182
Mahabir Agarwal v. Gita Roy, (1962) 2 Cr LJ 528 (Cal)   273
Mahendra Kumar Gaikwad v. Gulabbhai, 2001 Cr LJ 2111 (Bom): 2000 (2) CCC 692:
   2000 (2) Mah LJ 378   265
Mahendra Nath Yadav v. Sheela Devi, II (2010) DMC 487 (SC)   391
Major Jogindar Singh v. Bibi Raj Mohinder Kaur, AIR 1960 Punj 249: ILR (1960) Punj 222:
   1960 Cr LJ 640   221
Mallappa Fakirappa Sanna Nagashetti v. Shivappa, AIR 1962 Mys 140: ILR 1962 Mys 196   361
Malti v. State of Uttar Pradesh, 2000 Cr LJ 4170 (All): 2000 All LJ 2116:
   2001 (1) Hindu LR 403   207
Mangal Singh v. Rattno, AIR 1967 SC 1786: (1967) 3 SCR 454: 1968 (1) SCA 191   345
Mangala Bhivaji Lad v. Dhondiba Rambhau Aher, AIR 2010 Bom 122:
   2010 (4) All MR 716: 2010 (4) Mah LJ 486   212, 214
Mangat Mal v. Punni Devi, (1995) 6 SCC 88: 1995 AIR SCW 3885:
   AIR 1996 SC 172   181, 345, 346
Manish Goel v. Rohini Goel, (2010) 4 SCC 393: AIR 2010 SC 1099:
   2010 AIR SCW 1277   107, 110, 112
Manisha Sandeep Gade v. Sandeep Vinayak Gade, AIR 2005 Bom 180:
   2005 (1) All MR 564: 2005 (1) Bom CR 554   41
Manisha Tyagi v. Capt. Deepak Kumar, (2007) I HLR 297   49
Manisha Tyagi v. Deepak Kumar, AIR 2010 SC 1042: 2010 AIR SCW 1306:
   (2010) 4 SCC 339   48, 49
Margaret v. Chacko, AIR 1971 Ker 1   285
Mary Roy v. State of Kerala, AIR 1986 SC 1011: (1986) 2 SCC 209: 1986 (2) Supreme 296   373
Mary Soniz Zacharia v. Union of India, 1990 (1) KLT 131   435
Master X v. Y, AIR 2003 Del 195: 2003 (69) DRJ 21: 2003 Mat LR 561   186, 188

Case	Page
Maung Tin v. Ma Hmin, 34 Cr LJ 815: AIR 1933 Rang 138	224
Mausami Moitra Ganguli v. Jayant Ganguli, (2008) 6 MLJ 128: (2008) 8 Scale 527: AIR 2008 SC 2262	295
Maya v. Brij Hath, AIR 1982 Del 240: I (1982) DMC 31: 1982 Marri LJ 160	44
McEwan v. McEwan, (1964) 108 Sol Jo 198 CA: 129 JPJ 783	44
McGrath Re, (1893) 1 Ch 143: 62 LJ Ch 208: 67 LT 636	295
Md. Abdul Zalil Ahmed v. Marina Begum, AIR 1999 Gau 28: 1999 (2) Gau LR 369: 1999 (2) Hindu LR 576	402
Md. Ahmad Khan v. Shah Bano, AIR 1985 SC 945: 1985 Cr LJ 875: (1985) 2 SCC 556	166
Md. Ikram Hussain v. State of Uttar Pradesh, AIR 1964 SC 1625: (1964) 2 Cr LJ 590: ILR (1964) 2 All 423	387
Md. Usman v. Sainaba Umma, AIR 1988 Ker 138: (1987) 1 Ker LJ 712: ILR (1988) 1 Ker 28	404
Md. Yunus v. Shamshad Bano, AIR 1985 All 217: 1985 All WC 386: (1985) 11 All LR 313	430
Meena Dutta v. Anirudh Dutta, II (1984) DMC 388: (1985) 1 Hindu LR 280	100
Meenatchi Ammal v. Karuppana Pillai alias Muthuswami Pillai, (XLVIII) ILR Mad 503	269
Meenu Chopra v. Deepak Chopra, AIR 2002 Del 131: 2002 (1) CCC 239: II (2001) DMC 264	224
Merlin Thomas v. C.S. Thomas, AIR 2003 Ker 232: 2003 (6) Ind LD 545: 2003 (1) Ker LJ 633	430
Mithilesh Shrivastava v. Kiran Shrivastava, AIR 2012 Chh 21	39
Mohan Lal Sharma v. Parveen, AIR 2010 P&H 65: 2010 (1) CCC 418: 2010 (1) ICC 212	390
Mohan Lal v. Nihal Singh, AIR 2001 SC 2942: 2001 AIR SCW 4409: (2001) 8 SCC 584	86
Mohd. Ahmad Khan v. Shah Bano Begum, AIR 1985 SC 945: 1985 Cr LJ 875: (1985) 2 SCC 556	413, 416, 421, 425
Mohinder Kaur v. Major Singh, AIR 1972 P&H 184: 73 Punj LR 952	12
Mohinder Singh v. Preet Kaur, 1981 HLR 321 (P&H): AIR 1981 JK 25: 1981 Marri LJ 118	137
Mohinder Singh v. Ravneet Kaur, 2008 MLR 68 (P&H)	240
Molly Joseph v. George Sebastian, AIR 1997 SC 109: 1996 AIR SCW 4267: (1996) 6 SCC 337	436
Monika Rana v. Yogeshwar Singh Sapehia, AIR 2011 HP 54	283
Moonshee Buzloor Ruheen v. Shumsoonissa Begum, (1867) 11 MIA 551	133
Mr. X v. Hospital Z, AIR 1999 SC 495: 1998 AIR SCW 3662: (1998) 8 SCC 296	1, 2
Mr. X v. Hospital Z, AIR 2003 SC 664: 2002 AIR SCW 5335: (2003) 1 SCC 500	2
Mt. Altafan v. Ibrahim, AIR 1924 All 116: 21 All LJ 811: 75 Ind Cas 502	398
Mt. Rajwarin v. Lagan Singh, AIR 1921 Pat 379: 61 Ind Cas 64: 22 Cr LJ 336	273
Muhammed Davood v. Hafsath, AIR 2010 Ker 21	448
Muhammed v. Sainabi, 1976 KLT 711	424
Mukund Martand Chitnis v. Madhuri Mukund Chitnis, AIR 1992 SC 1804: 1992 AIR SCW 2025: 1993 (1) Bom CR 401	181

N

Case	Page
N. Shankar v. S. Saraswathi, (2010) 1 MLJ 959 (Mad)	90
N.B. Bhikshu v. State of Andhra Pradesh, 1993 Cr LJ 3280 (AP): I (1994) DMC 396: 1993 (2) Hindu LR 697	266
N.E. Horo v. Jahan Ara Jaipal Singh, AIR 1972 SC 1840: 1972 (1) SCA 524: (1972) 3 SCR 361	329
N.G. Dastane v. S. Dastane, AIR 1975 SC 1534: (1975) 2 SCC 326: (1975) 3 SCR 967	44, 50, 53
Nagaraj v. Ammayamma, I (2002) DMC 439 (DB Kant)	448
Nagireddi Lakshmi v. Nagireddi Nagaraju, AIR 2005 AP 17	306
Nalini Ranjan Chakravarty v. Kiran Rani Chakravarty, AIR 1965 Pat 442: 1965 (2) Cr LJ 530: ILR 44 Pat 833	273
Nanak Chand v. Chandra Kishore, AIR 1970 SC 446: 1970 Cr LJ 522: (1970) 1 SCR 565	211, 273
Nand Kishore v. Suman, (Mat. Appeal No. 134/2009 dt. 15-12-2009)	111
Nanjamma v. State of Karnataka, 1999 AIHC 3003 (Kant): ILR 1999 Kant 1094	368

Table of Cases

Naraini Bai v. State of Haryana, AIR 2004 P&H 206: 2004 (17) All Ind Cas 367:
2004 (1) Hindu LR 478   370
Narashimaha Murthy v. Susheelabai, AIR 1996 SC 1826: 1996 AIR SCW 2120:
(1996) 3 SCC 644   351, 355
Narasimha Rao v. Y. Venkatalakshmi, (1991) 2 SCALE 1: (1991) 3 SCC 451   451, 454
Narayan Rath v. Kuntala Kumari Rath, AIR 2005 Ori 49: 2004 (2) CLR 748: 2005 Mat LR 263   19
Narayanaswami Naick v. Mangammal, (1905) ILR 28 Mad 315: 15 Mad LJ 143   324
Narinder Kumar v. Suresh Kumari, AIR 1988 Del 222: 1988 Mat LR 235:
(1987) 6 Reports 201   86
Narinder Pal Kaur Chawla v. Manjeet Singh Chawla, AIR 2008 Del 7:
2008 (2) Marri LJ 107: 2008 Mat LR 184   213
Narinderjit Kaur v. Union of India, AIR 1997 P&H 280: 1997 (1) Hindu LR 442:
1997 Marri LJ 331   313
Naseem v. State of Uttar Pradesh, 1999 Cr LJ 301: 1998 All LJ 2270:
1998 (37) All CriC 867 (All)   415
Naval Kishore Somani v. Poonam Somani, AIR 1999 AP 1: 1998 (3) AP LJ 244:
1999 (3) CCC 179   43
Naveen Kohli v. Neelu Kohli, AIR 2006 SC 1675: 2006 AIR SCW 1550:
(2006) 4 SCC 558   87, 90, 114
Navjot Kumar @ Dolly v. Ajit Singh Phull, I (2001) DMC 87 (Karn)   233
Nazir Ahmad v. Emperor, AIR 1936 PC 253: (1936) 37 Cr LJ 897: 63 Ind App 372   387
Neelam Dadasaheb Shewale v. Dadasaheb Bandu Shewale, I (2010) I DMC 344 (Bom)   192, 448
Neelamma v. Sarojamma, (2006) 9 SCC 612   196
Neelu Kohli v. Naveen Kohli, AIR 2004 All 1   87
Neeraja Saraph v. Jayant Saraph, (1994) 6 SCC 461   183, 451
Neeta Kirit Desai v. Bino Samuel George, AIR 2003 Bom 7: 2003 (1) Bom LR 310:
I (2003) DMC 151   80
Nemichand Shantilal Patni v. Basantabai, AIR 1994 Bom 235: 1996 (1) CCC 259:
1994 (2) Hindu LR 55   310
Nil Ratan Kundu v. Abhijit Kundu, (2008) 7 MLJ 248 (SC): AIR 2009 SC (Supp) 732   294
Nilesh Narin Rajesh Lal v. Kashmira Bhupenderbhai Banker, AIR 2010 Guj 3:
2010 (2) CCC 757: 2010 (1) Guj LH 499   9
Nilima Mukherjee v. Kanta Bhusan Ghosh, AIR 2001 SC 2725: 2001 AIR SCW 3062:
(2001) 6 SCC 660   325
Ningappa v. Shivappa, 1994 AIHC 2068 (Kant)   322
Nirmala Manohar Jagesha v. Manohar Shivram Jagesha, AIR 1991 Bom 259:
1991 Mah LJ 267: I (1992) DMC 180   43
Noor Bibi v. Pir Bux, AIR 1950 Sind 8: 1950 Pak Cas Sind 18   401
Noor Saba Khatoon v. Mohd Quasim, AIR 1997 SC 3280: 1997 Cr LJ 3972:
1997 AIR SCW 3343   273, 414

O

Om Prakash v. Radhacharan, (2009) 7 SCALE 51   360, 363, 372

P

P. Archana @ Atchamamba v. Varada Siva Rama Krishna, I (2009) DMC 265 (AP DB):
AIR 2008 AP 216: 2008 (69) All Ind Cas 742   240
P. Malleswaramma v. P. Prathap Reddy, AIR 2006 AP 4: 2006 (38) All Ind Cas 840:
2005 (5) Andh LT 319   45
P.E.K. Kalliani Amma v. K. Devi, AIR 1996 SC 1963: 1996 AIR SCW 2337: (1996) 4 SCC 76   196
P.L. Sayal v. Sarla Rani, AIR 1961 Punj 125: 63 Punj LR 377   21
P.T. Ramankutty Achan v. Kalyanikutty, AIR 1971 Ker 22: 1970 Ker LT 554: 1971 Cr LJ 318   221
P.V. Madhavi v. P.V. Balakrishnan, AIR 2010 Ker 111   303

Padmo v. Surat Ram, 2003 Cr LJ 237 (HP): I (2003) DMC 483: 2003 (1) Hindu LR 523   254
Panchadi Chitti Venkanna v. Panchadi Mahalakshmi, Transfer Appeal No. 578 of 1973   12
Panchireddi Appala Suramma v. Gadela Ganapatlu, AIR 1975 AP 193: (1975) 1 AP LJ 37: ILR (1975) AP 105   12
Pandit Dattaraya Kulkarni v. Laxmi Pandit Kulkarni, (2001) 1 Femi-Juris CC 47 (Bom)   232
Parakkattil Abu v. Pachiyath Beekkutty, AIR 2011 Ker 88   407
Paras Ram v. Kamlesh, AIR 1982 P&H 60: I (1982) DMC 184: ILR (1982) 2 P&H 33   43
Pathumma v. Cholamarakkar, I (2009) DMC 466 (DB Ker)   271
Pavithra v. Rahul Raj, AIR 2003 Mad 138: 2003 (4) All Ind Cas 283: 2003 (2) Hindu LR 680   445
Philips Alfred Malsvin v. V.J. Gonsalves, AIR 1999 Ker 187: ILR (1999) 2 Ker 43: 1999 (1) Ker LJ 247   305, 337
Pinki Jain v. Sanjay Jain, AIR 2005 Del 273: 2005 (2) CCC 795: I (2005) DMC 241   40
Pinninti Venkataramana v. State, AIR 1977 AP 43 (FB): 1977 Cr LJ 368: ILR (1976) AP 837   12
Pistonji Kekobund Bharucha v. Aloo, AIR 1984 Bom 75: I (1983) DMC 468: (1983) 2 Bom CR 312   455
Ponnuthayee Ammal v. Kamakshi Ammal, AIR 1978 Mad 226 (Mad): 1978 Mad LR 241: 1978 Hindu LR 222   464
Poolakkal Ayisakutty v. Parat Abdul Samad, AIR 2005 Ker 68: ILR 2005 (1) Ker 14: 2005 (1) Ker LJ 7   293, 429
Poonam Gupta v. Ghanshayam Gupta, AIR 2003 All 51   81
Poonam v. Sumit Tanwar, AIR 2010 SC 1384: 2010 AIR SCW 2084: (2010) 4 SCC 460   110
Popri Bai v. Teerath Singh, AIR 2004 Raj 128: 2004 (3) Civ LJ 107: 2004 (2) CCC 262   242
Prabhavati v. Sumatilal, AIR 1954 Bom 546   248
Pradeep Kumar Kapoor v. Shailja Kapoor, AIR 1989 Del 10: II (1988) DMC 110: (1988) 2 Hindu LR 397   228
Prafulla Bala Mukherjee v. Satish Chandra Mukherjee, AIR 1998 Cal 86   325
Prakash Alumal Kalandari v. Jahanvi, AIR 2011 Bom 119   108
Pratibha Rani v. Suraj Kumar, AIR 1985 SC 628: 1985 Cr LJ 817: (1985) 2 SCC 370   456
Pratiksha v. Pravin Tapaswi, 2002 (2) HLR 551 (MP)   191
Praveen Mehta v. Inderjit Mehta, AIR 2002 SC 2582: 2002 AIR SCW 2886: (2002) 5 SCC 706   31
Premi v. Daya Ram, AIR 1965 HP 15   12
Prithviraj Singh v. Pavanvir Singh, 1986 Cr LJ 1432 (P&H): ILR (1986) 2 P&H 205   252
Puran Chand v. Kamla Devi, AIR 1981 J&K 5: 1980 Marri LJ 473: 1981 Mat LR 222   202
Pushkar Navnitlal Shah v. Rakhi Pushkar Shah, AIR 2007 Guj 5: 2007 (55) All Ind Cas 505: 2007 (1) Guj LR 859   218

Q

Qayyum Khan v. Noorunisa, 1978 Cr LJ 1476 (AP): 1978 Mat LR 343   424

R

R. Lakshmi Narayan v. Santhi, AIR 2001 SC 2110: 2001 AIR SCW 1820: (2001) 4 SCC 688   94
R. Suresh v. Chandra, AIR 2003 Kant 183: ILR (2003) 3 Kant 1638: 2003 (2) Kant LJ 67   227
R.V. Srinath Prasad v. Nandamuri Jayakrishna, AIR 2001 SC 1056: 2001 AIR SCW 1033: (2001) 4 SCC 71   430
Radha Kumari v. Dr. K.M.K. Nair, AIR 1988 Ker 235   130
Radha v. Mohinder Kumar, (1998) 8 SCC 530   115
Rafiq v. Bashiran, AIR 1963 Raj 239: 1963 Raj LW 954: ILR (1963) 13 Raj 558   430
Raghubar Singh v. Gulab Singh, AIR 1998 SC 2401: 1998 AIR SCW 2393: (1998) 6 SCC 314   347
Raj Kumar Bansal v. Anjana Kumari, AIR 1995 P&H 18: 1994 (1) Hindu LR 417: 1995 (21) Marri LJ 302   143
Raj Kumar Karwal v. Union of India, AIR 1991 SC 45: 1991 Cr LJ 97: (1990) 2 SCC 409   387
Raj Kumari Awasthi v. State of Uttar Pradesh, (2008) 3 ALJ 100   273

Raj Kumari v. Yashodha Devi, 1978 Cri LJ 600	276
Raj Rani v. Bimla Rani, AIR 2011 Del 170	361
Rajan Vasant Revankar v. Shobha Rajan Revankar, AIR 1995 Bom 246: 1995 (1) Bom CR 47: I (1995) DMC 532	43
Rajesh K. Gupta v. Ram Gopal Agarwala, AIR 2005 SC 2426: 2005 Cr LJ 2581: 2005 AIR SCW 2418	290
Rajesh Kumar Singh v. Rekha Singh, AIR 2005 All 16: 2005 All LJ 102: 2004 (23) All Ind Cas 365	34
Rajeshbai v. Shantabai, AIR 1982 Bom 231: 1981 Bom CR 699: 1981 Mah LJ 820	208
Ram Das v. Gandiabai, AIR 1997 SC 1563: 1997 AIR SCW 317: (1997) 1 SCC 74	324
Ram Devi v. Raja Ram, AIR 1963 All 564: 1963 All LJ 658	72
Ram Kali v. Gopal Das, ILR (1971) 1 Del 6: 1971 Raj LR 10	119
Ram Krishna Ramchandra v. Shamrao, ILR (1902) 26 Bom 526: 4 Bom LR 315	321
Ram Narain Gupta v. Rameshwari Gupta, AIR 1988 SC 2260: JT (1988) 3 SC 621: (1988) 4 SCC 247	32, 44, 96
Ram Prasad v. State of Uttar Pradesh, AIR 1961 All 334: 1961 All LJ 383: 1961 All WR (HC) 252	157
Ram Singh v. State, AIR 1963 All 313	273
Rama Ananda Patil v. Appa Bhima Redekar, AIR 1969 Bom 205: 70 Bom LR 773: ILR (1969) Bom 252	361
Raman Khanna v. Sham Kishore Khanna, AIR 2009 HP 42	367
Ramchoddas Narottamdas v. Emperor, AIR 1949 Bom 36: 49 Cr LJ 630	269
Ramesh Babu v. Usha, AIR 2003 Mad 281: (2003) DMC 272: 2003 (1) Mad LJ 576	233
Ramesh Chander v. Savitri, AIR 1995 SC 851: 1995 AIR SCW 647: (1995) 2 SCC 7	113
Ramesh Chandra Ram Pratap Daga v. Rameshwari Ramesh Chandra Daga, (2005) 2 SCC 33: AIR 2005 SC 422: 2004 AIR SCW 6990	215, 385
Ramesh Kumar v. Sunita Devi, AIR 2005 P&H 55: II (2005) DMC 575: 2005 (1) Hindu LR 360	132
Rameshwari Devi v. State of Bihar, AIR 2000 SC 735: 2000 AIR SCW 273: (2000) 2 SCC 431	196, 460
Ranjana Gopalrao Thorat v. State of Maharashtra, 2007 Cr LJ 3866 (Bom): 2007 (5) AIR BomR 271: 2007 All MR (Cri) 2298	466
Ranjit Kaur v. Pavittar Singh, 1992 Cri LJ 262 (P&H): ILR (1992) 2 P&H 107: 1991 (2) Punj LR 421	238
Ranjit Kumar Bhattacharyya v. Sabita Bhattacharyya, AIR 1996 Cal 301: 1996 (1) Cal LJ 465: 1996 (1) Hindu LR 520	205
Ranjit Singh Dhillon v. Punjab School Education Board, AIR 2004 P&H 382: 2004 (24) All Ind Cas 920: 2005 (1) Marri LJ 314	328
Rashida Khatun v. SK. Islam, AIR 2005 Ori 56: 2005 (1) CLR 162: 2005 Mat LR 296	396
Ratneshwar Saikia v. Kalpana Saikia, Crl Rev No. 88/2006 Gau 20-5-11	215
Rattan Prakash v. Bela Sihare, AIR 1996 Del 356: 1997 (1) Hindu LR 204: 1997 Marri LJ 46	358
Ravi Kumar v. State and Shikha Sharma v. State, 2005 (1) DLT 124	15
Reema Aggarwal v. Anupam, AIR 2004 SC 1418: 2004 Cr LJ 892: 2004 AIR SCW 344	467
Reema Bajaj v. Sachin Bajaj, AIR 2012 Raj 8	142
Revti Devi v. Kishan Lal, 1970 Ren CJ 417 (Del): 1970 Ren CR 71	171
Reynold Rajamani v. Union of India, AIR 1982 SC 1261: (1982) 2 SCC 474: II (1982) DMC 268	432
Rita Nijhawan v. Balkishan Nijhawan, AIR 1973 Del 200: (1973) 75 Punj LR (D) 168	22
Rita Rani v. Ramesh Kumar, (1995) 2 HLR 338 (P&H): (1995) 2 Punj LR 434: AIR 1995 P&H 337	384
Robins v. Robins, 1960 (3) All ER 66: (1960) 1 WLR 1089	21
Rohtash Singh v. Ramdevi, (2000) 3 SCC 180: AIR 2000 SC 952: 2000 Cr LJ 1498	215

Roop Narayan Verma v. Union of India, AIR 2007 Chh 64: 2007 Mat LR 538:
 2007 (3) ALJ (NOC) 526 — 131
Roopa v. Santosh Kumar, AIR 2005 All 172: 2005 (25) All Ind Cas 672: 2005 (2) CCC 798 — 115
Rosy Jacob v. Jacob Chakramakkal, AIR 1973 SC 2090: (1973) 1 SCC 840 — 295
Rukhsana Parvin v. Shaikh Mohd. Hussein, 1977 Cr LJ 1041: 1977 Mad LJ 231:
 79 Bom LR 123 (Bom) — 424
Ruma Chakraborty v. Sudha Rani Banerjee, JT 2005 (12) SC 134: AIR 2005 SC 3557:
 2005 AIR SCW 4938 — 171
Rupalli Masthanamma v. Thota Sriramulu, (1982) 1 Andh WR 393 — 277
Rupinder Kaur v. Gurjit Singh Sandhu, (1997) 117 Punj LR 553: (1998) 1 Marri LJ 424 — 48

S

S. Hanumantha Rao v. S. Ramani, AIR 1999 SC 1318: 1999 AIR SCW 1012: (1999) 3 SCC 620 — 28
S. Khushboo v. Kanniammal, (2010) 5 SCC 600: 2070 AIR SCW 2770: 2010 Cr LJ 2828 — 198
S. Narayanan v. Meenakshi, AIR 2006 Ker 143 — 352
S. Ranawat v. State of Gujarat, II (2010) DMC 730 (Guj) — 240
S. Thangavelu v. S. Kannammal, AIR 2005 Mad 106: 2005 (25) All Ind Cas 496:
 2004 (4) Mad LJ 508 — 187, 188
S.P.S. Balasubramaniyam v. Suruttayam @ Andali Padayachi, AIR 1992 SC 756:
 1992 AIR SCW 441: 1992 (3) SCJ 468 — 196
S.R. Batra v. Taruna Batra, AIR 2007 SC 1118 (Del): 2007 AIR SCW 1088:
 (2007) 3 SCC 169 — 170, 177, 280
S.S. Bindra v. Tarvinder Kaur, AIR 2004 Del 442: 2004 (23) All Ind Cas 189:
 II (2004) DMC 297 — 226
Sachdeva Rice Mills v. Raj Anand, AIR 1988 P&H 136: (1986) 90 Punj LR 576: 1987 ACJ 821 — 457
Salamat Ali v. Majjo Begum, AIR 1985 All 29 — 430
Samar Ghosh v. Jaya Ghosh, (2007) 4 SCC 511 — 90, 114
Samar Roy Chowdhury v. Snigdha Roy Chowdhury, AIR 1977 Cal 213: (1976) 2 Cal LJ 322:
 ILR (1977) 1 Cal 44 — 74
Sampa Karmakar v. Dr. Sanjib Karmakar, AIR 2012 Gau 32 — 96
Sandhya v. Union of India, AIR 1998 Bom 228: I (1999) DMC 143: 1998 (1) Hindu LR 653 — 330
Sangeeta B. Kadam v. Balkrishna Ramchandra Kadam, AIR 2005 Bom 262:
 2005 (2) Bom CR 515: I (2006) DMC 296 — 150
Sangeeta Balkrishna Kadam v. Balkrishna Ramchandra Kadam, AIR 1994 Bom 1:
 1994 (2) Civ LJ 424: 1994 (1) Hindu LR 605 — 151
Sanghmitra Ghosh v. Kajal Kumar Ghosh, (2007) 2 SCC 220: 2006 AIR SCW 5983 — 106
Sangitaben Jaiswal v. Sanjay Jaiswal, I (2001) DMC 19 (Guj) — 233
Sanjay Singh v. Garima Singh, (1998) 8 SCC 375 — 69
Santana Banerjee v. Susanta Kumar Banerjee, AIR 2012 Cal 16 — 140
Santosh Kumar Diwan v. Sitabai, AIR 2011 MP 161 — 362
Santosh Kumari v. Surjit Singh, AIR 1990 HP 77: 1990 Cr LJ 1012: (1989) 2 Hindu LR 111 — 159
Santosh Kumari v. Virender Kumar, AIR 1986 Raj 128: 1986 Raj LW 207: I (1986) DMC 377 — 100
Sarabjit v. Piara Lal, AIR 2005 P&H 237: 2005 (35) All Ind Cas 236: 2005 (3) CCC 179 — 299
Saraswathibai Shripad v. Shripad Vasanji, AIR 1941 Bom 103: 43 Bom LR 79:
 ILR (1941) Bom 455 — 295
Sarita Sharma v. Sushil Sharma, JT 2000 (2) SC 258: AIR 2000 SC 1019: 2000 Cr LJ 1459 — 288
Sarla Mudgal v. Union of India, AIR 1995 SC 1531: 1995 AIR SCW 2326:
 1995 Cr LJ 2926 — 165, 167
Saroj Rani v. Sudarshan Kumar Chadha, AIR 1984 SC 1562: (1984) 4 SCC 90:
 1984 Marri LJ 499 — 123, 130, 135, 136
Satinder Pal Singh v. Daman Preet, I (2009) DMC 196 (Del) — 104
Satish Sitole v. Ganga, AIR 2008 SC 3093: 2008 AIR SCW 5190: (2008) 7 SCC 734 — 114
Satya v. Teja Singh, AIR 1975 SC 105: 1975 Cr LJ 52: (1975) 1 SCC 120 — 450, 454

Saumya Ann Thomas v. Union of India, II (2010) DMC 526 (Ker) 438
Savitaben Somabhai Bhatiya v. State of Gujarat, AIR 2005 SC 1809: 2005 Cr LJ 2141:
  2005 AIR SCW 1601 198, 210, 215
Savitri Devi v. Manorama Bai, AIR 1998 MP 114: 1998 (1) Hindu LR 544:
  1998 (1) MPLJ 254 382
Savitri Pandey v. Prem Chandra Pandey, AIR 2002 SC 591: 2002 AIR SCW 182:
  (2002) 2 SCC 73 64, 107
Savitri v. Govind Singh, 1986 Cr LJ 41 (SC): AIR 1986 SC 984: (1985) 4 SCC 337 250
Sawan Ram v. Kalawanti, AIR 1967 SC 1761: (1967) 3 SCR 687: 1968 (2) SCJ 316 319
Sayeed Khan Faujdar Khan v. Zaheba Begum, AIR 2006 Bom 39: II (2006) DMC 294:
  2006 Mat LR 261 238, 258, 420
Saygo Bai v. Cheeru Bajrangi, AIR 2011 SC 1557 161
Seema v. Ashwani Kumar, AIR 2006 SC 1158: 2006 AIR SCW 858: (2006) 2 SCC 578 3, 4, 5
Seethalakshmi Ammal v. Muthuvenkatarama Iyengar, AIR 1998 SC 1692:
  1998 AIR SCW 1462: (1998) 5 SCC 368 364
Seth Badri Prasad v. Kanso Devi, (1969) 2 SCC 586 345
Shabana Bano v. Imran Khan, AIR 2010 SC 305 (MP): 2009 AIR SCW 7490:
  2010 Cr LJ 521 420, 423
Shaikh Ahmad v. Bai Fatima, AIR 1943 Bom 48: 44 Cr LJ 334: ILR (1943) Bom 38 273
Shamim Ara v. State of Uttar Pradesh, (2002) 7 SCALE 183 404
Shantabai Alias Gourabai v. Tarachand, AIR 1966 MP 8: 1965 MP LJ 615: 1965 Jab LJ 770 73
Shantha v. B.G. Shivananjappa, AIR 2005 SC 2410: 2005 Cr LJ 2615: 2005 AIR SCW 2613 234
Sharda v. Dharampal, AIR 2003 SC 3450: 2003 AIR SCW 1950: (2003) 4 SCC 493 187
Shataram Tukaram Patil v. Dagubai Tukaram Patil, AIR 1987 Bom 182:
  (1987) 2 Hindu LR 343: II (1987) DMC 100 208
Sheela Rani v. Jagdish Chander Sharma, AIR 2004 Del 158: 2003 (107) DLT 309:
  2003 (71) DRJ 122 229
Sheldon v. Sheldon, 1966 (2) All ER 257: (1966) 2 WLR 993: 110 SJ 269 44
Shobha Rani v. Madhukar Reddy, AIR 1988 SC 121: (1988) 1 SCC 105:
  JT 1987 (5) SC 433 24, 44, 50
Shobha Srinivas Bodigar v. Srinivas Veeranna Bodigar, AIR 2002 Kant 256 28
Shobha Suresh Jumani v. Appellate Tribunal, Forfeited Property, AIR 2001 SC 2288:
  2001 Cr LJ 2583: 2001 AIR SCW 2051 461
Siddaramappa v. Gouravva, AIR 2004 Kant 230: 2004 (2) Hindu LR 438:
  ILR (2004) 3 Kant 3611 315
Simpson v. Simpson, (1951) 1 All ER 955: (1951) 1 TLR 1019: 1951 P 320 411
Smruti Pahariya v. Sanjay Pahariya, (2009) 13 SCC 338: AIR 2009 SC 2840:
  2009 AIR SCW 4267 107
Sofia Begum v. Zaheer Hasan, AIR 1947 All 16: 230 Ind Cas 239 411
Somu Bai Yashwant Jadav v. Balagovind Yadav, AIR 1983 Bom 156:
  (1983) 1 Bom CR 632: (1983) 2 Civ LJ 58 363
Squire v. Squire, (1948) 2 All ER 51 21
Sridevi v. Jayaraja Shetty, AIR 2005 SC 780: 2005 AIR SCW 605: (2005) 2 SCC 784 377
Srinivas Managaonkar v. Sunanda, AIR 2001 SC 1285 130
Stanhope v. Stanhope, (1886) 11 PD 103 (CA) 251
State Bank of India v. Shweta Sahu, (2010) 3 SCALE 44 335
State of Haryana v. Bhajan Lal, AIR 1992 SC 604 : 1992 Cr LJ 527: (1992) Supp 1 SCC 335 465
Subramani v. M. Chandralekha, AIR 2005 SC 485: 2004 AIR SCW 7099: (2005) 9 SCC 407 388
Sucheta Singh Ghate v. Dilip Shanta, Ram Ghate, AIR 2003 Bom 390 261
Sudha Suhas Nandanvankar v. Suhas Ramrao Nandanvankar, AIR 2005 Bom 62:
  2005 (26) All Ind Cas 801: 2005 (1) Hindu LR 130 246
Sugden v. Sugden, (1957) 1 All ER 300: (1957) 2 WLR 210 251

Suman Kapur v. Sudhir Kapur, (2009) 1 SCC 422: 2008 AIR SCW 7730: AIR 2009 SC 589   90
Suman v. Surendra Kumar, AIR 2003 Raj 155: 2003 Mat LR 428: 2003 (1) CCC 393   103
Sumitra Devi v. Bhikan Choudhary, AIR 1985 SC 765: 1985 Cr LJ 528: (1985) 1 SCC 637   378
Suneer Sharma v. Madhurlata Sharma, AIR 2000 MP 26: 1999 (2) MP LJ 603:
2000 (1) CCC 315   29
Sunil Trambake v. Leelavati Trambake, AIR 2006 Bom 140: 2006 (42) All Ind Cas 527:
II (2006) DMC 461   187
Sunita Rajendra Nikalje v. Rajendra Eknath Nikalje, AIR 1996 Bom 85: 1996 (1) All MR 446:
1996 (2) Bom CJ 47   121
Sunita Shankar Salvi v. Shankar Laxman Salvi, AIR 2003 Bom 431: 2003 (1) All MR 267:
2003 (3) Bom LR 424   148
Surabhai Ravi Kumar Minawala v. State of Gujarat, AIR 2005 Guj 149:
2005 (31) All Ind Cas 472: 2005 (2) Civ LJ 554   291
Surendra Kumar Bhansali v. Judge, Family Court, AIR 2004 Raj 257:
2004 (19) All Ind Cas 685: 2004 (3) CCC 194   203
Suresh Khullar v. Vijay Khullar, AIR 2002 Del 373   204
Sureshta Devi v. Om Prakash, AIR 1992 SC 1904: 1991 AIR SCW 373:
(1991) 2 SCC 25   99, 106, 107
Surinder Kaur Sandhu v. Harbax Singh Sandhu, AIR 1984 SC 1224: (1984) 3 SCC 698:
(1984) 2 SCWR 116   295, 454
Suryakant alias Suresh Laxmishankar v. Indu, 1973 Guj LR 169   221
Sushil Kumar v. Minto Kumari, AIR 2012 Raj 1   71
Sushila Viresh Chhawda v. Viresh Nagshi Chhawda, AIR 1996 Bom 94:
1996 (2) Bom CR 531: 1996 (1) CCC 700   201
Sushma Chourie v. Hetendra Kumar Borkar, AIR 2010 Chh 30: 2010 (2) Cg LJ 37   5
Swaraj Garg v. K.M. Garg, AIR 1978 Del 296: 1978 Hindu LR 332: 1978 Raj LR 525   61
Swarajya Lakshmi v. G.G. Padma Rao, AIR 1974 SC 165: (1974) 1 SCC 58: (1974) 2 SCR 97   92
Swati Verma v. Rajan Verma, (2004) 1 SCC 123: 2003 AIR SCW 5841:
AIR 2004 SC 161   106, 114

T

T. Kochappi v. R. Sadasivam Pillai, AIR 2006 Mad 330: 2007 (1) ALJ (NOC) 69:
2007 (1) Rec CivR 209   293
T. Sareetha v. T. Venkata Subbaiah, AIR 1983 AP 356: II (1983) DMC 172:
(1983) 2 Civ LJ 158   133, 135, 136
T.P.S.H. Selva Saroja v. T.P.S.H. Sasinathan, 1989 Cr LJ 2032 (Mad)   262, 271
Tarun Ranjan Majumdar v. Siddhartha Datta, AIR 1991 Cal 76: (1990) 2 Cal LJ 306:
I (1991) DMC 14   295
Taruna Batra v. S.R. Batra, AIR 2005 Del 270: 2005 (2) CCC 692: I (2005) DMC 282   177
Taylor v. Fields, (1986) 224 Cal Rpr 186   198
Tejinder Kaur v. Gurmit Singh, AIR 1988 SC 839: JT 1988 (1) SC 395   153
Thambuswamy v. Ma Lone, 10 Bur LT 209: 37 Ind Cas 311: 18 Cr LJ 103   273
Thilothama v. Kunjappan, 1983 Cr LJ 273 (Ker): I (1983) DMC 241: 1983 Ker LT 90   423
Thoombath Haris v. K. Sherbin, AIR 2010 (NOC) 230 (Ker)   448
Thota Sesharathamma v. Thota Manikyamma, (1991) 4 SCC 312: JT 1991 (3) SC 506:
(1991) 3 SCR 717   345
Thrity Hoshie Dolikuka v. Hoshiam Shavaksha Dolikuka, AIR 1982 SC 1276:
(1982) 2 SCC 544: II (1982) DMC 288   285, 295
Thulasi Ammal v. Gowri, 1964 (1) MLJ 228: AIR 1964 Mad 118: ILR (1964) 1 Mad 65   464

U

Ugre Gowda v. Nagegowda, AIR 2004 SC 3974: 2004 AIR SCW 4308: (2004) 12 SCC 48   333
Ujagar Singh v. Mst. Jeo, AIR 1959 SC 1041: ILR 1959 Punj 1735: (1959) Supp 2 SCR 781   309

Uma Prasad v. Padmavati, (1999) AIHC 3494 (MP) 310
Umashankar Prasad Singh v. Radha Devi, AIR 1967 Pat 220 189, 191
Urmila Ginda v. Union of India, AIR 1975 Del 115: (1975) 1 Serv LR 419: 1975 Lab IC 1044 329
Urvashi Sibal v. Government of NCT of Delhi, AIR 2010 Del 157 111
Usharani Lenka v. Panigrahi Subhash Chandra Dash, AIR 2005 Ori 3:
2004 (23) All Ind Cas 583: 2005 (1) Marri LJ 476 37

V

V. Bhagat v. D. Bhagat, AIR 1994 SC 710: 1994 AIR SCW 45:
(1994) 1 SCC 337 26, 42, 44, 50, 90, 107
V. Mallikarjunaiah v. H.C. Gowramma, AIR 1997 Kant 77: ILR 1997 Kant 964:
1997 (1) Kant LJ 570 14
V. Muthusami v. Angammal, AIR 2002 SC 1279: 2002 AIR SCW 1083: (2002) 3 SCC 316 357
V.D. Grahalakshmi v. T. Prashanth, AIR 2012 Mad 34 3, 69
Vallikannu v. R. Singaperumal, AIR 2005 SC 2587: 2005 AIR SCW 2820: (2005) 6 SCC 622 365
Vandana v. Suresh Charan, AIR 2005 Raj 193: 2005 (2) CCC 142: 2005 (2) Hindu LR 628 96
Vankamamidi Venkata Subba Rao v. Chatlapalli Seetharamaratna Ranganayakamma,
AIR 1997 SC 3082: 1997 AIR SCW 3122: (1997) 5 SCC 460 346
Varsha Pravin Patil v. Pravin Madhukar Patil, AIR 2009 Bom 60: I (2009) DMC 649:
2009 (2) Hindu LR 121 46, 48
Veena Kalia v. Jatinder Nath Kalia, AIR 1996 Del 54: 1995 (59) DLT 635: 1996 Marri LJ 423 453
Veena Kapoor v. Varinder Kumar Kapoor, AIR 1982 SC 792: (1981) 3 SCC 92:
1982 Cr LJ 680 292
Velamuri Venkata Sivaprasad v. Kothuri Venkateswarlu, AIR 2000 SC 434:
1999 AIR SCW 4583: (2000) 2 SCC 139 348
Venkatacharyulu v. Rangacharyulu, 1891 ILR 14 Mad 316: 1 Mad LJ 85 12
Vidyut Kumar Verma v. Manju, AIR 2011 Pat 110 68
Vijay Kumar Prasad v. State of Bihar, AIR 2004 SC 2123: 2004 Cr LJ 2047:
2004 AIR SCW 2276 266
Vijay Lakshmi Devi v. Gautam Krishna Mishra, AIR 2010 Pat 56: 2010 (3) Civ LJ 231 141
Vijaya Manohar Arbat v. Kashirao Rajaram Sawai, AIR 1987 SC 1100: 1987 Cr LJ 977:
(1987) 2 SCC 278 276
Vijayalakshmamma v. B.T. Shankar, AIR 2001 SC 1424: 2001 AIR SCW 1347:
(2001) 4 SCC 558 323
Vijaykumar Ramchandra Bhate v. Neela Vijaykumar Bhate, AIR 2003 SC 2462:
2003 AIR SCW 2530: (2003) 6 SCC 334 32
Vikas Sharma v. Anita Sharma, AIR 2011 Utr 43 66
Vikram Aditya Singh v. Union of India, II (2006) DMC 689 (Del DB): AIR 2007 Del 101:
2006 (133) DLT 369 4
Vikram Vir Vohra v. Shalini Bhalla, AIR 2010 SC 1675 (Del): 2010 AIR SCW 2261:
(2010) 4 SCC 409 298
Vilayat Raj v. Sunila, AIR 1983 Del 351: (1983) 23 DLT 434: II (1983) DMC 164 23
Vimalben Ajitbhai Patel v. Vatslaben Ashokbhai Patel, (2008) 4 SCC 649:
AIR 2008 SC 2675: 2008 AIR SCW 4475 279
Vimla v. Veeraswamy, (1991) 2 SCC 375: 1991 AIR SCW 754 198
Vinita Saxena v. Pankaj Pandit, AIR 2005 Del 243: 2004 (113) DLT 884: II (2004) DMC 602 44
Vinita Saxena v. Pankaj Saxena, AIR 2006 SC 1662: 2006 AIR SCW 1585: (2006) 3 SCC 778 44
Vishnu Kumar v. State of Uttar Pradesh, 2006 (65) ALR 888 (All): AIR 2007 All 31:
2007 (1) ALJ 152 383, 389
Vishwambar v. Laxminarayana, AIR 2001 SC 2607: 2001 AIR SCW 2616: (2001) 6 SCC 163 302
Visnu Dutt Sharma v. Manju Sharma, AIR 2009 SC 2254: 2009 AIR SCW 2984:
(2009) 6 SCC 379 89, 114, 163
Viswambharan v. Dhanya, AIR 2005 Ker 91: ILR 2005 (1) Ker 374: 2005 (1) Ker LJ 330 270

W

Wazid Ali v. Rehana Anjum, AIR 2005 MP 141: 2005 (2) Hindu LR 562: 2005 (3) MPLJ 319 428

X

X v. Z, AIR 2002 Del 217: 2002 (96) DLT 354: I (2002) DMC 448 185

Y

Yallawwa v. Shantavva, AIR 1997 SC 35: 1996 AIR SCW 4185: 1997 (11) SCC 159 458
Yamanaji H. Jadhav v. Nirmala, AIR 2002 SC 971: 2002 AIR SCW 674: (2002) 2 SCC 637 381, 389
Yamunabai Anantrao Adhav v. Anantrao Shivaram Adhav, AIR 1988 SC 644: JT 1988 (1) SC 193: 1988 Cr LJ 793 204, 211, 213, 350, 387
Yamunbai v. Anant Rao, (1988) 1 SCC 330 11
Yashpal Singh Thakur v. Anjana Rajput, AIR 2001 MP 67: 2000 (3) MPLJ 127: 2001 (2) CCC 472 283
Yusuf v. Sakkeena, 1998 (2) KLT 573: AIR 1999 Ker 54: ILR (1999) 1 Ker 277 430

Z

Zynab Bi alias Bibijan v. Md. Ghouse Mohideen, AIR 1952 Mad 284 430

MARRIAGE

HIV Status of Person: Right to Marry whether Absolute
Mr. X v. Hospital Z,
AIR 1999 SC 495: 1998 AIR SCW 3662: (1998) 8 SCC 296

Issue: Does a person have an absolute right to marry? Can this right be "suspended"? Does divulgence of person's HIV status amount to breach of confidentiality and privacy?

Facts: The appellant, a surgeon in the Nagaland State Health service was directed by the State Government to accompany a patient to Madras for treatment. The patient required surgery and there was shortage of blood. The appellant agreed to donate blood. His blood sample taken by the respondent hospital revealed that he was HIV+. This was in June, 1995. In August, 1995 the appellant proposed marriage to Ms. Y and the same was scheduled to be held in December. The facts of the case do not indicate whether the appellant was even aware of his HIV+ status when he proposed to Ms. Y. The marriage was however called off because of the disclosure of the test report. Why, when, how and to whom the disclosure was made is also not clear. Cancellation of the marriage and divulgence of his HIV+ condition obviously caused a lot of embarrassment and agony to the appellant. He was ostracised by the community and had to leave his home State and reside in another State. He approached the Consumer Dispute Redressal Commission claiming damages against the hospital for disclosing his blood reports and breaching confidentiality. The same was dismissed. He then approached the Supreme Court. It was argued that 'duty of care' in the medical profession includes duty to maintain confidentiality and since this was violated by the respondent hospital, it was liable to pay damages. The Court went into the details of the ethics of confidentiality based on Hippocratic oath and the national and international codes of medical ethics. It was held that the duty to maintain secrecy is not absolute. "The proposed marriage carried with it the health risk to an identifiable person who had to be protected. The right to confidentiality, if any, vested in the appellant was not enforceable in the present situation," according to the court. (at p. 500)

As regards his right to privacy the court observed (at p. 501):

> "Having regard to the fact that the appellant was found to be HIV+, its disclosure would not be violative of either the rule of confidentiality or the appellant's right to privacy as Ms. Y with whom the appellant was likely to get married was saved in time by such disclosure, or else, she

too would have been infected with the dreadful disease if the marriage had taken place and consummated."

Order: The Court held that the right to marry is not absolute and remains suspended until the afflicted person is cured. Referring to some provisions under the Indian Penal Code, 1860, the Court observed that if he had married the lady, he would have committed offences under sections 269 and 270 of the Indian Penal Code *viz*., negligent act likely to spread infection of disease dangerous to life and malignant act likely to spread infection of any disease dangerous to life, respectively.

Comment: An extremely harsh and insensitive judgment—Its remarks "AIDS is the product of indisciplined sexual impulse"—are highly unsavoury and defamatory.

Marriage is the foundation of a stable family and civilised society; it accords status and security to the parties and their offspring. In fact, the right to marry is a component of the right to life under article 21 of the Constitution of India which says, "no person shall be deprived of his life or personal liberty except according to procedure established by law." This right has been recognised even under the Universal Declaration of Human Rights, 1948. Article 16 of the same states:

(1) Men and women of full age, without any limitation due to race, nationality or religion, have the right to marry and found a family. They are entitled to equal rights as to marriage, during marriage and at its dissolution.

(2) Marriage shall be entered into only with the free and full consent of the intending spouses.

(3) The family is the natural and fundamental group unit of society and is entitled to protection by the society and the State.

There are however, certain pre-requisites and conditions which need to be complied with to enter into and solemnise a legal marriage. This section of the book deals with some of these aspects and select cases thereunder.

Mr. X v. Hospital Z,
AIR 2003 SC 664: 2002 AIR SCW 5335: (2003) 1 SCC 500

Issue: AIDS patient's right to marriage and confidentiality.

Facts: Three-Judge Bench of the Apex Court partly overruled its earlier decision in *Mr. X v. Hospital Z*, AIR 1999 SC 495: 1998 AIR SCW 3662: (1998) 8 SCC 296 on whether there is a bar for marriage if a healthy spouse gives an informed consent to marriage with spouse found to be HIV+.

Order: The Court held that the two-Judge Bench in the 1999 judgment had gone further than was warranted by declaring generally as to "what rights and obligations arise in such context, as right to privacy and confidentiality or whether such persons are entitled to be married or not, or in the event such persons marry they would commit an offence under law or whether such right is suspended during the period of illness". It, however, reiterated the basis of its earlier decision and held that a person's right to privacy was not affected in any manner by revealing his HIV+ status to the relatives of his fiancee.

Comment: Bolting the door after the horse has escaped serves no useful purpose. The damage to the rights and psyche of AIDS patients has already been done by the 1999 judgment and no effective damage control can be done by the present judgment, except that it has conceded that the judgment (of 1999) had gone further than was warranted.

Registration of Marriage
Seema v. Ashwani Kumar,
AIR 2006 SC 1158: 2006 AIR SCW 858: (2006) 2 SCC 578

The Supreme Court made the directions that the marriages of all persons who are citizens of India belonging to various religions should be made compulsorily registrable in their respective States, where the marriage is solemnized. The Supreme Court directed the States and Central Government to take following steps:

(i) The procedure for registration should be notified by respective States within three months, by amending the existing rules or framing new rules. However, before bringing the said rules into force, the objections from members of the public shall be invited by due publicity and matter shall be kept open for objections for a period of one month.

(ii) The officer appointed under the said rules shall be duly authorised to register the marriages. Registration clearly states age and marital status of the parties. The consequences of non-registration or filing false declaration should also be provided in the said rules.

(iii) As and when the Central Government enacts a comprehensive statute, the same shall be placed before the court for scrutiny.

(iv) Counsel for various States and Union Territories shall ensure that the directions are carried out immediately.

Note: See *V.D. Grahalakshmi v. T. Prashanth*, AIR 2012 Mad 34. It was held in this case that a marriage registration certificate is not substantial proof of marriage (Hindu marriage in this case) if one party repudiates the same. The marriage either solemnised under section 7 or 7A of the Hindu Marriage Act is to be proved independently and the registration of such Hindu marriage is only for the purpose of facilitating the proof of the marriage and nothing more. Registration certificate, however, may be a proof for all other purposes concerning third parties to the marriage.

Jurisdiction of Registrar: Whether Residence of Parents Compulsory

Vikram Aditya Singh v. Union of India,
II (2006) DMC 689 (Del DB): AIR 2007 Del 101:
2006 (133) DLT 369

Issue: The issue involved was as to whether it is compulsory that one of the parents of the parties to the marriage should be residing within the jurisdiction of the Registrar for more than thirty days to get the marriage registered.

Facts: The marriage was solemnised in Delhi and the parties sought registration of the same. The petitioner was having difficulty in getting it registered in view of sub-clause (vi) of clause 7 of the Delhi Hindu Marriage Registration Rules, 1956 which requires that "one of the parties or his/her parents is residing within the jurisdiction of the Registrar for more than thirty days. The registration was refused on the specious plea that parents or one of the parties to the marriage is not residing in Delhi. On appeal to the High Court, reference was made to the Apex Court order in *Seema* v. *Ashwani Kumar,* AIR 2006 SC 1158: 2006 AIR SCW 858: (2006) 2 SCC 578. In this case the court has enjoined that the registration of marriage of persons who are citizens of India belonging to various religions should be made compulsory in their respective States where the marriage is solemnised. The High Court held that no rule or form could stipulate terms contrary to what the Apex Court has said.

The rule making power under section 8 of the Hindu Marriage Act could not be utilised to add sub-clause (vi) to clause 7 in Form A under the Delhi Hindu Marriage Registration Rules because it is contrary to the Supreme Court judgment.

Order: The court held that registration of marriage of parties where the marriage has been solemnised in Delhi cannot be denied whether or not their parents are residents of Delhi: Directions were issued accordingly.

Comment: Unnecessary technicalities should not come in the way of registration of marriages. In fact the process of registration should be simplified so as to facilitate rather than discourage parties to get their marriage registered.

Whether Presence of Parties is Mandatory

Chiranjit Kaur Nagi v. Government of NCT, Delhi,
I (2008) DMC 45 (Del)

Issue: Whether presence of parties before the Registrar and affixing of their signatures in the Register in the presence of the Registrar *vide* rules 3 and 4 of the Marriage Registration Rules, read with Forms A and B thereof was mandatory.

Facts: The husband was in America and the wife required a marriage certificate for purposes of obtaining immigration visa. The same was refused by the Registrar of Marriages on the ground that under section 8 of the Hindu Marriage Act both the applicant and her spouse have to appear before the Registrar. Hence wife's appeal. The rules which required the personal appearance of the parties even when they are separated by long distances, was assailed. The court held that indeed such rules were unfair and out dated. They act as impediments for parties to register their marriage. The court suggested that suitable mechanism should be evolved with mix of technology by incorporating video conferencing authentication of identities by Embassies and attestation of signatures and use of other internet facilities. Requiring the husband to come from America simply to appear before the Registrar would involve huge expense and loss of time the court held.

Order: Suitable directions were given to the Registrar to dispense with the husband's personal appearance for issuance of marriage certificate.

Comments: Technicalities and hassles should not come in the way of achieving the goal of compulsory registration of all marriages as enjoined by the Apex Court as well *vide* its judgment in *Seema* v. *Ashwani Kumar,* AIR 2006 SC 1158: 2006 AIR SCW 858: (2006) 2 SCC 578.

Marriage of Woman Already Married is Void
Sushma Chourie v. *Hetendra Kumar Borkar,*
AIR 2010 Chh 30: 2010 (2) Cg LJ 37

Issue: This was a case under section 5(i) coupled with section 11 of the Hindu Marriage Act where the issue involved was as to the validity of the marriage of the respondent wife who was an already married woman.

Facts: According to the petitioner husband, the wife was having illicit relations with one R.K., had two abortions as a result of this relationship and then married him; she was also residing with R.K. as his wife. Apart from that she had also filed a petition for resolution of conjugal rights under section 9 of the Hindu Marriage Act against R.K. – a petition where marriage is a pre-requisite. The petitioner alleged that the respondent showed herself as an unmarried woman and solemnised marriage with him. The respondent wife conceded that she had illicit relations with R.K., there were marriage negotiations also but there was no marriage. She further stated that in order to resolve the dispute between them (R.K. and respondent) they had filed a civil suit and all these facts were within the knowledge of the husband and his parents. The Family Court, however, came to a finding that she was an already married woman before she entered into marriage with the petitioner and hence the marriage was void being bigamous. Hence the wife's appeal. It was argued on her behalf that the husband has not proved the allegation of her first marriage with R.K. and, therefore, the present marriage was not in violation of the provision of section 5(i) of the Hindu Marriage Act. Both parties adduced oral as well as documentary evidence in support of their respective claims. The husband succeeded in discharging the burden of proof of the appellant's first marriage at the time of her marriage with the petitioner husband by documentary evidence which included:

(i) evidence of some judicial proceedings between the appellant wife and R.K., and

(ii) copy of application for restitution of conjugal rights filed by her under section 9 of the Hindu Marriage Act against R.K.

The wife, however, failed to disprove her first marriage though she and R.K. specifically deposed that they had never married; they had however conceded that in view of the marriage negotiations between them, they did have illicit relations and with a view to resolve controversy, the appellant filed a civil suit in the civil court.

Order: The wife's appeal was dismissed. The High Court held that the petition for restitution on behalf of the appellant against R.K. was sufficient to draw presumption of lawful marriage between her and R.K. If they were not married "there was no propriety to file an application under section 9 of the Act...." the court remarked. (at p. 32) Also, the appellant wife neither pleaded nor proved that her first marriage with R.K. had been dissolved by any mode permissible in accordance with the law. Hence the only inference was that she was not unmarried when she married the petitioner/respondent and hence the marriage was void.

Comment: A mandatory condition for a valid marriage under the Hindu Marriage Act is that neither of the spouses should have a subsisting marriage. When the allegation of subsisting marriage is denied the burden of proving the alleged marriage is on the petitioner and that of disproving the same is on the respondent. The fact that a petition for restitution of conjugal rights has been filed by the defendant herself against some other person is evidence enough of a pre-existing marriage of the petitioner with another person.

BOTH PARTIES SHOULD BE HINDU

Pre-marriage Convert to Hinduism is Hindu: Marriage not Void

Madhavi Ramesh Dudani v. *Ramesh K. Dudani,*
AIR 2006 Bom 94: 2006 (40) All Ind Cas 446:
I (2006) DMC 386

Issue: Wife was born Catholic Christian but later converted to Hinduism before marrying a Hindu man. Can the marriage be declared void under the Hindu Marriage Act for want of proof of performance of *Shudhi Karan* ceremony?

Facts: The wife, a born Christian but later converted to Hinduism and the husband, a Hindu, were married in 1983 according to Hindu rites under the Hindu Marriage Act. Two daughters were born who were given Hindu names. The wife participated in all Hindu religious ceremonies and pujas and was living with her husband in the Hindu family for more than eight years. When differences arose, the wife filed a petition, *inter alia*, for judicial separation. The husband filed a suit for declaration that the marriage was void since the wife was not a Hindu prior to the marriage and that she had not converted to Hinduism any time prior to the marriage. The Family Court judge accepted this contention and held that he had no jurisdiction to entertain the wife's petition for judicial separation, nor the one filed by the husband seeking declaration of nullity since neither of these petitions were maintainable under the Hindu Marriage Act. The wife appealed against this.

Order: It was held that the marriage between the parties cannot be said to be void merely for want of proof of *Shudhi Karan* ceremony, *i.e.*, conversion to Hinduism, before marriage. It can be presumed that the priest must not have performed the marriage without conversion. As to the relief, the court held that the marriage had clearly irretrievably broken down due to acts of cruelty by both parties. In the circumstances, it would be of no use to confine the relief only to Judicial separation. Consequently, instead of Judicial separation sought by the wife, counter-claim of divorce filed by the husband was decreed and the marriage between the parties was dissolved after making appropriate arrangements for alimony and house for wife and education and marriage expenses of daughters.

Comment: Under the Hindu Marriage Act, both parties to the marriage must be Hindus. Where a non-Hindu by birth converts to Hinduism before marriage and all facts and circumstances indiate that the converted spouse practised Hinduism, the plea of absence of proof of conversion ceremony cannot be raised to seek declaration of nullity of marriage on the ground that the other spouse was a non-Hindu. Further, by granting a decree of divorce instead of Judicial separation, the court adopted a practical approach. A separation decree does not provide meaningful relief—the parties live separately but legally married. The court, in its wisdom, made proper financial arrangements in the interest of wife and daughter and disolved the marriage by a decree of divorce.

Marriage between Christian and Hindu not Valid under Hindu Marriage Act

Gullipilli Sowria Rai v. Bhandaru Pavani,
AIR 2009 SC 1085: 2009 AIR SCW 244: (2009) 1 SCC 714

Issue: The issue involved in the case was as to the validity of a marriage between a Hindu and a non-Hindu under the provisions of the Hindu Marriage Act.

Facts: This was a civil appeal by special leave against an order of the High Court. The appellant, a Roman Catholic Christian male and the respondent a Hindu female got married under the provisions of the Hindu Marriage Act on 24-10-1996 in a temple, by exchange of 'thali' in the absence of anyone from their families. The marriage was also got registered under section 8 of the Act on 2-11-1996. A few months later, on 13-3-1997, the wife filed a petition in the Family Court at Vishakapatnam, under section 12(1)(c) of the Act for nullity of the marriage on the ground that the husband had misrepresented regarding his social status that he was a Hindu whereas, after marriage it transpired that he was a Christian. The husband admitted that he was a Roman Catholic but contended that such marriage could be solemnised under the Hindu Marriage Act. The Family Court accepted his argument and dismissing the wife's petition held that the marriage was valid. On appeal against this, the High Court reversed the order on 12-9-2002 and held that the marriage was void *ab initio* and, therefore, a nullity. On 23-1-2003 the respondent wife remarried. Thereafter the husband filed an SLP on 23-4-2003. It was argued that the words "marriage *may* be solemnised between any two Hindus" in section 5 of the Act indicates that the condition of both being Hindus is only directory and not mandatory and indicates permissibility of a marriage between a Hindu and a non-Hindu. As to section 11 of the Act which refers to void marriage, it was argued that a marriage is void under this section "if it contravenes any one of the conditions specified in clauses (i), (iv) and (v) of section 5" *i.e.*, subsisting marriage, parties within degrees of prohibited relationship, or parties being *sapindas* of each other, and in this case, none of these conditions were contravened and so the marriage would not be void. The marriage would at best be voidable and the High Court order declaring it to be void *ab initio*, was erroneous, it was contended. On behalf of the wife it was argued that the Preamble to the Hindu Marriage Act was very clearly worded and makes it clear that the Act was promulgated to amend and codify law relating to marriage amongst Hindus and the Act applies only to Hindus as defined in section 2(1)(c) of the Act; further that each religious community has its own form of marriage which excluded members of other religious communities.

Order: After hearing the argument on both sides the court came to the conclusion that the conditions indicated in section 5 were to apply in respect of marriage between two Hindus only: that a Hindu marriage could be solemnised only between two Hindus. The term "may" in section 5, according to the court, refers to marriage and not to a party's religion. Further, since the marriage did not fall within categories of void marriage under section 11, the wife had no option but make application under section 12(i)(c) that the marriage was a nullity on the ground that she was beguiled into marriage by fraudulent consideration that he was a Hindu and since valid marriage can be performed only between two Hindus, the marriage has rightly been declared to be a nullity by the High Court; it clarified that registration under section 8 could not and did not validate such marriage. The question of wife's subsequent marriage was of no relevance in view of the fact that the marriage between the appellant and the respondent was declared a nullity, the husband's appeal was thus dismissed.

Comment: India is a land of diversities with people from various religious faiths. The law makers, in their wisdom, have provided for different personal laws governing people belonging to different religions. Thus Hindus, Christians, Parsis and Muslims, all have their own personal laws apart from a secular law, the Special Marriage Act, 1954, which applies to all. Therefore, when parties purport to marry under, as in this case, the Hindu Marriage Act it is necessary that they should be Hindus or else they marry under the Special Marriage Act. Thus a marriage between a Hindu and a non-Hindu cannot be a legal marriage under the Hindu law, *i.e.,* the Hindu Marriage Act, 1955.

Marriage between Hindu and Christian not Valid under Act even if Registered

Nilesh Narin Rajesh Lal v. *Kashmira Bhupenderbhai Banker,* AIR 2010 Guj 3: 2010 (2) CCC 757: 2010 (1) Guj LH 499

Issue: Can a court dismiss a suit for declaration of nullity of marriage even while conceding that the marriage is a nullity?

Facts: The appellant, a Christian and the respondent, a Hindu entered into marriage which was solemnised according to Hindu rituals; the same was also got registered under the Hindu Marriage Act. Four years after marriage and three years after the birth of a child, the wife deserted the husband whereafter the latter filed a suit for declaration that the marriage was void. His contention was that the respondent was already married at the time of her marriage with the appellant and her first marriage was subsisting.

After going through the pleadings and evidence, the Family Court held that the respondent was married earlier but that marriage had been dissolved by a divorce deed before she married the appellant. The court therefore refused to declare the marriage void. Furthermore, the court held that the marriage between the appellant and the respondent was not valid, it was void under section 11 of the Hindu Marriage Act because it was not in consonance with the provisions under sections 5 and 7 of the Act *viz* – both parties were not Hindus. That being so, according to the court, the suit for declaration of nullity under the Act was not maintainable. The husband filed an appeal against this. It was argued on his behalf that the appellant being a Christian and the respondent a Hindu, the marriage was void under section 5 read with sections 7 and 11 of the Hindu Marriage Act and the court below was required to pass a decree for declaration as sought by the husband. Reference was made to the Andhra Pradesh judgment in *Bandaru* (alias *Gullipili Pavani* v. *Gullipilli Sowria Raj* (Appeal against order No. 2024/1998 decided on 12-9-2002) and upheld by the Supreme Court in *Gullipilli Sowria Rai* v. *Bhandaru Pavani*, AIR 2009 SC 1085: 2009 AIR SCW 244: (2009) 1 SCC 714) where, in similar circumstances, the marriage was held to be void *ab initio* and declared a nullity. The following observations of the Supreme Court in that case are pertinent:

" ..... Section 5 of the Act .... makes it clear that a marriage may be solemnised between two Hindus if the conditions contained in the said section were fulfilled. The usage of the expression "may" in the opening line of the section .... does not make the provision of section 5 optional. On the other hand, it in positive terms, indicates that a marriage can be solemnised between two Hindus if the conditions indicated were fulfilled. In other words, in the event of the conditions remaining unfulfilled, a marriage between two Hindus could not be solemnised. The expression "may" .... is not directory .... but mandatory and non-fulfilment thereof would not permit a marriage under the Act between two Hindus......."

In view of the above, the Gujarat High Court in *Nilesh Narin Rajesh Lal* held that the marriage was void.

Order: Relying on the Apex Court judgment as also the clear provisions of the Act the marriage was held to be void *ab initio*. "The court below erred in non-suiting the appellant though it did find that the marriage between the appellant and the respondent was not a legal and valid marriage", the court observed (at p. 4) A decree of nullity declaring the marriage as *null* and *void* was, accordingly, granted.

Comment: Section 5 of the Hindu Marriage Act which provides for the conditions for a valid marriage under the Act is very specific that both the parties need to be Hindus at the time of the marriage. A marriage between persons belonging to different religion can be solemnised under the Special Marriage Act, 1954, but not under the Hindu Marriage Act. A marriage between a Hindu and a non-Hindu according to Hindu rituals would not be valid notwithstanding its registration under the Act and if a declaration of its nullity is sought, the court cannot deny it.

Wife, a Born Hindu, Converted to Islam and then Reconverted to Hinduism: Marriage with Hindu valid

Flg Officer Rajiv Gakhar v. Bhavna @ Sahar Wasif, AIR 2011 SC 2053 (P&H)

Issue: Is a marriage between a Hindu male and a female who is originally a Hindu, converted to Islam and then reconverted to Hinduism, valid under the Hindu Marriage Act?

Facts: The parties were married in 1999 in a temple as per Hindu rites. At the time of marriage, the wife gave an affidavit that she was a Hindu and a spinster. However at a later stage during an interaction with her father, the petitioner husband came to know that the respondent wife had converted to Islam, changed her name to Sahar Wasif and married a Muslim and also had two children from him. He then filed a petition for nullity of marriage alleging misrepresentation, fraud and cheating and further on the ground that she being a Muslim and he a Hindu, there could be no valid marriage under the Hindu law as under section 5 of the Hindu Marriage Act only a marriage between "two Hindus" could be solemnised. The Trial Court accepted his case and declared the marriage a nullity and also directed the husband to pay rupees 2,000 as maintenance. The wife went in appeal against this which was allowed by the High Court and the husband's petition was dismissed. Hence the present appeal before the Apex Court.

Order: The husband relied on several cases, *inter alia, Yamunbai v. Anant Rao,* (1988) 1 SCC 330; *M.M. Malhotra v. Union of India,* AIR 2006 SC 80: 2005 AIR SCW 5497: (2005) 8 SCC 351 and *Gullipilli Sowria Rai v. Bhandaru Pavani,* AIR 2009 SC 1085: 2009 AIR SCW 244: (2009) 1 SCC 714, in support of his claim. On the other hand the wife led oral and documentary evidence in support of her case that here was no cheating, the husband was aware of all the facts and further, after her talaq she reverted to her original name and also underwent *shudhikaran* ceremonies thereby reverting to Hinduism. All these facts were testified by witnesses. The husband's argument that pursuant to marriage and conversion to Islam, she could not have returned to Hindu fold was not accepted. The court accordingly held that once the respondent wife had successfully established her claim that on the date of marriage with the appellant, she was a Hindu, there was no bar to her marriage with a Hindu *vide* section 5 of the Hindu Marriage Act.

Comment: The judgment explicitly reiterates that the crucial time to determine the religious status of the parties to the marriage is the date of the marriage. It is of no significance that prior to the marriage a party was a non-Hindu so long as on that crucial date of marriage he/she was a Hindu.

MARRIAGE BELOW THE LEGAL AGE

Marriage not Void

Pinninti Venkataramana v. *State,*
AIR 1977 AP 43 (FB): 1977 Cr LJ 368: ILR (1976) AP 837

Issue: Whether a Hindu marriage governed by the provisions of the Hindu Marriage Act, 1955 where the parties to the marriage or either of them, are below their respective ages as set out in clause (iii) of section 5, is void *ab initio*?

Facts: A wife filed a complaint in the court of the First Class Judicial Magistrate against her husband and ten others, alleging that the husband had committed an offence punishable under section 494 of the Indian Penal Code and that the other ten were a party to it. The husband's defence was that at the time of the marriage, *i.e.*, in 1959, he was 13 years of age and the complainant wife was nine years old and hence the marriage between them being void marriage and no marriage in the eye of the law, he had not committed any offence under section 494 by marrying another girl. The Magistrate, however, held that the marriage was legal and an offence was committed by his marrying again and so convicted them.

The convictions were confirmed in appeal, though with slight modifications. Against their convictions, the petitioners filed a revision in the High Court. *Panchireddi Appala Suramma* v. *Gadela Ganapatlu*, AIR 1975 AP 193: (1975) 1 AP LJ 37: ILR (1975) AP 105, was relied upon where the Division Bench had held that a marriage which is in contravention of clause (iii) of section 5 of the Hindu Marriage Act is void *ab intio* and is no marriage in the eye of law. Since it was felt that the view taken by the D.B. was not in accordance with the provisions of the Hindu Marriage Act the matter was referred to a larger Bench. Thereafter, the matter came up before Chinnappa Reddy and Punnayya, JJ. and by their order dated March 22, 1976 they referred the matter to a Full Bench. Relevant provisions of the Hindu Marriage Act Child Marriage Restraint Act sections 494 and 495 of the Indian Penal Code and several cases were referred to [*E.g.*, B. *Sivanandy* v. *P. Bhagavathyamma*, AIR 1962 Mad 400: 75 Mad LW 161 which relied upon *Venkatacharyulu* v. *Rangacharyulu*, 1891 ILR 14 Mad 316: 1 Mad LJ 85; *Panchadi Chitti Venkanna* v. *Panchadi Mahalakshmi*, Transfer Appeal No. 578 of 1973 and T.A. No. 546 of 1972; *Krishni Devi* v. *Tulsan Devi*, AIR 1972 P&H 305: 1972 Cur LJ 434: 74 Punj LR 561; *Mohinder Kaur* v. *Major Singh*, AIR 1972 P&H 184: 73 Punj LR 952 which found support from *Kalawati* v. *Devi Ram*, AIR 1961 HP 1; *Premi* v. *Daya Ram*, AIR 1965 HP 15; *Ma Hari* v. *Director of Consolidation*, 1969 All LJ 623: 1969 All WR (HC) 303; *Buddhi Sahu* v. *Lohusani Sahuni*, ILR 1970

Cut 1215 and *Gindan v. Barelal*, AIR 1976 MP 83: 1976 MPLJ 102: 1976 Hindu LR 270].

After a detailed analysis of the above, the court came to the conclusion that a marriage in contravention of the minimum age prescribed by the Act was not a void marriage. Had the law makers intended that, they would not have inserted clause (iv) in sub-section (2) of section 13 which gives to a wife married before the attainment of the age of 15 years, an option to repudiate her marriage after attaining the age of 15 but before attaining the age of 18. This clause clearly indicates the mind of the Legislature that the violation of clause (iii) of section 5 would not render the marriage either void or voidable but give an option to the girl to repudiate the marriage if solemnized before the age of 15. Also if each of the clauses in section 5 were to be treated as a condition precedent, the violation of which would render the marriage void *ab initio*, the Legislature itself would not have given out its mind by providing for contravention of the different clauses of section 5 differently. Neither under section 11 nor under section 12 of the Hindu Marriage Act is there any mention of a marriage in contravention of section 5(iii), thus meaning that such marriage is neither void nor voidable. If the view expressed in *P.A. Saramma* (supra) were to be accepted, then according to the court, the children of such marriage would be rendered bastard even under section 16 of the Hindu Marriage Act which provides for legitimisation of children of marriage which is void or voidable under section 16. It held:

> "It is well-settled principle of the law relating to marriages that the court should lean against the interpretation of any provision of law which is liable to render innocent children of the marriage as bastards."

Order: The Court clearly ruled that a marriage where the parties or any one of the parties is under the minimum prescribed age, is legal marriage. The only consequence of such marriage is that the persons concerned are liable to punishment under section 18, and under clause (iv) of sub-section (2) of section 13 an option to repudiate the marriage has been given to the wife. The appeal against conviction was accordingly, dismissed as the husband had committed an offence under section 494 of I.P.C.

Comment: The judgment seeks to protect the interests of children who would otherwise be rendered illegitimate if the under-age marriage is to be treated as void *ab initio*. However, it is over a quarter century since the judgment and a time has come to give serious thought to ban child marriages altogether.

Comment: It is significant to note that the Prohibition of Child Marriage Act, 2006, *vide* section 3 provides that a child marriage shall be voidable at the option of the contracting party who was a child at the time of marriage; marriage of a minor is void under section 12 of the Act if deceit or forceful means are used or if a minor is sold for purpose of marriage.

V. Mallikarjunaiah v. H.C. Gowramma,
AIR 1997 Kant 77: ILR 1997 Kant 964: 1997 (1) Kant LJ 570

Issue: Is a marriage where parties are below the minimum age requirement under the Hindu Marriage Act void?

Facts: A husband sought declaration that his marriage was void on the ground that he had not completed the age of 21 at the time of marriage, as required under section 5(iii) of the Hindu Marriage Act. According to him, he was 20 years, one month and twelve days old when the marriage was solemnized. The issue whether such marriage was valid, void or voidable was discussed at great length. The trial judge dismissed the husband's petition as it found no cause of action. In appeal, the arguments raised on behalf of the husband were that section 11 which provides for the grounds for void marriage, should be read with section 5 and any marriage in breach of conditions laid down in section 5 should be declared null and void. It was further contended that the law should not be so interpreted so as to defeat its provisions. On the other hand, for the wife it was contended that the Legislature specifically excluded section 5(iii) from the purview of section 11 (void marriage), section 12 (voidable marriage) and section 13 (divorce) and this exclusion was neither accidental nor by oversight, but deliberate. After detailed analysis and arguments of law and cases, the court held that such marriage is legal. The socio-cultural conditions of the society and the consequences of invalidating such marriages, on the girls specially, were highlighted thus:

> "Having regard to the strata in which such marriages were likely to take place, the Legislature was cautious of the fact that such provision should not have the result of rendering a large number of girls or young women virtually unmarried or destitute. The only security that a girl or woman in such a situation is entitled to is within the framework of the marriage and if that marriage can be loosely undone or if it is not recognised by the law, it would result in disastrous social consequences which is the only reason why this section was specifically excluded from sections 11 and 12 of the Act."

Order: The court held that the marriage was not void but valid even though the petitioner-husband had not completed the age of 21 at the time of the marriage. According to the court, the law does seek to discourage marriage of under-age boys and girls but not to the extent of making the marriage void or voidable. The court, however, suggested that in order to discourage such marriages, there is a need to provide for harsher penalties, particularly for those responsible for it.

Comment: The ultimate goal is to completely ban child marriages. However, in view of our socio-cultural conditions, child marriages are rampant in our society. It is only when safety and security of girls against exploitation is assured and a congenial atmosphere built up; when opportunities for education, job and economic security for girls are created along with awareness about the banes of child marriage—its effect on the couple—girls specially—and their children, is spread, will the incidence of under-age marriage come down. Under the Parsi law (Parsi Marriage and Divorce Act, 1936) such marriage is not valid (section 3), and under section 24 read with section 4(c) of the Special Marriage Act, 1954, such marriage is void.

Note: See also *Gajara Naran Bhura* v. *Kanbi Kunverbai Parbat*, AIR 1997 Guj 185: 1998 (1) MarriLJ 198: 1998 Mat LR 306 where a husband sought to defeat a wife's claim for maintenance on the ground that the marriage being in contravention of the minimum age requirement was void and so the wife had no right to seek maintenance. The court held that child marriage *per se* is not invalid nor a nullity unless there has been fraud or force, in which case provisions of section 12(1)(c) of the Hindu Marriage Act would be attracted. Such marriage (child marriage) being valid, the right and obligations that arise of the marriage cannot be avoided by not recognizing the marriage at all.

Ravi Kumar v. *State* and *Shikha Sharma* v. *State*, 2005 (1) DLT 124

Issue: What is the legal status of a marriage in contravention of legally prescribed age?

Facts: These petitions were in the nature of *habeas corpus*. R, a 28-year-old vegetable seller and S, a girl aged 16 plus, fell in love and got married. The elder sister, unhappy with the alliance and suspecting that S had been enticed and kidnapped by R lodged an F.I.R. Both R and S were apprehended. R was arrested on charge of kidnapping and S being a minor, was sent to Nari Niketan since she was not willing to go to her parents. Meanwhile, on statement of S that she and R loved each other and it was she who had called R and got married of her own choice, R was granted bail. R's application for custody of S was, however, dismissed. Subsequently, S filed a petition though R. Both were called in the court alongwith complainant who stated that she had lodged the complaint under a mis-apprehension and later realised that S had married R by her choice. The complainant accordingly, sought that the case against R be quashed. R was granted acquittal. In the other case, a writ of *habeas corpus* was filed by a mother and uncle of a minor girl aged 16 alleging that she had been kidnapped. It transpired, however, during the course of the proceedings that the accused was a tenant in the house of girl's mother and they started liking each other and got married. According to the girl's statement, it was she who suggested the boy (the accused) to leave home and get married since parents would not have agreed to their marriage. The complainant (mother) wanted the girl to stay with her at least till she attained majority but the girl refused. The girl, who was in the family way, wanted to live with the accused and until that time she expressed a desire to live in the Nari Niketan, rather than go to her parents.

The issue before the court was whether the marriages in both the above cases, were illegal; whether the girls, who though minor but had reached the age of discretion, could be sent in protective custody to a Remand Home against their will; whether in a *habeas corpus* petition, the court should entertain the prayer for quashing of the criminal proceedings for abduction, rape, kidnapping etc., in exercise of jurisdiction under articles 226 and 227 of the Constitution.

The main issue involved was, however, as to the status of the marriage because in both the cases, the girls were below the age of 18, though above 15.

Order: After analysing the case law on the issue, the court held that the marriage was neither void nor illegal on account of the girls being less than 18 years of age and being over 15 years. It accordingly held that the minor girls cannot, in the circumstances of the case, be directed to be detained in a Remand Home against their wishes. Criminal proceedings against the boys were quashed too.

Comment: While one does understand the rationale behind not invalidating non-age marriages, yet, the goal should be to completely ban child marriages in a phased manner. The court in this case has salvaged the situation by giving an order keeping in view the best interests of the parties in the circumstances of the case. It could, however, have added a rider or a word of caution against under-age marriages.

MATRIMONIAL RELIEFS AND GROUNDS

All the personal laws provide for certain matrimonial reliefs in situations where there are problems in marriage. These are restitution of conjugal rights, judicial separation and divorce. Apart from these a marriage may be annulled on certain specified grounds. Until such annulment, the marriage bond subsists with all the rights and liabilities which flow from a marriage. A marriage which is not in accord with the mandatory conditions specified in the statutory or personal laws of parties, is void. In other words, it has no legal status and will not be recognised by law whether or not the parties resort to legal proceedings and obtain a decree to that effect. The grounds for matrimonial reliefs under all the personal laws are more or less the same except the Muslim law, which is different.

This section of the Book contains cases on the various grounds for matrimonial reliefs, divorce specially.

ADULTERY

Wife Continuing to Live in Adultery Despite Promise that Would not Repeat: Marriage Dissolved

K.J. v. Smti K. w/o K.J.,
AIR 1952 Nag 395: ILR (1952) Nag 570

Issue: Would a husband, who leaves his young wife in the house in the company of a young man, be guilty of conniving his wife's adultery with the young man?

Facts: The parties were married at Nagpur under the Special Marriage Act on March 17, 1945. They had a son born of this marriage on June 4, 1948. The husband filed a suit for divorce against the wife alleging adultery with the co-respondent who was a student and staying in their house as a paying guest from September, 1948. The petitioner, who was connected with Trade Union Movement used to travel frequently. In March 1949, he went to Jodhpur where he was detained till January 30, 1950. After his return to Nagpur he found his wife had committed adultery with the co-respondent several times during his absence. The wife admitted to this and promised that she would not do that again. However, in spite of her promise, she continued to live a life of adultery with the co-respondent which was established by her letters. The wife alleged that the letters produced by the husband were obtained from her by force. The court, however, felt that in the circumstances of the case where the wife is an educated lady, the argument that she was forced to write these letters cannot be accepted. Also, the language of the letters shows that it was written voluntarily without any presure from anybody.

Thus, adultery was established. The court then delved on the issue of connivance. "Whether a reasonable person in such circumstances could have foreseen that a marital offence of this character was probable on the wife being alone in the company of another young man?"

According to the court, there is no presumption that there is connivance on the part of the husband. The husband, though he was moving in and out frequently, was always away on short visits and he had no reason to suspect illicit relation between his wife and the co-respondent. The wife, described her conduct admitting adultery, in these words:

"Your very absence proved instrumental in intensifying whatever such ordinary connection I had (with him) and in the end that intimacy took me so close to him that all those things changed into, *i.e.*, assumed the form of feeling of love and my condition became such that I began to feel the separation of any kind and I surrendered myself completely."

The court held, that the husband was in jail and so not a free agent as though he could have written to the paying guest to leave his house. This, however, does not prove that he connived. The wife's act of adultery was not induced by any voluntary or deliberate act on his part, the court said.

Further, as to condonation, the husband had forgiven her when she promised not to repeat her offence but despite her promise, she continued to have illicit relations with the co-respondent. And once the offence is repeated, the original guilt of the erring partner is revived, the court held.

Order: It was held that the wife was guilty of adultery and the husband had neither colluded nor condoned her act. The decree dissolving the marriage was confirmed.

Comment: Collusion and condonation are two important bars to a petitioner's claim. The idea is to ensure that by colluding, parties do not hood-wink the court. As to condonation, once the petitioner condones, the defendant's offence is wiped off unless it is repeated, in which case the original is also revived.

Adultery-Finding in Maintenance Proceedings Under Section 125, Cr. P.C., Can Be Used In Subsequent Divorce Proceedings

Narayan Rath v. *Kuntala Kumari Rath,* AIR 2005 Ori 49: 2004 (2) CLR 748: 2005 Mat LR 263

Issue: Can findings arrived at in maintenance proceedings under section 125 of the Cr. P.C., be used in subsequent divorce proceedings between the parties?

Facts: A husband filed a petition for divorce on the ground of wife's adultery. His case was that they were married in 1959 and were blessed with a daughter in 1963. He discovered letters received by his wife from her paramour, from the language of which it was evident that she was leading an adulterous life with one K. After discovery of these letters in 1963, the wife stayed in her parent's house and in 1974 she instituted proceedings under section 125 of the Cr. P.C., for maintenance for herself and the daughter. The Judicial Magistrate rejected her claim on the ground that she was leading a life of adultery; maintenance was, however, granted to the daughter. Both parties preferred criminal revisions which were dismissed and the order of the Judicial Magistrate was confirmed. Thereafter, the appellant-husband sought divorce on ground of adultery. To prove his case, he relied on certified copies of the letters and the deposition of the respondent wife in proceedings under section 125 and examined himself, his elder brother and the nephew of K. On assessment of the pleadings and evidence, the subordinate judge held that the case of adultery was not proved and hence dismissed the petition for divorce. Hence, the husband's appeal.

Order: For the appellant, it was argued that the basis for rejection of his petition by the subordinate court was that the letters were not proved in original in the civil proceedings and certified copy of the proceedings under section 125, Cr. P.C., are not sufficient to prove the fact that *K* had written these letters nor from the narration in the letter, adultery is proved; that deposition of the respondent wife in maintenance proceedings cannot be accepted as evidence to prove the case of adultery; that appellants' silence from 1963 to 1977 improbabilises the story of discovery of the letters from the wife's trunk; that the statement of the nephew that the writing is of his uncle *K* cannot be accepted as he did not prove that he had seen his uncle while writing and secondly, being the nephew he should not have spoken against his uncle. The court in the present appeal found these reasons as illogical and irrational. It was emphasised that in proceedings under section 125, Cr. P.C., both the trial magistrate as well as High Court in revision rejected the wife's claim for maintenance on the ground of proof of her adultery. These findings, unless rebutted by strong evidence, goes against the respondent.

Consequently, it was held that "adulterous conduct of the respondent is proved from the evidence adduced by the appellant and that has not been rebutted by the respondent. Under such circumstances, this court grants the decree of divorce by setting aside the impugned judgment and decree of the Trial Court".

Comment: When certain findings have been made by the courts in proceedings under section 125 of the Cr. P.C. and these are not rebutted, then such findings can be used in a suit for divorce also to establish the point or issue raised by the petition.

Note: See section on "paternity tests and adultery".

CRUELTY

Intention to be Cruel Immaterial

P.L. Sayal v. Sarla Rani,
AIR 1961 Punj 125: 63 Punj LR 377

Issue: Is *mens rea* or intention to cause cruelty essential to constitute mental cruelty so as to entitle the petitioner to a matrimonial relief. This was the issue involved.

Facts: The parties were married in 1948 and had two children. According to the petitioner husband, from mid 1949 the wife started ill-treating him and her real intention was that he leaves his parents house and set-up a home in Ludhiana with her parents. This unhappy situation reached climax when, on the advise of a 'faqir', she administered a potion in 1951, with ostensible object of bringing peace and harmony in the family. However, after this potion was given to him, he started having various health problems and his health started deteriorating. The husband construed this as cruelty and sought judicial separation on the ground of cruelty under section 10 of the Hindu Marriage Act. The wife resisted the same. Her argument was that the plea of cruelty is a mere camouflage and the real intention of the husband was to get rid of her to marry another girl. She agreed that the husband undoubtedly suffered health problems but denied that she had any malignant intention in giving that potion to him. The issue raised was whether the act of the respondent constitutes such cruelty as to cause a reasonable apprehension in the mind of the petitioner that it will be harmful or injurious for him to live with her. According to the district judge, it would not. Hence the husband's appeal. It was clear from the facts that the husband had suffered health problems and the wife also said that she had committed an evil act on the instigation of others and had she known about the ill-affects she would not have done it. The court analysed various English cases to determine how far intention is relevant in such cases. E.g., in *Squire* v. *Squire*, (1948) 2 All ER 51 where a wife suffered from insomnia and compelled her husband to remain awake to give her company at the cost of his health, it was held that though there was no evil intention on the part of the wife, yet, the act constituted cruelty. Reference was also made to other cases, like *Lissack* v. *Lissack*, 1950 (2) All ER 233: 1951-P 1; *Kaslefsky* v. *Kaslefsky*, 1950 (2) All ER 398: 66 TLR (Pt. 2) 616; *Jamieson* v. *Jamieson*, 1952 AC 525: (1952) 1 All ER 875: (1952) 1 TLR 833; *Robins* v. *Robins*, 1960 (3) All ER 66: (1960) 1 WLR 1089; and so on. Admitting the husband's appeal, a decree of judicial separation on the ground of cruelty was passed. The following observations of the court are pertinent (para 8) "The respondent's administration of the "love potion" may have emanated from the laudable object of bringing about domestic amity ……..but it had produced deleterious effect on the husband who is entitled to say now that it produced condition which he should not be called upon to endure. No doubt, man and wife take each other in marriage for better or worse, in sickness and in health but a spouse is not thereby entitled to put the life of the other in jeopardy, no matter what the real intention may be. The person whose life is put in jeopardy is entitled to seek protection of the court."

Order: The husband's appeal was allowed and a decree of judicial separation on the ground of cruelty by the wife was passed.

Comments: It is not the intention but the impact of the respondents act/ behaviour on the petitioner which determines whether cruelty is caused to the petitioner so as to entitle him/her to a matrimonial relief. "The court is not to wait for the recurrence of the peril again to afford remedy to the petitioner." If there is reasonable apprehension of recurrence of such conduct, the petitioner is entitled to protection by way of decree.

Husband's Debility and Sexual Weakness – Cruelty on Wife – Decree of Separation Sought by her Granted

Rita Nijhawan v. Balkishan Nijhawan, AIR 1973 Del 200: (1973) 75 Punj LR (D) 168

Issue: Does mental cruelty include sexual weakness? And, is a delay of 13 years for filing a petition for annulment on ground of husband's impotence, fatal to the case?

Facts: A wife filed a petition for annulment of marriage under section 12(1)(a) of the Hindu Marriage Act on the ground of husband's impotency or in the alternative for grant of decree of judicial separation under section 10(1)(a) and (b) (prior to the 1976 amendment) on the ground of desertion and cruelty. The parties were married in Delhi in 1954. In 1959, a son was born to them. In 1967, the wife filed the above mentioned application before the Additional District Judge, Delhi. The Judge gave the order against the petitioner. An appeal was made in the High Court and the order of the lower court was affirmed by a Single Judge. On the Letters Patent Appeal, the wife alleged impotency of the husband and that the marriage could not, therefore, be consummated. The birth of a child was attributed to the effect of medicines but all that "the respondent was able to do was to rub his organ on her organ and get discharged in the mouth of the vagina without any penetration". The court, however, found that it could not be believed that "there was not even one occasion when proper penetration took place during all the period from 1954 to 1967 more especially when the appellant became pregnant". Thus, the plea that the husband was impotent at the time of the marriage and continued to be so till the institution of the suit was not accepted. However, judicial separation was decreed on the ground of cruelty caused by the respondent's sexual debility. Reference was made to several cases to show that sex plays a significant part in marriage and intention of the respondent to cause harm is not the *sine qua non*.

As to the objection of delay of 13 years by the wife in filing the case, the court held that in view of the conditions of the society and the social background to which the parties belonged, such delay is not unusual.

Order: The wife's petition for judicial separation was decreed. According to the court, even though there was consummation and a child was born too, the husband's debility and sexual weakness was sufficient ground for causing mental cruelty to the wife.

Comment: There can be no fixed yardstick in the matter. It is a question of subjective satisfaction and each case has to be decided in the context of its own facts and desires/expectations of the parties.

Spouse Ceasing to be Hindu – *Locus* to File Petition under Hindu Marriage Act

Vilayat Raj v. *Sunila*,
AIR 1983 Del 351: (1983) 23 DLT 434: II (1983) DMC 164

Issue: Whether a marriage performed under the Hindu law can be dissolved under the Hindu Marriage Act by a spouse who ceases to be a Hindu by conversion to another religion?

Facts: The parties were Hindus at the time of marriage in 1978. They separated in 1980, and in 1981 the husband filed a petition for divorce under section 13(1)(ia) on the ground of cruelty. In the petition, he stated his religion as Mohammedan at the time of filing the same. The wife challenged his right to file a petition under the Hindu Marriage Act on the ground that he was no longer a Hindu. The Trial Court accepted the wife's plea but on appeal to the High Court, the order was reversed. It was held, that the relevant date on which both the parties are required to be Hindus in order to file a petition under the Hindu Marriage Act is the date of marriage and not the date of filing the petition.

The court observed:

> "Conversion.......does not *per se* operate to deprive the party of rights which may be otherwise available to him under the Act.... A party is not entitled to take advantage of his own wrong or disability and gain from a situation which he has brought about resulting in detriment to the other spouse.... But if the aggrieved party does not seek dissolution on this ground does it debar the other party from approaching the court on other grounds which are available to him under the Act? It would appear not."

The court made reference to the provisions of the Dissolution of Muslim Marriages Act, 1939. Under section 4 of the Act, renunciation of *Islam* by a married Muslim woman or her conversion to a faith other than *Islam*, shall not by itself, operate to dissolve her marriage. However, by a proviso to the section it is clarified that after such renunciation or conversion, the woman shall still be entitled to obtain a decree for the dissolution of her marriage on any of the grounds mentioned in section 2 of that Act. According to the Delhi High Court, even though the Hindu Marriage Act does not make any specific provision to this effect, the converted spouse would nevertheless be entitled to file a suit under it because he is not seeking any relief on the ground of conversion, nor is his case based on it in any manner.

Order: The husband's appeal was admitted and his conversion to *Islam* was held to be no bar to his filing petition under Hindu Marriage Act.

Dowry Demand – *Per se* is Cruelty

Shobha Rani v. *Madhukar Reddy*,
AIR 1988 SC 121: (1988) 1 SCC 105: JT 1987 (5) SC 433

Issue: Whether demand for dowry *per se* would amount to cruelty?

Facts: The parties were highly educated—the wife a post-graduate in biological sciences and the husband, by profession a doctor. Their happiness in marriage was, however, shortlived. Though at one point they thought of ending the relationship by mutual consent but that did not materialise. Ultimately, the wife moved the court for divorce on the ground of cruelty.

Cruelty simpliciter is a ground for divorce under section 13(1)(ia) of the Hindu Marriage Act; however, the same is not defined. It is a course of conduct of one which is adversely affecting the other. The cruelty may be mental or physical, intentional or unintentional. If it is physical cruelty, the court will have no problem to determine it. It is a question of fact and degree. Difficulty arises when it is a case of mental cruelty. In such cases the enquiry must begin as to the nature of the cruel treatment, and the impact of such treatment on the mind of the spouse. Ultimately, it is a matter of inference to be drawn by taking into account the nature of the conduct and its effect on the complaining spouse. There may, however, be cases where the conduct complained of itself is bad enough and *per se* unlawful or illegal. Then the impact or the injurious effect on the other spouse need not be enquired into or considered. In such case, the cruelty will be established if the conduct itself is proved or admitted.

The court pointed put the need for subjectivity while arriving at a conclusion whether the conduct complained of is cruelty or not. A set of facts stigmatised as cruelty in one case may not be so in another case. It cautioned(at page 123):

> "We, the judges and lawyers, therefore should not import our own notions of wife. We may not go parallel with them. There may be a generation gap between us and the parrties. It would be better if we keep aside our customs and manners. It would be also better if we less depend upon precedents."

In the case, the wife had several grievances but the only one with which the court was concerned was her complaint about the demand of dowry made by the husband and his parents. Dowry is a deep rooted evil in our society. It started as customary presents to the bride and bridegroom and his family as a mark of respect and affection. There was another aspect also to it *viz.*, various socio-economic considerations like less opportunities for high education or employment of girls and absence of legal right to a share in properties. This practice, however, has taken an ugly turn leading to torture and harassment to the bride. The court referred to the provisions of the Dowry Prohibition Act, 1961 as amended in 1984, and to section 498A of the Indian Penal Code penalizing a husband or his relatives who subject her to cruelty. It, however, confined itself to matrimonial conduct which constitutes cruelty as a ground for divorce. Such cruelty, if not admitted, requires to be proved on the preponderance of probabilities as in civil cases and not beyond a reasonable doubt as in criminal cases.

The wife's allegations of dowry demand by the husband and his parents was established, *inter alia*, by one of the letters written by the husband in which he had accepted that there was nothing wrong in his parents' asking for a few thousand rupees. "It is quite a common thing for which my parents are being blamed as harassment", the husband stated in his letter. The Trial Court or the High Court did not state that there was no demand for money. The case of the wife was, however, rejected on the ground that there was no satisfactory evidence that the demands were such as to border on harassment. According to the Trial Court (at p 125).

> "Though one would not Justify demand for money, it has to be viewed in this perspective. The respondent is a young doctor. There is nothing strange in his asking his wife to give him money when he needed it. There is no satisfactory evidence that the demands were such as to border on harassment".

The High Court also went on the same lines and said that the wife appears to be hypersensitive and she imagines too much and to unnatural things. It found that there was nothing wrong or unusual in the respondent, who is a doctor, asking his rich wife to spare some money.

The Supreme Court, on appeal, held that the High Court misunderstood the case and proceeded on the ground that the husband wanted money from the wife whereas the fact is that he himself had admitted in his letter that his parents demanded the money. It pointed out (at p. 126).

> "If the demand was only of such nature [i.e. the husband demanded money for help from the wife only] we would have thrown this appeal away. The wife must extend all help to husband and so too the husband to wife..... But case on hand is not a failure on that front...... It has been admitted by the husband himself in his letter dated August 28, 1983, addressed to the wife that his parents demanded dowry and...... that there was nothing wrong in that demand of the parents."

The court also made it clear that intention to harm is not an essential ingredient of matrimonial cruelty. It observed (at p. 127).

" There may be instances of cruelty by the unintentional but inexcusable conduct of any party....... The relief to the party cannot be denied on the ground that there had been no deliberate or wilful ill-treatment..... . The demand for dowry is prohibited under law. That by itself is bad enough. That in our opinion, amounts to cruelty entitling the wife to get a deree for dissolutions of marriage."

Order: The wife's appeal was granted and a decree for dissolution of marriage was passed in her favour on the ground of cruelty. The conduct that was held to amount to cruelty was the demand for dowry made by the husband and his parents. Thus, dowry demand *per se* has been held to constitute cruelty.

Comment: In our society today where dowry demands are increasing day by day, the judgment is a positive step. Cruelty is a vague and wide concept which cannot be established easily. However, as in this case, when the fact of dowry demand is established, it is construed as cruelty. also, intention to harm is immaterial.

Cruelty based on Allegations made in Written Statement

V. Bhagat v. D. Bhagat,
AIR 1994 SC 710: 1994 AIR SCW 45: (1994) 1 SCC 337

Issue: (i) Can a decree of divorce be passed in favour of the petitioner even when the allegations of the petitioner are recordedly "not proved"?

(ii) Can allegations made by the respondent in the written statement and other pleadings constitute cruelty so as to pass a decree of divorce?

Facts: The husband, a practising advocate in the Supreme Court, filed a petition for divorce on the ground of wife's adultery, under section 13(1)(i) of the Hindu Marriage Act. In the written statement filed by the wife and in questions put by her counsel to him in cross-examination, allegations were made that the husband was a mental patient. Statements like he is "suffering from mental hallucination" and "paranoid disorder", has a "morbid mind and needs psychiatric treatment", were made. In the cross-examination, the counsel appearing for the wife suggested that several members of his family, including his grandfather, are lunatics and that a streak of insanity is running in the entire family. When the petitioner objected to such questions, the wife's counsel made the following statement in the open court: "all of your family including your grandfather and others are lunatics with streaks of insanity running in the entire family; this is the respondents' case and that is why these questions have been asked". These questions and statements were made by the advocate on the instructions of the respondent wife. The courts below came to a finding that allegations of adultery levelled by the petitioner against his wife were "not proved" and so his petition was dismissed. Against this, the husband came in appeal.

Order: The court analysed the law and the authorities on the point in great detail. It exercised its inherent powers under article 142 of the Constitution to give relief to the petitioner. Without going into these details, reference may be made of the very practical, logical and erudite observations and findings of the Court. It observed (at p. 719):

> "The obvious conclusion is that she had resolved to live in agony only to make life a miserable hell for the petitioner as well. This type of callous attitude in the context of the facts of this case leaves no manner of doubt in our mind that the respondent is bent upon treating the petitioner with mental cruelty. It is abundantly clear that the marriage between the parties has broken down irretrievably and there is no chance of their coming together, or living together again. Having regard to the peculiar features of this case, we are of the opinion that the marriage between the parties should be dissolved under section 13(1)(ia) of the Hindu Marriage Act and we do so accordingly."

The husband in this case was fighting the battle for 13 long years and the wife was not only contesting the same, but as is obvious, at the same time levelling humiliating and false allegations. Even though the husband's ground of adultery was not proved yet the allegations and the conduct of the wife was held to amount to cruelty. Apart from that, the court found that there was no substance left in their relationship. When it was contended on behalf of the wife that the plea of irretrievable breakdown of the marriage is not sustainable, the Court aptly remarked (at p.721):

> "Before parting with this case, we think it necessary to append a clarification. Merely because there are allegations and counter-allegations, a decree of divorce cannot follow. Nor is mere delay in disposal of the divorce proceedings by itself a ground. There must be really some extraordinary features to warrant grant of divorce on the basis of pleadings (and other admitted material) without a full trial. Irretrievable breakdown of the marriage is not a ground by itself. But while scrutinising the evidence on record to determine whether the ground(s) alleged is made out and in determining the relief to be granted, the said circumstance can certainly be borne in mind. The unusual step as the one taken by us herein can be resorted to only to clear up an insoluble mess when the court finds it in the interest of both the parties."

Comment: This is indeed a very extraordinary but practical judgment. The Court ignored the technicalities of the law which require that the ground on which relief is sought has to be established before the relief is granted; it also invoked irretrievable breakdown of the marriage though it is not a ground available under the Act. The court took a holistic view and the cumulative effect of the entire circumstances to "clear up an insoluble mess".

Acts Alleged to Constitute Cruelty – Not Serious Enough – No Cruelty

S. Hanumantha Rao v. S. Ramani,
AIR 1999 SC 1318: 1999 AIR SCW 1012: (1999) 3 SCC 620

Issue: It is important to view the facts in totality so as to come to a finding of mental cruelty.

Facts: A husband filed a petition for divorce under section 13 of the Hindu Marriage Act on the ground of mental cruelty. Allegations in support of his claim included, *inter alia*, that the wife removed her *mangal sutra*; she kept copies of letters which she wrote to him and that has shaken his confidence; her parents made a representation to the women's protection cell for reconciliation and he had to take anticipatory bail.

The Trial Court held that the above incidents/conduct constituted cruelty by the wife and hence passed the decree in favour of the husband. The wife's appeal against this order to the High Court of Andhra Pradesh was allowed and the Trial Court order reversed. It is against this that the present appeal has come up before the Supreme Court.

Order: The court analysed the facts and circumstances of the case and came to a finding that the case of mental cruelty was not established by the allegations made by the husband. It conceded that while a *mangal sutra* around a wife's neck is a sacred symbol of married state, but in this case the wife had removed the same in privacy at the instance of the husband and so he cannot complain about it. Regarding retention of copies of letters by her, it was the wife's arguments that she had written various letters to the husband and he never cared to reply, so she started keeping copies. This, according to the court, is a natural thing to do in the circumstances of the case. As regards representation to the women's cell, the court found no evidence to indicate that the husband or his family was harassed by the cell whose intervention was sought for reconciliation through one of her relatives who was earlier Superintendent of Police. If, out of panic, the husband and his family members sought anticipatory bail, the wife could not be blamed for that, the court observed. The husband's appeal was, accordingly, dismissed.

Comment: Mangal sutra and bindi are considered to be important symbols of marriagehood. A woman who shows disrespect for these symbols is viewed as committing an affront to the dignity of the husband so as to give him cause of action to plead mental cruelty. While some courts have considered the 'offence' serious enough, others have not given it undue importance except as one incident amongst others. In this case, suppose the wife had not removed the *mangal sutra* at the instance of the husband, would she have been guilty of mental cruelty? In *Shobha Srinivas Bodigar* v. *Srinivas Veeranna Bodigar*, AIR 2002 Kant 256, a wife who removed her *mangal sutra* and threw it on the road was held to be guilty by the Trial Court. Fortunately, the High Court, in appeal, differed. Are there no symbols of married state for husbands which they need to honour? One wonders!

Note: *See* also *Gourab Datta* v. *Arundhati Majumdar,* AIR 2011 Gau 183 – A wife who used to earn money by tuitions from 6 a.m. and working in a school followed by tuitions again and therefore returning home at 10 p.m. is no indication of any adverse conduct on her part. Her late return home does not constitute cruelty to her husband.

Wife Unable to Conceive – Ill-treated – Husband Married Again – Held Cruelty by Husband

Suneer Sharma v. *Madhurlata Sharma,*
AIR 2000 MP 26: 1999 (2) MP LJ 603: 2000 (1) CCC 315

Issue: Second marriage of the husband is *per se* enough ground to establish the wife's plea of cruelty and desertion.

Facts: The appellant husband and the respondent wife; both belonged to the medical profession, the wife being more qualified than the husband. When after two years of the marriage the wife did not conceive, she was subjected to various medical tests which indicated that there was some problem because of which chances of her conceiving were poor. Thereafter, she was allegedly ill-treated and taunted as a *banjh* (barren woman). Once the mother-in-law suggested to her that she should end her life so that the appellant could go in for another marriage. She was forcibly turned out of the house and thereafter the appellant entered into another marriage and had three children from this marriage. The wife filed a suit for dissolution of marriage under section 13 of the Hindu Marriage Act on the ground of mental and physical cruelty, desertion and his second marriage. The Trial Court, after recording evidence, passed a judgment in favour of the wife; an appeal against this order by the husband was also decided against him by a single judge, hence the present Letters Patent Appeal.

Order: Dismissing the husband's appeal, the court said that there was no cause for interference with the orders of the earlier courts. It observed (at p. 28):

> "........when he has contracted a second marriage and is living with his second wife and children for last so many years, the respondent wife has a just and reasonable cause to live separately from him. Contracting a second marriage in itself is an act of causing mental torture and tantamounts to cruelty for purpose of section 13 of the Hindu Marriage Act."

Comment: While, there were other facts and circumstances as well to establish the ground of cruelty and desertion, the very fact of the husband contracting a second marriage by itself was held to be an act of cruelty sufficient to give relief in favour of the wife.

Mental Cruelty to be Assessed having Regard to Various Factors Like Status, Education etc., of Parties

G.V.N. Kameswara Rao v. G. Jabilli,
AIR 2002 SC 576: 2002 AIR SCW 162: (2002) 2 SCC 296

Issue: Dimensions of cruelty, specially, mental cruelty cannot be circumscribed. Each case would have to be assessed on its own facts and circumstances.

Facts: A husband filed a petition for divorce on the ground of wife's cruelty. The litigation went on for 15 years. While the Family Court granted him divorce, the High Court reversed the same holding that it was the husband who was at fault and he was trying to take advantage of his own wrong.

The husband was an academically highly qualified person with two doctorates and the wife also was a post-graduate and working as lecturer at the time of marriage. He was working in the U.S.A. and the wife joined him later, after six months. There were problems and tensions right from the beginning. The husband alleged that the wife was always quarrelling and behaved in a very insulting manner, humiliating him in the presence of outsiders and creating scenes, not doing any household work, refusing to share bed, etc. After sometime she returned to India with their daughter and the husband did not even know where they were until he made enquires and found out. When he went to fetch them, he was insulted and not allowed to enter the house. He further alleged that she filed criminal complaints against him and his mother and they were called to the police station where they were detained for more than ten hours. Though the police refused to register any complaint as they did not find any *prima facie* case, it caused a lot of agony and embarrassment to the petitioner husband and his mother. On the basis of these allegations, he sought divorce on the ground of mental cruelty. After analysing the evidence and the nature of complaints, the Court held that cruelty was established.

Order: The High court order dismissing the husband's petition for divorce on the ground of wife's cruelty was set aside. The Supreme Court held that the mental cruelty faced by the petitioner is to be assessed having regard to his status in life, educational background and the environment in which he lived. In this case, the husband who was holding a position in life must have suffered humiliation, and acute mental cruelty in the hands of the wife and so was entitled to a decree of divorce. It observed:

> "The police did not register any case evidently as it was a domestic quarrel and not of a serious nature, and the incident shows the innate lack of self-control which had driven the respondent to this exorable conduct. But the humiliation and agony suffered by the appellant and his mother, considering their status in life and the social circumstances, was too much."

Comment: Cruelty, not being defined, the inference of cruelty—mental cruelty specially, has to be drawn from the circumstances of each case. Its dimensions and parameters cannot be circumscribed.

Non-consummation of Marriage and Rude & Abusive Behaviour is Cruelty

Praveen Mehta v. *Inderjit Mehta,*
AIR 2002 SC 2582: 2002 AIR SCW 2886: (2002) 5 SCC 706

Issue: In an appeal against divorce by the wife, the fact of husband's second marriage which was perfectly legal in the circumstances of the case, is an important consideration in dismissing the appeal.

Facts: A husband filed a divorce petition against his wife on the ground of mental cruelty. The acts and behaviour alleged included wife's non-cooperation in conjugal relations as a result of which the marriage was not consummated, her abusive and rude behaviour in the presence of elders and outsiders, police complaints against the petitioner and his parents, making false statement that she had conceived and there was a miscarriage, etc. The couple had lived together for hardly six months after marriage and at the time of filing the petition by the husband, they had been living separately for ten years. All efforts by him to bring her around failed. The cumulative effect of all these on the mind of the husband was considered.

Order: The court held that the acts alleged by the husband were grave enough to constitute mental cruelty. It remarked:

"Mental cruelty is a state of mind and feeling with one of the spouses due to the behaviour pattern by the other.........feeling of anguish, disappointment and frustration in one spouse caused by the conduct of the other can only be appreciated on assessing the attending facts and circumstances taken cumulatively."

The court emphasised the fact that in case of mental cruelty, an isolated instance of behaviour cannot be picked up to assess whether or not such behaviour constitutes mental cruelty.

Comment: Combination of factors constitute mental cruelty. In this case, the husband had entered into another marriage two years after the judgment of the single judge and nearly four months after the judgment of the division bench of the High Court, both decreeing dissolution. There were no legal impediments to the husband's second marriage.

Not Any or Every Abnormal Act Would Constitute Mental Cruelty

B.N. Panduranga Shet v. S.N. Vijay Laxmi,
AIR 2003 Kant 357: ILR (2003) 3 Kant 1852: 2003 (3) Kant LJ 247

Issue: Can any and every abnormal act of the other party be viewed as mental cruelty or schizophrenic so as to entitle the petitioner to a matrimonial relief?

Facts: A husband sought dissolution of the marriage on the ground of mental cruelty by the wife. He alleged that the wife was suffering from schizophrenia, and behaved in a manner which caused him mental cruelty. The acts and incidents alleged by him were, such as, removing *mangalsutra* and *kumkum*, throwing bangles and other abnormal behaviour. He further averred that she had started showing her "true colours" and abnormal behaviour just 15 days after the marriage.

Order: The court held that these acts were not sufficient to prove cruelty; the further fact that the husband stayed with her in this condition for four years before he took her to the doctor, and also had two children indicate that he did not notice any serious abnormality which necessitated medical treatment. The wife's condition and conduct was, therefore, held to be not such that the husband could not be expected to live with her and it would be unreasonable to ask him to do so. The mere fact that the marriage had broken down or that the parties may not be able to live together henceforth cannot be a ground for the court to brand a person as one suffering from schizophrenia. The following observations of the Supreme Court in *Ram Narain Gupta* v. *Rameshwari Gupta*, AIR 1988 SC 2260: JT (1988) 3 SC 621: (1988) 4 SCC 247 were relied upon:

> "All mental abnormalities are not recognised as grounds for grant of decree. If the mere existence of any degree of mental abnormality could justify dissolution of marriage, few marriages would indeed survive."

The husband's petition was thus dismissed.

Comment: In cases where plea of mental disorder or unsoundness of mind is taken for obtaining dissolution of marriage, courts are very cautious. Every person suffers from some degree of unusual or abnormal behaviour. The court would not take notice of every aberration unless it is of a serious or grave nature.

Mental Cruelty – Retraction of Charges Once Levelled – Damage Already Done – Does not Absolve Party of Mental Cruelty

Vijaykumar Ramchandra Bhate v. Neela Vijaykumar Bhate,
AIR 2003 SC 2462: 2003 AIR SCW 2530: (2003) 6 SCC 334

Issue: Would allegations of unchastity against the wife absolve the husband of mental cruelty to the wife if he later retracts his allegations?

Facts: A wife filed a divorce petition against her husband on the ground of cruelty, alleging incidents of harassment and nagging which caused her mental agony, thereby affecting her health. The Family Court viewed these to be normal wear and tear of matrimonial life. However, the allegations made by the husband in his written statement against her character with enumeration of incidents and instances and branding her as an unchaste woman having illicit relations with the son of a neighbour were held to be "grave assault on character, honour, reputation, status as well as health of the wife". Even though these allegations were later withdrawn by amending the written statement, the court held that the husband could not be absolved of levelling the outrageous allegations. The divorce decree in favour of the wife was upheld in appeal. On the issue whether the averments, accusations and character assassination of the wife by the appellant husband in his written statement constituted mental cruelty, the Court observed:

> "The position of law in this regard has come to be well-settled and declared that disgusting accusations of unchastity and indecent familiarity with a person outside wedlock and allegations of extra-marital relationships is a grave assault on the character, honour, reputation, status as well as the health of the wife. Such aspersions or perfidiousness attributed to the wife..........would amount to worst form of insult and cruelty sufficient by itself to substantiate cruelty in law, warranting the claim of the wife being allowed."

The husband's plea that once the allegations were withdrawn by an amendment, they should not form the basis for consideration and should in fact be considered to have never been on record, was rejected with the following remarks:

> "A conscious and deliberate statement levelled with pungency and that too, placed on record through the written statement cannot so lightly be ignored or brushed aside to be of no consequence, merely because it came to be removed from the record only..........the indelible impact and scar it initially would have created, cannot be said to have got *ipso facto* dissolved, with the amendment ordered."

Order: The husband's appeal against the divorce decree was dismissed as the court held that even retracted allegations of the husband would constitute mental cruelty on the wife. The retraction cannot absolve the husband of the mental cruelty inflicted by him by allegations in his written statement.

Another point clarified by the court was that the section on cruelty does not stipulate any particular period or duration to be necessary to constitute cruelty. It is not the length nor the numerical count of such incident nor continuous course of such conduct but "the intensity, gravity and stigmatic impact of it when meted out even once and the deleterious effect of it on the mental attitude, necessary for maintaning a conducive matrimonial home".

The husband's further plea that if the divorce decree is set aside, there may be fresh avenues and scope for reconciliation, was brushed aside by the court as "too desolate, merely born out of despair rather than based upon any real concrete and genuine purpose or aim."

Comment: It is a positive judgment which gives a message that a spouse cannot play clever by first hurling accusations and then, as an eye-wash, withdraw them. The pain and mental torture caused by the allegations has been duly recognised.

Wife Gang Raped: No Cruelty on Husband

Rajesh Kumar Singh v. *Rekha Singh,*
AIR 2005 All 16: 2005 All LJ 102: 2004 (23) All Ind Cas 365

Issue: Can a husband claim cruelty on the plea that he has to live with his wife who is a victim of gang rape?

Facts: The parties were married on May 11, 1999 and lived together for some days after marriage whereafter, the husband who is in defence services (not in the officer category, though) joined back his duties. In between they lived together from time to time when the husband used to come home. The time when they were not together, the wife used to reside at her father's residence and visited her in-laws off and on.

An unfortunate incident with the wife took place during April 11-13, 2000 whereafter the husband filed a suit for divorce on ground of adultery and cruelty by the wife. His allegations were that the wife had illicit relations with respondent 2; she had been missing during the period April 11-13, 2000 for which an FIR was lodged by her father on April 12, 2000 and she was found in unconscious state on April 13, 2000 near a railway track. He further alleged that she had left her father's residence on April 11, 2000 with respondent 2 for abortion but later on respondent 2 duped her and she was gang-raped during April 11-13, 2000. The wife denied that she was missing; that she had any illicit relationship with respondent 2 or anyone else; she alleged that her in-laws used to ill-treat her and her husband had promised to take her with him; she was informed that he was coming and she was to meet him at his sister's house where the appellant husband's father and his sister were present; they gave her tea mixed with some intoxicant; she became unconscious and thereafter she was left near the railway track. She does not know what had happened with her during April 11-13, 2000.

The Trial Court dismissed the husband's petition. It held that the wife had no illicit relationship with respondent number 2 or anyone; and moreover, rape was not a ground for divorce. Hence the husband's appeal. During the examination, the husband and his father made no complaints about her character or general behaviour/conduct. However, photostat copies of some letters were filed which the court disbelieved. There was no other evidence to establish her illicit relations with anyone. The court came to a conclusion that some unfortunate incident happened and as the husband himself had stated—the wife was gang raped. The husband's counsel suggested that it was not possible for the appellant (husband) to move in the society with a person who has been gang raped and it is a kind of cruelty and so he is entitled to a decree of divorce.

Order: The husband's appeal was dismissed. The court was, in fact, shocked at the counsel's submission. It stated:

> "We have no words to describe this submission. The least we can say: We are appalled. It is beyond our comprehension that anyone can even make such suggestion. It shows lack of understanding regarding rape, trauma and emotional needs of a rape victim."

The court further remarked:

> "............adultery is a ground for divorce, rape isn't. There is a fundamental difference between the two; one is with consent, the other is without consent. There is no evidence that the contesting respondent was a consenting party or she has committed adultery."

Thus, the court clearly held that the wife had no illicit relations with anyone; rape is not a ground for divorce; the husband could not claim cruelty because he had to live with a rape victim; and there was no cruelty on the part of the wife.

Comment: The court has shown immence sensitivity to the issue. Today when cases of rape are increasing each day, the plight of the victim who has suffered the trauma of rape can well be imagined if the courts view it as a 'matrimonial offence'. "The rape victim doesn't require divorce suit slapped on her; she doesn't require court room; she requires counselling, understanding, compassion and moral support".

Mere Bald Statements, Routine Wear and Tear Vague Allegations: No Cruelty

Asha Gupta v. Rajiv Kumar Gupta, AIR 2005 P&H 134: 2005 (2) CCC 106: 2005 (2) Punj LR 45

Issue: Would concealment of correct age; approaching women's organisation or lodging criminal complaint, by themselves be sufficient to establish cruelty by a wife so as to entitle the husband to a decree of divorce?

Facts: A husband filed a petition for divorce under section 13 of the Act on the ground of cruelty by the wife. The incidents and facts which allegedly constituted cruelty on him were, *inter alia*, that she had stated on the first night of the marriage that she married him against her wishes and she was forced to do so by her parents and brother; that for a few days after marriage she avoided consummation; that she had concealed her real age; that she was dyeing her hair which fact was not revealed before marriage; that she misrepresented that she was the youngest child of her family; that she compelled him to separate from his parents and live separately; that she was very aggressive; that she approached women's organisation which harassed him; that she lodged a report with police for offences under sections 406 and 498A of the IPC; that she threatened suicide; that she went to his workplace and insulted him; that she would sit in the balcony and tell her child that his father (the child's) was dead; that they were living separately for eleven years, etc. The additional district judge passed a decree of divorce on the above allegations. Hence the wife's appeal, which was accepted.

Order: Most of the acts alleged by the husband were held to be bald statements by him. The allegations were vague and too general and nothing concrete was brought on record to show that the wife had caused cruelty. Her approaching the *Mahila Sangathan* or filing criminal complaints was held not to be cruelty, especially when husband was having dowry articles with him even on the date of filing of petition. As to the issue of age, it was found that both the parties had tried to conceal their exact ages and not disclosing correct age would not be sufficient to prove allegation of cruelty especially when husband himself was guilty of not giving his true age. It was also held that merely living separate for eleven years would be no ground for holding that the marriage had irretrievably broken and even assuming that it had irretrievably broken down, the divorce could not have been granted since breakdown of marriage is not a statutorily recognised ground for divorce. Thus, the ADJ's decree was set aside and the wife's appeal allowed.

Comment: Mere bald statements or routine wear and tear of married life would not constitute cruelty. However, cruelty is a very wide and vague term and its parameters cannot be defined. Each case would have to be decided on the basis of its own facts and circumstances.

Note: See also *Jagalur Madhukeshwar* v. *B.G. Kamalakshi*, AIR 2012 Karn 22 where husband's allegations of cruelty consisted only of acts of omission on the part of wife, like not doing household work or taking care of children, and no overt acts of cruelty were alleged, the court held no case of mental cruelty entitling him to relief was made out.

Cruelty by Wife's Parents – Whether Cruelty by Wife

Kamlesh Kumar Agarwal v. *Mamta Devi,*
AIR 2005 Jhar 10: II (2004) DMC 706: 2004 (4) Civ LJ 535

Issue: Can behaviour of the relatives of the wife be considered to be act of cruelty on the part of the wife?

Facts: The parties were married on April 27, 1996 and also had a son. The husband filed a petition for divorce under section 13(1)(i-a) of the Hindu Marriage Act on the ground of cruelty. He alleged that after six months of marriage, differences arose and the wife started behaving cruelly towards him and denied him her company. She left him and went to her parents' house though she returned after sometime, and then again left with the child. The wife denied all allegations and submitted that she had never behaved cruelly and was willing to live with her husband and in-laws. The husband examined five witnesses. The court relied on evidence of two witnesses who had no axe to grind—the landlady of the building where the couple were residing and a friend of the elder brother of the petitioner. According to their statements there was no serious misunderstanding between the husband and the wife and there was nothing amiss in their relationship. In sum, the court below found no evidence of the wife ill treating her husband amounting to cruelty within the meaning of section 13(1)(i-a) of the Hindu Marriage Act and so dismissed the husband's petition; hence the husband's appeal.

Order: The court held that there was no sufficient evidence to support the husband's plea. It held, "The behaviour of the relatives of the wife cannot be considered to be an act of cruelty on the part of the wife though no doubt she could have resisted their attempts to disturb the matrimonial home and continued to stay with her husband." The husband's appeal was accordingly dismissed and the Trial Court order confirmed.

Comment: It is true that the behaviour of relatives of the wife cannot be considered to be act of cruelty on part of wife but each case has to be decided on its own facts. If their behaviour is too objectionable and the wife either acquiesces or supports them then its impact on the marriage and the husband's mind may be serious. Likewise, if the behaviour of husband's relatives is bad, it could amount to cruelty on the wife.

Refusal to have Sex and Long Separation etc., is Cruelty

Usharani Lenka v. Panigrahi Subhash Chandra Dash,
AIR 2005 Ori 3: 2004 (23) All Ind Cas 583:
2005 (1) Marri LJ 476

Issue: (i) Would mere allegations by the husband of wife's pre-marriage pregnancy and abortion just before marriage without cogent evidence, entitle him to a decree under section 12?

(ii) Does wife's refusal to have sexual intercourse with the husband and living away from him for seven years; and filing of criminal cases, amount to mental cruelty?

Facts: The parties were married on May 22, 1997 according to Hindu rites, but, as alleged by the husband, the same was never consummated as the wife refused sexual relationship. He also suspected that the wife was pregnant by some other person and she terminated the pregnancy just before the marriage. His further allegation was that the wife had permanent gynaecological problem due to which she refused sexual relations with him. He accordingly sought annulment of the marriage under clause 12(1)(a) (non-consummation owing to impotence) and 12(1)(d) (wife's pregnancy at time of marriage through someone other than petitioner).

In addition, the husband sought a decree of divorce under section 13 of the Hindu Marriage Act on the ground of mental cruelty alleging that she had refused sexual intercourse, deserted him soon after marriage and filed several criminal cases against him, thus causing him intense mental pain and psychological agony. The wife challenged the arguments. Her case was that soon after marriage, the husband and his family members started making demands for dowry and when these demands were not acceded to, she was tortured and ill-treated by them. According to her, the husband had filed the case on false grounds only to protect himself and his family from criminal prosecution for dowry demand and torture.

The Family Court granted a decree of divorce subject to the husband paying her permanent alimony of ₹ 40,000. Both the parties were aggrieved and hence the appeal.

Order: The court found that there was no evidence on record to indicate that the wife was pregnant by some other person before the marriage or that she had undergone abortion before the marriage. There was also no specific evidence that she had any gynaecological problem rendering her unfit for sexual intercourse. Contrarily, there was a medical report which stated that she was sexually healthy and not suffering from any gynaecological problem. Bald statements of the husband cannot be taken to be sufficient to satisfy the requirements of section 12(1)(a) and (d) of the Act the court held (at p. 5). However, in regard to divorce under section 13, the court found that the wife's refusal to have sexual intercourse and also leaving the matrimonial home shortly after marriage and continuing to be away for 7 years did amount to mental cruelty. Besides, she also filed criminal cases and the husband had to defend these cases for a considerable time. All these factors must have been very humiliating and thus amounted to mental cruelty, the court said. The husband was thus held to be entitled to decree of divorce. The amount of permanent alimony of ₹ 40,000 granted by the Family Court was raised to ₹ 1 lakh. The husband's plea that since the wife was erring party, she was not entitled to maintenance was not accepted. According to the court:

> "This plea does not appear legally convincing to us for the simple reason that the marriage between the parties is admitted and the indigenous status of the wife is established. The conduct of the husband in the civil proceeding has also to be taken note of. He made allegations of adultery and impotency against the wife which were found to be baseless."

Thus the Family Court divorce decree was confirmed and alimony raised from ₹ 40,000 to one lakh.

Comment: Allegations of pre-marriage pregnancy and abortion are very serious and defamatory and courts should take serious note of them. Parties should not be allowed to resort to ground-hunting in a desperate bid to get out of a relationship. False allegations involving character of a spouse are not only socially stigmatic but also cause great agony and trauma.

Filing of criminal cases /complaints *per se* is not cruelty

Kamleshwari Bai v. *Peeluram Sahi,* AIR 2010 Chh 16

Issue: A wife seeking resort to protective legal provisions leading to harassment or other consequences for husband/his family would not *per se*, be guilty of cruelty unless these complaints or cases were malicious, false or motivated.

Facts: In this case, there were problems in the marriage and the wife alleged ill-treatment, dowry demand and harassment by the husband. The husband was also living in a relationship with another woman. The wife thus was compelled to bane the matrimonial home to stay with her parents. She also filed complaint under the criminal law for dowry demand. However, when the husband left the company of the other woman, the wife was prepared to go back to the matrimonial home but the husband refused to take her back and filed a case for divorce on ground of cruelty and desertion. He alleged that she misbehaved with him and his family, did not do household work and preferred to stay at her parents house who were financially in a better position. Her fling of complaint was construed as cruelty. On the basis of above averments, the Trial Court decreed his suit and granted divorce.

Order: Against this order, the wife filed an appeal. Allowing the same, the court held, "invoking legal remedy by parties cannot be termed as cruelty unless the same is launched mala fidely and with a view to harass and torture the other party. "The decree of divorce was consequently set aside.

Comment: Protective laws for women do have the potential of misuse by unscrupulous people the courts are not unaware of this. In any case, the mere resort to these remedies without any *mala fides* would not constitute cruelty.

Note: See also *Deeplakshmi Zingade* v. *S.R. Zingade*, AIR 2012 Bom 16 where court held, "when an Act (protection of Women from Domestic Violence Act, 2005, in this case) permits a wife to approach court under provisions of the Act and if that remedy is availed of such act should not be treated as cruelty otherwise in no case can a lady file a complaint if it is to be treated as cruelty." Also See *Goka Kameswari* v. *Goka Venkataramaiah*, AIR 2012 AP 23; *Mithilesh Shrivastava* v. *Kiran Shrivastava*, AIR 2012 Chh 21.

Filing False Criminal Cases and Resiling From Agreement to Withdraw Criminal Cases after taking Substantial Amounts under the Agreement is Cruelty

Pinki Jain v. Sanjay Jain,
AIR 2005 Del 273: 2005 (2) CCC 795: I (2005) DMC 241

Issue: Filing of criminal cases leading to arrest which are admittedly false, and resiling from an agreement after taking a substantial amount to sign papers for divorce by mutual consent are clear instances of cruelty.

Facts: A husband filed a petition for divorce on the ground of cruelty under section 13(1)(i-a), Hindu Marriage Act against his wife. Amongst the allegations amounting to cruelty, it was stated, *inter alia*, that the wife had filed false complaints against him, his father and uncle, and criminal cases were registered in the court of the CJM, Meerut under various sections of the Indian Penal Code and Dowry Prohibition Act. On the basis of this, they were arrested and remained in jail for about ten days. Even their bail application was strongly opposed by the wife. Ultimately, there was a mutual settlement between the parties and under that the wife agreed to receive ₹ 5,25,000 towards full and final settlement for divorce by mutual consent. She also received Kisan Vikas Patra valuing ₹ 3 lakh, ₹ 35,000 in cash and balance amount of ₹ 1,90,000 to be paid by way of two FDRs of ₹ 95,000 each in the name of son and daughter.

The criminal cases were found to be baseless and the husband and his relatives were acquitted. Also the wife, after receiving Rs 3 lakh by way of Kisan Vikas Patra and ₹ 35,000 in cash from the husband, resiled from the settlement and did not agree for divorce by mutual consent. This, according to the Additional District Judge, was a clear instance of cruelty and so he passed a decree for divorce. Hence the wife's appeal.

Order: Dismissing the wife's appeal, the High Court held that the criminal complaints filed by the wife were "admittedly" not based on true facts; in other words, they were false. As remarked by the court this "one single instance of cruelty which stands admitted between the parties takes the wind out of appellant's sails". Besides, after receiving a heavy amount as per agreement, she resiled from the agreement and refused to sign divorce papers as agreed by her under the agreement. The conduct of the wife was thus held to be a clear case of cruelty.

Comment: Filing of false criminal cases by the wife leading to arrest and confinement in jail, of the husband and his relatives is cruelty; and so also resiling from an agreement after taking part of amount under the agreement under which she agreed to divorce by mutual consent. The husband thus succeeded in obtaining divorce on ground of cruelty.

Note: See also *Dinesh Nagda v. Shantibai*, AIR 2012 MP 40 where false prosecution of the husband and his family members for offences under section 498A and 494 of the I.P.C leading to trial for seven long years causing them extreme agony and humiliation was construed as cruelty.

Cruelty Based on Allegations Made in Written Statement
Manisha Sandeep Gade v. *Sandeep Vinayak Gade,*
AIR 2005 Bom 180: 2005 (1) All MR 564: 2005 (1) Bom CR 554

Issue: (i) Can divorce be granted on ground of cruelty merely on the basis of allegation made by the respondent in the written statement?

(ii) Is it mandatory to amend the petition and raise the plea that the petitioner has suffered cruelty in view of the allegations made in the written statement?

Facts: The parties were married in December 1997, but stayed together for hardly two years as differences developed between them. There was no child of the marriage. Both were working – wife was self-employed with monthly income of ₹ 6,000 and the husband, a teacher with salary of ₹ 3,000. The husband filed a petition for divorce under section 13(1)(i) of the Hindu Marriage Act on the ground of cruelty and the wife filed a petition seeking permanent maintenance under section 18 of the Hindu Marriage Act.

The case of the husband was that the wife treated him with cruelty and the following instances were enumerated to substantiate the case, *viz*. (i) refusal to do domestic work, (ii) insulting and abusive behaviour, (iii) insistence on having a separate residence; (iv) not returning home on a number of days every week, (v) threatening and terrorizing the husband and his parents, (vi) not disclosing that she had some gynaecological problem prior to marriage and concealing her miscarriage. While denying all these allegations, the wife made her own allegation in the written statement which were, that (i) he behaved with her perversely and harassed her sexually; (ii) he would indulge in obscene talk with his girl friends on phone and in person and would behave immodestly with the girl friends to torture her; (iii) he had illicit relationship with one 'L', wife of 'V' and in fact he wanted to marry her. Apart from these allegations against the husband, she made the following allegations against her father-in-law as well, *viz*. (i) he would touch her unnecessarily, and (ii) he would barge into the kitchen if she was changing her clothes.

On analysing the evidence, the Family Court came to the conclusion that the husband had failed to establish the six specific instances of cruelty. He, however, stated that the allegations made by the wife in the written statement were baseless and amounted to cruelty. As to her allegation about the illicit relationship with L, there was no other evidence except her own bare words in the affidavit. In fact it was her duty to examine L's hudband V which was not done. Likewise, no details about her allegations against the father-in-law were given. Thus, a decree of divorce was granted in favour of the husband. As to the wife's entitlement to alimony under section 25 of the Hindu Marriage Act, the court noted that the wife's income was more than the husband's and so she was not entitled to permanent alimony. As far as the wife's petition for maintenance under section 18 of the Hindu Adoptions and Maintenance Act was concerned, the court held that since the marriage was being dissolved, the wife could not claim relief under section 18, as sub-section (1) of section 18 given right of maintenance to a Hindu wife whose marriage is subsisting. The section also provides for the right of residence to a wife, which, however, would be available if the husband is guilty of cruelty. That apart, on the facts of the case, the judge was of the view that the husband did not have such capacity to provide any separate residence, and accordingly dismissed the wife's petition under the Hindu Adoptions and Maintenance Act. The wife filed an appeal against these orders; the husband did not file any cross-objection to the finding of the family Court that the six instances of cruelty alleged by him were not established. The High Court observed that, he not having challanged this, it can be taken that he has accepted that he has failed to establish the allegations of cruelty on those grounds.

Order: The main issue for consideration in the appeal was as to whether the Family Court was right in granting divorce merely on the basis of the allegations made by the appellant wife in her written statement. Also, it was contended on behalf of the wife that the least he should have done was to amend his petition and raise the plea that he had suffered cruelty in view of the allegations made in the written statement; thereafter specific evidence on that behalf should have been led before any conclusion was arrived at. *In the absence of any such plea being raised by amending the petition, the respondent should not have been allowed to argue the plea of cruelty merely on the basis of the allegations made in the written statement,* it was argued (at p. 183—emphasis added). On the other hand, for the husband it was argued that the allegations were so wanton that they had only to be noticed to examine whether they will constitute cruelty or not. If that was so, the decree of divorce ought to follow inasmuch as section 13(1)(i-a) of the Hindu Marriage Act speaks of "treating the other party with cruelty". The phrase is wide enough and would cover a cruel treatment even subsequent to the filing of the petition by making baseless allegations in the written statement. The High Court analysed the judgments of the Apex Court in *V. Bhagat* v. *D. Bhagat*, AIR 1994 SC 710: 1994 AIR SCW 45: (1994) 1 SCC 337 and *Chanderkala Trivedi* v. *Dr. S.P. Trivedi*, (1993) 3 SCALE 541: (1993) 4 SCC 232: JT (1993) 4 SC 644, to come to a finding that where serious allegations are made in pleadings, the consequent irretrievable breakdown of the marriage, though not a ground by itself, will be a very important circumstance to be considered while deciding whether divorce should be granted or not. Once such serious allegations are made, it becomes clear that there is no chance of parties coming together or living together again. The following observations of the court in *V. Bhagat* v. *D. Bhagat*, AIR 1994 SC 710: 1994 AIR SCW 45: (1994) 1 SCC 337, were referred to:

> "Making of the allegations and yet opposing divorce would mean a resolve to live in agony only to make the life miserable for both the parties."

Likewise, referring to *Chanderkala Trivedi* it was stated that once serious allegations are made in the pleadings of husband and wife, it is obvious that the marriage between the parties is dead and continuing the litigation further is nothing but an exercise in futility and continuing the agony.

As for allegations in the written statement themselves amounting to cruelty, realiance was placed on *Jaishree Mohan Otavnekar* v. *Mohan Govind Otavnekar*, AIR

1987 Bom 220: 1987 Mah LJ 160: 1987 Mah LR 617; *Nirmala Manohar Jagesha* v. *Manohar Shivram Jagesha,* AIR 1991 Bom 259: 1991 Mah LJ 267: I (1992) DMC 180; *Rajan Vasant Revankar* v. *Shobha Rajan Revankar,* AIR 1995 Bom 246: 1995 (1) Bom CR 47: I (1995) DMC 532; for the wife's argument that it was imperative that an amendment ought to have been carried out to the petition to contend that the allegations in the written statement constituted cruelty, *Gurbachan Kaur* v. *Sardar Swaran Singh,* AIR 1978 All 255: 1978 All LJ 284: 1978 All WC 371; *Paras Ram* v. *Kamlesh,* AIR 1982 P&H 60: I (1982) DMC 184: ILR (1982) 2 P&H 33 and *Naval Kishore Somani* v. *Poonam Somani,* AIR 1999 AP 1: 1998 (3) AP LJ 244: 1999 (3) CCC 179 were relied upon.

After analysing the cases referred to by the counsels of both the parties, as also the evidence, facts and circumstances of the case, the court held that the Family Court's order was correct. It was observed (at p. 193):

"When one party to the petition has sough divorce on some ground and the respondent to that petition does not merely defend it to get it defeated but makes further serious allegations against the petitioner, it becomes a clear step towards the dissolution of the marrigae".

The court further pointed out that "in a case where the petitioner makes the grievance of cruelty on the basis of some instances and fails to establish the same but the respondent comes up with serious allegations (such as adultery, insanity or unchastity) and proves the same, would it not amount by itself to cruelty by the respondent? Will it be expected of the court to tell the petitioner to amend his petition in view of those allegations in the written statement and send him back to the Trial Court when on the face of it those allegations constitute cruelty and particularly when the respondent produces no credible evidence in support thereof. ....in a situation like this, the court will be failing in its duty if the parties are directed to amend the pleadings and again spend much more time in a re-trial where the conclusion is foregone and obvious", the court observed. In any case, in the facts of the present case, even though no amendment was carried out in the petition, the parties had led their evidence on the allegations made by the appellant wife. All the findings of the Family Court were upheld, *viz.* (i) allegations made by the appellant wife were baseless and false and constituted cruelty (ii) petition for maintenance under section 18 of the Hindu Adoptions and Maintenance Act could not be maintained as divorce was granted; and (iii) no permanent alimony could be awarded to the appellant wife under section 25 of the Hindu Marriage Act in as much as it was clearly established that the income of the appellant wife was better than the respondent-husband's.

Comment: The court has given a very practical and logical judgment. True it is that irretrievable breakdown is no ground for divorce, but in cases such as these where baseless, false and atrocious allegations are made in a written statement, it is clear evidence that the respondent does not wish to live with the petitioner but at the same time wants to defeat the petition. This serves no useful purpose except prolonging the litigation, increasing acrimony and wasting court's time. Also, the court has rightly rejected the technical plea of need to amend the petition in view of the allegation of the respondent in the written statement.

Mental Cruelty Alleged: Decree Granted on Humanitarian Ground as Marriage was Practically Dead

Vinita Saxena v. Pankaj Saxena,
AIR 2006 SC 1662: 2006 AIR SCW 1585: (2006) 3 SCC 778

Issue: Can the ground of mental cruelty be invoked in situation where the marriage is practically dead and withholding divorce would be inhuman?

Facts: This was a wife's petition for divorce under section 13 of the Hindu Marriage Act on the ground of cruelty. She alleged that the respondent husband was suffering from paranoid schizophrenia and was incompetent to perform sex as a result of which the marriage was not even consummated. Her further allegation was that the husband used to beat her on several occasions on the instigation of his mother. The Trial Court came to a finding that the incidents of cruelty as alleged by the wife do not come within the scope of cruelty as she failed to give specific dates of incidents when she was beaten and also that she did not report the matter to the police. After considering the evidence of the witnesses, the allegation that the respondent was suffering from paranoid schizophrenia was also rejected. The wife's petition was thus dismissed. Against this she filed an appeal before the Delhi High Court *Vinita Saxena v. Pankaj Pandit*, AIR 2005 Del 243: 2004 (113) DLT 884: II (2004) DMC 602. The High Court referred to several English as well as Indian cases where cruelty was explained and analysed [*King v. King*, 1952 (2) All ER 584: 1953 AC 124: (1952) 2 TLR 429; *Horton v. Horton*, 1940 (3) All ER 380: 163 LT 314: 109 LJP 108; *McEwan v. McEwan*, (1964) 108 Sol Jo 198 CA: 129 JPJ 783; *Gollins v. Gollins*, 1964 AC 644: (1963) 3 WLR 176: (1963) 2 All ER 966; *Sheldon v. Sheldon*, 1966 (2) All ER 257: (1966) 2 WLR 993: 110 SJ 269; *Maya v. Brij Hath*, AIR 1982 Del 240: I (1982) DMC 31: 1982 Marri LJ 160; *N.G. Dastane v. S. Dastane*, AIR 1975 SC 1534: (1975) 2 SCC 326: (1975) 3 SCR 967; *Shobha Rani v. Madhukar Reddy*, AIR 1988 SC 121: (1988) 1 SCC 105: JT 1987 (5) SC 433; *V. Bhagat v. D. Bhagat*, AIR 1994 SC 710: 1994 AIR SCW 45: (1994) 1 SCC 337] After analysing the cases and evidence the High Court came to the conclusion that the wife failed to prove her case. Mere branding of a spouse as schizophrenic is not enough, the court held, relying on *Ram Narain Gupta v. Rameshwari Gupta*, AIR 1988 SC 2260: JT (1988) 3 SC 621: (1988) 4 SCC 247. Degree of mental disorder of the spouse must be proved to be such that petitioner spouse cannot reasonably be expected to live with the other and in this case, according to the court, there was insufficient evidence on record to establish the case of cruelty. On wife's special leave petition under article 136 of the Constitution however, the Apex Court reversed the High Court judgment. Several human aspects of life were taken note of which, according to the court were sufficient to allow the wife's appeal and "entitle her to be relieved from the shackles and chains of the respondent husband and live her own life, if nothing else but like a human being," some of these aspects *inter alia*, were:

> (i) The appellant wife was only 24 when she got married and the spouses lived together for hardly 4 to 5 months.

(ii) The marriage was not even consummated as the husband was not in a position to do so.

(iii) The parties have been living separately since long and have not even seen each other for thirteen years.

(iv) There is no workable solution and parties cannot reconcile themselves to live together ever again.

(v) If divorce is not granted or the wife were expected to stay with the husband it would be injurious to her health.

(vi) The wife is highly educated and the husband is not gainfully employed anywhere.

(vii) The husband has not pursued the case and after leaving his deposition incomplete during the trial he has neither appeared before the Trial Court nor even before the High Court.

Order: The wife's appeal was allowed and a decree of divorce granted. The following observations of the court are pertinent (at p. 1674).

"In our view, the orders of the courts below have resulted in grave miscarriage of justice to the appellant who has been constrained into living with a dead relationship for over 13 years. The resultant agony and injustice that has been caused to the appellant, it is a fit case for interference under article 136 of the Constitution of India and reversal of findings of the courts below which have resulted in grave miscarriage of justice."

Comments: The marriage having completely broken down was viewed as mental cruelty and divorce was seen as deliverance from an unbearably unhappy situation.

Wife's Allegations of Bigamy and Dowry Demand and Against Husband's Potency in Reply to his Allegations Against her – Held Does not Amount to Cruelty

P. Malleswaramma v. P. Prathap Reddy, AIR 2006 AP 4: 2006 (38) All Ind Cas 840: 2005 (5) Andh LT 319

Issue: (i) Whether mere fact of filing criminal cases for bigamy and dowry demand against husband by the wife would amount to cruelty?

(ii) Whether allegations by wife against potency of husband in reply to allegations of impotency of wife by husband, would amount to cruelty?

Facts: Parties were married for nine years at the time when the husband sought divorce against the wife. He alleged that the wife denied him conjugal society, that she was violent, adamant and aggressive; that she had initiated two criminal cases—one alleging dowry demand and the other alleging bigamy, both of which ended in his acquittal. The wife, on the other hand, contended that she was prepared to join her husband and give him conjugal society. She further contended that the husband accused her of being impotent as they had no child, and when she asked the husband for a medical check up, he did not pay any heed. The Trial Court granted a decree of divorce in favour of the husband, hence the wife's appeal.

Order: Dismissing the appeal, the court held: "marital tie between the wife and husband has been considered to be a holy relationship and courts in all cases shall not grant divorce for mere asking, which would in our considered view, be contrary to the age-old faith in the very system of marriage. Therefore, on an over all view of the matter, we are of the view that the husband did not make any attempt to establish his case, except making self-serving statement, that too, nine years after the marriage, and further mere fact that several years have elapsed and the husband has been living with another woman, which fact is off the record, cannot be factors leading to the conclusion that the relationship cannot be retrieved or that it is a case of prolonged incompatibility, in which event, courts may have to exercise discretion to grant relief of divorce".

The court also observed that a mere ground of not begetting children cannot be treated as an act of cruelty, particularly when the husband did not make any complaint at all the first time when he filed a petition seeking a divorce is indicative of the fact that he had something in his mind and thought than what actually meets the eye, not certainly denial of conjugal society to the husband.

Comment: Courts are not inclined to decree divorce to parties on their asking. The goal is to preserve the sanctity of the relationship as far as possible. No party can seek *alibis* to come out of it.

Absence of Formal Complaints to Police etc., no Reason to Dislodge Allegations of Cruelty

Varsha Pravin Patil v. *Pravin Madhukar Patil,*
AIR 2009 Bom 60: I (2009) DMC 649: 2009 (2) Hindu LR 121

Issue: Can a wife's version of cruelty by the husband be disbelieved simply because the wife had made no formal complaints against it?

Facts: This was a husband's petition for divorce against the wife on the ground of cruelty and desertion. The wife's contention was that it was the husband's behaviour which was cruel which impelled her to leave. The husband's main defence against the wife's allegation was that if he had treated her with cruelty, she would have made a formal complaint to the police, or her parents would have made a complaint to her in-laws and since she had made no such complaint, her allegations cannot be believed. The Trial Court disbelieved the wife's version and granted a divorce decree in favour of the husband. Hence her appeal. Reversing the Trial Court order the court observed (at p. 64):

> "…. It is not at all expected that a newly married young woman would immediately rush to police station to lodge any complaint or to otherwise commence tirade of allegations against her husband and his relations, for there is a danger to spoil matrimonial relationships for ever if such action is taken.

.... Conversely it could be inferred that she did not ventilate grievance..... because she harboured under the impression that one day or the other there will be reconciliation. The tolerance of such newly married young woman cannot be treated as her intention to permanently abandon the matrimonial relationship."

Order: The Trial Court decree granting divorce to the husband was set aside.

Comment: It is common knowledge that protective laws against cruelty in matrimonial relationships are double-edged weapons. While they seek to protect the interests of the wives, their misuse is not unknown either. Also, once formal complaints are made to any authorities, the police specially, chances of rapprochement if any, are almost gone. In view of this many wives refrain from making police complaints or even to their parents so that the matter does not get aggravated and in a hope that with time problems will be sorted out. In this context, the present Bombay High Court order is significant.

Hemwanti Tripathi v. *Harish Narain,*
AIR 2012 Del 1

Issue: Parameters of cruelty are too wide to admit of any strait-jacket formula. The married life should be reviewed as a whole and the ill-conduct must be persistent and deleterious enough to the relationship. The simple fact that no close relative or neighbour has been produced to prove acts of cruelty is no ground to demolish the plea of cruelty.

Facts: This was a case of extreme cruelty perpetrated by the husband on his wife; his acts and behaviour constituted mental and physical cruelty and torture of the worst kind which included casting aspersions on the wife's, character physical beatings, abuses, insults, throwing the wife and daughter out of the house etc. The wife, unable to endure any further, filed a petition for divorce on the ground of cruelty. The Trial Court, however, dismissed the same on the ground that she had failed to produce any close relative including her uncle who was living in neighbourhood, to prove the beatings and torture by the husband, as alleged by her. Hence the wife's appeal.

Order: The court analysed several cases and discussed the wide dimensions of cruelty so as to constitute matrimonial offence entitling the applicant to relief. In this case, the Trial Court had given clear findings in favour of the wife but still passed judgment against her on the ground that the acts alleged by her can at best be termed as wear and tear of daily life and further that she failed to produce any close relative including her uncle who lived in neighbourhood, to prove her case. Allowing the wife's appeal, the High Court observed (at p. 8):

"This court fails to comprehend as to how such a view could be taken by the learned Trial Court as clearly serious and malicious allegations of the appellant having relationship with one Sadhu and her staying out of the house during rights also levelled by the respondent and as per the settled legal position casting such aspersions on the character of the other spouse has the effect of causing deleterious effect on the mind of such spouse and the same is worse form of cruelty."

It is significant to note that the husband did not deny the fact that no evidence was led by him to prove that the appellant wife used to go out during night and stay with that Sadhu. The Trial Courts order was held to be "perverse and illegal on the very face of it" and set aside. Divorce was accordingly granted in favour of the wife.

Comment: When the alleged acts of cruelty are on the face of if so obvious and atrocious, the mere fact that close relatives or neighbours were not produced to testify or that no formal complaints were made to police (as alleged in *Varsha Pravin Patil* v. *Pravin Madhukar Patil*, AIR 2009 Bom 60: I (2009) DMC 649: 2009 (2) Hindu LR 121, see *supra*) is no ground to dislodge the wife's testimony and charge so as to defeat her case.

Cruelty Alleged: Middle Path Adopted

Manisha Tyagi v. *Deepak Kumar,*
AIR 2010 SC 1042: 2010 AIR SCW 1306: (2010) 4 SCC 339

Issue: The issue of conduct that would constitute cruelty and that of adopting, in a case of a petition for divorce, a middle path by granting judicial separation instead of divorce to enable parties to think about it once again, was subject matter of consideration in this case.

Facts: The case had a long and chequered history where parties, well-settled and educated, fell out soon after marriage. The husband, an army officer, filed a petition for divorce under section 13 of the Hindu Marriage Act alleging cruelty by the wife. As instances and examples of cruelty, he alleged that the wife was rude, ill-mannered, quarrelsome and schizophrenic making his life a living hell; she shouted, made scenes and humiliated him in front of his officers and jawans; she further made disgusting allegations of sodomy against him and of molestation against his old and infirm father. Further, the husband alleged that she filed various criminal cases against him which ended either in his acquittal or discharge, or were quashed thereby indicating that these were false. Besides, she also hurled filthy abuses on him and his family members, compared him to a barking dog; he also complained about her erratic sexual behaviour. The wife on the other hand made equally vile allegations of dowry demand, sodomy and mental and physical torture by the husband and his family members. In sum, both parties displayed equal show of strength in respect of accusations and allegations against each other. Efforts were made towards reconciliation without success. The Trial Court, on evaluation of the entire evidence, came to the conclusion that even though it is a clear case where marriage has irretrievably broken but under the law as it exists, the marriage cannot be dissolved on this ground. Reference was made to *Rupinder Kaur* v. *Gurjit Singh Sandhu*, (1997) 117

Punj LR 553: (1998) 1 Marri LJ 424 where it was held that even if the marriage has irretrievably broken, it is no ground for divorce. The court however found (in *Manisha Tyagi's* case) that both the parties were at fault and the husband could not prove that the wife had treated him with cruelty of the nature as to entitle him to a decree of divorce. The petition was thus dismissed; hence the husband's appeal before a single Judge of the Punjab and Haryana High Court. According to the judge the wife had crossed "Lakshmana Rekha" and exceeded all limits of decency when she went to the extent of lodging a false FIR and when she tried to humiliate him in the eyes of his superiors. He observed (at p. 1045):

> "I do not deny that a woman has no [sic?] rights after the lawful marriage. She expects love and affection, financial and physical security, equal respect and lots more but at the same time, the wife must remain within the limits. She should not perform her acts in such a manner that it may bring incalculable miseries for the husband and his family members. She should not go to that extent that it may be difficult for her to return from that point."

The single Judge however found that both the parties were at fault and adopted a middle path by granting a decree of judicial separation; it hoped that the parties might ponder over and think of reuniting at least for the sake of their daughter; and if they do not reunite within the statutory period of one year, it will be open to either of them to seek a decree of divorce. The husband accepted the verdict but the wife went in appeal before the Division Bench (*Manisha Tyagi v. Capt. Deepak Kumar*, (2007) I HLR 297. On re-evaluation of the entire evidence, the Court, surprisingly, on the wife's appeal against judicial separation granted divorce in favour of the husband. It observed (at p. 301) of (2007) 1 HLR 297 and quoted by Supreme Court at p. 1046 of *Manisha Tyagi v. Deepak Kumar*, AIR 2010 SC 1042: 2010 AIR SCW 1306: (2010) 4 SCC 339):

> "The allegations and counter-allegations had flown thick and proper in this case .... The learned single Judge chose a middle path by holding that both the parties were at fault and accordingly granted decree of judicial separation instead of divorce. To what effect and what difference it has made to the lives of the parties cannot really be made out.....Both the parties continue to differ and have refused to patch up....What is left of his marriage?

The court also observed that even though the marriage had irretrievably broken but since this is not a ground for divorce under the statutory law, the court proceeded on the basis of allegations of cruelty; it was more than convinced that the wife's behaviour amounted to cruelty of the worst type. Her making complaints and FIR's ending in his discharge or acquittal were also construed as cruelty. The court took a very serious view of her allegations of being molested by her father-in-law. "A daughter-in-law making an allegation against her old and infirm father-in-law of molesting her would certainly be an intolerable behaviour, which can be termed nothing but an act of immence cruelty for a son......." the court observed.

Thus the Division Bench reversed the single Judge order and granted divorce to the husband on the ground of wife's cruelty. Against this, the wife came in appeal to the Supreme Court. If was held that the High Court had erred in granting the divorce decree to the husband. The wife had come before the Division Bench of the High Court complaining against the decree of separation granted by the single judge, therefore even if her appeal had been dismissed, the finding in her favour (that no cruelty was proved against her) would have remained intact. The effect of the Division Bench order is as if an appeal by the husband against the decree of judicial separation has been allowed. According to the Apex Court, it was not a case where it was necessary for the D.B. to correct any glaring and serious errors committed by the courts below which bad resulted in miscarriage of injustice. "In our opinion, there was no compelling necessity, independently placed before the Division Bench to justify reversal of judicial separation. In such circumstances, it was wholly inappropriate for the Division Bench of the High Court to have granted a decree of divorce to the husband", the Court held (at p. 1050).

Order: The order of the Division Bench of the High Court granting divorce was set aside and that of the single Judge granting judicial separation was upheld.

Comment: Reference was made to a few cases to explain what would constitute cruelty [*e.g.*, *N.G. Dastane* v. *S. Dastane*, AIR 1975 SC 1534: (1975) 2 SCC 326: (1975) 3 SCR 967; *Shobha Rani* v. *Madhukar Reddy*, AIR 1988 SC 121: (1988) 1 SCC 105: JT 1987 (5) SC 433; *V. Bhagat* v. *D. Bhagat*, AIR 1994 SC 710: 1994 AIR SCW 45: (1994) 1 SCC 337]; in view of these, the court observed that to constitute cruelty, the conduct complained of is no longer required to be so atrociously abominal which would cause a reasonable apprehension that would be harmful or injurious to continue the cohabitation with the other spouse. However, in this case, both the Trial Court and the appellate court had come to a finding that the conduct of the wife did not constitute cruelty of such nature so as to entitle husband to a decree of divorce. While strictly speaking the ground may not have been proved nonetheless, the parties had gone too far in their break-up; they had been living apart for several years and fighting. Withholding divorce in such situation may be technically correct but pragmatically? One wonders?

Wife Undergoing Abortion without Consent/ Knowledge of Husband is Cruelty

Anjali Bhan v. Ajay Kumar Bhan, AIR 2011 J&K 54

Issue: This was a case under section 13 of the Jammu and Kashmir Hindu Marriage Act (4 of 1980). The main issue involved was whether a wife aborting child without knowledge and consent of husband would amount to cruelty; and whether temporary rapprochement could be construed as condonation. The fact that the marriage had irretrievably broken down was also taken note of by the court in this case.

Facts: This was an appeal against decree of divorce granted to the husband on his petition before the Additional District Judge. The grounds initially taken by the husband were desertion and cruelty but the plea of desertion did not hold ground as it could not be established. However, various incidents to establish mental cruelty by the wife were spelt out in the petition; these *inter alia*, were the wife misbehaving with him and his family members, not performing household chores, threatening, maligning and insulting the husband, lodging of false and frivolous complaints and most serious of all, aborting foetus without consent and knowledge of the husband and his family. The wife denied all these allegations. The Trial Court, on appreciation of evidence and survey of the case law held that the wife was guilty of desertion and cruelty and also there being no chances of patch-up granted a decree of divorce in favour of husband; it also awarded an amount of ₹ 2 lakhs as permanent alimony to the wife and ₹ 1 lakh to the child. Hence the wife's appeal against the divorce decree.

Order: The wife's argument was that the plea of mental cruelty based on her unilateral decision to the abortion, could not be taken since, after the alleged cruelty, the parties had lived together and also had a child which means that the earlier act of her alleged cruelty was condoned; she further argued that the Trial Court erroneously took the marriage as broken though no such ground was urged in the petition. After a detailed analysis of the facts and law the wife's appeal was dismissed. The following observations of the court are pertinent (at p. 60):

> "The decision to abort a child and that also taken unilaterally by a wife is a grave matter not to be taken to have been condoned by the husband by making an unsuccessful effort to go for rapprochement. A brief lull in marital affairs possibly because of intervention and advice of elders may generate a hope that time may prove a great healer, but cannot be taken indicative of condonation of conduct that has left the husband tormented and shattered. If a spouse treats other spouse with cruelty and peace is broken temporarily by the parents and other relations whereafter the erring spouse continues with cruelty, the cause to seek divorce re-emerges and the wound cannot be said to have healed and the complaining spouse estopped from bringing a fresh action for divorce.

And further (at p. 62):

> "Such a unilateral act (wife undergoing abortion) is bound to leave psyche of the husband bruised and battered, give rise to a host of questions in the mind of the husband, sow seeds of suspicion and lead to life-long frustration and mental depression."

The court also dismissed the appellants argument that in the absence of specific averment by the husband, the Trial Court could not have considered the aspect of breakdown of the marriage. It (the High Court) remarked (at p. 63):

> "In a family dispute ..... the court is bound to assess and evaluate how wide is the gulf of disagreement between the parties, explore the chances of reconciliation and wherever even a meager chance of rapprochement and reconciliation is visible, to persuade the parties to bury the hatchet, give their relationship a second chance, and also to declare the marriage irretrievable where no chance of reconciliation is visible. Long separation between the parties as in the present case and cessation of marital relationship for a long period may be the factors that contribute to the view that there is no hope of the parties coming together notwithstanding any amount of effort made by the Trial Court and all those interested in reconciliation between the parties."

Consequently, it was held that there was no infirmity in the Trial Court order made "after mapping out milestones in the marital life of the parties, holding that there was no chance of reconciliation." Hence the wife's appeal against divorce order was dismissed; the amount of Rs. 1 lakh towards maintenance for the child was, however raised to ₹ 2 lakhs.

Comment: While a condoned act of cruelty should not form the basis of divorce decree, it is equally true that too much insistence on technicalities where human relations and emotions are involved, are to no one's advantage. In this case, the wife even at the appellate stage, instead of denying the averments in the husband's petition, has accused him of cruelty and levelled serious counter-charges to justify her conduct. This, according to the court, is enough and more evidence that the marriage is not workable.

CRUELTY AND CONDONATION

No Decree, if Cruelty is Condoned

N.G. Dastane v. S. Dastane,
AIR 1975 SC 1534: (1975) 2 SCC 326: (1975) 3 SCR 967

Issue: Can a decree of judicial separation on ground of cruelty be granted when cruelty is established but the same is condoned and even while the respondent has not specifically pleaded condonation?

Facts: The parties, who were highly educated and belonged to elitist class, were married on May 13, 1956. Two daughters were born in 1957 and 1959. Between May and October of 1960 there were tensions between them and each blamed the other of cruelty and harassment. On February 27, 1961 the wife left the home while she was three months pregnant. In August, 1961, the third daughter was born. The matrimonial suit was filed by the husband on February 19, 1962. He sought—(i) annulment under section 12(1)(c) of the Hindu Marriage Act on the ground that his consent to the marriage was obtained by fraud, alternatively, (ii) divorce under section 13(1)(iii) on the ground that the respondent was incurably of unsound mind and in the alternative, (iii) judicial separation under section 10(1)(b) on the ground that the respondent had treated him with such cruelty as to cause a reasonable apprehension in his mind that it would be harmful or injurious for him to live with her. (After the amendment in 1976 the petitioner has simply to establish that the respondent has 'treated the petitioner with cruelty'.)

The husband alleged that prior to the marriage, the respondent wife was treated in the Yeravad Mental Hospital for schizophrenia but her father fraudulently represented that she was treated for sunstroke and cerebral malaria. The Trial Court rejected this contention. It also rejected the contention that the respondent was of unsound mind. It however held that the respondent was guilty of cruelty and on that ground it passed a decree for judicial separation. Both went in appeal to the District Court; the husband's appeal was dismissed and the wife's allowed. The appellant husband then filed a second appeal in the Bombay High Court which was also dismissed. The High Court drew an inference that the words of abuse or insult used by the wife must have been in retaliation to the abuses, insults and rebukes made by the husband. On further appeal by the husband to the Supreme Court, the approach of the High Court was termed as erroneous and its findings vitiated. However, in view of the fact that the litigation has been pending for 13 long years, the Supreme Court, instead of remanding the matter to the High Court, proceeded with the case itself. The court discussed the concept of cruelty in great detail. It agreed with the warning given by Lord Denning L.J. in *Kaslefsky* v. *Kaslefsky,* 1950 (2) All ER 398 (403): 66 TLR (Pt. 2) 616, that "if the doors of cruelty were opened too wide, we should soon find ourselves granting divorce for incompatibility of temperament. This is an easy path to tread, especially in undefended cases. The temptation must be resisted lest we step into a state of affairs where the institution of marriage itself is imperilled". However, Justice Chandrachud felt that, "to hold in this case that the wife's conduct does not amount to cruelty is to close for ever the door of cruelty so as to totally prevent any access thereto. This is not a case of mere austerity of temper, petulence of manners, rudeness of language or a want of civil attention to the needs of the husband and the household".

Amongst the acts alleged and construed as cruelty were:

1. She would indulge in every sort of harassment and would blurt out anything that came into her mind like, " I want to see the ruination of the whole Dastane dynasty", "You are not a man", "You are a monster in a human body", "burn the book written by your father and apply the ashes to your forehead" or " pickle them (daughters) and preserve them in jar" and so on.
2. Threats to pour kerosene on her body and set fire to herself and the house.
3. Lock the husband out when he was due to return from office.
4. Mercilessly beat children, put chillies in their eyes.

In one of the letters addressed by him to his father who offered to mediate, he (husband) stated.

" She is a hot headed, arrogant, merciless, thoughtless, unbalanced girl devoid of sense of duty. Her ideas about a husband are: He is a dog tied at doorstep, who is supposed to come and go at her beck and call whenever ordered . She behaves with the relatives of her husband as if they were her servants. When I see her besides herself with furry, I feel afraid that she may kill me at any moment. I have become weary of her nature of beating the daughters, secolding and nagging me every night uttering abuses and insults".

The court found that there was enough proof to establish cruelty. It pointed out that the burden of proving the case undoubtedly lies on the petitioner, but it is not proof beyond reasonable doubt. "Proof beyond reasonable doubt is proof by a higher standard which generally governs criminal trials involving inquiry into issues of *quasi-*criminal nature. A criminal trial involves the liberty of the subject which may not be taken away on a mere preponderance of probabilities." In other words, in matrimonial cases, the guilt can be proved by "preponderance of probabilities" and not by proof beyond reasonable doubt.

However, while cruelty was proved, the court felt that the same was condoned by the husband. Even though condonation was pleaded as a defence by the respondent, the court felt that it was their duty, in view of the provisions of section 23(1)(b) to find whether cruelty was condoned. Referring to D. Tolstoy's,

The Law and Practice of Divorce and Matrimonial Cause, Sixth ed., p. 75, the court held that condonation means forgiveness of the matrimonial offence and the restoration of offending spouse to the same position as he or she occupied before the offence was committed. It clarified that " condonation of matrimonial offence is not to be like to full presidential pardon under article 72 of the Constitution which, once granted, wipes out the guilt beyond the possibility of revival. It is always subject to implied condition that the offending spouse will not commit a fresh matrimonial offence".

However, in this case the Court found that "the evidence of condonation was as strong and satisfactory as the evidence of cruelty". The continual cohabitation between the parties since the major allegations of cruelty and the subsequent birth of a daughter was one indication. The husband did allege subsequent acts of cruelty by the wife, but, according to the Court, they were provoked by him and also, they were not serious enough to revive the old acts of cruelty committed by her.

Order: The Court held that there was condonation of the wife's cruelty by the husband and after the condonation, there was no serious allegation against her which would revive her earlier cruel acts. Thus, even while cruelty initially was proved but in view of it being condoned by the husband, it was held that he was not entitled to the decree. His appeal was accordingly dismissed.

Comment: It is a very unfortunate case where parties had been litigating for over a decade with all sorts of allegations and counter allegations against each other. The marriage was practically dead but on the technical ground of condonation, relief was refused to the petitioner. The parties, thus, were neither legally separated, nor in fact together.

Wife Enduring Cruelty is not Condonation of Cruelty

K. Preetha v. N. Bhaskaran,
AIR 2011 Ker 27

Issue: Can the mere fact of a wife enduring cruelty by husband for ten years and thereafter filing suit for divorce on this ground be construed as her having 'condoned' the cruelty. Further, can a wife who is unemployed at the time of marriage but later gets employed and seeks divorce be said to be guilty of a "wrong" within the meaning of section 23 of the Hindu Marriage Act.

Facts: The parties in this case were married in 1998 and lived together till 2008. The wife endured the husbands acts of cruelty for all these years but unable to tolerate any longer, she was constrained to leave the matrimonial home in 2008 and filed a petition for dissolution of marriage on ground of cruelty under section 13(1)(ia) of the Hindu Marriage Act. She alleged acts of physical cruelty, assaults, splashing of chilly water on her face, pushing her out of the house, not caring to even contact her when her mother died etc. The husband made no appearance and an *ex parte* order dismissing the wife's petition was made. According to the Trial Court, the wife's claim for divorce on the ground of cruelty was not made out. It appears to have felt that a decree of divorce cannot be granted in view of section 23 of the Act, *viz.*, "condonation" by the wife of husband's cruelty and "wrong" committed by her. Hence the wife's appeal, which was allowed. The following observations of the High Court are pertinent (at p. 29):

> "Section 23 of the Hindu Marriage Act can have no application in the facts .... The court below appears to have assumed that the conduct of the wife living with the husband for about a decade and complaining later about the cruelty shows "wrong" on her side. The court below, without any material appears to have assumed that the improved financial position of the wife – she was unemployed when she entered matrimony but subsequently entered Government service as a nurse – was prompting her to claim divorce .... according to us, this assumption is not justified and cannot be reckoned as "wrongs" for the purpose of section 23 to turn down relief under section 13(1)(ia). It would be anachronistic to reject the evidence of cruelty on the ground that the wife had suffered such conduct without demur for a long time. In the Indian context the woman is culturally resigned to endure and tolerate inconvenience and impropriety in matrimony of her spouse to the extent possible. If after a decade she asserts that she is not able to live with such a spouse any longer, that cannot be reckoned by a compassionate court as "wrong". The mere evidence/admission for enduring cruelty cannot be reckoned as condonation under section 23. Economic dependence may be compelling many a wife to endure matrimonial cruelty of the contumacious variety without demur. That she makes the claim for divorce on the ground of cruelty after she has attained economic independence cannot by itself be held to be sufficient to dub her conduct as "wrong" or "condonation" under section 23.... Section 23 cannot at all justify the rejection of the claim for divorce in this case."

Order: The wife's appeal was allowed and a decree of divorce under section 13(1)(ia) passed in her favour.

Comment: This was a case where a wife's tolerance and endurance was misconstrued by the Trial Court. It is common knowledge that a wife resorts to matrimonial litigation only when situation reaches a point beyond endurance. Until then she keeps hoping that things will improve. The case also is indicative of the fact that economic dependence of a wife often impels her to live in the matrimonial home despite cruelty and torture by the husband or in-laws. It is not a wife's improved financial position which "prompts her to claim divorce" as held by the Trial Court, but her financial security surely equips her to be on her own and say quits to torture and mental/physical cruelty at the hands of the husband.

DESERTION

Bipinchandra Jaisinghbai Shah v. Prabhavati,
AIR 1957 SC 176: 1957 SCR 838: 1957 SCC 48

Issue: Does mere physical departure of one spouse from the company of another without any intention to put an end to cohabitation, constitute desertion?

Facts: This is a classic case under the Bombay Hindu Divorce Act, 1947, on 'desertion' where the law and concept of desertion was discussed in great detail. It was an appeal by special leave against the judgment and decree of the High Court of Judicature dated August 22, 1952, reversing the order of a single Judge of that court, by which he had granted a decree for dissolution of marriage between the appellant and the respondent on the ground of desertion.

The husband, appellant in this case, was the petitioner. Misunderstandings and problems cropped up in the marriage because of a friend of the husband with whom the wife became intimate when the husband was on a short trip abroad. There were letters also to establish the intimacy. The defendant wife having been discovered in her clandestine amorous correspondence with her supposed paramour, she could not face her husband and his family and went to her parents' place on May 24, 1947 on the pretext of a marriage in the family. The husband was quick to send solicitor's letter to her charging her of the intimacy and asking her to send back the child to him. He also sent a telegram to his father-in-law asking him not to send the defendant back. On July 4, 1951 the husband filed a petition for divorce on the ground that the defendant had been in desertion ever since May 24, 1947, without reasonable cause and without his consent and against his will for a period of over four years (four years of separation was a statutory requirement under the Bombay Hindu Divorce Act, 1947). The wife pleaded constructive desertion by the husband alleging that she was forcibly turned out of the house. The husband denied this. He had succeeded at the Trial Court but lost on appeal by the wife at the High Court. In the present appeal to the Supreme Court also, he did not succeed as he failed to discharge the burden of proof of desertion thoughout the whole period of four years. There was evidence to establish that "the wife had left the husband's place in shame not having the courage to face him after the discovery of her intimacy with another man; but that, according to the court will not render her in the eye of the law, a deserter."

The court lucidly defined and explained the concept of desertion. It held that if a spouse abandons the other in a state of temporary passion, for example, anger or disgust without intending permanently to cease cohabitation, it will not amount to desertion. It held:

"For the offence of desertion, so far as the deserting spouse is concerned, two essential conditions must be there, *viz.*, (i) the factum of desertion, and (ii) the intention to bring cohabitation permanently to an end (*animus deserendi*). Similarly, two elements are essential so far as the deserted spouse is concerned. These are: (i) the absence of consent, and (ii) absence of conduct giving reasonable cause to the spouse leaving the matrimonial home to form the necessary intention aforesaid. The petitioner for divorce bears the burden of proving those elements in the two spouses respectively..... Desertion is a matter of inference to be drawn from certain facts which may not in another case be capable of leading to the same inference..... If, in fact, there has been a separation, the essential question always is whether that act could be attributable to an *animus deserendi*. The offence of desertion commences when the fact of separation and the *animus deserendi* co-exist. But it is not necessary that they should commence at the same time. The *de facto* separation may have commenced without the necessary *animus* or it may be that the separation and the *animus deserendi* coincide in point of time; for example, when the separating spouse abandons the marital home with the intention, express or implied, of bringing cohabitation permanently to a close..... if a deserting spouse takes advantages of the *locus penitentiae*....and decides to come back to the deserted spouse by a *bona fide* offer of resuming the matrimonial home with all implications of marital life before the statutory period is out or even after the lapse of that period (unless proceedings for divorce have been commenced), desertion comes to an end and if the deserted spouse unreasonably refuses the offer, the latter may be in desertion and not the former. Hence, it is necessary that during all the period that there has been a desertion, the deserted spouse must affirm the marriage and be ready and willing to resume married life on such conditions as may be reasonable. It is also well-settled that in proceedings for divorce, the plaintiff must prove the offence of desertion like any other matrimonial offence, beyond all reasonable doubt. Hence, though corroboration is not required as an absolute rule of law, the courts insist upon corroborative evidence, unless its absence is accounted for to the satisfaction of the court."

Several authorities like, Rayden on *Divorce* (6th Edn., p. 128); *Halsbury's Law of England* (3rd Edn., Vol. 12, pp. 241-43); Lord Goddard, C.J. in *Lawsen* v. *Lawsen*, 1955 (1) All ER 341 (342): (1955) 1 WLR 200; Privy Council in *Lana* v. *Lana*, 1955 AC 402 (417): (1954) 3 All ER 571: (1954) 3 WLR 762, were referred to in support of the above propositions.

Order: The husband lost the appeal as he failed to prove his case of desertion. On the contrary there was evidence that there was no *animus* on the part of the wife to permanently leave the husband as she had stayed with her mother-in-law and father-in-law on several occasions and asked them to intercede on her behalf to bring about reconciliation. All attempts by the wife's father and brother also failed as the husband refused to take her back.

Comment: This was a case under the Bombay Hindu Divorce Act, 1947 which required a statutory period of four years of unreasonable separation by the withdrawing spouse to establish the matrimonial offence of desertion by the petitioner. The concept of desertion has been discussed in great detail with all its ingredients and details and is relied upon by the courts in all cases where desertion is an alleged ground for the relief.

Wife's Refusal to give up Job & Join Husband – Whether Amounts to Desertion

Kailash Wati v. *Avodhia Parkash*, (1977) 79 Punj LR 216: 1977 Hindu LR 175

Issue: Whether a wife, who was gainfully employed at a place away from her matrimonial home, would be justified in law to refuse to leave her job and join her husband to live in the matrimonial home despite the insistent demand of the husband to do so?

Facts: The appellant wife was married to the respondent on June 29, 1964 and at the time of marriage both were employed as teachers in different places. After the marriage the wife was transferred to the station of her husband's posting and they stayed together for about 8-9 months. Thereafter, the wife got herself transferred back to her original place of posting and started living there with her parents against the wishes of her husband. Except for a paltry spell of 3 or 4 days in September 1971, the couple did not live together. The husband thereupon filed a petition for restitution of conjugal rights under section 9 of the Hindu Marriage Act. The wife took the plea that she has never refused to honour her matrimonial obligations but was firm in her stand that she would not resign. According to her, the husband knew at the time of marriage that she was working and posted in a different place and therefore she was under no obligation to live with her husband because considerations of employment prevented her to do so. She reiterated that she has never denied access to her husband as and when possible at her place of posting where she was residing with her parents. The spouses are employed at a place more than eighty miles apart; hence the practical position is that the husband might visit on an alternative week and perhaps, at her option, the wife if so inclined, may return a visit in similar circumstances.

The direct issue which arose in these circumstances was, according to the court, whether the hallowed concept of the matrimonial home can be whittled down to a weekend or an occasional nocturnal home meeting at the unilateral desire of the wife to live separately?

The court examined three situations in this context, *viz*

(i) where the husband marries a woman who is already working;
(ii) where the husband encourages or at least allows his wife to take up employment after marriage;

(iii) where a wife, against the wishes of her husband accepts [or continues?] employment away from the matrimonial home and unilaterally withdraws therefrom.

In all these three situations, the court's view was that it is the right of the husband to claim the wife's society and companionship within the matrimonial home. It observed:

"The true position in law appears to be that any working woman entering into matrimony by necessary implication consents to the obvious and known marital duty of living with a husband as a necessary incident of marriage."

Two exceptions, however, were conceded by the court. *Firstly*, the husband must actually establish a matrimonial home wherein he can maintain his wife in dignified comfort in accordance with the means and standards of living of the parties; and *secondly*, it must be crystal clear that the husband while claiming the society of his wife in the marital home should be acting in good faith and not merely to spite his wife.

Apart from these exceptions, a wife is not entitled to unilaterally withdraw from the matrimonial home and live elsewhere merely by taking shelter behind the plea that she would not deny access to the husband as and when possible. Considerations only of employment elsewhere also would not furnish her reasonable ground for withdrawal from the society and companionship of the husband which in practical terms is synonymous with withdrawal from the matrimonial home.

The reason and rationale behind giving the right to decide upon the *locus* of matrimonial home is the fact that the legal duty or burden to maintain the wife and children vests on the husband. Usually, if not invariably, he is the wage earner of the family and is thus compelled to live near his place of work. It stands to reason, therefore, the court observed, that the right of choosing a home wherefrom he can effectively discharge his legal duty of being the bread earner of the family, should fall upon him.

It was argued that the approach of the court is tilted a little in favour of the husband which the court denied. It remarked:

"A closer and incisive analysis would.............. show that this is not necessarily so. Indeed a contrary view or even a vacillate statement of the law would be more burdensome not only to one but to both the spouses. The concept of the Hindu marriage of earlier times has slid down from its high altar of being sacramental to the more mundane concept where the rights and duties of the wife are governed by status; though as yet it has not reached the stage of being a mere civil contract as in western countries.............. It is best perhaps that in present time it should be a silken bond between affectionate spouses or at least co-operative partners."

Order: After analysing the facts and other authorities and propositions, the court held that the wife had deliberately and ingeniously secured her transfer away from the matrimonial home. For the last nearly one decade, the wife had virtually refused to live with her husband and was categorical in her stand that she would not leave her job even though the husband was in a position to support her in reasonable comfort. According to the court, *the wife has to make a choice betwixt the job and the husband.* (emphasis added) The wife's withdrawal was held to be unilateral and without reasonable excuse. "The respondent husband here has waited patiently in the wings for the best part of his life and it would perhaps be bordering on the cruelty to require him to keep on waiting in suspense".

Comment: The judgment can no longer be sustained as good law in view of the changing times when more and more women are working and wish to be financially secure. The law is also gradually recognising that along with rights, women have duties too, to maintain children, parents and in some cases the husbands as well. It cannot, however, be denied that the prime obligation still continues to be the man's. Also, the need to maintain a balance in the interest of children and the family as a whole cannot be underscored. However, these are matters best left to the good sense of the parties. Law cannot compel them in the matter for where compulsion comes, relationships are bound to go sour.

The court in this case also made a plea for introducing irretrievable breakdown of marriage as a ground for divorce. It very aptly observed:

"Where both of them cannot even mutually agree upon something so basic as either living apart (may be for reasons of the wife's employment) or even upon a common place to live together, then it is plain that the marriage has reached dangerously near that precipice which, in legal terminology has been summarised as that it has irretrievably and irrevocably broken down. In such situation, it is obviously in the interest of both that they should clearly and determinedly make their choice and decide to part and go their individual ways rather than be condemned by the law to live together unhappily ever afterwards."

Locale of Matrimonial Home when Both Spouses Working at Different Places – Wife's Withdrawal not Unreasonable

Swaraj Garg v. *K.M. Garg,*
AIR 1978 Del 296: 1978 Hindu LR 332: 1978 Raj LR 525

Issue: When the husband and the wife are both gainfully employed at two different places from before their marriage, where will be the matrimonial home after the marriage?

Facts: The wife was working as a teacher at Sunam, District Sangrur since 1956 and was headmistress of Government High School when she was examined as witness in 1969. The parties were married on July 12, 1964 at Sunam. The husband was not well-employed and had a very low income job in Delhi with no allowances nor did he have any house of his own at Delhi. There was no discussion between them at any time as to where their matrimonial home should be after the marriage. Hence, even after marriage the wife continued to live at Sunam and the husband at Delhi. Between 1964 and 1965 the wife came to live with her husband twice for couple of months but after returning back to Sunam or February 2, 1965, she did not return to Delhi. Hence the husband's petition under section 9 of the Hindu Marriage Act for restitution of conjugal rights. According to him the causes of her estrangement from him were:

(a) She felt the separation from her parents keenly and longed to go back to them;
(b) She pressed the husband that his aged father should not live with him;
(c) The parents of the wife wanted to live on her income and urged her to return to their home.
(d) The wife was abusive, short-tempered and quarrelsome.
(e) She was irritable and frigid.

The wife defended the petition and denied all the allegations. According to her, it was he who treated her badly; he was bent upon extracting maximum amount of money from her and her parents; that he had taken huge dowry from her parents and had deprived her of jewellery, clothes and other valuables given to her by her parents. She further alleged that he never provided her with proper medical treatment when she was ill and in the family way and during delivery. Because of his cruelty she could not join her husband.

The husband's petition was dismissed by the Trial Court but was allowed in appeal by a single judge of the Delhi High Court. Hence the Letters Patent Appeal by the wife. Two points were discussed in detail in this appeal, *viz.*, the choice of matrimonial home and, the conduct of the husband. As to the former, the court was of the opinion that the basic principles on which the location of the matrimonial home is to be determined by the husband and the wife are based on common convenience and benefit of the parties. Reference was made to the law in England as stated in *Halsbury's Laws of England*, Fourth Edn. (1975-76), para. 623, and repeated in Rayden on *Divorce*, 12th Edn., para. 93, which is as follows:

> "*Choice of matrimonial home.*—It is a husband's duty to provide his wife with a home according to his circumstances. There is no absolute rule whereby either party is entitled to dictate to the other where the matrimonial home shall be; the matter is to be settled by agreement between the parties, by a process of give and take and by reasonable accommodation............. The location of a husband's work is a most important consideration to be borne in mind in selecting the situation of the matrimonial home although in some cases the wife's business and livelihood may be a predominant consideration............. Neither party............. has a casting vote............. if the parties are both unreasonable each might be entitled to a decree on the ground of the other's desertion, but this proposition has been doubted and disapproved. The parties should so arrange their affairs that they spend their time together and not apart; and where there is a difference of view, reason must prevail."

The spouses cannot live on love alone, as remarked by the court. They have to eat, be clothed, have shelter and have such other amenities of life as may be obtained from the income of that spouse who is earning more. If, as in this case it is the wife who alone has the job which is also a good job and the husband does not have sufficient income, can it be said that even then the husband has a right to decide that the matrimonial home must be at the place where he happens to reside and the wife must resign her job and come to live with him there? There is absolutely no principle or authority in law which compels the wife to do so, the court said. On this issue, the court differed from the view of the Punjab and Haryana High Court full Bench in *Kailash Wati* v. *Avodhia Parkash*, (1977) 79 Punj LR 216: 1977 Hindu LR 175. Referring to Mulla's *Hindu Law*, 14th Edn., para. 442, which enjoins upon the wife an absolute duty to follow her husband and submit to his authority, the court observed that these propositions and the cases cited thereunder are of 1898 and 1901 and need to change with the changing times. Reference was also made to K.T. Bhashyam Aiyangar's work *Women in Hindu Law*, (1928) wherein he stated that "we must give back their rights and privileges in law of which we have robbed them. The injustices perpetrated on them in the name of law should be remedied and even as we honour them in life so must we make them equal to us in law. Then shall law be really a reflection of life."

Likewise were the remarks made by Mr. Justice Krishnaswamy Iyengar in *Durgaprasada Rao* v. *Sudarsanaswami*, AIR 1940 Mad 513: ILR 1940 Mad 653 which were quoted with approval:

> "We cannot shut our eyes to changes almost revolutionary in character and extent which have been for a considerable time past taking place in the structure of the Hindu social order and in the ideals and sentiments which govern it. The old sanctions seem to have all but disappeared, sweeping away before them the old faith and the old institutions which did constitute in the past an integral condition of the indigenous fabric."

Order: In the instant case (*Swaraj Garg*) the court found no substance in allegations made by the husband against his wife. It found that the conduct of the husband, as was evident from correspondence made to the wife, was such as to frighten her from joining him and thus giving her a reasonable excuse for not joining him.

The court also referred to article 14 of the Constitution which guarantees equality before the law and equal protection to both. Any law which gave the exclusive right to the husband to decide upon the place of matrimonial home without considering the merits of the claim of the wife would be contrary to article 14 and unconstitutional for that reason, the court remarked.

After going through the entire facts and submissions, the court came to the following conclusion:

> "Due to the financial difficulties of the husband and comfortable position of the wife and also due to the discouraging conduct of the husband towards the wife, we are of the view that the wife had a reasonable excuse

for not resigning her job and for not coming to live with the husband in Delhi. The question of the wife withdrawing herself from the society of the husband did not arise at all because the husband and the wife had not been able to decide where the matrimonial home should be set-up. The fault, if any, for the lack of any agreement between them on this point was not of the wife and may be said to be of the husband."

Thus, the decree granted in favour of the husband by the single judge was set aside and the Trial Court order dismissing the petition of the husband was restored.

Comment: This is a progressive judgment in consonance with the needs of the changing times. While conceding equal right to both the spouses, the court has expressed due concern to the need for maintaining reason and balance.

It has also made a plea for introducing breakdown of marriage as a ground for divorce where there is stalemate and the marriage hangs in a state of limbo.

There can be no Desertion without Cohabitation

Savitri Pandey v. *Prem Chandra Pandey*, AIR 2002 SC 591: 2002 AIR SCW 182: (2002) 2 SCC 73

Issue: (i) Can there be desertion without cohabitation?

(ii) Need to raise limitation period for appeal from 30 days to 90 days.

Facts: A wife sought divorce on the ground of desertion and cruelty under section 13 of the Hindu Marriage Act. The Trial Court and the High Court found, on facts as also on evidence led in support of cruelty, that she failed to establish that she was treated with cruelty. The courts emphasised that ordinary wear and tear of family life cannot be equated with cruelty. The acts complained of were not acts of cruelty but sensitivity of the wife with respect to such conduct complained as cruelty. "Cruelty", according to the court "cannot be decided on the basis of the sensitivity of the petitioner and has to be adjudged on the basis of the course of conduct which would, in general be dangerous for a spouse to live with the other". (at p. 595)

The Family Court, however, granted divorce on the ground of desertion. On appeal, the High Court set aside the decree. It is against this that the wife filed an appeal to the Supreme Court.

A very significant aspect of this case was that there was no cohabitation between the parties and this fact was admitted by the wife. The court emphasised that there could be no desertion without cohabitation. It remarked (at p. 597):

"Cohabitation by the parties is an essential [ingredient] of a valid marriage as the object of the marriage is to further perpetuation of the race by permitting lawful indulgence in passions for procreation of children. In other words, there can be no desertion without previous cohabitation by the parties. The basis for this theory is built upon the recognised position of law in matrimonial matters that no one can desert who does not actively or wilfully bring to an end the existing state of cohabitation. However, such a rule is subject to just exceptions which may be found in a case on the ground of mental or physical incapacity or other peculiar circumstances of the case. However, the party seeking divorce on the ground of desertion is required to show that he/she is not taking advantage of his or her own wrong."

In this case, it was the wife herself who had declined and did not permit the husband to have cohabitation for consummating the marriage, thus implying that it is she who deserted.

Another significant fact in the case is that the wife re-married pending husband's appeal in the High Court. The court took serious note of this and remarked (at p. 598):

"If despite pendency of appeal the appellant chose to solemnize the second marriage, the adventure is deemed to have been undertaken at her own risk and the ultimate consequences arising of the judgment in the appeal pending in the High Court. No person can be permitted to flout the course of justice by his or her overt or covert acts."

A plea of irretrievable breakdown of the marriage was also taken on behalf of the petitioner wife but the same was dismissed as, according to the court, a party cannot be allowed to take advantage of his/her own wrong and then plead breakdown of the marriage.

Order: The wife's appeal was dismissed. She was refused decree of divorce on ground of desertion as the same was not established. There being no cohabitation, there could be no desertion by the husband. Desertion, according to the Court, cannot be equated with separate living of the parties. The court also made a strong plea for raising the limitation period for appeal which is 30 days under section 28(4) of the Hindu Marriage Act. This according to the court was inadequate and facilitated the frustration of the marriage by the unscrupulous litigating spouses. A minimum period of 90 days was suggested and any marriage solemnized during this period would be deemed void.

Comment: Cohabitation is essential before there can be desertion. However, cohabitation does not mean only "permitting lawful indulgence in passions for procreation of children" (at p. 597). Plea for raising limitation period for appeal is very logical. It would prevent second marriages pending appeal which, according to the court, would be deemed void.

Note: Vide an amendment in 2003, this period has been raised to 90 days.

Wife Refusing to Stay with Husband's Parents: No Desertion

Vikas Sharma v. Anita Sharma,
AIR 2011 Utr 43

Issue: Would a wife who refuses to stay with the husband's parents in a different place, though is ready to stay with the husband, guilty of desertion so as to entitle the husband to a decree for divorce? This was the issue involved in the case.

Facts: The husband in this case was a rifle man in Indian Army and posted in Manipur whereas his parental house was at Mussorie. He wanted his wife to stay with his parents which the wife was not inclined to do. The husband thereupon filed a petition for divorce under section 13 of the Hindu Marriage Act, 1955 on the ground of desertion. The wife filed a counter-claim for restitution. The Trial Court dismissed the husband's petition and decreed restitution of conjugal rights in favour of the wife. It is against this that the husband filed the present appeal.

Order: It was held that there was no desertion on the part of the wife. "Merely not obliging the petitioner to stay in his parents' house where he himself is not residing, in our opinion, cannot be said to be desertion", the court observed (at p. 44). The husband's appeals were consequently, dismissed.

Comments: Upon marriage, the parties are normally obliged to live with each other; this obligation does not extend to living with the parents or any other place, where the other spouse is not residing. Compelling a wife to live with husband's parents where he himself is not residing, is by no means fair and her refusal to do so would not constitute desertion.

FRAUD

Misrepresentation about Boys' Particulars Made by Father to Girl's, Mother – Held Fraud on Girl – Annulment Decreed

Babui Panmato v. *Ram Agya Singh,*
AIR 1968 Pat 190

Issue: Does a misrepresentation about the particulars of a bridegroom made by the father to the mother of the bride and over heard by the bride, amount to fraud so as give to the bride, a ground to seek annulment based on false representation?

Facts: The petitioner was a little over 18 years of age at the time of marriage which took place in May 1959. Just before her marriage she had overheard her father telling her mother that he had fixed up a husband for her who was financially affluent and aged between 25 and 30. Having heard these particulars, she raised no objection to the proposed marriage and in a way, she impliedly consented to the marriage. At the time of marriage, she was, as is customary in Hindu family, specially in rural areas, under heavy veil and so could not see the bridegroom. When she saw her husband for the first time after the marriage, she discovered that he was aged even more than her father, *i.e.*, over 60 years. She wept and insisted upon being sent back to her parents house whereupon the respondent beat her. However, she stealthily escaped to her father's house where she was not allowed, so she took shelter at her uncle's place. Thereupon the defendant husband started criminal proceedings under section 498 of the Indian Penal Code against her uncle and parents. He succeeded in taking her to his house where she was confined in a room and she again escaped. Ultimately in March, 1961, she filed a petition for dissolution of the marriage on the ground of fraud in the matter of procurement of her consent to the marriage. The Trial Court rejected her petition on two counts: (i) that there was no misrepresentation to the petitioner inasmuch as the particulars of the bridegroom were not conveyed to her directly and these had been merely overheard by her while her father was mentioning them to her mother and (ii) the fraudulent representation within the meaning of section 12(1)(c) must be made at the time of the solemnization of the marriage and not earlier, that is to say, at the time of settling the marriage. Hence the appeal by the wife. The court referred to the definition of 'fraud' in section 17 of the Contract Act *viz.*:

> "Fraud" means and includes any of the following acts committed by a party to a contract, or with his connivance or by his agent, with intent to deceive another party thereto or his agent, or to induce him to enter into the contract:—

(1) the suggestion, as a fact, of that which is not true, by one who does not believe it to be true;

(2) the active concealment of a fact by one having knowledge or belief of the fact.

(3) ....

(4) any other act fitted to deceive.

In this case, the petitioner was *sui juris* and her consent to the marriage should have been obtained directly but that was not done; in order to procure her consent the particulars of the bridegroom were conveyed by the father to the mother, within the hearing of the bride. Thus, the father made suggestions to the petitioner's agent, *viz.*, the mother, of certain facts which he himself knew were not true. He not only misrepresented but actively concealed true facts. As to Trial Court's finding that there was no fraudulent misrepresentation to the petitioner, the Appellate Court pointed out that in an average Hindu family talks about marriage between father and daughter are not carried on directly but through the agency of a female relative, particularly the mother. Hence, the father's discussion with the mother did amount to fraudulent misrepresentation to the petitioner, intended to procure her consent to the marriage.

As to Trial Court's ruling that the fraudulent representation envisaged in section 12(1)(c) of the Act must be made at the time of solemnization of the marriage and not earlier, the High Court pointed out that while in sub-clause (a) and (d) of section 12(1) the expression "at the time of marriage" is found, the same is non-existent in sub-clause (c), thus meaning that under clause (c) it is not necessary to prove that consent was obtained by force or fraud at the time of marriage.

Order: The order of the lower court was set aside and a decree of annulment of the petitioner's marriage with the respondent under clause (c) of section 12(1) was passed.

Comment: The judgment is a reflection of the plight of a girl (which is not unusual) where she is lured into marriage by false representation by none other than her own father. She was bold enough to escape and seek relief through the court, but she is an exception. Innumerable girls in her position suffer in silence.

Misrepresentation as to Age

Vidyut Kumar Verma v. *Manju,*
AIR 2011 Pat 110

Issue: Is misrepresentation or concealment of age and/or qualification of a party of such vital significance so as to give a ground to the other party, to seek annulment of the marriage under section 12(1)(c) of the Hindu Marriage Act on ground of fraud? This was the point involved in this case.

Facts: This was a wife's petition for having her marriage declared as *null* and *void* under section 12(1)(c) of the Hindu Marriage Act, 1955 on the ground that consent to the marriage was obtained by fraud and misrepresentation. She alleged that her consent to the marriage was obtained by the husband (the appellant in this case) stating that he was a computer engineer whereas he was not so, further, there was misrepresentative as to his age as it was disclosed to be 25 while he was only 19 years old. The Trial Court, on appreciation of evidence, allowed the wife's application and the marriage was declared void. The husband filed the present appeal against this order. He denied all the allegations and argued that nothing was concealed and moreover, even if the age of the appellant was represented to be 25, the girl admittedly being 32, there was already so much age difference and that being so, according to the appellant, it was immaterial whether the boy was below 25 or 25. As to qualification, it was argued that concealment of qualification is not of such vital significance so as to dissolve the marriage.

Order: It was held that any misrepresentation as to qualification is of vital significance and would vitiate consent; and further, as alleged, disclosure of true qualification to the bride's father, even if it were true (in this case it was not so established) would be of no significance. The husband's appeal was thus dismissed and the marriage declared *null* and *void*.

Comment: When two persons enter into marriage alliance, it is presumed that they have an informed consent as to the, *inter alia*, material fact or circumstances conserning the party. When one party misleads, misrepresents or defrauds another as to any material factors, and qualification is one such, then obviously, the aggrieved party has a right to call off the marriage.

Note: See also *V.D. Grahalakshmi v. T. Prashanth,* AIR 2012 Mad 34 where it was held that suppression of the fact of registration of earlier marriage by the wife is a material fact amounting to fraud which comes under section 12(1)(c) of the Act thereby rendering the marriage voidable.

Fraudulent Divorce Petition through Impostor

Sanjay Singh v. *Garima Singh,* (1998) 8 SCC 375

Issue: A fraud was played upon the court by getting an impostor to file a divorce petition.

Facts: A suit for divorce was allegedly filed by the husband in the name of the wife or on behalf of the wife. An *ex parte* decree was hurriedly obtained. When the wife came to know about it, she filed a suit for declaration that the *ex parte* decree was null and void as she had never filed any suit for dissolution of the marriage. The High Court held that even assuming that the suit was filed by the real respondent, *i.e.,* the wife, "when the suit proceeded in hot haste and resulted in *ex parte* decree in quick succession of events which were spread over a period of one month, it became clear that the *ex parte* decree was a result of complete non-application of mind and.......it reflected a clear case of fraud on the court as it amounted to snatching a decree of divorce from the court in the absence of any real case being made out by either side". Besides, it appeared to the court that the appellant had obtained the decree by getting an impostor to file the suit. The husband filed an appeal before the Supreme Court.

Order: The husband's appeal against this order was dismissed and the *ex parte* decree was set aside. The court remarked: "Divorces are not granted for the asking but the parties are put to trial to prove the ingredients for grant of the divorce as provided in the Hindu Marriage Act." The court held, that the petition in this case was clearly collusive and the decree was passed without application of mind.

Comment: This was a clear case of fraud upon the court where a husband sought a divorce through an impostor who filed the suit as the petitioner wife.

Concealment of Vasectomy by Husband is Fraud

Best Morning v. *Nirmalendu,*
AIR 1987 Gau 63: II (1987) DMC 214: (1987) 2 Gau LR 324

Issue: This was a case for annullment of the marriage under section 12(1)(d) of the Hindu Marriage Act on the ground that the respondent wife was, at the time of the marriage, pregnant by some person other than the petitioner.

Facts: A child was born within five months and six days of the marriage which implies that the wife was pregnant at the time of the marriage. The husband consequently filed a petition for declaring the marriage a nullity on this ground. A DNA test was conducted which established that the petitioner husband was not the biological father of the child nor the child the biological child of the petitioner but that the wife was the biological mother of the child as the report. The Trial Court however dismissed the husband's petition on the ground that there could have been a possibility of the wife coming into contact with the petitioner and getting conceived.

Order: The husband filed an appeal against this: Allowing the same the court held that even assuming that there was a finding of access (between the spouses) in favour of the wife, yet in view of the scientific tests and the DNA report, it has been categorically proved that the husband is not the biological father of the child, whereas the mother is the biological mother of the child. This is sufficient to prove that the wife was pregnant at the time of marriage by some person other than the petitioner husband.

Comment: While courts would not lightly concede to arguments against a wife's character nor to the status of a child born within marriage, yet, when there are strong indications supported by scientific tests, the courts would not deny relief to a husband under the provision of section 12(1)(d) of the Hindu Marriage Act.

Sushil Kumar v. Minto Kumari, AIR 2012 Raj 1

Issue: This was a case for annullment of the marriage under section 12(1)(d) of the HMA on the ground that the respondent wife was, at the time of the marriage, pregnant by some person other then the petitioner.

Facts: A child born within five month six days of the marriage which implies that the wife was pregnant at the time of the marriage. The husband consequently filed a petition for declaring the marriage a nullity on this ground. A DNA test was conducted which established that the petitioner husband was not the biological father of the child nor the child the biological child of the petitioner but that the wife was the biological mother of the child as per the report. The Trial Court, however, dismissed the husband's petition on the ground that there could have been a possibility of the wife coming into contact with the petitioner and getting conceived.

Order: The husband filed on appeal against this allowing the same the court held that even assuming that there was a finding of access (between the spouses) in favour of the wife, yet in view of the scientific test and the DNA report, it has been categorically proved that the husband is not the biological father of the child whereas the mother in the biological mother of the child. This is suffcient to prove that the wife was pregnant at the time of marriage by some person other than the petition husband.

Comment: While courts would not lightly concede to arguments against a wife's character nor to the status of a child born within marriage yet, when there are strong indications repported by scientific tets, the courts would not deny relief to a husband under the provision of section 12(1)(d) of the HMA.

IMPOTENCY

Impotency *Per se* does not Render Marriage a Nullity

Ram Devi v. Raja Ram,
AIR 1963 All 564: 1963 All LJ 658

Issue: The issue involved in this case was whether a marriage with an impotent woman or impotent man would be a nullity with no binding ties of matrimony.

Facts: The parties belonged to Vaishya community and were married according to the Hindu rites. This was a wife's suit for maintenance on the ground of husband's cruelty, remarriage and desertion. The husband resisted the same alleging that since the wife was impotent she could not be legally married to him. According to him she was unfit for cohabitation and procreation and consequently the marriage was a nullity. The wife was medically examined and on the basis of evidence adduced, the Trial Court came to the conclusion that the wife was neither impotent nor incapable of having children; rather it was the husband who was held to have ill-treated her and remarried. The wife was consequently awarded maintenance. On appeal, the order was reversed and the wife was held to be impotent and sterile and the marriage a nullity according to the Hindu law. Hence the wife's appeal.

Order: The court discussed at length the issue of whether a marriage with an impotent man/woman would be a nullity with no binding ties of matrimony despite sacramental rites. If discussed and distinguished between two situations *viz.:* (a) where a male or female falls in the category of being neither a male nor a female and (b) where a male or female suffers from some physical deformity which incapacitates him or her from consummating the marriage. While in the former case there could be a point in holding the marriage a nullity, in the latter, according to the court, there could be no reason for this. Various cases and texts were analysed and while admitting that sexual intercourse for procreation is important in marriage, the court categorically ruled out against nullity of a sacramental marriage where there was a physical incapacity. It observed (at p. 567):

> It was not uncommon in this country and it is not even uncommon now for children to get married by their parents and elders. Under the Child Marriage Restraint Act while it is an offence to get such children married, it has not been laid down by the Act that the marriage itself would be a nullity. There may be cases where children were married during infancy and it may not be possible to find out the physical condition of the girl. She may be normal for a child of her age at the time of marriage and subsequently on attaining majority meet with an accident and get such deformity which may make the act of cohabitation impossible. Could it be said that in such a case the marriage itself would be a nullity and the

matrimonial ties between them had no effect in the eye of law? There may be cases where a woman because of a peculiar temperament may refuse to permit intercourse by husband, could it be said that the marriage tie by itself could be a nullity? There have been cases where the husband and wife have lived together without having any sexual relations between them. Could that by itself dissolve the marriage tie?

Consequently, it was held that impotency does not render marriage a nullity and married status is not disturbed until dissolution is sought. The Trial Court order was thus restored.

Comment: A marriage on ground of impotency is not void but only voidable under section 12(1)(a) of the Hindu Marriage Act and so long as the healthy spouse does not choose to have it dissolved the parties continue to be husband and wife with all rights and obligations attached to the relationship.

Person could be Impotent event if Structurally Normal

Shantabai Alias Gourabai v. *Tarachand,*
AIR 1966 MP 8: 1965 MP LJ 615: 1965 Jab LJ 770

Issue: Can a decree of annulment on ground of impotency be passed even though the 'other party' is medically and structurally normal?

Facts: The parties were married in 1960 and lived together for two years. During this period she occasionally visited her parents. The husband filed a petition for annulment of the marriage under section 12(1)(a) of the Hindu Marriage Act on the ground of wife's impotency. He alleged that despite innumerable efforts, the marriage could not be consummated because of resistance on the part of the wife. The wife denied this and according to her, it was the husband who avoided her. The Trial Court granted the decree hence the wife's appeal. On medical examination of the parties, both were found to be structurally and medically normal for consummation. Unlike the English law where either party to a marriage can seek dissolution on the ground of impotency (even the party who suffers from the infirmity), under the Indian law it is the non-petitioner who must be impotent. Since in this case both were medically normal, it became the duty of the court to make every endeavour to reach the truth. After sifting the evidence and statements of the parties, the court reached a conclusion that the statements of the wife could not be believed, specially her statement that on the third day of her marriage she complained to her father of the husband's incapacity to consummate the marriage. After going through certain authorities, the court came to the conclusion that a marriage can be annulled not only in case of absolute incapacity but also where the impotency is of a relative type, *viz., quoad hunc.*

Order: The court dismissed the wife's appeal and held that although the appellant is not structurally or psychologically incapable of allowing sexual intercourse generally, yet she has an uncontrollable aversion to allowing coitus to the petitioner-husband. This case belongs to the rare variety of frigidity—*quoad hunc*.

Comment: Under section 12(1)(a) as amended in 1976, the petitioner has just to prove non-consummation of the marriage at the time of the institution of the suit.

Impotency – Need not be Incurable to get Relief

Samar Roy Chowdhury v. *Snigdha Roy Chowdhury*, AIR 1977 Cal 213: (1976) 2 Cal LJ 322: ILR (1977) 1 Cal 44

Issue: Does impotency have to be of incurable nature in order to give a ground for annulment to the other party? Does cure subsequent to filing of petition, affect the petitioner's claim?

Facts: The parties were married on May 13, 1973. On December 13, 1973, the husband filed a petition under section 12, Hindu Marriage Act for annulment of the marriage. His case was that the marriage could not be consummated despite several attempts by him. Because of the repeated refusals by the wife to consummate the marriage, he persuaded the wife to be examined by a doctor and the doctor, after due examination found that she was suffering from malformation of the organs. The husband alleged that the respondent is impotent and her mental and physical condition makes consummation of the marriage a practical impossibility and such condition existed at the time of marriage and continued to be so until the institution of the proceedings.

He further stated, "that the respondent is physically, mentally and psychologically impotent of the type known as *quoad hunc* or *quoad hanc* or in other words, the respondent is at least impotent to the petitioner and the marriage cannot be consummated".

The wife denied all allegations. After going through the averments of the parties, the lower court dismissed the husband's petition. According to him, from the medical evidence it appears that the respondent is suffering from painful "vaginismus" or "narrow vaginal introitus", but she was not suffering from any defect of permanent nature. The Trial Court accordingly held that the wife was not impotent as the defect was curable; that the wife was willing to have the operation done as suggested by the doctors but the husband and his parents were not agreeable to this; that the wife was eager to make the marriage a success and so even after the husband's petition, she got herself operated. On these facts the husband's petition was dismissed. Against this order, the husband filed an appeal. The main point for consideration was whether there was consummation of the marriage, and if not, whether the non-consummation was due to impotency of the wife.

While the matter was pending, the Marriage Laws (Amendment) Act of 1976 came which made some changes in section 12 of the Hindu Marriage Act. Prior to the amendment, section 12(1)(a) read as follows:

"That the respondent was impotent at the time of marriage and continued to be so until the institution of proceedings."

By the 1976 amendment, it says:

"That the marriage has not been consummated owing to the impotency of the respondent".

After hearing both the parties and going through the authorities relied upon by them, Justice Banerjee held:

"We are of the opinion that the marriage has not been consummated due to the impotency of the respondent. .... In our opinion the curability of impotency is not a consideration for the purpose of deciding the case whether the marriage is voidable under section 12(1)(a) of the Act...."

According to the court, the omission on the aspect of curability in section 12(1)(a) is not accidental but deliberate. Had the Parliament intended to make only *incurable* impotency a ground for relief, it would have said so. A reference was made to section 13(iii) and (iv) of the Act which says '*incurably* of unsound mind' and 'virulent and *incurable* leprosy' respectively as grounds for divorce. Thus, in case of impotency, the court is not to enquire whether the condition can be cured in future. It has only to see "whether the ends of marriage have been attained or not when the action was initiated".

Order: The husband's appeal against the lower court's order dismissing the husband's petition for annulment on the ground of wife's impotency was allowed and a decree passed in his favour. Neither the issue of incurability or curability of the condition, nor the fact that the respondent has been cured of the disability since the filing of the petition, are relevant considerations.

Comment: In a country where child marriages are rampant and children get married much below the age when consummation can take place, how would the courts apply the law, one wonders. Would there be a different yardstick in such cases. Technically or medically, the child may not be 'impotent' but could be incapable of consummation due to incomplete development of the organs.

Vasectomy is not Impotency but Concealment of Same is Fraud Entitling Wife to Decree of Annulment

Best Morning v. *Nirmalendu*,
AIR 1987 Gau 63: II (1987) DMC 214: (1987) 2 Gau LR 324

Issue: Can vasectomy be equated with impotency? Does concealment of vasectomy prior to marriage amount to fraud on the wife so as to entitle to a decree of annulment?

Facts: A wife filed a petition for annulment of marriage, under section 19 of the Indian Divorce Act, 1869. She alleged that the husband had undergone vasectomy operation prior to the marriage and this fact had not been disclosed to her. She pleaded that the marriage be declared null and void because of the husband's incompetence to enter into the pretended marriage by reason of his impotency and further, on the ground of cheating. In confirmation proceedings, the question was raised whether vasectomy on the male renders him impotent so as to provide a ground for a decree under section 19(1) of the IDA, declaring the marriage *null* and *void*.

Order: It was held that no case for impotency can be made out because impotency and disability to have children because of the vasectomy, are two different things; the latter does not make a man impotent. However, the court held that a fraud was committed on the wife. It observed:

> "Maternity is the natural inclination of a woman, C.A. Stoddard said, 'there can be no higher ambition for a Christian woman than to be a faithful wife and a happy and influential mother'. It is the place which God has given woman, and she who fills it well, is as honourable and honored as the most 'illustrious man can be'........ Not that every barren marriage is to break down but that there should be no deception or fraud perpetrated on the wife by the husband in this regard."

The decree of nullity was, accordingly, confirmed on this ground.

Comment: Concealment of the fact that the husband had undergone vasectomy operation prior to marriage is indeed a very serious fraud on the wife. It not only gives to a wife a right to dissolve the marriage on ground of mental cruelty, but also to have the marriage annulled on the ground of fraud.

Wife's Virginity is no Proof of Husband's Impotency

Bhaswati Sarkar v. *Angshuman Sarkar*,
AIR 2000 Cal 210: 2000 (2) Cal LJ 219: II (2001) DMC 237

Issue: Just as non-conception and/or inability to conceive are no proof of non-consummation likewise mere fact that wife is a virgin is not enough proof of husband's impotency.

Facts: Under section 24(ii) of the Special Marriage Act, 1954, any marriage solemnized under this Act shall be null and void and may, on a petition by either party thereto against the other be so declared by a decree of nullity if, *inter alia*, the respondent was impotent at the time of the marriage and at the time of the institution of the suit. And under section 27(1)(d), a divorce can be sought on the ground that the other party has treated the petitioner with cruelty. Wilful refusal of the respondent to consummate as a result of which the marriage could not be consummated renders a marriage voidable. In this case, the wife filed a petition seeking a decree of nullity under section 24(ii) of the Act, and for divorce under section 27(1)(d) of the Act. She alleged that the husband was impotent at the time of marriage and continued to be so at the time of the institution of her case.

Order: The husband denied impotency but conceded non-consummation of the marriage. However, according to him, the non-consummation was due to the wife's attitude since she did not want to conceive. He offered to undergo medical examination to disprove the wife's allegation of the his impotency. The court held that the initial *onus* to establish that the marriage was not consummated because of husband's impotency and also that such impotency continued till the filing of her petition, lies with the wife. It is only after such burden is discharged by the wife that the husband has to prove that he was not impotent both at the time of the marriage and till the institution of the wife's suit and further, that the marriage could not be consummated owing to the wife's conduct. Mere fact that wife was virgin is no proof of husband's impotency, the court held.

Comment: In order to prove the ground of impotency, a wife has to lead other evidence as well in support of her case and not only the fact that she was a virgin.

IRRETRIEVABLE BREAKDOWN OF MARRIAGE

Broken Marriage – Divorce Decreed

Chanderkala Trivedi v. *Dr. S.P. Trivedi,*
(1993) 3 SCALE 541: (1993) 4 SCC 232: JT (1993) 4 SC 644

Issue: Can a court ignore strict technicalities of the law and give relief after assessing the circumstances and equities of the case?

Facts: The husband filed a petition for divorce on the ground of cruelty by the wife. The wife filed a written statement attributing adultery to the husband. In the counter-reply the husband put forward another allegation against the wife that she was having undesirable association with young boys. In the light of these pleadings a decree of divorce was granted. The wife filed an appeal before the Supreme Court.

Order: The decree of divorce was upheld. The following observations and findings of the Court are pertinent to indicate that the theory of irretrievable breakdown of the marriage as a ground for divorce, has indeed made a backdoor entry into the matrimonial law. It said:

> "Once such allegations are made by the husband and wife as had been made.........it was obvious that the marriage of the two cannot in any circumstance be continued any further."

It was submitted that there was an error in the finding of the High Court but the Apex Court did not propose to examine it as it was satisfied that the marriage was dead and sending back the matter to division bench to decide it again would mean another exercise in futility leading to tortuous litigation and continued agony of the parties. And further, the Court remarked (at p. 233):

> "We do share the feelings of the wife expressed by the learned counsel that a conservative Hindu lady would not prefer to be known as a divorcee in the society. At the same time, we cannot be oblivious of the impossible situation in which the parties have landed themselves which indeed is unfortunate."

Viewing the facts and circumstances in totality, the Court, under its inherent powers to do complete justice, upheld the divorce decree. It held (at p. 233):

> "Whether the allegations of the husband that she [the wife] was in the habit of associating with young boys and the recording by the three courts are correct or not, but what is certain is that once such allegations are made by the husband and wife as have been made in this case, then it is obvious that the marriage of the two cannot in any circumstances be continued any further. The marriage appears to be practically dead........"

Comment: The courts have started taking a holistic view of the situation and circumstances of the case rather than clinging to proof of technical grounds. The inherent powers of the courts are wide enough to interpret the circumstances in such a way as would impart "complete justice" to the parties in a given case. The equities, however, need to be seriously and sensitively worked out in such cases.

Irretrievable Breakdown – Divorce Granted
Kanchan Devi v. Promod Kumar Mittal,
AIR 1996 SC 3192: 1996 AIR SCW 1933: (1996) 8 SCC 90

Issue: Can a divorce be granted on the ground of irretrievable breakdown of the marriage?

Facts: The case had a chequered history with wife filing successive applications for maintenance and the husband obtaining an *ex parte* divorce which was later set aside. There was a short stint of reconciliation and differences again. The parties were practically living separate for over a decade and all attempts at reconciliation failed. Both the parties also agreed that they could not live together hence they arrived at a settlement. The court found that there was no possibility of reconciliation.

Order: Invoking its jurisdiction under article 142 of the Constitution which empowers the court to pass "any decree or order as is necessary for doing complete justice in any case or matter pending before it.........." the court passed a decree of divorce. Though the statements made by the parties and the memorandum of settlement clearly indicated that it was a case of divorce by mutual consent, the following observations reinforced the fact that irretrievable breakdown of the marriage as a ground for divorce has imperceptibly found a place in the Hindu Marriage Act:

> "In view of the peculiar facts and circumstances of the case and being satisfied that the marriage between the appellant and the respondent has irretrievably broken down and that there is no possibility of reconciliation, we in exercise of our powers under Article 142 of the Constitution of India, hereby direct that the marriage..........shall stand dissolved by a decree of divorce." (at p. 3193)

Comment: There is no point in withholding divorce when the marriage has broken beyond repair. Since it is not a statutory ground for divorce, the courts try to fit the case into some statutory ground available to the parties so that meaningful relief could be given.

Lengthy Litigation *Per Se* – No Ground for Considering Marriage as Broken

Neeta Kirit Desai v. *Bino Samuel George,*
AIR 2003 Bom 7: 2003 (1) Bom LR 310: I (2003) DMC 151

Issue: Can a marriage, where litigation has been going for long, be dissolved on the ground of irretrievable breakdown because of the long litigation?

Facts: The wife was a Hindu and the husband was a convert to Hinduism. The marriage, however, did not work and soon after marriage, litigation started. The wife prayed for a decree of annulment and declaration to that effect under section 5 combined with sections 11 and 12(c) of the Act, *viz.*, that the consent was obtained by fraud and force. There were no details about the alleged fraud or force. After a full trial, the petition was dismissed. The wife made one appeal after the other upto the Supreme Court, but failed. Thus, the findings on the absence of any force or fraud were final and conclusive and the marriage was held to be legal and valid. The wife then started a second round of litigation seeking divorce on the ground of cruelty alleging that the husband had demanded ₹ 25 lakh from her for signing consent to divorce and also defamed her in society by spreading damaging rumours against her which made it difficult for her to live in society. The pleadings were vague and general and were not accepted. Ultimately, she took the plea that the marriage was dead for all practical purposes having lasted for only seven days. The court did not accept this plea either.

Order: The court dismissed the wife's petition for divorce. It found that not a single allegation made by the wife was worthy of investigation so much so that even if the husband had remained *ex parte*, the wife could not have succeeded.

According to the court, the litigation was *prima facie* frivolous and vexatious, instituted and fought under pressure from some family members. The plea that litigation had been going on for long and so the marriage should be treated to have been irretrievably broken down was not accepted. Acceptance of such an argument, according to the court:

> "[W]ill mean that in all matters wherever matrimonial litigation went on for five to ten years, the divorce must follow. In Indian Courts any litigation howsoever minor it may be, takes years for decision in the original court, then appeals take their own share of time; under these circumstances, mere lengthy period of litigation cannot be pressed into service to contend that marriage is dead for all practical purposes.... The lapse of time in litigation alone cannot be a ground to hold that the marriage is dead."

Comment: It is a case of a completely broken marriage. However, since irretrievable breakdown of the marriage, *per se*, is no ground for divorce unless the facts and allegations made by the petitioner fit into one of the statutory grounds provided for the relief, no meaningful relief can be given by the courts.

The court has, in this case, made an honest statement and admitted that even minor litigation takes years to be settled. It is important, however, to find a way out and ensure that, at least in matrimonial cases where lives and hapiness of parties are involved, there should be expeditious disposal so that where possible, parties can restart or reorganise their lives.

Divorce Granted Despite Petitioner Husband's own Fault Simply Because Relationship Broken Beyond Repair

Poonam Gupta v. *Ghanshayam Gupta*, AIR 2003 All 51

Issue: (i) Can a marriage be dissolved on the sole ground of irretrievable breakdown of the marriage?

(ii) Can a husband take advantage of his own wrong to obtain a decree of divorce?

Facts: The husband filed a petition for divorce alleging cruelty etc., against the wife, and obtained an *ex parte* decree. Soon after the decree, he remarried and also had a child. The wife challenged the *ex parte* order before the division bench which was admitted and the case was remanded to the Family Court for expeditious disposal. The Family Court held that even though cruelty on the part of the wife, as alleged by the husband, was not established yet, considering the fact that both parties were levelling allegations and counter-allegations against each other, it was not possible for them to live together. Thus, a decree of divorce subject to the husband paying rupees five lakhs to the wife, was passed. On appeal against this by the wife, the court made efforts for reconciliation and while the wife was still prepared to go back, husband *categorically refused*.

Order: The court dismissed the wife's appeal. It observed:

"Since there are allegations and counter-allegations of misbehaviour and physical and mental torture by both the parties, we find that it would not be actually possible for the two to live together. Besides, there is also the fact that during the pendency of the petition for divorce, the husband has remarried and has two children."

And further:

"Taking advantage of the *ex parte* divorce, he immediately remarried making a situation impossible for the wife to return and live together. In fact, the circumstances indicate that the plaintiff-husband was responsible for creating a situation in which the court may not be left with any other alternative but to grant a decree of divorce as under no circumstances can the marriage now be retrieved."

The wife thus lost the appeal and a decree of divorce against the husband was confirmed.

Comment: It is a disappointing judgment where the husband, even though he could not establish the ground on which he sought divorce, was granted decree because *"during the pendency of the petition, he remarried and had two children from this marriage"*. (emphasis added) His own fault became a ground to give him the relief he wanted. But perhaps that was the demand of expediency in this case.

Marriage Broken – Divorce Granted with View to do "Complete Justice"
A. Jayachandra v. Aneel Kaur,
AIR 2005 SC 534: 2005 AIR SCW 163: (2005) 2 SCC 22

Issue: Can a court grant a decree of divorce to shorten the agony of the spouses engaged in long drawn litigation, on the ground of irretrievable breakdown of the marriage?

Facts: The parties, both doctors by profession, were married on October 10, 1978. They were blessed with two children. The parties were working in the same hospital which was established by the appellant's father. According to the husband, the respondent's behaviour was "obnoxious, humiliating and amounting to mental cruelty". He sent a notice to the wife seeking divorce by mutual consent to avoid unnecessary complications. It was stated therein that they had not had any physical relations for over two years; that she had treated him with cruelty and her conduct amounted to desertion for two years and that it was neither safe, desirable nor advisable to continue marital relationship. The parties did discuss the issue but with no results, hence, the husband filed a petition for divorce under section 13 of the Hindu Marriage Act in the Family Court. He alleged that the respondent ill-treated him, abused him in vulgar language in the home and at the hospital and other places thereby causing mental agony, damage and loss personally and professionally and also in the social circles; that she made allegations about his character; caveats were filed at different places with a view to forestall legal action and create an impression of innocence. After the husband filed the petition, the wife filed a suit for injunction in respect of right to practise in the hospital. The suit was not objected by the husband and the same was decreed. Subsequently, an execution petition was filed praying for attachment of hospital equipments belonging to him and for his civil detention for alleged disobedience of the order of injunction. An application for maintenance was also filed before the Family Court though, admittedly, she herself was a professional doctor. After going through the evidence the Family Court found that unfounded allegations which caused mental agony were made by the wife which amounted to mental cruelty; however, keeping in mind the welfare of the children, a decree of judicial separation instead of divorce was passed by the Family Court. Both parties appealed—the husband against grant of separation instead of divorce and the wife questioning the legality of the decree for judicial separation. The Division Bench of the High Court dismissed the husband's appeal. It held that the materials on record were not sufficient to prove any mental cruelty. "The entire evidence led by the appellant did not even emit smell of cruelty", the court remarked.

According to the High Court, even if it was a fact that the respondent was using abusive language and making allegations of adultery with nursing staff, the husband ought to have examined some witnesses from the hospital and since it was not done, cruelty was not established. Hence the husband's appeal. The Supreme Court disagreed with the High Court's view that some witnesses from the hospital were necessary to be examined. That alone should not have been made the determinative factor to discard evidence on record. "On that ground alone the judgment of the High Court is vulnerable", the court remarked. The evidence as led and which was practically undisputed was that the respondent had asked the husband to do certain things which could not be termed to be simple advise for proper behaviour. For example, in her evidence, she clearly accepted that she had said five things to be followed by him. Surprisingly most of them related to ladies working in the hospital. These were clear manifestations of her suspecting the husband's fidelity, character and reputation. For instance, the first so-called advise was not to ask female staff members to come and work off-duty hours when nobody was available in the hospital. Second was, not to work behind the closed doors with certain members of the staff. This according to the court was nothing but casting doubt on the reputation, character and fidelity of the husband. *"Constant nagging on those aspects, certainly amounted to causing indelible mental agony and amounts to cruelty"*, the court said.

Another point of significance in the case was that the court pointed out that "if acts subsequent to the filing of the divorce petition can be looked into to infer condonation of the aberrations, acts subsequent to the filing of the petition can be taken note of to show a pattern in the behaviour and conduct". In this case, after the husband's divorce petition, the respondent wife filed a suit for injunction and went to the extent of seeking his detention. She also filed a maintenance petition which was dismissed; she lodged several caveat petitions too.

Order: The Court came to a clear finding of mental cruelty in this case. It also deduced from the facts and circumstances of the case that the marriage had irretrievably broken down. While conceding that irretrievable breakdown of marriage is not one of the statutory grounds on which court can direct dissolution of marriage, it held that it had with a view to do complete justice and shorten the agony of the parties engaged in long drawn battle, directed dissolution of the marriage in certain cases. A decree of divorce was accordingly passed in favour of the husband.

Comment: A very practical approach has been adopted by the Court. Indeed it serves no useful purpose to prolong the agony of the parties where there is not even an *iota* of their ever living happily again.

Where no Alleged Ground Proved – Relief cannot be Granted on Ground of Irretrievable Breakdown of Marriage

Ajay Sayajirao Desai v. Rajashree Ajay Desai,
AIR 2005 Bom 278: 2005 (3) All MR 577:
2005 Bom CR Sup 793

Issue: When the grounds alleged for divorce are not established, the petitioner cannot plead irretrievable breakdown of the marriage, more so when the non-petitioner has all through expressed a desire, which according to the court, was genuine, to live with the husband.

Facts: The parties were married in 1994 and had a child. The petitioner-husband's case was that right from the beginning of marriage, the wife's behaviour was strange and rude. He also alleged desertion by the wife because she went for delivery to her parents house and never returned. He, however, filed a petition for restitution of conjugal rights under section 9 of the Hindu Marriage Act. The wife, in reply, sought to justify her withdrawal in her written statement and alleged cruelty by the husband and his mother. Within three days of the wife's filing the written statement, the husband withdrew his petition for restitution without assigning any reason whatsoever. After three months, he filed a petition for divorce on the ground of cruelty and desertion and also for child's custody. As instances of cruelty the husband stated: (i) non-disclosure of the hereditary disease that the wife was allegedly suffering, *viz.* white spot on her waist (leucoderma); (ii) the wife slapped him when he made an attempt to touch the waist of the wife where she had the spot. (This was at the time of honeymoon); (iii) soon after returning from honeymoon, she insisted for separate residence; (iv) her rude behaviour with his parents and mentally challenged sister; (v) threats given by the wife of serious consequences; (vi) insulting and humiliating treatment meted out to him and his relatives whenever they visited her at her parents' house with a view to bring her back; (vii) false allegations made against him and his mother in the written statement filed in reply to husband's petition for restitution of conjugal rights; (viii) threats given by her to him and his relatives on phone and through letters.

The Family Court, after extensively dealing with the evidence led by the parties, held that the allegations which allegedly caused mental agony and cruelty were unfounded; nor was desertion established. Prayer for custody of the child was also rejected. Hence the appeal.

Order: The court analysed the pleadings and evidence of the parties in great detail and came to the following conclusions:

> (i) The husband came to know about the white spots on the wife's body quite early in marriage and, according to his own statement, they had no discussion on it. Thereafter, they admittedly had healthy sexual relationship. He also stated in his pleading that he had no grievance regarding the white spot. Thus, it cannot be said that the disease was

suppressed at the time of marriage and it caused him mental cruelty when he noticed it after two months of marriage.

(ii) The white spot seems to have been consciously accepted by the husband probably because he also had a fully grown up mentally challenged sister in the house and his parents wanted the wife to take care of her.

(iii) As to wife's misbehaviour with the sister and parents of the husband, except for his bare words there is no material on record.

(iv) The fact that the petition for restitution was filed in 1996 and efforts were allegedly made to bring her back show that the husband and his mother had no grievance against the wife whatsoever.

(v) As to threats of serious consequences, there was no material in support except bare words. If this had been true why were efforts made to bring her back?

(vi) As to insistence on separate residence, the court remarked, if this were to be construed to amount to mental cruelty, "probably every petition coming to this court for divorce on such ground will have to be allowed". Unless the intensity of such insistence goes to the extent of making it impossible for the husband to live without mental agony, torture or distress, such allegation cannot be taken to constitute cruelty.

(vii) As to allegations made in the written statement (in reply to husband's petition for restitution) amounting to cruelty, according to the court, these were made only as a defence to justify her withdrawal. Also there was no occasion to prove the truth or falsity of these allegation of the wife because the husband, for reasons best known to him, withdrew his restitution petition.

Thus, the court held that no cruelty was established. Likewise, the allegation of desertion was also held to be false. There was no intention of the wife to desert. She was all through not only willing but made efforts to join the husband. In fact the husband changed his residence and did not even inform his new address to her. When she went to his house, the same was locked. She approached an organisation 'Asha Sanstha' to intervene and tried to resume cohabitation but all invain.

The plea of irretrievable breakdown of the marriage was also taken by the husband but the same too was turned down on the ground that the wife was all through ready to go back; it is the husband who refused to take her back.

The husband's petition for divorce was thus rejected by the Family Court and then in appeal, by the High Court.

Comment: The court saw through the *mala fides* of the husband who first filed a petition for restitution, even in the face of averments that the wife's behaviour was cruel, and then within three days of wife's written statement, withdrew that petition and filed for divorce. He pleaded desertion, cruelty and irretrievable breakdown of the marriage, hoping perhaps, that some ground might click. The court, however, found that his case was not genuine.

Alleged Ground not Proved but Marriage Broken – Relief Granted

Dinesh Kumar Mandal v. Mina Devi, AIR 2005 Jhar 77: 2005 (27) All Ind Cas 752: 2005 (3) Civ LJ 339

Issue: When an alleged ground is not proved, can the court grant divorce on another ground specified in the Act on the plea that factually the marriage has broken down and withholding the decree will not in any case bring them together?

Facts: The parties were married in 1994. However, their bliss did not last long and the husband filed a petition for divorce on the ground of adultery. According to the husband, the wife frequently left his house without his permission to go to her parents; she often used a stay in the house of several persons, and that she was living in adultery. He even impleaded the alleged adulterer as co-respondent. On the basis of adduced evidence, however, the Trial Court found that adultery was not proved and so dismissed the husband's petition. Hence the husband's appeal.

Order: The court held that even though the case of adultery was not proved yet it is an admitted fact by the wife that she lived in the houses of several persons. Also, the parties had been living separately for seven years which indicated breakdown of the marriage with no chances of rapprochement. In fact they started living separately very soon after the marriage. The court relied on *Narinder Kumar* v. *Suresh Kumari*, AIR 1988 Del 222: 1988 Mat LR 235: (1987) 6 Reports 201 and *Mohan Lal* v. *Nihal Singh*, AIR 2001 SC 2942: 2001 AIR SCW 4409: (2001) 8 SCC 584, where separate living of the parties for long years was held to be enough evidence that the marriage had irretrievably broken down and therefore divorce was granted. In the instant case also, parties were living separately and according to the court even if the divorce was not allowed, still they would live separately. Hence, the court held that even though adultery is not proved, a case of desertion is made out and so a decree of divorce was granted on the ground of desertion.

Comment: Parties living separately for long years soon after marriage is enough evidence to establish breakdown of the marriage. Thus, while the ground alleged, *viz.* adultery, was not established, the court held that desertion was proved and hence a decree of divorce sought by the husband was granted.

Broken Marriage – Divorce Granted – Support of "Cruelty" Taken by Court
Naveen Kohli v. Neelu Kohli,
AIR 2006 SC 1675: 2006 AIR SCW 1550: (2006) 4 SCC 558

Issue: Can irretrievable breakdown of the marriage be the basis for grant of decree of divorce under the Hindu Marriage Act?

Facts: This was a matrimonial case with a chequered history. A husband sought divorce on the ground of mental cruelty. His allegations were, *inter alia*, that the wife, who was the sole proprietor of a company holding 94.5 percent shares wherein the husband was an employee, got a news item published that the husband was acting against the spirit of Articles of Association and had caused immense loss of business and ill-will. Further, business associates were cautioned to avoid dealing with him. Besides criminal proceedings, an FIR was launched alleging cheating, forgering and enticing married women with criminal assault. All this, according to the husband, lowered his image and caused mental cruelty. On the basis of pleadings and evidence, the Trial Court passed a decree of divorce on the ground of mental cruelty. The wife filed an appeal against this. The Division Bench of Allahabad High Court discussed the concept of cruelty as a matrimonial wrong in great detail. While it conceded that acts and conduct amounting to mental cruelty in matrimonial life abound, it observed. (*Neelu Kohli v. Naveen Kohli*, AIR 2004 All 1 at 12):

> "Mere fact that the erring spouse is moody, whimsical, mean, stingy, selfish, boorish, irritable, and inconsiderate, etc., will not be sufficient. Similarly, merely neglect or want of affection, expression of hatred will not be a conduct constituting cruelty. The idiosyncrasies of the wife sometime may not amount to cruelty even though they may make the husband unhappy. There may be occasion where conduct may lead to unpleasantness but such unpleasantness alone may not be cruelty and may reasonably fall within ambit of ordinary wear and tear of matrimonial life which is not sufficient to establish cruelty as envisaged under the Act."

In this case, according to the High Court, a news item issued to protect the interests of its employees and major share holders cannot be said to be illegal or motivated, nor would initiating criminal proceedings and lodging FIR in the circumstances of the case, be enough to warrant divorce on husband's petition. The Trial Court decree allowing divorce was thus, set aside. The husband thereupon filed a special leave petition under article 136 of the Constitution.

Order: After analysing the facts and circumstances of the case and various decisions on cruelty by the various courts in India and other countries, the court dissolved the marriage. The following observations are pertinent (at p. 1688):

> "Once marriage has broken down beyond repair, it would be unrealistic for the law not to take notice of the fact and it would be harmful to society and injurious to the interest of the parties."

Even after making all sorts of allegations and filing criminal cases against the husband, the wife, in this case was still challenging the divorce. The court observed (at p. 1689):

> From the analysis and evaluation of the entire evidence, it is clear that the respondent (wife) has resolved to live in agony only to make life a miserable hell for the appellant (husband) as well. This type of adamant and callous attitude....leaves no manner of doubt....that the respondent is bent upon treating the appellant with mental cruelty. It is abundantly clear that the marriage between the parties has been broken down irretrievably and there is no chance of their coming together or living together again.... there has been a total disappearance of the emotional substratum in the marriage. The course which has been adopted by the High Court [*viz.*, setting aside the decree passed by the Family Court] would encourage continuous bickering, perpetual bitterness and may lead to immorality.

And further, the court observed (at p. 1690):

> "The marriage has been wrecked beyond the hope of salvage; public interest of all concerned lies in the recognition of the facts and to declare *defunct de jure* what is already *defunct de facto* to keep the sham is obviously conducive to immorality and potentially more prejudicial to the public interest than the dissolution of the marriage bond."

The husband's appeal consequently was allowed and a decree of divorce sought by him was granted. It is significant to note that ostensibly, the decree was based on the matrimonial ground of 'cruelty' but as is evident from the entire approach and reasoning of the court, the court found no reason to keep the practically dead marriage which is in "insolublemess" only legally alive. A strong plea for incorporating irretrievable breakdown of marriage as ground for divorce was made by the apex court.

Comment: The futility of retaining a bond simply for the sake of keeping it legally alive has been an issue of debate and discussion since several years now. Time and again courts have also expressed their views on it. In the instant case, a copy of the judgment was sent to the Secretary, Ministry of Law and Justice, Department of Legal Affairs, with recommendation that the Government gives serious thought to it. It may be pointed out that the Marriage Laws (Amendment) Bill, 2010 seeks to incorporate irretrievable breakdown of the marriage as an additional ground for divorce. Needless to say that this will be hedged with several safeguards against abuse.

Note: The Bill has since been passed.

Ground Statutorily not Provided so no Relief though Hard Case

Visnu Dutt Sharma v. *Manju Sharma,*
AIR 2009 SC 2254: 2009 AIR SCW 2984: (2009) 6 SCC 379

Issue: Can a court dissolve a marriage on a ground not provided under the Hindu Marriage Act *viz.,* simply on ground that the marriage has been irretrievably broken?

Facts: A husband filed a petition for divorce under section 13(1)(ia) against his wife alleging cruelty. In support of his case he alleged several instances and incidents; however, he failed to prove the allegations as a result of which the Trial Court dismissed his petition. His further appeal to the High Court was also dismissed, hence he approached the Supreme Court. It was argued that the parties had stayed together for hardly 25 days and the marriage was over for all practical purposes, and that being so, divorce be granted on the ground of irretrievable breakdown of the marriage. The court declined to concede to this argument. It held that section 13 of the Hindu Marriage Act which provides for several grounds on which divorce may be obtained makes no provision for divorce on this ground. This court cannot add such a ground as, according to the Court, doing so would amount to amending the Act which is the function of the Legislature. It was argued by the appellant husband that this court had, in fact in some cases dissolved marriage in circumstances where it found that the marriage had irretrievably broken down and there was no point in refusing the divorce. To this argument the court observed:

"In our opinion, those cases have not taken into consideration the legal position...and hence they are not precedents. A mere direction of the Court without considering the legal position is not precedent.

Order: Decree of divorce was refused on ground of irretrievable breakdown of the marriage as no such ground is statutorily provided under the Hindu Marriage Act.

Comment: A plea for introducing irretrievable breakdown of the marriage as a ground for divorce was strongly made by academicians, jurists and judges and, the Law Commission. Consequently the Marriage Laws (Amendment) Act 2010 has been introduced incorporating this ground.

Both Parties at Fault – Marriage Broken but Relief Based on 'Cruelty'

N. Shankar v. S. Saraswathi, (2010) 1 MLJ 959 (Mad)

Issue: Can a High Court grant a decree of divorce when both spouses are at fault, ostensibly on the ground of cruelty but in reality on ground of breakdown of the marriage.

Facts: The parties in this case were well educated – the husband was an engineer and the wife an advocate who left practice after marriage; however, they could not adjust in their marital life and the husband filed a petition for divorce on the ground of cruelty under section 13(1) of the Hindu Marriage Act. He alleged various acts of cruelty perpetrated by the wife on him, *inter alia*, that she used to force him to have sexual intercourse even when he was not well and was suffering a wheezing problem; if he refused her demand, she would become hysterical, abusive and physically violent and scratch him with her nails; she would pick up quarrels over petty things and even threaten to commit suicide. The parties had lived together for only four years and separated for 12 years and litigating. According to the wife, however, the husband had extra-marital affairs and wanted her to agree to a divorce by mutual consent and on her refusal to do so, used to beat her. Further, she alleged that when her only 27 years old brother died, the appellant/husband even refused to convey his condolence to the bereaved family. After hearing the averments of both the parties, the Trial Court came to the conclusion that no cruelty, as alleged by the husband, was established and hence dismissed his petition. Against this the husband filed the present appeal. After making unsuccessful attempts for reconciliation, the court passed a divorce decree. It observed that the Trial Court failed to take into consideration the wild and reckless allegations made against each other; there was denial of marital comforts to each other for long period which undoubtedly would amount to mental cruelty; the fact that the husband refused to visit the bereaved family on the death of wife's young brother was an instance not only indicating bitterness against each other but also that normal human feelings and emotions had been lost. In view of all this, the court was of the opinion that it was impossible to preserve or save the marriage and any effort to keep it alive would prove to be totally counter-productive. The court referred to various cases where relief was sought on ground of cruelty – mental cruelty specially – and decrees were granted not so much on the basis of this ground as on the fact that marriage in these cases had irretrievably broken down – whether due to fault of petitioner or respondent. (*Suman Kapur* v. *Sudhir Kapur*, (2009) 1 SCC 422: 2008 AIR SCW 7730: AIR 2009 SC 589; *V. Bhagat* v. *D. Bhagat*, AIR 1994 SC 710: 1994 AIR SCW 45: (1994) 1 SCC 337; *Chanderkala Trivedi* v. *Dr. S.P. Trivedi*, (1993) 3 SCALE 541: (1993) 4 SCC 232: JT (1993) 4 SC 644; *Samar Ghosh* v. *Jaya Ghosh*, (2007) 4 SCC 511; *Naveen Kohli* v. *Neelu Kohli*, AIR 2006 SC 1675: 2006 AIR SCW 1550: (2006) 4 SCC 558.

In the present case, N. Shanker, also the court found that both the spouses were at fault and the marriage had completely broken down; the marriage had become a fiction and ceased to exist in spirit though remaining on papers.

Order: The husband's appeal was allowed and a decree of divorce granted. However, as if by way of a disclaimer, it observed (at p. 965):

"We make it clear that our opinion is not rested upon irretrievable breaking down of marriage but based on section 13(1) [(*viz.*, cruelty)] of the Act."

Comments: This is yet another case indicating how in the absence of statutory ground of irretrievable breakdown, the courts seek *alibis* to fit the case within parameters of a statutorily recognised ground. Surprisingly, even when both the parties are admittedly guilty of a matrimonial offence, the petitioner's plea of cruelty by the other forms the basis for the decree. The real reason for the decree is breakdown though. It is significant to note that all the cases referred to by the court in *N. Shankar* in support of its case were decided by the Apex Court. In any case it is the Supreme Court alone vide its extra ordinary powers which has the competence to pass a decree to do complete justice even in the absence of statutory ground; no other court has such powers. It may, however, be pointed out that the Marriage Laws (Amendment) Bill, 2010 makes a provision for adding irretrievable breakdown of the marriage as a ground for divorce.

LEPROSY

Decree Granted

Swarajya Lakshmi v. *G.G. Padma Rao,*
AIR 1974 SC 165: (1974) 1 SCC 58: (1974) 2 SCR 97

Issue: Should emotional considerations come in the way of a husband who seeks divorce on the ground of wife's leprosy?

Facts: The husband was a doctor and both the parties were young. After marriage they lived together for one-and-a-half year and had a child. Thereafter, the husband petitioned for divorce on the ground that the wife was suffering from lepramatous form of leprosy and tuberculosis. The Additional Chief Judge of the city Civil Court was of the view that the wife was suffering from virulent and incurable form of leprosy for a period of not less than three years preceding the petition. The husband's petition was however dismissed on the ground that it was premature as three years had not elapsed since the date of the marriage. (Prior to 1976, *vide* section 14 of the Act a petition for divorce could not be filed unless three years had elapsed since the date of marriage; (this has now been reduced to one year). The husband filed an appeal against this which was allowed. The husband, alongwith his main petition for divorce, also filed a petition under section 14 of the Act for relaxing the three years period on the ground that the case was one of exceptional hardship to him. His arguments were that—(i) the wife was suffering from leprosy and close contact with her carried the risk of his contracting the disease himself; and (ii) the wife was also suffering from tuberculosis, which would detrimentally affect his health and professional practice. On behalf of the wife, it was argued that in view of the revolutionary nature of sulphone treatment, leprosy should no longer be regarded as an incurable disease. Mukherjee J., who delivered the judgment, pointed out that even the sulphone treatment or even the discovery of CIBA – 1906, which was less toxic, did not guarantee complete cure.

Order: The court upheld the High Court order granting divorce to the husband under section 13(1)(iv) of the Act. It observed:

> "Sociologists insist and they do so very correctly that we should not allow our minds to be swayed by feelings of emotional loathing and revulsion with which leprosy patients have been treated throughout human history in all countries throughout the world and that we should take up a very humane and balanced outlook and accept leprosy 'as simply another disorder that requires medical attention'. We have no doubt that this is absolutely correct about what should be the social approach but to our

minds we should not provide any justification for compelling a husband to live with a wife who is suffering from an aggravated form of leprosy and who can give him and his children leprosy almost any moment in their daily life.....we have no doubt in our mind that the law makers do not treat the subject of divorce lightly and must have taken into consideration the consequences of one spouse being compelled to live intimately with another who suffers from leprosy when they provided for a way out for the former."

Comment: The courts and law makers should take due note of the advancements in medical science and treatment of the condition. The judgment is over three decades old and the parties were married over 40 years ago. There have been great strides in medical science since then.

MENTAL DISORDER

Non-cohabitation for a Month – No Inference of Mental Disorder

R. Lakshmi Narayan v. Santhi,
AIR 2001 SC 2110: 2001 AIR SCW 1820: (2001) 4 SCC 688

Issue: Can an inference of mental disorder be drawn merely from the fact that there was no cohabitation for a period of about a month.

Facts: The parties to the marriage had met each other before the marriage. In other words, it was an arranged marriage after parties were satisfied of the alliance. After staying together for about 25 days, they parted company and the husband sought annulment of the marriage on the ground of wife's mental abnormality. In fact, he sought a declaration that the marriage was void as the wife was suffering from chronic and incurable mental disorder and was not fit to lead a married life. The allegations to substantiate the ground were, *inter alia*, that on the night of marriage, the husband found her drowsy; she refused cohabitation; she said she was suffering from mental disorder since childhood; she did not want to have any conjugal relationship and stated that she was married under pressure from her parents. There was no allegation that she was incapable of giving valid consent to marriage owing to unsoundness of mind at the time of marriage. A marriage sought to be annulled on the ground pleaded is not *per se* void but voidable and strict standard of proof is required with heavy burden on the party who approaches the court for annulment of a marriage already solemnized. According to the court, to draw an inference of mental disorder merely from the fact that there was no cohabitation for a short period of about a month, is neither reasonable nor permissible. To brand the wife as unfit for marriage and procreation on account of mental disorder, it needs to be established that the ailment suffered by her is of such kind or such extent that it is impossible for her to lead a normal married life.

Order: The husband's appeal was dismissed as he failed to establish his case for declaring the marriage *null* and *void* under section 12(1)(b) read with section 5(ii) of the Hindu Marriage Act.

Comment: The burden of proving mental disorder of the respondent is heavy and the courts do not lightly concede to the petitioner's plea unless it is satisfied that the case is established medically and factually.

Psychological Depression is not Mental Disorder

Hema Reddy v. Rakesh Reddy,
AIR 2002 AP 228

Issue: Is psychological depression synonymous to mental disorder so as to provide a ground for matrimonial relief?

Facts: The husband filed a petition for divorce on the ground of mental disorder of the wife. He alleged that the wife had strange habits of scratching her hands and head in a very irritating manner, had bouts of silence, never mixed up with family members, was also depressed and keen to go to her parental house. He further alleged that she ridiculed him and taunted him about his meagre salary and also had suicidal tendencies. In fact, the wife had lost her mother 3-4 years prior to her marriage and was under a psychiatrist's treatment since then. The Trial Court passed a decree in favour of the husband, hence the wife's appeal. The court held that the conditions and incidents narrated by the petitioner do not amount to mental disorder.

Order: The wife's appeal was allowed and the husband's case for divorce on the ground of wife's mental disorder was rejected. The court held:

> "The depression by itself is no ground under the Hindu Law to grant decree of divorce. The petitioner has to prove by leading medical evidence that psychological depression is synonymous to mental disorder."

The husband did not lead any evidence to that effect. In fact, even the fact of mental depression was not proved by leading cogent evidence.

Comment: Courts in India are very cautious and careful in granting relief to the petitioner on the ground of respondent's mental disorder. Apart from the other consequences of a divorce, an element of stigma is also attached when a decree is passed on this ground.

Minor Aberrations – No Mental Disorder

Devi Sharma v. Chandra Mohan Sharma,
AIR 2003 P&H 327: 2003 (2) Hindu LR 259:
2004 (1) Marri LJ 385

Issue: Acts like not wearing *mangal sutra* etc., are not so grave so as to constitute mental disorder or cruelty.

Facts: A husband filed a petition for annulment and in the alternative, for divorce on the following facts. He alleged that the marriage ceremony could not be completed as during the course of the *'saptapadi'*, the wife fell unconscious and the *'pheras'* (the sacred rounds around the fire) could not be completed; the marriage therefore was *null and void* and hence a decree under section 12 of the Hindu Marriage Act be passed. Though he lived with her for one-and-a-half-year, but, his defence to this was that he was not aware of this infirmity and the legal requirement of a valid marriage until his lawyer told him about it.

As regards divorce on grounds of mental disorder and cruelty, he alleged that she often used to get unconscious and when this fact was brought to the notice of her parents, he was informed that she had fallen ill prior to marriage and was being treated by the doctor; and further according to the husband, she had abnormal habits. She used to spoil all her clothes while taking meals, behaved strangely and shouted, was not wearing *mangal sutra*, was not applying *bindiya*, was not cooking meals and as a result he often had to go to office or sleep without any food. She also asked him to commit suicide so that she could get the job in his place. All this, according to the husband constituted mental cruelty. After perusing through the entire evidence, the Trial Court held that the marriage was complete and there was no infirmity in that; also her conduct did not establish mental cruelty. On the contrary, it was the husband who maltreated her thereby forcing her to file criminal cases against him under sections 406 and 498A of the I.P.C. It, however, held that the wife was suffering from schizophrenia which was incurable and hence dissolved the marriage under section 13(1)(iii) of the Act. The wife appealed against grant of divorce on the ground of mental disorder.

Order: The High Court affirmed the Trial Court's finding that there was a complete marriage and also that there was no cruelty on the part of the wife; as to mental disorder, the court found that the records of the Medical Board and the government psychiatric clinic in the foreign country (Surinam) where the parties stayed after marriage, stated that the wife was not suffering from any mental illness, nor was there any indication to that effect during the lengthy cross-examination. Thus, the Trial Court's order granting divorce was set aside.

Comment: While the law recognises the fact that conjugal harmony and happiness is not possible if either of the parties suffers from serious mental deficiency or mental disorder but, at the same time, the courts are very discreet in awarding relief on this ground. As aptly observed by the Supreme Court in *Ram Narain Gupta* v. *Rameshwari Gupta*, AIR 1988 SC 2260: JT (1988) 3 SC 621: (1988) 4 SCC 247:

> "If the mere existence of any degree of mental abnormality could justify dissolution of marriage, few marriages would indeed survive."

Note: See also *Sampa Karmakar* v. *Dr. Sanjib Karmakar*, AIR 2012 Gau 32.

Alleged Conduct need not be Abnormally Excessive

Vandana v. *Suresh Charan*
AIR 2005 Raj 193: 2005 (2) CCC 142: 2005 (2) Hindu LR 628

Issue: The words "abnormally aggressive or seriously irresponsible conduct" in the explanation to sub-clause (iii) of section 13(1) of the Hindu Marriage Act do not limit the scope of the main provision in section 13(1)(iii).

Facts: The parties were married in 1994. The husband filed a petition for divorce under section 13(1)(iii) of the Hindu Marriage Act on the ground of mental illness of the wife. The husband alleged that even during the performance of the marriage rites, the wife had no control over her body and she was not in a position to perform *saptapadi*. She was given some tablets a few times during the course of the rites. She hardly stayed with him for four days and even during that time her behaviour, conduct and talk was very abnormal. The husband tried to bring her back from her parent's house but she was not sent. After about six years, her brother brought her to the plaintiff-husband's village and at that time she started using abusive language in presence of many people and the entire village came to know that she was suffering from a mental disorder. Her brother also admitted this fact and stated that she was under treatment. The wife, even at that time, stayed with the husband for just about 5-6 days but the marriage was never consummated. The husband's petition for divorce was resisted. It was contended that since he was busy preparing for some competitive exams, he did not want to be disturbed and so he left her at her parents house; that after he cleared the exam, he started disliking her and wanted to marry a more beautiful girl; she also alleged that he used to make sarcastic remarks as she did not bring enough dowry.

The husband sought amendment of his petition for divorce so as to include ground to challenge the marriage itself. He alleged that the marriage was void because the defendant was mad prior to and at the time of marriage and the consent for the marriage was obtained by suppressing this material fact. He, accordingly, sought declaration that the marriage was void under section 12 of the Hindu Marriage Act. This decree, however, was not granted as it was time-barred. The suit for annulment was filed after six years as against one year, which is the limitation period under the section. The court, however, proceeded with the divorce petition. The wife was found to be suffering from schizophrenia and mentally sick by the Medical Board. After considering the evidence and facts of the case, the Trial Court decreed divorce. Hence the wife's appeal.

Order: It was argued that the plaintiff-husband did not plead that the wife is suffering from any mental disease which is incurable or a mental disorder of such kind and to such extent that he cannot live with her because of that disorder nor was it alleged that her behaviour was aggressive or violent. The court considered the provision of section 13(1)(iii) at great length and also referred to some judgments. It held that *Explanation* (b) to sub-clause (iii) of sub-section (1) of section 13 uses the words "abnormally aggressive or seriously irresponsible conduct" on the part of the other party, in the context of 'psychopathic disorders' but this does not limit the scope of the main provision *i.e.*, section 13(1)(iii).

The court also emphasised the fact that in the language used in sub-clause (iii), care has been taken by using the word " reasonably" before "expected to live with respondent". The word could have been "difficult" or "impossible" before "expected to live" but that has not been done. The petitioner is, therefore, required to prove that as a reasonable person, he cannot live with the non-petitioner because of the latter's mental sickness. If it is to be construed that decree of divorce can be granted only in cases where the respondent has aggressive or violent conduct, then there was no need for using the words 'petitioner cannot *reasonably* be expected to live with the respondent' in the main sub-clause (iii).

The mental illness of the wife, could with fact that all these years, the marriage could not even be consummated because of the mental illness was need enough to establish that the wife failed to discharge the matrimonial obligations and created the situation of their separation as the husband could not be expected to live with her. The delay, as alleged by the respondent, was also held to be satisfactorily explained. *The decree was thus granted and the wife's appeal dismissed.*

Comment: While unsoundness of mind and mental sickness is no fault of oneself yet, the other person cannot be expected to suffer if, because of the respondent's condition, a situation has been created that it would be unreasonable to expect the petitioner to live with him/her. The courts, however, are required to examine the totality of the facts of each case. The court in this case emphasised the need for extra care to ensure that the provision is not misused; the sufferer also needs sympathy and consideration, the court observed.

MUTUAL CONSENT

Can Consent, Once given, be Unilaterally Revoked

Sureshta Devi v. *Om Prakash*,
AIR 1992 SC 1904: 1991 AIR SCW 373: (1991) 2 SCC 25

Issue: Whether a party to petition for divorce by mutual consent under section 13B of the Hindu Marriage Act can unilaterally withdraw the consent or whether the consent once given is irrevocable?

Facts: The parties were married in November, 1968 and lived together for about six to seven months. On January 8, 1985 they moved a petition under section 13B for divorce by mutual consent in the District Court at Hamirpur. On January 9, 1985 the court recorded the statements of the parties. On January 15, 1985 the wife filed an application in the court stating, *inter alia*, that her statement dated January 9, 1985 was obtained under pressure and threat of the husband and she was not even allowed to meet her relatives to consult them before filing the divorce petition. She, therefore, prayed for dismissal of the petition. The District Judge made certain orders which were taken up in appeal before the High Court and the High Court remanded the matter to the District Judge for fresh disposal. Ultimately, the District Judge dismissed the divorce petition. On appeal by the husband, the High Court reversed the order and granted a decree for dissolution of the marriage by mutual consent. According to the High Court, a spouse who has given consent to a petition cannot unilaterally withdraw the consent and such withdrawal would not take away the jurisdiction of the court to dissolve the marriage by mutual consent; the court further found that the wife had given her consent without any force, fraud or undue influence and so was bound by that consent. Hence the wife's appeal to the Supreme Court. The Supreme Court referred to the requisites of section 13B(1), *viz*.:

   (i) parties have been staying separately for a period of one year;

   (ii) they have not been able to live together; and

   (iii) they have mutually agreed that marriage should be dissolved.

The court elucidated the meaning of the expression "living separately" thus:

> "The expression..................connotes............not living like husband and wife. It has no reference to the place of living. The parties may live under the same roof by force of circumstances, and yet they may not be living as husband and wife. The parties may be living in different houses and yet they could live as husband and wife. What seems to be necessary is that they have no desire to perform marital obligations and with that

mental attitude, they have been living separately for a period of one year immediately preceding the presentation of the petition."

The second requirement, *viz.*, they have not been able to live together seems to indicate that the marriage is broken down and it would not be possible for the parties to reconcile.

The third requirement is mutual agreement to dissolve the marriage.

Under sub-section (2) of section 13B there is a requirement of second motion, not earlier than six months after the filing of the petition. The court, after satisfying itself about the genuineness of the averments in the petition, as also that there was no force, pressure or undue influence, shall pass a decree on the joint motion of both the parties.

The issue was whether it was open to one of the parties at any time till the decree of divorce is passed, to withdraw the consent given to the petition. Reference was made to *Jayashree Ramesh Londhe* v. *Ramesh Bhikaji Londhe*, AIR 1984 Bom 302: (1984) 1 Bom CR 586: 1984 Mah LJ 308; *Chander Kanta* v. *Hans Kumar*, AIR 1989 Del 73: I (1988) DMC 509: (1988) 14 DRJ 337; and *Meena Dutta* v. *Anirudh Dutta*, II (1984) DMC 388: (1985) 1 Hindu LR 280, wherein the courts held that the crucial time for consent for divorce under section 13B was when the petition was filed, and to *K.I. Mohanan* v. *Jeejabai*, AIR 1988 Ker 28: 1986 Ker LJ 833: (1986) 2 Hindu LR 467; *Harcharan Kaur* v. *Nachhattar Singh*, AIR 1988 P&H 27: (1987) 2 Hindu LR 184: II (1987) DMC 305; and *Santosh Kumari* v. *Virender Kumar*, AIR 1986 Raj 128: 1986 Raj LW 207: I (1986) DMC 377, where a contrary view was taken. After analysing the cases and the statutory provision, the Supreme Court came to the conclusion that the section does not provide that if there is a change of mind it should not be by one party alone but by both. "If one of the parties at that stage [*i.e.,* at the time of the second motion] says that 'I have withdrawn my consent' or 'I am not a willing party to the divorce', the court cannot pass a decree of divorce by mutual consent. If the court is held to have the power to make a decree solely based on the initial petition, it negates the whole idea of mutuality and consent for divorce. Mutual consent to the divorce is a *sine qua non* for passing a decree for divorce under section 13B", the court remarked.

Order: The wife's appeal was allowed and the decree for dissolution of marriage passed by the High Court was set aside. The court was categoric that consent must continue till the time of the decree and not just the time of filing the petition.

Comment: The judgment has resolved the controversy on the issue of unilateral withdrawal of consent by one of the parties. The whole idea of providing for an *interregnum* is to give time to the parties to think over. If meanwhile, for whatever reasons, one of the parties withdraws consent then a divorce by mutual consent cannot be decreed; besides, the court has elucidated the meaning of separate living. Thus, parties may be living separately even if they are residing in the same place and conversely, they may not be living separate even if they are residing at different places. "Living separately" has no reference to the place of living of the parties.

Consent Decree even after Consent Withdrawn by One of the Parties
Ashok Hurra v. Rupa Bipin Zaveri,
AIR 1997 SC 1266: 1997 AIR SCW 1314: (1997) 4 SCC 226

Issue: Can a divorce decree by consent be passed even after consent has been withdrawn by one of the parties?

Facts: The parties were married in 1970. Fourteen years later, they filed a joint petition for divorce under section 13B of the Hindu Marriage Act, 1955. About eight months after filing the petition, the husband alone moved the court and pressed his application for divorce. Notice was sent to the wife and on application of both the parties, the case was adjourned. There were several adjournments and unsuccessful attempts by the Trial Court for reconciliation. Within one year of the filing of the petition, the husband remarried and also had a child. The wife filed criminal cases for declaring the marriage (second marriage) illegal and the child illegitimate.

After about 19 months [under section 13B(2), the second motion cannot be made earlier than six months and *later than eighteen months* after the presentation of the divorce petition (emphasis added)] of the filing of the petition for divorce, the wife withdrew her consent and sought dismissal of the petition. The husband objected and contended that she had no right to withdraw after eighteen months had elapsed. The Trial Court, however, held that since the wife withdrew her consent, the divorce decree could not be granted. Against the Trial Court order, the husband filed an appeal before a Single Judge of the Gujarat High Court. After going through the entire facts and law, the court came to the conclusion that since the wife had not withdrawn the petition within the period of eighteen months, and also as the marriage had irretrievably broken down, the divorce should be granted. The decree of dissolution of the marriage was made effective from the date of filing of the petition. Under section 13B(2), a decree dissolving the marriage under this section shall be passed *with effect from the date of the decree* (emphasis added). Thus, an order made on March 3, 1996, was given retrospective effect from August 21, 1984, *i.e.*, the date of filing the petition.

Against this order, the wife filed a Letters Patent Appeal before the Division Bench of the Gujarat High Court which was admitted and the Single Judge order was set aside. The grounds for setting aside the order were:

(i) The consent should continue till the decree of divorce is passed; in this case there was no consent as the wife had withdrawn her application.

(ii) Irretrievable breakdown of marriage is no ground for divorce.

(iii) Even if it was a case where a decree could have been granted, the same could not have been granted with retrospective effect from the date of the petition but only from the date of the decree.

(iv) As regards the discretion of the court to exercise its special powers, a court would not like to exercise jurisdiction in a case where the party's conduct is reprehensible. In this case, the husband had remarried during the subsistence of the first marriage at a time when the divorce petition was pending. Besides, he had participated in reconciliation proceedings knowing well that he could not accept the party as his wife.

The court also invoked the clean hands maxim, *i.e.*, the party who comes to court must come with clean hands, which obviously, the husband did not in this case. The Division Bench, accordingly, refused to grant the divorce.

Against this, the husband approached the Supreme Court. A two-judge bench of the court invoked its jurisdiction under article 142 of the Constitution where in exercise of its jurisdiction, the court may pass such decree or make such order as is necessary for doing complete justice. The court conceded that the husband had clearly committed a wrong by entering into a bigamous marriage pending divorce proceedings. It remarked:

> "We have not lost sight of the fact that the conduct of the husband is blameworthy in that he married a second time and got a child during the pendency of the proceedings but that factor cannot be blown out of proportion or viewed in isolation nor can deter this court to take a total and broad view of the realities of the situation when we deal with adjustment of human relationships."

Exercising its jurisdiction under article 142 of the Constitution, the court proceeded to grant a divorce conditional on the husband paying an amount of ₹ 10 lakh plus ₹ 50,000 as litigation expenses to the wife.

The legal issues discussed were:

(i) The marriage had irretrievably broken and there was no point in prolonging the agony of the couple who were fighting like "Kilkenny cats" and litigating in various courts.

(ii) There was a long delay in the disposal of the matter.

(iii) The wife had failed to withdraw the petition within the period of eighteen months; also no case was made out for revocation of consent, like fraud, undue influence, etc.

(iv) That all reconciliation efforts made by the court had failed.

(v) The husband had remarried and also had a child from the second marriage.

Order: The court took notice of the cumulative effect of the various circumstances and facts and came to the conclusion that the marriage was dead "emotionally and practically" with no chance of revival. It felt that this was a case where jurisdiction could be exercised under article 142 of the Constitution and granted divorce by mutual consent in order to meet the ends of justice. The decree was made conditional on the husband paying ₹ 10 lakh plus ₹ 50,000 as litigation expenses to the wife.

Comment: One fails to understand how divorce by "mutual consent" could be granted when one of the parties had withdrawn the consent. Also, the court gave relief to the husband who had committed a wrong and an offence under the Indian Penal Code by marrying during pendency of divorce proceedings. It also amounts to an affront to the dignity of the court and court process that even while proceedings were pending, the husband remarried. A decree cannot be bargained by money power. Also, a marriage cannot be dissolved with retrospective effect.

Unilateral Silence at Time of Second Motion is not Withdrawal of Consent: Divorce Granted

Suman v. Surendra Kumar,
AIR 2003 Raj 155: 2003 Mat LR 428: 2003 (1) CCC 393

Issue: Whether a party who has initially consented to a divorce by mutual consent, could, just by his silence at the time of second motion, frustrate the proceedings so as to deny divorce to the other party?

Facts: The parties had filed a joint consent petition for divorce. After recording the statements of the parties, the next date of hearing was fixed. The husband did not appear. There were several adjournments but the husband remained absent. He neither appeared nor sent any information. The wife made an application for summoning the husband as witness to record his statement but the same was rejected as, according to the court, there was no such provision for recording of evidence of a party who fails to appear. The Family Court held that no divorce decree could be passed in the absence of both the parties. Hence the appeal by the wife.

Order: The Family Court order was set aside in appeal. It was held that if, during the period of *interregnum i.e.,* six months to eighteen months, either party wishes to withdraw, he/she can approach the court and convey the same to the court but this cannot be left as a matter of inference to be drawn by the court. The court observed:

> "When the husband has himself left the matter for inference, the inference ought to be drawn in favour of consent rather than for absence of consent."

The words "on the motion of both the parties", have to be read as meaning that consent of both the parties is available at the stage of the second motion, the court held:

> "Silence cannot be taken to amount to withdrawal of consent.... If he was withdrawing his consent for dissolution of marriage by a decree of divorce by way of mutual consent, nothing prevented him from taking that stand before the Family Court at the stage of second motion. The husband, on the other hand, decided to adopt a course of silence in order to further harass the wife. We are not inclined to take a too technical view of sub-section (2) of section 13B of the Act and fall in the same error as the Family Court did. Merely because the second motion was not signed

by both the parties, it cannot be said that the consent of the husband was missing at the second stage. On account of absence of the husband, rather we would like to take a view that the consent to decree of divorce being granted has to be presumed. What is important is consent of the parties. Format is not important. Substance is to be seen."

Divorce by mutual consent was accordingly decreed in favour of the wife.

Comment: The court has adopted a logical and practical approach. While explicit withdrawal of consent before or at the time of second motion defeats the other party's claim to divorce by consent, the recalcitrant spouse should not be allowed the liberty to frustrate the proceedings by mere silence and non-cooperation.

Mala fide Retraction

Satinder Pal Singh v. Daman Preet, I (2009) DMC 196 (Del)

Issue: Section 13B of the Hindu Marriage Act provides for divorce by mutual consent. However, between the two motions there is on interregnum of six months the idea behind which is to provide the parties time and occasion to rethink whether they really want a divorce. The issue involved in this case was whether *mala fide* retractions after giving an informed and free consent during the first motion, can be allowed.

Facts: A husband filed a petition for divorce under section 13 of the Hindu Marriage Act but during the course of the proceeding the same was converted into a joint petition by mutual consent on certain terms and conditions; the husband agreed to pay an amount of rupees eight lakhs to the wife and the wife would withdraw maintenance proceedings filed by her under section 125 Cr. P.C., she had also lodged some FIRs under sections 498A, 406/34 of the Penal Code against him and *vide* the terms of settlement she agreed to co-operate in having them quashed. After signing the compromise agreement when she was asked to sign the joint divorce petition, she resiled. In fact the husband had also got the drafts for the agreed amount prepared but she was dilly dallying on one pretext or the other; her intention was to extract more and more without any basis by changing her advocates. First she raised the issue of the *stridhana* which was in the custody of the Investigating Officer the husband raised no objection and asked her to take it; she again changed her stand and demanded more *stridhana* without specifying which *stridhana*; then she stated that even if the *stridhana* is returned she is not prepared to abide by the agreement. Obviously she had resiled from her commitment. The court conceded that it cannot force the respondent to sign or make a statement for divorce but looking at the tendency of using courts as a tool to extract money, it decided to give the following directions.

(i) The Metropolitan Magistrate in whose court her application for maintenance under section 125 of the Cr. P.C. is pending will not proceed with it unless she abides by the compromise.
(ii) The court of session where the trial of FIR is pending will not proceed and in terms of the compromise, the wife has to join for quashing the FIRs and until that time, the proceedings will be stayed.
(iii) The Addl. Dist. Judge where the divorce petition is pending shall continue with the suit.
(iv) No interim maintenance will be paid to the respondent wife because of her non-abiding of the compromise.
(v) Proceedings in the case would be conducted on day-to-day basis and the wife's conduct in resiling and trying to extract more and more after changing advocates should be kept in mind.

Order: While there was no decree of divorce by mutual consent, regular proceedings in original divorce suit filed by the husband would continue with above directions.

Comment: This is a very significant judgment and would prevent misuse of law and judicial process. Cases where a party initially gives consent for mutual divorce and later resiles without any justification whatsoever are not unknown. This judgment is bound to send signals of caution to those who seek to hoodwink the judicial process.

Extra-ordinary Powers of Apex Court to Dispense with Consent

Anil Kumar Jain v. *Maya Jain*, AIR 2010 SC 229 (MP): 2009 AIR SCW 5899: (2009) 10 SCC 415

Issue: In a petition for divorce by mutual consent under section 13B of the Hindu Marriage Act is the requirement of subsisting consent till the end an absolute requirement or can it be dispensed with in the circumstances of the case? This was the issue involved in the case.

Facts: This was a petition for divorce by mutual consent filed by the parties. As per the requirement under section 13B the date for consideration of the petition was fixed for after six months. When after this period the matter was taken up the husband reiterated his stand but for the wife it was submitted that despite serious differences between them she did not want the marriage to be dissolved. In view of the wife's withdrawal of the consent the district judge dismissed the petition. Against this the husband went in appeal to the Madhya Pradesh High Court at Jabalpur. The wife was categoric here also that she would neither live with the husband nor agree to a divorce; however the High Court dismissed the appeal since, it had no powers, unlike the Supreme

Court which, in similar circumstances can exercise its extra-ordinary powers under article 142 of the Constitution and under exceptional circumstances grant decree even without the other party's consent at a later Stage. Hence the present appeal before the Supreme Court. The following facts and circumstances of the case are significant:

(i) The petition was filed by mutual consent of both the parties.

(ii) The parties had entered into an agreement whereunder the appellant husband had transferred valuable property rights in favour of the wife and it was only after registration of such property that she withdrew her consent.

(iii) She continues to enjoy the property and is adamant that she would not live with him nor agree to divorce.

(iv) The parties have been living separately for seven years and the marriage is irretrievably broken down.

After analysing the facts and circumstances of the case as also various judgments (*inter alia* – *Ashok Hurra* v. *Rupa Bipin Zaveri,* AIR 1997 SC 1266: 1997 AIR SCW 1314: (1997) 4 SCC 226; *Sureshta Devi* v. *Om Prakash,* AIR 1992 SC 1904: 1991 AIR SCW 373: (1991) 2 SCC 25; *Anita Sabharwal* v. *Anil Sabharwal,* (1997) 11 SCC 490; *Kiran* v. *Sharad Dutt,* (2000) 10 SCC 243; *Swati Verma* v. *Rajan Verma,* (2004) 1 SCC 123: 2003 AIR SCW 5841: AIR 2004 SC 161; *Sanghmitra Ghosh* v. *Kajal Kumar Ghosh,* (2007) 2 SCC 220: 2006 AIR SCW 5983) the court invoked its extra-ordinary powers under article 142 of the Constitution held that it would be a travesty of justice to continue with the marriage. It emphasised that while under the existing laws the consent given initially has to subsist till the second stage when the petition comes up for orders and a decree is finally passed, only in special circumstances can the Supreme Court exercise its jurisdiction under article 142 of the Constitution to waive the statutory requirements to do complete justice in a given case. In this case, the court found admitted facts which made it a fit case for exercising its special powers; the parties had been living separately for over seven years, the husband had transferred some properties to her which she was still enjoying pursuant to settlement at the time of filing of the petition, the wife retracting her consent and not agreeing to either live with the husband nor give consent for the divorce.

Order: Allowing the husband's appeal, the judgment of the High Court was set aside and the marriage dissolved by a decree of divorce under section 13B of the Hindu Marriage Act. The court, however, made it explicit that as a general rule, the law as it stands is that consent of both the parties is required and such consent should subsist till the divorce; and further that it is only the Supreme Court, and neither the civil courts nor even the High Courts, which is competent to waive this requirement.

Comment: Retractions after initial consent for a divorce by consent are not unknown. While the idea behind the six-month *interregnum* is to give an opportunity to the parties to rethink yet, if pursuant to a settlement before filing a petition benefits are taken under that settlement and thereafter the party withdraws consent, then the court, the Supreme Court alone, will take a holistic view of the facts and circumstances of the case and waive this requirement to meet the ends of justice. Parties cannot be allowed to make a mockery of the legal provisons and the judicial process.

Withdrawal of Consent: Apex Court Refuses Decree
Hitesh Bhatnagar v. Deepa Bhatnagar, AIR 2011 SC 1637

Issue: Can a decree of divorce by mutual consent under section 13B of the Hindu Marriage Act be passed notwithstanding withdrawal of consent by one of the parties? This was the issue involved in the present case.

Facts: The parties were married in 1994 and had a daughter. Due to some temperamental differences they started living separately since the year 2000 and in 2001 they filed a petition for divorce by consent under section 13B of the Hindu Marriage Act. However, before the second motion, the wife withdrew her consent and the petition was dismissed by the district court on this ground. The husband's appeal against such dismissal before the Punjab and Haryana High Court was also dismissed in 2006, hence the present appeal before he Supreme Court.

Order: The court referred to several cases, inter alia, *Sureshta Devi* v. *Om Prakash*, AIR 1992 SC 1904: 1991 AIR SCW 373: (1991) 2 SCC 25; *Smruti Pahariya* v. *Sanjay Pahariya*, (2009) 13 SCC 338: AIR 2009 SC 2840: 2009 AIR SCW 4267 and came to the conclusion that consent of both the parties until the final decree is mandatory. The court observed (at p. 1643):

> "In the present fact scenario, the second motion was never made by both the parties as is a mandatory requirement of the law, ... the non-withdrawal of consent before the expiry of the said eighteen months has no bearing....[this period] was specified only to ensure quick disposal of divorce by mutual consent, and not to specify the time period for withdrawal of consent, as canvassed by the appellant."

The husband then sought to invoke the fact that the marriage having irretrievably broken, should be dissolved notwithstanding withdrawal of consent by the wife; for this, he sought support from *Anil Kumar Jain* v. *Maya Jain*, AIR 2010 SC 229 (MP): 2009 AIR SCW 5899: (2009) 10 SCC 415 wherein though consent for mutual divorce was withdrawn yet a decree of divorce was granted under article 142 of the Constitution on the ground that the marriage had irretrievably broken down. The court, however, refused to accept this plea in the instant case and held that powers under article 142 of the Constitution can be exercised only in exceptional cases. It referred to its judgments in *Manish Goel* v. *Rohini Goel*, (2010) 4 SCC 393: AIR 2010 SC 1099: 2010 AIR SCW 1277; *V. Bhagat* v. *D. Bhagat*, AIR 1994 SC 710: 1994 AIR SCW 45: (1994) 1 SCC 337; *Savitri Pandey* v. *Prem Chandra Pandey*, AIR 2002 SC 591: 2002 AIR SCW 182: (2002) 2 SCC 73 in support of its view that irretrievable breakdown alone cannot be the sole ground for dissolving the marriage.

Order: The husband's appeal was dismissed as the court thought that it would be a travesty of justice to dissolve this marriage as having broken down. "Though there is bitterness amongst the parties and they have not even lived as husband and wife for the past 11 years, we hope that they will give this union another chance, if not for themselves, for the future of their daughter."

Comment: While it is true that once consent by one of the parties is withdrawn within permissible parameters a decree by consent under section 13B may not be in order, however, where a marriage has been practically broken and is subsisting only in law and nothing more, then expediency demands that the same be legally buried. The recent amendment in the marriage laws seeks to achieve that purpose.

Withdrawal of Consent without Substantial Ground: Divorce Granted

Prakash Alumal Kalandari v. *Jahanvi,*
AIR 2011 Bom 119

Issue: Whether consent to a petition for divorce by mutual consent under section 13B of the Hindu Marriage Act could be unilaterally withdrawn by one of the parties without any substantial or logical basis, was the issue involved in the case.

Facts: This was a wifes petition for divorce on the ground of cruelty which was contested by the husband who also sought custody of children. Pending these proceedings the parties sought to convert the same and seek divorce by mutual consent; consent terms were executed and signed before the Family Court on 6-10-2008, which included issues of custody, visitation, maintenance, etc. However, on 13-2-2009, the appellant husband withdrew his consent and the reason he gave for such withdrawal was that the wife had failed to comply with terms of visitation and did not provide access to children. The Family Court dismissed his plea and held that the husband could not withdraw his consent in the fact situation of the present case. The wife's contention was that the children were not keen to meet the father; that she never denied access and infact the husband was in jail and so could not meet the children; she further contended that the husband was not paying the maintenance agreed upon and was in arrears; further, that pursuant to the terms and conditions, she facilitated disposal of criminal cases under section 498A of the Indian Penal Code, filed against him. In view of the above, the husband was refused withdrawal of consent. Hence his appeal before the High Court.

Order: Dismissing the appeal, the High Court held that there was no strong reason given by the husband to withdraw his consent. "If the husband is allowed to withdraw, it would be nothing short of husband resorting to fraud and misrepresentation which cannot be permitted by courts of law and equity....a party cannot be allowed to withdraw unless it is able to substantiate just cause to court's satisfaction" the court observed. In this case, the sole ground given by the husband for withdrawing was not substantiated; the husband was in jail and so was unable to meet the children and not that the wife was obstructing access and denying him visitation.

Comment: The idea behind the provision of divorce by mutual consent is to provide an expedient and amicable way out of an unworkable marriage. There is a cooling off period before the final decree is passed and a party can withdraw consent within this time. However, at times, a party who has initially given consent voluntarily and without any force or pressure, at a later stage seeks to withdraw the consent without any cogent reason, simply to harass the other party. The courts are therefore cautions in allowing such withdrawal and would not grant such permission unless there are cogent and convincing reasons for the same.

Waiver of Six Months Waiting Period when Divorce Petition Already Pending

Dineshkumar Shukla v. *Neeta,* AIR 2005 MP 106: 2005 (2) Civ LJ 709: 2005 (2) CCC 161

Issue: Is the waiting period of six months under clause (2) of section 13B of the Hindu Marriage Act mandatory even when the divorce petition is pending and ultimately, after efforts for reconciliation fail, the parties decide to obtain a divorce by mutual consent?

Facts: The parties were married in 1987 and had a child. The relations between them soured and the husband filed a petition for divorce under section 13(1)(ia) and (ib) of the Hindu Marriage Act on the ground of cruelty and desertion in 1996. All efforts at reconciliation failed. During the pendency of the petition, both husband and wife made a joint petition under section 13B of the Hindu Marriage Act for dissolution of marriage by mutual consent. The Trial Court refused to pass the divorce decree immediately on the ground that the waiting period of six months was mandatory.

Order: The matter first came to a Single Judge but in view of "diametrical opposite views taken by co-ordinate benches" in several cases, the Chief Justice constituted a division bench to hear the matter. During the pendency of the revision, the period of six months was over and the Trial Court passed the divorce decree; in fact both the parties remarried and were living with their respective spouses. However, in view of the conflicting views taken by different single Bench of the court, the division bench proceeded with the matter in order to resolve the conflict "to iron out the creases". After hearing the submission of the parties and going through the case law, it was held that the provisions of sub-section (2) of section 13B of the Hindu Marriage Act are directory in nature and the waiting period can be brought down from six months when a divorce on mutual consent is sought in a divorce petition already pending and all efforts at reconciliation have failed, provided the mandatory requirements of section 13B(1) are fulfilled.

Comment: If the parties are already litigating and there is no iota of their reconciling, no purpose would be served by waiting for six months after their joint petition for divorce. The purpose of the waiting period is to give them chance to reconsider their decision but when the case is past that stage, it is futile to wait.

Note: See however *Gurpinder Kaur Sahsi* v. *Ravinder Singh Sahsi*, AIR 2005 P&H 187: 2005 (2) Hindu LR 118: 2005 (3) CCC 66 where a decree was passed just 24 days after filing of the petition for divorce by consent, the court on appeal set it aside. The petition was filed on October 1, 2002; it was adjourned to April 5, 2003 for recording of statements of parties but meanwhile parties sought waiver of the waiting period and the Trial Court passed the decree on October 24, 2002. The High Court set it aside holding that, this on the very face of it, was contrary to statutory provisions.

Waiver of Waiting Period Sought: Not Granted

Poonam v. *Sumit Tanwar*, AIR 2010 SC 1384: 2010 AIR SCW 2084: (2010) 4 SCC 460

Issue: The issue of waiver of six months' waiting period for divorce by mutual consent was involved in this case.

Facts: The parties in this case were married on 30-11-2008 and separated just two days after the marriage. They filed a petition for divorce by mutual consent under section 13B(1) of the Act on 9-9-2009 and the same was disposed of by the Family Court on 25-11-2009 asking them to wait for six months as per the statutory requirement. Aggrieved by this they filed a writ petition under article 32 of the Constitution for issuance of direction to waive the statutory waiting period of six months. The court analysed and referred to a few cases to explain when and under what circumstances these special powers can be invoked. Referring to *Manish Goel* v. *Rohini Goel*, (2010) 4 SCC 393: AIR 2010 SC 1099: 2010 AIR SCW 1277 it observed that this Court, in exercise of its power under article 142 of the Constitution, generally should not issue any direction to waive the statutory requirements. Courts are meant to enforce the law and therefore, are not expected to issue a direction in contravention of law or to direct the statutory authority to act in contravention of law.

Order: The petition for waiver of the waiting period was dismissed. The Court clarified that appropriate relief under article 32 can be given only if it is shown to Court and the court is satisfied that a Fundamental Right has been violated. In this case, the court held (at p. 1389):

> "The petition has been filed without any sense of responsibility either by the parties or their counsel. Such a practice is tantamount to not only disservice to the institution but it also adversely affects the administration of justice. Conduct of all of them has been reprehensible."

Comment: While courts would generally not waive the waiting period but the Marriage Laws (Amendment) Bill, 2010 seeks to do away with this waiting period of six months.

Waiver of Statutory Period of One Year Sought: Refused as High Court has no such Power

Urvashi Sibal v. *Government of NCT of Delhi,* AIR 2010 Del 157

Issue: Can proviso to section 14 of the Hindu Marriage Act, 1955, be invoked to seek waiver of statutory period of one year for divorce by mutual consent under section 13B of the Act?

Facts: Differences between the parties arose within one month of the marriage and they started living separately. The marriage having broken down they wanted to have a divorce by mutual consent. However, since a year had not elapsed from the date of separation, they filed an application under section 14 of the Act for waiver of the one year statutory period for filing a divorce by mutual consent under section 13B of the Act. The Trial Court dismissed the application in view of the Supreme Court clear ruling in *Anil Kumar Jain* v. *Maya Jain,* AIR 2010 SC 229: 2009 AIR SCW 5899: (2009) 10 SCC 415 where it was held that it was the Supreme Court alone, which in exercise of its extraordinary powers under article 142 of the Constitution, could waive the statutory period and pass a decree of divorce by mutual consent under section 13B(2) of the Act. Nether the Civil Court nor even the High Court can pass an order before the expiry of period prescribed under the provisions of the section, the Supreme Court clarified. Thus, it did not confine itself to the question of waiver of six months period between the two motions but to waiver of any statutory period under any of the provisions of the Act. Hence the appeal. The counsel for the petitioners argued that the marriage had irretrievably broken down and the court is within its right to invoke proviso to section 14 of the Act and permit parties to file a petition for divorce under section 13B before the expiry of one year; the argument, however, found no favour with the court. The court referred to, *inter alia,* its own judgment in *Nand Kishore* v. *Suman,* (Mat. Appeal No. 134/2009 dt. 15-12-2009) where it distinguished the provisions contained in section 13B(1) and section 14 of the Act for waiving the statutory period of one year before filing a petition under section 13 or 13B of the Act and observed:

> "....requirement under section 13B(1) of the Act is separation for a period of one year or more beside others to file a petition whereas under section 14 of the Act court has the power to condone the statutory period of one year, required for filing a petition under section 13 of the act or any provision contained in the said Act from the date of marriage. Therefore, under no circumstances, section 14 of the Act can be invoked in the proceedings initiated under section 13B of the Act.

Order: Dismissing the present appeal (*Urvashi Sibal*) the court held (at p. 159):

> "...the statutory period of one year required to be maintained by the parties for filing a petition under section 13B of the Act are independent of the provisions contained in section 14 of the Act. Section 13B when read is a complete code in itself and, therefore, for filing a petition under section 13B of the Act parties cannot be allowed to invoke section 14 seeking waiver of the statutory period of one year from separation for filing a petition under section 13B of the Act."

Comment: Statutory waiting periods have been prescribed for filing petitions for divorce on available grounds under section 13 and for divorce by mutual consent under section 13B of the Act. The idea is to prevent recourse to hasty divorce petitions. However, there may be exceptionally hard cases where flexibility may be required to meet the ends of justice. In such situations, *vide* the Supreme Court order in *Anil Kumar Jain* (2010 supra) it is the Supreme Court alone which, in exercise of its extra-ordinary jurisdiction under article 142 of the Constitution can permit waiver or relaxation of the period. It may however be pointed out that by the time the parties approach the Apex Court for such waiver, it would have been long past the prescribed statutory period.

No Waiver of Statutory Period in Circumstances of the Case

Manish Goel v. Rohini Goel,
(2010) 4 SCC 393: AIR 2010 SC 1099: 2010 AIR SCW 1277

Issue: The issue involved in the case was as to the exercise of special powers by the Apex Court under article 136 and article 142 of the Constitution and the circumstances in which they could be exercised.

Facts: The case is an example of the proverbial "hurry makes curry" situation where the parties, highly qualified, fell out soon after marriage. The husband filed a petition for annulment of the marriage under section 12 of the Hindu Marriage Act at Gurgaon and the wife filed petitions under the Protection of Women Against Domestic Violence Act, 2005 at Delhi, she also filed FIR's against the husband and his family members under sections 498A, 406 and 34 of the Indian Penal Code. However, on the intervention of family members and friends, they entered into compromise and prepared a Memorandum of Understanding in the proceedings pending before the Mediation Centre in Delhi whereby they agreed to settle all their disputes and have the marriage dissolved by mutual consent. A petition was consequently filed in the Family Court at Delhi and their statement was recorded on 16-11-2009. They then moved another application for waiver of the six months period for filing the second motion, which was turned down *vide* an order dated 1-12-2009. The Family Court observed that it was not competent to allow such waiver, as *vide* directions of the Apex Court in *Anil Kumar Jain v. Maya Jain,* (2009) 10 SCC 415, only the Supreme Court was competent to give directions for such waiver. Thereupon, a special leave petition was filed by the petitioner/appellant in the Supreme Court where it was argued that there is no prohibition in law in entertaining the petition under article 136 of the constitution against the order of the Family Court and as such there was no occasion for the petitioner to approach the High Court as the relief sought by him could not be granted by any court other than the Supreme Court. Hence, according to the petitioner, he has a right to approach the Apex Court against the order of the Family Court and cannot be non-suited. The court expressed its unhappiness in the manner in which the matter was handled and argued. Its sarcasm is evident in the following observations (at p. 1100):

"....the parties merely being highly qualified, have claimed even to be higher and above the law, and have [claimed] a vested right to use, misuse and abuse the process of the court."

During pendency of petition for dissolution of marriage before a competent court at Gurgaon, they filed a petition for divorce by mutual consent before the Family Court in Delhi. "Such procedure adopted by the petitioner amounts to abuse of process of the court", the court remarked.

As to the jurisdiction of the Supreme Court under article 136 of the Constitution the court agreed that a plenary jurisdiction exercisable on assuming appellate jurisdiction has been conferred in the widest possible terms under this article, it however, went to clarify that "it is an extra-ordinary jurisdiction vested by the Constitution in the court and therefore extra-ordinary care and caution has to be observed while exercising this jurisdiction. There is no vested right of a party to approach this Court for the exercise of such a vast discretion; however such a course can be resorted to when this Court feels that it is so warranted to eradicate injustice." (p. 1101)

The court thus clarified that such powers can be exercised to see that injustice is not perpetrated or perpetuated or there should be a question of law of general public importance or a decision which shocks the conscience of the court. In other words, "unless it is shown that exceptional and special circumstances exist that substantial and grave injustice has been done and that the case in question presents features of sufficient gravity warranting review of the decision appealed against, such exercise should not be done" (at 1101). Such power cannot be used to "short circuit the legal procedure prescribed in overriding power" the court remarked.

Exercise of special powers under article 142 of the Constitution was sought as, according to the appellant, the case presents special features warranting such exercise. The court conceded that it had been exercising such power for dissolving a marriage which is "totally unworkable, emotionally dead, beyond salvage and has broken down irretrievably, even if the facts of the case do not provide a ground in law on which the divorce could be granted. Divorce decree has been granted to put quietus to all litigations between the parties and to save them from further agony." The court referred to various of its own judgments on the issue. (*inter alia, Ramesh Chander* v. *Savitri,* AIR 1995 SC 851: 1995 AIR SCW 647: (1995) 2 SCC 7; *Kanchan Devi* v. *Promod Kumar Mittal,* AIR 1996 SC 3192:

1996 AIR SCW 1933: (1996) 8 SCC 90; *Anita Sabharwal* v. *Anil Sabharwal*, (1997) 11 SCC 490; *Ashok Hurra* v. *Rupa Bipin Zaveri*, AIR 1997 SC 1266: 1997 AIR SCW 1314: (1997) 4 SCC 226; *Kiran* v. *Sharad Dutt*, (2000) 10 SCC 243; *Swati Verma* v. *Rajan Verma*, (2004) 1 SCC 123: 2003 AIR SCW 5841: AIR 2004 SC 161; *Durga Prasanna Tripathy* v. *Arundhati Tripathy*, AIR 2005 SC 3297: 2005 AIR SCW 4045: (2005) 7 SCC 353; *Naveen Kohli* v. *Neelu Kohli*, AIR 2006 SC 1675: 2006 AIR SCW 1550: (2006) 4 SCC 558; *Samar Ghosh* v. *Jaya Ghosh*, (2007) 4 SCC 511; *Satish Sitole* v. *Ganga*, AIR 2008 SC 3093: 2008 AIR SCW 5190: (2008) 7 SCC 734.)

The court, however, also referred to some of its judgments where a contrary view was taken e.g., *Chetan Dass* v. *Kamla Devi*, AIR 2001 SC 1709: 2001 AIR SCW 1660: (2001) 4 SCC 250; *Visnu Dutt Sharma* v. *Manju Sharma*, AIR 2009 SC 2254: 2009 AIR SCW 2984: (2009) 6 SCC 379. In these cases the court had held that where the legal ground for grant of divorce is missing, exercising such power tantamounts to legislation and thus transgression of the powers of the Legislature, which is not permissible in law.

The court stated that generally, no court has competence to issue a direction contrary to law nor can it direct an authority to act in contravention of statutory provisions. "Courts are meant to enforce the rule of law and not pass orders or directions which are contrary to what has been injected by law." (at 1103) it clarified. In sum, the court held that in exercise of the powers under article 142, this Court generally does not passion order in contravention of, or ignoring statutory provisions nor is the power exercised merely on sympathy.

Order: In this case the petitioner abused the process of the court by approaching different forums for the same relief; further, according to the Court, the statutory period of six months for the second motion under section 13B(2) of the Act has been provided to give an opportunity to the parties to rethink; and more significantly, in this case there has been no obstruction to the stream of justice nor any injustice caused which required to be eradicated, nor even any question of general public importance involved. Since none of these contingencies existed in this case, the court refused to entertain the petition and the same was accordingly dismissed.

Comment: Section 13B was inserted in the Hindu Marriage Act in 1976 with a view to liberalise the divorce law and mitigate hardship of couples impelled to continue in the relationship even though they wished to be out of it. In order to prevent any hasty and impulsive step in this direction, the Legislature has provided for a six-month period between the two motions. During this period the parties can think over and if they wish, they may withdraw the petition; and if they are decided to part ways, they can go ahead after six months. There may however be hard or exceptional cases warranting waiver of any waiting period. To meet such hard contingencies the Supreme Court may exercise its special power under article 136 or article 142 of the Constitution. However, as observed by the court, this is an extraordinary jurisdiction and has to be exercised exceptionally and only in extraordinary situations. In any case nobody has a vested right to invoke such jurisdiction.

Annulment Decree in Appeal Converting to Consent Divorce
Radha v. Mohinder Kumar,
(1998) 8 SCC 530

Issue: Can the parties make a joint request for converting a decree of annulment which is in appeal – into a decree of divorce by mutual consent?

Facts: It is very short order, where a husband had obtained an annulment of the marriage. The wife filed an appeal before the Supreme Court. During the course of appeal the parties entered into a compromise and requested the court that the marriage between them may be kept dissolved but not on annulment and instead by "mutual consent" effective from the date of the High Court order (which was 29-7-1984).

Order: The court acceded to this "reasonable" request and substituted the order of the High Court as if from the date of its judgment, the marriage between the parties stood dissolved by a decree of divorce by mutual consent.

Comment: An annulled marriage wipes out all the incidents and rights in marriage and vitally affects the status of the spouses and the children. Though the short order in the case mentions no details whatsoever, the court, in converting the annulment decree into a decree of divorce by mutual consent must have taken note of this factor.

Exemption from Personal Appearance on Medical Grounds
Roopa v. Santosh Kumar,
AIR 2005 All 172: 2005 (25) All Ind Cas 672: 2005 (2) CCC 798

Issue: Can the Family Court reject an application seeking exemption from appearance on ground of illness in proceedings for divorce by mutual consent under section 13B of the Hindu Marriage Act?

Facts: The parties filed a joint petition for divorce by mutual consent under section 13B of the Hindu Marriage Act. Prior to that, there were other petitions, application and complaints filed by the parties against each other. Later they decided to ultimately settle the matter by mutual consent. September 27, 2004 was fixed for passing order. However, on that date, the wife could not appear and she filed an application seeking exemption from appearance disclosing her illness as the ground for her absence. This application, however, was rejected by the Family Court on the ground that there was no provision for moving an application for exemption of appearance. The joint petition for divorce was, accordingly, rejected. Hence the appeal by the wife.

Order: The appeal was allowed. The court held that the Family Court ought to have considered the application on merit. "Family Court Act does not allow advocates to appear before Family Court. Technicalities cannot be allowed to prevail upon substantial interest of justice. Procedures are made to achieve ultimate object to dispense justice", the court remarked (at p. 174). Also, there was nothing to indicate that the husband was not agreeable to the consent or that he wished to resile from what he had stated in the petition signed jointly by him and his wife. There was, therefore, no reason to reject the consent petition. The wife's appeal was accordingly allowed; the Family Court decree was set aside and the original petition for divorce was restored and remanded to the Family Court for being decided on merits.

Comment: While it is true that technicalities should be avoided in proceedings before the Family Court and that is one of the reasons why lawyers are, as a matter of rule, not allowed, but that should not be done at the cost of justice. The Family Court has, under section 10 of the Family Courts Act, 1984, all the powers of a Civil Court, and that includes the power to accept an application for exemption from appearance or adjournment as well.

NON-RESUMPTION OF COHABITATION AFTER A DECREE OF JUDICIAL SEPARATION OR RESTITUTION

Non-resumption of cohabitation after a decree of judicial separation or non-compliance of a decree for restitution of conjugal rights is a ground for divorce under several personal law matrimonial statutes *viz*. The Hindu Marriage Act, 1955 (section 13(1A)(i) & (ii)); Special Marriage Act, 1954 (section 27(2)(i) & (ii)); Parsi Marriage and Divorce Act, 1936 (section 32A); Under the Divorce Act, 1869 as amended in 2001 (10(i)(viii)) however, only non-compliance of restitution decree for two years or above is a ground for dissolution of the marriage.

The idea behind incorporating the above grounds for divorce is to end stalemate in marriages; when parties have been judicially separated for a year or above and there has been no resumption of cohabitation or where, despite a restitution decree the parties have not come together, of is a strong indication that the marriage is dead for all practical purposes. This affords a ground to the parties – both the decree holder and the judgment debtor – to seek dissolution of the marriage. The Divorce Act which applies to Christians is different under section 10(1)(viii) of this Act if the respondent *i.e.*, the person against whom a decree of restitution of conjugal rights is passed fails to comply with the decree for two years or above then the ground for divorce becomes available to the petitioner in whose favour the decree of restitution is passed further, there is no provision affording a ground for divorce on non-resumption of cohabitation after a decree of judicial separation.

The ground of non-resumption of cohabitation after decree of separation on restitution has given rise to certain issues for judicial consideration. Significant selected cases in this context have been discussed and analysed in this section.

Separation Decree – Mere Absence of Efforts to Resume Cohabitation is no Wrong so as to Disentitle Relief

Madhukar Bhaskar Sheorey v. *Saral Madhukar Sheorey*, **AIR 1973 Bom 55: 1972 Mah LJ 762: ILR (1973) Bom 113**

Issue: After a decree of judicial separation obtained by a wife, the husband makes no efforts to resume cohabitation. Does he commit a "wrong" within the meaning of section 23 of the Hindu Marriage Act?

Facts: The wife obtained a decree of judicial separation on the grounds of cruelty and desertion in 1965. In 1968, the husband filed a petition seeking divorce under section 13(1A) of the Hindu Marriage Act on the ground that there was no resumption of cohabitation between the spouses for over two years (this period of two years has been reduced to one year by amendment in 1976) from the date of the decree of judicial separation. The husband's petition was dismissed by the lower court on the ground that section 13(1A) is controlled by section 23 of the Act under which a petitioner to a relief cannot take advantage of his or her own wrong or disability. Further, according to the court, since the wife had obtained the decree of judicial separation on grounds of cruelty and desertion, the husband "should have assured the respondent that he would treat her well". Also there was no evidence that he had asked her to come back and stay with him and the wife refused the offer. This, according to the court, amounted to taking advantage of his own wrong and so he was held not to be entitled to relief under section 13(1A) of the Act. Hence the husband's appeal.

Order: The court reviewed the earlier cases on the point and tracing the history of the amendment as also the relationship between section 13(1A) and section 23 concluded (at p. 58):

> "Section 13(1A) refers to the existing state of affairs and has no reference to a wrong committed by a party to the marriage or by whom the wrong is committed. This provision is totally different from the provisions of section 13(1)(viii) and (ix) which gave the right to apply for divorce only to the wronged party and not to the wrongdoer. It is undoubtedly true that any relief granted by the court will have to take into consideration the conduct of the party applying for divorce by virtue of section 23(1). But such conduct must, in any case after the amendment of section 13 in 1964, necessarily be the conduct subsequent to the passing of the decree of judicial separation or restitution of conjugal rights and not prior conduct. There is no obligation to remedy the wrong which led to the decree for restitution of conjugal rights or judicial separation."

Comment: Where a husband takes no initiative or steps to resume cohabitation with a wife who has obtained a decree of separation against him, no wrong is committed by the husband so as to disentitle him to relief under section 13(1A).

Decree of Restitution – Mere Non-compliance or Non-inclination to Join not a Wrong so as to Deny Divorce

Dharmendra Kumar v. *Usha Kumar*,
AIR 1977 SC 2218: 1977 (2) SCJ 471: (1978) 1 SCR 315

Issue: Is a wife, who has obtained a decree for restitution of conjugal rights, who does not respond to her husband's invitation to come and stay with him, disentitled to decree of divorce under section 13(1A), Hindu Marriage Act in view of section 23 of the Act?

Facts: A wife obtained a decree for restitution of conjugal rights under section 9 of the Act on August 27, 1973. A little over two years after the decree, on October 28, 1975, she presented a petition under section 13(1A)(ii) for dissolution of the marriage on the ground that there has been no restitution of conjugal rights as between the parties to the marriage for a period of two years (this period has been reduced to one year after the amendment in 1976) or upwards after the passing of the decree. The husband admitted that there was no restitution of conjugal rights between them after the restitution decree but stated that he had made attempts to comply with the decree "by writing several letters to the petitioner" and "otherwise", inviting her to live with him, but the petitioner, "refused to receive some of the letters and never replied to those which she received". Thus, according to the husband, the petitioner "has herself prevented the restitution of conjugal rights she prayed for and now seeks to make a capital out of her own wrong". It was contended on his behalf that in view of the provision in section 23(1)(a) she cannot be allowed to take advantage of her own wrong and disability for the purpose of obtaining the relief. The Additional District Judge, who relied on several cases [*e.g.*, *Ram Kali* v. *Gopal Das*, ILR (1971) 1 Del 6: 1971 Raj LR 10; *Gajna Devi* v. *Purshotam Giri*, ILR (1977) 1 Del 725: AIR 1977 Del 178: 1978 Hindu LR 116] held that no such circumstance has been alleged from which it could be said that the petitioner wife was trying to take advantage of her own wrong. The husband's appeal against this to the Delhi High Court, was summarily dismissed. Hence the appeal. It was held that mere non-compliance with the restitution decree does not constitute wrong within the meaning of section 23(1)(a). Had the Parliament intended that a party which is guilty of a matrimonial offence and against whom a decree for judicial separation or restitution has been passed, would, in view of section 23 of the Act, not be entitled to obtain divorce, then it Could have inserted an exception to section 13(1A) and with such exception, the provision of section 13(1A) would practically become redundant as the guilty party could never reap benefit of obtaining divorce, while the innocent party was entitled to obtain it even under the statute as it was before the amendment.

Section 23 of the Act therefore, cannot be construed so as to make the effect of amendment of the law by insertion of section 13(1A) nugatory. Also, according to the court, the expression "taking advantage of his or her own wrong" occurring in clause (a) of section 23(1) of the Act does not apply to taking advantage of the statutory right to obtain dissolution of marriage which has been conferred on him/her, by section 13(1A). "In such a case, a party is not taking advantage of his own wrong, but of the legal right following upon the passing of the decree and the failure of the parties to comply with the decree," the court said.

Order: The husband's appeal against the High Court order granting decree of divorce to the wife on the ground of non-compliance of restitution decree, was dismissed. "In order to be a wrong within the meaning of section 23(1)(a) the conduct alleged has to be something more than a mere disinclination to agree to an offer of union; it must be misconduct serious enough to justify denial of the relief of which the husband or the wife is otherwise entitled." In this case, the allegations made by the husband, even if true, do not constitute wrong or amount to misconduct grave enough to disentitle the wife of the decree of divorce, the court held.

Comment: Judgments such as this, are only back door entry to the concept of irretrievable breakdown of the marriage. The wife in all likelihood, had no intention to honour the restitution decree which she had obtained against the husband. And while even the husband may not have been sincere in his offers to call back the wife, it provided an easy spring-board to get out of the marriage and get a divorce on a statutorily recognised ground.

Long Separation – No Divorce but Judicial Separation Granted

Angrez Kaur v. *Baldev Singh*,
AIR 1980 P&H 171: 1979 Hindu LR 561: 1980 Marri LJ 54

Issue: Would a long period of separation ripen into a right to seek divorce?

Facts: The husband filed a suit for restitution of conjugal rights under section 9 of the Hindu Marriage Act on the ground that the wife had left him without any reasonable cause. He, however, lost the case as the court found that the wife had a reasonable ground to live separately. After 29 years of marriage and 15 years of virtual separation the husband petitioned for divorce on the ground that they were living separate since long and both the parties stated that they could not live together. The District Court granted the decree but on appeal, the High Court found that it was the husband who was at fault and so could not be given a divorce.

Order: The court held that the husband could not prove any ground on which divorce could be given. However, in view of the long separation and no prospects of immediate reconciliation, the High Court granted judicial separation under section 13A, *i.e.*, alternative relief.

Comment: The case is a reflection of the sorry state of affairs where parties neither live together nor get legally free to restart their lives. The petition in the appeal stage could have been converted to a petition for divorce by mutual consent in view of the fact that both the parties admitted that they were living separately for long and there are no prospects of rapproachement.

Restitution Decree – Non-Compliance of – Spouse Thwarting Attempts to Comply – Cannot take Advantage

Sunita Rajendra Nikalje v. Rajendra Eknath Nikalje, AIR 1996 Bom 85: 1996 (1) All MR 446: 1996 (2) Bom CJ 47

Issue: Can a husband who thwarts wife's attempts to comply with a restitution decree take advantage of his wrong and seek divorce on the ground of non-compliance of restitution decree?

Facts: A husband filed a petition for restitution of conjugal rights under section 9 of the Hindu Marriage Act after his wife made an application for maintenance under section 125 of the Cr. P.C. The petition was granted. However, all attempts by the wife to join him were thwarted by him and his mother and so the decree of restitution remained uncomplied. The husband then filed a petition for divorce under section 13(1A)(ii) on the ground that there was no cohabitation for over a year since the passing of the restitution decree. The wife resisted the petition on the ground that he could not be allowed to take advantage of his wrong. The Trial Court found that no wrong was committed and so the decree was passed. Hence the wife appealed.

Order: It was held that there was enough evidence to prove that the wife had made attempts to go back but she was not allowed by the husband and his mother to join the husband. In fact, the wife also filed a complaint to the police. The court held that the husband, on whom lies the burden of proving that he was not taking advantage of his wrong, failed to discharge the burden. Divorce was consequently denied.

Comment: While mere disinclination of a party to effect reunion after a decree of restitution may not be a wrong within the meaning of section 23 of the Hindu Marriage Act [*Dharmendra Kumar* v. *Usha Kumar*, AIR 1977 SC 2218: 1977 (2) SCJ 471: (1978) 1 SCR 315], thwarting attempts by a party to comply with the decree is a wrong so as to disentitle the petitioner to a decree under section 13(1A).

No Vested Right to Divorce on this Ground

Hirachand Srinivas Managaonkar v. Sunanda, AIR 2001 SC 1285: 2001 AIR SCW 1196: (2001) 4 SCC 125

Issue: Does a petitioner have a vested right to get relief under section 13(1A), Hindu Marriage Act by merely showing that the ground for such relief exists?

Facts: The wife had obtained judicial separation on the ground of husband's adultery. The court also ordered the husband to pay maintenance to the wife and minor daughters. The husband did not comply with this order; he also continued to live in adultery. He filed a petition for divorce under section 13(1A)(i) on the ground that there has been no cohabitation after the separation decree. This was dismissed as, according to the court, he could not be allowed to take advantage of his own wrong. The court remarked that even after a decree of judicial separation, it is the duty of the parties to do their part for cohabitation. The husband was expected to act as a dutiful husband towards the wife and the wife was expected to act as a devoted wife towards the husband. The husband, in refusing to pay maintenance to the wife, failed to act as a dutiful husband and thereby committed a wrong within the meaning of section 23(1)(a) of the Act. Further, living in adultery is a continuing matrimonial offence. The offence does not get frozen or wiped out merely on passing of a decree for judicial separation which merely suspends certain duties and obligations of the spouses without legally breaking the matrimonial tie. The husband's living in adultery without any remorse was held to be yet another "wrong" which he deliberately committed to thwart any attempt to reunite so as to justify rejection of his divorce application.

Order: The husband's petition for divorce on the ground of non-cohabitation after a decree of judicial separation (obtained by the wife in this case) was rejected on the ground that the husband could not be allowed to take advantage of his wrong *viz.*, not paying maintenance which was ordered; and continuing to live in adultery. "Once cause of action for getting decree of divorce under section 13(1A) arises, it does not crystallise into a right which the court is bound to concede", the court remarked (at p. 1290).

Comment: A wrong which is the basis on which an earlier decree is passed—judicial separation in this case—should not logically come in the way of relief subsequently sought under section 13(1A). Also to expect, as was done in this case, that even after a court battle which ended in a decree of judicial separation, the husband should act as a dutiful husband and the wife as a dutiful wife, appears to be too unrealistic. As for the 'wrong' of non-payment of maintenance, the court should take it up independently and ensure that the order is complied with; in any case her right to the maintenance does not get frozen on the court's dismissing the husband's petition under section 13(1A) on the ground *inter alia* of his not paying the maintenance.

Consent Separation Decree: Non-cohabitation thereafter – Ground for Divorce

M. Aruna Kumari v. *A.V. Janardhan Rao*, 2003 (5) SCALE 290

Issue: Can a decree of judicial separation passed with consent of both the parties, provide a ground for divorce under section 13(1A)(i) of the act, *viz.* non-cohabitation after a separation decree?

Facts: The wife filed a petition for judicial separation; the husband contested the same. However, in order to end the tension, he indicated in his written statement that he had no objection if the decree was granted to the wife. After making efforts for reconciliation, the court passed the decree on 23-12-1995. On 28-12-1996 *i.e.*, after the lapse of one year, the husband sought divorce under section 13(1A)(1). The wife resisted the same and contended that she was never interested in separation and that she got the decree in the hope that there might be a positive change in the husband's attitude and behaviour. The husband's petition was rejected by the Family Court on the ground that the decree of judicial separation was without contest and literally a consent or collusive decree and he could not be allowed to take advantage of his own wrong. On appeal, the Andhra Pradesh High Court considered the entire evidence and relying on *Saroj Rani v. Sudarshan Kumar Chadha,* AIR 1984 SC 1562: (1984) 4 SCC 90: 1984 Marri LJ 499 held that a consent decree *per se,* in matrimonial matters, cannot be treated as collusive (*A.V. Janardhan Rao v. M. Aruna Kumari,* AIR 2000 AP 127: 2000 (1) CCC 690: II (2000) DMC 118). Hence the wife's present SLP challenging the same. Her contention was that the evidence on record was not scrutinised by the High Court and therefore its finding should not be binding and the matter remitted to High Court for reconsideration. Her further plea was that there was ample evidence on record to indicate that her husband had been visiting her even after the decree of separation and even staying with her. The court, however, on the basis of facts and evidence found no justification to interfere with the High Court order in exercise of its power under article 136 of the Constitution.

Order: The wife's appeal against grant of divorce by the High Court was rejected. However when it was brought to the courts notice that their daughter had attained marriageable age and that the father was not taking any interest or responsibility towards that, the court directed that he should make some provision for the marriage. He was asked to pay ₹ 50,000 and his office was directed to deduct ₹ 5,000 per month from his salary every month for ten months and send the amount to her.

Comment: The wife's plea in the case was not justified. She cannot misuse the Court's time and resources on a superficial plea that she had sought the court decree of judicial separation only in the hope that the husband would mend his ways but that in fact she was not interested in the separation. Once having obtained the decree she cannot thwart the husband's claim to rely on the decree to seek a divorce on ground available to him under the Act. Along with granting divorce to the husband, the court also directed him to make same financial contribution towards the marriage of their daughter.

Consent Restitution Decree not *per se* Collusive

Saroj Rani v. Sudarshan Kumar Chadha,
AIR 1984 SC 1562: (1984) 4 SCC 90: 1984 Marri LJ 499

Issue: (i) Would a decree for restitution of conjugal rights passed with the consent of parties, amount to collusion?

(ii) Can a husband seek divorce on ground of non-compliance of restitution decree obtained by consent?

(iii) Would this amount to taking advantage of his own wrong?

Facts: This was a wife's petition for restitution of conjugal rights. The parties were married in 1975; had two daughters in quick succession (unfortunately the second daughter died when she was just six months old) and as alleged by her, in May, 1977, the husband allegedly turned her out of the house and withdrew himself from her society. The wife also alleged several mal-treatments, both by the husband as well as by her in-laws. The husband denied the allegations but made a statement in the Trial Court that the wife's application for restitution be granted. Accordingly, a decree for restitution was passed in March, 1978. A little over a year later in April, 1979, the husband filed a petition for divorce under section 13(1A)(ii) on the ground that one year had passed since the decree of restitution but no actual cohabitation had taken place between the parties. The wife denied this and stated that she was taken to the husband's house by her parents but the husband turned her out after two days. She further stated that she had also filed an application under section 28A of the Hindu Marriage Act in the court of Sub-Judge, Jalandhar in 1979, with the request that the husband should be directed to comply with the restitution decree. The District Judge, while holding on the basis of evidence that there was no resumption of conjugal rights between the parties after the decree, held that in view of the provision of section 23 and in view of the fact that the restitution decree was a consent decree and at that time there was no provision like provision in section 13B *i.e.*, divorce by mutual consent—the husband was not entitled to relief by way of divorce decree. Against this, the husband filed an appeal before the Punjab and Haryana High Court which held that, in view of the decision in *Dharmendra Kumar* v. *Usha Kumar*, AIR 1977 SC 2218: 1977 (2) SCJ 471: (1978) 1 SCR 315, it could not be said that the husband was taking advantage of his "wrong". The conduct alleged to be a wrong has to be something more than mere disinclination to agree to an offer of reunion; it must be misconduct serious enough to justify denial of the relief to which the petitioner is otherwise entitled. It, however, held that the decree for restitution of conjugal rights could not be passed with the consent of the parties and, therefore, being collusive disentitled the husband to a decree for divorce. The matter then came up before a Division Bench, which held that a consent decree could not be termed to be a collusive decree so as to disentitle the husband to relief. The Full Bench decision of the Punjab and Haryana High Court in *Joginder Singh* v. *Pushpa*, AIR 1969 P&H 397: ILR (1968) 2 P&H 714, was relied upon wherein it was held that a consent decree in all cases could not be said to be a collusive decree.

On wife's appeal to the Apex Court, it was held that a consent decree cannot be said to be collusive in all cases; further it did not accept the wife's contention that the conduct of the husband amounted to a wrong within the meaning of section 23(1)(a) of the Hindu Marriage Act. The court remarked:

> "We reach this conclusion without any compunction because it is evident that *whatever be the reasons this marriage has broken down and the parties can no longer live together as husband and wife; if such is the situation it is better to close the chapter.*" (emphasis added)

The court's attention having been drawn to *T. Sareetha*, AIR 1983 AP 356, it expressed its views on the constitutional validity of section 9. Approving

Harvinder Kaur, AIR 1984 Del 66, the court observed that financial sanction by way of attachment of properties which has been provided for disobedience of the restitution decree (Rule 32, Order 21 of the C.P.C) is only an inducement for the parties to live together in order to give them an opportunity to settle their differences amicably. Agreeing with Justice Avadh Behari of the Delhi High Court in *Harvinder Kaur*, Justice S. Murtaza Fazal Ali and Justice Sabyasachi Mukherji held that "the right of the husband or the wife to the society of the other spouse is not merely a creature of the statute. Such a right is inherent in the very institution of marriage itself............ There are sufficient safeguards in section 9 to prevent it from being a tyranny".

The court further remarked: It serves a social purpose as an aid to the prevention of break-up of marriage. It cannot be viewed in the manner the learned judge of the Andhra High Court has viewed it and we are therefore unable to accept the position [proposition?] that section 9 is violative of article 14 or article 21 of the Constitution if the purpose of the decree for restitution of conjugal right..................is understood in its proper perspective and if the method of its execution in cases of disobedience is kept in view.

Order: The wife lost the appeal and the court found that there was no collusion in a consent decree of restitution of conjugal rights; there was no wrong committed by the husband and since there was no cohabitation for a year since the passing of the decree, the husband was within his legal right to seek divorce on that ground; a decree of restitution does not infringe any of the provisions of the Constitution; it rather aims at encouraging and motivating parties to live together, the Court observed.

Comment: While the legality of section 9 cannot be assailed, it cannot be denied that it serves *practically* no purpose as an order for restoring conjugal rights. It is only a circuitous route to obtaining a divorce. It would be a useful study to find out how many restitution orders really end up to meaningful resumption of cohabitation.

Non-cohabitation after Restitution or Seperation Decree

Bijaya Lakshmi Kundingi v. *Kamala Lochana Kundingi*, AIR 2005 Ori 120: 2005 (33) All Ind Cas 580: 2005 (2) Ori LR 23

Issue: Is a court obliged to grant a divorce decree to the applicant on the simple ground of non-cohabitation after a decree of restitution or judicial separation, for a year or above?

Facts: The parties were married in 1976. The husband ill-treated the wife and also developed illicit relationship with another woman. When the wife objected to this, the husband deserted her and withdrew from her society. When all efforts to bring him back failed, the wife filed a suit for restitution of conjugal rights in 1987. She also sought maintenance *pendente lite* and litigation expenses which was allowed. A decree of restitution of conjugal rights was also passed in favour of the wife. In order to avoid the decree, the husband left his service and went to another place. The wife followed him there and discovered that he was living with the other woman. She filed proceedings for execution of the restitution decree but before the decree was executed, the husband, after a lapse of more than one year from the date of decree of restitution, filed a suit for divorce under section 13(1A)(ii) the Hindu Marriage Act on the ground that there has been no reunion between the parties for over a year, pursuant to the decree for restitution of conjugal rights. He also filed a memo before the executing court to drop the execution proceedings as not maintainable. The executing court, accordingly, dismissed the execution proceedings against which the wife filed a revision before the District Judge. This was also dismissed as infructuous on the ground that the suit for divorce having been decreed in favour of the husband, the revision became infructuous. The husband also failed to pay her maintenance.

The Trial Court had decreed divorce despite wife's objection that the husband frustrated all her attempts to unite and so he could not be allowed to take advantage of his wrong within the meaning of section 23(1)(a) of the Hindu Marriage Act. The court held that the husband was not guilty of any "serious misconduct" so as to disentitle him to the decree to which he was legally entitled to under section 13(1A)(ii) of the Hindu Marriage Act. The wife's appeal against this before the Additional District Judge was dismissed. Hence the second appeal.

Order: After hearing the rival contentions of both the parties and analysing some judgments, the court held that courts below went wrong in applying the ratio of the decision in *Dharmendra Kumar* v. *Usha Kumar*, AIR 1977 SC 2218: 1977 (2) SCJ 471: (1978) 1 SCR 315, which was relied upon, under which in order to be a "wrong" within the meaning of section 23(1), the conduct alleged has to be something more than a mere disinclination to agree to an offer of reunion; it must be serious misconduct to justify refusal of relief to which the applicant is otherwise entitled. In this case, it could not be said that no serious misconduct has been committed by the husband. The court held:

> "The unshaken testimony of the appellant wife........which has been illegally discarded by the courts below clearly shows that the action of the respondent-husband to frustrate the steps taken by the appellant wife for reunion is a "wrong" within the meaning of section 23(1) of the Act. Coupled with this....non-payment of maintenance as directed by the courts below as well as this court........also amounts to commission of a wrong within the meaning of section 23 of the Act."

The following observations of the Supreme Court in *Hirachand Srinivas Managaonkar* v. *Sunanda*, AIR 2001 SC 1285: 2001 AIR SCW 1196: (2001) 4 SCC 125, which also were referred to by the court in the instant case (*Bijaya Lakshmi Kundingi*, at p. 124) are pertinent:

> "In this connection, it is also necessary to clear an impression regarding the position that once a cause of action for getting a decree of divorce under section 13(1A) of the Act arises, the right to get a divorce

crystallizes and the court has to grant the relief......This impression is based on misinterpretation of the provision in section 13(1A). All that is provided............is that either party........may present a petition.........The section..........only enables either party to file an application [and not that] the court has no alternative but to grant a decree of divorce."

Comment: Section 13(1A) only enables a party to file petition for divorce and it is not as if the court is bound to pass a decree. Whether or not to grant relief would depend on the facts and circumstances of each case. "It would be too hazardous to lay down a general principle of universal application."

Husband Continuing to Live with Another Woman: Not Entitled to Relief

Kanchan Sanjay Gujar v. *Sanjay Gujar*, AIR 2009 Bom 151: 2009 (4) CCC 509: II (2009) DMC 566

Issue: In a petition for divorce under section 13(1A)(ii) of the Hindu Marriage Act the *onus* of proof that the petitioner was not guilty of "wrong" or "misconduct" for the non-resumption of cohabitation lies on the petitioner and not on the respondent.

Facts: The parties were married in the year 1980 and had three children. In 1991 the husband moved out of the matrimonial home and started living separately with another woman. In 1995 the wife filed a petition for restitution of conjugal rights and in 1996 the husband filed a divorce petition under section 13 of the Hindu Marriage Act on the grounds of cruelty and desertion. By a common judgment in 1999 the Family Court granted decree of restitution in favour of the wife and dismissed the husband's petition for divorce. In 2001, the husband filed a divorce petition under section 13(1A) stating that after the decree of restitution passed in 1999 there had been no resumption of cohabitation between the parties and therefore the marriage be dissolved. The Family Court granted the divorce against which the wife filed the present appeal. She contended that the husband was living in an adulterous relationship before the decree of restitution and even after the decree he continued to live with that other woman as her husband. It was thus the husband who was responsible for the non-resumption of cohabitation and therefore, in view of section 23(1)(a) of the Act, was not entitled to decree as he was trying to take advantage of his own wrong. The respondent husband on the other hand supported the impugned order claiming that the only issue before the Family Court was whether there had been restitution of conjugal rights between the parties for a period of one year after passing of the decree of restitution in 1999.

His further contention was that as per the settled position of law mere non-compliance of decree for restitution *per se* could not amount to taking advantage of his own wrong under section 23(1)(a) as there is no obligation placed by the statute on him under the Act for compliance before seeking relief under section

13(1A). Furthermore, it was contended that the wife failed to show that he has taken advantage of his own wrong; also to constitute a "wrong" in terms of section 23 of the Act there has to be a positive act and/or action/conduct which is more than disinclination to cohabit and no such case has been made out by the appellant wife. The Apex Court judgment in *Dharmendra Kumar* v. *Usha Kumar*, AIR 1977 SC 2218: 1977 (2) SCJ 471: (1978) 1 SCR 315 was relied on.

After detailed analyses of the statutory provisions and case-law, the court held that it was imperative for the party applying under section 13(1A) of the Act to prove that he/she was not guilty of committing a "wrong" or "misconduct" in resumption of cohabitation pursuant to decree of restitution. "The *onus* is clearly on the party applying to Family Court for divorce under section 13(1A) of the Act and it is not for the opponent party to prove what steps he/she had taken for resumption of cohabitation...."the court observed (at p. 158). Besides, the fact that the husband continued to live with another woman as her husband even after a decree of restitution, thereby making resumption of cohabitation impossible for the wife would be a "wrong" or "misconduct" within of section 23(1)(a) of the Act.

Order: The wife's appeal was allowed and the divorce decree passed by the Family Court was set aside. The husband's conduct of continuing to live with another woman despite the wife's obtaining a restitution order was a wrong disentitling him to relief.

Comment: The idea behind section 13(1A) of the Act is merely to enlarge the right to apply for divorce; however, mere maintainability of a petition does not make it compulsive that the petition must be allowed and divorce granted. The court has to satisfy itself that the petitioner is not trying to take advantage of any wrong committed by him.

REPUDIATION OF MARRIAGE

Court to be 'Satisfied' that Wrong-doer does not take Advantage

M. Ajith Kumar v. K. Jeeja @ Sanila,
AIR 2009 Ker 100: 2009 (78) All Ind Cas 372:
2009 (1) Ker LT 634

Issue: Would mere reluctance on the part of a spouse to cohabit after a decree of restitution against him/her constitute a wrong so as to disentitle the spouse to relief under section 13(1A)(ii) of the Hindu Marriage Act.

Facts: The parties to the marriage lived together for a very short period of two and a half months and thereafter the husband left for the gulf. A son was born of the marriage. According to the husband, when he returned from Gulf, the wife, who was taken to her parents house for delivery, was not allowed to live with him by her parents. After about a year, the wife filed a petition for restitution of conjugal rights which was decreed with a direction to resume cohabitation within two months. Prior to this decree the wife had also filed a petition for maintenance for self and child which was allowed by mutual consent. The husband further stated that despite several attempts made by him, the wife did not resume cohabitation and they were living separately for 9½ years. Hence he filed a petition for divorce under section 13(1A)(ii) on ground of non-resumption of cohabitation after a restitution decree. The wife's contention was that it was the husband who stood against the resumption of cohabitation despite the restitution decree. After hearing the rival contention, the Family Court considered the entitlement of the husband under section 13(1A)(ii) in the light of section 23(1)(a) of the Hindu Marriage Act *viz.*, that the petitioner seeking relief cannot be allowed to take advantage of his own fault or wrong. It held that on the basis of evidence on record it was clear that the husband had no intention to resume cohabitation and hence he is not entitled to the decree of divorce. Hence the husband's appeal. The High Court held that the relief can be denied even if the ground under the statute is available if the court is satisfied that the petitioner-appellant is taking advantage of his or her own wrong within the meaning of section 23(1)(a) of the Act. The word 'satisfied' used in the section has to be construed as 'satisfied on the basis of the legal evidence' adduced before the court that the petitioner is not taking advantage of his or her own wrong or disabilities. Certain aspects of law are also to be borne in mind while considering the question of "wrong" on the part of the petitioner. The court also clarified that mere non-compliance of the decree of restitution *per se* would not amount to taking advantage of one's own wrong. In other words as stated by the court (at p. 103) "mere reluctance on the part of the spouse in resuming cohabitation cannot be construed as a "wrong" so as to disentitle him or her to get a decree of divorce under section 13(1A)(ii) of the Act notwithstanding section 23(i)(a) of the Act".

Order: In this case the High Court found that the Family Court had not discharged the obligation of satisfying itself whether the appellant-husband was the wrongdoer and if so whether his conduct would amount to a wrong within the meaning of section 23(1)(a) of the Act so as to disentitle him to a decree of divorce. The Family Court should have considered the question as to whether there was any obstacle for the wife to join the husband who could be regarded as the "wrongdoer". In view of this, the matter was remanded to the Family Court for disposal in accordance with law.

Comment: Some significant judgment of the Apex Court were referred to in this case viz., *Srinivas Managaonkar* v. *Sunanda*, AIR 2001 SC 1285 where the court emphasised that mere fulfilment of the requirement under section 13(1A)(ii) does not mean that the court is bound to grant the divorce decree to the applicant. Such an interpretation would run counter to the provisions of sections 23(1)(a) and (b) of the Act. In other words, a period of separation or non-compliance after a decree of restitution does not *ipso facto* ripen into a right to get divorce on that basis. On the other hand, in *Dharmendra Kumar* v. *Usha Kumar*, AIR 1977 SC 2218: 1977 (2) SCJ 471: (1978) 1 SCR 315 and *Saroj Rani* v. *Sudarshan Kumar Chadha*, AIR 1984 SC 1562: (1984) 4 SCC 90: 1984 Marri LJ 499 *see also Radha Kumari* v. *Dr. K.M.K. Nair*, AIR 1988 Ker 235, the Court held that the failure of the husband in not enforcing the decree of restitution will not disentitle him from getting divorce under section 13(1A)(ii) unless there is evidence to prove that his conduct amounted to a wrong within the meaning of section 23(1)(a) of the Act disentitling him to the relief.

In *Ajith Kumar's* case, the parties had been litigating for over a decade; the husband contested the wife's petition for restitution but she succeeded in obtaining it; there was, however, no resumption of cohabitation despite the decree- for whatever reasons – fault or no fault of any party – and ultimately the husband sought divorce which was rejected by the Family Court on the ground that the husband had committed a wrong because he had no intention to resume cohabitation. One wonders what practical purpose would be served by remanding the case back to Family Court to ascertain whether indeed he was at fault. Parties in such case cannot be compelled to resume cohabitation. As a saying goes, a horse can be taken to the water but cannot be made to drink it. Cohabitation is not something which can be thrusted by force on any party. Even if the husband is ultimately denied divorce in view of section 23(1)(a), that is not going to save the marriage.

Constitutional Validity of the Provision

Roop Narayan Verma v. Union of India,
AIR 2007 Chh 64: 2007 Mat LR 538: 2007 (3) ALJ (NOC) 526

Issue: Under section 13(2)(iv) of the Hindu Marriage Act, a wife may file a petition for divorce *inter alia*, on the ground that "her marriage (whether consummated or not) was solemnized before she attained the age of fifteen years and she has repudiated the marriage after attaining that age but before attaining the age of eighteen years." The issue of constitutional validity of this clause was involved in this case.

Facts: The parties in this case were married in 1969 while they were little kids-the boy being seven and the girl just four. After 23 years the wife filed an application for maintenance of ₹ 1,000 under section 125 of the Cr. P.C. The husband contested it on the ground, *inter alia*, that the marriage had not been solemnised in accordance with mandatory provision under section 5 of the Hindu Marriage Act and the Child Marriage Restraint Act as both the parties were below the prescribed age for marriage and hence there was no legally enforceable obligation against each other. He also contended that the State was under obligation to restrain such marriages and since the State Authorities failed in its obligation it is the State's responsibility and he cannot be compelled to maintain the wife. Furthermore, it was argued that the provision was discriminatory *vide* article 15 of the constitution since the option of repudiating an underage marriage is available only to a wife and not to a husband who also could be a victim of child marriage. The Magistrate, after an enquiry into all the above allegations directed the husband to pay ₹ 750 per month towards maintenance of wife. The husband's revision as well as the present appeal were dismissed. The court conceded that non-compliance of the provisions against child marriage indeed gives rise to various evils and the State should ensure to come through if by appropriate legislation or by making other legal devices. However as to the constitutional validity of section 13(2)(iv) the court held that in view of article 15(3) of the Constitution, the State has powers to make special provisions for the benefit of women and children.

Order: A marriage between underage parties not being void, the husband was directed to pay maintenance to the wife. His plea that the provision enabling only the wife to repudiate such marriage was unconstitutional was dismissed and so also the contention that State having failed to prevent such marriages it is the responsibility of the State and not his, to provide for the wife.

Comment: It is common knowledge that despite laws against child marriages and awareness campaigns, child marriages still thrive. However the provisions of the Prohibition of Child Marriage Act, 2006 are more stringent and one hopes that it helps curbing such marriages. Also, the right to avoid such marriage which is hitherto provided only to the wife has now been given to the husband also. Section 3(1) of the Act says, "Every child marriage whether solemnised before or after the commencement of this Act shall be voidable at the option of the contracting party who was a minor at the time of the marriage."

Minor Girl Filing Petition for Repudiation Through Brother even while Father Alive

Ramesh Kumar v. Sunita Devi,
AIR 2005 P&H 55: II (2005) DMC 575: 2005 (1) Hindu LR 360

Issue: (i) Can a minor file a petition for divorce under section 13(2)(iv) through her brother even though father was alive?

(ii) Can the plea of *res judicata* apply to a subsequent petition for divorce where the earlier petition, which was premature, was dismissed as withdrawn?

Facts: The petitioner, a minor girl, was married when she was about 11 years old. The law, *vide* section 13(2)(iv) of the Hindu Marriage Act gives to a girl married before the age of 15, an option to repudiate the marriage after she attains the age of 15 but before attaining the age of 18. In this case, she filed a petition to repudiate the marriage while she was about 13 years of age. The same was, however, dismissed as withdrawn. Later she filed the petition through her brother when she became legally competent to exercise her right. The same was decreed by the matrimonial court and the marriage was dissolved. Hence, the husband's appeal. In appeal it was contended that the earlier petition having been dismissed, the later petition was barred by the principle of *res judicata* and *secondly*, the petition should have been filed through the father who was alive but the same being filed through the brother, was not competent.

Order: Both these contentions were overruled and it was held that the earlier petition being premature, it being dismissed as withdrawn was no bar to the petitioner's filing the second petition when she became competent to file the same. *Secondly*, a minor can sue either through her mother, father or brother who has no adverse interest against her. So, in this case the brother was not incompetent to file the divorce petition on behalf of the petitioner.

Comment: The provision under section 13(2)(iv) was incorporated about three decades back. If marriage of minors is to be seriously prohibited, such provisions should not find a place in the statute. Their existence sends wrong signals. Also, if a non-age, *i.e.*, marriage between, or of, minors is solemnized under customary law, can the provision of the statute be invoked to later have the marriage dissolved? Can the parties take recourse to custom as well as the statute? Or would the court in such case refuse to dissolve the marriage since the custom under which they were married, allows child marriage?

RESTITUTION OF CONJUGAL RIGHTS

The right or entitlement to consortium is the most significant component of marital bond. When one spouse leaves the other or withdraws or abandons the company of the other without any reasonable cause, the aggrieved spouse may seek court intervention. The idea behind relief by way of restitution of conjugal rights is to aim restoring a relationship which has got estranged for whatever reasons. This remedy has been statutorily provided under all personal laws, viz., section 9 Hindu Marriage Act sections 32-33 Divorce Act section 36 Parsi Marriage and Divorce Act and section 22 of the Special Marriage Act. While the Muslim law has no statutory provision but, on the basis of texts and principles of Mulla (Principles of Mohammedan Law (1972) Para 28; See also Fyzee, *Outlines of Mohamedan Law* (1974) p. 121) that "where a wife, without lawful cause ceases to cohabit with her husband, the husband may sue the wife for restitution of conjugal rights" and "the wife has the right to demand the fulfilment by the husband of his marital duties, the relief of restitution of conjugal rights is fairly established. (*See* also Moonshee Buzloor Ruheen v. Shumsoonissa Begum, (1867) 11 MIA 551)

This section of the Book contains and analyses cases on restitution of conjugal rights and the various aspects and issues involved therein.

Constitutional *Vires* of Restitution Provision
T. Sareetha v. T. Venkata Subbaiah,
AIR 1983 AP 356: II (1983) DMC 172: (1983) 2 Civ LJ 158

Issue: Whether section 9 of the Hindu Marriage Act which provides for restitution of conjugal rights is violative of articles 14, 19 and 21 of the Constitution?

Facts: The husband filed a petition for restitution of conjugal rights under section 9 of the Hindu Marriage Act against his star wife Sareetha. The wife filed an objection as to the jurisdiction of the Cuddapah Court. The Trial Court held that the Cuddapah Court had jurisdiction to try the petition and against this the wife went in revision to the High Court. Justice Choudary of the High Court affirmed the lower court's order on the point of jurisdiction. It discussed the issue of constitutional validity of section 9. The judge termed the provision of restitution of conjugal rights as "uncivilised," "barbarous", "engine of oppression" and assailed section 9 as being violative of articles 14, 19 and 21 of the Constitution. "Sexual cohabitation is an inseparable ingredient of a decree for restitution of conjugal rights", according to the court. The result is that the decree holder gets a right not only to the company of the other but also to have marital intercourse with her/him. This would result in transferring the choice of whether to have or not to have marital intercourse to the State and not to the individual concerned. As a natural corollary, it also meant the surrender of the choice "to allow or not to allow one's body to be used as a vehicle for another human being's creation".

Since a restitution decree is capable of being enforced, the court felt that it is "to coerce through judicial process the unwilling party to have sex against the person's consent and free will with the decree-holder". In the words of Justice Choudary, "nothing can conceivably be more degrading to human dignity and monstrous to human spirit than to subject a person by the long arm of the law to a positive sex act".

Holding a restitution decree violative of article 21 of the Constitution which guarantees rights to life and personal liberty, the judge held that right to privacy is a part of article 21 and is bound to include body's inviolability and integrity and intimacy of personal identity, including marital privacy. A decree for restitution of conjugal rights constitutes the grossest form of violation of an individual's right to privacy; it denies to the woman her free choice whether, when and how her body is to become the vehicle for the procreation of another being.

Section 9, according to the court, was also in violation of article 14 of the Constitution. It agreed that in form section 9 does not offend the classification test inasmuch as it makes no discrimination between husband and wife and makes the remedy available to both equally. However "bare equality of treatment regardless of the inequalities of realities is neither justice nor homage to the constitutional principle".

The remedy is, in social reality, almost exclusively used by the husband and reasons for this are obvious. A restitution decree, if enforced against a wife, would change her whole life pattern whereas the husband's position remains more or less the same. This is so because of the different biological roles of the two. "As a result, this remedy works in practice only as an engine of oppression to be operated by the husband for the benefit of the husband against his wife. By treating the wife and the husband who are inherently unequals as equals, section 9 of the Act offends the rule of equal protection of the law."

The section was also assailed on the touchstone of 'minimum rationality'. It promotes no legitimate public purpose based on any conception of the general good and hence is arbitrary and void.

According to the court, the only advantage of a restitution decree was that it provides a ground for divorce at a later stage but the price for this was very high *viz.*, human dignity.

Order: Section 9 of the Hindu Marriage Act was termed as 'savage', 'barbarous' and 'uncivilised' and as offending constitutional provisions and hence declared as *null* and *void*.

Comment: The judgment is no longer good law in view of the Supreme Court judgment in *Saroj Rani* v. *Sudarshan Kumar Chadha*, AIR 1984 SC 1562: (1984) 4 SCC 90: 1984 Marri LJ 499.

Harvinder Kaur v. *Harmander Singh Choudhry*, AIR 1984 Del 66: ILR (1984) 1 Del 546: 1984 Raj LR 187

Issue: Does the provision of restitution of conjugal rights in section 9 of the Hindu Marriage Act violate constitutional provisions of equality and privacy?

Facts: The petitioner husband filed a petition for restitution of conjugal rights against the wife on the ground of her unreasonable withdrawal from his company. The same was decreed by the Trial Court. Aggrieved by the order, the wife came in appeal to the High Court. She challenged the constitutional validity of section 9 by relying, *inter alia*, on *T. Sareetha* v. *T. Venkata Subbaiah*, AIR 1983 AP 356: II (1983) DMC 172: (1983) 2 Civ LJ 158. The same was, however, dismissed.

Justice Avadh Behari denounced the introduction of constitutional law in family law as "introducing a bull in a China shop". The meaning and idea of cohabitation and consortium, and the purpose behind a restitution decree were discussed in detail and it was held that restitution aims at cohabitation and consortium and not merely sexual intercourse. "A disproportionate emphasis on sex, almost bordering on obsession has, according to the Delhi High Court, coloured the views of the judge in *T. Sareetha*. Various authorities were quoted to support the contention that sex is not the be-all-and-end-all of a marriage relationship. The essence of marriage is cohabitation and according to Justice Avadh Behari, "the court cannot enforce sexual intercourse but only cohabitation, and restitution of conjugal rights cannot be ordered where the respondent refuses sexual intercourse but continues to cohabit with the petitioner".

The court held that section 9 is in a way an extension of section 23(2) and (3) which aims at stabilising a marriage and encouraging reconciliation. A restitution decree "acts as an index of connubial felicity. It is a sort of litmus paper. If the decree is disobeyed it is an indicia that the parties have reached a stage of no return. In this case the parties get a ground for divorce after a lapse of one year. "It is a peg on which to hang a divorce. It is a foothold and handhold for section 13(1A)", according to the court.

Further, according to the court, sections 9 and 13(1A) are inseparable as the latter comes into existence because of the former. In declaring section 9 as *ultra vires*, section 13(1A) will also have to be struck down so the good will be thrown away with the bad.

Order: Holding the *vires* of section 9 the court denounced the induction of constitutional law in the home. "In the privacy of the home and the married life neither article 21 nor article 14 have any place. In a sensitive sphere which is at once most intimate and delicate, the introduction of the cold principles of constitutional law will have the effect of weakening the marriage bond......In the home the consideration that really obtains is the natural love and affection which counts for so little in these cold courts. Constitutional law principles find no place in the domestic code."

Comment: The court has taken a very logical view of the provision. The Supreme Court, in *Saroj Rani* v. *Sudarshan Kumar Chadha*, AIR 1984 SC 1562: (1984) 4 SCC 90: 1984 Marri LJ 499, accepted the views of the Delhi High Court as against the views of the Andhra High Court in *T. Sareetha* v. *T. Venkata Subbaiah*, AIR 1983 AP 356: II (1983) DMC 172: (1983) 2 Civ LJ 158.

REASONABLE CAUSE FOR WITHDRAWAL

Husband's Blindness: Reasonable Cause for Wife's Withdrawal

Mohinder Singh v. Preet Kaur,
1981 HLR 321 (P&H): AIR 1981 JK 25: 1981 Marri LJ 118

Issue: Is blindness of a husband after marriage a reasonable ground for a wife to withdraw from his society so as to defeat his petition for restitution of conjugal rights under section 9 of the Hindu Marriage Act?

Facts: The parties were married for six months. The husband met with violence from his brother and as a result lost his eyesight and became totally visually handicapped. The wife went back to her parents and never returned. The husband filed a suit for restitution of conjugal rights under section 9 of the Hindu Marriage Act but lost. Hence his appeal.

Order: The court held that the wife had a reasonable ground to withdraw from the society of her husband. It observed:

> "The conjugal relations are meant for happiness and not for disaster and misery; no situation can afford happiness when she is forced to live as a wife of a blind unprotected man..........she is not devoid of compassion but, she is asked to pay too high a price for this compassion. The husband too is expected to have sympathy for her. The sympathy of the wife cannot restore eyes to the husband but the sympathy of the husband can restore the charm of life to the wife."

Comment: Though cruelty was neither directly alleged nor pleaded, yet, it is obvious that according to the court it would amount to cruelty on the wife to expect her to live with a husband who has become totally handicapped visually just after six months of the marriage.

Wife's Employment

Geeta Jagdish Mangtani v. Jagdish Mangtani,
AIR 2005 SC 3508: 2005 AIR SCW 4755: (2005) 8 SCC 177

Issue: Would a wife's insistence on not leaving her job to join her husband amount to desertion thereby entitling the husband to a decree of divorce on the ground of desertion?

Facts: This was a husband's petition for divorce against his wife under section 13(1)(ia) and (ib) of the Hindu Marriage Act on the grounds of cruelty and desertion. The parties were married in 1992 at Ulhasnagar (Mumbai) where the husband resided with his parents. The wife also stayed there for sometime but in between returned to her parents at Bhuj (Gujarat) to join her service as a school teacher in a government school at Gandhidham. In 1993 she left for her parent's house for delivery and thereafter never returned to the matrimonial home. She was earning about ₹ 8,000 per month whereas the husband was earning just ₹ 1,400 from a private job. Her plea was that until the husband is able to provide her financial security she would not join him by leaving her job. For the husband it was argued that the wife knew about his meagre salary even at the time of marriage so she cannot take the plea of his inadequate income and financial insecurity. Further it was argued that in 1993 she left the matrimonial home on the pretext of delivery and never returned nor agreed to return thereby deserting him; there was thus the *factum* as well as *animus* of desertion. The Trial Court granted divorce on the ground of cruelty and desertion. On wife's appeal before the Joint District Judge, the decree was set aside as being "improper and illegal". It held (see *Jagdish Mangtani* v. *Geeta Jagdish Mangtani*, XLIV(i) 2003 Guj LR 309 (315):

> "If a woman gets good designation or good job on the strength of her education and if the husband is not earning good income and is residing at another place after marriage, wife cannot be compelled, according to orthodox Hindu mythology, to leave her good service or status and to stay at the husband's place. If she refuses to do so, she cannot be called upon to be ready for divorce. If it is so acted upon, it would be an insult to the woman's pride and it would amount to denial of woman's right to equality."

Against this the husband filed an appeal before the Gujarat High Court which confirmed the decree of the Trial Court and reversed that of the first Appellate Court, on the ground of desertion only as ground of cruelty was not pressed. The wife's argument was that she was prepared to resign if the husband earned at least ₹ 5,000 per month, but due to financial instability and growing liabilities specially after the birth of a child, she could not leave her government job to join her husband; her staying in Gandhidham was therefore with a reasonable cause and would not constitute desertion under the provisions of the Act it was argued. The husband on the other hand contended that after 1997 there was a clear case of *factum* of desertion as the wife was not prepared to go to Mumbai and he was not prepared to go to Gandhidham. It was further argued that he was not at fault since the wife was aware of his salary at the time of marriage and there was no reason for her now to demand that she would not join him unless he started earning more. A large number of cases were cited by both the parties in support of their respective contentions. After considering all the facts, evidence and case-law as also vain attempts by the court to bring about reconciliation, the court came to the conclusion that the husband was entitled to divorce. It remarked (at p. 329 of XLIV(i) 2003 Guj LR 309):

> "The court has no alternative but to pass the order for divorce to see that both people can be free to have their own houses in this behalf because to keep both husband and wife when one stays at Mumbai and another at Gandhidham, without intention to stay together, would serve

no purpose. Therefore the marriage is completely broken down and no useful purpose would be served by dismissing the second appeal."

The wife filed an appeal against this before the Supreme Court which was dismissed.

Order: The Supreme Court and discussed the wife's appeal against grant of divorce to the husband found no infirmity in the High Court order. The court particularly took note of the fact that the parties knew even before marriage whatever they were earning. Wife was earning more than double than what the husband earned and she entered marriage with full knowledge of this fact; they stayed together only for a brief period of seven months whereafter there was exchange of notices etc., and husband's divorce petition; the wife made no attempts to stay with the husband even during the long summer vacation in school. All this, according to the court, indicated *animus deserendi* and this was not with reasonable cause, "such course of conduct amounts to total abandonment and cannot be justified on monetary considerations alone as a reasonable cause to desert. It also amounts to wilful neglect of husband by the wife", the court observed, confirming the decree of divorce.

Comment: The observations of the courts, the High Court specially, indicate that the fact that the marriage had irretrievably broken down weighed heavily in the granting of the divorce decree though other factors supported and supplemented the plea of desertion. It is also significant to note that the judgment has a potential of sending signals that wives ought not to take up jobs – even if their financial condition so demands – at a place other than where the husband is working or residing. Each case, however, has to be assessed on its peculiar facts and circumstances. After all there are happy marriages despite husband and wife living at different places due to job exigencies and conversely, there are disastrous marriages too where both are working at the same place. There cannot, therefore, be any absolute rule.

Wife Subjected to Mental/Physical Torture: Reasonable Ground for Withdrawal

Kuldeep Kumar Dogra v. *Monika Sharma,* AIR 2010 HP 58

Issue: Is a husband who subjects his wife to mental and physical cruelty entitled to seek restitution against her?

Facts: A husband filed a petition for restitution of conjugal rights under section 9 of the Hindu Marriage Act against his wife. His allegations were that the wife left the matrimonial house without any reasonable excuse, that she wilfully refused to cohabit with him and perform her duties as a wife. The same was resisted by the wife on several grounds, primarily on the ground that he deliberately and intentionally created a situation which was not congenial for her to live in. She alleged extreme mental harassment and physical violence. In sum, that her withdrawal was not without reasonable cause. Infact, she was a very religious woman who performed 'pujas' in a temple, was revered by the public and known as "Sandhoori Mata". Her popularity did not go down well with the husband who tried to prevent her from going to the temple by burning the wooden bridge connecting the road to the temple. He compelled her to hand over the offerings of the temple where she performed "puja – archna", by subjecting her to physical and mental cruelty. He also got the electricity and phone connection of her room disconnected. All of this was testified by their 12 years old son.

Order: The Additional District Judge dismissed the husband's petition who then filed the present appeal. The court analysed the facts, circumstances and the evidence and also referred to various cases on the subject. If came to the conclusion that there was reasonable cause for the respondent/wife to withdraw from the husband's company. It observed (at p. 61):

> "A conjoint reading of the evidence of the parties leaves no room for doubt that it would not be possible for the wife.... to live with the husband. She has been subjected to beatings and threats by him and she reasonably apprehends that it is not safe for her to live with the appellant".

The husband's appeal was consequently, dismissed.

Comment: While normally a husband and wife are expected to live together but there is no absolute rule that come what may, once they are married they are bound to live together even though the situation and circumstances may be very hard and harsh. The matrimonial relief of restitution of conjugal rights is available to the petitioner only if the other party has withdrawn without any reasonable excuse.

If the withdrawing party has enough and more convincing grounds to leave the petitioner, the relief will be refused. And as, very aptly held by the court in *Kanna alias Mahalakshmi Ammal* v. *Krishnaswami Achari,* AIR 1972 Mad 247: 84 Mad LW 755 the ambit of "reasonable excuse" extends to a "practical impossibility for the parties to live together." In that case the judge applied the standard of modern women instead of that expected by Manu to judge "whether the misbehaviour or misconduct of the husband is such as will entitle the wife to refuse to cohabit with him." The relations between the husband and the wife's father were strained and the transference of this bitterness from the father to the daughter, according to the judge, made it," a practical impossibility for the parties to live together....and totally improper under the circumstances to order restitution."

Santana Banerjee v. Susanta Kumar Banerjee,
AIR 2012 Cal 16

Issue: Can baseless apprehensions of a wife of future torture in the matrimonial home be treated as a reasonable cause for her deserting the husband?

Facts: This was a husband's petition for restitution of conjugal rights under section 9 of the Hindu Marriage Act against his wife who left the matrimonial home alongwith their infant daughter barely two years after the marriage. The husband had an old disabled father, old mother and a handicapped brother. The wife wanted the husband to live away from them which it was not possible for him to do, so she left the matrimonial home. She also alleged mental and physical harassment, torture and dowry demand. Despite efforts by the husband to bring her back, she refused; hence his petition for restitution. He was prepared to take her back inspite of the fact that pursuant to her criminal complaints, he had to face humiliation of imprisonment for a day. The wife agreed to return on the condition that, the husband went to her father's place to bring her back. The husband conceded to that also. However, inspite of that, the wife refused to return and alleged apprehensions torture if she returned.

Order: The Trial Court decreed the husband's suit against which the wife filed the present appeal. The same was dismissed the court observed (at p. 19):

> The apprehension of wife of further torture on her return to her matrimonial home, resulting in her death is found to be a myth as she herself deposed that she would return to her matrimonial home if husband went to her fathers place to bring her back."

Comment: The reasons for withdrawal from consortium must be weighty enough to defend a suit for restitution filed by the aggrieved spouse. When there are no compelling circumstances for the non-applicant spouse to desert the other, the courts would decree restitution. How effective it would be to restore union is a different matter but the endeavour of the courts is to retain the bond of matrimony.

Alternate Relief in Petition for Restitution
Vijay Lakshmi Devi v. *Gautam Krishna Mishra,* AIR 2010 Pat 56: 2010 (3) Civ LJ 231

Issue: Two issues involved in the case were:
  (i) In a petition for restitution of conjugal rights, can an alternative prayer for divorce be made?
  (ii) If the respondent remains *ex parte*, would the petitioner be absolved from discharging the *onus* to prove his case?

Facts: This was a husband's petition for restitution of conjugal rights or, in the alternative for a decree of divorce on the ground of desertion. His contentions were that the wife left for her parental house soon after marriage and despite all efforts on his part to bring her back she refused and even misbehaved with him. It was further alleged that she was in the habit of demanding money for her maintenance and on query, she abused the entire family of the petitioner and also threatened to divorce him. Notices were issued to the wife for appearance but she did not appear; notice by publication in daily newspapers was also issued but she chose not to contest. The Family Court consequently held an *ex parte* hearing where it was deposed by the petitioner and his three witnesses that the wife never co-operated with him in leading a happy conjugal life; did not perform her duties towards him and his ailing parents; there was no compatibility in the marriage; that she threatened to seek divorce and all efforts to sustain the marriage had failed. The Family Court was satisfied that the husband deserved a decree of divorce and consequently granted the same. Hence the wife's appeal. It was contended on her behalf that when an application was filed for restitution, the Family Court could not have passed a decree of divorce; and further that there was no evidence on record to justify a divorce and no proper finding has been recorded while passing the decree.

After hearing the contentions of both sides, the court, relying on *Bhavna Adwani* v. *Manohar Adwani*, AIR 1992 MP 105: I (1992) DMC 286: 1992 (1) Hindu LR 549 held that there was no legal prohibition under the provisions of the Hindu Marriage Act for filing a petition for restitution or in the alternative for divorce on the ground of desertion. As to the other objection the High Court held that the Family Court passed the decree on the ground that the wife chose not to appear thereby implying that she is not desirous to resume conjugal life which according to the court was not sufficient ground to pass the decree. "True it is, the appellant wife remained *ex parte* but that would not absolve the husband to discharge the *onus* for making out a case for divorce which was the alternative prayer", the court held (at p. 57).

Order: The Family Court order was set aside with a direction to proceed afresh and record appropriate finding in law regard being had to the ground on which relief is sought.

Comment: In the context of this case a reference may be made of a High Court judgment in *Baldev Raj* v. *Bimla Sharma*, AIR 2006 HP 33 where the court had held that a husband who seeks restitution by filing a petition under section 9 of the Hindu Marriage Act cannot, in the alternative, also make a prayer for divorce on the ground of desertion under section 13(1). According to the court these two are "diametrically opposite and mutually destructive" and so cannot be made together. This approach, it is submitted, is not fair. The court should have gone into the merits of the case; if the wife's withdrawal from his company, was reasonable then the husband's petitions for restitution and in the alternative for divorce could have been rejected but if the husband's case of desertion by the wife was established then he should have been granted relief. The parties in this case were living apart for over ten years and the marriage was allowed to be kept in a state of limbo.

Note: *See* also *Reema Bajaj* v. *Sachin Bajaj*, AIR 2012 Raj 8.

RECONCILIATION EFFORTS

Termination of a marriage could be one of the most traumatic experiences in a person's life with enormous social, psychological and emotional repercussions on the spouses, their children, the entire family as also on the society at large. It is therefore, the endeavour of the courts to try possibility of saving the marriage as far as possible. Provisions to this effect are incorporated in the personal law statutes as well whereunder a duty is cast on the courts to attempt reconciliation between the parties who are litigating.

Select cases on this aspect have been enumerated in this section.

No Divorce Decree on Basis of Conciliator's Recommendations

Raj Kumar Bansal v. Anjana Kumari,
AIR 1995 P&H 18: 1994 (1) Hindu LR 417:
1995 (21) Marri LJ 302

Issue: Can a court pass a decree of divorce on the recommendation of the conciliators or arbitrators?

Facts: It is the duty of the court to make every endeavour to bring about reconciliation between the parties before proceeding to grant dissolution or separation. In view of the mandate contained in section 23(2) of the Hindu Marriage Act the courts used to hold chamber meetings with the parties and try conciliation. However, because of the heavy work load and other constraints these sessions used to be often short and perfunctory. Realising these problems, sub-clause (3) was added to section 23(2) in 1976 and now the court may refer the matter for reconciliation to any persons named by the parties or to any person nominated by the court. In this case, the court referred a matter to arbitrators chosen by both the parties for possible settlement of their dispute. The arbitrators gave an award that the marriage should be dissolved and on that basis the Trial Court passed a decree. On appeal against this by the husband, the decree was set aside.

Order: The court held, that though a matter may be referred to a person or persons of the choice of the parties, but if their attempts for reconciliation fail the matter has to be sent back to the court. In view of the statutory laws, matrimonial disputes cannot be decided by arbitrators (except under customary law). The arbitrators have no power to recommend divorce and the court cannot pass a decree on that basis.

Comment: Reconciliators or arbitrators can only try to reconcile and settle their differences as neutral persons who have the time to discuss the problems with the parties at length. This serves a useful purpose specially when there is a communication gap between the parties but this cannot form the basis of a divorce decree.

Failure to Appear in Reconciliation Proceedings – Court cannot Strike Down Defence

Love Kumar v. *Sunita Puri*,
AIR 1997 P&H 189: ILR (1997) 2 P&H 79: II (1998) DMC 711

Issue: Can a court strike down party's defence in a divorce petition for not appearing for reconciliation proceedings under section 23(2) of the Hindu Marriage Act?

Facts: A wife filed a petition for divorce on the ground of cruelty and desertion. The husband filed his written statement. *Vide* the provision in section 23(2) of the Hindu Marriage Act the court sought to make endeavour to bring about reconciliation between the parties. However, on three dates fixed by the court, the husband did not appear. The Trial Court thereupon struck down his defence and without framing issues, adjourned the case for wife's evidence and after recording her evidence immediately granted the divorce. The husband filed an appeal against this order.

Order: It was argued on the part of the appellant that failure to appear for reconciliation did not authorise the court to strike off his defence. For the wife, it was argued that on the husband's failure to appear for reconciliation the court was left with no choice except to strike off his defence and once the defence was struck off, the framing of issues was not necessary. In support of wife's case, reference was made to section 24 where also, in proceedings for maintenance *pendente lite*, there is no provision explicitly providing for striking down the defence if the respondent fails to pay maintenance and yet it is the settled law that the court can strike off defence of the respondent. The court, however, did not accept this argument. A comparison was made between the provisions under section 23(2) and section 24 of the Hindu Marriage Act. Under the former, it is incumbent on the court to endeavour to bring about reconciliation but neither any liability is cast nor right created. Under section 24, on the other hand, a liability is imposed on one party and a right is created in favour of the other. Non-compliance of orders under section 24 has legal consequences and impedes further progress of the case. It was, accordingly, held that the Trial Court was in error in striking down the husband's defence and in "unwarranted hot haste decided the divorce petition in her favour".

Comment: Reconciliation proceedings are only an attempt by the court to talk over to the parties and try reconciliation, whereas an order under section

24 explicitly imposes a duty on one party and gives a right to the other. If the party on whom a liability is imposed fails to comply with the court order, the court is competent to strike off his defence in the main proceedings.

Wife Allegedly Duped: *Ex Parte* Divorce – Appeal Rejected – Court Ought to have Tried Reconciliation and Allowed Appeal

Balwinder Kaur v. Hardeep Singh, AIR 1998 SC 764: 1998 AIR SCW 474: (1997) 11 SCC 701

Issue: Can a court reject an appeal in case of *ex parte* divorce decree where even the requirements of section 23 have not been complied with and the judgment-debtor alleges fraud in obtaining the decree?

Facts: A wife was duped by the husband into signing a divorce petition and appearing in court as a witness. The husband did not appear and an *ex parte* divorce decree was passed. The wife filed an appeal against this. She alleged that a fraud was played on her and stated that she never wanted a divorce. The High Court rejected the appeal and directed her to file a separate suit in the civil court. Hence her appeal to the Supreme Court.

Order: The court held, that the Trial Court erred in not making any endeavour to secure the husband's presence when it was required and try conciliation; also that by rejecting the wife's appeal, the High Court failed to exercise power of superintendence under article 227 of the Constitution. Grant of *ex parte* divorce without satisfying itself whether the requirements of section 23 were complied with was held to be not proper. A party cannot defeat the provisions of sub-sections (2) and (3) of section 23 simply by remaining *ex parte*. The court remarked (at p. 768):

> "The court can, in such a situation, require the personal presence of the parties. Though the proceedings were *ex parte*, in the case like this the court cannot be a silent spectator and it should itself endeavour to find out the truth by putting questions to the witnesses and eliciting answers from them."

Comment: In case of *ex parte* divorce decree, the court has to be all the more cautious to ensure that there is no fraud etc. Rejecting wife's appeal against divorce where she was duped into signing the divorce papers, even while she alleged fraud and denied having sought divorce, was unfair indeed. The Supreme Court, however, allowed the wife's appeal.

Issuance of Non-bailable Warrants to Try Reconciliation

Jagraj Singh v. Birpal Kaur,
AIR 2007 SC 2083: 2007 AIR SCW 3201: (2007) 2 SCC 564

Issue: Vide section 23(2) of the Hindu Marriage Act a Matrimonial Court is under duty to make every endeavour to bring about reconciliation between the parties before if grants any relief. The issue involved in this case was as to whether a court can go to the extent of issuing non-bailable warrants against a party to procure his/her appearance in order to try reconciliation?

Facts: This was a wife's petition for divorce under section 13 of the Act on grounds of desertion and cruelty. The Trial Court dismissed her petition as the allegations were not proved. Thereupon the wife filed an appeal. The husband, who was out of the country, appeared through his attorney-holder. The High Court directed the husband to appeal before the court in person. On the stipulated date again he did not appear but his attorney-holder assured the court that he would appear personally on the next date. He remained absent again. Taking a serious view of this, the court issued non-bailable warrants to be executed through the Ministry of External Affairs. This was challenged before the Supreme Court. It was argued that personal appearance of the party to the proceedings was not mandatory and the court had no jurisdiction to issue non-bailable warrants under the Act. The court dismissed this argument and analaysing the ambit of courts duty under section 23(2) Hindu Marriage Act it observed (at p. 2086):

> "Conjugal rights are not merely creature of statute but inherent in the very institution of marriage; the matrimonial disputes should not be allowed to be driven to a bitter legal finish. Every possible effort must be made so as to restore the conjugal home and bring back harmony between the husband and wife and the court must endeavour by directly involving the parties in such manner so that 'possible irritations and misapprehensions should not be allowed to vitiate the [conjugal] atmosphere. Hence the approach of the court should be much more constructive, affirmative and productive rather than abstract, theoretical and doctrinnaire".

The court should not give up its efforts merely because there is no chance of parties reconciling, or one or the other says so; it is obliged to determine the reasonability of their stands and this is not possible without a personal interaction with the couple.

The court had granted interim stay against the non-bailable warrants issued by the High Court in order that he overcomes the apprehension that he might be arrested the moment he landed in India; however, since the husband's counsel reiterated that no such order could be passed, the Supreme Court dismissed his appeal. It held:

> "The husband is bent upon to disobey and flout the order passed by the court which is in consonance with section 23(2), he cannot claim as of right the equitable relief from the court."

According to the court, conceding to the husband's plea would "virtually make the benevolent provision nugatory, ineffective and unworkable, defeating the laudable objective of reconciliation in matrimonial disputes."

Order: The husband's appeal against issue of NBW by the High Court was dismissed and he was enjoined to appear in person.

Comment: There is no doubt that the institution of marriage is very sacrosanct and divorce should be the last resort; also that courts should do their best to endeavour reconciliation. But how far should courts go would depend on the facts and circumstances of each case.

Reconciliation Efforts even when Ground for Relief is Conversion

Bini v. Sundaran K.V.,
AIR 2008 Ker 84: ILR (2008) 1 Ker 203: 2008 (1) Ker LJ 162

Issue: The issue involved in this case was whether reconciliatory efforts by the court are mandatory in all divorce cases irrespective of the grounds for the petition?

Facts: This was a husband's petition for divorce on the ground that the wife had ceased to be a Hindu by conversion to another religion. The wife admitted her conversion and on that basis a decree of divorce was granted to the husband. Aggrieved by this, the wife filed an appeal contending that simply because she had converted to another religion should not be a ground for granting divorce to the husband; she also argued that the court made no efforts to try reconciliation and explore the possibility of rapprochement. It is significant to note that under section 23(2) of the Hindu Marriage Act when divorce petition is filed on the ground, *inter alia*, of conversion reconciliation efforts are not mandatory. The Kerala High Court, however, accepted the wife's appeal and set aside the divorce decree. It held that even though under the provisions of the Hindu Marriage Act reconciliation efforts are not mandatory in the present context yet after the enactment of the Family Courts Act 1984 even in grounds excepted by the Hindu Marriage Act the Family Court is bound to make such endeavour. Passing of a decree on mere admission of conversion by a spouse was against the spirit and mandate of the provisions of the Family Court Act the court held.

Order: The Family Court order granting divorce was set aside and the case was remitted to Family Court to proceed afresh in accordance with law.

Comment: Though religion is a very personal issue yet efforts at reconciliation should be made by the court; it is not unlikely that parties might see reason and not insist on divorce simply on this ground when there is no other serious problem in the marriage.

DIVISION OF MATRIMONIAL ASSETS

Section 27, Hindu Marriage Act *vis-a-vis* Wife's Right to a Flat when She is Co-owner on Record

Sunita Shankar Salvi v. *Shankar Laxman Salvi*,
AIR 2003 Bom 431: 2003 (1) All MR 267: 2003 (3) Bom LR 424

Issue: When a wife is a co-owner of a flat on papers, has she a fifty per cent. share in it?

Facts: A flat was allotted to the parties by way of alternate accommodation to them without any consideration, by the builder and developer of the building in lieu of the accommodation surrendered by them which they were occupying as residential accommodation. The share certificate issued by the housing society, showing membership and interest in the flat was in the joint names of both the husband and wife; they were shown as joint owners. In fact, the husband himself admitted that the wife's name was incorporated as co-owner of the flat on his request. On wife's petition under section 27 of the Hindu Marriage Act, read with section 115 of the Civil Procedure Code for a share in the flat, the Family Court held that since the wife had no interest, title or right as she had paid no consideration or cost towards the flat and *secondly*, since the right to acquire the flat arose out of tenancy right which the husband had surrendered in favour of the builder, therefore the wife was not entitled to any share in the flat. Hence the wife's appeal.

Order: The Family Court's order was reversed. The High Court held that even though there was no tenancy in the wife's name, the same was for the benefit of the family and she occupied the premises as member of the family. Moreover, there was an "unambiguous unequivocal admission" by the husband that the wife be treated as co-owner. Thus, by his own conduct, he is estopped from contending to the contrary. The court, accordingly, ordered that the wife was entitled to equal share in the flat and in case equitable division was not possible, the parties should be given right to purchase 50% of the share of the other party and further, in case none of the parties wish to purchase the share of the other, then the court ordered that the flat should be put to sale and the proceeds shared equally.

Comment: The court decided in favour of the wife's 50% share in the flat in this case because the flat stood in the joint names of the parties; however, in most cases it may not be so. What would be the approach of the court in such situation where the wife has neither financially contributed nor is the flat in their joint names?

Matrimonial Court's Jurisdiction to Dispose of Even Such Properties which are not Joint of the Spouses

Hemant Kumar Agrahari v. Lakshmi Devi,
AIR 2004 All 126: 2004 All LJ 972: 2004 (2) CCC 50

Issue: Does the Matrimonial Court have jurisdiction under section 27 of the Hindu Marriage Act to dispose of even those properties which are not joint of the spouses?

Facts: Wife filed a petition for divorce on the ground of adultery and cruelty of the husband. She also prayed for relief of return of goods valued at ₹ one lakh and cash of ₹ 75,000 given to the husband at the time of marriage. The Trial Court decreed divorce and also return of goods and cash in part. Both filed appeal against the order—the wife against the order of not returning the remaining goods and the husband against the order asking him to return the goods. The significant point for adjudication was whether court could order disposal of exclusive properties of the spouses.

Order: The court held that under section 27 of the Act the Matrimonial Courts have jurisdiction to dispose exclusive property of the spouses, provided it was presented at or about the time of marriage. The section uses the phrase "property presented at the time of marriage, which may belong jointly to both husband and wife". Thus one pre-requisite of the section is that the property must be connected with the marriage. So far as the question of property being jointly owned by the parties is concerned, the section no where uses mandatory word "must" but uses the word "may". The use of the word "may", includes within its penumbra the property which may not belong jointly to the parties. In other words, the court ruled that section 27 does not confine or restrict the jurisdiction of the courts to deal only with joint property but permits disposal of exclusive property of parties as well, provided these properties were presented at or about the time of marriage.

Comment: The court has done well to enlarge the concept of joint property "presented at or about the time of marriage" to include even exclusive properties of the spouses. Thus, it would imply that a wife may claim even her *stridhan* under the section rather than resorting to other dilatory court procedures.

Note: The Matrimonial Court has no jurisdiction to make order in respect of property presented subsequent to the marriage (*M.D. Krishnan v. M.C. Padma*, AIR 1968 Mys 226: (1967) 2 Mys LJ 432: 12 Law Rep 209). Also articles, properties, furniture etc., acquired by the couple by their own efforts after marriage are not covered by this section. An order of the Family Court granting relief under section 27 of the Hindu Marriage Act in respect of such articles was held to be without jurisdiction in *Kamlakar v. T.K. Sambhus*, AIR 2004 Bom 479.

Jurisdiction of Family Courts under Section 7(1)(c), Family Courts Act *vis-à-vis* section 27 of Hindu Marriage Act

Sangeeta B. Kadam v. Balkrishna Ramchandra Kadam, AIR 2005 Bom 262: 2005 (2) Bom CR 515: I (2006) DMC 296

Issue: A suit for recovery by wife of her ornaments and property which is her own is not maintainable under section 27, Hindu Marriage Act but is so under section 7(1)(c) of the Family Courts Act, 1984.

Facts: This case had a long history. The parties were married in 1969 but within a few months relations became strained. Both had their own versions and grievances. In between their rough times, three children were also born to them. Ultimately, in 1982, the husband filed a petition for divorce. The wife contested the same and also claimed her ornaments which she had left behind and also various household articles and furniture in the matrimonial home. [It is pertiment, to note that the wife was working with far better salary than the husband.] The husband did not file any counter to this claim.

In the wife's written statement, she denied all the allegations of the husband and contended that it was he who had treated her with cruelty. She therefore filed a petition for judicial separation. Both these petitions (of husband and wife) were heard together and the city civil court judge at Mumbai dismissed the husband's petition and granted a decree of judicial separation to the wife. As to ornaments and articles claimed by the wife, the court was of opinion that these were either purchased or acquired by the wife and so he did not have jurisdiction to go into the entitlement of the same under section 27 of the Hindu Marriage Act which governs disposal of marital property *i.e.*, property acquired at or about the time of marriage which may belong jointly to both the husband and the wife.

After the lapse of one year since the decree for judicial separation, the husband filed a petition for divorce under section 13(1A)(i), before the Family Court. The proceedings were filed in the Family Court since these courts were set up in Mumbai in 1989 pursuant to the passing of the Family Courts Act, 1984. The wife opposed the divorce petition but the same was granted in 1991. Meanwhile, the wife had also filed an appeal against the order of the judge, city Civil Court, rejecting her claim for ornaments and other articles on the ground that it was not maintainable under section 27 of the Hindu Marriage Act. The single Judge, however, held that the appellant had claimed these items as her own property, therefore, it is not possible to hold that these ornaments and other articles were presented to her "at or at about the time of marriage or to show that it had become the joint property of both the husband and wife".

The wife filed an appeal against this order as well as against the grant of divorce. These were heard together by the Division Bench which held that section 27 of the Hindu Marriage Act did not cover the claim of ornaments and properties which were not presented to a wife at the time of marriage. It, however, held that it can grant relief in respect of such properties by invoking section 151 of the Civil Procedure Code. This order is reported in AIR 1994

Bom 1: 1994 (2) Civ LJ 424: 1994 (1) Hindu LR 605, as *Sangeeta Balkrishna Kadam v. Balkrishna Ramchandra Kadam.* Thus, her claim for ornaments and articles was allowed; the decree of divorce in favour of the husband was, however, confirmed.

The husband, aggrieved by the order allowing her claim for articles, filed an appeal in the Apex Court in 1993 which held that section 27 of the Hindu Marriage Act does not include only the property given at the time of marriage but would also include the property given before or after the marriage to become their joint property. However, according to the court though section 27 was attracted to the present claim but since no proper trial was held on this issue the matter was sent back to the Family Court. This order forms the judgment in *Balkrishna Kadam v. Sangeeta Kadam,* AIR 1997 SC 3562: 1997 AIR SCW 3667: (1997) 7 SCC 500. Thus proceedings were revived in the Family Court. The parties gave an application that they did not want to lead any fresh evidence and the evidence led earlier on the issue which was remanded to the Family Court, be considered. However, after hearing the arguments, the judge held that since the wife had not adduced any evidence to establish her claim, her contention could not be accepted. Hence the wife's appeal.

Order: It was contended by the wife's counsel that the Supreme Court had already held that section 27, Hindu Marriage Act did apply to the fact situation of the present case. As for evidence, it was argued that the evidence was already led when the matter was contested before the city civil court and when the matter was remanded an application had been filed before the Family Court stating that the evidence led earlier be considered and so the Family Court judge should have looked into that evidence. The present court looked into the evidence recorded earlier in great detail and came to the conclusion that "in the absence of adequate evidence on record and on probabilities, it is not possible to accept her claim for the items of furniture and other articles"........ In regard to ornaments, the wife's claim was conceded; the value of gold and silver ornaments was assessed at Rs. 1,20,000. According to the court:

> "......... from his (husband's) deposition, it is clear that the ornaments were either given to the wife by her parents or from the husband's side at the time of marriage and they belong to her and form part of her *stridhana*, which surely belongs to her only."

Another significant aspect of the matter was pointed out by the counsel. As far as the question of jurisdiction of the court to deal with the claim of ornaments was concerned—when the wife filed her claim, it was decided by the city civil court. Now the matter is with the Family Court. Her claim mentioned that the ornaments and articles were either purchased by her or belonged to her. While it could be argued that section 27, Hindu Marriage Act, was a restricted section and it covered only the property presented at or after marriage; property owned by the spouses separately required an independent civil suit. The jurisdiction of the Family Court, however, is wide. Under *Explanation* (c) to section 7(1) of the Family Courts Act, 1984, it has the jurisdiction to decide a suit or proceeding between the parties to a marriage with respect to the property of the parties or either of them. In other words, the court, clarified:

"Now that the matter is decided by the Family Court after remand, it is decided by a court vested with wider jurisdiction and even if it is contended that the ornaments were acquired or purchased by the appellant herself, they would still fall within the concept of property belonging to either of the parties under section 7(1), *Explanation* (c) of the Family Courts Act, 1984."

After the matter was remanded to the Family Court, the wife had moved an amendment in 1998 to claim ownership of the flat. She submitted that this flat had been sold by her husband to a third party in 1991 though it formed a part of her property. This was rejected by the Family Court on the ground that the matter remanded to him was for a limited purpose to decide the issue of *stridhana* and the claim for ownership of the flat would mean widening the scope of the proceedings and the fundamental character thereof will change. The wife filed a writ to challenge this order which was rejected by a single judge. The present Division Bench also did not accept this claim. She was advised to file separate proceedings for this claim.

Hence the wife's appeal was allowed in part in so far as the husband was directed to pay an amount of ₹ 1,20,000 with interest at the rate of 10% from the year 1982.

Comment: The case had a long chequered history. It depicts the hassles and agony of parties whose relationship became strained soon after the marriage but the litigation has been going on for over quarter century. The fate of the children born during the tug-of-war between the parents can be imagined. The basic dispute in the present case concerned ornaments and property. The wife's claim to *stridhana* was allowed because the case had passed on to the Family Court which was set up during the course of the litigation and the Family Court having wider jurisdiction was competent to decide the wife's claim to *stridhana* under section 7(1)(c) of the Family Court (as against section 27 of the Hindu Marriage Act). However, Family Courts do not exist everywhere. Would a wife (or the husband as the case may be) have to file a civil suit in the ordinary courts with all the delays, expenses and harassment in order to claim her properties?

RE-MARRIAGE

Re-marriage Pending Appeal of Divorce Decree

Tejinder Kaur v. Gurmit Singh,
AIR 1988 SC 839: JT 1988 (1) SC 395

Issue: After a decree of dissolution of marriage, is it open for a party to remarry pending an application for special leave to appeal by the other party in terms of section 15 of the Hindu Marriage Act?

Facts: A husband obtained a decree of dissolution of the marriage on the ground of cruelty from the court of the Additional District Judge, Patiala, on March 29, 1986. The wife filed an appeal before the High Court but the same was dismissed *in limine* on July 16, 1986. The wife, thereupon, filed a special leave petition. The preliminary objection raised against the appeal was that the petition had become infructuous as the respondent husband had in the meanwhile, remarried on August 17, 1986 i.e., just after a month of the dismissal of her appeal. The issue raised was whether the condition pre-requisite under section 15 of the Hindu Marriage Act before a lawful marriage can take place after a decree of dissolution has been complied with or not. Under section 15, it is only after the time for filing an appeal, if there is such a right, has expired without any appeal having been filed or an appeal has been filed but dismissed, can the parties remarry.

Reference was made to several cases, notably, *Lila Gupta* v. *Laxmi Narian*, AIR 1978 SC 1351: (1978) 3 SCC 258: 1978 (2) SCJ 428 and *Chandra Mohini Srivastava* v. *Avinash Prasad Srivastava*, AIR 1967 SC 581: (1967) 1 SCR 864: 1967 (1) SCJ 42. In *Lila Gupta*, the court had held that a marriage contracted in contravention of the rule relating to one year waiting laid down in the proviso to section 15 (prior to 1976) would not be void. ".........viewing the successive Marriage Act, it appears that prohibitory words without a declaration of nullity, were not considered by the legislature to create a nullity," the court observed. And further, an incapacity for second marriage for a certain period does not have the effect of treating the former marriage as subsisting.

In *Chandra Mohini*, the court held that even though section 15, in terms does not apply to a case of special leave to appeal to Supreme Court, a spouse who has won in the High Court and got a decree of dissolution of marriage cannot, by marrying immediately after the High Court judgment, take away the right of presenting an application for special leave from the other spouse. According to the Court, the successful party must wait for a reasonable time and make sure whether an application for special leave has been filed in this court.

In the instant case (*Tejinder Kaur*), the husband denied knowledge of any appeal in the High Court or its dismissal, and so it was argued that he was justified in contracting a second marriage on August 17, 1986, *i.e.*, immediately after the expiry of one month from the date of decree by the High Court. The wife, however, placed on record a copy of the registered notice dated May 31, 1986, intimating him of the appeal.

Order: The court held that the husband should have enquired about the fate of the appeal. At any rate, the High Court having dismissed the appeal on July 16, 1986, the petitioner wife could have presented a special leave petition within 90 days therefrom under article 133C of the Limitation Act, 1963. Until that period, it was not lawful for either party to marry again, the Court held.

It remarked (at p. 840):

> "Under the law laid down in this enactment, monogamy is the rule and a party can only contract a valid second marriage after the first ceases to exist in the manner envisaged by section 15. The rule laid down in this section is an integral part of the proceedings by which alone both the parties to the decree of divorce can be released from their incapacity to contract a fresh marriage."

Comment: Thus, it implies that the second marriage was void. Such cases give rise to many problems. The first marriage is *practically* no longer subsisting but only technically still alive as there is scope for appeal or chances of the decree of dissolution passed earlier being set aside. However, if any of the parties out of ignorance of law (which though is no defence) rushes to enter into a fresh alliance, the second spouse specially becomes the worst victim, and if there are children born of the second marriage—they suffer too. Perhaps the pre-1976 proviso to section 15 which put a bar to re-marriage within a year of dissolution was safer and more explicit (though problems of this kind have arisen even when that proviso existed – *Chandra Mohini's* case is an example).

Re-marriage after Annulment Decree

Lata Kamat v. *Vilas*,
AIR 1989 SC 1477: (1989) 2 SCC 613: JT 1989 (3) SC 48

Issue: Does section 15 of the Hindu Marriage Act (re-marriage of divorced persons) apply to a decree of annulment passed under Sections 11 and 12 of the Act, in this case, under section 12(1)(d)?

Facts: The respondent husband instituted a petition on March 7, 1984, for a declaration that the marriage of the respondent with the appellant wife was a nullity under section 12(1)(d) of the Hindu Marriage Act on the ground that at the time of the marriage the appellant wife was pregnant by some one other than the respondent. The wife contested the allegation but the Trial Court granted a decree in favour of the respondent by judgment dated May 3, 1985, declaring the marriage to be a nullity. The wife filed an appeal before the Additional

District Judge on July 19, 1985. Before this appeal could be filed, the husband re-married on June 27, 1985 and in the appeal filed by the wife, he raised a preliminary objection contending that after the Trial Court judgment on May 3, 1985, he has re-married on June 27, 1985, and when he re-married there was no impediment to the marriage as the appeal period of 30 days was already over. The husband's objection was allowed and the wife's appeal was dismissed as infructuous. The wife filed a second appeal before the Bombay High Court but that also was dismissed by a judgment dated February 20, 1987 (*Lata v. Vikas*, AIR 1987 Bom 231: I (1987) DMC 484: (1987) 1 Hindu LR 440), on the ground that as the appeal was filed by the wife after re-marriage of the respondent, it had become infructuous. The wife's application for maintenance *pendente lite* was also dismissed. Thus, after obtaining special leave, the appellant wife filed the appeal in the Supreme Court. It is pertinent to note that according to the lower courts, section 15 will apply only when there is a decree under section 13 (divorce) and not to a decree under section 12. In the Supreme Court, it was contended on behalf of wife, that the language of section 15 clearly shows that it refers to a marriage which is dissolved and it also talks of right of appeal; hence it is not possible to distinguish between a decree of nullity under sections 11 or 12 and a decree of divorce under section 13. Further, in support of this contention, it was argued that section 28 of the Act provides for appeals against all decrees made by the court in proceedings under the Act thus implying that section 28 applies to orders under sections 11 and 12 also. On the other hand, for the respondent-husband, it was argued that the language of section 15 refers to "marriage dissolved by decree of divorce", whereas in the instant case, the marriage was not dissolved by a decree of divorce but declared a nullity under section 12 of the Act.

The court, however, after analysing the cases referred to by the parties in support of their respective contentions and the provisions of the Act came to the conclusion that section 15 applies to proceedings under sections 11 and 12 as well. It held that if the contention of the husband were to be accepted, it would mean that as soon as decree is passed the party aggrieved may appeal, but the other party by re-marriage would make the appeal infructuous and, therefore, the right to appeal of one of the parties to the decree under section 28 will be subject to the act of the other party in cases where decree is passed under sections 11 or 12. If that were to be so, the court pointed out, the Legislature would have provided a separate provision for appeal when there is a decree under section 13 and a different provision for appeal when there is a decree under section 11 or 12. The fact that section 28 confers a right of appeal which is unqualified, unrestrictive and not depending on the mercy or desire of a party, against "all decrees", clearly indicates that decrees under sections 11 and 12 are also included. "The phrase marriage has been 'dissolved by decree of divorce' will only mean where the relationship of marriage has been brought to an end by the process of court by a decree," the court said.

Order: The court allowed the wife's appeal and the judgment passed by the High Court as well as by the lower courts was set aside. The case was remanded back to the first Appellate Court.

Comment: The applicability of section 15 to decrees of dissolution under section 11 seems to be erroneous. A marriage dissolved under section 11 is a void marriage—it is void *ab initio* where parties never had any status of marriage. They need not even have gone to court to get such marriage annulled by any decree because the marriage has no legal status. However, having obtained a decree, it would not be correct to hold that the parties should be subject to the provision of section 15 for re-marriage.

It is suggested that by dropping the word divorce from the phrase, "when a marriage has been dissolved by a *decree of divorce*" the confusion can be avoided. Simply the fact that "marriage has been dissolved by decree", should suffice. Decrees under section 11 should be taken out of the purview of the section.

BIGAMY

Constitutional Validity of Anti-bigamy Provisions in Hindu Marriage Act

Ram Prasad v. State of Uttar Pradesh,
AIR 1961 All 334: 1961 All LJ 383: 1961 All WR (HC) 252

Issue: Whether the provisions prohibiting bigamy under the Hindu Marriage Act are invalid as being violative of the right of religion guaranteed under article 25 of the Constitution?

Facts: The appellant, claiming to be a Hindu, was an engineer employed in the State of Uttar Pradesh in the Public Works Department. He was married in 1934 and had a daughter. Thereafter, his wife had several miscarriages and according to the doctors, she could not bear a child again. Both the appellant and his father believed that according to Hindu *Dharma Shastras* salvation was not possible without a son and in the absence of a male child in the family, a number of religious obligations would remain unfulfilled so the appellant husband decided to marry in the hope of getting a male child. Initially, the wife consented to this, but later changed her mind. She made a complaint to his office. Relying on Rule 27 of the Government Servants' Conduct Rules, the State Government directed the appellant not to marry a second wife without obtaining its permission. Accordingly, an application requesting for permission to marry again was submitted to the State Government. Meanwhile the Hindu Marriage Act, 1955, came into force, which prohibited a second marriage during the subsistence of the first marriage. The permission sought for was, accordingly, refused. The husband filed a writ petition under article 226 of the Constitution challenging the validity of rule 27 of the Government Servants' Conduct Rules as well as the provisions of the Hindu Marriage Act which prohibited bigamy on the ground that they infringed the freedom of religion guaranteed by article 25 of the Constitution. He prayed that the orders of the State Government refusing permission for his second marriage be quashed and that a direction be issued that his application be decided in accordance with the personal law as laid down in the *Dharma Shastra*. The petition was, however, dismissed by Justice Mehrotra who held that the impugned provisions of the Hindu Marriage Act and the Government Rule, were saved by clause (2)(b) of article 25 of the Constitution which does not prevent the State from making any law providing for "social welfare and reform.........". Further, according to the court, it cannot be said that it was an obligatory or integral part of the Hindu religion to marry a second wife in the life-time of the first if the latter had no male child. The Hindu religion permitted the adoption of a son and an adopted son was, for all purposes, as good as a natural born son, the court observed. Hence, the appeal was dismissed. The court held that if some of the sections of the Hindu Marriage Act have been enacted as a measure of social welfare and reform, nothing in the first clause of article 25 of the Constitution can be allowed to affect that enactment. "The legislature of the country is the best judge of what is necessary for the welfare or reform of a particular community at any particular stage", the court said.

Order: The court dismissed the husband's appeal and held that the provisions of the Hindu Marriage Act which are being challenged, do not infringe article 25 of the Constitution and are clearly protected by Clause (2)(b) of it. Rule 27 of the Government Servants' Conduct Rules only gives effect to those provisions, the court said.

Comment: Barring Muslim personal law, all personal laws enjoin monogamy. Infact there is a lot of debate on the need for having a uniform civil code, which would, *inter alia*, prohibit bigamous marriages permitted presently under some communities. By no stretch of logic can welfare measures or provisions such as these, be challenged as infringement of any rights of an individual.

Bigamous Marriage – Second Marriage should be Legally Valid for Conviction

Bhaurao Shankar Lokhande v. State of Maharashtra, AIR 1965 SC 1564: 1966 (1) SCJ 298: (1965) 2 SCR 837

Issue: Is it essential for a conviction for bigamy under section 494, I.P.C, that the second bigamous marriage should be a legally valid marriage?

Facts: Bhaurao Shankar Lokhande, appellant 1, was married to the complainant Indubai in about 1956. In February 1962, he married Kamlabai during the life-time of Indubai. On Indubai's complaint under section 494 of the penal code, he was convicted. His appeal to the sessions judge was dismissed and so also the revision to the High Court, hence the appeal by special appeal to the Supreme Court. The only contention raised in appeal was that in law, it was necessary for the prosecution to establish that the alleged second marriage had been duly performed in accordance with the religious rites applicable to the form of marriage gone through. It was contended that the essential ceremonies for a valid marriage had not been performed when the appellant and Kamlabai married each other. The prosecution, however, argued that the marriage was performed in accordance with the customs prevalent in the community of the appellant for *gandharva* form of marriage, and therefore, the second marriage was a valid marriage. Besides, according to the prosecution, it is not necessary for the commission of the offence under section 494 of the Indian Penal Code, that the second marriage be a valid one and that a person going through any form of marriage during the life-time of the wife would commit the offence of bigamy under section 494, I.P.C, even if the later marriage be void according to the law applicable to that person.

The court, however, did not accept the contentions of the prosecution and held that if the marriage is not a valid marriage, it is no marriage in the eyes of law. "The bare fact of a man and woman living as husband and wife does not, at any rate, normally give them the status of husband and wife even though they may hold themselves out before society as husband and wife and the society treats them as husband and wife," the court remarked. Reference was made to Sections 5 and 17 of Hindu Marriage Act *viz.*, conditions for a valid marriage and punishment for bigamy and it was held that unless the marriage was performed in accordance with the requirement of the law applicable to a marriage between the parties, the marriage cannot be said to have been solemnized and hence no offence under section 494 is committed.

Order: The court found that the prosecution had failed to establish that the marriage between the appellant and Kamlabai was performed in accordance with customary rites as required by section 7 of the Hindu Marriage Act, and therefore, does not come within the expression "solemnize marriage" occurring in section 17. Consequently, section 494 of the Indian Penal Code is not attracted. The conviction was accordingly, set aside.

Comment: It is an unhappy judgment and has been assailed by academics and jurists, alike. In fact the word 'solemnized' in sections 7 and 17 of the Hindu Marriage Act should not be strictly construed and if the parties have gone through some form of marriage and have been living as husband and wife and so acknowledged by the society, the marriage should be presumed and recognised under the law.

Bigamous Marriage not Legal even if Spouse Consents

Santosh Kumari v. *Surjit Singh,*
AIR 1990 HP 77: 1990 Cr LJ 1012: (1989) 2 Hindu LR 111

Issue: Can a Hindu husband take a second wife even if the first wife consents to it? Court exercises revisional jurisdiction under article 227 of Constitution on basis of newspaper report.

Facts: This is an interesting case which was initiated on the basis of a news item published in the Punjab Kesari, a daily from Jallandhar, stating that a Judicial Magistrate in District Kangra had permitted one 'S' to contract a second marriage on the ground of non-fulfilment of his sexual desire from his weak and ailing wife; further, under that order, the first wife would continue to be the legally wedded wife and the husband would provide all facilities and maintenance to her and the daughter. This news item was brought to the notice of the High Court Registrar by the District and Sessions judge, for being placed before the Chief Justice to consider if any action under revisional jurisdiction or Constitution could be taken up. The matter was thereupon taken up and registered under article 227 of the Constitution.

Order: The admitted facts are, *inter alia*, that the first wife had filed a civil suit for giving a declaration that her husband be allowed to marry another woman as she was weak and ailing, and the decree to that fact was passed by the sub-judge. The order started:

> "Keeping in view the admission of the defendant, I accordingly proceed to grant declaration to the effect that due to ill and weak health of the plaintiff and thereby unable to satisfy the sexual desire of the defendant, the defendant is permitted to solemnise second marriage and the plaintiff will be entitled to be called as legally wedded wife of the defendant who will provide the plaintiff and his daughter all amenities like clothings, boarding lodging till death, and marriage of the daughter will also be performed by the defendant...."

The High Court held that such order was absolutely wrong and illegal and against the clear provisions of the Hindu Marriage Act which clearly lays down that neither party should have a spouse living at the time of marriage. Further, section 494 of the Indian Penal Code also makes the act of marrying again during the lifetime of husband or wife as a punishable offence. The court expressed its displeasure against the order in these words:

> "The sub-judge is expected to know such elementary principle of law and it is a gross mistake on his part to have ignored such principle of law and to have given a decree contrary to the provision of the Hindu Marriage Act and perpetuate a criminal offence of bigamy punishable under the Indian Penal Code."

The order of the sub-judge was accordingly, set aside.

Comment: Physical debility, illness or weakness is no ground for matrimonial relief and in any case, in this case no matrimonial relief of divorce or annulment was obtained or even sought. A husband (or wife) cannot take another wife (or husband) during the subsistence of the first marriage even if the first spouse gives consent for the same. A court declaration giving such permission is a much more serious matter which was rightly set aside and also criticized by the High Court.

When First Marriage Void, Subsequent Marriage not 'Plural Marriage' but Reprehensible Conduct

M.M. Malhotra v. Union of India,
AIR 2006 SC 80: 2005 AIR SCW 5497: (2005) 8 SCC 351

Issue: Would a husband married to an already married woman be guilty of plural marriage if he subsequently marries another woman?

Facts: The appellant husband was an officer in the Air Force. He married the complainant in 1973. In 1990, she filed complaints against the husband alleging that he had illicit relations with another woman; that he tortured her brutally and also used criminal force on her by slapping, kicking and beating her. She also alleged that he had married the other woman and had committed the offence of bigamy. It is significant to note that in around 1993, the husband had filed a suit for a declaration, *inter alia*, that the complainant was not his wife as she already had a subsisting marriage on the date they started living as husband and wife. His suit was decreed. The husband's argument was that since the marriage with the complainant was null and void *vide* section 5(i) read with section 11 of the Hindu Marriage Act and no marriage in the eyes of the law, his subsequent marriage was not a case of plural marriage. This argument was accepted by the authorities and it was held that while the appellant could not be held guilty for the offence of plural marriage, his conduct overall, was reprehensible and involved moral turpitude. Punishment by way of order of compulsory retirement, was thus passed. Husband's appeal against this to the High Court was dismissed, hence the present appeal.

Order: The court went through the various provisions of the Hindu Marriage Act and cases thereunder to establish that a void marriage is no marriage in the eye of the law; it also analysed provisions of Air Force Act, 1950 and Air Force Rules and Regulations. After considering all these as also the facts and circumstances of the case, the Apex Court came to the conclusion that the appellant's conduct was highly reprehensible and unbecoming of his position and hence the punishment of compulsory retirement was not at all disproportionate. The appeal was accordingly, dismissed.

Comment: This is yet another case where a man lives with another woman as his wife for about twenty years, but later wriggles out of matrimony on the plea that her first marriage was subsisting. While technically it is a void marriage but very often, women may be duped into such alliances to be later abandoned. In this case, since the husband belonged to the Air Force services, the authorities took strict action by ordering his compulsory retirement, but what about cases in ordinary circumstances? The 'illegitimate' wife has hardly any relief and the man, hardly penalised.

Wife Leaving House: No Justification for Husband to take Second Wife "for the sake of his family"

Saygo Bai v. *Cheeru Bajrangi*,
AIR 2011 SC 1557

Issue: The issues involved in the case were *firstly*, would the mere fact that the wife has left the matrimonial home and has not returned since 4-5 years enough ground to defeat her right of maintenance under provision of section 125 Cr. P.C. and *secondly*, is a wife's leaving the matrimonial home for some years enough justification for a husband to enter into a second marriage?

Facts: This was a wife's application for maintenance under section 125 of the Cr.P.C. She alleged that the husband, who was a constable in police department, neglected to maintain her and the children; that he married a second wife and the wife (the appellant) and her children were thrown out of the house. The husband contested the same and argued that the wife had left him for no rhyme or reason and that despite his efforts, she did not return to the matrimonial home; when she did not come back for 4-5 years then he was left with no choice but to marry again for the sake of his children. Further, he alleged that the application for maintenance was filed only after five years of abandonment of the matrimonial home. The Trial Court held that the husband was compelled to marry second wife because of the appellant's (first wife) refusing to join him; it also gave a finding that the appellant had not come to court with clean hands as she had no justification to leave the matrimonial home; the fact that she never tried to hold a *panchayat* nor made public the reason for her living with her parents was also held against her. The wife's revision against this was dismissed as the revisional court held that the "respondent husband had become helpless and therefore, got married only for his family" (at p. 1559). The wife's appeal against this, before the High Court met with similar fate with rather strange observation that, "the appellant had not left the house on the grand of second marriage performed by the respondent but the respondent had contracted the marriage on the ground that the appellant left the house and failed to discharge her matrimonial obligation" (at p.1559). Hence the wife's present appeal before the Supreme Court.

Order: "To say that we are shocked by the orders passed by all the three courts below would be an understatement" the Apex Court observed (at page 1559). It held that the fact of appellants leaving the matrimonial home is no justification for husband's second marriage and also that courts below were in error in holding that even if the husband had remarried, the appellant wife was not entitled to maintenance as she had left the matrimonial home before the remarriage. Regarding the wife's not calling a *panchayat*, a fact which was adversely construed against her, the Supreme Court held that even if she had not called the *panchayat* it did not mean that the respondent was justified in throwing her out and getting married again. The wife's appeal was allowed and maintenance awarded to her.

Comment: The attitude and approach of all the three lower courts was indeed very unfair. The fact that the wife had left the matrimonial home 4 or 5 years earlier is no reason to *ipso facto* hold that she loses her right to claim maintenance, moreso, as in this case, the husband had admittedly entered into second marriage. Infact, the explanation to section 125(3) clearly states that a husband's second marriage would be a fit ground for a wife to refuse to live with him and claim maintenance.

Court Acquiesing in Husband's Bigamous Marriage
Kiran Devi v. *Batul Kumar Verma*,
AIR 2011 Pat 16

Issue: This is a very queer case where the question is (though not raised in the court, or the order) whether the court should so easily allow a husband to enjoy his bigamous marriage even while the first lawful wife is a victim but succumbs to social compunctions and forgives him.

Bigamy

Facts: Parties were married in 1994 and a son was born in the year 1995. In 1999 the wife filed a suit for restitution of conjugal rights and the husband made a counter-claim for a divorce decree on ground of desertion and cruelty. According to the wife she was forced to leave the matrimonial home. The Trial Court, after hearing the parties, held that in view of the allegations and counter allegations between them and the fact that they have been living separately for the last 14 to 15 years the marriage had irretrievably broken down; the claim of the wife for restitution was accordingly rejected and a decree of divorce was granted in 2009 after allowing maintenance for the wife and son. The wife filed an appeal against this. On the date of hearing, the parties arrived at a settlement and the wife agreed to go back to the matrimonial home. She however sought some time to collect her belongings. A short order to this effect was also passed and ten days time was given to the parties to be present in the court, allowing with the child and then proceed to the matrimonial home from there. However, in July 2010 – another date when parties were required to be present in court – the wife disclosed that on the date which was fixed for them to go to the matrimonial home – the husband disclosed to her counsel that he had already entered into a second marriage and also has an eight year old son. The husband endorsed this by way of counter affidavit and claimed that he had contracted second marriage in May, 2009. There is nothing to indicate whether he remarried after the period of appeal against the divorce decree available to the wife had elapsed or within that period. However, in view of all these developments, efforts for reconciliation were dropped. The wife took a categorical stand that even though the husband had concealed everything from her, including the date when he remarried, yet, she does not want to be a divorcee and to avoid such a stigma she is prepared to compromise and forgive him by not taking any further civil or criminal action against him provided he agrees to pay 50% of his salary to her by way of maintenance to her and the son. It was also agreed that she will stay separately from him and they will not interfere with each other's life. On conditions acceptable to be the parties, an order was made accordingly. The court specially made a note of the fact that the decree of divorce passed by the Trial Court was granted on a ground not permissible in law in view of the Apex Court judgment in *Visnu Dutt Sharma* v. *Manju Sharma*, AIR 2009 SC 2254: 2009 AIR SCW 2984: (2009) 6 SCC 379 where it was held that irretrievable breakdown cannot be invoked for dissolving a marriage as it is not a ground provided under the Hindu Marriage Act.

Order: The decree of divorce was set aside; the appellant wife would continue to be legally wedded wife of the respondent; however, in view of the agreement between the parties, she would not insist on restitution of conjugal rights provided the husband fulfils his obligations.

Comment: The judgment is a vivid reflection of our social attitudes. The wife was impelled to leave the matrimonial home and when she sought relief by way of restitution, the husband filed a counter-petition for divorce. He even had the audacity to enter into a second marriage. The court did not delve into the issue whether the second marriage was illegal – having been contracted within the appeal period available to wife, or it was legal. The only reason why the wife agreed to compromise was that she did not want to be stigmatised as a divorcee. While maintenance she would have got in any case, even after a divorce, but the fear of social stigma and its repercussions on the child are issues that haunt women and impel them to live under the facade of marriage. While there can be no estoppel against the law, the wife in this case even surrendered what is her legal right – a right to seek restitution of conjugal rights against the errant husband.

CONVERSION AND BIGAMY

Hindu Husband Embracing Islam, Solemnizing a Second Marriage during Subsistence of First Marriage – Second Marriage is Void

Sarla Mudgal v. *Union of India,* AIR 1995 SC 1531: 1995 AIR SCW 2326: 1995 Cr LJ 2926

Issue: Whether a Hindu husband married under the Hindu law could, by embracing Islam, solemnize a second marriage; whether such marriage is valid and whether the husband would be guilty of bigamy?

Facts: This was a set of four petitions filed by two organisations, under article 32 of the Constitution. The first petition involved a Hindu wife Meena Mathur whose Hindu husband Jitender Kumar became a Muslim and married a Hindu woman converted to Islam, named Sunita Narula *alias* Fatima. In another petition, Sunita *alias* Fatima, alleged that after their conversion to Islam and subsequent marriage, her husband came under the influence of his first wife and reconverted to Hinduism and also ceased to maintain her. Her further contention was that she continued to be a Muslim and was not being maintained under either of the personal laws. In the third petition, a Hindu wife Geeta Rani, alleged that her husband embraced Islam to marry another woman Deepa. The fourth petition was by a Hindu wife Sushmita Ghose alleging that her husband after conversion intended to marry another woman, Vanita Gupta.

The issues involved were:

(i) Whether a Hindu husband married under the Hindu law, by embracing Islam, can solemnize a second marriage?

(ii) Whether such marriage, without having the first marriage dissolved under the law, would be a valid marriage *qua* the first wife who continues to be a Hindu?

(iii) Whether the apostate husband would be guilty of the offence under section 494 of the Indian Penal Code, 1860 (bigamy)?

The court referred to various decisions on the subject and came to the conclusion that a marriage celebrated under one personal law cannot be dissolved by the application of another personal law. Where a marriage takes place under the Hindu law, the parties acquire a status and certain rights by the marriage itself under the law governing the Hindu marriage. If one of the parties is allowed to dissolve the marriage by adopting and enforcing a new personal law, it would tantamount to destroying the existing rights of the other spouse who continues to be a Hindu. According to the Court, a Hindu marriage can be dissolved on any of the grounds specified in the Act. Until the marriage is so dissolved none can marry again. Conversion to Islam and marrying again would not, by itself, dissolve the Hindu marriage. Consequently, the second marriage of the apostate would be a marriage in violation of the provisions of the Act, and an illegal marriage *qua* his wife who married him under the Act and continues to be a Hindu. According to the Court:

> "The real reason for the voidness of the second marriage is the subsistence of the first marriage which is not dissolved even by the conversion of the husband. It would be giving a go-by to the substance of the matter and acting against the spirit and statute if the second marriage of the convert is held legal."

Apart from this, according to the court, such marriage is violative of the principles of justice, equity and good conscience.

The Court also addressed the need for a uniform civil code as envisaged by article 44 of the Constitution. Justice Kuldip Singh noted the earlier observation of the Supreme Court to enact a uniform civil code in *Md. Ahmad Khan* v. *Shah Bano*, AIR 1985 SC 945: 1985 Cr LJ 875: (1985) 2 SCC 556, and the observations of Justice O. Chinnappa Reddy in *Jordan Diengdeh* v. *S.S. Chopra*, AIR 1985 SC 935: (1985) 3 SCC 62: II (1985) DMC 42. The Court remarked:

> "Since in the absence of a uniform civil code there is an open inducement to a Hindu husband wanting to enter into another marriage to become a Muslim, courts need to adopt a construction of the laws resulting in denying the Hindu husband converted to Islam the right to marry again without having his existing marriage dissolved in accordance with law."

Order: The Court held that under the Hindu personal law, a marriage continued to subsist even after one of the spouses converted to Islam; the second marriage of the apostate would be a marriage in violation of the provisions of the Act and illegal marriage *qua* his wife who married him under the Hindu law and continues to be a Hindu; and the second marriage of a Hindu husband after his conversion to Islam is void in terms of section 494 of the Indian Penal Code and the apostate husband would be guilty of the offence of bigamy.

Comment: It is a welcome judgment which seeks to stop back-door entries to bigamous relationships under the garb of conversion.

Hindu Husband Converting to Islam and Marrying during Subsistence of First Marriage – Guilty of Bigamy

Lily Thomas v. *Union of India*,
AIR 2000 SC 1650: 2000 AIR SCW 1760: 2000 Cr LJ 2433

Issue: Can a married Hindu man convert to Islam and marry again during the subsistence of his first marriage? Would he be guilty of the offence of bigamy notwithstanding the fact that his new religion permits polygamy?

Facts: This case was a batch of writ review petitions filed by various persons and the Jamiat-Ulemi Hind and Muslim Personal Law Board; the judgment in *Sarla Mudgal v. Union of India*, AIR 1995 SC 1531: 1995 AIR SCW 2326: 1995 Cr LJ 2926 was also sought to be reviewed, set aside, modified, and quashed by way of review. It was contended that the judgment in *Sarla Mudgal* is contrary to fundamental rights as enshrined in articles 20, 21, 25 and 26 of the Constitution. The court found that no case for reviewing the judgment was made out. "The petition is misconceived and bereft of any substance", the Court remarked. The argument that the law declared in *Sarla Mudgal* cannot be applied to persons who have solemnized marriages in violation of the mandate of law prior the date of judgment, was also not accepted. The decision in that case holding that the second marriage of a Hindu husband after conversion to Islam without having his first marriage dissolved under law would be invalid, the second marriage would be void in terms of the provisions of section 494 of the I.P.C and the apostate-husband would be guilty of the offence under section 494, I.P.C does not lay down any new law, according to the court. The court had not laid down any new law but had only interpreted the existing law which was in force. It ruled:

> "It is settled principle that the interpretation of a provision of law relates back to the date of the law itself and cannot be prospective from the date of the judgment because concededly the court does not legislate, but only gives an interpretation to an existing law. We do not agree with the argument that the second marriage by convert male Muslim has been made offence only by judicial pronouncement. The judgment has only interpreted the existing law after taking into consideration various aspects argued at length before the Bench which pronounced the judgment. The review petition alleging violation of article 20(1) of the Constitution is without any substance and is liable to be dismissed on this ground."

The alleged violation of other fundamental rights was also held to be misconceived. Thus, in short, the review petition in respect of *Sarla Mudgal's* judgment was dismissed.

As regards the other petitions, the brief facts are: A Hindu man G.C. Ghosh, already having a subsisting marriage with Sushmita Ghosh under the Hindu Marriage Act and a Hindu woman Vanita Gupta, embraced Islam and got married under Islamic rites. For all practical purposes, they continued to be Hindus as was indicated from electoral records, records of the maternity hospital where the child was born to them and the visa application forms. The complainant wife alleged that her husband had only feigned conversion to solemnize a second marriage. She also stated that "though freedom of religion is a matter of faith, the said freedom cannot be used as a garb for evading other laws where the spouse becomes a convert to 'Islam' for the purpose of avoiding the first marriage". According to the court, the conversion was apparently not the result of exercise of the right of freedom of conscience but was feigned "subject to what is ultimately held by the Trial Court where G.C. Ghosh is facing the criminal trial, to get rid of his first wife to marry a second wife". The court remarked that in order to avoid the clutches of section of 17 of Hindu Marriage

Act if a person renounced his Hindu religion and converts to another religion and marries a second time, what would be the effect on his criminal liability? This is the question which the court took upon itself to consider. In other words, the *Court considered the effect of the second marriage* qua *the first marriage which continued to subsist in spite of the conversion of the husband to Islam, for the limited purpose of ascertaining his criminal liability under section 17 of the Hindu Marriage Act read with section 494 of the Indian Penal Code* (punishment for bigamy, and remarrying again during life time of husband or wife, respectively).

Order: The court referred to several judgments in great detail and held that if a husband already married under a monogamous law (the Hindu law in this case) marries a second wife under some other religious faith after converting to that religion, the offence of bigamy alleged by the Hindu wife would have to be investigated and tried in accordance with the provisions of the Hindu Marriage Act. Under the Hindu Marriage Act a bigamous marriage is prohibited and constitutes an offence under section 17, hence any marriage solemnized by the husband during the subsistence of that marriage, notwithstanding his conversion, would be an offence triable under section 17 of the Hindu Marriage Act read with section 494 of the Indian Penal Code. The court clarified that "the position under the Mohammedan Law would be different as, in spite of the first marriage, a second marriage can be contracted by the husband [subject to certain religious restrictions, *e.g.*, capacity to do justice between co-wives]........... This is the vital difference between Mohammedan Law and other personal laws. Prosecution under section 494 in respect of second marriage under Mohammedan Law can be avoided only if the first marriage was also under the Mohammedan Law and not if the first marriage was under any other personal law where there was prohibition on contracting a second marriage in the life-time of the spouse".

Thus *a distinction was made between a polygamous marriage by a Muslim under Muslim Law and one contracted by a non-Muslim after his conversion to Islam.*

The following observations of the court are pertinent in this context:

"Religion is a matter of faith stemming from the depth of the heart and mind. Religion is a belief which binds the spiritual nature of man to a supernatural being, it is an object of conscientious devotion, faith and pietism. Devotion in its fullest sense is a consecration and denotes an act of worship. Faith in the strict sense constitutes firm reliance on the truth of religious doctrines in every system of religion. Religion, faith or devotion are not easily interchangeable. If the person feigns to have adopted another religion just for some worldy gain or benefit, it would be religious bigotry. Looked from this angle, a person who mockingly adopts another religion where plurality of marriage is permitted so as to renounce the previous marriage and desert the wife, he cannot be permitted to take advantage of his exploitation as religion is not a commodity to be exploited."

As to the argument on behalf of the Jamaat-e-Ulema Hind and the Muslim Personal Law Board that the finding of the court in *Sarla Mudgal* to the effect that second marriage after conversion to Islam would be void would render the status of the second wife as that of a concubine and children born of that wedlock as illegitimate, the court clarified that the "issue is not involved in the present case". The court held:

> What we are considering is the effect of second marriage *qua* the first marriage which subsists in spite of conversion of the husband to Islam, for the limited purpose of ascertaining his criminal liability under section 17 of the Hindu Marriage Act read with section 494 I.P.C. As and when this question is raised, it would be open to the parties to agitate the legitimacy of such wife and children and their rights in appropriate proceedings or forum."

Camment: The cumulative effect of *Sarla Mudgal* and *Lily Thomas* is that upon conversion to Islam, the first marriage solemnized under monogamous law is not affected, and the second marriage after conversion to a religion which permits polygamy is void and punishable under section 17 of the Hindu Marriage Act and section 494 of the Indian Penal Code. This will put a check on conversions with ulterior motive. However, provision on the lines of sections 4 and 52 of the Parsi Marriage and Divorce Act, 1936 and section 43 of the Special Marriage Act, 1954 explicitly providing that such second marriage would be void, needs to be incorporated in the Hindu Marriage Act. The Hindu Marriage Act is silent on the status of the second wife of a man who converts and re-marries during the subsistence of his first Hindu marriage. All that section 17 says is that any marriage between two Hindus, solemnized after the commencement of this Act is void if at the date of such marriage either party had a husband or wife living, and the provisions of sections 494 and 495 of the Indian Penal Code shall apply.

MATRIMONIAL HOME/PROPERTIES/ RIGHT OF RESIDENCE

The issue of matrimonial home and division of matrimonial properties is a natural fall-out of any divorce litigation. The statutory law on the subject is, however, far from satisfactory. Several cases have come up before the courts, including the Apex Court, where courts have had occasion to decide on the issue. The recently enacted Protection of Women from Domestic Violence Act, 2005 seeks to provide protection to women in the context of matrimonial home. Several cases involving issue of division of matrimonial assetts/properties and matrimonial home have been discussed and analysed in this section of the book. The controversy/vagueness surrounding the concept of shared-household has been set at rest by the Apex Court in *inter alia, S.R. Batra* v. *Taruna Batra*, AIR 2007 SC 1118 (Del): 2007 AIR SCW 1088: (2007) 3 SCC 169.

Does a Husband have a Legal Right to Stay in Accommodation Allotted to his Wife?

B.R. Mehta v. *Atma Devi,*
AIR 1987 SC 2220: (1987) 4 SCC 183: JT 1987 (4) SC 474

Issue: Does a husband have a legal right to stay in a house allotted to the wife? Can a landlord evict the tenant/husband whose wife has been allotted government accommodation, under clause (h) of section 14(1) of the Delhi Rent Control Act?

Facts: Under section 14(1)(h) of the Delhi Rent Control Act, 1958, one of the grounds on which a landlord can seek eviction of his tenanted premises is that "the tenant has......built, acquired vacant possession of, or been allotted a residence............" In this case the wife, a government employee, was allotted a house. The landlord of the premises filed a suit for eviction on the said ground against the husband who was the tenant. The question before the court was whether the allotment of a house to the wife, in all circumstances disentitled her husband to retain the tenanted premises. The Additional Rent Controller, the rent Tribunal and even the High Court held that the husband, against whom the landlord had filed an eviction suit, was disentitled to retain the disputed premises as in view of the wife's getting government accommodation, he had acquired vacant possession of the residence, within the meaning of proviso (h) of section 14(1) of the Delhi Rent Control Act. Hence the husband's appeal.

Order: The court reversed the earlier orders and held that the wife's house was not the matrimonial house over which the husband could have a right, domain or occupation. Reference was made to *Revti Devi* v. *Kishan Lal*, 1970 Ren CJ 417 (Del): 1970 Ren CR 71, in which the Delhi High Court held that mere occupation of a new residence by the tenant without any legal right to do so would not be covered by the proviso. It stated:

> "If he goes to stay in the house of his wife, legally speaking, he has no right as such to stay and can be turned out from the house at any time by its legal owner, namely, the wife. There was no law according to which the husband and the wife could be deemed to be one person. Therefore, where proviso (h) required that the tenant himself should acquire vacant possession of another residence before he can become liable to eviction, the effect of its language cannot be whittled down by arguing that proviso (h) would apply even if it is not the tenant himself but his wife........were to acquire such residence."

Comment: With more and more women holding government jobs and entitled to government accommodation, and also going in for purchase of flats, the judgment is bound to create confusion. Can a wife evict a husband from her government or private accommodation if she has strained relations with him; and likewise, can a husband ask her wife to vacate, because as per the judgment of the Supreme Court, the wife's house is not the husband's and "legally speaking, he has no right as such to stay and *can be turned out from the house at any time by its legal owner, namely the wife*". It follows that the same rule would apply if the house belongs to the husband. It is important that the concept of matrimonial home and the rights of spouses therein be statutorily recognised as under the English law.

Divorced Wife's Right to be Impleaded as Respondent in Eviction Proceedings Filed by Landlord against her Husband

Ruma Chakraborty v. *Sudha Rani Banerjee*, JT 2005 (12) SC 134: AIR 2005 SC 3557: 2005 AIR SCW 4938

Issue: Does a divorced wife have a right to be impleaded as a respondent in eviction proceedings filed by a landlord against her husband?

Facts: A landlady filed a suit for eviction under section 13(1)(a) of the West Bengal Premises Tenancy Act, 1956, on the ground of subletting the premises without her consent. Her case was that the tenant's marriage with his wife having been dissolved by a decree of divorce, the wife was no longer a part of the tenant's family and therefore her (divorced wife's) occupation of the suit premises was in contravention of the statutory provisions of the Act. The husband had, admittedly left the suit premises but his minor children along with their mother as the custodian (*i.e.* the divorced wife) were living there. The tenant husband's defence, consequently, was that his children are entitled to the tenancy right and virtually can step into the shoes of the recorded tenant who is still alive and contesting even though he has walked out of the premises parting with exclusive legal possession to the wife. The appellant-wife filed an application under Order 1, rule 10(2) of the Civil Procedure Code for being impleaded as a defendant almost 8 years after the institution of the suit. Her application was dismissed by the Civil Judge. She then moved the Calcutta High Court in civil revision but her application was rejected there also; hence the appeal to the Apex Court.

It was argued on behalf of the appellant that being the divorced wife, she continued to enjoy the status akin to that of a licensee under her husband in respect of tenancy of her husband pursuant to the provisions of sections 3 and 18 of the Hindu Adoptions and Maintenance Act. (Under section 3, Hindu Adoptions and Maintenance Act, maintenance includes provision for residence; and under section 18 thereof, a Hindu wife is entitled to be maintained by her husband during her life-time).

Further, that by precluding her from contesting the suit, the suit would be decreed *ex parte* to the detriment of the appellant and her minor children who even after the decree of divorce, continue to have a right of residence in the suit premises and cannot be dispossessed except in accordance with law.

Another argument for the appellant was that the High Court had failed to appreciate that even after the divorce decree, the wife still has a right of maintenance which includes right of residence. Consequently, the appellant had a right of residence *vis-à-vis* her husband and so their stay in the rented accommodation of her husband could not be treated as illegal.

Another fact brought to the court's notice in support of the appellant's case was a notice issued by the landlady sent to the appellant stating that the appellant has been paying rent on behalf of the tenant and occupying the said accommodation. The appellant was, herein, requested to get a confirmation in writing from her husband that he had no interest in the said premises of the house and surrender the possession of the same to the landlady so that the agreement could be entered into with the appellant on fresh terms and conditions if she proposed to continue to stay. The letter/notice further stated that so long as these formalities were not completed, the occupation by the appellant was illegal and unauthorised. This letter, according to the appellant's counsel, amounted to recognition of the appellant as a sub-tenant by the landlady.

For the tenant, it was argued that there was no infirmity in the orders of the Trial Court and the High Court and *vide* Order 1, rule 10(2) of the CPC the appellant wife was not a necessary party whose presence was necessary for complete and effective adjudication of the case. It was further stated that, only parties notified as sub-tenants were to be made parties under section 13(2) of the Act *i.e.*, when the tenant obtains the prior written consent of the landlord under section 114 of the Act and both the tenant and sub-tenant have been notified under section 16(1). This was not the case of the appellant, it was argued. As to proper party, it was contended that the appellant had to show a direct legal interest as opposed to commercial or indirect interest in the subject-matter of litigation, especially in a suit relating to immovable property. In this case the appellant, not being a party to the contractual tenancy, could not claim any right, title or interest through her divorced husband and consequently she had totally failed to demonstrate any legal interest which would entitle her to be impleaded as a proper party also.

Order: After going through the various cases referred by the parties in support of their respective arguments, as also the statutory provisions in the C.P.C and the various laws entitling a wife to maintenance with right to residence as a component of maintenance, the court came to the following conclusions:—

(i) The husband, as the pleadings also indicated, never allowed his wife to occupy the suit premises and that she was in possession of the suit premises only as a custodian of the minor children of the defendant/husband/tenant and that the monthly rents payable were being paid on account and on behalf of the defendant.

(ii) The defendant himself was contesting the suit by filing a written statement and therefore the appellant wife had no *locus standi* to be impleaded in the suit either as a necessary or proper party in whose presence the suit ought to be or should be heard.

(iii) The mere payment of rent by her on behalf of the defendant could not create a jural relationship of landlord and tenant.

(iv) Since the original tenant was alive and contesting, the question of representing the interest of minor children did not arise.

(v) The court also held that the letter produced by the appellant in support of her argument that the landlady had recognised her as a sub-tenant, in fact did not support her case as she (the landlady) had clearly stated that unless the formalities were completed, the occupation of the premises by the appellant were illegal and unauthorised.

The court analysed the case of *B.P. Achala Anand v. S. Appi Reddy*, (2005) 2 SCALE 105: AIR 2005 SC 986: 2005 AIR SCW 934, in great detail in support of its finding that a divorced wife stands on a different footing than a deserted wife as divorce brings to an end the status of a wife as such. Whether or not she has the right of residence in the matrimonial home would depend on the terms and conditions on which the decree of divorce has been granted and provision for maintenance (including residence) has been made. In the instant case (*Ruma Chakraborty*) which was a divorce by mutual consent, the husband was ordered to pay a sum of ₹ 200 p.m. for maintenance of the minor children only. The appellant-wife, in the opinion of the court, by such consent order, had expressly waived her right to maintenance. In the words of the court:

"We are of the opinion that the court has no jurisdictional power to add a person as a party who is neither a necessary party nor a proper party. The appellant in the status of a divorcee cannot claim interest in the suit premises either independently or through her erstwhile husband and, as such, she cannot be held to say that she is a party without whose presence the court cannot adjudicate and pass a decree.......... The appellant is also not a person whose presence is necessary to enable the court to effectually and completely adjudicate all the questions involved in the suit."

Comments: This is yet another judgment by the Apex Court which indicates the need and urgency for adequate and effective law to protect a wife's requirement for shelter after divorce. Award of nominal amounts by way of maintenance do not meet such need.

Deserted Wife's Right to Contest Eviction Proceedings Filed by Landlord against her Husband

B.P. Achala Anand v. S. Appi Reddy,
(2005) 2 SCALE 105: AIR 2005 SC 986: 2005 AIR SCW 934

Issue: (i) Can a deserted wife be permitted to become a party to an eviction suit filed by the landlord against her husband-tenant if she apprehends that the husband is contesting out or not contesting diligently so as to prejudicially affect her interests.

(ii) Does a divorced wife have no right whatsoever to continue occupying the tenanted premises which has been the matrimonial home?

Facts: The appellant was the legally wedded wife of the respondent. When their relationship got estranged, he deserted her. The matrimonial home was a tenanted premises owned by defendant. The husband left behind his wife and children in the tenanted premises and walked away to reside in a lodge. In 1991, proceedings for dissolution of marriage by decree of divorce were initiated and on December 3, 1998, the marriage stood dissolved by a decree of divorce by mutual consent. In November 1991, the landlord served a notice upon the tenant-husband for eviction and proceedings initiated on the ground of *bona fide* self- requirement and also, that the rent was in arrears. However, because of the strained relations with his wife and the fact that he himself had discontinued living in the tenanted premises, the husband was not serious in contesting the eviction suit. The appellant-wife, therefore, moved an application under Order 1, rule 10 of the C.P.C, seeking her own impleadment in the eviction proceedings so as to defend the same. This application was rejected by the Trial Court; hence the wife's appeal to the High Court which was allowed. The wife was permitted to be brought on record as a defendant subject to her depositing a sum of Rs 10,000 towards arrears which she did. The eviction suit was disposed of by the Trial Court which ordered partial eviction of the tenants. Feeling aggrieved, the landlord preferred a revision petition in the High Court. The High Court held that there is no relationship of landlord and tenant between the landlord and the 'wife' (appellant); that tenancy vested only in the 'husband' who had given away the contest. Accordingly, the order of partial eviction was set aside and an order of eviction under section 21(1)(a) of the Karnataka Rent Control Act, 1961, made. The appellant wife, thereupon, filed the present appeal by special leave. The husband did not file any appeal.

Order: The main issue for determination was whether the deserted wife had a right to contest the eviction suit. A Hindu wife is entitled to be maintained by her husband; she is also entitled to remain under his roof and protection; and also separate residence if by reason of the husband's conduct or by his refusal to maintain her in her own place or residence, or for other just cause, she is compelled to live apart from him. Right of residence is a part and parcel of wife's right to maintenance. This has been statutorily recognised by section 18 coupled with section 3(b) of the Hindu Adoptions and Maintenance Act. As to wife's right to maintenance (which includes residence) *vis-a-vis* the provisions of the Rent Control law, the latter makes provision for protection of tenant not only for his own benefit but also for the benefit of all those who are entitled to reside therein. A decree or order for eviction would deprive not only the tenant of such protection but members of his family (including the spouse) will also suffer eviction. So long as the tenant defends himself, the interests of the family members merges with that of the tenant and they too are protected. The tenant cannot, by collusion or by deliberate prejudicial act, give up the protection of the law to the detriment of his family members. According to the court, so long as a decree of eviction has not been passed, the members of the family are entitled to come to the court and seek leave to defend and thereby contest the proceedings and such leave may be granted by the court if the court is satisfied that the tenant was not defending—by collusion, connivance or neglect—or was acting to the detriment of such persons. While no Indian authority on the point of wife's right to contest eviction proceedings was brought to notice, the court referred to various English authorities on the point. On the issue of a wife's right to residence in the matrimonial home, the court referred to a few cases. *Dr. Abdur Rahim Undre* v. *Padma Abdur Rahim under*, AIR 1982 Bom 341: I (1982) DMC 204 is significant. The marriage between the parties was subsisting in law but broken down irretrievably. The husband filed a suit, *inter alia*, for injunction, restraining the wife from entering the matrimonial house. The court held that an injunction subject to certain terms and conditions could be granted. The parties, on account of seriously estranged relations between them could not be forced to live together. The flat was big enough to allow the parties to live there separately. The court earmarked separate portions for the husband and the wife to live separately and restrained the wife from entering the portion in occupation of the husband who was an eminent surgeon, so that he could have peace of mind to enable him to discharge his duties as a surgeon. [How would the court have decided if the flat was not big enough? One wonders !]. In addition, the husband was directed to pay a certain amount of money by way of maintenance to the wife.

In *Bharat Heavy Plates and Vessels Ltd.*, AIR 1985 AP 207: (1985) 2 Andh LT 127: (1985) 3 Com LJ 1, the husband was an employee in a company and was allotted a quarter in which he lived with his wife and children. When differences developed between the spouses, the husband left the company quarter and also wrote to the company to terminate the lease which was in his favour. Apprehending eviction, the wife went to court for protection seeking injunction restraining the company from evicting her and the children, which was granted.

The High Court upheld the order. It held that the quarter was meant to be used by the employee husband who was under an obligation to provide shelter to the wife and children. The husband and the company had both recognised the quarter to be the matrimonial home wherein the wife too was residing. The amount of rent was directed to be deducted from the salary of the husband.

After referring to the above mentioned cases and a few more, the court held that a deserted wife, who has been or is entitled to be in occupation of the matrimonial home, is entitled to contest the suit for eviction filed against her husband in his capacity as tenant subject to satisfying two conditions, *viz.*, (i) that the tenant has given up contest or is not interested in contesting the suit and such giving up by the tenant-husband shall prejudice the deserted wife who is residing in the premises, and (ii) the scope and ambit of the contest or defence by the wife would not be on a footing higher or lower than that of the tenant himself.

So long as, by availing the benefit of the provisions of the Transfer of Property Act and rent control legislation, the tenant would have been entitled to stay in the tenancy premises, the wife too can continue to stay exercising her right to residence as a part of right to maintenance, subject to compliance with all such obligations including the payment of rent to which the tenant is subject. This right of the wife, however, comes to an end with the wife losing her status as wife consequent upon decree of divorce and the right to occupy the house as part of right to maintenance coming to an end. The court remarked (at p. 995):

> "Divorce is termination of matrimonial relationship and brings to an end the status of wife as such. Whether or not she has the right of residence in the matrimonial home, would depend on the terms and conditions in which the decree of divorce has been granted and provision for maintenance (including residence) has been made. In the event of the provision for residence of a divorced wife having been made by the husband in the matrimonial home situated in the tenanted premises, such divorced wife too would be entitled to defend in the eviction proceedings, the tenancy rights and rights of occupation thereunder in the same manner in which the husband-tenant could have done and certainly not higher or larger than that."

In the present case, during the pendency of the eviction proceedings in the High Court, a decree of dissolution of marriage by mutual consent was passed on December 3, 1998. The terms and conditions of such settlement have not been brought on record by the appellant wife. It is not the case of the wife that she is entitled to continue her residence in the tenanted premises by virtue of an obligation incurred by her husband to provide residence for her as a part of maintenance. Consequently, it was held that she cannot be allowed to prosecute the appeal and defend her right against the claim for eviction made by the landlord.

Comment: It is a very significant judgment which makes one point very clear and that is, that a deserted wife can be a party to eviction proceeding filed by the landlord against her husband-tenant if she apprehends that the husband is acting in a manner which is prejudicial to her interests. However, as for a divorced wife, it would only depend on the terms and conditions of settlement made by the husband. If the husband had not made any provision for her residence in the tenanted matrimonial home, then she has no right whatsoever. As to a wife's right to stay in the tenancy premises, according to the court, she can continue to stay exercising her right to residence as a part of right to maintenance, but that right comes to an end with the wife losing her status as wife consequent upon divorce and *the right to occupy the house as part of right to maintenance coming to an end. Thus, it has been made explicit that the wife has no right to stay in the matrimonial home after divorce.* It is time that serious thought be given to provide a law to protect the interests of divorced women in this regard.

Property Belonging to In-laws: Estranged Wife cannot Re-enter as Matter of Right

S.R. Batra v. Taruna Batra,
AIR 2007 SC 1118 (Del): 2007 AIR SCW 1088: (2007) 3 SCC 169

Issue: Issues of great significance in the context of matrimonial home and shared household were involved in this case, *viz*:

(i) Would the matrimonial home shift after the husband has shifted to another place leaving the wife?

(ii) Can an estranged wife who has left the home and also removed her belongings therefrom, as of right, re-enter the house belonging to her in-laws even if the husband is no longer residing there?

(iii) Is the property belonging to the in-laws a "shared-household" within the meaning of sections 2(5), 17 and 19(1) of the Protection of Women from Domestic Violence Act, 2005 so as to entitle the wife to re-enter into it as a matter of right in view of the fact that after marriage she had lived there with her husband for sometime and even though the husband is no longer living there but has shifted to another house owned by him?

These were the issues in this special leave appeal before the Apex Court against the judgment of the Delhi High Court, *Taruna Batra* v. *S.R. Batra*, AIR 2005 Del 270: 2005 (2) CCC 692: I (2005) DMC 282.

Facts: The parties were married in the year 2000 and started living in the house belonging to the husband's parents. After sometime, the couple shifted to the second floor of the house. However, relations between them deteriorated and the wife moved to her parent's house whereas the husband shifted to his own flat in Ghaziabad. Thereafter, the husband filed a divorce petition. The wife, on the other hand filed FIR's against the husband, his parents and the married sister-in-law under provisions of sections 406, 498A, 506 coupled with section 34 of the India Penal Code pursuant to which they were arrested and were bailed out only after three days. Later when the wife tried to enter the house she found the main entrance locked. She consequently filed a suit for mandatory injunction directing the respondents in-laws, their son-in-law and her husband, to open the main entrance to allow her in; she also applied for permanent injunction restraining them from breaking open the locks of her second floor matrimonial home and removing her goods therefrom. The respondents contested the suit and applied for a mandatory direction to the petitioner to hand over possession of the second floor of the property. They argued, *inter alia*, that:

(i) The petitioner was not residing in the second floor of the house since 2002; on the contrary, she trespassed upon the property and on inspection of the portion it was noted on February 23, 2003 that except for a blanket, there was nothing else there.

(ii) The son had purchased some property in Ghaziabad and had shifted there and hence that was now the matrimonial home of the petitioner.

(iii) In law, the use of the second floor property by the petitioner was merely permissive as the entire property was owned by the respondent (parents) and the petitioner had no right to reside in that property, except with their permission.

After going through the facts and hearing the contentions of the parties, the Trial Court held that the petitioner was "admittedly" in possession of the second floor and both the parties should refrain from interfering in each other's right to have access to the common passage. On appeal against this order, the senior civil judge held that the petitioner was not residing in the second floor as her goods were not there, nor did the premises have electricity and water, further, he held that since the husband of the petitioner was not there but living elsewhere, the matrimonial home cannot be where only the wife was residing. Also, that the wife had no right over the property belonging to persons other than her husband and therefore the wifes application for interim injunction deserved to be dismissed. It was, however, directed that the wife may visit the property "once or twice in a month alongwith local police to see that the locks in suit premises were intact or not". The parties were directed to maintain *status quo*. Both the parties were aggrieved by the order and hence filed respective petitions before the High Court under article 227 of the Constitution.

The court proceeded on the assumption that the wife was not residing in the second floor of the house but her constructive possession was not seriously doubted; the court also believed that the husband was now not residing there. On these assumptions, the issue was whether the second floor of the house was the petitioner wife's matrimonial home or not. If so, then she had a right to stay there, otherwise not. The court pointed out that unlike as in England where the Matrimonial Homes Act, 1983 protects the interests of the spouses, there is no law in India. This fact was also pointed out by the Supreme Court in *B.R. Mehta v. Atma Devi*, AIR 1987 SC 2220: 1987 4 SCC 183: JT 1987 (4) SC 474.

According to the court in *Taruna Batra*, the accepted practice in India is that after marriage the bride resides with her husband, usually in the parental home of the husband. A woman would, therefore, have a right to remain in that matrimonial home as long as she is married and if she is 'obliged' to leave that home, she would be entitled to obtain an injunction from an appropriate court protecting her right and preventing her from being thrown out. Consequently, according to the court, going by the general accepted practice, the ground floor of the house was the matrimonial home of the petitioner and her husband Amit Batra where they stayed after marriage even though the entire building belonged to the husband's mother, and later on they shifted their matrimonial home to the second floor of that house with the consent of the owners/appellants. It was argued on behalf of the appellants that the husband having shifted to Ghaziabad that would be the matrimonial home now and he was prepared to have the petitioner reside with him there.

Dismissing this argument the High Court held that in view of the husband's divorce petition (which was dismissed in default) "it is extremely unnatural to expect the petitioner to treat Amit Batra's Ghaziabad residence as her matrimonial home." In other, words, the, court ruled, "Amit Batra shifting from the second floor of the said property to Ghaziabad would not *ipso facto* shift the petitioner's matrimonial home to Ghaziabad." The court also relied on *Anu Seth* v. *Rohit Narain Seth*, (2000) 87 DLT 486: 2001 (3) Civil LJ 308 where it was held that mere fact that the husband shifts out of the matrimonial home to set up a home somewhere else does not, in all cases, mean that his new place of residence becomes the matrimonial home.

The respondents (in the High Court) had contended that the property was owned by then and they had only permitted the petitioner to reside there-in and such permissive user did not give her a right to reside in that property. Dismissing the argument the court held that the respondents were no strangers but parents of the husband and parents-in-law of the petitioner. The theory of permissive user could not be advantageously used by them in the Indian context particularly when the son and the petitioner actually lived with them on the ground floor and thereafter on the second floor of the same house with full knowledge and consent with a view to shift their matrimonial home from the ground floor to the second floor. The court consequently held that the petitioner was entitled to continue to reside in that house which was her matrimonial home and nobody could deny her access or interfere in her possession thereof.

Hence the present appeal before the Apex Court. Referring to *B.R. Mehta* v. *Atma Devi*, AIR 1987 SC 2220: 1987 4 SCC 183: JT 1987 (4) SC 474 it was held that, unlike the Matrimonial Home Act, 1967 in England there is no law in India. The court in that case however hoped that (at p. 196):

"it may be that with change of situation and complex problems arising it is high time to give the wife or the husband a right of occupation in a truly matrimonial home, in case of strained relationship between the husband and the wife."

These observations of Justice Sabyasachi Mukharji (for himself and Justice G.L. Oza) were, however, according to Justice Markandey Katju in the present case, "merely an expression of hope and it does not lay down any law. It is only the Legislature which can create a law and not the court. The courts do not legislate, and whatever may be the personal view of a judge, he cannot create or amend the law, and must maintain judicial restraint" (at para 15)

In view of this, it was held that the rights which may be available to a wife can only be against the husband and not against the father-in-law or mother-in-law. In this case the house belonged to the mother-in-law and not to the husband and hence the wife could not claim any right to live in that house.

Further, support was sought by the wife under the provisions of the Protection of Women from Domestic Violence Act, 2005 which protect a woman from being evicted from the shared household, and shared household is wide enough to include a household where the person aggrieved lives or at any stage had lived in a domestic relationship. [*see* sections 2(5), 17 and 19(1) of the Act]

If was contended that in this case since the respondent wife had in the past admittedly lived in the property in question so the said property is her shared household. Rejecting this argument the Court held that if such pleas were to be accepted it will mean that wherever the husband and wife lived together in the past would become shared household and the wife can well insist in living in these houses merely because at some stage she had stayed there with her husband. "Such a view would lead to chaos and would be absurd," the Court remarked.

Order: Allowing the appeal the Court held that shared household would mean only a house belonging to or taken on rent by the husband or the house which belongs to the joint family of which the husband is a member. In this case the property neither belonged to the husband nor was it taken on rent by him nor a joint property of which the husband is a member. Hence it is not a shared household and the respondent cannot claim any right therein, the Court held.

Comment: The Protection of Women from Domestic Violence Act, 2005 seeks to protect the interest of women no doubt but, in the words of the Apex Court "it needs to be given an interpretation which is sensible and which does not lead to chaos in society." The need to have a proper law on matrimonial home and the separated wife's right therein, however, cannot be underscored.

Estranged Wife's Right of Residence in the Matrimonial House

Komalam Amma v. *Kumar Pillai Raghavan,* AIR 2009 SC 636: (2008) 14 SCC 345: 2008 AIR SCW 7799

Issue: Can a husband defeat an estranged wife's right of residence in the house after obtaining a decree of declaration of ownership and possession of the house?

Facts: A husband filed a suit for declaration of ownership/title in respect of property where the wife and their two daughters were residing, and for recovery of possession. The Trial Court and the first appellate court decreed the suit of the husband for declaration of title over the property on the ground that the said property was purchased by him out of his own funds and no funds were provided by the wife. The order was challenged before the High Court.

It was argued that being the wife she was entitled to reside there along with the daughter. It was also contended that she had obtained a charged decree for maintenance over the property and the impugned decree will result in conflicting decrees defeating the statutory charge under section 39 of the Transfer of Property Act, 1882. The High Court however did not accept this plea and held that the decree for possession passed in favour of the husband would not come in the way of the wife's right to enforce the charge. It was further held that in view of the estranged relations between the spouses, the wife cannot still claim a right of residence in the matrimonial home so as to resist a decree for possession. Thus, the second appeal was dismissed. Hence the present appeal. For the appellant, reference was made to *Mangat Mal* v. *Punni Devi*, (1995) 6 SCC 88: 1995 AIR SCW 3885: AIR 1996 SC 172 where the issue was whether maintenance encompasses provision for residence. The case was considered in the context of section 14(1) of the Hindu Succession Act, 1956 and it was held that the concept of maintenance must include provisions for food and clothing and take into account basic need of roof over the head. Provision for residence may be made either by giving a *lump sum* in money or property in lieu thereof. Reference was made to section 3(b)(i) of the Hindu Adoptions of Maintenance Act, 1956 which defines maintenance to include "in all cases, provision for food, clothing, residence, education and medical attendance and treatment."

B.P. Achala Anand v. *S. Appi Reddy*, (2005) 2 SCALE 105: AIR 2005 SC 986: 2005 AIR SCW 934 was also relied upon where the Court observed:

> "A Hindu wife is entitled to be maintained by her husband. She is entitled to remain under his roof and protection; she is also entitled to separate residence if by reason of the husband's conduct or by his refusal to maintain her in his own place of residence or for other just cause, she is compelled to live apart from him. Right to residence is a part and parcel of a wife's right to maintenance. This right has come to be statutorily recognised with the enactment of the Hindu Adoptions and Maintenance Act. Section 18 provides for maintenance of wife. Maintenance has been so defined as to include therein provision for residence amongst other things.

Order: The court held that these aspects were not considered by the High Court. The matter was therefore remitted to the High Court to consider the issue by re-hearing the appeal in the light of *Mangat Mal's* and *Achala Anand's* cases.

Damages to Wife

Mukund Martand Chitnis v. *Madhuri Mukund Chitnis*, AIR 1992 SC 1804: 1992 AIR SCW 2025: 1993 (1) Bom CR 401

Issue: A husband who resorts to mudslinging and character assassination of the wife is liable to be criminally prosecuted and also pay damages to the wife.

Facts: The relations between the husband and wife were not cordial. The husband continually resorted to mudslinging and character assassination; he also lodged a complaint of theft of ornaments against her. Upon his complaint, the wife's house was searched and all this caused a great deal of embarrassment, harassment and mental agony to her. She filed a complaint under section 498A of the Indian Penal Code (cruelty by husband or his relatives) and also under section 500 of the Indian Penal Code (for defamation). The Trial Court sentenced the husband to imprisonment for six months and a fine of ₹ 3,000. The sessions court set aside the sentence of imprisonment and imposed a fine of ₹ 6,000. On further appeal, the High Court convicted the husband under section 498A (IPC) and sentenced him to pay a fine of ₹ 30,000 and in default, to suffer rigorous imprisonment for two months and a fine of ₹ 6,000. It remarked *Madhuri Mukund Chitnis v. Mukund Martand*, 1992 Cr LJ 111: 1991 (1) Bom CR 683: 1991 Bom LR 157:

> "....the charges made against the present petitioner by the husband and criminal proceedings instituted by him and the vigour with which these were repeated and carried on, constituted cruelty of an intense degree. It is the horrifying number of atrocities committed in the name of dowry and unfortunate number of wife burning incidents that brought section 498A of the I.P.C on the statute book. The section however is specially worded in order to encompass even this class of cruelty committed through the litigative process."

Against this, the husband filed an appeal before the Supreme Court.

Order: The court advised the parties to arrive at an amicable settlement. The husband agreed to deposit ₹ 30,000 and the appeal against conviction under section 500 of the IPC was compounded on the husband paying ₹ 1 Lakh. The husband was also required to file an unqualified apology in the Court within a week "for the mental strain and stress caused to the wife on account of various defamatory allegations made against her." In addition to this, the husband's brother was asked to file an undertaking that the husband will not file any proceedings – civil or criminal – against her for any averments, allegations or statements made by her in any of the proceedings. The court further ordered that if the husband failed to file the apology, or the brother failed to file the undertaking and also, if they failed to deposit the amount within the prescribed period, then the conviction orders passed by the High Court would be confirmed and the husband would be liable to be arrested.

Comment: The judgment is indicative of the court's concern to protect the honour and dignity of a wife against a husband who makes reckless allegations to harass her. As aptly remarked by the court. "This should prove to be an eye-opener to those who believe that they can get, away by casting aspersions on a woman to serve their ends and silence her" (at p. 1806).

Damages to Deserted Wife by NRI Husband

Neeraja Saraph v. Jayant Saraph,
(1994) 6 SCC 461

Issue: This was a suit for damages by a wife married to an NRI who later deserted her and obtained annulment of the marriage from an American Court.

Facts: A non-resident Indian man got married in India and deserted the wife after the honeymoon. Initially, he persuaded her to give up her job and join him. After a few months he obtained an annulment decree from an American court. The wife filed a suit for damages in *forma pauperis* for ₹ 22 lakh against the husband and father-in-law. The same was decreed *ex parte* by the Trial Court. The father-in-law filed an appeal in the High Court which stayed the operation of the decree subject to the father-in-law depositing rupees one lakh in a bank, within a month and permitting the wife to withdraw ₹ 50,000. Dissatisfied, the wife filed an appeal before the Supreme Court.

Order: The Supreme Court gave an interim relief and directed that a sum of rupees three lakhs be deposited within two months. She was entitled to withdraw rupees one lakh without any security and the remaining amount was to be deposited in a nationalised bank with interest thereupon to be paid to her. It was further stated that if the case was not decided within a reasonable time, she would be entitled to withdraw further amounts. Justice Sahai suggested the need for enacting a law to deal with situations where NRIs marry in India and desert their wives. A reference was made to the Foreign Judgment (Reciprocal Enforcement) Act, 1993 under section 1 of which the UK issued Reciprocal Enforcement of Judgment (India) Order, 1958, and the Indian and Colonial Divorce Jurisdiction Act, 1940. The court suggested legislation incorporating the following provisions:

(a) no marriage between an NRI and an Indian woman solemnized in India may be annulled by a Foreign Court;

(b) provision for adequate alimony to the wife in the property of the husband, both in India and abroad;

(c) decree of Indian courts should be executable in foreign courts, both on principle of comity and by entering into reciprocal agreement like section 44A of the Civil Procedure Code which makes foreign decrees executable.

Comment: The judgment assumes significance in view of growing number of NRI marriages. The glamour attracts the parties but not unoften only to suffer later.

Paternity/DNA Tests

Gautam Kundu v. State of West Bengal,
AIR 1993 SC 2295: 1993 AIR SCW 2325: 1993 Cr LJ 3233

Issue: Can a court order a blood group test to determine paternity of a child as a matter of course.

Facts: The parties were married in 1990 according to Hindu rites. They lived together for sometime whereafter the wife left the matrimonial home to reside with her parents to prepare for her Higher Secondary Examination. Meanwhile, she conceived. When the husband and his parents came to know about it they insisted that she undergoes abortion which she refused and a female child was born. She was meted out cruel treatment both physically and mentally. She filed a petition for maintenance under section 125 of the Cr. P.C. for herself and the daughters which was granted *ex parte* by the Chief Judicial Magistrate @ of ₹ 300 p.m. for the petitioner wife and ₹ 200 for the child. A revision filed against this by the husband was dismissed. Thereafter, he filed an application for blood group test of the child to prove that he was not the father of the child. This application was dismissed on the grounds that there were other methods in the Evidence Act to disprove paternity-*viz.*-non-access etc., and moreover it is settled law that medical test cannot be conclusive of paternity. The husband again filed a revision against this before the High Court which was dismissed too holding that birth of a child during the continuance of marriage is a conclusive proof of its legitimacy *vide* section 112 of the Evidence Act except where non-access is proved. Hence the special leave petition by the husband.

Order: The husband's petition was dismissed. The court significantly analysed the legal position in U.K. and U.S.A. as also several cases along with statutory and judicial position in the Indian context. Wherever such application – for blood group test – is made in order to have roving enquiry, such prayer cannot be entertained, the court held, approving *Bhartiraj v. Sumesh Sachdeo*, AIR 1986 All 259. Section 114 read with section 4 of the Evidence Act debars evidence except in cases of non-access, for disproving presumption of legitimacy and paternity; the presumption is rebuttable though. The court must carefully examine as to what would be the consequences – whether it will have effect of branding the child a bastard and mother as unchaste. Reference was made to *Dikhtar Jahan v. Md. Farooq*, AIR 1987 SC 1049: 1987 Cr LJ 849: (1987) 1 SCC 624. In the present case (*Gautam Kundu*), the only purpose for seeking the test was to avoid maintenance. Dismissing the husband's application, the court observed, "the stigma of illegitimacy is very severe and we have not any of the protective legislations as in England to protect illegitimate children. No doubt, this may in some cases require a husband to maintain children of whom he is probably not their father, but the Legislature alone can change the rigour of the law and not the court."

Further, according to the court, such test involves restraint on personal liberty and no one can be compelled for the same. In any case, in this case the only purpose seeking the test was to avoid paying maintenance and hence it could not be allowed.

Comment: Doubting a child's paternity and seeking blood group test is a serious matter which could have far reaching consequences on the child's psychology and his/her social and legal status; it also amounts to casting aspersions on the woman's character. Hence, courts are not inclined to easily grant permission for such tests.

DNA Test on Discharged Foetus to Establish Paternity
X v. Z,
AIR 2002 Del 217: 2002 (96) DLT 354: I (2002) DMC 448

Issue: Can a party seek and obtain from the court, permission to have a DNA test conducted on a foetus conceived and aborted during the subsistence of the marriage? This was the issue involved in this case.

Facts: This was a wife's petition for divorce under section 9 of the Divorce Act on grounds of cruelty and adultery by the husband. The husband denied the allegations and made a counter-charge against the wife alleging adultery. According to him, the wife had an affair with one J resulting in her pregnancy. It was a tubular pregnancy which was got aborted and due to an abnormality the tubular foetus was preserved by the All India Institute of Medical Sciences (AIIMS) for medical research. When the husband came to know that the records and slides had been preserved, he filed an application for directing the pathology department of the AIIMS to prepare slides containing her blood cells and blocks of the operation case of wife's abortion and order DNA test to ascertain if he was the father. The wife resisted the same on the ground that it would be an invasion of her constitutional right to liberty and privacy under articles 20(3) and 21 of the Constitution of India.

Order: After going through the entire evidence and case-law, the court held that the right of privacy is not absolute, and moreover, in this case the foetus had already been discharged and no more a part of her body. There was therefore no question of invasion of her personal liberty or privacy. Allowing the husband's application, the court directed that requisite slides and blocks be prepared for conducting the DNA test for ascertaining if the petitioner was the father.

Comment: DNA test can be allowed in exceptional cases; further, right of privacy is not absolute moreso when the fetal material is already discharged and not a part of the person's body.

Child's Application for DNA Test to Establish Parentage

Master X v. Y,
AIR 2003 Del 195: 2003 (69) DRJ 21: 2003 Mat LR 561

Issue: Can a DNA test be ordered as a matter of course to determine the paternity of a child in an application seeking declaration of child's legitimacy?

Facts: This was an application by a minor through his next friend and mother seeking interim maintenance and also seeking declaration that the defendant is his father and thus the minor is entitled to all rights and interests as his son. A direction that the defendant should undergo a DNA test to establish paternity was also sought so that "the cloud over the plaintiff's parentage is removed and the child is able to lead a normal life".

The plaintiff's case was that his mother and the defendant were working in the same office and developed intimacy; the mother was allured into marriage by the defendant who was an already married man; the marriage was kept secret as per the defendant's desire; and that he later deserted her and disowned them. It was argued that the plaintiff was in his adolescent years and going through anguish and trauma, and suffering from a feeling of insecurity, he is socially ostracized and questions regarding his father are asked by his friends and all this is having adverse psychological impact on the child and affecting his all round development.

Order: The court went through the entire evidence available in the case. Documentary evidence by way of medical records of the hospital where the son was born was also available. These records indicated that the plaintiff's mother was married to someone else and in the hospital records the name of the mother was mentioned as the plaintiffs', but the defendant was not named as the father. The court held that the "documentary evidence falsify averments in the plaint and raises considerable doubt on the conduct and credibility of the plaintiff's mother". The court accepted the defendant's plea that "........merely because a scientific test is available to determine parentage, the same is not to be directed to be undergone by the parties unless there is overwhelming evidence and circumstances to justify such a direction; a test such as the 'DNA test' cannot be directed on bold allegations." The application of the plaintiff was accordingly dismissed as no case for direction to the defendant to undergo DNA test or pay interim maintenance to the defendant was made out.

Comment: It is a very unfortunate case where the child has to suffer because of the [mis]deeds and irresponsible conduct of the parents – Law, however, has to take its course.

Court's Power to Order DNA Test – Discretionary

S. Thangavelu v. S. Kannammal,
AIR 2005 Mad 106: 2005 (25) All Ind Cas 496:
2004 (4) Mad LJ 508

Issue: Can a court direct parties to undergo medical tests or give sample of blood for DNA test for establishing paternity of a child?

Facts: The parties were married in 1984 and a male child was born in 1988. The husband filed a petition for dissolution of marriage in 1998. Pending this, he filed an application under section 45 of the Indian Evidence Act and section 151 of the CPC for DNA test. According to him, the marriage with the respondent was never consummated and the respondent's minor son was not his offspring. The subordinate judge found that there was no *bona fide* in the claim and dismissed the petition. Hence the appeal. The husband's counsel relied on *Sharda* v. *Dharampal*, AIR 2003 SC 3450: 2003 AIR SCW 1950: (2003) 4 SCC 493, which held that the court had ample power to order for medical examination like DNA test and it would not affect or interfere with the personal liberty as enshrined in article 21 of the Constitution.

Order: The court held that even though it had ample powers to direct the parties to undergo medical tests or give sample of blood for DNA test, but the party who seeks such relief must have a strong *prima facie* case. In this case, no strong *prima facie* case was made out. The present petition was filed by the husband after 14 years of marriage alleging that the minor son was not his. Besides, it was in evidence that the wife had filed a suit for partition claiming share for her son in the joint family property well before he filed the divorce petition. The petitioner, according to the court, had raised a defence disputing the paternity of the child to get over the claim made in the said partition suit. It was only a desperate attempt to harass the respondent, the court observed. The order of the subordinate judge refusing the husband's application was upheld.

Comment: DNA test for establishing paternity of a child is a sensitive matter which affects the mind and psychology of the child too. It is correct on the part of the court not to concede to these applications unless there is a strong *prima facie* case.

DNA/paternity Test to Establish Adultery

Sunil Trambake v. Leelavati Trambake,
AIR 2006 Bom 140: 2006 (42) All Ind Cas 527:
II (2006) DMC 461

Issue: Is denial of paternity a good ground to order paternity test on a child, more so when the child is not even a party to the matrimonial proceedings.

Facts: The husband filed a petition for divorce against the wife under section 13 of the Hindu Marriage Act. The wife resisted the same and alleged that the husband was leading a life of adultery after deserting her; she further alleged that he had married one, Meena and also had a son Rupesh from this marriage. She therefore filed an application for a DNA test to prove her allegations. The Trial Court ordered the test on the ground that in the interest of justice the DNA test was necessary to give on opportunity to the wife to establish her case that the petitioner husband was living in adultery. The husband filed an appeal against it.

Order: It was argued by the appellant that the scope of enquiry in the matrimonial petition was limited and the Trial Court will have to decide whether he is entitled to divorce as prayed for and for that DNA test to determine paternity was not required; further, that such test cannot be ordered as a matter of routine and in this case, Meena and Rupesh were not a party to the proceedings filed by him and ordering the test is violation of principles of natural justice. The wife on the other hand justified the Trial Court order stating that the test was necessary to prove that the husband was living in adultery, had deserted her and so was not entitled to the divorce he had sought; further, that if he is not submitting to the paternity test, an adverse inference may be drawn. The High Court rejected her arguments. It held that such test can be allowed only in exceptional cases in the interest of the child. In this case, the wife was seeking the test not in the interest of the child but in her own interest to establish her case against the husband's divorce petition. Further, according to the court, the second wife and the son were not even party to the case. An order made behind their back is a clear violation of principles of natural justice. The husband's appeal was thus allowed and the Trial Court order directing DNA test was set aside.

Comment: Tests to establish the paternity of a child is a very sensitive issue and should indeed not be ordered as a matter of routine. These can affect the psyche of the child and have far reaching consequences on his social and legal status. There can be other documentary and evidentiary proofs to establish paternity and resort to DNA testing should be the last option when the interests of the child so demand.

Note. *See* also *Gautam Kundu* v. *State of West Bengal,* AIR 1993 SC 2295: 1993 AIR SCW 2325: 1993 Cr LJ 3233; *Master X* v. *Y,* AIR 2003 Del 195: 2003 (69) DRJ 21: 2003 Mat LR 561; *S. Thangavelu* v. *S. Kannammal,* AIR 2005 Mad 106: 2005 (25) All Ind Cas 496: 2004 (4) Mad LJ 508.

INJUNCTIONS

Injunction Against Second Marriage: Not Allowed

Umashankar Prasad Singh v. Radha Devi,
AIR 1967 Pat 220

Issue: Whether a wife's suit for injunction restraining the husband to marry another girl is maintainable under any of the provisions of the Hindu Marriage Act, 1955?

Facts: A wife filed a suit for injunction alleging that her husband was contemplating to marry another lady, in contravention of the Hindu Marriage Act, 1955. The reliefs she sought were that the defendant first party, *i.e.*, the husband, should be permanently injuncted from marrying any other girl, specially the second defendent whom he was about to marry and *secondly*, that the defendant second party be permanently restrained from marrying the defendant first party. She also impleaded the father and the grandfather of the intended wife of defendant 1 as defendants 3 and 4 and against them also asked for a permanent injunction restraining them from giving defendant 2 in marriage to defendant 1.

The husband raised objections to the jurisdiction and maintainability of the suit. The District Judge, Muzaffarpur, however, held that the petition was maintainable and the court had jurisdiction to proceed with the case. Hence the appeal by the husband.

The question that was considered was whether the petition filed by the wife can be said to be a petition under the Hindu Marriage Act. She had described that as matrimonial suit and called that as a complaint. According to the court, under sections 9, 10, 11, 12, 13 and 14 of the Act a petition can be filed under different circumstances and for different kinds of reliefs and purposes. "None of those petitions can cover one of the present nature", the court observed.

For the wife it was argued that her plaint or petition was under section 17 of the Act which says:

> "Any marriage between two Hindus solemnized after the commencement of this Act is void if at the date of such marriage either party had a husband or wife living, and the provisions of sections 494 and 495 of the Indian Penal Code shall apply accordingly."

This argument was repelled on the ground that the section (section 17) does not authorise any petition to be filed in regard to any marriage between two Hindus, either party having a spouse living. The provision under this section makes such marriage, if solemnized after the commencement of the Act to be void from the date of such marriage and makes that act punishable under sections 494 and 495 of the Indian Penal Code. "This is a declaratory provision and not a remedial one", according to the court.

Order: The court held that, under the scheme of the Hindu Marriage Act the reliefs available are, restitution of conjugal rights, judicial separation, divorce, or a decree of nullity in case of a void or voidable marriage. The petition filed by the wife does not claim any of these above mentioned reliefs and does not fall in any of the aforesaid categories. The District Court as defined in section 3(b) of the Act, is a court of exclusive jurisdiction for only matters falling within the Act. Hence the petition filed by the wife is not maintainable and the District Judge had no jurisdiction to either entertain or try the same.

Comment: Prior to 1978, *vide* sub-section (5) of section 6, there was a provision for injunction in cases where the consent of a guardian was required for an intended marriage and in the interest of the bride the court thought it necessary to prohibit the intended marriage. The court made a reference to this provision to establish the point that where the Legislature thought appropriate to provide for injunction, it did so, and in a situation as the one in the present case, there was no provision for injunction.

It may be pointed out that section 6 of the Act has been repealed in 1978.

Injunction Against Second Marriage: Allowed

Kirti Sharma v. Civil Judge, Senior Division, Etah,
AIR 2005 All 197: 2005 (59) All LR 53: 2005 (2) All WC 1741

Issue: Whether an injunction restraining a spouse to remarry can be issued even though the Hindu Marriage Act, 1955, makes no provision for it?

Facts: The plaintiff filed a suit for restitution of conjugal rights under section 9 of the Hindu Marriage Act alongwith an application for interim injunction restraining the defendant (wife) from contracting second marriage. An interim injunction was issued. This order has been challenged in the present writ petition under article 226 of the Constitution.

Order: The writ petitioner's case was that she was kidnapped at gun point and that she was not married to the plaintiff and as such the suit was not maintainable and the injunction could not be granted. The court found, on evidence and statements made by witnesses, that the defendant admittedly stayed with the plaintiff after a marriage ceremony under Arya Samaj rites for more than one month but the marriage was not consummated as both parties had decided not to consummate the marriage till their relationship was approved by wife's parents. Allegations that the defendant was kidnapped and held by force, was not substantiated, according to the court.

Further, for the wife it was argued that the Hindu Marriage Act was a special legislation and the provision under Order 39, Rule 1 would not apply for granting injunction restraining a wife from remarrying. The court, however, did not accept this argument also and held: "No doubt Hindu Marriage Act is a special Act but if it is silent on the issue of injunction, the place can be occupied by general legislation especially so to restrain a party from performing a void act." [*viz.*, second marriage which is void under section 11 if performed in contravention of section 5(i) (already subsisting marriage)]

Comment: Even though the Hindu Marriage Act makes no provision for issuing injunctions, yet, that does not prevent the court from restraining a party from doing an act which is illegal or void under the provision of the Hindu Marriage Act.

Injunction Against Forced Entry into Matrimonial Home
Pratiksha v. Pravin Tapaswi,
2002 (2) HLR 551 (MP)

Issue: Can a wife be restrained from forcibly entering the matrimonial house?

Facts: A husband filed a divorce petition against his wife on the ground of cruelty. Alongwith this, he also filed an application under Order XXXIX, rules 1 and 2, read with section 151 of the Civil Procedure Code (CPC), 1908, praying that the wife be restrained from forcibly entering the house. His allegation was that the wife had left the house without his knowledge, taking away her jewellery, and apprehends that she may come again and create problems and also attempt/commit suicide and implicate him. The Trial Court allowed his application and an injunction was granted against the wife in exercise of its inherent powers under section 151 of the C.P.C. Against this, the wife filed the present appeal.

Order: It was argued for the wife that under the Hindu Marriage Act the only reliefs available are restitution of conjugal rights, judicial separation, divorce or nullity (or other ancillary reliefs) but no declaratory relief or relief by way of injunction has been provided. For this argument the counsel for the appellant wife relied on *inter alia, Umashankar Prasad Singh* v. *Radha Devi*, AIR 1967 Pat 220 wherein it was held that there was no provision in the Hindu Marriage Act for granting an injunction against the other party restraining him or her from contracting another marriage. As against this, it was argued by the defendant that by virtue of section 21 of the Hindu Marriage Act the provisions of the C.P.C. are applicable to the petitions under the Hindu Marriage Act and all proceedings under the Hindu Marriage Act shall be regulated, as far as may be, by the C.P.C. Thus in view of section 21 of the Hindu Marriage Act, the injunction application under section 151 of the C.P.C. would be tenable before the court hearing the petition and the court can exercise the powers for grant of injunction. A court under section 151 of the C.P.C. has inherent powers to pass such orders as may be necessary to meet the ends of justice or to prevent abuse of the process of the court [Relying on *Braj Kishore Sinha* v. *Rekha Sinha*, I (1992) DMC 331: AIR 1992 Pat 173: 1991 (2) BLJR 990; *Bajrang Rai* v. *Ismail Mian*, AIR 1978 Pat 339: 1978 BLJR 497: 1978 Pat LJR 519; *Chitra Sengupta* v. *Dhruba Jyoti Sengupta*, AIR 1988 Cal 98: II (1987) DMC 162: 1987 Mat LR 306; *Anita Karmokar* v. *Birendra Chandra Karmokar*, AIR 1962 Cal 88: 65 Cal WN 786: ILR (1962) 2 Cal 23]. After analyzing the cases and the facts and circumstances of the case, the court held that the provisions contained in the CPC have been, by virtue of section 21 of the Hindu Marriage Act made applicable to different types of petitions under the Act and, by virtue of this section, the court is not powerless or precluded to issue temporary injunctions. According to the court, an injunction can be issued to a Hindu husband or wife from contracting a second marriage during the subsistence of the first. The Hindu Marriage Act does not expressly create any bar on seeking preventive relief of injunction in proceedings filed under the Hindu Marriage Act. Dismissing the wife's appeal, it was held that under inherent powers, the courts hearing petitions regarding conjugal rights and matrimonial obligations can issue injunctions and preventive orders.

Comment: Notwithstanding that the Hindu Marriage Act makes no provisions for injunctions or restraining orders, courts do have inherent powers to pass such orders in the interest of justice of the case.

Injunction Against Using Husband's Surname after Divorce

Neelam Dadasaheb Shewale v. *Dadasaheb Bandu Shewale*, I (2010) DMC 344 (Bom)

Issue: The issue involved in this case was whether a husband could seek injunction restraining his wife from using his surname after divorce and whether this was a matter which the Family Court could take cognizance of. Another issue involved was whether a party (in this case the wife) could be granted permission to be represented by his constituted attorney.

Facts: This was a husband's interim application on wife's application for enhancement of maintenance under section 25 of the Hindu Marriage Act, 1955. The husband sought injunction restraining his divorced wife from using his surname. His argument was that by using the ex-husband's name or surname there is always a possibility of people being misled that she is still the wife when in fact she is not. He was in the police department and alleged that the wife, after divorce was misusing his name. The suit was resisted on the grounds, *inter alia*, that the Family Court had no jurisdiction in the matter to issue injunction; and further that she had filed an appeal against the divorce decree obtained by the husband and until that decree becomes final, she continues to be his wife and so entitled to use his name as well. The wife also sought permission to be represented by her constituted attorney on the ground that she was ill, does not know English, that she has been mentally and physically tortured by her husband and would not be able to stand court proceedings. The Family Court conceded the husband's application and refused the wife's application for being represented by her constituted attorney. Hence her appeal.

Order: The High Court confirmed the Family Court order and held that the matter of injunction in this case was clearly one arising out of marital relationship within the meaning of section 7(1)(d) of the Family Courts Act and so the Family Court had jurisdiction to entertain it. It also confirmed the injunction restraining the appellant wife from using the husband's surname after divorce. As to the wife's application for permission to be represented by her constituted attorney, the court held that under section 13 of the Family Courts Act, no party is entitled, as of right, to be represented by a legal practitioner; however, if the court considers it necessary in the interest of justice, it may seek assistance of legal expert as *amicus curiae*. This right however does not extend to the parties' constituted attorney. The general law of procedure under Order 3, rule 1 of the Civil Procedure Code as also the special laws contained in Bar Councils Act and Bombay Pleaders Act would apply in the Family Court. The court observed; "if constituted attorney of all the parties are allowed to appear, the court would be overrun by any number of unqualified unenrolled persons." Thus, the wife's appeal was dismissed and the orders of the Family Court, Baroda, were upheld.

Comment: The order injuncting the woman from using her husband's surname after divorce does not sound to reason. A wife legally and legitimately acquires the husband's surname after marriage she lives by that name for considerable period and builds up an identity by that name. Stripping her of that name and identity because of apprehension of misuse of husband's name after divorce, is unfair. If there are apprehensions of misuse or *mala fides*, there are other recourses available to prevent them. Orders such as these would surely dissuade wives from ever adopting the husband's surname after marriage. Though no one hopes, expects or foresees break up of the marriage yet, there is no guarantee against it. A female should not be made to keep changing her names with change in her marital status. This would also give rise to anomalous situations where the mother and the children of marriage have different surnames.

LIVE-IN RELATIONSHIPS

Right to Maintenance in a Live-in Relation
Chanmuniya v. *Virendra Kumar,*
(2010) 10 SCALE 602: 2010 AIR SCW 6497

Issue: The significant issue involved in this case was as to the interpretation of the term 'wife' for purposes of maintenance in the context of live-in relationships.

Facts: This was a claim for maintenance under section 125 of the Cr. P.C. by the claimant who was living with the respondent for a considerable period of time. The same was resisted on the ground that the claimant was not the wife and so not entitled to maintenance.

Order: In a detailed analysis of the case law and statutory provisions, the provisions of the Protection of Women from Domestic Violence Act, 2005, in particular, the court held that a broad and expansive interpretation should be given to the term "wife" to include even those cases where a man and woman have been living together as husband and wife for a reasonably long period of time and strict proof of marriage *vide* section 7 of the Hindu Marriage Act should not be a pre-condition for maintenance under section 125 of the Cr. P.C. so as to fulfil the true spirit of the beneficial provisions of maintenance under section 125. The court further observed that such an interpretation would be a just application of the principles enshrined in the Preamble to our Constitution, namely social justice and upholding the dignity of the individual.

Drawing support from the provisions of the Protection of Women from Domestic Violence Act, 2005, the court pointed out that this Act gives a very wide interpretation to the term "domestic relationships" as to take it outside the confines of marital relationship in the nature of marriage. Therefore a woman in live-in relationships is also entitled to all the reliefs in the said Act. According to the court if relief by way of maintenance can be awarded in cases of live-in relationships, they should also be allowed in proceedings under section 125 of the Cr. P.C. In other words, a man who lived with a woman for a long time even though without having undergone legal necessities of a valid marriage, should be made liable to pay if he deserts her. The man should not be allowed to benefit from the legal loopholes by enjoying the advantages of a *de facto* marriage without undertaking duties and obligations. However, in view of the divergence of judicial opinion on the interpretation of the word "wife", the court requested the chief justice to refer the issue to a larger Bench. The questions to be decided are whether long period of living together would raise presumption of valid marriage; whether strict proof of marriage is essential for maintenance claim under section 125 Cr. P.C. having regard to the provisions of the DVA; and whether marriage performed according to customary rites and ceremonies without strictly fulfilling requisites of section 7(1) of the Hindu Marriage Act or any other personal law, would entitle a woman to maintenance under section 125 Cr.P.C.

Comment: While the Protection of Women from Domestic Violence Act, 2005, has endorsed and recognised live-in relationships, yet, as held by the Apex Court in *D. Velusamy* v. *D. Patchaiammal,* AIR 2011 SC 479 *infra,* the relationship should be within the parameters of the law and not in violation of the same.

Property Rights of Children of Live-ins
Bharatha Matha v. *R. Vijaya Renganathan,*
AIR 2010 SC 2685: 2010 AIR SCW 3503: (2010) 6 SCALE 53

Issue: Live-in relationships are being gradually accepted socially and even legally recognised under the provisions of the Protection of Women from Domestic Violence Act, 2005. The issue involved in this case was as to the property rights of children born of such relationship.

Facts: This was a suit for property by a sister 'P' claiming, share of her brother 'M' on the ground that he died unmarried and intestate. The opposite party 'R' on the other hand claimed the same on the ground that she had a live-in relationship with 'M' and had two children from him and so they are legal heirs entitled to property of M. The fact was that 'R' was an already married female with the marriage subsisting and she entered into a live-in relationship with 'M'. It was contended on her behalf that a presumption of marriage could be drawn in view of their long live-in relationship and the children born to them would be legitimate and hence entitled to coparcenary properties of their father 'M'. The Trial Court and the first appellate court recorded a categoric finding of fact that since 'R' was already married, her husband was alive and there had been no legal separation between them, therefore the question of live-in-relation of 'R' with 'M' could not arise nor a presumption of marriage based on long cohabitation. On appeal, however, the Madras High Court reversed the factual findings of the courts below and held that live-in relationship between the said two parties would lead to a presumption of marriage between them. Hence the present appeal before the Apex Court which held that the High Court erred in interfering with the factual findings of the courts below which were based on appreciation of the entire evidence. A reappraisal of findings is permissible only if the findings recorded by the lower courts is perverse or suffers from the vice of irrationality which was not the case here. Further, according to the Supreme Court it was not appropriate for the High Court to re-appreciate the evidence in second appeal as no substantial question of law was involved therein. Thus it was held that there could be no presumption of marriage.

As regards rights of children in the property, the Court analysed section 16 of the Hindu Marriage Act and a few cases, inter alia, S.P.S. Balasubramaniyam v. Suruttayam @ Andali Padayachi, AIR 1992 SC 756: 1992 AIR SCW 441: 1992 (3) SCJ 468; P.E.K. Kalliani Amma v. K. Devi, AIR 1996 SC 1963: 1996 AIR SCW 2337: (1996) 4 SCC 76; Rameshwari Devi v. State of Bihar, AIR 2000 SC 735: 2000 AIR SCW 273: (2000) 2 SCC 431; Jinia Keotin v. Kumar Sitaram Manjhi, (2003) 1 SCC 730; Neelamma v. Sarojamma, (2006) 9 SCC 612 and held that the fiction of legitimacy created by section 16 of the Hindu Marriage Act is limited to the extent of right in property of parents only. In the instant case (Bharatha Matha) it was nowhere pleaded that the suit property was the self-acquired property of 'M'; further, it was evident from the records that there was no partition of the joint family properties; in other words, that the property was copercenary property and as such the children were not entitled to the same.

Order: Children born of a live-in relationship where even long cohabitation cannot lead to presumption of marriage between their parents in view of non-compliance of mandatory provisions of the Hindu Marriage Act, were held not to be entitled to the coparcenary property of 'M' in this case. In the context of inheritance, section 16 of the Hindu Marriage Act confers only limited rights to children born of void or voidable marriage.

Comment: Even while long cohabitation might give rise to presumption of marriage and the Protection of Women from Domestic Violence Act, 2005 recognises live-in relationships yet these have to be within the parameters of law. A relationship in contravention of statutory requirements does not confer legal status on the parties.

Maintenance Rights in Live-in Relationship
D. Velusamy v. D. Patchaiammal,
AIR 2011 SC 479

Issue: The issue involved in this case was as to maintenance right under section 125 of the Cr.P.C. of a woman who had lived for some years with an allegedly married man.

Facts: The respondent, D, filed a petition for maintenance under section 125 of the Cr.P.C. alleging that she was married to V in 1986 and that two or three years thereafter, he deserted her. The appellant V however resisted the same alleging that he was already married to one Lakshmi as per the Hindu Marriage Act and also has a grown up son and so there was no question of marriage with the respondent. The Family Court, however, came to a finding that D was indeed married to V and so entitled to maintenance. This findings was upheld by the Madras High Court, hence the appeal. To begin with, the finding of the Family Court and High Court were arrived at without making Lakshmi a party to the suit. According to the court, no such declaration about Lakshmi not having been married to 'V' could be made without making her a party and hence such declaration as to her marital status is wholly *null* and *void* as it would be violative of the rules of natural justice. Consequently, no declaration could be validly given holding that the appellant was married to 'V' because if Lakshmi was his wife then he could not have married 'V' without divorcing Lakshmi. Even though the definition of "wife" is wide enough to include a divorced wife too but a second wife whose marriage is void on account of subsistence of first marriage is not a wife who could be deserted or divorced so as to be covered under section 125 of the Cr. P.C. Furthermore, the court referred to the provisions of the Protection of Women from Domestic Violence Act, 2005 also, specially the definition of "domestic relationship" which includes not only the relationship of marriage but also a relationship in the nature of marriage. Thus the law recognises not only relationship of marriage but also relationship in the nature of marriage; this, according to the court has been done by Parliament taking notice of a new social phenomenon which has emerged in our country known as live-in relationship. Though rare yet in India, but common in some other countries. The Apex Court pointed out that relationship in the nature of marriage is akin to common law marriage which too require compliance with certain conditions, *viz.*

(a) The couple must hold themselves out to society as being akin to spouses.

(b) They must be of legal age to marry.

(c) They must be otherwise qualified to enter into a legal marriage, including being unmarried.

(d) They must have voluntarily cohabited and held themselves out to the world as being akin to spouses for a significant period of time.

Thus, according to the court, not all live-in relationships will amount to a relationship in the nature of marriage to get the benefits of the Act of 2005, *inter alia*, maintenance.

In the present case there was no finding by the Family Court on the question of whether the appellant and the respondent had lived together for a reasonably long period of time in a relationship which was in the nature of marriage; *secondly*, the declaration that the appellant was married to the respondent and not to Lakshmi was also held to be *null* and *void*; and *thirdly*, there was no satisfactory explanation for the delay of twelve years in filing the maintenance petition. The defendant was allegedly deserted in 1988 and she filed the maintenance petition in 2001.

Order: In view of all the above, the impugned judgment of the High Court and the Family Court was set aside and the matter remanded to Family Court judge to decide the matter afresh in accordance with law and in the light of the observations made by the Supreme Court.

Comment: The Protection of Women from Domestic Violence Act, 2005 has endorsed and given legal recognition to live-in relationships in the nature of marriage. Such relationships, however, have a potential of confusion and uncertainty on various issues, which though might get streamlined in due course with more and more judicial pronouncements. However to recognise a relationship to be one "in the nature of marriage" strict compliance of conditions for a valid marriage need to be adhered to.

If may be pointed out that the court in this case, analysed various cases from America *e.g., Taylor* v. *Fields,* (1986) 224 Cal Rpr 186; *Devaney* v. *L'Esperance,* 195 NJ 247 (2008), and also from India, *e.g., Vimla* v. *Veeraswamy,* (1991) 2 SCC 375: 1991 AIR SCW 754; *Savitaben Somabhai Bhatiya* v. *State of Gujarat,* AIR 2005 SC 1809: 2005 Cr LJ 2141: 2005 AIR SCW 1601; *S. Khushboo* v. *Kanniammal,* (2010) 5 SCC 600: 2070 AIR SCW 2770: 2010 Cr LJ 2828.

Note. Palimony (Maintenance) decisions of courts in USA have also been discussed in this judgment at paras 24 to 31, pages 482-483.

———

MAINTENANCE

Matrimony entails certain rights and obligations and maintenance is one of them. A wife is entitled to claim maintenance under the personal laws as well under the provisions of the Code of Criminal Procedure, 1973. While under the personal laws an application for maintenance can be made only if there are matrimonial proceedings under the statute, in case of maintenance under the provisions of the Cr. P.C., there need not be any matrimonial litigation. It may be mentioned here that under the Hindu personal law, there is an additional statute – the Hindu Adoptions and Maintenance Act, 1956. Under section 18 of the Act a Hindu wife is entitled to live separately from her husband without forfeiting her claim to maintenance, provided her separate living is justified as provided in the statute.

Apart from maintenance for wives our laws provide for maintenance for parents children and other dependents. The Hindu personal laws make provision for maintenance of husbands as well.

The present section of the case book enumerates various cases on maintenance for wives, parents, children and other dependents.

MAINTENANCE FOR WIVES AND ALLIED ISSUES

Order of Dismissal of Main Decree not "any decree" under Section 25

Chand Dhawan v. Jawaharlal Dhawan,
(1993) 3 SCC 406: 1993 AIR SCW 2548: 1993 Cr LJ 2930

Issue: Do the words "any decree" in section 25 of the Hindu Marriage Act include an order of dismissal of the main petition?

Facts: The parties were married in 1972 and had three children. In 1985, a petition for divorce by mutual consent was filed in the court purported to have been filed jointly by the consent of both the spouses. As per the requirement of section 13B of the Act the petition was kept pending for six months. On coming to know of the petition, the wife filed objections. According to her, she never consented to the divorce and the husband had duped her into signing some blank papers on a false pretext, which he used in the petition. However, some understanding was arrived at, under which the wife agreed to join the husband. Both the parties gave a joint statement and the divorce petition was got dismissed. Barely three months later, the husband filed a divorce petition on several grounds. The wife filed an application under section 24 for litigation expenses and maintenance *pendente lite*, which was granted. Since the husband did not make the payments, the divorce proceedings initiated by him were stayed under orders of the High Court of Allahabad. The wife then filed a petition under section 25 for grant of permanent alimony on the ground that she was facing starvation whereas the husband was a multi-millionaire. She also filed a petition under section 24 for maintenance *pendente lite* and litigation expenses. The Additional District Judge allowed her petition and granted a sum of ₹ 6,000 as litigation expenses and ₹ 2,000 per month as maintenance *pendente lite* from the date of application. The husband filed a revision petition against it in the High Court. The wife also approached the court seeking enhancement of the amount. Both the revision petitions were referred to a larger Bench. The husband's objection was that the wife's application was not maintainable since there was no decree under the Act and in the absence of "any decree" no order under sections 24 or 25 of the Act could be passed. This objection was sustained whereupon wife filed an appeal in the Supreme Court. The issue was whether the words "any decree" in section 25 includes an order of dismissal of petition. Reference was made to several cases. Some courts held that permanent alimony can be granted only when any decree is passed and the relief sought is given; if the relief is not granted then it means that there is no decree and in such situation maintenance cannot be awarded. On the other hand, there were cases supporting the argument that the words "passing any decree" imply both—the allowing as well as dismissal of the main petition. After an analysis of the case law, the Supreme Court came to the conclusion that the wife's application for maintenance was not maintainable as the wife had withdrawn her consent to the divorce petition and the same was dismissed. An order of dismissal of a petition, does not disturb the marriage nor confers or takes away any legal character or status.

According to the court (at p. 416):

"Without the marital status being affected or disrupted by the Matrimonial Court under the Hindu Marriage Act, the claim of permanent alimony was not to be valid as ancillary or incident to such affectation or disruption."

Order: The wife's claim for maintenance under the Hindu Marriage Act was dismissed. The court, however, held that the wife's claim in such a situation can be agitated under the Hindu Adoptions and Maintenance Act, 1956 since section 18(1) of this Act entitles a wife to maintenance even without any disruption in her marital status. It observed (at p. 418):

"Like a surgeon, the matrimonial court, if operating, assumes the obligation of the post-operatives, and when not, leaves the patient to the physician."

Comment: The judgment is bound to create problems for wives whose husbands want to get rid of them and file petitions which, for whatever reasons, get dismissed. The dismissal of the petition may only go to show that the case of the husband against the wife is unfounded. What is the fault of the wife in such case? *Secondly*, while Hindus have a law like the Hindu Adoptions and Maintenance Act where a wife can seek maintenance even without any disruption of her marital status, what about women from other communities. They have to bank upon the provisions of the Cr. P.C. only.

Petition for Nullity of Marriage – Whether Maintenance *pendente lite* can be Claimed

Sushila Viresh Chhawda v. *Viresh Nagshi Chhawda*, AIR 1996 Bom 94: 1996 (2) Bom CR 531: 1996 (1) CCC 700

Issue: Can litigation expenses and interim maintenance under section 24 be claimed, even when the main petition is for nullity of the marriage?

Facts: A husband filed a suit for nullity of marriage under the Hindu Marriage Act on the ground of fraud. His allegation was that the wife was suffering from a big ovarian tumour which had to be surgically removed along with ovary just eight days after the marriage and this fact of the tumour was concealed at the time of marriage. The wife filed an application for interim maintenance under section 24 of the Hindu Marriage Act. This was opposed by the husband on the ground that the marriage was void and in view of the fraud committed by her, she was not entitled to interim maintenance. The Family Court rejected the wife's application without even going into its merits. Hence her special leave petition under article 227 of the Constitution.

Order: The High Court set aside the order of the Family Court. It held that the wording of section 24 is very clear that an application for maintenance can be filed in any proceeding under the Act. It observed:

> "When a fact of marriage is acknowledged or proved, alimony follows subject, of course, to the discretion of the court in the matter having regard to the means of the parties and it would be no answer to the claim....... that the marriage was void *ipso jure* or was voidable."

The court further remarked:

> "The direction of interim alimony and expenses of litigation under section 24 is one of urgency and it must be decided as soon as it is raised and then only the matters in controversy can be gone into.......and the law sees that nobody is disabled from prosecuting or defending the matrimonial case by starvation or lack of funds........."

Comment: The purpose of section 24 is to provide sustenance and financial assistance for pursuing the litigation. The provision is available in case of any proceeding under the Act and not confined to any particular proceeding.

Whether Proceedings under Limitation Act are "Proceedings" for Purpose of Section 24

Ghari Lal v. Surjit Kaur,
AIR 1997 J&K 72: 1997 Marri LJ 434

Issue: Can proceedings under section 5 of the Limitation Act, 1963 for condonation of delay be termed as proceedings for purposes of section 24 of the Hindu Marriage Act?

Facts: The husband obtained an *ex parte* restitution decree against the wife. The wife filed an application for setting aside the same after the period of limitation had expired. She also filed an application under section 5 of the Limitation Act for condonation of the delay. Pending this application, she filed an application under section 30 of the Jammu and Kashmir Hindu Marriage Act (4 of 1980) for maintenance. (This section of the Jammu and Kashmir Act is in *pari materia* with section 24 of the Hindu Marriage Act.) The husband objected to her application on the ground that proceedings under section 5 of the Limitation Act could not be considered as proceedings for purposes of grant of maintenance. His plea was, however, rejected. Hence his appeal.

Order: The husband's appeal was admitted. The High Court relied on *Puran Chand* v. *Kamla Devi*, AIR 1981 J&K 5: 1980 Marri LJ 473: 1981 Mat LR 222, where it was held that maintenance is awardable on monthly basis "during the proceedings" which connotes that maintenance is admissible from the time of commencement of the proceedings till their termination. According to the court, proceedings in Trial Court would naturally commence from the date on which issues are framed and since there can be no stage of framing of issues in an application seeking condonation of delay in proceedings under section 5 of the Limitation Act, section 30 of the J&K Hindu Marriage Act cannot apply. Accordingly, the court held that application for condonation of delay was not a proceeding within the meaning of section 30 of the Jammu and Kashmir Hindu Marriage Act (or section 24 of the Hindu Marriage Act). While conceding that this provision seeks to help a litigating spouse who does not have sufficient means to maintain himself/herself, the court observed:

"But at the same time, this provision cannot be used in such a way that it acts as a weapon of sword for harassment of the other party."

Comment: Strict interpretation of the provision can work hardship on the party sometimes. Suppose a wife obtains an *ex parte* order and the husband files an application for setting aside and condonation of delay for seeking restoration of the order only to harass the wife, would the court deny her expenses to fight out the application? Each case needs to be decided on its own facts and circumstances.

Maintenance under Section 25, when Appeal against Divorce Pending

Surendra Kumar Bhansali v. *Judge, Family Court,*
AIR 2004 Raj 257: 2004 (19) All Ind Cas 685: 2004 (3) CCC 194

Issue: Is an application under section 25 of the Hindu Marriage Act maintainable while an appeal against divorce is pending?

Facts: A husband obtained a decree of divorce against his wife. After the decree, the wife filed an application for permanent alimony under section 25. She also filed an appeal against the divorce decree. The husband challenged the maintenance application on the ground that in view of an appeal against the divorce decree which was pending, no order for maintenance under section 25 of the Hindu Marriage Act could be passed. A maintenance order was, however, passed. He filed a writ petition in the High Court under articles 226 and 227 of the Constitution with a prayer that the order passed by the Family Court allowing maintenance be quashed.

Order: The husband's appeal was dismissed and the High Court held that an application under section 25 can be made at the time of passing of the decree or at any time subsequent thereto. In this case, since the divorce petition by the husband was decreed and the marriage dissolved, the wife's application was held to be tenable. According to the court, the relief could have been refused if the main petition had been dismissed as per the decision of the Supreme

Court in *Chand Dhawan* v. *Jawaharlal Dhawan*, (1993) 3 SCC 406: 1993 AIR SCW 2548: 1993 Cr LJ 2930, but not simply on the ground that an appeal against the divorce decree was pending.

Comment: An appeal against a decree of divorce does not disentitle a party from filing an application for maintenance under section 25 of the Hindu Marriage Act. Such application, in terms of the provision of section 25, can be filed at the time of the passing of the decree or *at any time subsequent thereto*. An appeal against the decree does not take away this right.

Marriage Void: No Maintenance

Yamunabai Anantrao Adhav v. *Anantrao Shivaram Adhav*, AIR 1988 SC 644: JT 1988 (1) SC 193: 1988 Cr LJ 793

Issue: A woman who marries an already married man is not entitled to maintenance under the provision of section 125, Cr. P.C., because such marriage is void, even though the wife was kept in the dark of the husband's earlier marriage.

Facts: The petitioner got married to a person who had a living spouse. She filed an application for maintenance under section 125 of the Cr. P.C.

Order: Since the husband already had a lawful living, spouse, he could not have married the petitioner under the law which enjoins monogamy. The marriage being void under section 11, being in contravention of the provision of section 5(1) of the Hindu Marriage Act the wife was not entitled to maintenance, according to the court. The expression "wife" under section 125 means a legally wedded wife. The explanation to the section includes a divorced wife also but, according to the court, a woman could not be a divorcee unless there was a marriage in the eyes of law preceding that status. The fact that the wife was not informed of the first marriage, did not in the opinion of the court, make any difference. Thus, in view of the voidness of the marriage, the wife was held to have no status and hence not entitled to maintenance from the husband. Even though she was defrauded she could not rely on the principle of estoppel so as to defeat the provisions of the Act.

Comment: This is a very unfair interpretation of the law. A man who conceals or misrepresents that he is unmarried cannot be allowed to take advantage and then say that since he was already married, he owes no liability towards the second wife.

N.B.: In *Bakulbai* v. *Gangaram*, 1988 (1) SCALE 188, also the Apex Court held that a wife whose marriage was void because of the subsistence of the husband's earlier marriage, was not entitled to maintenance from the husband. This was also a wife's petition for maintenance under section 125 of the Cr. P.C., *See* also *Suresh Khullar* v. *Vijay Khullar*, AIR 2002 Del 373.

Marriage Void: No Maintenance but Damages Granted

Ranjit Kumar Bhattacharyya v. *Sabita Bhattacharyya,*
AIR 1996 Cal 301: 1996 (1) Cal LJ 465: 1996 (1) Hindu LR 520

Issue: Is a woman who is not a legal wife but has lived with a married man as his wife, entitled to damages even though not for maintenance?

Facts: A married man lived with a woman for several years inducing her to believe that she was his wife, and also had children from her. Later they fell apart. The woman filed a suit for maintenance under section 18 of the Hindu Adoptions and Maintenance Act, 1956 and also under section 125 of the Cr. P.C. The man denied marriage and his liability to maintain her. The Additional District and Sessions Judge held that in view of the long and continuous cohabitation between the parties, there was a strong presumption of marriage and that mere absence of proof regarding marriage rites could not dislodge the presumption unless there was proof of insurmountable obstacles to a valid marriage. A decree of maintenance for ₹ 500 per month was thus passed. Hence the husband's appeal.

Order: It was argued that section 18 of the Hindu Adoptions and Maintenance Act makes no provision for maintenance from a 'husband' with whom a woman has entered into a void marriage. This contention was accepted by the court and it was held that the applicant was not entitled to maintenance. The court, however, ordered the man to pay damages. According to the court, it is obvious that the man must have induced her to believe that she is his wife; "for such immoral activities, the appellant should not be spared altogether, though the damage that had been caused, both physically and mentally, could not be compensated in any way," the court remarked. He was, accordingly, directed to pay Rs. 30,000 by way of damages.

Comment: This case is yet another example of how a woman can be defrauded and duped into a relationship and the man can just get away because under the law they are not husband and wife. There is a need for a law which should impose liability on such erring males who defraud women into a legally void marriage only to abandon them later and then take advantage of their own illegal/immoral act. As rightly remarked by the court in this case, no amount of damages can compensate the damage caused to the woman.

Compliance of All Essential Ceremonies to Establish Legal Marriage not Essential under Section 125 Cr. P.C

Dwarika Prasad Satpathy v. *Bidyut Prava Dixit,*
2000 Cr LJ 1 (SC): AIR 1999 SC 3348: 1999 AIR SCW 3844

Issue: Whether compliance of essential ceremonies is necessary to establish legal marriage, in maintenance proceedings under section 125 Cr. P.C.? The courts have held that some form of marriage is enough to uphold a wife's right for maintenance under this section.

Facts: The wife became pregnant by the non-applicant before she was married to him. When after conceiving she insisted that the non-applicant should marry her, he was reluctant. However, on the intervention of some relatives and friends, a marriage was performed in presence of witnesses in Lord Jagannath Temple. The wife was in advanced stage of pregnancy and there was no observance of customary rites and ceremonies for the marriage. Immediately after the impugned marriage, the wife was left at the house of her parents where she delivered within one week of the marriage. Ever since they stayed separately. On the wife's petition for maintenance under section 125 of the Cr. P.C., for herself and the child, the husband denied the existence of a valid marriage though he did not dispute the paternity of the child. The issue of validity of the marriage was the crux of the case. After analysing the facts, circumstances and the law, as also cases on the point, the court ruled in favour of the petitioner wife.

Order: The court held that the validity of the marriage for the purpose of summary proceedings under section 125 of the Cr. P.C., is to be determined on the basis of evidence brought on record by the parties. It observed that the standard of proof of marriage in such proceedings is not as strict as is required in a trial of offence of bigamy under section 494 of the I.P.C. Once it is admitted that the marriage procedure was followed, then it is not necessary, according to the court, to further probe into whether the said procedure was complete as per Hindu rites. If the wife, in proceedings under section 125 Cr. P.C., succeeds in showing that the parties lived together as husband and wife, and the husband admits that there was imperfect marriage ceremony but does not deny the child's paternity and the Magistrate is *prima facie* satisfied with regard to performance of marriage then strict proof of performance of essential rites is not required. The Court remarked:

> "After not disputing the paternity of the child and after accepting the fact that marriage ceremony was performed, though not legally perfect as contended, it would hardly lie in the mouth of the appellant to contend in proceedings under section 125, Cr. P.C., that there was no valid marriage as essential rites were not performed at the time of the said marriage. The provision under section 125 is not to be utilised for defeating the rights conferred by the Legislature to the destitute women, children or parents, who are victims of social environment."

Thus, the wife was awarded maintenance of ₹ 400 in her favour and ₹ 200 to the child till she attained majority. Significantly, the application took 11 years to be decided.

Comment: The case shows the plight of a woman who foolishly succumbs to promises of a man to be abandoned later. The court, however, showed sensitivity by not accepting the plea of incomplete marriage – though it took as long as 11 years till the award came.

Woman Living with a Man cannot be Equated as Wife

Malti v. State of Uttar Pradesh,
2000 Cr LJ 4170 (All): 2000 All LJ 2116: 2001 (1) Hindu LR 403

Issue: Can a woman living with a man under the same roof, be equated with a 'wife' in terms of the maintenance provisions under section 125, Cr. P.C.?

Facts: The applicant was working in the house of the man as a cook. She stayed with him in the same house and shared an intimate physical relationship. After sometime, he pushed her out and also refused to give her any financial support. Thereupon, she filed a petition for maintenance. Her plea was that they were living together as husband and wife for quite sometime, so her 'paramour' was under an obligation to maintain her. The man admitted to the intimacy but stated that he was never married to her, and therefore, he was under no duty to maintain her. The Trial Court, however, held that since they were both living together under one roof and shared intimate physical relationship which the man admitted, he was liable to maintain her. Hence, the appeal by the man.

Order: The High Court reversed the Trial Court order. The trial judge had failed to note that the word used in section 125, Cr. P.C., is "wife" and not an unwed partner. Also, there was no reference or evidence of any ceremony, whether complete or incomplete of any marriage. It was, therefore, held that the grant of maintenance solely on the ground of parties living under one roof and having illicit relationship is not proper. If a man and a woman choose to live together and indulge in sex, no marital status is conferred upon them automatically by their so living. The two may also agree to live together to satisfy their animal needs, but such union is never called a marriage nor is a woman leading such life bestowed with the sacrosanct honour of a wife, the court ruled. "Thus, in law it is not enough to declare any woman a legally wedded wife. Wife means a legally wedded wife. According to section 125 of the Cr. P.C., there ought to be a marriage according to the custom or religion prevalent among the community. A marriage carries a legal, social or religious sanction behind it", according to the court.

Comment: While it is fair to stretch the meaning of the word "wife" to include a woman where the man and the woman have gone through a form or some ceremonies of marriage (though technically incomplete or wrong) for purposes of conceding her claim for maintenance under the provisions of section 125 of the Cr. P.C. it cannot be stretched so far as to include a woman staying with a man in a live-in relationship with no ceremony or form of marriage, whatsoever. She may fight for her right in a different forum (*e.g.*, compensation) but not claim maintenance as a 'wife' under section 125 of the Cr. P.C.

Note: It is significant to note that under the provisions of the Protection of Women from Domestic Violence Act, 2005, even a woman in a live-in relationship with a man, is entitled to maintenance. *See* also *Chanmuniya* v. *Virendra Kumar*, (2010) 10 SCALE 602: 2010 AIR SCW 6497; *D. Velusamy* v. *D. Patchaiammal*, AIR 2011 SC 479.

If Marriage Void – Wife not Entitled to Maintenance

Bhau Saheb v. Leelabai,
AIR 2004 Bom 283 (FB): 2004 (13) All Ind Cas 948:
2004 (1) Hindu LR 615

Issue: (i) Whether an order dismissing a wife's petition seeking declaration that her marriage was valid can come under the term "any decree" so as to entitle her to claim maintenance under section 25, Hindu Marriage Act?

(ii) Whether a wife whose marriage is void, is entitled to maintenance?

Facts: Shortly after marriage, the wife filed criminal cases under sections 498A, 323, 504 and 506 of the Indian Penal Code against the husband. She also filed case for maintenance under section 125 of the Cr.P.C. This was dismissed by the Family Court on the ground that she was not legally wedded wife of the opposite party. Meanwhile, she filed an application before the Family Court seeking declaration that the marriage was valid and the child is legitimate. Along with that she sought maintenance for the daughter.

Her petition seeking declaration regarding validity of the marriage was dismissed by observing that she was not legally wedded wife since her husband was an already married man. Maintenance, however, was granted in favour of the child. In the backdrop of this legal battle she filed a petition under section 25 of the Hindu Marriage Act for permanent alimony which was allowed by the Family Court and the husband was ordered to pay ₹ 1,000 per month to the wife w.e.f. the date of application. The Family Court drew support for its order from several judgments, *e.g., Shataram Tukaram Patil* v. *Dagubai Tukaram Patil*, AIR 1987 Bom 182: (1987) 2 Hindu LR 343: II (1987) DMC 100; *Rajeshbai* v. *Shantabai*, AIR 1982 Bom 231: 1981 Bom CR 699: 1981 Mah LJ 820; *Govindrao Ranoji Musale* v. *Sou. Anandibai*, AIR 1976 Bom 433: 1977 Hindu LR 465: (1977) 79 Bom LR 73 and *Krishnakant Mulashankar Vyas* v. *Reena Krishna Vyas*, AIR 1999 Bom 127: 1999 (1) CCC 423: II (1999) DMC 221.

The husband appealed against the Family Court order. He denied solemnization of marriage and in the alternative claimed that he was already married on the alleged date of marriage with the petitioner and so the marriage if any, was void in view of section 5(i) read with section 11 of the Hindu Marriage Act and so the 'wife' was not entitled to any maintenance. The High Court delved on the issue as to whether "any decree" could mean "every decree", in great detail. It referred to various cases decided by the High Court as well as by the Apex Court. It also considered some hypothetical situations to indicate that the term "any decree" cannot be expanded or stretched too liberally to include any court order. For instance, if the husband approaches the court for restitution of conjugal rights against his wife and the court believes his case that the wife's withdrawal from his society was without reasonable cause, will the court grant permanent alimony in favour of the wife while granting a decree of restitution in favour of the husband which the wife refuses to obey?

The court pointed out that the conduct of the parties and also other circumstances of the case are important considerations and they cannot control the discretion conferred upon the court by the expression "court may". If there can be cases of denial of maintenance to even legally wedded wife, the liberal construction of section 25 so as to entitle an illegitimate wife to maintenance would not be proper.

According to the court, it is a fundamental principle of law that in order to claim a relief from the court of law, there must be a legal right based on a legal status. When status of a woman as wife is not recognised by the provisions of the Act which confers the right of permanent alimony, she cannot be entertained for grant of relief in the absence of recognition of her status by the Act. If the construction of the word "wife" is not accepted uniformly for same remedy provided in special legislation i.e., section 125, Cr. P.C. and personal law, anomalous position may occur. A woman who is denied maintenance under section 125, Cr.P.C. for reason that she is not the legally wedded wife would successfully pray and obtain permanent alimony in total disregard of earlier judgment pronounced as also provision for legitimacy of marriage as contained in personal law. The court observed:

> "Even while considering section 25 to be a "welfare legislation", it cannot be ignored that a liberal construction although may benefit the second wives who are drawn into the form of marriage by keeping them ignorant about illegitimacy of the same, may encourage bigamous marriages with full knowledge and in spite of existence of a legislation in the field, preventing bigamous marriages."

Further, the court made a distinction between a marriage which is void and one which is voidable. The court may consider granting of maintenance while declaring the nullity of a voidable marriage as the relationship would be legal in law until annulled, but not in case of nullity of marriage which is void *ipso jure*.

Order: The wife lost her case. The court held that any decree would not mean every decree so as to entitle a wife to claim maintenance; and further that wife of a void marriage is not entitled to maintenance.

Comment: Absolving a husband of the liability to maintain his second wife who was kept in the dark about the fact of his first marriage would encourage, rather than discourage a man to enter into such bigamous marriage. A wife would rarely enter into a marriage with an already married man with full knowledge of this fact simply because she would not be denied maintenance.

No Maintenance to Wife where Marriage Void

Savitaben Somabhai Bhatiya v. State of Gujarat,
AIR 2005 SC 1809: 2005 Cr LJ 2141: 2005 AIR SCW 1601

Issue: (i) Can an already married man who defrauds a woman to enter into a relationship, be absolved of the liability to maintain her under section 125, Cr. P.C., on the ground that his second wife was not his legal wife because he was an already married man, which fact he concealed from her?

(ii) Can an award of maintenance made prior to 2001, when there was a maximum limit, be later raised without formal amendment in the claim petition?

Facts: The appellant was married to the respondent in 1994 according to customary rites and rituals of their caste. Though initially all went well, after sometime she was subjected to mental and physical torture. The reason for this change in husband's attitude, the appellant wife alleged, was the fact that he developed illicit relations with a lady named Veenaben. The respondent neglected his wife and child; hence, she filed an application for maintenance under section 125 of the Cr. P.C. The husband opposed this application on the ground that the appellant was not his legally wedded wife and the child born to her was not his. According to him, Veenaben was his wife whom he had married 22 years back and had two children also. The Trial Court, however, granted maintenance; on husband's appeal the additional sessions judge set aside the order and remanded the matter to the Trial Court for fresh adjudication after affording the husband an opportunity to cross examine the witnesses of the appellant. After considering the matter afresh, the Trial Court again awarded maintenance to both the appellant and the child. A criminal revision application was again filed by the husband which was dismissed by the Additional District Judge. The husband then filed a special criminal application before the Gujarat High Court which held, that the appellant was not legally wedded wife of the respondent; this finding was substantiated by documentary proofs of the fact that the respondent was already married to Veenaben before the alleged date of marriage between the appellant and the respondent. However, maintenance granted to the child was maintained and the amount of ₹ 350 p.m. awarded to her was enhanced to ₹ 500 p.m.

On wife's appeal to the Supreme Court against the finding that the marriage was not legal, it was contended on her behalf that the High Court had taken too technical a view and that strict proof of a valid marriage is not the *sine qua non* for getting maintenance under the provisions of section 125 of the Cr. P.C. It was further argued that the documents produced by the husband to substantiate the plea of his earlier marriage with Veenaben should not have been given primacy over the clinching evidence adduced by the wife to show that she was unaware of the alleged marriage. Also, since the husband is guilty of fraud and misrepresentation, the equity should not weigh in his favour. Law is intended to protect destitute and harassed women and rigid interpretation given to the word "wife" goes against the legislative intent, it was argued.

Order: The court refused to accept this plea. It conceded that "there may be substance in the plea........that law operates harshly against the woman who unwittingly gets into relationship with a married man and section 125 of the Code does not give protection to such woman. This may be an inadequacy in law, which only the Legislature can undo. But as the position in law stands presently, there is no escape from the conclusion that the expression "wife" as per section 125 of the Code refers to only legally married wife". (p. 1811)

Reference was made to a few cases (*Nanak Chand* v. *Chandra Kishore*, AIR 1970 SC 446: 1970 Cr LJ 522: (1970) 1 SCR 565; *Yamunabai Anantrao Adhav* v. *Anantrao Shivaram Adhav*, AIR 1988 SC 644: JT 1988 (1) SC 193: 1988 Cr LJ 793) in support of the proposition that personal law of the parties is relevant for deciding the validity of the marriage and any attempt to exclude altogether the personal law applicable to the parties from consideration is improper. The fact that the wife was not informed about the earlier marriage was held to be of no significance as, "the principle of estoppel cannot be pressed into service to defeat the provision of section 125 of the Code". According to the court:

"........ the legislature considered it necessary to include within the scope of the provision an illegitimate child but it has not done so with respect to woman not lawfully married. However desirable it may be............to take note of the plight of the unfortunate woman, the legislative intent being clearly reflected in section 125 of the Code, there is no scope for enlarging its scope by introducing any artificial definition to include woman not lawfully married in the expression wife."

Thus, the wife not being legally married wife was held not to be entitled to maintenance under section 125 of the Code. However, as regards maintenance for the child the amount of ₹ 350 was raised to ₹ 500 by the High Court and that was the maximum which could be awarded prior to the amendment in 2001, which has done away with any limits. Hence, the amount was raised to Rs. 850. The argument of the husband that there was no amendment made to the claim petition seeking enhancement was rejected as being too technical a plea.

Comment: If judges feel too constrained and tied down by the letter of the law even in the face of glaring injustice to an innocent wife "who unwittingly gets into relationship with a married man", it is time that the law should be expeditiously and suitably amended so as to provide relief to such women. Also, it sounds harsh and illogical that a man who misrepresents and defrauds another woman to enter into a relationship, should later be allowed to get out of the relationship on the basis of his own wrong or misrepresentation or fraud. Such an approach would only encourage unscrupulous men to enter into bigamous or legally defective marriages. It is a pity that the hands of the judges should be tied down to strict application of law with all its technicalities, rather than imparting justice.

Marriage Void: Inherent Powers under CPC cannot be Invoked

Mangala Bhivaji Lad v. *Dhondiba Rambhau Aher*, AIR 2010 Bom 122: 2010 (4) All MR 716: 2010 (4) Mah LJ 486

Issue: The issue involved in this case was as to right of maintenance of a Hindu woman who is married after coming into force of the Hindu Marriage Act to a Hindu male having a legally wedded wife, in other words, a wife whose marriage is void being bigamous. The provisions invoked in this case were sections 5, 11 and 25 of the Hindu Marriage Act, section 18(2)(d) of the Hindu Adoptions and Maintenance Act 1956; (HAMA) and section 151 of the Civil Procedure Code, 1908.

Facts: The appellant in this case married in 1983, a man who already had a wife. They got their marriage registered and lived together for 17 years before they separated in 1999. Thereafter the respondent husband filed a petition in the Family Court for a declaration that his marriage with the appellant was *null and void* under section 5(i) coupled with section 11 of the Hindu Marriage Act, and for an injunction to restrain her from representing herself as his wife and from visiting his residence and work place. The appellant wife resisted the same on grounds that the husband had concealed his earlier marriage; and that there was a proper marriage between her and the petitioner which was registered as well. She also sought provision for separate residence and permanent alimony under section 18 of the Hindu Adoptions and Maintenance Act. The Family Court found that the marriage was void but refused the declaration to that effect in view of section 23(a) and (d) of the Hindu Marriage Act on the ground that the husband cannot be allowed to take advantage of his own wrong. It, however, refused to grant maintenance on the ground that the marriage was void and so she was not entitled to maintenance under section 25 of the Hindu Marriage Act nor under section 18 of the Hindu Adoptions and Maintenance Act. It also restrained the appellant from visiting the respondent's place of residence as well as work. The wife filed on appeal against the Family Court order on grounds, *inter alia,* that:

 (i) Since the Family Court declined to declare the marriage as *null and void,* her status as a "wife" was not affected and hence she has a right to maintenance.

 (ii) The term 'wife' has not been defined anywhere so there cannot be a restrictive meaning attached to it thereby depriving her of a right to claim maintenance, which is a provision for social justice and protection.

 (iii) The narrow interpretation of the provision of maintenance under section 25 read with section 24 of the Hindu Marriage Act may render section 23 of the Act ineffective. The court refused to accept these arguments. It held that:

   (a) In view of the clear provisions in section 5(i) and section 11 of the Hindu Marriage Act a marriage where a spouse already has a subsisting marriage is void *ipso jure* and does not require a declaration to that effect.

(b) Absence of such declaration does not, by default, give her the status of a legally wedded wife. Reference was made to the following observation of the Supreme Court order in *Yamunabai Anantrao Adhav* v. *Anantrao Shivaram Adhav*, AIR 1988 SC 644: JT 1988 (1) SC 193: 1988 Cr LJ 793.

"The marriages covered by section 11 are void *ipso jure*, that is void from the very inception, and have to be ignored as not existing in law at all if and when such a question arises. Although that section permits a formal declaration to be made on the presentation of a petition, it is not essential to obtain in advance such a formal declaration from a court in proceedings specifically commenced for the purpose.

(c) The expression 'wife' means a legally wedded wife only in terms of the law applicable to the parties. In case of Hindus, the law relating to marriage is codified by the Hindu Marriage Act and therefore unless the marriage is valid under the provisions of this Act, the parties cannot describe themselves as "husband" and "wife" for purpose of application of different statutes, like, Hindu Adoptions and Maintenance Act (section 18) or Criminal Procedure Code (section 125) for deriving the benefits available thereunder."

The argument on behalf of the appellant that section 18 of the Hindu Adoptions and Maintenance Act entitles a Hindu wife, whether married before or after the commencement of this Act to maintenance by her husband even upon living separately "if he had another wife living", was also repelled by the court. It held that the expression "any other wife" means any other legally wedded wife, *i.e.*, where both marriages had taken place prior to the Hindu Marriage Act when second marriage was legal.

As regards the contention that the Hindu Adoptions and Maintenance Act is a piece of beneficial legislation and should be liberally construed, the court held that while a provision may be liberally construed but liberality cannot overstep legislative limits of interpretation putting into the legislation something which is not there. The counsel for the wife sought relief by referring, *inter alia*, to a judgment of the Delhi High Court in *Narinder Pal Kaur Chawla* v. *Manjeet Singh Chawla*, AIR 2008 Del 7: 2008 (2) Marri LJ 107: 2008 Mat LR 184 wherein the court held that a Hindu husband is estopped from challenging validity of the second marriage if he has not disclosed to the second wife the factum of his first marriage, otherwise, according to the Delhi High Court, it would amount to giving premium to the husband for defrauding the second wife. The Legislature never intended that a woman who is in the position of a second wife, be not treated as the "wife" at least for the purposes of section 18 of the Hindu Adoptions and Maintenance Act and deprived of her right to seek maintenance. The court gave relief to the second wife by invoking the provisions of section 151 of the C.P.C. It observed that when laws' terms are inadequate and lead to loose ends, the court can rely on its inherent powers to do justice. The following observations of the Delhi High Court in *Narinder Pal Kaur* are pertinent:

"Strictly, the statutory entitlement of the court may not apply but having the recognised right and necessity to enforce it, the court can, in exercise of its inherent powers reach out justice by giving remedial and such salutary reliefs. Justice after all is another name of fairness. It cannot be blind to the facts in a given case and should reach out in its mercy those results which would be necessary to avoid ruinous consequences like economic or moral destitution."

Consequently, the wife of a void marriage in this case was given maintenance not on the provision of section 18 of the Hindu Adoptions and Maintenance Act but in exercise of inherent powers under section 151 of the C.P.C.

Reverting to *Mangala Bhivaj Lad* case, the wife's counsel's plea for involving inherent powers under section 151 of C.P.C was turned down by the Bombay Court. It remarked (p. 129).

"with respect, we do not agree with such course of action because it is well-established that the inherent powers are required to be exercised by the court only in the absence of statutory provisions and not to circumvent statutory provision. Besides, inherent power of section 151 C.P.C is only a source of power to the court to make such order as may be necessary for the ends of justice or to prevent abuse of the process of the court. It cannot be a source of right to claim maintenance."

Order: The wife's appeal was dismissed and the court held that she was not entitled to any maintenance as, the expression "Hindu wife" used in section 18 of the Hindu Adoptions and Maintenance Act means legally wedded wife and no less and the appellant not being the legally wedded wife of the respondent, cannot resort to section 18 of the Hindu Adoptions and Maintenance Act. The court relied on the Andhra Pradesh High Court judgment in *Abbayolla M. Subba Reddy* v. *Padmamma*, AIR 1999 AP 19: 1998 (3) CCC 426: I (2000) DMC 266. It may be mentioned that in *Mangala Bhivaj Lad* the court had also found that, *firstly*, the claimant knew about the husband's earlier marriage when she married him and *secondly*, she had sufficient income and means of support of her own though these were not the factors on which the judgment was based.

Comment: Hindu law enjoins monogamy and hence any marriage in breach of this mandatory provision is void and confers no rights to the parties *qua* each other. The issue of maintenance for a wife who is already married and marries again or whose husband is already married and then married her has been differently decided by the courts; there have been cases where wives have been trapped into marriage by the husband's concealing the fact of their earlier marriage. While some courts have conceded the moral duty of the husband to support the wife in such cases, there are others who have held that the wife has no right to claim maintenance even in such cases. The argument of inherent powers of the court on grounds of sympathy or mercy to do justice to a wife who has been defrauded into a bigamous marriage has also been rejected by courts, as was done in the case-in-hand. While law needs to be respected and monogamy enforced yet there needs to be a way out to guard the interests of a wife who is not at fault at all and the husband tries to take advantage of his own wrong.

Marriage Complete Nullity: No Maintenance under Section 125 Cr. P.C.

Ratneshwar Saikia v. Kalpana Saikia, Crl Rev No. 88/2006 Gau 20-5-11

Issue: This was a petition for maintenance under section 125 of the Cr. P.C. where the issue of validity of the marriage of the applicant who was an already married woman, was involved.

Facts: The applicant had filed a maintenance application under section 125, Cr. P.C. contending that she was married to the non-applicant according to Hindu rites and rituals and being ill-treated by him was forced to leave the house; that she had to seek police help to re-enter; further that she was under prolonged medical treatment and the husband gave her no financial support. Though the husband denied the marriage, the Family Court held that the petitioner was a legally married wife and hence entitled to maintenance. The husband was accordingly directed to pay ₹ 1200 per month to her by way of maintenance. Against this, the husband filed a revision before the Gauhati High Court. His argument was that the applicant was already married to one B.N. and also had a female child, that she was ill-treated by B.N. and sought temporary accommodation from the non-applicant who, on humanitarian grounds agreed to do but when after some time he asked her to vacate the room, she, with ill-motive and ill-advise of others insisted that she was his wife and would not leave. It was therefore argued that she not being his wife as she had not obtained any decree of dissolution of her marriage with B.N., he had no liability to maintain her. Reference was made to several cases in support of this plea *e.g., Rohtash Singh* v. *Ramdevi,* (2000) 3 SCC 180: AIR 2000 SC 952: 2000 Cr LJ 1498; *Savitaben Somabhai Bhatiya* v. *State of Gujarat,* AIR 2005 SC 1809: 2005 Cr LJ 2141: 2005 AIR SCW 1601; *Ramesh Chandra Ram Pratap Daga* v. *Rameshwari Ramesh Chandra Daga,* (2005) 2 SCC 33: AIR 2005 SC 422: 2004 AIR SCW 6990. The prayer on behalf of the wife that the case be remanded to Family Court for fresh hearing to decide question regarding dissolution of her earlier marriage, was not allowed.

Order: After going through the evidence, the case-law as well as statutory law, the court held that under section 125(b) of the Cr. P.C., "wife" includes a woman who has been divorced or obtained a decree of divorce from the husband and has not remarried. In this case, there was evidence to prove that the respondent was married to one B.N. before she allegedly married the present petitioner which fact she had suppressed in her application for maintenance. After the respondent disclosed this fact in the written statement, the petitioner conceded that she was married to B.N. but that the latter had married second wife who was also made nominee in his pension papers. On the basis of this fact she was trying to persuade the court that she had already been divorced by B.N. and as such the present marriage with the petitioner was valid. The court refused to accept this argument and held that a Hindu marriage could be dissolved only under the provisions of section 13 of the Hindu Marriage

Act and there being no evidence to establish that any divorce was obtained, it must be accepted that the earlier marriage was subsisting. Hence the marriage being a complete nullity, she was not entitled to maintenance from the present respondent.

Comment: Law gives no legal status to an alleged marriage undergone during the subsistence of an earlier marriage of either of the parties. Mere fact that nomination etc., is made in favour of some other person is no proof of dissolution of the earlier marriage.

INCOME OF CLAIMANT

Claimants Income not to be Ignored

Bhagwan Dutt v. Kanta Devi,
AIR 1975 SC 83: 1975 Cr LJ 40: (1975) 2 SCC 386

Issue: Is the husband's liability to maintain his wife under section 488 of the Cr. P.C. (now 125), absolute or is wife's income an important determinant?

Facts: A wife was earning rupees eight hundred per month while the husband's salary was rupees six hundred per month. The wife sought maintenance under section 488, Cr. P.C. (prior to the 1973 amendment). The same was granted without taking the wife's income into account. The husband filed a revision before the additional sessions judge who held that since the wife's income was "substantial" and "enough to maintain herself", she was not entitled to maintenance from the husband. A single judge of the High Court who heard the reference, held that section 488 of the Cr. P.C. does not contemplate taking into consideration the income of the wife. Hence, the husband's appeal.

Order: The court held that the income of the wife could not be ignored; it has to be taken into account in arriving at the amount payable to her as maintenance. The section does not confer an absolute right on a wife to get an order of maintenance against the husband nor does it impose an absolute liability on the husband to support her in all circumstances. The right to maintenance is circumscribed by certain factors, *viz.*, (a) relationship of husband and wife, (b) inability of wife to maintain herself, (c) sufficient means of husband, and (d) proof that husband has neglected or refused to maintain her.

Comment: It is but fair and logical that there should be no absolute liability nor right in the matter. The whole idea is to provide maintenance to the needy applicant keeping in view the circumstances of the case and position of the parties. The wife's own income is a significant factor to be considered while making the maintenance order.

Young Educated Lady – Whether Expected to be Capable of Own Maintenance

Chandana Guha Roy v. Gautam Guha Roy,
AIR 2004 Cal 36: 2004 (17) All Ind Cas 790: I (2005) DMC 607

Issue: Should an educated young lady be expected to be capable of maintaining her own self?

Facts: A husband filed a petition for divorce and the wife applied for maintenance under section 24, Hindu Marriage Act and also under section 125, Cr. P.C. Thereafter, the husband also filed an application under section 24, Hindu Marriage Act. The applications of both the parties were dismissed by the Trial Court. Against the wife's application, it was held that the husband was no longer in service as, consequent to his arrest after wife's criminal complaints against him, his services were terminated. The court further observed that it was a settled principle of law that an educated lady cannot be encouraged to sit idle expecting any allowance from the husband. The wife filed an appeal against the order.

Order: It was held that the ground for rejection of the wife's application was not proper. The income of the husband must be within his special knowledge; he did not make any attempt to prove either his actual income or his dismissal from job. Besides, when his application for maintenance was rejected he did not challenge the same and this implied that he was not prejudicially affected by the order. Above all, according to the court, the husband had filed the divorce suit which also incurred expenditure which goes to show that he did have some income. In view of all these facts, the matter was remanded for fresh trial.

Comment: In these times of equality, a wife is as much liable to maintain her husband as the husband is to maintain his wife—depending on the circumstances of the case. However, the Trial Court's observation in this case that an educated young lady cannot be expected to sit idle expecting allowance from the husband, did not find favour with the High Court. There can, however, be no hard and fast rule in this respect, and each case would have to be decided on its own facts and situations.

Husband cannot seek Production of Documents of Family Assets to Establish Wife's Means

Pushkar Navnitlal Shah v. *Rakhi Pushkar Shah*, AIR 2007 Guj 5: 2007 (55) All Ind Cas 505: 2007 (1) Guj LR 859

Issue: After the amendment of section 6 of the Hindu Succession Act, 1956 and insertion of section 29A by Maharashtra in the Hindu Succession Act in 1994 a female has acquired equal rights as a coparcener in the property and business of her father. Can a husband seek production of documents of the family assets/incomes in which a wife has a share, in defence to the wife's application for maintenance and litigation expenses to establish that the wife has enough means and so is not entitled to any maintenance and litigation expenses under section 24 of the Hindu Marriage Act, 1955.

Facts: A wife filed an application for maintenance and litigation expenses under section 24 of the Hindu Marriage Act. In order to establish that she has sufficient means of her own and therefore not entitled to maintenance from him, he filed an application under Order XI, rule 14 of the Civil Procedure Code for production of some documents by her. Such documents were sought in view of the fact that by insertion of section 29A in 1994 in the Hindu Succession Act, 1956 by Maharashtra, and also other amendments in the Hindu Succession Act, notably, amendment of section 6 (whereby female has been given equal coparcenary rights) and deletion of section 23 (whereby she can seek partition of dwelling house), a female's rights have been brought at par with the males'. To establish the fact that the wife has considerable assets in the joint family properties and business and therefore her application under section 24 was not tenable, he filed the above mentioned application under Order XI, rule 14 which provides:

Order XI, rule 14 "*Production of documents.* It shall be lawful for the court, at any time during the pendency of any suit, to order the production by any party thereto, upon oath of such of the documents in his possession or power, relating to any matter in question in such suit, as the court shall think right; and the court may deal with such documents, when produced, in such manner as shall appear just."

The Trial Court rejected his application, hence his present petition under article 227 of the Constitution. His argument was that these documents were required to support his defence that the wife was having considerable share in the movable as well as immovable ancestral property of parental family including rights in business as well as assets of father's business. The documents sought pertained to family business in which the wife had a legal share; the husband's contention was that section 24 of the Hindu Marriage Act gives equal right to both so the Trial Court ought to have considered sources of income of either party and then decide; further it was argued that procedural law had to be interpreted so as to advance the object of substantive provision – section 24, Hindu Marriage Act in this case – and therefore the High Court should exercise its jurisdiction and direct production of documents. The husband also contended that wife's application for production of salary certificate etc., of the husband was allowed but similar application by him to establish wife's income was refused.

Order: The court dismissed the husband's petition. It held that the court has to see whether the documents sought to be produced are in the power and possession of the person from whom these are sought. Merely because the wife's application for production of documents which were admittedly within the possession of the husband was granted is no reason to grant husband's present application. No such parity can be claimed merely because of the provision of section 24 without fulfilling requisite conditions laid down in rule 14, Order XI of the C.P.C, the court observed. It held that the provision in Order XI, rule 14 gives discretion in the matter to the court. "The provision is not available to an applicant to make a fishing or roving inquiry and in case of such an application like the present one, the court is justified in rejecting such application."

It further clarified that the High Court's jurisdiction under article 227 of the Constitution is limited to examining whether the impugned order suffers from any jurisdictional error or is perverse in any manner. Justifying the Trial

Court order, it held that even if on same facts and circumstances and evidence on record it is possible for High Court to take different view of the matter, that by itself would not be sufficient to permit intervention in exercise of powers under article 227. The High Court is not expected to function as an appellate court in these proceedings.

As to the provisions of section 29A of the Maharashtra Amendment to the Hindu Succession Act and the enlargement of female's rights under the Act the court recorded that it was not possible to express any opinion as, "admittedly these provisions are not applicable *inter vivos* and come into play only at the stage of opening of succession. Even if a daughter is equated with coparceners of Hindu undivided family, it is well-settled that no coparcener can predicate his share in joint family property till actual partition takes place. Thus, the contention in the context of present proceeding is, to say the least, misconceived".

The petition was thus summarily rejected.

Comment: The whole purpose behind section 24 proceedings is to ensure that a party to matrimonial proceedings should not, during the course of the litigation, suffer from want of funds both in respect of his/her sustenance as well as in fighting the legal battle. The court should take due notice of the assets and incomes/earnings of both the parties. In this case, however, the issue was primarily confined to the husband's right to seek production of documents pertaining to family assets, business and other incomes in which the wife was a sharer under the law. The application was rejected. If allowed this would have helped husband to defend his case and establish that it was not a case where the wife has no sufficient income for her support and necessary expenses of proceedings.

INCOME/CAPACITY OF NON-APPLICANT

Relevance of Non-applicant's Income and Capacity

K.M.P. Kovilamma v. Moopil Eradi,
(1973) Cr LJ 1878: 1973 Ker LT 757: 1972 Ker LJ 893

Issue: Is a husband liable to maintain his wife under section 488 (now section 125) of Cr. P.C., irrespective of wife's income and capacity?

Facts: A second wife aged 68 and in affluent position, filed an application for maintenance against her husband who was 80 years old and in poor mental and physical health. The husband had, in fact, distributed all his properties between the children of his first wife, the applicant wife and her children. The lower court rejected her application holding that the purpose of enacting section 488 (now section 125) of the Cr. P.C. is only to prevent vagrancy, and it cannot be used as a lever for ulterior purposes. The wife went in appeal.

Order: It was argued on behalf of the appellant that in proceedings under section 488, the wife's capacity to maintain herself is irrelevant, and so even if she is affluent, she is entitled to claim maintenance from her husband. Rejecting this argument, the court held:

> "If a change in the pecuniary circumstances of the parties subsequent to the passing of the order is a matter which can be taken into account by the Magistrate to reduce the maintenance, it appears to us that the pecuniary position of the parties is a matter which the Magistrate can take into account even at the initial stage of passing the order for maintenance."

Comment: Prior to the amendment in 1973, the income of the non-applicant was not an important consideration in maintenance claims. The income or the ability of the wife to earn and maintain herself was, thus, irrelevant (*Suryakant* alias *Suresh Laxmishankar* v. *Indu,* 1973 Guj LR 169; *Major Jogindar Singh* v. *Bibi Raj Mohinder Kaur,* AIR 1960 Punj 249: ILR (1960) Punj 222: 1960 Cr LJ 640). In *P.T. Ramankutty Achan* v. *Kalyanikutty,* AIR 1971 Ker 22: 1970 Ker LT 554: 1971 Cr LJ 318), however, a more realistic approach was adopted. After the amendment in 1973, the Code specifically lays down that only a wife who is unable to maintain herself is entitled to maintenance from her husband.

Capacity to Maintain – Presumption

Dasarathi Ghosh v. Anuradha Ghosh,
1988 Cr LJ 64 (Cal): II (1986) DMC 120: 1986 (2) Hindu LR 165

Issue: Can a husband with little or no visible income be absolved from his liability to maintain his wife under section 125, Cr. P.C., if otherwise he is healthy and able bodied?

Facts: A wife filed a petition for maintenance under section 125 of Cr. P.C. The petition was allowed and an allowance of ₹ 100 per month was decreed. The husband challenged the Magistrate's findings both in respect of his capacity to pay the maintenance as well as the quantum. The sessions judge held that the husband's capacity to pay ₹ 100 per month was not established satisfactorily. He, therefore, reduced the amount to ₹ 75 per month. The husband, thereupon, moved the High Court under article 227 of the Constitution.

Order: It was argued on his behalf that the courts below had erred in holding without evidence, that he had sufficient means to pay maintenance to the wife. The wife's contention was that the husband had vast landed property, that he also had a business in paddy and rice and thus earned between ₹ 800 and ₹ 900 per month.

The court, however, accepted the husband's appeal. It held (at p. 65):

> "To saddle the husband with the burden of paying maintenance to the respondent, it must be established first that the petitioner has sufficient means to pay the same. All that has been established in this case is that the petitioner has only 3 *bighas* of land. There is no material, whatsoever, to show how much is left of the produce of these 3 *bighas* after meeting all the costs of cultivation. It cannot be considered proper to come to any definite finding on the point of one's means merely on the basis of what one may be found to be wearing at a particular point of time........from mere fact that the husband had 3 *bighas* of agricultural land or that he wore a wrist watch, a gold ring and clothes worth about ₹ 150, it cannot be said that he had sufficient means."

It was urged on behalf of the wife that the petitioner being an able-bodied young man, it is to be presumed that he is capable of earning sufficient means so as to be able to reasonably maintain his wife and that it is for him to establish cogent grounds for holding that he is unable for reasons beyond his control, to earn enough to maintain her. For this proposition, *Chander Prakash* v. *Sita Rani*, AIR 1968 Del 174: 1968 Cr LJ 1153: 71 Punj LR (D) 167, was relied upon. The court, however, did not agree with this argument and held (at p. 66):

> "There is really no such presumption in law and such presumption cannot also be spelt out from the language of section 125, Cr. P.C. Marriage is the normal state in this country and people who habitually live below the poverty line (their number is quite substantial) and even beggars marry in this country. Ordinarily, such people cannot even maintain themselves in a proper way. Marriage does not endow then with any

ability not only to maintain their own selves but also their wives, in a proper way. In that view of the matter it is difficult to understand why from the very fact that a person is able-bodied it is to be presumed that he is in a position to pay sufficient maintenance to his wife, whether in fact he is in such a position or not. That will be going against the provision of the section itself which only saddles the husband with the burden of maintenance to his wife when he has sufficient means and yet neglects to do so."

In this case, the amount had been reduced from ₹ 100 to ₹ 75 by the first appellate court and the husband's advocate suggested that it be further reduced to ₹ 50. Since the difference was not much and in any case the order was temporary, the High Court decided not to interfere in the quantum.

Comment: This is not a happy judgment. A person who is not able to maintain his wife has no moral right to marry. The duty to maintain a wife is one of the most important obligations imposed on the husband by the *Shastras* as well as by law. The word "means" in section 488 (now 125) of the Cr. P.C. has generally been construed by the courts to signify not only visible means such as real property in the shape of income, revenue or estate, but includes the capacity to earn; and a healthy able-bodied man must be presumed to have the means or capacity to earn and support his wife or children. The *onus* is on him to show that by accident, disease or other reasons beyond his control he is not able to earn. Otherwise, the presumption is that he has the capacity to earn and means to support the wife.

Husband Becoming *Sadhu* not Absolved of Liability to Maintain Wife

Hardev Singh v. State of Uttar Pradesh, 1995 Cr LJ 1652 (All): II (1995) DMC 624: 1995 All LJ 446

Issue: Can a husband, on becoming a *sadhu* be absolved of his liability to maintain his wife and children under the provision of section 125 of the Cr. P.C.?

Facts: A wife, along with two children filed an application for maintenance under section 125 of the Cr. P.C. Since the husband did not contest, an *ex parte* decree was passed whereunder the husband was directed to pay ₹ 500, ₹ 300 and ₹ 200 to each respectively by way of maintenance. In recovery proceedings by the wife, the husband made an application under section 482, Cr. P.C., for staying further proceedings and for dismissing the maintenance application. His argument was that the award of an amount of ₹ 1,000 (₹ 500 + ₹ 300 + ₹ 200) was illegal as the maximum limit permissible under section 125 was ₹ 500, and *secondly*, since he had renounced the world and become a *sadhu*, he was not liable to pay any maintenance.

Order: Both these contentions were over-ruled by the court. Relying on *Capt. Ramesh Chander Kaushal* v. *Veena Kaushal*, AIR 1978 SC 1807: (1978) 4 SCC 70: 1978 Cr LJ 3, it was held that the words 'in the whole' in section 125 of the Cr. P.C. do not refer to all the members of the family but only to the items of maintenance. In other words, each applicant is entitled to a maximum amount of ₹ 500. As regards the second contention, there was no proof of the husband having became a *sadhu* but even assuming that he had, it does not absolve him from the duty to maintain. The following observations of the Rangoon High Court in *Maung Tin* v. *Ma Hmin*, 34 Cr LJ 815: AIR 1933 Rang 138, were quoted with approval:

> "A man is not, and ought not to be, permitted by his own voluntary act to free himself from the elementary duty of maintaining his wife and children and he is amenable to the provisions of section 488, notwithstanding the fact that he has adopted the yellow robe and become a member of the Sangha."

Also, relying on *Dhani Ram* v. *Ram Devi*, 1954 All LJ 626, the court held that 'means' includes earning capacity and a healthy able-bodied man is presumed to have the means to support his wife.

Comment: The issue as to the maximum amount which may be awarded under section 125 of the Cr. P.C. has been settled by removing any upper limit by an amendment in the Cr. P.C. in 2001.

On the question whether a husband can, by his own voluntary act, be absolved of his liability to maintain his wife and children, the court has clearly ruled that he cannot.

Maintenance claim by Wife – Status of Husband and not her Parents to be Considered

Meenu Chopra v. *Deepak Chopra*, AIR 2002 Del 131: 2002 (1) CCC 239: II (2001) DMC 264

Issue: Is the amount of maintenance in favour of the wife, to be fixed according to the financial status of the husband, or that of the wife's parents?

Facts: A wife filed an application for maintenance under sections 18 and 20 of the Hindu Adoption and Maintenance Act, 1956, as an 'indigent person' under provisions of Order XXXIII read with section 151 of the Code of Civil Procedure. On being satisfied that she was not possessed of sufficient means to pay court fee, her prayer to sue as indigent person was allowed by the court. In her maintenance claim, the wife averred that her husband was earning not less than rupees two lakh per month. Before filing the suit, she sent him a legal notice demanding maintenance at the rate of ₹ 20,000 per month to which the husband replied stating that the amount of maintenance claimed is dependent on the status of the parties and the needs of the claimant. He further stated in his reply, "a person whose father at the time of retirement earned only ₹ 3,000 per month is demanding maintenance of ₹ 20,000 per month is most amusing. Obviously their parasitical intention is to fleece me out of my hard earned income so that these people can live a life of debauchery. I am truly amazed at the demand". (at p. 132) He did not state in his reply that the demand was excessive nor that he was not possessed of sufficient means to pay the amount. His only argument to refute her claim was that she came from a family with modest means and so was not having a status entitling her to maintenance at this high rate. He, however, remained *ex parte* at the trial.

Order: On being *prima facie* satisfied with the averments made by the wife about his income, the court fixed interim maintenance at the rate of Rs. 20,000 per month. It observed (at p. 132):

> "The status of the parents of the plaintiff is totally irrelevant consideration. After the marriage, it is the status of the husband which is determinative of the quantum of maintenance to be given to the wife. After the marriage, a girl adopts matrimonial home and gets attuned to the living standard of her husband.......... If she has to suffer his miseries, she has a right to enjoy his affluence also. Therefore, if the husband is wealthy and leading opulent life, his wife also has a right to be the partner in his property and live with the same standards and equal dignity. It does not lie in the mouth of the husband, after separation of the spouses, to say that the wife is no longer entitled to the standard on which she has been living with the husband and that she should re-adopt the standard of her parental home."

Comment: The tone and tenor of the husband's reply to the notice was most unbehoving. The court very aptly remarked that if a wife can be a partner with her husband in times of misery, she has a right to share his affluence as well. In any case when quantum of maintenance is fixed for a wife, the means, capacity and the financial status of the husband are the important factors to be considered.

Can Wife claim Maintenance for Husband's Mother also

Amit Kumar Sharma v. VIth Addl. District and Sessions Judge, Bijnor,
AIR 1999 All 4: 1999 All LJ 25: 1999 (1) CCC 272

Issue: Can a husband's mother's needs be taken care of in a wife's application for maintenance when the mother is staying with her?

Facts: The husband filed a petition for divorce. Thereupon, the wife filed application for maintenance under sections 24 and 25 of the Hindu Marriage Act claiming maintenance for herself, two minor children and ailing mother of the husband who too was staying with her. The same was allowed by the Trial Court and affirmed by the additional district judge in appeal. The husband filed an appeal against the order.

Order: The court held that section 24 contemplates maintenance either to wife or husband and the mother is in no way connected with the *lis* relating to marriage between the husband and wife. The court observed (at p. 7) that "the Indian social fabric involves maintenance of parents with religious scruples and devotion but the court is called upon to interpret the law and not the religious or social duties". Section 125 of the Cr. P.C. and section 20 of the Hindu Adoptions and Maintenance Act are there to take care of the parents' maintenance rights, according to the court. The court further held (at p. 7):

> "Where there is a specific provision of law on the basis of religious scruples or social system, it could not be permissible to stretch section 24 to the extent of taking the place of section 125, Cr. P.C. and section 20 of the Hindu Adoptions and Maintenance Act nor it can overlap the said sections............section 24 does not postulate the scope of granting maintenance to the mother of the husband *even when she is ailing and lives with the applicant.*" (emphasis added)

Maintenance award in favour of the mother was accordingly set aside by the High Court.

Comment: The court has taken a very rigid and technical view. While awarding maintenance in an application the court considers, *inter alia*, the needs of the applicant. Besides, under section 25 "any other circumstances of the case" is a relevant consideration. When the husband's mother, whom in any case he is liable to maintain, is staying with his estranged wife who is taking care of her needs, including medical treatment, the court should have given due consideration to these needs rather than driving her (the mother) to file separate suits for maintenance under the provision of the Cr. P.C. or Hindu Adoptions and Maintenance Act.

Assessing the Income – What is the Crucial Time

S.S. Bindra v. Tarvinder Kaur,
AIR 2004 Del 442: 2004 (23) All Ind Cas 189: II (2004) DMC 297

Issue: In a claim for maintenance *pendente lite* what is the crucial time for assessing the income of the non-claimant – time of petition of claimant or time of order?

Facts: A husband filed a petition for divorce and the wife filed maintenance application under section 24 of the HMA for herself and children. She claimed ₹ 30,000 per month plus ₹ 33,000 as litigation expenses. The Trial Court assessed the husband's income at ₹ 1,30,000 per month and accordingly ordered him to pay ₹ 75,000 per month plus rupees one lakh as litigation expenses. Against this, the husband filed a revision challenging the quantum. It was also argued that at the time of the wife's petition, the income of the husband was much less and so the applicants were entitled to live in style commensurate with the husband's income at that time. Further, it was argued that the trial judge granted almost double of what was claimed by the wife. He awarded ₹ 75,000 as against ₹ 30,000 and rupees one lakh as against ₹ 33,000. The court agreed as a matter of general principle that in awarding interim maintenance, one of the considerations is that the wife and children shall enjoy the same standard of living as the husband, but emphasised that "the intention was not to peg it or freeze it to the date of separation". If in terms, orders are to be pegged to a particular point in time then if income of the earning spouse were to suffer a drastic reduction for any reason including deterioration in his/her health, the court would be precluded from making any adjustment because of these factors.

Order: According to the court "the vicissitudes of family income must always be translated and infused into orders granting maintenance". The court does not grant exactly what is prayed for but usually much less. By that very yardstick it is not precluded to grant *more if the circumstances call for it.* (at p. 245)

Comment: A very logical interpretation indeed. If the income of the husband increases mani-fold between the time of application and order, the judge should not be precluded to fix the amount on that basis; and so also if it decreases. It should not be left to the claimant or non-complainant to file fresh application for reassessment.

Whether Medical Expenses to be Included
R. Suresh v. Chandra,
AIR 2003 Kant 183: ILR (2003) 3 Kant 1638:
2003 (2) Kant LJ 67

Issue: Can medical expenses incurred by a wife be claimed under section 24 of the Hindu Marriage Act?

Facts: A wife had already obtained an order under section 24 of the Hindu Marriage Act for ₹ 3,000 per month as interim maintenance and ₹ 10,000 by way of litigation expenses. Subsequently, she claimed ₹ 35,000 which she spent for a surgery she had undergone. The husband challenged the same on two counts: *Firstly*, that since he was already paying interim maintenance there was no occasion to pay further amount over and above that; and *secondly*, that as a government servant he was entitled to reimbursement, but only if the treatment was got done in specified government hospitals. In this case, since the wife had got treatment in a private nursing home and that too outside the State where he was employed, he would not get the reimbursement.

Order: The court rejected both these arguments of the husband. It was held that since the word "support" in section 24 of the Hindu Marriage Act was not defined, it should be given dictionary meaning or as understood in general parlance. Further, the court can draw inspiration from the word "maintenance" as defined in section 3(b)(i) of the Hindu Adoptions and Maintenance Act which includes provision for food, clothing, residence, education, *medical attendance and treatment*. Though this definition too is not exhaustive but only inclusive, medical attendance and treatment have been specifically mentioned. Referring to *Pradeep Kumar Kapoor* v. *Shailja Kapoor*, AIR 1989 Del 10: II (1988) DMC 110: (1988) 2 Hindu LR 397, it was held that the word "support" and "maintenance" are synonymous and the definition of "maintenance" as given in the Hindu Adoptions and Maintenance Act equally applies to the word "support" in section 24 of the Hindu Marriage Act. As far as the issue of reimbursement from office was concerned, the court held that the issue is not of *his* reimbursement from office but the wife's claim for reimbursement from him. The wife was, accordingly, held to be entitled for reimbursement of her medical expenses from the husband under section 24 of the Hindu Marriage Act.

Comment: This is a significant judgment where the court has elucidated the concept and meaning of the term "support" in the context of section 24 of the Hindu Marriage Act, and held that expenses incurred on medical treatment would also be covered in the word "support".

Maintenance – Whether Includes Right to Reside in Tenanted Premises

Ajit Bhagwandas Udeshi v *Kumud Ajit Udeshi*, AIR 2003 Bom 120: 2003 (3) Bom CR 224: I (2003) DMC 602

Issue: Can a court, in maintenance proceedings by a wife, award tenanted residential premises in favour of a wife?

Facts: A husband obtained divorce on the ground of wife's desertion. The Family Court also granted permanent alimony at the rate of ₹ 1,000 per month and residential premises in favour of the wife. The husband objected to the grant of residential premises. In fact the premises in which the parties stayed together were hired by the wife's grandmother as tenant. After the grandmother's death, the landlord sought eviction against the wife. There was a compromise at the instance of the husband and after negotiations, the wife vacated after taking ₹ 35,000 from the landlord by way of compensation and goodwill. The wife alleged that this amount was retained by the husband who agreed to buy a residential accommodation in her name with that amount along with amount she received after selling her ornaments which she had received from her grandmother as her legal heir. However, instead of purchasing accommodation, he kept the money with himself and started harassing her. Ultimately they took a house on rent after paying *pagdi* and started living there along with their children. Because of the differences between them, the wife started staying on the ground floor of the house and the husband occupied the mezzanine. The husband also got involved with another woman and started pressurising the wife for divorce which she refused. Thereafter, the husband started the divorce proceedings which culminated in the impugned order of the Family Court.

Order: It was held that even though the accommodation was rented in the name of the husband, a substantial amount towards the *pagdi* was paid by the wife. Also, he was not staying in the house and was only retaining possession of the mezzanine; in fact he was staying elsewhere and did not need that accommodation. On the other hand, the wife had no alternate accommodation. The husband's appeal was, accordingly, dismissed.

Comment: Though maintenance under the definition in section 3(b)(i) of the Hindu Adoptions and Maintenance Act includes residence, this provision is practically very inadequate. In the instant case, the court gave meaningful relief to the wife. It aptly observed that the wife cannot be left without shelter.

Right of Residence as Part of Maintenance – A Personal Right; is not Heritable

Sheela Rani v. Jagdish Chander Sharma,
AIR 2004 Del 158: 2003 (107) DLT 309: 2003 (71) DRJ 122

Issue: The right of residence as part of maintenance is a personal right and the legal representatives of the wife cannot have a vested interest in the matter.

Facts: 'Maintenance' includes, within its ambit, provision for residence. This, however, is a personal right and not heritable. In this case, according to the husband, his wife and children had forcibly entered the premises belonging to him. He, therefore, filed a suit for possession of property which was decreed by the Trial Court. Against this, the wife filed an appeal but pending appeal, she died. The other defendants, *viz.* the children (sons, daughter and daughter-in-law) sought to proceed with the appeal.

Order: The court held that the appeal became infructuous on the death of the wife since the right of residence under section 18 of the Hindu Adoptions and Maintenance Act was personal to her and the legal representatives do not have a vested interest in the matter.

Comment: An order of maintenance, including the right of residence, is personal to the wife and is not inheritable by her adult children on her death.

MALA FIDE TRANSFERS
Mala fide Transfer of Property cannot Defeat Wife's Claim for Maintenance
Hari Lal v. Balvantia,
AIR 1998 All 211: 1998 All LJ 1371: 1998 (3) CCC 275

Issue: Where property is transferred with *mala fide* intentions to defeat a claim for maintenance, such property is liable for maintenance in the hands of the transferee.

Facts: A wife filed a suit for maintenance against the property of her husband alongwith a prayer that he may be restrained by permanent injunction from transferring the property. The same was decreed by the Trial Court. The husband, however, transferred the property in favour of the defendants. After the death of the husband, the wife claimed maintenance from the property. She alleged that despite knowledge of the fact that the burden of maintenance was on the property, the defendants, in collusion got the same transferred in their name. The defendants contested the claim and argued that the husband was a cancer patient and *in lieu of* the financial help rendered to him by the defendants, he executed a sale-deed in their favour. They, accordingly, claimed to be *bona fide* purchasers with valuable consideration.

Order: After analysing the facts and circumstances of the case, the court found that the evidence of consideration in the transfer was not of definite nature so the same could only be treated as gratuitous. It was held, that the wife was entitled to maintenance under section 18 of the Hindu Adoptions and Maintenance Act coupled with section 39 of the Transfer of Property Act, 1882 (TPA), under which, where a third party has a right to receive maintenance and such property is transferred, the right may be enforced against the transferee in certain circumstances.

Comment: Section 28 of the Hindu Adoptions and Maintenance Act and section 39 of the TPA, seek to protect the right of claimants for maintenance, against *mala fide* transfer of properties.

Maintenance – Protection Against *Mala Fide* Transfers

Kangal v. *Atwariya Devi,*
AIR 2002 All 77: 2002 All LJ 603: 2002 (2) CCC 210

Issue: Section 28 of the Hindu Adoptions and Maintenance Act, 1956, seeks to protect the right of claimants against *mala fide* transfers by persons liable to maintain. *Bona fide* transfers, however, are not effected.

Facts: Under section 28 of the Hindu Adoptions and Maintenance Act where a dependant has a right to receive maintenance out of an estate and such estate or any part thereof is transferred, then the right to receive may be enforced against the transferee. This right can be enforced only if—(i) the transfer is for consideration and (ii) the transferee knew about the right of maintenance attached to the property. In this case, a wife filed a suit for maintenance under section 18 of the Hindu Adoptions and Maintenance Act against her husband, including past maintenance. She also made a prayer for creating a charge for maintenance on a plot owned by him. However, before the order, the husband sold the plot by a sale-deed. Pending suit, the husband died and the wife claimed maintenance against the purchaser (the revisionist in this case). The District Court ordered in favour of the wife and held that she could proceed against the transferee. Hence, the revision.

Order: The court admitted the revision and held that the plot was sold by the deceased husband for consideration and before it was attached or any charge created, and therefore, the property was not liable for maintenance. The claim of the wife for maintenance from the husband was a personal obligation of the husband and on his death the claim does not survive. The revisionist who purchased the plot before court order, for consideration and without notice of any right of maintenance attached to it, was held not liable.

Comment: The idea behind section 28 of the Hindu Adoptions and Maintenance Act is to protect the right of claimants against mala fide transfers only to defeat their right. However, if the transfer is bona fide, for consideration and the transferee had no knowledge of any such right of the claimant, then the transferee is not liable.

BARS TO MAINTENANCE CLAIM

Decree of Restitution against Wife – No Absolute Bar to her Maintenance Claim

Pandit Dattaraya Kulkarni v. *Laxmi Pandit Kulkarni*, (2001) 1 Femi-Juris CC 47 (Bom)

Issue: Is a decree of restitution of conjugal rights against the wife, a bar to her claim for maintenance from the husband under section 125 of the Cr. P.C.?

Facts: A husband obtained a decree for restitution of conjugal rights against his wife in 1972, on the ground of her withdrawal from his society without reasonable cause. In 1990, the wife filed an application for maintenance under section 125 of the Cr. P.C., on the ground that the husband had contracted marriage with another woman, therefore, she could not stay with him and comply with the decree for restitution. The Trial Court, after considering the evidence on record, awarded maintenance. Hence, the husband's appeal.

Order: It was argued on behalf of the appellant-husband that once a Civil Court had held that the wife had no reasonable ground to stay away from the husband, she would not be entitled for grant of maintenance as the findings of the civil court in restitution order would be binding in criminal proceedings under section 125, Cr. P.C. However, according to the court, the said finding could not be binding on the Criminal Court or on the parties for all times to come. If in criminal proceedings, the court finds that the husband had subsequently taken a second wife or was living with another woman, the wife is entitled to claim separate maintenance as she is not obliged to resume cohabitation with the husband if he is living with another woman. The defence under sub-section (4) of the section 125 of the Cr. P.C. (that the wife is, *inter alia*, without any sufficient reason, refusing to live with her husband), would not be available to the husband and the decree of restitution passed against the wife cannot stand as a bar against her claim for separate maintenance, in this case, the court held. The maintenance order was accordingly, upheld.

Comment: A wife may claim maintenance from the husband notwithstanding a decree of restitution of conjugal rights obtained by the husband. If the wife has sufficient grounds for not joining the husband despite a restitution order, such restitution order would not stand in the way of her seeking maintenance under the provision of section 125 of the Cr. P.C.

WHEN FREE LEGAL AID

Litigation Expenses when Free Legal Aid Available

Ramesh Babu v. Usha,
AIR 2003 Mad 281: (2003) DMC 272: 2003 (1) Mad LJ 576

Issue: Can an applicant who is entitled to free legal aid, seek litigation expenses under section 24 of the Hindu Marriage Act, 1955?

Facts: A husband filed a petition for annulment of marriage. The wife claimed interim maintenance and litigation expenses under section 24 of the Hindu Marriage Act. The Family Court ordered ₹ 2,500 towards litigation expenses and ₹ 1,250 per month as interim maintenance. Both were dissatisfied and filed appeals – the husband against the maintainability of the litigation expenses and the wife against inadequacy of the amount of interim maintenance.

Order: The husband's argument was that the wife was entitled to free legal aid and, therefore, he was not liable to pay her litigation expenses. The court, however, did not accept this argument and held (at p. 283):

> "Though free legal aid is available..... I am of the view that on this ground the claim of the deserving person cannot be rejected or non-suited when the statutory provision enables the parties to the said proceedings to apply for interim maintenance as well as litigation expenses."

The amount of interim maintenance was also raised from ₹ 1,250 to ₹ 3,000 per month as the wife had no independent source of income and the carry home salary of the husband was assessed at around ₹ 9,000 per month.

Comment: It is common knowledge that the procedure for getting legal aid as well as services available under it may not be satisfactory. To deny litigation expenses under section 24 only on the ground that legal aid is available to the applicant is not justified, as was done by the Gujarat High Court in *Kalaben Kalabhai Desai v. Alabhai Karamshibhai Desai*, AIR 2000 Guj 232: I (2001) DMC 295: 2001 (1) Hindu LR 493. In that case the court rejected a wife's claim for litigation expenses on the ground that she could avail free legal aid which is provided by the State. According to the court, the burden cannot be put on the husband merely because the wife was ignorant of her right to avail legal aid. The view adopted by the court in *Ramesh Babu* is more realistic and logical.

Note: *See* also *Navjot Kumar @ Dolly v. Ajit Singh Phull*, I (2001) DMC 87 (Karn); for a different view, see *Sangitaben Jaiswal v. Sanjay Jaiswal*, I (2001) DMC 19 (Guj); *A.K. Rathod v. B.A. Rathod*, I (2001) DMC 87 (Guj).

LIMITATION

Bar of Limitation – When Applicable

Shantha v. *B.G. Shivananjappa*, AIR 2005 SC 2410: 2005 Cr LJ 2615: 2005 AIR SCW 2613

Issue: Can the bar of limitation under proviso to section 125(3) of the Code of Criminal Procedure apply when the decree-holder has already initiated execution proceedings within time and that execution application is still pending?

Facts: A petition for maintenance under section 125 of the Cr. P.C. was filed by the appellant wife claiming maintenance for herself and her minor daughter. The same was allowed by the Trial Court on January 20, 1993, awarding a sum of ₹ 500 p.m. to the wife and ₹ 300 p.m. to the daughter. The appellant filed application for issuance of warrant for ₹ 5,365 as arrears of maintenance from the period January 20, 1993, till August 31, 1993. This application was very much within the period of limitation of 12 months as prescribed in the proviso to section 125(3) of the Cr. P.C. The husband filed appeals and revisions against the Trial Court order which were dismissed. By that time, the arrears had piled up further. The appellant, therefore, filed an interim application claiming arrears from the period from January 20, 1993, till the date of the filing of the interim application, *viz*. June 16, 1998, for an amount of ₹ 46,000. The husband thereupon deposited a sum of ₹ 5,365 towards maintenance from January 20, 1993, upto August 31, 1993. The rest of the arrears amount was objected to as being time-barred. The session judge over-ruled the objection holding that once an application was filed and was pending no fresh application was required for claiming maintenance which had fallen due for the period past application. According to the sessions judge (at p. 2410), "it is implicit in the powers of the court to make an order directing the husband to make payment of arrears of maintenance upto the decision while disposing of the application for recovery of arrears of maintenance". Fresh application would only lead to multiplicity of litigation, the session judge observed. The High Court, however, allowed husband's revision against this order and held that the application was barred by limitation. Hence, the applicant wife's appeal.

Order: The court held, that the first application for recovery of arrears was filed within one year. As no amount was paid and the application was pending, the purpose of the subsequent interim application filed on September 1, 1998, was only to mention the amount due upto date. This does not mean that the application was fresh application made for the first time. The Court held (at p. 2412) that "the main petition filed in 1993 was pending and kept alive and the filing of subsequent interim application in 1998 was only to specify the exact amount which accrued due upto that date. Such application is only supplementary or incidental to the petition already filed in 1993 admittedly within the period of limitation." Thus, the court held that the High Court had erred in reversing the order of the sessions judge. The wife's appeal was allowed with the following observations (at p. 2412):

> "It must be borne in mind that section 125, Cr. P.C., is a measure of social legislation and it has to be construed liberally for the welfare and benefit of the wife and daughter. It is unreasonable to insist on filing successive applications when the liability to pay the maintenance as per the order under section 125(1) is a continuing liability."

Comment: The idea behind the proviso to section 125(3), is that the decree-holder should not allow the arrears to pile up for too long so as to make payment by the judgment-debtor difficult. However, once the process of execution is initiated well within the limitation period, the bar of limitation cannot be taken if the first application is still pending and meanwhile time has passed and arrears piled up.

SETTLEMENT/CONSENT WHETHER BAR TO SUBSEQUENT CLAIM

Surrender of Right to Claim Maintenance *vide* Settlement Deed – No Bar to Subsequent Claim

Bai Laxmiben v. Bharatbhai Vechatbhai Patel,
1986 Cr LJ 1418 (Guj): I (1986) DMC 129: 1986 (27) Guj LR 272

Issue: Is a wife who has surrendered her right to claim maintenance under a settlement-deed, debarred from claiming maintenance under section 125 of the Cr. P.C.?

Facts: A wife filed an application for maintenance under section 125 of the Cr. P.C. Thereafter, the parties obtained a divorce by compromise. Under the deed of divorce, the wife agreed to drop maintenance proceedings upon the husband paying her a *lump sum* amount of ₹ 901 for future maintenance. After about two years, the wife again filed an application under section 125. Both the courts below dismissed her claim; hence her appeal to the High Court.

Order: The husband's contention was that under section 127(3)(c), her application was barred. Section 127(3)(c) says where any order has been made under section 125 in favour of a woman who has been divorced by or has obtained a divorce from her husband, the Magistrate shall, if he is satisfied that:

   (a) ....
   (b) ....
   (c) The woman has obtained a divorce from her husband and that she had voluntarily surrendered her right to maintenance after her divorce, cancel the order from the date thereof.

The High Court dismissed the husband's plea and held that for the applicability of this provision the pre-requisite is that there should be an order under section 125 of the Cr. P.C. In this case, there was no order under section 125; the parties had just arrived at a settlement and the proceedings under section 125 had been dropped without any order. The wife was thus entitled to seek maintenance under section 125, the court held. The court also reiterated the stand taken by the courts earlier in cases of lump-sum settlements. It was the duty of the court to examine whether the amount so paid had any rational connection with the necessities of life or was it just an illusory amount. In this case, an amount of ₹ 901 was, in no way, considered to be sufficient for her entire life. After assessing the husband's income, an amount of ₹ 130 per month was fixed for her maintenance.

Comment: The provision for cancellation of maintenance under section 127(3)(c) is applicable only when the earlier maintenance is awarded under section 125 of the Cr. P.C. If the maintenance is settled by a mutual agreement then section 127(3)(c) is not applicable. Also, the amount by way of settlement needs to be a realistic amount, not just illusory.

EARLIER COMPROMISE

Earlier Compromised Agreement – No Bar to Subsequent Claim for Enhancement

Joydel Kumar Biswas v. *Madhuri Biswas*, 1994 Cr LJ 3342 (Cal): I (1996) DMC 12: 1996 (2) Hindu LR 290

Issue: A compromise agreement arrived at by the parties in respect of maintenance is no bar to a wife's subsequent claim for enhancement.

Facts: In enhancement proceedings under section 127 of the Cr. P.C. by the wife, the parties entered into a compromise under which the husband agreed to pay ₹ 6,000 for the marriage expenses of the daughter and ₹ 100 per month to the wife. After some time, the wife again applied for enhancement of the allowance, which was allowed. Hence, the husband's present revision against it.

Order: It was argued on his behalf that since the amount was settled by way of a compromise agreement, the wife was now estopped from moving the court for enhancement. The court relied on several cases and held that an application for modification of maintenance order in changed circumstances cannot be barred by any agreement. The following observations made by the Punjab and Haryana High Court in *Ranjit Kaur* v. *Pavittar Singh*, 1992 Cri LJ 262 (P&H): ILR (1992) 2 P&H 107: 1991 (2) Punj LR 421, were relied upon:

> "The statutory right of wife to maintenance cannot be barred, done away with or negatived by the husband by setting up an agreement to the contrary. Such an agreement, in addition to it being against public policy would also be against the clear intendment of this provision......... Thus, the agreement whereby this statutory right of wife to maintenance was relinquished may not *per se* be illegal but it cannot be given effect to being a negation of the statutory right as provided for in this section and being opposed to public policy."

Comment: While it is understandable that in the event of changed circumstances a settlement arrived at by compromise should not stand in the way of a wife seeking enhancement of the allowance, it is important that courts should not take the agreements lightly either. If agreements were to have no value after some time, the non-claimants would be discouraged to make compromise settlements.

Note. *See* however *Sayeed Khan Faujdar Khan* v. *Zaheba Begum*, AIR 2006 Bom 39: II (2006) DMC 294: 2006 Mat LR 261 where it was held that a consent settlement made under section 125 Cr. P.C. operates as estoppel against filing subsequent application for maintenance under a different Act.

WIFE CONSENTING TO GIVE UP CLAIM

Wife Agreeing to give up Claim under Consent Divorce Decree – No Bar to Claiming Maintenance in Future

Geeta Satish Gokarna v. *Satish Gokarna,*
AIR 2004 Bom 345: 2004 (20) All Ind Cas 839:
2004 (3) Mah LJ 159

Issue: Can a wife under a consent divorce decree agree to give up her claim for any maintenance in future and would this debar her from claiming any maintenance from her husband thereafter?

Facts: A marriage was dissolved by mutual consent of the parties and as one of the terms of the consent decree, the wife agreed not to claim any maintenance/alimony from the husband. However, two years after the decree, she filed an application under section 25 of the Hindu Marriage Act for permanent alimony at the rate of ₹ 25,000 p.m. from the date of application. The Trial Court held that the wife's application was maintainable despite the consent clause whereunder it was agreed that "the petitioner [wife] will not claim any maintenance or alimony in future from the respondent [husband]". Accordingly, it ordered the husband to pay ₹ 2,000 per month as maintenance to the wife. Both the parties appealed—the wife against the quantum and the husband against the very maintainability of the wife's claim. The appeals were dismissed. The High Court found no material on record which could justify enhancement of the amount in favour of the wife, and as to the husband's objection, it held that the power to grant maintenance has been conferred on the court by Parliament under the Act and the parties cannot, by agreement, oust the court's jurisdiction. The court further stated that permanent alimony and maintenance are a larger part of the right to life. These provisions according to the court are included "to enable a person unable to maintain herself (or himself) to be protected..... Therefore, any clause in a contract or consent terms providing to the contrary would be against public policy". (at p. 349)

Reference was made to a Bombay High Court decision in *Hirabai Bharucha* v. *Pirojshah Bharucha*, AIR 1945 Bom 537: 47 Bom LR 514, which was a case under section 40 of the Parsi Marriage and Divorce Act, 1936 where the wife had given up her right of maintenance in terms of an agreement. The court, in that case held (quoted in *Geeta Satish Gokerna* at p. 348):

> "The principle is that where on grounds of public policy, wife cannot enter into such contract then the contract is void and the court will take no notice of that and ignore that part of the order though it was made by consent because as remarked by Lord Atkin 'the wife's right to

future maintenance is a matter of public concern which she cannot barter away'......."

Order: An agreement in a consent divorce decree not to claim maintenance cannot close the doors for a wife to claim maintenance thereafter. Maintenance has been construed as an integral part of right to life.

Comment: While it cannot be denied that maintenance is an integral part of right to life one really wonders whether it is fair to allow a consenting party to retract. The view taken by the court has the potential of discouraging mutual settlement of issues and consent divorces since consent agreements are package where parties agree to barter certain rights and claims to buy peace. If terms and conditions of the consent agreement are fair and reasonable, the courts should honour such agreement and discourage retraction.

Note: *See* also *P. Archana @ Atchamamba* v. *Varada Siva Rama Krishna*, I (2009) DMC 265 (AP DB): AIR 2008 AP 216: 2008 (69) All Ind Cas 742. Where however there was a "full and final" settlement made by parties in Civil Court in 1983, the wife's subsequent application for maintenance in 2002 was held to be not *bona fide* in *S. Ranawat* v. *State of Gujarat*, II (2010) DMC 730 (Guj).

Parents cannot Barter Away Children's Right
Mohinder Singh v. *Ravneet Kaur,*
2008 MLR 68 (P&H)

Issue: An issue of great significance involved in this case was whether, while setting their own matrimonial claims, parents can barter rights of children.

Facts: In a matrimonial dispute between the parents they arrived at a settlement whereunder it was agreed that the father would not press for the custody of the children and they will stay with the mother, and the mother, in return, will not claim any maintenance for them. However, after some time the children filed an application for maintenance under section 20 of the Hindu Adoptions and Maintenance Act, 1956 and the same was allowed by the Trial Court. Against this the father filed an appeal. His contentions *inter alia*, were:

(i) in view of the settlement agreement at the time of divorce, the mother who had the custody of the children had agreed that the children would not ask for any maintenance from him and so now the children are estopped from making such claim;

(ii) that the children were not unable to maintain themselves which is the basis for eligibility to seek maintenance – as they were already being maintained by the mother;

(iii) *vide* section 20(2) of the Act a child may claim maintenance from his or her father *or* mother thereby implying that the children can claim only against one of them – either the mother or the father; and in this case since they were already being maintained by the mother, it was not open to them to file a maintenance application against the father as well.

Order: The father's appeal was dismissed and the court held that maintenance is a statutory right of the children and parents cannot amongst themselves enter into any agreement whereunder they barter away this right of the children. Such an agreement being against the interests of the minors cannot be enforced in law and hence the father cannot be absolved of his duty to give maintenance for the children.

As to the argument that children can seek maintenance only against one of the parents the court held that if the amount paid by way of maintenance by one of the parents is not sufficient, there is nothing to prevent the children from enforcing their claim against the other parent as well. The other parent cannot seek exemption on the plea that the children are already being provided by one parent. The father was thus held liable to pay maintenance to the children.

Comment: While it is logical that parents should not be allowed to barter away the rights of children yet it is significant to note that agreements in matrimonial proceedings must be holistically viewed. The terms of settlement are by way of a package where parties compromise on certain things. A husband or wife may give up a right or entitlement in lieu of something and if that is fair, it should be honoured. True it is that rights of children should not be bartered away by parents in order to secure settlement of their matrimonial disputes yet the same cannot be ignored altogether. Each case needs to be decided on its own peculiar facts and circumstances, the prime consideration undisputedly being the interests of the children.

DATE OF AWARD

Maintenance *pendente lite* – Date from which to be Awarded
Popri Bai v. Teerath Singh,
AIR 2004 Raj 128: 2004 (3) Civ LJ 107: 2004 (2) CCC 262

Issue: Should the court award maintenance *pendente lite* from the date of order or from the date of application?

Facts: A husband filed a petition for restitution of conjugal rights against his wife on February 3, 1999. On July 15, 1999, the wife filed an application under section 24 of the Hindu Marriage Act for interim maintenance for herself and the minor son. On April 11, 2001 the Trial Court directed the respondent husband to pay ₹ 1,000 per month till the decision of the husband's application. No mention, however, was made as to the date from which the same was to be paid. On June 1, 2001, the husband got his restitution petition dismissed for non-prosecution. On August 23, 2001, the wife filed an application for execution of the order dated April 11, 2001, for recovery of amount from the date of filing the petition. The execution court held that she was entitled to maintenance only from the date of the order and not from the date of application. The wife filed a revision against this. The court held that the husband played a trick by deliberately getting his petition dismissed. If the court were to go by the facts of the dates, then the wife would be entitled to maintenance only for one month and a few days *viz.*, from April 11, 2001 to June 1, 2001. According to the court, in awarding maintenance under section 24, the court has a discretion to order maintenance either from the date of application or from the date of order or from any other date; however, this is a judicious order and where a court decides not to grant maintenance from date of filing of the application then it needs to record the reasons therefor. In this case no reasons were recorded for not granting maintenance from the date of application. It remarked:

> "In these facts and circumstances of the case, if the respondent-husband is permitted to do injustice and play tricks with the poor petitioner wife, it will result in failure of justice to her. Not only this, unscrupulous husbands, like the present one, will get success in their oblique motives and *mala fide* intentions."

Order: The court, in exercise of its powers under article 227 of the Constitution to do complete justice, modified the order dated April 11, 2001 by awarding interim maintenance *w.e.f.* the date of filing the application, *viz.*, July 15, 1999. It held:

"It is a case where, if order of the........Trial Court is allowed to stand, it will not only result in failure of justice to the poor wife but it will cause serious prejudice to her. Not only this, it will encourage these unscrupulous litigants who make attempts to befool or play tricks with their wives."

Comment: This case is a vivid example of how some unscrupulous husbands try to harass their wives and use the court process for achieving this. The court, however, saw through the husband's tricks. It is suggested that a maintenance order should be made from the date of application unless there are justifiable reasons to do otherwise. In such cases reasons should be recorded.

CONDUCT OF PARTIES

Husband Allowing Dismissal of his Main Petition – Liable to Pay Arrears of Maintenance

Lataben Y. Goswami v. *Yogendra Kumar Shankargir Goswami*,
AIR 1996 Guj 103: 1996 (1) CCC 188: 1996 (1) Hindu LR 712

Issue: Can a husband be absolved of the liability to pay arrears of interim maintenance to the wife after allowing dismissal of his main petition under the Act?

Facts: A husband filed a petition for restitution of conjugal rights under section 9 of the Hindu Marriage Act whereupon the wife applied for maintenance under section 24, Hindu Marriage Act. The same was allowed and the court allowed ₹ 200 per month as interim maintenance and ₹ 300 towards litigation expenses on April 1, 1988. The husband challenged this but his application was rejected. He was given sufficient time for making the payment which he failed to do. In the main petition also, he made no appearance on subsequent dates either in person or through counsel, hence the same was dismissed for non-prosecution on August 5, 1993. The wife filed an application for recovery of arrears of maintenance amount *w.e.f.* April 1, 1988 to August 5, 1993. The same was turned down as being not maintainable in view of the dismissal of the main petition of the husband. Hence the wife's revision.

Order: It was argued on behalf of the wife that under the provision of section 28A of the Hindu Marriage Act all decrees and orders made by it in any proceeding under the Act are enforceable in the same manner as decrees and orders of the court made in the exercise of its original civil jurisdiction. And further, it was contended that an order for maintenance *pendente lite* remains in force during pendency of proceedings and in this case the proceedings under section 9 for restitution remained pending till the application was dismissed on August 5, 1993 and so the wife was entitled to the arrears.

After going through the contentions of both the parties, the wife's revision was allowed. The court observed:

> "The finding of the learned Trial Court that the interim order passed in any proceedings would itself get extinguished or lost the sanctity with the ultimate fate of the main proceedings is perverse on the face of it. In case such interpretation is given.........then the whole purpose of enacting the aforesaid section in the Act will be frustrated.....Not only this but it will be easy for a spouse who does not want to pay the amount of the maintenance or the cost of litigation despite the order of the court to deny the same

by allowing the dismissal of the petition for non-prosecution. Section 28A was substituted in the Act of 1955 to mitigate the hardships........"

Comment: A husband cannot be allowed to defeat the claim of the wife to the arrears of maintenance by simply dropping or not proceeding with the main petition. This would not only be unfair on the wife but also defiance of court order.

Husband's Remarrying Sufficient Cause for First Wife's Withdrawal & Claiming Maintenance

Ashabi B. Takke v. *Bashasab Takke,*
AIR 2003 Kant 172: ILR 2003 (1) Kant 737: 2003 (2) Kant LJ 420

Issue: Is a wife's refusal to join her husband who has remarried sufficient justification for her withdrawal from him and claiming maintenance?

Facts: A wife filed an application for maintenance under section 25 of the Hindu Marriage Act on the ground that her husband had driven her out of the house and had also contracted a second marriage. The facts of the case are not clear as to the main relief sought by her except that she alleged ill-treatment; desertion and second marriage. The husband's contention was that he was prepared to take her back and offered her to return which she declined. The Trial Court held that the wife having turned down the husband's offer to return, she was not entitled to maintenance; hence her petition was dismissed. The wife appealed against this.

Order: The fact of second marriage was established. The husband, however, argued that she had refused to join his company earlier and so was guilty of desertion. His other defence was that she had, earlier also, filed an application for maintenance under section 125 of the Cr. P.C. which was dismissed. In view of the above mentioned circumstances, the Trial Court's refusal to grant her maintenance was justified, the husband contended. The High Court, however, did not accept these arguments and held (at p. 173):

> "The question of the wife deserting the husband or the husband deserting the wife pales into insignificance in the light of this development [*i.e.,* the husband's second marriage]. The fact that the wife could not get maintenance earlier under section 125, Cr. P.C. proceedings also cannot have any bearing in a suit for maintenance filed subsequent to the defendant husband having contracted a second marriage. This is so even if the personal law of the defendant permits him to contract more than one marriage."

Comment: The second marriage of the husband *per se* is sufficient justification for a wife to leave him and claim maintenance. When that is proved, nothing else needs to be established.

Wife Taking Advantage of own Wrong

Sudha Suhas Nandanvankar v. Suhas Ramrao Nandanvankar,
AIR 2005 Bom 62: 2005 (26) All Ind Cas 801:
2005 (1) Hindu LR 130

Issue: Can a wife whose conduct demonstrates that she is trying to take advantage of her own wrong or fraud to harass the husband, be awarded permanent alimony?

Facts: The parties were married in 1995 according to Hindu rites. The marriage was annulled by a decree of nullity in 1996 on the ground that the wife was suffering from epilepsy at the time of marriage which fact was not disclosed to the husband and hence a fraud was committed on him prior to the Marriage Laws (Amendment) Act, 1999 epilepsy was a ground on which a marriage could be avoided and a decree obtained under section 11, coupled with section 5(ii)(c) of the Hindu Marriage Act. The word epilepsy in section (c) of section 5(ii) has now been deleted.] Even though the decree was *ex parte*, it was not challenged by the wife. However after the decree the wife first claimed return of articles which were presented to her by her parents at the time of marriage. Further, she claimed expenses incurred at the marriage. During pendency of this application she again submitted application for return of articles and jewellery presented to her by her in-laws at the time of marriage. She further claimed permanent alimony. The wife's application was only partly allowed by the Family Court. Hence she filed an appeal in respect of part rejection of her application. The main issue for consideration was in respect of alimony claimed by her.

Order: The court conceded that a wife is entitled to claim alimony even though a decree of nullity is passed at the instance of the non-applicant. This, however, according to the court is not an absolute right. If a wife's conduct is such that the court feels that she should not be granted maintenance, the court may refuse her application. In this case, according to the court:

> "The non-disclosure by the parents of the appellant, and the appellant's accepting the decree as it is, without making any grudge in respect of the ground that the appellant was suffering from epilepsy prior to the marriage reflects upon the conduct of the appellant, and if we take into consideration this aspect what we find is that the appellant is trying to take advantage of her wrong or fraud and is trying to harass the respondent by claiming the amount of alimony."

And further, the court held:

> "What we find is that after a decree of annulment, the respondent has married and he is having a child. Now this appears to be an attempt on the part of the appellant and her parents to disturb the marital life of the respondent which he has tried to settle after annulment of the marriage. This is an attempt to shift the liability of maintenance by the appellant-wife on a husband who was not at fault and who has not consummated the marriage. *Even though the law permits the right of alimony in favour of*

the appellant, however, the conduct and circumstances involved in the present case does not permit us to pass an order of permanent alimony in favour of the appellant." (Emphasis added).

The wife's appeal was, thus, dismissed.

Comment: If a married man defrauding a woman into entering a bigamous relationship and then seeking annulment on that ground, can be absolved from paying maintenance to the defrauded wife [*Bakulbai* v. *Gangaram,* 1988 (1) Scale 188] where is the fairness or justification to deny maintenance to a wife whose major misconduct is the concealment of her epilepsy before marriage on the basis of which the husband has already obtained annulment. This is not to justify "wrong", "misconduct" or "fraud" on the part of any spouse but only indicates how subjective approach/attitude can lead to varying interpretations in order to deny or grant a relief. In both the cases, *Bakulbai* and *Sudha Suhas Nandanvankar* (examples can be multiplied) the fraud is serious but the victim is the wife only—whether the husband is the defrauder or it is she who is guilty of the fraud.

QUANTUM

Quantum of Maintenance

Capt. Ramesh Chander Kaushal v. Veena Kaushal,
AIR 1978 SC 1807: (1978) 4 SCC 70: 1978 Cr LJ 3

Issue: Whether the amount of ₹ 500 "in the whole" (prior to amendment) which could be awarded to a claimant under section 125, Cr.P.C., means the total award for wife, children and parents taken together?

Facts: The husband filed a petition for divorce and the wife claimed maintenance under section 125 of the Cr..P.C. As an interim measure, the District Court awarded maintenance and the High Court fixed the rate at ₹ 400 as a provisional figure. Meanwhile the Magistrate, on the evidence before him, ordered *ex parte* monthly maintenance at ₹ 1,000 for mother and the two children together. This was challenged on the ground that the maximum amount which could be awarded to the mother and children, as a whole, under section 125 of the Code was ₹ 500. Dismissing the argument, the court held:

> "This provision is a measure of social justice and specially enacted to protect women and children and falls within the constitutional sweep of article 15(3) reinforced by article 39. We have no doubt that sections of statutes calling for construction by courts are not petrified print but vibrant words with social functions to fulfil. The brooding presence of the constitutional empathy for the weaker sections like women and children must inform interpretation if it has to have social relevance. So viewed, it is possible to be selective in picking out that interpretation out of two alternatives which advances the cause—the cause of the derelicts." (para. 9)

The court referred, *inter alia*, to the following remarks of Chagla, C.J., in *Prabhavati* v. *Sumatilal*, AIR 1954 Bom 546:

> "The intention of the Legislature was clear, and the intention was to cast an obligation upon a person who neglects or refused to maintain his wife or children to carry out his obligation towards his wife or children. The obligation is separate and independent in relation to each one of the persons whom he is bound in law to maintain. It is futile to suggest that in using the expression "in the whole", the Legislature was limiting the juridiction of the Magistrate to passing an order in respect of all the persons whom he is bound to maintain, allowing them maintenance not exceeding a sum of one hundred rupees." (This was the amount prior to 1973 Code.)

Order: The order of the Magistrate was upheld and the Court held that there was no illegality in the Magistrate's order in awarding ₹ 1,000 for mother and children, all together.

Comment: The case now has an academic value only, since, by an amendment in 2001, there is no upper ceiling. The judgment, however, is indicative of the court's sensitivity to interpret the provisions so as to promote the cause of justice and the weaker parties.

INTERIM MAINTENANCE

Interim Maintenance Order

Savitri v. Govind Singh,
1986 Cr LJ 41 (SC): AIR 1986 SC 984: (1985) 4 SCC 337

Issue: Can a court in maintenance proceedings under section 125 of the Cr. P.C. make interim orders for maintenance in the absence of any express provision to that effect? (The controversy is settled in view of the amendment of the Cr. P.C. in 2001.)

Facts: A wife made an application for maintenance under section 125 of the Cr. P.C. Immediately thereafter, she made another application for interim order directing the husband to pay reasonable sum by way of maintenance pending disposal of the main application. Her application was refused by the Magistrate on the ground that there was no express provision in the code which empowered the Magistrate to make such order. Thereafter, the wife filed a special leave petition under article 136 of the Constitution before the Supreme Court.

Order: The Supreme Court held, that in the absence of any express prohibition preventing a Magistrate to pass an interim order of maintenance, it is appropriate to construe the provisions in Chapter IX as conferring an implied power on the Magistrate to direct the other party to pay reasonable sum pending final disposal of application under section 125 of the Cr. P.C. In the absence of interim orders, applicants without any means of subsistence are likely to suffer grave hardships. The court observed that generally an application for maintenance takes several months for being disposed of finally. In order to enjoy the fruits of the proceedings of maintenance, the applicant should be alive till the date of the final order and that the applicant can do so, in a large number of cases, only if an order for payment of interim maintenance is passed by the court.

It was argued on behalf of the husband that such orders might cause prejudice to the party against whom it is passed. Negativing this contention, the court held that such prejudice is minimal and can be set right after hearing both the parties. Also, the Magistrate may insist upon affidavit being filed by the applicant stating grounds in support of his or her claim for interim maintenance in order of satisfy itself that there is a *prima facie* case for making such order.

Comment: The Code of Criminal Procedure (Amendment) Act, 2001, makes an express provision for interim maintenance orders, so now there is no controversy on the point. It is a fact that final orders take long time and the whole purpose of seeking maintenance would be lost if the applicant is not provided with maintenance during the interim period.

EXECUTION OF MAINTENANCE DECREE

Maintenance Already Due: Widow can Proceed Against Assets of Deceased Husband

Aruna Basu Mullick v. *Dorothea Mitra*, AIR 1983 SC 916: (1983) 3 SCC 522: II (1983) DMC 289

Issue: Does an order for alimony get extinguished with the death of the judgment-debtor?

Facts: A wife filed an application for maintenance under section 37 of the Special Marriage Act, 1954. An order for ₹ 300 per month was made. In execution proceedings, the decree was compromised and the husband agreed to pay the arrears in instalments. On March 31, 1965, he executed a Will but made no provision for satisfaction of the maintenance decree. On April 3, 1965, he died. The appellant, who was the executrix under the Will, got it duly probated. She paid maintenance for some period after the death of the judgment-debtor but thereafter since no payment was made, the wife filed a suit for recovery of arrears of ₹ 19,500. The appellant filed an objection and argued that the order of alimony was not made a charge and so the liability was extinguished on the death of the judgment-debtor. This objection was over-ruled by the executing court. The appellant then went in revision and the Division Bench of the Calcutta High Court agreed with the finding of the executing court. The appellant was, however, granted a certificate of appeal; hence the present appeal to the Supreme Court.

Order: On behalf of the appellant some English authorities were sought to be relied upon to show that no cause of action subsists after the death of husband and so an order for alimony would be extinguished. [*e.g.,* 13 *Halsbury's Laws of England* (4th Edn., Para. 891 at 419-30, 1975); *Sugden* v. *Sugden,* (1957) 1 All ER 300: (1957) 2 WLR 210; *Stanhope* v. *Stanhope,* (1886) 11 PD 103 (CA)]. The court, however, did not agree with this argument of the appellant and held that the Special Marriage Act was an Indian statute passed after Independence and there was no warrant to be guided by English authorities in the interpretation of its provisions. It was, accordingly, held that the assets left behind by the husband were liable to be proceeded against in the hands of his legal heirs for the satisfaction of the decree of maintenance.

Comment: When an amount by way of maintenance has already become due to the widow, she can proceed for its recovery from the assets left behind by her deceased husband.

ARREARS TILL LIFE OF HUSBAND

Only Arrears Till Husband's Life can be Recovered

Prithviraj Singh v. *Pavanvir Singh*, 1986 Cr LJ 1432 (P&H): ILR (1986) 2 P&H 205

Issue: A deceased husband's estate is liable for maintenance due to the wife till his death and not for any period beyond his death.

Facts: The husband had bequeathed all his properties to his nephew. The wife filed execution proceedings for recovery of arrears of maintenance. The nephew approached the court contending that after the death of the deceased, he became the sole owner, and therefore, the process of recovery of arrears for maintenance had become invalid. The Magistrate thereupon called back the warrants of attachment which had been issued, and dismissed the wife's application. In revision filed by the wife, it was held that the amount of maintenance allowance for a period for which the husband was alive could be realised by her as provided under section 421(1)(b) of the Code (*i.e.*, procedure in respect of levying fines) and restored the wife's application. Against this, the deceased husband's nephew filed the present revision.

Order: The court held, that the estate of the husband could not be burdened with enforcement of maintenance order under the Code for any period beyond the date of the husband's death, but was enforceable against it till his death.

Comment: When maintenance order in favour of a wife has been made and the amount is in arrears, upon the death of the husband, his estate is liable only for the period till his death. The deceased husband's estate cannot be burdened for recovery, for period beyond his death.

Wife's Claim for Maintenance does not Stand Satisfied after Defaulting Husband's Imprisonment for Non-payment

Kuldip Kaur v. *Surinder Singh*, 1989 Cr LJ 794 (SC): AIR 1989 SC 232: (1989) 1 SCC 405

Issue: Does a wife's claim for arrears of maintenance stand satisfied upon the husband being sent to jail for non-payment of the same?

Facts: Upon a clear finding of cruelty by the husband, the Trial Court awarded maintenance to the wife. The amount not having been paid, the husband was in arrears. The wife sought enforcement of the orders and the husband was sentenced to imprisonment for non-payment. The wife moved an application for recovery of arrears which was rejected by the Magistrate on the ground that the claim for arrears stood satisfied upon the husband being sent to jail. The wife's revision application in the High Court was summarily rejected without a speaking order, hence her appeal to the Supreme Court.

Order: The Supreme Court held that sentencing a person to jail was a "mode of enforcement" and not a "mode of satisfaction" of a decree. The liability could be satisfied only by making actual payment of the arrears. The purpose of sending a judgment-debtor to jail was not to wipe out the liability which he had failed to discharge; it was only a means for achieving the end *viz.*, enforcement of the order. The Court consequently directed that the defaulting husband be put to jail till he made the payment.

Comment: The court pointed out the difference between 'mode of enforcement' and 'mode of satisfaction'. So, until the judgment-debtor makes the payment he will keep on going to jail. But this mode of enforcement may go on endlessly: what if the husband prefers going to jail rather than making the payment?

Note: *See* also *Ajith Kumar* v. *Shaima*, AIR 2010 (NOC) 229 (Ker).

ORDERS BY GRAM PANCHAYAT

Execution of Maintenance Orders Made by *Gram Panchayat*

Padmo v. Surat Ram,
2003 Cr LJ 237 (HP): I (2003) DMC 483: 2003 (1) Hindu LR 523

Issue: Can an order of maintenance under section 125 of the Cr. P.C., passed by the *Gram Panchayat* under the H.P. Panchayati Raj Act, 1994, be executed by the Chief Judicial Magistrate?

Facts: A wife filed an application for maintenance under section 125 of the Cr.P.C., alleging desertion by the husband. The Additional Chief Judicial Magistrate at Theog referred the matter to the *Gram Panchayat*, Tehsil Theog, Shimla. The *Gram Panchayat* passed a maintenance order at the rate of ₹ 300 each for the wife and one child and ₹ 200 each for two other children. On the husband's failing to pay, the wife filed for execution of the maintenance order and arrears which amounted to ₹ 3,400. The *Gram Panchayat* issued notice to the husband to deposit the amount within ten days, but he failed to do so. Under the Himachal Pradesh Panchayat Raj Act, 1994, a *Gram Panchayat* is not empowered to issue a warrant for levying the amount due in the manner provided for levying fines under section 125(3) of the Cr. P.C. It can, however, impose a fine of ₹ 100. Besides, it can also forward the order of maintenance for execution, to the court of the Judicial Magistrate having jurisdiction. The *Gram Panchayat*, accordingly, sent the file to the Judicial Magistrate for execution of the order but the same was returned with observation that there was no provision to send the file to this court. The wife thereupon filed an application in the court of the Additional Chief Judicial Magistrate under section 125 Cr. P.C., seeking fresh order since the order passed by the *Gram Panchayat* could not be executed. This was also returned by the court on the ground that since the earlier order existed, no new order could be passed. Hence, the wife's appeal.

Order: The court examined the Himachal Pradesh Panchayati Raj Act, 1994. Under this Act general powers are given to the *Gram Panchayat* to entertain civil, criminal and other revenue matters, and maintenance is one of them. The Chief Judicial Magistrate was accordingly, directed to execute the order passed by the *Gram Panchayat*. The court observed that "since the matter is pending for the last more than four years the said court is directed to expedite the matter and provide justice and succour to helpless wife and children left in the lurch by the husband to fend for themselves".

Comment: The idea behind empowering *Gram Panchayats* to entertain and decide certain cases is to expedite relief. It is, however, unfortunate that the case had to oscillate between the *Gram Panchayat* and the courts before the applicant wife could finally get relief.

NON-COMPLIANCE OF ORDER TO PAY LITIGATION EXPENSES

Defence can be Struck Down

Bani v. Parkash Singh,
AIR 1996 P&H 175: I (1997) DMC 5: ILR (1997) 1 P&H 118

Issue: In case of non-compliance of an order under section 24 of the Hindu Marriage Act can the defence of the defaulter be struck down?

Facts: A husband obtained a decree of divorce against the wife on the ground of cruelty. She filed an appeal against it. During pendency of appeal, she sought maintenance and litigation expenses under section 24 of the Hindu Marriage Act. The court decreed ₹ 500 per month as maintenance *pendente lite* and ₹ 2,200 as litigation expenses.

Order: The husband failed to comply with this order despite several notices over a period of two years. His defence was therefore struck down. The court observed (at p. 176):

> "Law is not that powerless as not to bring the husband to book. If the husband has failed to make the payment of maintenance and litigation expenses to the wife, his defence can be struck out."

Comment: The purpose behind this is to ensure that a husband provides for the wife and children while the litigation is on. If he fails to do so, his defence will be struck out and the case will proceed.

Note: See also *Anupama* v. *Ashwani Kumar*, I (2002) DMC 665 (P&H); *Hema* v. *Parthasarthy*, 2003 (1) HLR 8.

Order under Section 24, Non-compliance by Husband: No *ex parte* Divorce in his favour Because of Wife's Non-filing Written Statement

Dinesh Kumar v. Santosh Devi,
AIR 2007 All 30: 2007 (1) ALJ 138: 2006 (65) All LR 889

Issue: The issue involved in the case was whether an *ex parte* divorce decree could be passed in favour of the husband against the wife who fails to file her written statement as the husband had failed to comply with an order of maintenance under section 24 of the Hindu Marriage Act made in her favour.

Facts: The husband sought and got an *ex parte* divorce decree against his wife. The wife went in appeal and the lower appellate court set aside the divorce decree. Against this the husband came in appeal. His argument was that there was no justification on the part of the lower appellate court to have set aside the divorce order simply because there was non-compliance on his part of directions given under section 24 of the Hindu Marriage Act. An order under this section was passed by the Trial Court directing the husband to deposit litigation expenses amounting to ₹ 2,000 and also pay an amount of ₹ 5,000 per month to the wife. The husband had failed to deposit the said amounts. In revision against the order under section 24, no stay was obtained either.

Order: It was held that in case such litigation expenses are not paid to the wife, the court cannot compel her to file written statement or pronounce an *ex parte* judgment under Order 8, rule 10 of the Civil Procedure Code. The Trial Court should have, in fact dismissed the divorce petition itself for non-compliance of the order under section 24. The court remarked that the defendant wife is not expected to be in a position to file the written statement and contest the suit in such circumstances when the litigation expenses, as directed by the court, had not been paid to her by the husband. In such case, if the court proceeds to pass an *ex parte* divorce order, it would be nothing but making mockery with the procedure provided for that purpose. The husband's appeal was consequently, dismissed.

Comment: The purpose of section 24 is to provide financial assistance to a spouse to fight/contest legal proceedings. When a court passes an order to that effect, the defaulting party cannot take advantage of that and seek matrimonial relief.

Mode of Divorce Immaterial to Claim for Maintenance by Wife

Kongini Balan v. M. Visalakshy,
1986 Cr LJ 697 (Ker)

Issue: Can a wife who has obtained divorce by mutual consent seek maintenance in view of the provision of section 125(4) of the Cr. P.C.?

Facts: A wife who had obtained a divorce by mutual consent filed an application for maintenance under section 125 of the Cr. P.C. The husband's objection was that under the provisions of section 125(4) of the Cr. P.C., a wife who is residing separately by mutual consent is not entitled to maintenance, and by that logic, a divorcee by mutual consent cannot be placed in a more advantageous position. His plea was that a wife could become a divorcee by different ways, *viz.*, by being divorced by the husband, by obtaining divorce from the husband and by divorce by mutual consent and that it was only under the first two situations that she would be entitled to maintenance and not in case of a divorce by mutual consent.

Order: This argument was rejected by the court and it was held (at p. 698):

> "The respondent's status as divorced wife does not depend upon the mode of divorce. The code does not say that a divorced wife is not entitled to maintenance in case the divorce has been obtained by mutual agreement."

It was further held that the fact that under section 125(4) of the Cr. P.C., a wife living separately from the husband by mutual consent without divorce was not entitled to maintenance does not mean that a wife upon divorce would not be entitled to maintenance either, merely because she obtained divorce by mutual agreement. Had that been the intention of the Legislators, it would have been made explicit, the court held.

Comment: Under the Cr. P.C., even a divorced wife is entitled to maintenance. Mode of divorce is immaterial. Thus, even if the divorce is obtained by mutual consent, she is not debarred from claiming maintenance under the Code.

Note. See however *Sayeed Khan Faujdar Khan v. Zaheba Begum*, AIR 2006 Bom 39: II (2006) DMC 294: 2006 Mat LR 261 in section of Muslim law.

SIMULTANEOUS REMEDIES

Army Officer's Wife may Claim Maintenance under Army Act as well

Capt. Suneel v. Union of India,
AIR 2004 Del 95: 2003 (12) All Ind Cas 915: 2003 (107) DLT 224

Issue: Does an army officer's wife have a right to claim maintenance under the provisions of the Army Act even while she has a remedy under section 125 of the Cr. P.C. and section 24 of the Hindu Marriage Act?

Facts: The parties were married in 1995, but after some time their relations strained and in 2001, the husband filed a petition for divorce under section 13 of the Hindu Marriage Act. The wife, on the other hand, filed criminal complaints under sections 406 and 498A of the I.P.C, against the petitioner husband and his parents and a case was registered. She also made an application to the Army Commander, Headquarters, for grant of maintenance allowance. After hearing the husband, the Army Commander (AC) made an order sanctioning deduction of 22% from the pay of the petitioner towards wife's maintenance. Against this, the husband filed the present writ petition.

The husband's contentions in appeal were that:

  (i) he never neglected to maintain the respondent;
 (ii) he had made sufficient provision by depositing sum of ₹ 2 lakhs in fixed deposit out of which she has fraudulently withdrawn ₹ 1 lakh;
(iii) she is having her own income of ₹ 5,000 per month;
(iv) the respondent, instead of making an application for maintenance under section 125 Cr. P.C., or under section 24 of Hindu Marriage Act in the proceedings for divorce, made an application to the Army Commander for grant of maintenance, and,
 (v) the General Officer Commanding-in-Chief (one of the respondents) has passed the order for deduction at the rate of 22% from his pay and allowances without considering the merit of the case and recommendations of the Commanders in the charge of Command.

The respondents sought to justify the impugned order. There was only one significant issue to be decided. The court held that the powers to grant maintenance under the Army Act are independent of the provisions of the Cr. P.C. (section 125), and section 24 of the Hindu Marriage Act. Section 90(i) of the Army Act makes provision for deductions from pay and allowances of an officer of any sum required by order of the Central Government or any prescribed officer to be paid for the maintenance of his wife or his legitimate or illegitimate child. In terms of rule 193 of the Army Rules, the prescribed officer for purposes of clause (i) of section 90 is the Chief of the Army Staff or the Officer Commanding the Army. Further, Army Order 23/94 provides a detailed procedure to be observed before ordering for deductions of any amount from the pay and allowances of an officer. In view of all these provisions and rules, the wife was held not to be debarred from claiming maintenance by making application to the Army authorities.

Order: The Army Order 23/94, ensures, *inter alia*, that on account of the deductions, the officer concerned is not put to undue financial hardship; hence a ceiling is provided which is 22% in respect of wife and in no case the amount of maintenance allowance sanctioned to the wife and/or child is to exceed 30% of the officer's pay and allowances. In this case, deduction of 22% per month were allowed. However, in view of arrears the monthly amount calculated for deductions to clear the arrears was far above 33% (it was about 42.6%) which is not permissible. This mistake was rectified; consequently, in order to compensate the petitioner for overpayment, further deductions from pay and allowances were directed to be paid at a reduced rate till the amount paid in excess is liquidated. Other than that, the husband's petition was dismissed.

Comment: Under the Army Act, there are specific and detailed provisions and procedure for granting maintenance to wives of the army officers. A wife who seeks maintenance under these provisions instead of the provisions in the Hindu Marriage Act or the Cr. P.C., is very much within her right. In other words, maintenance provisions in the Cr. P.C., and the Hindu Marriage Act do not debar an army officer's wife to claim maintenance under the provisions of the Army Act.

JURISDICTION

Maintenance Claim by Wife – Jurisdiction of Court

Sucheta Singh Ghate v. Dilip Shanta, Ram Ghate,
AIR 2003 Bom 390

Issue: Can a maintenance petition by a wife under the Hindu Adoptions and Maintenance Act be filed at a place where the wife resides?

Facts: A wife filed a petition for maintenance under the Hindu Adoptions and Maintenance Act, 1956, in the Family Court at Pune. The parties were married under the Special Marriage Act, 1954 at Pune and after marriage lived in Ahmedabad. After difference arose between the couple, the wife came back to her father's place at Pune. The issue was as to the maintainability of the petition in Pune Family Court. The husband challenged the Pune Family Court jurisdiction. The Hindu Adoptions and Maintenance Act has no provision on the question of jurisdiction.

Order: Under section 20(c) of the Code of Civil Procedure, a suit is to be filed at a place where the cause of action wholly or in part arises. According to the court, the circumstances forming infraction of the right of the wife continued in Pune where she returned to her father as her suffering due to lack of maintenance continued while she lived with her father; consequently, cause of action also arose in Pune. The provisions of the Hindu Adoptions and Maintenance Act are beneficial in nature and the aim is to benefit the wife and old infirm parents. The whole purpose would be defeated if the person in need has to chase the non-applicant who keeps changing residence or prefers to reside at a place far away from the claimants. The Family Court at Pune was, thus, held to have jurisdiction to entertain the wife's petition for maintenance under the Hindu Adoptions and Maintenance Act.

Comment: When a statute has no provision as to jurisdiction, the provisions of the C.P.C in the matter would be applicable in civil matters. In maintenance claims under the Hindu Adoptions and Maintenance Act jurisdiction would lie with the court at a place where the claimant resides. Even going by the analogy of the Hindu Marriage Act the parties, in this case having been married in Pune, the Pune court is competent to entertain the wife's maintenance application. Also a wife's suffering due to lack of maintenance where she resides would imply that cause of action lies where she resides.

RIGHTS AND DUTIES OF PARENTS

Father not Unable to Maintain Himself – Not Entitled

Attar Singh Jain v. Amit Singh Jain, (1982) Cr LJ 211 (Del)

Issue: A father could not establish neglect by the son nor that he was unable to maintain himself; his application under section 125(1)(d) of the Cr. P.C. was, therefore, dismissed.

Facts: A father had four sons. He was staying with the respondent but some differences developed and he left the son to stay with another son. He, however, filed a maintenance claim against him. The same was dismissed, hence this appeal.

Order: The court dismissed his appeal. It was held, that the applicant could neither prove that he was being neglected by his son nor that he was unable to maintain himself. On the contrary, there was evidence that another son was sending him a regular allowance which he was depositing in a bank as saving. Under these circumstances, the father's claim was negatived.

Comment: An applicant has to establish both—that he was being neglected (by the son in this case) and also that he was unable to maintain himself. If this is not established, the application for maintenance fails.

Mother's Liability to Maintain Children

T.P.S.H. Selva Saroja v. T.P.S.H. Sasinathan, 1989 Cr LJ 2032 (Mad)

Issue: Is a mother liable to maintain her children under section 125 of the Cr. P.C.?

Facts: A daughter aged 31, filed a petition for maintenance under section 125 of the Cr. P.C., against her mother. Her claim was under section 125(1)(c) *viz.*, "inability to maintain herself by reason of any physical or mental abnormality". Her ground was based on the facts that she was living away from her widowed mother because the movements of her mother with another person had caused a great damage to the reputation of her family and also caused injury to her mind. The mother invoked the inherent powers of the High Court under section 482 of the Code, to have the maintenance proceedings quashed. Her argument was that under section 125 of the Code, a daughter who had attained majority and who did not suffer any physical or mental abnormality or injury which incapacitated her from maintaining herself, would not be entitled to maintenance.

Order: The court held, that mere physical or mental abnormality or a mere injury will not be covered under clause (c) of section 125(1) of the Cr. P.C. The word injury will have to be read in the context of inability to maintain. Injury to the minor as alleged by the claimant in this case did not come within the scope of the injury contemplated under the clause, the court held. However, on the issue whether the mother can, at all, be directed to pay maintenance to her daughter, the court observed:

> "The question need not have to be gone into this petition. However, one cannot overlook that in the context of the social purpose and the moral obligation cast on the mother, she could not be easily excluded from her liability, once it is shown that she has sufficient means of her own, independent of the father and the child would come within the purview of section 125(1)(b) or (c)."

Comment: Though the daughter lost her case in view of the facts but, in principle, the court conceded that a mother with independent means, would be as much under a duty to maintain children, as the father.

Mother does not Include Step-Mother

Kirtikant D. Vadodaria v. *State of Gujarat,*
(1996) 4 SCALE 44: (1996) 4 SCC 479: JT 1996 (6) SC 244

Issue: Does the expression 'mother' in clause (d) of section 125(1) of the Code of Criminal Procedure include 'step-mother'.

Facts: A father filed maintenance petition against his son from his first deceased wife. After his wife's death, he had re-married and had three sons and two daughters from the second marriage. The maintenance application was contested and the same was dismissed by the Trial Court, but in the revision court, a settlement was arrived at and that was recorded as full and final settlement. Notwithstanding this settlement, the father and his second wife filed a joint maintenance petition. The claim of the father was dismissed in view of the earlier settlement but the claim of the step-mother was conceded and maintenance awarded to her. All the courts upheld this order, and hence the appeal to the Apex Court.

Order: After considering the dictionary meaning of the expression mother and the position under the *Shastric* law, the court found that 'mother' means only natural mother and does not include 'step-mother'. As regards the rights of a step-mother to claim maintenance from the step-son, the court held that in view of the "dominant purpose behind the benevolent provisions contained in section 125.........a childless step-mother may claim from her step-son, provided she is a widow or her husband if living, is also incapable of supporting and maintaining her". In the facts and circumstances of the present case, it was held that the step-mother was not entitled to the maintenance.

Comment: The case has set the controversy on the point at rest. Prior to this, there was divergence of opinion by the High Courts—some holding that mother would include step-mother whilst others holding a view that mother includes a natural or adoptive mother but not a step-mother. The Hindu Adoptions and Maintenance Act, 1956, specifically provides that a parent includes a childless step-mother and has a right of maintenance (*Explanation* to section 20).

Mother's Right to 'stay' in 'sons' House

Anandi D Jadhav v. *Nirmala Ramchandra Kore*, AIR 2000 SC 1386: 2000 AIR SCW 1161: (2000) 3 SCC 703

Issue: Does a mother have a "legal right" to reside in the house of the sons; do the sons have a duty to provide her residence in their house along with their families?

Facts: This was a case under the Bombay Rents, Hotel and Lodging House Rates Control Act, 1947. A mother who was the tenant, was living in the suit premises with her sons for 30 years. On the sons' constructed his own house, the landlord sought to evict the tenant on the ground that she had acquired alternate accommodation which was a ground for eviction under the above mentioned Act. The provision under section 20 of the Hindu Adoptions and Maintenance Act, 1956, was invoked in support of the eviction case stating that the mother had a right to be maintained by her sons and since maintenance includes "residence" [section 3(b) of the Act] she was entitled to live in their house and consequently a suitable alternative accommodation was available to her, entitling the landlord to seek her eviction.

Order: The court dismissed the landlord's plea. It held that the mother was not liable to be evicted on the ground of having acquired "vacant possession" because the house built by her sons was not her house over which she had any legal right to reside. Though it was conceded that the old mother has a right to be maintained by the sons but observed that this "does not mean, that she is entitled to live along with her son's families". It remarked (at p. 1389):

> "..........morally, they [sons] are obliged to take care of the aged mother by accommodating her in their house, yet, in law we cannot enlarge that obligation to legal duty to provide her residence in the house along with his family."

Comment: In the facts of the case, the mother was held not to be liable to be evicted and so the order was to her advantage; however, the observations of the Court that she had no "legal right" to reside in the house built by her sons and the sons have no "legal duty" to provide her residence in the house along with their family have the potential of being invoked to the disadvantages of the parents in some cases. Each case, however, would have to be decided on its own facts and circumstances.

Parent may Claim Maintenance from any one of their Children

Mahendra Kumar Gaikwad v. *Gulabbhai,* 2001 Cr LJ 2111 (Bom): 2000 (2) CCC 692: 2000 (2) Mah LJ 378

Issue: Can a parent with more than one child seek maintenance from any one child?

Facts: A mother filed an application for maintenance against her son, under section 125(1)(d) of the Cr. P.C. She had no income of her own, and her husband who was a pensioner with small income, was a diabetic patient and had to spend lot of money on his medicines alone. The son and his wife were gainfully employed and financially in good position. The son, however, contested the mother's application on three counts, *viz.*, (a) maintenance of the mother is, primarily, the responsibility of the father and not the son, and since the father was receiving pension, she cannot claim maintenance from him (the son); (b) she has two more sons, one of whom was earning very well, and thus it was not his (respondent's) sole responsibility to maintain his mother; and (c) the parents had not discharged their parental duties towards him, and therefore, they had forfeited their right to claim maintenance from him.

Order: The court did not accept the plea of the son and held that the parent has an option to seek maintenance from any of his or her children. The parent may have his or her own legitimate reasons for the choice.

Comment: While it is the option of the parent to seek maintenance from a particular child, the court would definitely go into the circumstances of the case to ensure that parents do not, by sheer whim or fancy, spare a son who has sufficient means and proceed against another whose means are limited.

Note. See also *A. Ahathinamiligai* v. *Arumughnam,* 1988 Cr LJ 6 (Mad): 1987 Mad LW (Cri) 278 where it was held that there was no violation of article 14 of the Constitution (right to equality) if the parent (father in this case) seeks maintenance against only one of the several children.

Court of Jurisdiction where Claimant is a Parent

(i) *Ananth Gopal* v. *Gopal Narayan,*
1985 Cr LJ 152 (Kant): 1985 (1) Hindu LR 222:
ILR 1985 Kant 2607

(ii) *Ganga Sharan Varshney* v. *Shakuntala Devi,*
1990 Cr LJ 128 (All): 1990 All LJ 34: I (1990) DMC 71

(iii) *N.B. Bhikshu* v. *State of Andhra Pradesh,*
1993 Cr LJ 3280 (AP): I (1994) DMC 396: 1993 (2) Hindu LR 697

(iv) *Vijay Kumar Prasad* v. *State of Bihar,*
AIR 2004 SC 2123: 2004 Cr LJ 2047: 2004 AIR SCW 2276

Issue: The issue involved in all these cases was as to the court of jurisdiction where a parent seeks maintenance from his/her children under section 125 of the Cr. P.C. Can the parent file the application where he/she resides or is it to be filed at a place where the non-applicant resides? Judicial opinion on this has been divided.

Facts: In *Ananth Gopal* v. *Gopal Narayan,* a father filed a petition for maintenance under section 125 Cr. P.C. against his son in the court having jurisdiction where he (the applicant father) resided. The son raised objection to the jurisdiction and argued that the petition would lie only in Bangalore where he (the non-applicant son) resided. He referred to the provision under section 126(1) whereunder proceedings for maintenance under section 125 may be taken against any person in any person in any District:

(a) where he is, or

(b) where he or his wife resides or,

(c) where he last resided with his wife, or as the case may be, with the mother of the illegitimate child.

According to the son the provision of section 126(1) refers only to husband and wife or the mistress and not the parents or children. Hence a father can file a petition only where the son resides. The court, however, conceded in favour of the father.

Ganga Sharan Varshney v. *Shakuntala Devi,* was a mother's application for maintenance against her son at a place where she resided. The same was opposed by the son on the ground of lack of jurisdiction. His plea, however, was rejected.

In *N.B. Bhikshu* v. *State of Andhrà Pradesh,* however, where the applicant father resided in Hyderabad and the non-applicant son in Bombay, the court accepted the son's objection that the father could not file the maintenance application in Hyderabad.

In *Vijay Kumar Prasad* v. *State of Bihar,* a father residing at Siwan filed a petition for maintenance under section 125 Cr. P.C. in the court of the Chief

Judicial Magistrate at Siwan against his son who resided at Patna which was allowed. The appellant son filed an application in the High Court for transfer of the case from Siwan to Patna. His plea was that due to undue influence of the politicians, "he would not get justice if the case is tried at Siwan as he could not even arrange a lawyer to represent him." His second contention was that the court at Siwan had no jurisdiction to entertain the application in view of the provisions contained in section 126(1) of the Cr. P.C. The High Court rejected the son's application primarily on the ground that the apprehensions of undue influence of politicians was not established. As to the issue of jurisdiction, although the same was not explicitly adverted to but it can be inferred from the High Court decision that the judicial magistrate had been held to have jurisdiction to entertain the father's application for maintenance. Against this the son successfully filed a special leave appeal before the Apex Court.

Orders: As mentioned above, the opinion of the courts on the issue of court of jurisdiction in case of maintenance application by a parent under section 125 of Cr. P.C., has been divergent. Thus in *Ananth Gopal* it was held that in view of the beneficial nature of the proceedings, a liberal interpretation should be given and therefore the father could file a maintenance petition at a place where he resided. So also in *Ganga Sharan Varshney* where also the court held that the provision under section 126(1)(b) of the Cr. P.C. should be liberally construed and should be interpreted to include any claimant whether it was the wife, child, mother or father. The idea behind these provisions is to give facility to a helpless and indigent person to claim maintenance at the place where he/she resides. The court observed (at pp. 130-131) *Ganga Sharan Varshney supra.*

"A statute has to be construed in a manner to carry out the intention of the Legislature and even a modification or contradiction of the language of the Legislature is permissible in order to square with the intention. If the destitute or vagrant mother is compelled to institute proceedings only at a place where the son resides she may not at all be in a position to pursue her case. On the other hand, the son having pecuniary resources can certainly contest the case against her at the place where the mother resides."

In *N.B. Bhikshu* and *Vijay Kumar Prasad* however, the Andhra Pradesh High Court and the Supreme Court respectively, took a different view. In the former case, it was held that the court in Bombay where the son was residing and not the court in Hyderabad where the father resided, had jurisdiction to entertain father's petition for maintenance and in the latter the court at Siwan where the father was residing was held to have no jurisdiction when the son resided in Patna.

The Supreme Court, in *Vijay Kumar Prasad*, after analysing the provisions of section 488, clauses (6) and (8) and the earlier judgment in *Jagir Kaur* v. *Jaswant Singh*, AIR 1963 SC 1521: (1963) 2 Cr LJ 413: (1964) 2 SCR 73, came to the conclusion that clauses (b) and (c) of section 126 of the present Cr. P.C. which correspond to section 488(6) and (8) of the old code, relate to wife and children. In other words, the benefit given to the wife and children to initiate proceedings at the place where they reside is not given to the parents. The court observed (at p. 2123) that' "a base reading of the section makes it clear that the parents cannot be placed on the same pedestal as that of the wife or children for the purpose of section 126 of the Code". Consequently, it was held that an application by the father or mother claiming maintenance has to be filed at the place where the non-applicant lives. In this case since the son was practicing in Patna, the court at Siwan where the father resided was held to have no jurisdiction.

Comment: With due respect to the Court, the Apex Court judgment in *Vijay Kumar Prasad* neither sounds to reason nor is if fair. The approach adopted by it defeats the whole purpose behind the beneficial provision. Under the Code of 1895 as amended in 1898, Chapter XXXVI was entitled "of maintenance of wives and children." Under the 1973 amended code, Chapter IX is titled, "Order for maintenance of wives, children and *parents*" (emphasis added). While consequential changes were made in section 125 by incorporating right of parents, no change was made in section 126 dealing with procedure and thus it continues to correspond to the provisions of section 488, clauses (6) and (8) of the old code. The omission to make consequential changes in section 126 of the code could not be deliberate if one goes behind the spirit of adding parents along with wives and children in section 125. It is an inadvertent omission; the court seems to have taken a very literal and technical view. Parents in old age could be equally helpless and indigent and may not be in a position to travel distances to file their claim where the children reside. Normally both in terms of their physical as well as pecuniary resources, they may be in a weak position to file/contest the case where the non-applicant resides. However, in view of the provisions of the Maintenance and welfare of Parents and Senior Citizens' Act, 2007, a parent can now file an application for maintenance where he/she resides [section 6(1)(a)]

RIGHTS AND DUTIES OF DAUGHTERS

Married Minor Daughter's Right to Claim Maintenance

Ramchoddas Narottamdas v. *Emperor,*
AIR 1949 Bom 36: 49 Cr LJ 630

Issue: Does a minor daughter, upon marriage, *ipso facto* lose her right to maintenance under section 488 (now section 125) of the Cr. P.C.?

Facts: A husband had been ordered to pay maintenance of ₹ 40 p.m. for his wife and four children (₹ 16 for the wife and ₹ 6 for each child). After some time the appellant father made an application praying that the amount be reduced as the eldest daughter had been married. On the other hand, the wife and daughters prayed for enhancement of the allowance on the ground that the husband's or father's salary had been raised. The Magistrate enhanced the amount for the wife and three children without disturbing the claim of the married daughter who was 15. The father thereupon filed a revision and argued that once a daughter is married, she gets an enforceable right to be maintained by her husband, and therefore, she cannot be said to be unable to maintain herself within the meaning of section 488, and therefore, the liability of the father ceases. *Chantan* v. *C. Mathu*, AIR 1917 Mad 276: ILR 39 Mad 957: 17 Cr LJ 16, was referred to in support of the contention that where a child possesses a right to be legally maintained from the mother's *tarwad*, then he is not entitled to an order to maintenance under section 488. Disagreeing with this argument Justice Jahagirdar observed that "a daughter does not, on marriage, *ipso facto* lose her right of maintenance from the father. The real and only test is whether that child is unable for maintain itself. It may be that the husband himself is a child or poor to maintain her". (at p. 37)

Support was drawn for this proposition from *Meenatchi Ammal* v. *Karuppana Pillai* alias *Muthuswami Pillai*, (XLVIII) ILR Mad 503, where the court held that the question really turns upon whether the altered circumstances are such that the child is able to maintain herself by reason of her marriage and ceased to depend on the original maintenance. (She was already getting a maintenance allowance from her father.) (at p. 504)

Order: The court set aside the order directing the applicant to pay maintenance to his married daughter and remitted the case to the Magistrate to pass fresh orders after ascertaining whether in spite of her marriage she is still unable to maintain herself either because her husband is too poor to maintain her or for any other good reason.

Comment: After the amendment of 1973, the Cr. P.C. has conceded the right of maintenance to a minor married daughter under certain circumstances. An adult married daughter has, however, been explicitly excluded whatever her circumstances.

Adult Unmarried Daughter's Right to Maintenance (under HAMA)

Viswambharan v. Dhanya,
AIR 2005 Ker 91: ILR 2005 (1) Ker 374: 2005 (1) Ker LJ 330

Issue: Is an unmarried major daughter entitled to claim maintenance from her father under section 20 of the Hindu Adoptions and Maintenance Act?

Facts: Two daughters who had attained majority—one was already a major at the time of filing the application, the other attained majority during the pendency of the proceedings—claimed maintenance from their father under the provisions of section 20 of the Hindu Adoptions and Maintenance Act. Their case was that the father was not maintaining them; he was residing separately and the claimants were unable to maintain themselves. According to the claimants, the father's monthly income exceeded ₹ 4,500 so they claimed ₹ 1,000 per month for each of them. The father disputed both—his liability to pay, as well as the quantum. The Family Court held that the father had the liability to maintain his daughters in this case. Accordingly, the father was directed to pay ₹ 500 per month to each of them till they get married. The father filed an appeal against this order.

Order: The order was challenged on the ground that both the daughters, having attained majority, are not entitled to maintenance in view of section 20(2) of the Hindu Adoptions and Maintenance Act and *secondly*, that the amount is excessive. It was contended that under sub-section (2) of section 20, the liability extends only to a minor child and further, in view of sub-section (3) in case of a daughter who is unmarried, *even during her minority she can claim maintenance only if she is unable to maintain herself out of her own earnings or other property*. Therefore, the claim of the daughters who have attained majority, though unmarried, is not legally sustainable. This argument according to the court "rebels against logic and common sense. It runs counter to the salutary legislative object, intent and purpose. It would be irrational to come to such a conclusion". Another significant aspect pointed out by the court was that if the argument of the appellant were to be accepted, then the female child would be subjected to greater fetter and restriction than a male child. An unmarried minor male child, if the contention was accepted, would be entitled to maintenance even when he was able to maintain himself out of his own earnings or property whereas, an unmarried minor female child would disentitle herself for maintenance if she was able to maintain herself. This, according to the court "would certainly offend the constitutional mandate relating to equality and prohibition of discrimination on the ground of sex under articles 14 and 15 of the Constitution". What article 15(3) of the Constitution permits is only protective discrimination in favour of a female and not hostile and unreasonable discrimination against her", the court emphasised. And yet another perspective was pointed out. Under the Child Marriage Restraint Act, 1929, as amended in 1978, the permitted age of marriage for a female child is 18 years so any marriage performed in accordance with law will have to be performed only after the girl attains the age of 18. If that be so, the stipulation in section 3(b)(ii) of the Act that in the case of the unmarried daughter, maintenance will include reasonable expenses of and incident to her marriage would lose its meaning and content if the appellant-father's argument was accepted. The advantage of that expanded definition of maintenance would then be available only to those female children who violate the provision of the Child Marriage Restraint Act.

The court thus ruled that while normally the liability to maintain a child would continue until he/she attains majority irrespective of the fact whether the child is or is not able to maintain itself, but, in case of a male, his right to be maintained would cease when he attains majority and in case of a female child, such right will continue even after she attains majority until she gets married, provided she is unable to maintain herself out of her own earnings. The daughters were consequently held to be entitled to maintenance from the father; the quantum was also upheld as reasonable in view of the income of the father.

Comment: In this context, there is a very discriminatory provision in section 125(c) of the Cr. P.C. whereunder even a *major married son* is entitled to maintenance if he is unable to maintain himself by reason of some physical or mental infirmity, whereas, in case of a daughter, a married daughter who is a major, even if infirm is not so entitled. Simply because she is married, she is denied the right which her other sisters (if unmarried) and brothers (whether married or unmarried) have.

Adult Unmarried Daughter to Prove Physical or Mental Abnormality

(i) *T.P.S.H. Selva Saroja* v. *T.P.S.H. Sasinathan*, 1989 Cr LJ 2032 (Mad)

(ii) *Pathumma* v. *Cholamarakkar*, I (2009) DMC 466 (DB Ker)

Issue: Vide section 125(1)(c) of the Cr. P.C. an unmarried adult daughter is entitled to maintenance from her father or mother only when she is, by reason of any physical or mental abnormality or injury, unable to maintain herself. The issue in these cases was as to what would constitute mental injury so as to give entitlement to maintenance. In *T.P.S.H. Selva Saroja* the question as to whether a mother can at all be directed to pay maintenance to her daughter, was also raised.

Facts: In both the cases adult unmarried daughters claimed maintenance – one against the father and the other against the mother – on the ground of mental injury suffered by them. In the first case, the 31 years old daughter's claim was based on the facts that she was living away from her widowed mother because the movements of his mother with another person had caused a great damage to the reputation of his family and also caused injury to her mind. The mother invoked the inherent powers of the High Court under section 482 of the Cr. P.C. to have the maintenance proceedings quashed. Her argument was that under section 125 of the Cr. P.C. a daughter who had attained majority and who did not suffer any physical or mental abnormality or injury which incapacitated her from maintaining herself, would not be entitled to maintenance. The court agreed that mere physical or mental abnormality or a mere injury will not be covered under clause (c) of section 125(1) of the Cr. P.C. In the other case *Pathumma* v. *Cholamarakkar* there was a dispute regarding paternity of the claimant daughter. She alleged that this caused mental injury to her leading to a situation of remaining unmarried on account of the paternity dispute.

The emphasis by the daughter was on mental injury leading to her remaining unmarried and not to her inability to maintain herself owing to such mental injury. According to the court, unless it is pleaded and established before the court that on account of such mental injury she is unable to maintain herself, she cannot seek maintenance. What exactly is the scope and ambit of mental injury is yet a grey area under law in the context of entitlement for maintenance, the court observed.

Order: The claimants were refused relief in both the cases. In the first case the court held that the injury alleged will have to be read in the context of inability to maintain and the injury alleged by the daughter in this case did not come within the scope of injury contemplated under clause (c) of section 125(1) of the Cr. P.C. As regards the question whether a mother can at all be directed to pay maintenance, the court held that if she has sufficient means of her own, she cannot be excluded from such liability. In this case, however, in view of the facts, the daughter was held to be not entitled to maintenance.

In the other case also the court held that the daughter needs to establish that owing to the mental injury alleged by her due to the paternity dispute, she is unable to maintain herself. The matter was consequently remitted to the Family Court for fresh consideration in accordance with law.

Comment: While physical or mental abnormality or physical injury is not difficult to ascertain what would constitute mental injury in the present context would depend on the circumstances of the case and would have to be interpreted and ascertained in the context of inability caused to the claimant to maintain herself. Not every kind of tension, mental stress or injury would *ipso facto* or *per se* result in inability to maintain.

Maintenance of Adult Unmarried Daughter – Provisions of Cr. P.C. *vis-a-vis* Hindu Adoption and Maintenance Act

Raj Kumari Awasthi v. *State of Uttar Pradesh,*
(2008) 3 ALJ 100

Issue: The issue involved in this case was as to an adult unmarried daughter's right to claim maintenance from her father under the provision of section 125 of the Cr. P.C.

Facts: The applicants for maintenance who were the wife and daughter of the non-applicant, obtained a maintenance order under section 125 of the Cr. P.C., against the husband and father respectively from the Family Court. The court ordered Rs. 700 per month to each of them. This order was later modified under section 127 of the Cr. P.C. whereby grant of maintenance in favour of the wife was upheld but in case of the daughter, it was limited till she turned major. It is this modified order which was challenged before the High Court. It was argued that under section 127 of the Cr. P.C., grant of maintenance cannot be denied to an adult unmarried daughter who has no source of income and who being a student of class XII is in dire need of father's support for her upbringing and education. The court referred to and analysed the maintenance provisions under the Cr. P.C., the Hindu Adoption and Maintenance Act and the Law Commission Recommendations in its 41st Report (1969). It also referred to various cases on the issue, e.g., *Jagdish Jugtawat* v. *Manju Lata,* (2002) 11 UP Cr R 313 (Sup Cr): (2002) 5 SCC 422: 2002 (6) Bom CR 189; *Nanak Chand* v. *Chandra Kishore,* AIR 1970 SC 446: 1970 Cr LJ 522: (1970) 1 SCR 565; *Ram Singh* v. *State,* AIR 1963 All 313; *Mahabir Agarwal* v. *Gita Roy,* (1962) 2 Cr LJ 528 (Cal); *Nalini Ranjan Chakravarty* v. *Kiran Rani Chakravarty,* AIR 1965 Pat 442: 1965 (2) Cr LJ 530: ILR 44 Pat 833; *Mt. Rajwarin* v. *Lagan Singh,* AIR 1921 Pat 379: 61 Ind Cas 64: 22 Cr LJ 336; *Bhagat Singh* v. *Emperor,* (1910) 11 Cr LJ 427 (Punj): (1910) 6 Ind Cas 960; *Krishnaswami Ayer* v. *Chandravadana,* (1918) 25 MLJ 349: AIR 1914 Mad 594: ILR 37 Mad 565; *Thambuswamy* v. *Ma Lone,* 10 Bur LT 209: 37 Ind Cas 311: 18 Cr LJ 103; *Shaikh Ahmad* v. *Bai Fatima,* AIR 1943 Bom 48: 44 Cr LJ 334: ILR (1943) Bom 38; *Jagir Kaur* v. *Jaswant Singh,* AIR 1963 SC 1521: (1963) 2 Cr LJ 413: (1964) 2 SCR 73; *Noor Saba Khatoon* v. *Mohd Quasim,* AIR 1997 SC 3280: 1997 Cr LJ 3972: 1997 AIR SCW 3343.

The court in *Raj Kumari Awasthi* expressed deep disconcert and lamented that a reading of section 125(1)(c) makes it apparent that "a person having sufficient means is required to maintain her unmarried daughter who has turned major, only if her inability to maintain herself is due to any physical or mental abnormality or injury and not otherwise" (at p. 101). The court, however, stayed the order of the Family Court limiting the daughter's right to maintenance only till she reached the age of majority. It relied on a two judge decision of the Apex Court in *Jagdish Jugtawat* v. *Manju Lata,* (2002) 11 UP Cr R 313 (Sup Cr): (2002) 5 SCC 422: 2002 (6) Bom CR 189 where in similar circumstances, the father had prayed that daughter be allowed maintenance only till she attains majority and not thereafter. The Magistrate refused the prayer and the High Court upheld the same and declined to interfere with the order, even though it conceded that *vide* provision of section 125 Cr. P.C. the daughter was entitled to maintenance only until she attained the age of majority and not thereafter. It drew support from the provisions of the Hindu Adoption and Maintenance Act, 1956, under which, *vide* section 20(3) even a major daughter is entitled to seek maintenance from her father. Thus, in order to avoid multiplicity of litigation, the High Court order was not interfered with. The Supreme Court referred to the following observations of the High Court.

"....taking an overall view of the matter, I ... am of the candid view that the provisions require literal interpretation and a daughter would cease to have the benefit of the provisions under section 125 Cr. P.C. on attaining majority though she would be entitled to claim the benefits further under the statute/ personal law. But the court is not inclined to interfere as the order does not result in miscarriage of justice; rather interfering with the order would create great inconvenience [to the daughter] as she would be forced to file another petition under sub-section (3) of section 20 of the Act of 1956 for further maintenance etc. Thus in order to avoid multiplicity of litigation, the order impugned does not warrant interference."

Thus, the Supreme Court also in *Jagdish Jugtawat* was of the view that no exception could be taken to the judgment passed by the High Court in maintaining the order of the Family Court which was based on a combined reading of section 125 of the Cr. P.C. and section 20(3) of the Hindu Adoption and Maintenance Act as it was of the view that the right of a minor girl for maintenance from her parents after attaining majority till her marriage is recognised in section 20(3) of the Hindu Adoption and Maintenance Act. Drawing support from this, the Allahabad High Court in *Raj Kumari Awasthi* held that on a combined reading of section 125 of the Cr. P.C. and section 20(3) of the Hindu Adoption and Maintenance Act the right of a daughter to claim maintenance from her parents after attaining majority till her marriage is recognised in section 20(3) of the Hindu Adoption and Maintenance Act and consequently it stayed the operation of the order restricting the daughter's right only until the age of majority. According to the court, to expect that an unmarried daughter who is still going to college or staying at home awaiting marriage and who has no source of income, can be denied maintenance unless her inability to maintain herself is due to physical or mental abnormality is extremely harsh and oppressive, and "in all likelihood violative of articles 14 and 21 of the Constitution". This provision appears particularly anomalous and discriminatory the court observed because in the other clauses of section 125(1), *i.e.*, in clauses (a), (b) and (d), a person with sufficient means is required to maintain his wife, his legitimate or illegitimate minor child whether married or not or his father or mother who are unable to maintain themselves and there is no additional requirement for these categories of persons to demonstrate that their inability to maintain themselves is due to physical or mental abnormality or injury for claiming the benefit of this salutary social legislation. The provision, as it stands also seems contrary to the spirit of articles 15(3) and 39(e) and (f) of the Constitution which veritably enjoin the State to design laws for the welfare of women and children and for ensuring that children and youth are protected from moral and material abandonment," the court added. The court also referred to the provisions of the Muslim personal law whereunder a daughter is entitled to be maintained by the father till her marriage.

In view of the fact that salutary amendments have been introduced for making maintenance provisions more sensitive and responsive to the special needs and problems of females the retention of section 125(1)(c) in the present form according to court "appears to be the result of a oversight by the Legislature" (p. 106).

Order: The High Court stayed the operation of the Family Court order restricting the daughter right to maintenance only until she attains majority. Notice was issued to the Union of India through the Attorney-General and the State of Uttar Pradesh through the Advocate-General to show cause as to how they support the legal validity of section 125(1)(c) of the Cr. P.C. A plea was made to amend the same and give to all unmarried daughters a right to be maintained even after attaining majority if they are unable to maintain themselves.

Comment: A girl or a boy just 18, cannot be expected to be independent enough to earn and maintain herself/himself. Does the law expect them to give up studies and start earning livelihood once they reach the age of 18? While there is no absolute right nor any absolute duty, the law needs to address the issue more realistically. Not all personal laws have provisions like section 18(3) of the Hindu Adoption and Maintenance Act in their statutes.

DUTIES OF DAUGHTERS

Married Daughter's Liability to Maintain Parents

Vijaya Manohar Arbat v. Kashirao Rajaram Sawai,
AIR 1987 SC 1100: 1987 Cr LJ 977: (1987) 2 SCC 278

Issue: Is a married daughter liable to maintain her father under the provision of section 125(1)(d) of the Cr. P.C.?

Facts: The appellant Dr. Mrs. Vijaya Arbat was the married daughter of the respondent by his first wife. Her mother died in 1948 and thereafter he remarried and was living with his second wife. The father (respondent) filed an application for maintenance from his daughter on the ground that he was unable to maintain himself. At the outset, a preliminary objection was raised to the very maintainability of the application on the ground that section 125(1)(d) does not entitle a father to claim maintenance from his daughter. This objection was overruled by the Magistrate. The daughter then moved the Bombay High Court in revision. The order of the Magistrate was affirmed and the High Court held that the application of a father for maintenance, who was unable to maintain himself, was maintainable against his married daughter having sufficient means. The revision application was, thus, dismissed. Hence, the appeal by special leave.

Order: On behalf of the appellant, it was contended that under clause (d) of section 125(1), a father is not entitled to maintenance from his daughter—whether married or not; the use of the pronoun "his" in clause (d) indicated that it is only the son who is liable to maintain his parents; had the Legislature intended that maintenance could be claimed from daughters as well, it would not have used the pronoun 'his', it was argued. The court, however, did not accept this argument. It observed that section 2(y) of the Cr. P.C., provides that the words and expressions used herein and not defined in the Indian Penal Code (I.P.C) have the meanings respectively assigned to them in that Code. Section 8 of the IPC lays down that the pronoun 'he' and its derivatives are used for any person whether male or female. Thus, in view of section 8, I.P.C, read with section 2(y), Cr. P.C. the pronoun 'his' in Clause (d) of section 125(1), Cr. P.C. also indicates a female. Also, section 13(1) of the General Clauses Act, 1897, lays down that in all Central Acts and Regulations, unless there is anything repugnant in the subject or context, words importing the masculine gender shall be taken to include females. Therefore, the pronoun "his" as used in clause (d) of section 125(1), Cr. P.C., includes both a male and a female. The counsel for the appellant relied on *Raj Kumari* v. *Yashodha Devi*, 1978 Cri LJ 600, where the

Punjab and Haryana High Court held that the liability to maintain the parents (mother in this case) rests only on the son and not the daughter.

The Supreme Court in the present case, however, did not accept the contentions of the appellant that a married daughter had no obligation to maintain her parents even if they were unable to maintain themselves. A daughter after marriage does not cease to be a daughter of the father or mother. If the contentions of the appellant daughter were to be accepted, parents having no son and only daughter, could go destitute if the daughters, even though they had sufficient means, refused to maintain their parents, the court observed. The Court made reference to *M. Areefa Beevi* v. *K.M. Sahib*, 1983 Cr LJ 412 (Ker): ILR (1982) 2 Ker 49: 1982 Ker LJ 186, and *Rupalli Masthanamma* v. *Thota Sriramulu*, (1982) 1 Andh WR 393, where also the view taken was that where the parents are unable to maintain themselves, they can claim maintenance from their daughter also under section 125(1)(d). Thus, the Supreme Court, in the present case, held that the purpose of such enactment was to enforce social obligation and we do not think why daughters should be excluded from such obligation to maintain their parents. The case was accordingly remanded for disposal on merits.

Comment: It is a very progressive judgment and sends message of equality between boys and girls. If girls have been given equal rights, why not equal duties as well. One of the reasons for preference of son in our society is the notion that they will support the parents in their old age and need. If such duty is extended to daughters as well, such bias will change. In any case, it is not an absolute liability; the court will take various factors into consideration before making an order. What is important is that an application for maintenance by parents against daughters should be maintainable.

Note: It is significant to note that after the enactment of the Maintenance and Welfare of Parents and Senior Citizens Act, 2007 it is clear that adult daughters, including married daughters have a duty to maintain their parents; "maintenance" includes provision for food, clothing, residence and medical attendance and treatment.

WIDOWED DAUGHTER-IN-LAW

Widowed Daughter-in-law's Right to Maintenance

Balbir Kaur v. Harinder Kaur,
AIR 2003 P&H 174: 2003 (2) CCC 80: 2003 (2) Marri LJ 499

Issue: Is a widowed daughter-in-law entitled to maintenance under section 19 of the Hindu Adoptions and Maintenance Act from the self-acquired property of the father-in-law when the said property has been alienated (or irrespective of the alienation)?

Facts: F was the owner of a house consisting of more than five rooms. He had one son and four daughters. After marriage of his son, he gave one of the rooms to the son and daughter-in-law, D, for their residence. Though the relations between the son and his wife D were not good but D stayed with him all along. The son died in 1975. During the life-time of F, D continued to stay in that accommodation along with her three children. F gifted the entire house, including the room occupied by D, to one of his daughters (the plaintiff) in 1977. After a few months of the gift deed, the plaintiff sought possession of the room on the ground that the property was the self-acquired property of her father F who had gifted the same to her and so D should hand over its possession to her. D lost at the Trial Court and first appeal; hence, her appeal to the High Court.

Order: One of the issues was whether a widowed daughter-in-law was entitled to maintenance from her father-in-law or his heirs or his donees even if the property of the father-in-law was self-acquired property. The law on the point was analysed. The widowed daughter-in-law's right of maintenance and residence against her father-in-law existed even under the Shastric law and the same has been statutorily recognised by section 19 of the Hindu Marriage Act. This right under the Act is available against the father-in-law having in possession coparcenery property, out of which the widowed daughter-in-law has not obtained any share. However, under the old Hindu law prevailing before 1956, the widow had a right of maintenance even against self-acquired property of her father-in-law. *Gopal Chandra Pal* v. *Kadambini Dasi*, AIR 1924 Cal 364: 73 Ind Cas 235, was referred to where a Division Bench of the Calcutta High Court had held that though a widowed daughter-in-law had no legal right to maintenance as against self-acquired property of her father-in-law, but if her husband had died during the life-time of the father-in-law, then the latter was under a moral obligation to maintain his widowed daughter-in-law, even though he had no ancestral assets in his hands. When the father-in-law's estate passed to his heirs by inheritance, the moral obligation of the father ripened into a legal obligation of the heirs. The court accordingly held in *Balbir Kaur* case, that even though, under the Hindu Adoptions and Maintenance Act the right of the widowed daughter-in-law is limited to the extent of coparcenary property in the hands of the father-in-law, but under the old Hindu law prevailing before the Hindu Adoptions and Maintenance Act this right of the widowed daughter-in-law of the pre-deceased son is available against the father-in-law's self-acquired property also. The right, according to the court, will not cease to be in force because the same is not inconsistent with any of the provisions of the Hindu Adoptions and Maintenance Act. Thus, *D*'s appeal was allowed and she was allowed to remain in possession of the room *in lieu* of her pre-existing right of maintenance.

Comment: Under section 19 of the Hindu Adoptions and Maintenance Act a daughter-in-law can seek maintenance from the father-in-law only from out of the coparcenary property in his hands out of which she has not obtained any share. In this case, the father-in-law had gifted the entire house, which was self-acquired property, to his daughter, including the room occupied by the widowed daughter-in-law. While he should have provided for the daughter-in-law no doubt, but legally he was within his right to make the gift. Morally may be correct but one wonders whether it can be sustained if one goes by the strict law.

No Enforcement of Maintenance Against Property of Mother-in-law

Vimalben Ajitbhai Patel v. *Vatslaben Ashokbhai Patel*, (2008) 4 SCC 649: AIR 2008 SC 2675: 2008 AIR SCW 4475

Issue: Can a wife enforce maintenance ordered against her husband against her mother-in-law's property? This was the significant issue involved in this case.

Facts: 'S' was married to J in 1992. In 1993 they fell apart and 'S' filed various criminal complaints against her husband and her in-laws, the appellants. They were granted bail subject to the condition that they would not leave India without prior permission of the court; however, on the ground of getting medical treatment for the father-in-law, they left India after applying for permission but before the same was granted. S got their bail cancelled and standing warrant of arrests against the appellants was got issued. On wife's application the husband was declared an absconder and a public proclamation was issued for attachment of properties. In fact the property, which was given on rent, belonged to the mother of the husband, but the same was ordered to be attached and both the tenant and the auction purchaser were directed to deposit the rent and the sale proceeds in the court. The wife, who had earlier obtained a maintenance order in her favour against the husband for a monthly allowance of ₹ 10,000, got the same executed against the amount deposited in the court and withdrew arrears for a period of 10 months at the rate of ₹ 10,000 per month. The husband challenged the sale as invalid and contended that the property of the mother-in-law cannot be sold by the court even if the husband had defaulted and the daughter-in-law cannot claim maintenance from the mother-in-law's property. The wife, on the other hand, contended that her husband being the only son of his parents and properties having been acquired through ancestral funds and there being no assertion that these were self acquired properties, she had a right of maintenance out of the joint family property in terms of section 18 of the Hindu Adoption and Maintenance Act. On appeal, however, the Apex Court not only reversed the order but strongly criticised the High Court's judgment. It held that maintenance of a wife during the subsistence of the marriage is the duty of the husband. The obligation of the father-in-law to maintain her arises only when the husband has died *vide*, section 19 of the Hindu Adoption and Maintenance Act. Besides, such obligation cannot be enforceable if the father-in-law has not the means to do so from any coparcenary property in his possession out of which the daughter-in-law has not obtained any share. In other words, the deceased husband must have had a share in the property. Furthermore, the property in the name of the mother-in-law can neither be subject-matter of attachment, nor during the lifetime of the husband, his personal liability to maintain his wife can be directed to be enforced against such property, the Court held (at p. 660).

The court also referred to the provisions of Protection of Women from Domestic Violence Act, 2005 and observed that sections 17 and 20 thereof, provide for a higher right in favour of the wife *viz.*, she not only acquires a right to be maintained but also a right of residence which is a higher right. However, the court clarified that as per the legislation the right extends only to joint properties in which the husband has a share. As held by the Apex Court in *S.R. Batra* v. *Taruna Batra*, AIR 2007 SC 1118 (Del): 2007 AIR SCW 1088: (2007) 3 SCC 169 a wife cannot claim a right of even a residence in the property belonging to her mother-in-law.

Order: The judgment of the Gujarat High Court was set aside, the property of the mother-in-law was released from attachment and the wife was directed to refund the sum of rupees one lakh withdrawn by her, with interest, and costs were also imposed on her. The wife could pursue her remedies against her husband in accordance with law but in no case can the mother-in-law's property be attached for execution of maintenance decree it was held.

Comment: In view of absence of any clear and concrete provisions regarding matrimonial property and right of residence for a deserted/divorced wife, the number of cases where in-laws and their properties are implicated is on the rise. The enactment of the Domestic Violence Act with concepts of "shared household" etc., added to this phenomenon. In view of *S.R. Batra* (supra) however, it is settled that a wife cannot legally enforce her right of rasidence in the property belonging to her mother-in-law; the present case has also clarified that the husband's obligation of maintaining his wife cannot be enforced against the properties of the in-laws – the father-in-law in the absence of son being a co-sharer in the property and in case of mother-in-law, in no situation. The following observation of the Supreme Court in *Vimlaben* are pertinent (at p. 66):

> "Keeping in view entirety of the facts and circumstances of the case we are of the opinion that gross injustice has been caused to the appellant [mother-in-law]. She did not deserve such harsh treatments at the hands of the High Court. Respondent 3 [the wife] speaks of her own human rights, forgetting the human right of the appellant, far less the fundamental right to life and liberty conferred on an accused in terms of article 21 of the Constitution of India."

HUSBAND'S RIGHT TO MAINTENANCE

Husband Incapable of Earning Entitled to Maintenance under Hindu Law and Parsi Law

Lalit Mohan v. Tripta Devi,
AIR 1990 J&K 7: 1989 Kash LJ 96: II (1989) DMC 23

Issue: Can a husband claim maintenance from his wife?

Facts: The husband had met with a serious accident as a result of which he lost his mental equilibrium. Relationship between the spouses deteriorated and the wife obtained a decree for divorce on the grounds of cruelty and desertion. The husband's appeal against the divorce decree failed but he made an application for maintenance under sections 30 and 31 of the Jammu and Kashmir Hindu Marriage Act, 1955 (corresponding with sections 24 and 25 of the Hindu Marriage Act, 1955). The wife was working in the National Hydro Project Corporation and was earning. The husband contended that she had sufficient means whereas he was suffering from permanent impairment because of the head injury and so incapable of working. In view of this, he claimed permanent alimony at the rate of ₹ 500 per month from the wife.

Order: The husband's application was granted. The court held that the husband did not have an independent income whereas wife was in a position to pay maintenance to the husband in terms of sections 30 and 31 of the Jammu and Kashmir Hindu Marriage Act. However, since the wife was in temporary service, the court ordered that she should pay Rs. 500 as litigation expenses and a sum of ₹ 100 per month as permanent alimony. While granting maintenance, the court observed:

> "The object of the section is that none of the parties should suffer to get adequate justice from the court on account of his or her financial difficulties. The reasons for enacting the provisions is that a wife or husband who has no independent income sufficient for her or his support or enough to meet the necessary expenses of the proceedings may not be handicapped. Such a provision was made on social and moral grounds with the motive that the party should be able to maintain himself or herself during the pendency of the proceedings as there was no freedom of contracting another marriage.........the other spouse is under an obligation to provide the indigent spouse financial assistance so that the proceedings may be conducted and he or she be maintained during the pendency of the proceedings and not forced to starvation or moral degradation."

Comment: The Hindu Marriage Act, 1955 and the Parsi Marriage and Divorce Act, 1936 as amended in 1988 (sections 39 and 40) are the only statutes which recognise a husband's right to seek maintenance from the wife. Though cases of husband's claiming maintenance from wives are rare, there may be situation and circumstances as in the present case, where a husband is incapacitated from earning and a wife is earning. In such case, the Hindu Law and the Parsi Law statutorily recognise the husband's right. It is important, however, that the applicant husband should not voluntarily incapacitate himself by refusing to do work even though he is otherwise capable of earning. [*E.g., Govind Singh* v. *Vidya,* AIR 1999 Raj 304: 1999 (3) CCC 219: II (2000) DMC 693; *Yashpal Singh Thakur* v. *Anjana Rajput,* AIR 2001 MP 67: 2000 (3) MPLJ 127: 2001 (2) CCC 472; *Bhupinder Kaur* v. *Vijaya Singh,* 2003 AIHC 4033 (P&H).]

Monika Rana v. *Yogeshwar Singh Sapehia,* AIR 2011 HP 54

Issue: The case involved the issue of maintenance claim by a husband who incapacitates himself from earning and then seeks maintenance from his wife.

Facts: A husband, who was a B.Sc. B.Ed filed a petition for divorce under section 13 of the Hindu Marriage Act against his wife, on the ground of cruelty and desertion. He also filed on application for maintenance and litigation expenses under section 24, Hindu Marriage Act. His case was that he had no source of income nor any property whereas the wife, who was a trained J.B.T. teacher, was a government employee. The wife refuted his contentions and averred that the husband had sufficient income to support himself as his father was a retired principal from senior secondary school and his mother is also working as headmistress; besides, according to the wife, he had sufficient landed property and the husband was not interested to work and engage himself gainfully. She stated that she was prepared to maintain him if he lived with her. The additional district judge granted his application and ordered the wife to pay him monthly allowance of ₹ 500 and also litigation expenses of ₹ 2,000. The present case is an appeal against this by the wife.

Order: After going through the facts and case-law the court held that the husband himself has incapacitated himself from earning income; it is not that he had been looking for a job and could not find one. Mereover, support given by the parents can also be taken into consideration while assessing income. The offer given by the wife that she was ready and willing to maintain him in case he joins her was conditional on his staying with her and not otherwise. Thus the maintenance order was set aside.

Comment: Though under the Hindu Marriage Act even a husband is entitled to maintenance from the wife but a person who incapacitates himself cannot claim maintenance.

CHRISTIAN PARTIES

Maintenance under CPC Provisions

K. Kumar v. Leena,
II (2010) DMC 519 (Ker): AIR 2010 Kant 75: ILR 2010 Kant 1221

Issue: Is a Christian wife and the children entitled to maintenance by resorting to the provisions of section 9 of the Civil Procedure Code even though the Christian Marriage Act makes no provision for that? This was the issue involved in the present case.

Facts: The parties were married under the Christian Marriage Act. On husband's failing and neglecting to maintain her and the children the wife who had no means of survival, invoked the provisions of section 9 of the C.P.C for claiming maintenance. The husband resisted the same. It was argued that the Christian Marriage Act provides the procedure regarding performance of marriage and there is no provision for maintenance thereunder. He also pleaded incapacity to pay. Rejecting his argument the court held that even if the Christian Marriage Act makes no provision for maintenance, such right is available under the common law; wife and children are dependents and a suit by a Christian wife and children is not barred under the provisions of the C.P.C. Section 9 of the C.P.C says:

> "The court shall (subject to the provisions hereinafter contained) have jurisdiction to try all suits of a civil nature excepting suits of which their cognizance is either expressly or impliedly barred."

The court referred to the following observations of the Apex Court in *M.V. Elizabeth v. Harwan Investment and Trading Pvt. Ltd.*, AIR 1993 SC 1014: 1993 AIR SCW 177: (1992) 1 SCR 1003, para 87 in support of the case:

> "....where statute is silent and judicial intervention is required, courts strive to redress grievance according to what is perceived to be principles of justice, equity and good conscience."

Order: The right of the claimants to seek maintenance from the husband/father by invoking the provisions of section 9 of the C.P.C was conceded.

Comment: The duty to maintain wife and children is a social, legal and moral one. Even if no provision for such relief exists in the personal law of the concerned parties, the provisions of the C.P.C, which is an overarhing procedural law in civil matters, can be invoked to come to the rescue of the parties and seek relief.

CUSTODY AND GUARDIANSHIP

Custody to Parent Living Outside Court's Jurisdiction

Margaret v. Chacko,
AIR 1971 Ker 1

Issue: Can custody and care of a child be entrusted to a parent who is living outside the country and hence outside the court's jurisdiction?

Facts: An Indian, while studying in West Germany, married a German lady, domiciled and residing in Germany. Soon differences arose between them and their marriage was dissolved by a German Court. They had two children. The husband returned to India and secretly brought the children with him. When the mother came to know about it, she came to India and filed a writ of *habeas corpus* for the recovery of children and for an order that custody be handed over to her. The children were of tender age.

Order: The court held that if the court, as *parens patriae* feels that it is necessary in the paramount interest of the child that custody and care of the child be entrusted to one of the parents who is residing out of its jurisdiction, it has full powers to pass orders permitting the child to be removed out of jurisdiction. To ensure that future orders of the court will be complied with, the court ordered the mother to execute bond for the return of the child if and whenever required by the court to do so; it also took an undertaking from German Consulate Authority in Madras that they would render all possible assistance for the implementation of any order that might be passed by the court at a later stage. The court relied on the decision in *Karnot (in re:)*, (1964) 2 All ER 339, where under similar circumstances an English Court passed an order in favour of an Indian mother.

Comment: Where the welfare of the child so demands, the court can also permit the child to be taken out of the country by one of the parents, with proper safeguards.

Fact that Mother is Working – Not to Affect her Right to Child's Custody (Case under Parsi Law)

Thrity Hoshie Dolikuka v. Hoshiam Shavaksha Dolikuka,
AIR 1982 SC 1276: (1982) 2 SCC 544: II (1982) DMC 288

Issue: Is the fact that the mother is working and so will not be available to the child for long hours, such an important factor so as to deny the child's custody to her?

Facts: The case involved the custody of a minor daughter under section 49 of the Parsi Marriage and Divorce Act, 1936, and had a long and chequered history. The Bombay High Court had refused custody to the mother on the ground that she was a working woman and, therefore, would not be available to the child for most part of the day. Hence, the mother's appeal to the Supreme Court.

Order: The Court analysed the law and the entire facts of the case in very great detail. Keeping in view the well-established criterion of the best interests of the child, the court ordered that the child's custody be handed over to the mother. It held that the High Court was wrong in refusing custody to the mother on the ground that she was working and so would not be available to the child for long hours. However, since the custody battle was long drawn and the child had been under a great emotional strain and stress shuttling from court to court and from one parent to the other and witnessing the unhealthy court drama, the Supreme Court directed that the child be sent to a boarding school. The father was given visitation rights and also to have her with him for half the period of vacation.

Comment: The welfare of the child is the only consideration in awarding custody. A significant aspect of this case was that after the above order, the father flouted the custody order intentionally and without any reason, by retaining the child with him beyond the permissible period. The High Court found him guilty of contempt of court and directed his detention in civil prison for three months. Against this order, the husband appealed. The Supreme Court held (*Hoshie Shavaksha Dholikuka* v. *Thrity Hoshie Dholikuka*, AIR 1982 SC 1457: 1982 Cr LJ 1937: (1982) 2 SCC 577), that the father was guilty of contempt; however, in view of the fact that the child was attached to the father and sending him to prison would further disturb the child, the court let-off the father with a warning. Thus, even in the matter of imposing sentence on the father for flouting court order and committing contempt, the court kept in mind the impact of the sentence on the child's mind, and accordingly took a lenient view by not sending the father to prison.

Constitutional Validity of Some Sections under Hindu Minority and Guardianship Act and Guardians and Wards Act

Githa Hariharan v. *Reserve Bank of India* and *Vandana Shiva* v. *J. Bandhopadhyaya*,
AIR 1999 SC 1149: 1999 AIR SCW 811: (1999) 2 SCC 228

Issue: The constitutional validity of sections 6(a) of the Hindu Minority and Guardianship Act 1956 and 19(b) of the Guardians and Wards Act 1890 were challenged as being violative of articles 14 and 15 of the Constitution. Both the petitions were heard together.

Facts: In *Githa Hariharan*, the parents of a minor applied to the Reserve Bank of India for Relief Bonds in the name of their minor son. In the application, they stated that the mother would act as the guardian of the child for purpose of investments made with the money. Accordingly, in the prescribed form the mother signed as the guardian. The bank refused to entertain the application and asked the parents to produce the application form signed by the father or a certificate of guardianship from a competent authority, in favour of the mother. Against this, the mother filed a petition in the court.

In *Vandana Shiva*, divorce proceedings were already pending between the parties and the father prayed for the custody of their son. He was, as alleged by the petitioner, repeatedly writing to her and asserting that he being the only natural guardian of the child, no decision pertaining to the child should be taken without his permission. The petitioner consequently moved the Apex Court challenging section 6(a) of the Hindu Minority and Guardianship Act, 1956, and section 19(b) of the Guardians and Wards Act, 1890, as being violative of articles 14 and 15 of the Constitution, being discriminatory on the ground of gender.

Section 6(a) of the Hindu Minority and Guardianship Act says:

> "Section 6. *Natural guardians of a Hindu minor.*—The natural guardian of a Hindu minor, in respect of the minor's person as well as in respect of the minor's property (excluding his or her undivided interest in joint family property) are:
>
> (a) in the case of boy or an unmarried girl – the father, and *after him*, the mother provided that the custody of a minor who has not completed the age of five years shall ordinarily be with the mother.
>
> (b) ....
>
> (c) ....
>
> *Explanation*............................"

Section 19(b) of the Guardians and Wards Act says:

> "Section 19. *Guardian not to be appointed by the court in certain cases.*— Nothing in this chapter shall authorise the court ....to appoint or declare a guardian of the person—
>
> (a) ....
>
> (b) of a minor *whose father is living* and is not in the opinion of the court, unfit to be a guardian of the person of the minor; or
>
> (c) ...."

Hearing both the petitions together, the court observed that the wording of section 6(a) of the Hindu Minority and Guardianship Act. 'the father and after him the mother', do give an impression that the mother can act as a guardian only after the life-time of the father. However, instead of striking down this section as also section 19(b) of the Guardians and Wards Act as unconstitutional, it chose to construe the provisions in a manner so as not to offend the constitutional mandate of gender equality and non-discrimination. According to the court, the Constitution which came in 1950, prohibits gender discrimination and the Hindu Minority and Guardianship Act came six years later. The Parliament could not have intended "to transgress the constitutional limits or ignore the fundamental rights guaranteed by the Constitution which essentially prohibits discrimination on the grounds of sex".

Order: Adopting the rule of harmonious construction, it held that the word "after" in section 6(a) of the Hindu Minority and Guardianship Act need not necessarily mean "after the life-time", but "in the absence of". If the father is not in the charge of actual affairs of the minor, either because of his indifference or by virtue of mutual understanding between the parents, or because of some physical or mental incapacity, or because he is staying away from the place where the mother and the minor are living, then, in all such situations, the father can be considered as 'absent' under the impugned provisions and the mother, who, in any case is recognised natural guardian, can act validly on behalf of the minor as the guardian. The predominant consideration in every case, however, would be the welfare of the child, the court clarified.

Comment: The judgment has given an extended meaning to the word "after" to include certain situations wherein the mother can act as guardian even while the father is alive; however, the primary clause still stands and the mother will come only after the father. What if the father and mother are living together and the father is not "absent" within the meaning of the term as given by the court? The court has missed an opportunity to confer equal guardianship right on the mother. Needless to say, the prime consideration would and should always remain the welfare of the child.

Note. It is significant to note that *vide* the Personal Laws (Amendment) Act, 2010 the mother's right under section 19 of the Guardians and Wards Act has been brought at par with the fathers' and the court cannot appoint/declare a guardian of the person whose father *or mother* is living and is not unfit to be guardian.

Mother Flouting Court Custody Order – Yet Custody Awarded in View of Welfare of Children

Sarita Sharma v. *Sushil Sharma,*
JT 2000 (2) SC 258: AIR 2000 SC 1019: 2000 Cr LJ 1459

Issue: Can a mother who removes children from father's custody thereby flouting court orders, be denied custody on this single ground when, in view of other facts and circumstances, the welfare of the child requires that custody be given to her?

Facts: A couple having two children and living in the United States, had problems in their marriage. The husband sought dissolution of the marriage in a district court in Texas, U.S.A. By an interim order, the custody of the children was given to the father with visitation right to the mother. The mother picked up the children from the father's residence and brought them to India without any order from the American Court. The American Court passed the divorce decree sought by the petitioner husband and also give custody rights to the father (the petitioner) with not even visitation rights to the mother. With this order the father approached the Delhi High Court and custody was granted to him. The mother thereupon filed a special leave petition in the Supreme Court.

Order: The court perused through the facts of the case and the entire circumstances. It held that the welfare of the minor children should be the paramount consideration in deciding the issue of their custody; it observed that the court should not be guided entirely by the fact that the wife had taken the children from the father's custody despite the order of the American Court. The children also had expressed their desire to stay with the mother. While conceding that the decree passed by the American Court would be a relevant factor, it ruled that the same "cannot override the consideration of welfare of the minor children." The custody was awarded to the mother. The factors which weighed in making this order were—there was no one in the father's house other than his 80-year-old mother to look after the children; the father was in the habit of taking 'excessive alcohol', one of the children was a female child aged about five, and ordinarily, a female child should be allowed to remain with the mother; it would not be desirable to separate the siblings.

Comment: The act of the mother in removing the children from the father's house despite court's order of interim custody to the father, is objectionable indeed; the court, however, did not blow this negative factor against the mother, out of proportion because, in custody disputes, it is neither the preferential legal right of the contesting parties, nor their conduct (unless it has a bearing on the child's welfare) which is decisive, but the welfare of the children.

Guardianship given to Paternal Grandfather Despite Adoption by Maternal Grandfather

Jai Prakash Khadria v. *Shyam Sunder Agarwalla*, AIR 2000 SC 2172: 2000 AIR SCW 2341: (2000) 6 SCC 598

Issue: An adoptive father who was the grandfather of her widowed daughter's son, and became a natural guardian under section 7 of the Hindu Adoptions and Maintenance Act was displaced and paternal grandfather was appointed as guardian even though there was nothing ostensibly against him.

Facts: This was a battle between the maternal grandfather and the paternal grandfather, over the custody of a one-year old male child. The child had lost his father and was living with the maternal grandfather along with his (child's) mother. The paternal grandfather filed an application for being appointed as guardian and custodian of the child; he also sought an *ex parte* injunction against the mother, restraining her from giving the child in adoption to her father. A day after the petition, the mother gave the child in adoption to her father. The Family Court, however, granted guardianship and custody rights to the paternal grandfather, hence the appeal to High Court and having failed there, to the Apex Court.

Order: The order of the Family Court was affirmed by the High Court and the maternal grandfather was asked to handover the child to the paternal grandfather. On further appeal to the Supreme Court also, the order was not changed. The Court seems to be impressed by some considerations, which, *inter alia* were:

"The child was over-fondled when he was with the paternal grandfather whereas when with the maternal grandfather, he used to be left alone with the servants. Also, the paternal grandfather had revoked his Will executed earlier in favour of the daughters and made a fresh Will in favour of the child. The Will was, however, subject to the condition that the child comes and lives with them. Another factor which weighed with the courts was the fact of the mother's re-marriage and the second husband having two children from his previous marriage."

Comment: The factor of revoking the earlier Will and making a fresh one in favour of the child should not have been of any significance since a Will can again be revoked any time; moreover, financial security of the child was not an issue since even the maternal grandfather was affluent, and also, very loving to the child. It is also pertinent to note that under the law, the adoptive father becomes the natural guardian and he can be displaced from this position only if he is judicially disqualified. In this case, the mother, a widow, was fully competent to give the child in adoption which she did, and *secondly*, there was nothing to indicate that the adoptive father now *i.e.*, the maternal grandfather, was in any way unfit to be a natural guardian so as to warrant his displacement by giving guardianship or custody rights to the paternal grandfather. By appointing the paternal grandfather as guardian of a child who was legally given in adoption by the widowed mother to her father, the court has only weakened and diluted the widow's right to give her child in adoption. It may be pointed out that the court, in this case refrained from even commenting on the issue of validity of the adoption.

Legal Right of Party is Immaterial

Rajesh K. Gupta v. *Ram Gopal Agarwala*,
AIR 2005 SC 2426: 2005 Cr LJ 2581: 2005 AIR SCW 2418

Issue: The legal right of a party is immaterial in child custody disputes where the paramount consideration is the welfare of the child.

Facts: A writ of *habeas corpus* was filed by the appellant-father of a child in the High Court to produce the child and hand over her custody to the appellant. The father was an advocate-on-record in the Supreme Court. Differences arose between the couple and so the wife left him to stay with her parents. Their minor daughter was with the mother and the dispute revolved around her custody. The ground for seeking custody of the child was that, according to the husband, the child had been abducted by the wife's parents and further, that on account to mental ailment with which his wife (the mother of the child) was suffering, the custody of the child should be given to him. Considering the facts and circumstances of the case, the court held that the mother could continue with the child's custody. Hence the appeal by the father.

Order: It was argued that the mother was suffering from serious mental disorder of paranoid schizophrenia for almost two decades and was treated in U.S.A. where her father at that time was posted; and then in the All India Institute of Medical Sciences. It was further submitted that the life and health of the child would not be safe with the mother. According to the father, his mother will be living with him to look after the child. The Court, however, on the basis of medical records found that the mother was not suffering from any kind of serious mental ailment. It held, that the father was a lawyer and this profession is very exacting and time consuming. On the other hand, the wife's father was well educated and financially sound and could look after the needs of his daughter as well as the child. The maternal grandmother is also there to look after the child. Also, the judge of the High Court before whom the mother and child appeared and who also talked to the mother, recorded that the child was in perfect condition. The Supreme Court, after considering the submission of the counsels and the facts of the case, found no reason to interfere and hence dismissed the appeal.

Comment: In disputes regarding custody of a minor child, it is not the legal right of the parties but the welfare of the child which is the prime consideration while awarding custody.

Superior Financial Position of any Party – *Per se* no Consideration

Surabhai Ravi Kumar Minawala v. *State of Gujarat,* AIR 2005 Guj 149: 2005 (31) All Ind Cas 472: 2005 (2) Civ LJ 554

Issue: (i) Is superior financial position of a party any consideration for awarding custody of a minor to that party?

(ii) Would a writ of *habeas corpus* on mother's petition lie in case where the minor child is not in illegal custody of the father?

Facts: This was a mother's petition filed under article 226 of the Constitution, praying the court for issuance of writ of *habeas corpus* against the father of a minor child aged nine months, to produce the child in the court and direct him to handover its custody to her. The main objection to this petition was that it was not maintainable since an alternate efficacious remedy was available to the petitioner and further, that there was no need to issue writ of *habeas corpus* since the child was not in illegal custody of the father and the welfare of the child would be maintained in the best possible manner if the child remained with the father and his family. It was further averred that it was the petitioner who had left the family with her father and brother and she was not prepared to come back, and therefore, her petition should be dismissed. The petitioner's contention was that she was thrown out of the house when the child was just two months old.

Order: The court made all efforts to bring about settlement between the parties but that did not work. In these efforts, the court specifically stated that the petitioner was not at fault; rather it was the father who made things difficult. The argument that father's custody not being illegal, a writ of *habeas corpus* would not lie was also rejected. For this *Veena Kapoor* v. *Varinder Kumar Kapoor*, AIR 1982 SC 792: (1981) 3 SCC 92: 1982 Cr LJ 680, was relied upon. The main focus, however, was on the child's welfare. Under section 6 of the Hindu Minority and Guardianship Act the mother is the natural guardian of a minor and the custody of a child below age five would ordinarily be with the mother. The father's superior financial position was of no relevance as, according to the court (at p. 154)," no amount of wealth and 'mother-like-love' can take the place of mother's care and love for the child". And further, according to the court, "if the claim of the respondent (father) is to be weighed *vis-a-vis* the claim of the petitioner regarding safeguarding the interests of the child, it is very clear that petitioner can provide all the basic, necessary facilities and amenities to the child. Besides, from the father's affidavit it transpired that the child is likely to be with its grandmother and paternal aunts; and "between the mother on the one side and grandmother and the paternal aunts on the other, undoubtedly, the scale would tilt heavily in favour of the mother", the court remarked. The suggestion that the child be allowed to stay 15 days in a month with father was rejected as it would unnecessarily toss the child like a shuttlecock between the two families. This would adversely affect the child's health and make adjustment difficult for him. Custody was, accordingly, given to the mother.

Comment: In custody disputes, the prime consideration is always the welfare of the child and not the legal rights of the contesting parties. In the interest of the child, the court can issue a writ of *habeas corpus* to produce the child in the court and order handing over the child to the party with whom the child's interest is better safeguarded.

Mothers' Re-marriage does not Defeat her Right to Custody

Lekha v. *Anil Kumar*,
(2006) 12 SCALE 163

Issue: Would mother's remarriage defeat her claim to her child's custody.

Facts: The parties got separated just two and a half months after their marriage. Thereafter, the wife gave birth to a baby boy. She also filed a suit for divorce on ground of husband's cruelty which was granted by the Trial Court; custody of the child was also obtained by her. The husband filed an appeal before the Kerala High Court seeking custody of his now eleven-year-old son.

During pendency of this appeal the wife remarried. The High Court reversed the Trial Court order on the ground of the mother's remarriage and directed that the child's custody be handed over to the father even without interviewing the child. Against this order, the wife filed an appeal. The High Court order was set aside and that of the Trial Court restored.

Order: Admitting the wife's appeal, the Apex Court held that custody would lie with the mother notwithstanding her remarriage. The court held that even though under the Hindu law, the father is the natural guardian after the age of five, the predominant consideration is the welfare of the child. It remarked:

> "The fact that the mother had married again after the divorce of her first husband is no ground for depriving the mother of her parental right of custody. In cases like the present one, the mother may have shortcoming but that does not imply that she is not deserving of the solace and custody of her child. If the court forms the impression that the mother is a normal and independent young woman and shows no indication of imbalance of mind in her, then...the custody of the minor child should not be refused to her or else we would be really assenting to the proposition that a second marriage involving a mother *per se* will operate adversely to a claim of a mother for the custody of her minor child."

In this case, the child was bright and intelligent and wished to stay with his mother. He also stated that his mother treated him and the new born baby with same love and affection and that his step-father also loved him. Custody was thus granted to the mother with arrangements for father's visitation.

Comment: The Apex Court judgment comes as a reassurance to mothers who, after a divorce are wary of getting married again lest they lose custody of their child/children. A husband and wife may have problems amongst themselves even ending in their divorce but that surely does not make the mother less deserving of custody of her own child even if she remarried.

Note. *See* also *Keshav Ganpatrao Hedau* v. *Damodhar Udaramji Kandrikar,* AIR 2005 Bom 118: 2005 (2) Civ LJ 279: 2005 (1) Hindu LR 140 where the child's father died within six months of the child's birth and the mother remarried after some years, the paternal grandfathers application for custody and guardianship of the child was rejected; "second marriage, in no way disentitles the mother to have custody of her minor son and to act as a guardian", the court observed. Likewise in *T. Kochappi* v. *R. Sadasivam Pillai,* AIR 2006 Mad 330: 2007 (1) ALJ (NOC) 69: 2007 (1) Rec CivR 209; *see* also *K. Venkat Reddy* v. *Chinnapareddy Viswanadha Reddy,* AIR 2009 AP 1: 2009 (73) All Ind Cas 523: 2008 (6) Andh LT 360 where after the death of the mother children were with the father who remarried, the maternal grand father's application for custody of children on ground of father's remarriage was dismissed, *Poolakkal Ayisakutty* v. *Parat Abdul Samad,* AIR 2005 Ker 68: ILR 2005 (1) Ker 14: 2005 (1) Ker LJ 7 where father who had remarried was given custody over claim of maternal grandmother who was not in good health and was herself dependant on her other daughter.

"Positive Test" as to what is in Child's Interest
Nil Ratan Kundu v. Abhijit Kundu,
(2008) 7 MLJ 248 (SC): AIR 2009 SC (Supp) 732

Issue: The issue involved in this custody dispute was whether custody of a child can be given to the father merely because he is the natural guardian and suffers from no disqualification provided in the law.

Facts: This was a custody dispute between the father and the maternal grand parents of the child. The mother of the child was, allegedly, tortured to death by the father who was charged under sections 498A and 304 of the Indian Penal Code and arrested. The child was just 4½ years old at that time and was in ailing condition. His custody was handed over to the maternal grandparents who nursed him and brought him up with utmost love and care and also admitted to one of the best schools. After the father came out on bail he filed an application under the Guardians and Wards Act, 1890, seeking custody of the child which was strongly resisted by the maternal grandparents. They contended that the father of the child had killed the child's mother (*i.e.*, daughter of the defendants) and criminal cases were pending against him; that the child was handed over to them when he was in very bad state of health and now his custody should not be given to the father. The Trial Court, however, allowed the application observing that the fact that criminal cases were pending against him did not *ipso facto* disqualify him from being guardian and held that the father being the natural guardian "the present and future of Antariksh [the child] would be better secured in the custody of the respondent [father]" (p. 250)

An order was accordingly made to give over the custody of the child who was then about six years old, to the father "immediately". An appeal against this before the Calcutta High Court was dismissed. The Division Bench of the High Court held that the impugned order did not suffer from any infirmity and directed the appellants to hand over the child to the father with visitation rights to the appellants. Hence the present appeal. It was argued that both the lower courts had adopted a technical and legalistic rather than pragmatic and realistic approach and they had not taken into account the welfare of the child which ought to be the paramount consideration in such cases. They reiterated that the respondent-father of the child, and his family members tortured the child's mother for not bringing enough dowry; she was mentally and physically harassed and was admitted to the hospital by the appellants only; that after she was cured she again returned to the matrimonial home but she was again brutally assaulted by the respondent and his mother and succumbed. All this caused great mental shock to the child who become very ill and it was the appellants who nurtured him back to health and were looking after him. It was also argued that the child's wishes were never ascertained by courts below even though he was over six years old at that time and capable of independent opinion. Another significant contention raised by the appellant was that the courts below had not taken the fathers "character" into account.

The father's counsel however, as expected, supported the order of the Trial Court and High Court and urged that these courts had considered the relevant legal provisions and the fact that the respondent was the natural guardian and "there was no earthly reason to deprive him of custody of the minor" and that the minor should not be deprived of natural love and affection of his father in absence of mother; and further, that the courts below were conscious of the pending cases against his client and therefore had observed that if ultimately he is convicted and sentenced to jail, the appellants could move the court for change of custody. In view of all the above, the respondents counsel urged that the impugned order cannot be said to be illegal or contrary to law and the Apex Court, in exercise of its jurisdiction under article 136 of the Constitution, may not interfere with it.

These arguments, however, did not find favour with the Supreme Court. It analysed the statutory provisions and the case-law in great detail. Reference was made, *inter alia* to the following cases, viz., *Annie Besant v. G. Narayaniah*, AIR 1914 PC 41: 12 All LJ 1155; *Bimla Devi v. Subhash Chandra Yadav*, AIR 1992 Pat 76: 1991 (1) Civ LJ 471: II (1991) DMC 587; *Chandrakala Menon v. Vipin Menon*, (1993) 2 SCC 6: 1993 All CriC 144; *Elizabeth Denshaw v. Arvind M. Denshaw*, AIR 1987 SC 3: (1987) 1 SCC 42: 1986 (4) Supreme 487; *Goverdhan Lal v. Gajendra Kumar*, AIR 2002 Raj 148: 2001 (3) Raj LR 638: 2002 (1) WLC 419; *Howarth v. Northcott*, 152 Conn 460; *Kamla Devi v. State of Himachal Pradesh*, AIR 1987 HP 34: (1986) 3 Crimes 151; *Kirtikumar Maheshankar Joshi v. Pradipkumar Karunashanker Joshi*, AIR 1992 SC 1447: 1992 AIR SCW 1528: (1992) 3 SCC 573; *M.K. Hari Govindan v. A.R. Rajaram*, AIR 2003 Mad 315: 2003 (3) Ind LD 856; *Mausami Moitra Ganguli v. Jayant Ganguli*, (2008) 6 MLJ 128: (2008) 8 SCALE 527: AIR 2008 SC 2262; *McGrath Re*, (1893) 1 Ch 143: 62 LJ Ch 208: 67 LT 636; *Rosy Jacob v. Jacob Chakramakkal*, AIR 1973 SC 2090: (1973) 1 SCC 840; *Saraswathibai Shripad v. Shripad Vasanj*, AIR 1941 Bom 103: 43 Bom LR 79: ILR (1941) Bom 455; *Surinder Kaur Sandhu v. Harbax Singh Sandhu*, AIR 1984 SC 1224: (1984) 3 SCC 698: (1984) 2 SCWR 116; *Tarun Ranjan Majumdar v. Siddhartha Datta*, AIR 1991 Cal 76: (1990) 2 Cal LJ 306: I (1991) DMC 14; *Thrity Hoshie Dolikuka v. Hoshiam Shavaksha Dolikuka*, AIR 1982 SC 1276: (1982) 2 SCC 544: II (1982) DMC 288.

The following statement of Bailey in *Habeas Corpus* (Vol I p. 581) which was also referred to by the Apex Court (at p. 252) is worth special mention in the present context:

"The reputation of the father may be stainless as crystal; he may not be afflicted with the slightest mental, moral or physical disqualification for superintending the general welfare of the infant; the mother may have been separated from him without the shadow of a pretense of justification; yet the interests of the child may imperatively demand the denial of father's right and its continuance with the mother. The tender age and precarious state of its health make the vigilance of the mother indispensable to its proper care; ....every instinct of humanity unerringly proclaims that no substitute can supply the place of her whose watchfulness over the sleeping cradle, or waking moments of her offspring, is prompted by deeper and holier feeling than the most liberal allowance of nurses' wages could possibly stimulate."

Order: After a lengthy analysis, the court came to the conclusion that the orders passed by the courts below are short of the fundamental principles on more than one ground. For instance, they noted that the grand parents were giving all love and affection to the child, but that does not, according to the lower court, mean that the father will not give that love and affection; that the appellants gave the child education in good school does not mean that father would not, and so on. In fact, the courts below emphasised the fact of the father being the *natural guardian and not having invoked any disqualification provided in law* on the basis of which they granted custody in favour of the father. The Supreme Court however, held that it is not the "negative test" that the father is not unfit or disqualified to have custody but the "positive test" whether such custody would be in the interest of the child, which is material. The child is not a property or commodity and issues relating to custody of minors and tender aged children have to be handled with love, affection, sentiment and by applying human touch to the problem, the court held. The lower courts ought to have considered the allegations against the father and the pending criminal cases against him; a complaint against the father alleging and attributing death of the mother to him and the criminal cases against him are relevant considerations which were not considered by lower courts nor did these courts ascertain the wishes of the child. In view of all the above, the appeal of the grand parents was allowed and the father's application for the child's custody was dismissed. In fact the court called the child to ascertain his wishes and found that he was very happy with the grand parents.

Comment: The judgment reiterates the fundamental principle that in custody disputes, it is not the rights of the parties but the welfare of the child which is the decisive factor. A 'positive test' as to what is in child's best interest rather than 'negative test' that the claimant is not unfit, should be followed while awarding custody. The approach of the lower courts in this case was very insensitive, harsh and unrealistic; the Trial Court directing the grandparents to handover the child's custody to father *"immediately"* and the High Court ordering the handing over *"within twenty-four hours positively"* was rather cruel on both the child and the grand parents who lost their daughter in the hands of the child's father; and who then nursed back the child to health who was in a state of great mental shock; equally shocking was the courts remarks that custody be handed over to the father and should he be convicted and sent to jail on charge against him for the death of the child's mother the grant-parents can again apply for taking back the custody. As rightly remarked by the court, the child is not a chattel, property or commodity. It cannot be handled like a shuttle cock from one court to another; uprooted from one custodian to the other; shifting of the child impacts his personality, growth and peer relationships and hence his all round development.

Plea of Continuity
Gaurav Nagpal v. Sumedha Nagpal,
AIR 2009 SC 557 (Del): 2008 AIR SCW 7687: (2009) 1 SCC 42

Issue: Should custody of the child be not disturbed simply on the plea of continuity? This argument is often taken when custody is with one parent (or any guardian/custodian) and another seeks it. This was the issue involved in the case.

Facts: A two-year-old male child who was in the custody of the mother, was forcibly snatched away by the father. Ever since then the wife started rounds of courts including a writ of *habeas corpus* in the Delhi High Court which was dismissed for want of jurisdiction. Her application for child's guardianship before the civil judge in Gurgaon was dismissed. According to the judge, it would not be in the interest of the child to change his custody as he has already got so used to the love and affection of the father and his family. On revision, she got visitation rights but the father did not allow that, thereupon she filed a contempt petition in the District Court which granted custody to the mother. An unsuccessful appeal was made in the High Court where it was argued by him that the Trial Court had taken into consideration the fact that the child was with him for a continuous period of seven years and also that he (the father) did not suffer from any disability or infirmity, and made the order in his favour holding that the continuity should not be disturbed. The other arguments advanced in support of his claim were better financial position, big house, company of brother's children etc. The mere fact of being the mother should not be the basis for granting the custody and changing custody at this stage would traumatise him, it was contended. His arguments however, did not cut ice. For the mother, it was pleaded that the child was with her and the father forcibly took him away and thereafter thwarted all her attempts to get it back and even denied her visitation rights; further, that she is a school teacher and financially capable of bringing up the child. The child was poisoned against the mother but she was confident that he could overcome the same soon. In view of all the above, the High Court dismissed the husband's appeal. It observed that the daily trauma that the child faced in being tutored and poisoned against his mother could be far greater than the trauma he would face when united with his mother and the father who poisons the child against another parent cannot be said to have acted in the best interests or welfare of the child. Hence, the father's appeal before the Apex Court. The court analysed the issue in great detail and lamented on the increasing number of break ups in marriage which affect children most. It observed that in suits for custody, the court has not only to look at the issue on legalistic basis but from human angles; emphasis is not on what parties say but on what is in the best interest of the minor. Dismissing the husband's appeal, the court made the following significant remarks:

> "The trump card in the appellant's argument is that the child is living since long with the father. The argument is attractive. But the same overlooks a very significant factor. By flouting various orders, leading

even to initiation of contempt proceedings, the appellant has managed to keep custody of the child. He cannot be a beneficiary of his own wrongs."

Order: Paramount consideration in custody suits being the welfare of the child, and not the legal right of a parent, the court granted custody to the mother.

Comment: The court emphasised that the term "welfare" needs to be construed liberally so as to include moral, religious and ethical welfare of the child; financial and physical comforts should not be the sole factors to decide what is in the best interests of the child.

Variation of Custody Orders
Vikram Vir Vohra v. Shalini Bhalla,
AIR 2010 SC 1675 (Del): 2010 AIR SCW 2261: (2010) 4 SCC 409

Issue: The issue involved was as to whether an arrangement in regard to custody and visitation rights of a child agreed upon in the petition for divorce by mutual consent can be subsequently varied or altered by filing an application under section 26 of the Hindu Marriage Act.

Facts: The parents had obtained a divorce by mutual consent; and as regards the child, a seven-year-old son, there was a settlement between the parties incorporated in the divorce petition, whereunder the child's custody would be with the mother with the father having visitation rights. After some time both filed applications seeking modification of the terms and conditions about custody. The father sought permanent custody and the mother wanted to take the child to Australia where she got better job opportunities and so sought revocation of the visitation rights granted to the father. The Trial Court, the High Court and the Apex Court were all of the opinion that the welfare of the child lies with the mother and that orders as to custody and visitation being interlocutory, these can be moulded and changed as per the needs of the child; it was also held that absence of the terms and conditions in the divorce decree does not disentitle the wife to file an application under section 26 of the Hindu Marriage Act seeking revocation of the appellants visitation rights. Both the High Court as well as the Supreme Court had also personally interviewed the child who was categoric that he wished to be with the mother. "A child is not a chattel nor is he/she an article of personal property to be shared in equal halves, the Court observed" (at p. 1678)

The following observations of the court in the context of variation of the visitation rights of the father are pertinent:

"....this Court finds that the respondent-mother is getting a better job opportunity in Australia. Her autonomy on her parenthood cannot be curtailed by Court on the ground of a prior order of custody of the child. Every person has a right to develop his or her potential. In fact a right to development is a basic human right. The respondent-mother cannot be asked to choose between her child and her career. It is clear that the child is very dear to her and she will spare no pains to ensure that the child gets proper education and training in order to develop his faculties and ultimately to become a good citizen. If the custody of the child is denied to her, she may not be able to pursue her career in Australia and that may not be conducive either to the development of her career or to the future prospects of the child. Separating the child from his mother will be disastrous to both."

Order: The husband's appeal was dismissed; his visitation rights were not totally ignored but restructured so as to be compatible with the educational career of the child.

Comment: The primary consideration in custody cases is the welfare of the child. The court also recognised the mother's right to development in her career, and held that the welfare of both the mother and the child lies with keeping the child with the mother in Australia with modified visitation rights for the father in India. Thus a balance was struck between the rights and interests of all.

Jurisdiction in Child Custody Suit
Sarabjit v. *Piara Lal,*
AIR 2005 P&H 237: 2005 (35) All Ind Cas 236: 2005 (3) CCC 179

Issue: The expression "minor ordinarily resides" in section 9 of the Guardians and Wards Act, 1890 has to be construed to mean where the mother resides and not where the child is actually residing.

Facts: This was a suit for custody of a minor child by the widowed mother. The parties were married at H and stayed at A after marriage, where the son was born. The father of the child died when the child was just a year old. The petitioner mother stated that after her husband's death, she was turned out of the house at A by her in-laws and her child was forcibly and illegally snatched by them. Despite intervention of relatives and neighbours, neither she was allowed to stay at A nor was she allowed to take the child. She then went to H, her parental place. She filed a petition for custody of the child under sections 7 and 25 of the Guardians and Wards Act, 1890, read with section 6 of the Hindu Minority and Guardianship Act, 1956, at H.

The Guardian Judge, on the basis of objection raised by the respondent, held that such petition could be filed within the jurisdiction of District Courts where the minor "ordinarily resides" as provided by section 9 of the Guardians and Wards Act *viz.,* A, the petition was, accordingly returned for presentation in the competent court. Hence, the present petition.

Order: The mother had, during the pendency of this petition also filed application for grant of interim custody of the child, asserting that the custody petition was returned to her by the Guardian Judge after keeping it pending for two years. This, according to her counsel was a calculated attempt to ensure that the child attains the age of 5 so that they are out of the ambit of section 6(a) of the Hindu Minority and Guardianship Act under which the custody of a minor who has not completed the age of 5 shall, ordinarily be with the mother. On the main issue of jurisdiction the court held that the expression "minor ordinarily resides" in section 9 of the Guardians and Wards Act has to be interpreted to mean the residence of the mother. Once, under section 6(1) of the Hindu Minority and Guardianship Act it is mandatory that the child below the age of 5 years has to reside ordinarily with the mother, it is implied that the residence of the mother would be the residence of the child. Thus, the court, where the mother resides, would have jurisdiction to entertain the custody application and not the court where the child is actually residing. As to the claim of the mother on merits, the court held that the tender age of the child below 5 years would necessarily require the natural love and affection which the child is likely to get in the lap of his mother rather than that of grandmother and grandfather. Another aspect which the court considered was that it would be highly inconvenient for the mother to prosecute proceedings for the custody of her minor son at A.

The court accordingly set aside the order rejecting her application for custody of the child on the ground that court at place A alone would have jurisdiction to decide the application, and directed that custody be given to the mother.

Comment: When a minor is of an age when she or he is ordinarily expected to remain with the mother, the issue of jurisdiction has to be decided according to the place where the mother is residing. In cases such as this where a child of very tender age was allegedly, forcibly taken from the mother by her in-laws residing at place A, it would indeed be unfair to expect a mother, (widow in this case) staying with her parents at another place, to prosecute proceedings for custody of her child at place A.

Jurisdiction

Amal Saha v. *Basana Saha,*
AIR 1988 Gau 22: (1987) 2 Gua LR 84: (1987) 2 Civ LJ 238

Issue: This was a dispute involving custody of children where the issue involved was as to the jurisdiction of the court at a place where children resided as against the court where the non-applicant father resided.

Facts: Parents of two minor sons resided at Gauhati. After the husband/father deserted them, the mother put the children in a hostel at Digboi. The father removed the children from the hostel and took them away to Calcutta. The mother filed an application for custody at Gauhati. The father/husband raised an objection and argued that jurisdiction lay with the court in Calcutta.

Order: Deciding the issue in favour of the mother, the court observed (at pp. 23-24):

(i) The court must ignore recent removal, if any, from a place where the child ordinarily resides. If this fact of removal is taken into consideration, the provisions of the Act will be rendered nugatory.

(ii) There can be no presumption that minor is deemed to reside at the place where his natural guardian resides. In other words, the place of residence of natural guardian is not the determining factor in deciding the question of jurisdiction.

(iii) If in deciding the place where the minor ordinarily resides, the court comes to a finding that the minor was residing with any one of its parents, then the question of constructive custody may arise depending on the circumstances in the case.

(iv) If the minor has no permanent abode, he must be deemed to reside where he actually resides.

It was held, that the court at Gauhati had the jurisdiction to entertain the custody application filed by the mother.

Comment: In custody disputes, for purposes of conferring jurisdiction on courts the place where a child ordinarily resides is the place where the child actually resides.

No Third Party Intervention in Custody Dispute when both Parents Alive

Akash v. *State of Andhra Pradesh,*
AIR 2000 AP 261: II (2000) DMC 490: 2000 (2) Hindu LR 603

Issue: Can a third person intervene in a custody dispute when both parents of a minor child are alive?

Facts: In proceedings for divorce before the Family Court, custody of minor male child was awarded to the mother. Under the order, the mother was required to take the child to the father during holidays, vacations and other festivals failing which the custody order in her favour was liable to be modified. On the mother's (petitioner's wife) failure to comply with these directions, the father (husband) filed a petition for modification of the order and arrest of the wife for contempt of court order. The mother appeared before the court and tendered an unconditional apology; she explained the circumstances which prevented her from taking the child to the father. Her father was ill and in hospital and the child who was just nine years old, could not be sent alone to the father's place which was 1400 kilometres away. The mother's apology was accepted with directions that the orders should be complied with in future. The maternal grand-father filed a writ petition in the High Court praying that the child was not comfortable in the company of the father and that he was of an age where his wishes should be given due weight and accordingly he should not be forced to go to meet the father. It was further contended that the distance between the place of residence of the father and the mother was about 1400 kilometres and it was very inconvenient for the mother to take the child to the father.

Order: The court held that the maternal grandfather had no *locus standi* to file the petition since both the natural guardians of the child were alive. They alone can raise objections, if any. In this case, the mother never raised the question of inconvenience in the court; rather she had given an undertaking to the court that she would take the child to the father as per the directions. The mother could not be allowed to flout the Family Court orders and deny to the father the visiting rights, the court held.

Comment: When both the parents are alive and none of them is under any disability to have the child's custody, the intervention of any third party in the matter is barred. If any of the parents have reservation on the custody order made by the Trial Court, they alone can take up the matter for review and not any third party.

Hindu Minority and Guardianship Act: Alienation of Minor's Property

Vishwambar v. Laxminarayana,
AIR 2001 SC 2607: 2001 AIR SCW 2616: (2001) 6 SCC 163

Issue: An alienation of immovable property of minor by a mother without court permission is voidable. A suit for recovery of such property without prayer for setting aside the sale is not maintainable.

Facts: Under section 8 of the Hindu Minority and Guardianship Act, 1956, a natural guardian cannot alienate the estate of a minor without prior permission of the court. A sale without prior permission is voidable at the instance of the minor or any person claiming under him. In this case, the mother of the plaintiffs sold some properties while they were minors, without court permission; nor was there any legal necessity for the sale. Such alienations, under the law mentioned above, were voidable at the instance of the plaintiffs who after attaining majority, could have got the same cancelled if they wanted to recover the properties from the purchaser. The plaintiffs, however, on attaining majority, filed a suit for recovery of possession from the purchaser without making any prayer for setting aside the sale. Such prayer was added subsequently during the hearing of the suit by an amendment under Order 6, rule 17 of the Civil Procedure Code, 1908.

Order: The plaintiffs were the appellants before the Apex Court. By the time the prayer was made for setting aside the sale, the period of limitation as prescribed under section 60 of the Limitation Act, 1960, had elapsed. The appeal of the plaintiffs was, therefore, dismissed. According to the court, the claim for recovery of possession of the properties could not have been made without first setting aside the sale deeds which were voidable; the suit as initially filed by them was not maintainable and by the time the defect was rectified by amendment, the suit became barred by limitation.

Comment: In order to recover possession of properties alienated under a voidable transaction, first the transaction has to be set aside and then only can the suit for recovery be filed. A direct suit for recovery without having the sale-deed set aside is not maintainable.

Alienation of Minor's Property
P.V. Madhavi v. P.V. Balakrishnan, AIR 2010 Ker 111

Issue: This was a suit for setting aside the sale deed executed by the mother as the guardian of a minor without court permission.

Facts: The mother had sold certain properties belonging to the minor son without court permission. It was purported to have been sold for a sum of ₹ 6,000 for clearing the debts of the plaintiff's father and a part of the amount was paid towards consideration for purchasing another property in the name of the plaintiff. On attaining majority, the son filed a suit within the limitation period, for setting aside the alienation. He alleged that the alienation by his mother was wrongful and injurious to him and that the consideration was meagre; he further stated that the father had no debts and there was no necessity to sell the property. Besides, according to him he had no knowledge about the purchase of the property in his name. In view of all this, the alienation made by the mother was void and liable to be set aside, it was contended. The court conceded that the plaintiff in this case was competent to have the alienation set aside but clarified that equity requires that the minor should restore to the transferee any benefit he may have received under the transfer before he (the minor) can take the benefit of any decree in his favour. It held (pp. 114-115):

> "In cancelling the documents, the plaintiff need only surrender benefits received as justice may require. Such benefit required by the justice is the actual benefit received under the impugned transaction, which is avoided. It may not be conducive to justice to allow the minor to have double advantage by avoiding the transaction and at the same time retaining its benefits. ..... In a given case, the benefit may be only the actual consideration and its interest. But where the consideration for the impugned transaction itself is the purchase of another property in the name of the minor, that property must be taken as the benefit derived by the minor and it must be directed to be returned. Value of the properties might have gone up and return of the consideration in money alone may work out injustice to the defendant-purchaser and undue gain to the minor"

And it concluded "....the legal position is that whether the sale deed is void or voidable, the minor seeking to set it aside cannot claim interference of a court of law without making restitution. The law is clear that if a person sells or mortgages another's property having no legal or equitable right to do so and that other benefits by the transaction, the latter cannot have it set aside without making restitution to the person whose money has been applied for the benefit of the estate. The principle of restitution in such cases is based on the equitable maxim "he who seeks equity must do equity".

Order: The minor (now major) refused to make restitution of benefits derived under the sale deed, hence the court refused to grant him relief.

Comment: It is not the strict letter of the law or rigid application of statutory provisions but the equities in a given case which form the basis of court judgments.

ADOPTION

Adoption has been recognised for centuries but being a part of personal laws there is no uniformity among different communities. Infact, Hindu law is the only law which recognises adoption in the true sense and statutorily recognises the same. The Hindu Adoptions and Maintenance Act, 1956 makes detailed provisions regarding conditions for a valid adoption. The Parsis have no statutory law of adoption though a customary form of adoption known as *'palak'* is prevalent amongst them. Under this custom the widow of a childless Parsi can adopt a child on the fourth day of her husband's death for performing certain annual religious rites. The child does not acquire any property rights. The Muslims have no statutory law on adoption either and a Muslim who wishes to adopt may adopt if he can prove the existence of a custom permitting adoption. Likewise in the case of Christians, the parties may adopt if they can prove any custom which permits them to adopt. In *Philips Alfred Malsvin* v. *V.J. Gonsalves*, AIR 1999 Ker 187: ILR (1999) 2 Ker 43: 1999 (1) Ker LJ 247 however, the court upheld a Christian couples' right to adopt with all the rights to the adopted child as are enjoyed by a biological child According to the court the right to adopt is inherent in the right to life guaranteed under article 21 of the Constitution. In the context of adoption, the Juvenile Justice (Care and Protection of Children) Act, 2000 as amended in 2006 is equally significant. Under this Act, adoption is one of the ways recognised by Parliament to facilitate rehabilitation of surrendered children or children in need of care and protection. The Court invoked *inter alia*, provisions in article 21 of the Constitution also. Inter-country adoptions are on the increase; in the absence of any specific law in this regard, there are various guidelines provided by the Supreme Court *vide* its judgment in *Lakshmi Kant Pandey* v. *Union of India*, AIR 1984 SC 469: (1984) 2 SCC 244: (1984) 2 SCR 795: 1984 Marri LJ 249 and more recently in *Lakshmi Kant Pandey* v. *Union of India*, 2010 (6) SCALE 23.

Enactment of a uniform law of adoption still seems to be a far cry. Serious efforts by introducing Bills towards that in 1972 and in 1980 did not meet with any success.

In 1990 the Christian Adoption and Maintenance Bill was mooted by various organizations but that too could not make its entry in the statute book.

Customary law on adoption is recognised among Christian by Courts. Also Guardians and wards Act is there but that gives only rights of guardianship and is not the same as adoption.

This section of the Book deals with significant cases on the subject of adoption.

Applicability of Hindu Adoptions and Maintenance Act

Act not Applicable to Pre-Act Adoptions

Nagireddi Lakshmi v. *Nagireddi Nagaraju,*
AIR 2005 AP 17

Issue: Would the provisions of the Hindu Adoptions and Maintenance Act, 1956, be applicable to an adoption made prior to 1956?

Facts: The plaintiff was adopted by the first respondent and her husband with all necessary formalities and there was also a registered adoption-deed executed on November 15, 1955. After the father's death, the plaintiff and his adoptive mother jointly enjoyed the properties. However, as the plaintiff was a minor and the mother being a lady unable to manage the properties, the joint family properties were managed by the father of the first respondent. Gradually, due to instigation by the other relatives, the first respondent started disliking the plaintiff and also tried to alienate the plaint-schedule joint properties. Thereupon, the plaintiff filed a suit for partition of the properties. The same was decreed by the Trial Court but, on appeal, the District Court set aside the decree. Hence, the appeal. The main issue was as to the validity of the adoption of the plaintiff, which was the basis for the claim to the properties. The adoption was a pre-1956 (Act) adoption and the same was challenged as some of the requirements laid down in the 1956 Act were not complied with. It was contended, *inter alia*, that the adoptive father had not taken his wife's consent; that there was *sapinda* relationship between the plaintiff and the adoptive mother; that even after the adoption, the adoptive father's mother settled some properties in favour of the adoptive mother and not the plaintiff which is an indication that there was no valid adoption. The challenge was not accepted as, according to the court, the provisions of the Hindu Adoptions and Maintenance Act, 1956, have no application to the adoptions made prior to the said Act. Under the Act of 1956, there is a legal presumption under section 16 with regard to the validity of the registered documents relating to adoption. The court shall presume that the adoption has been made in compliance with the provisions of the Act unless and until it is disproved. Therefore, the general presumption is in favour of the adopted son and to treat the adoption deed as genuine document unless contrary is proved. Under section 30 of the 1956 Act the validity of the adoptions made before the commencement of the Act shall be determined as if the Act had not been passed. Thus, the provisions of the Act have no application to adoptions made prior to the commencement of the Act. No doubt, under the Hindu Adoptions and Maintenance Act a male Hindu cannot adopt a child without the consent of his wife; if a female is a minor (even a male) she is not entitled to adopt but admittedly, provisions of the Act has no application to pre-1956 adoption.

Under the old law, a person, though under 18, yet if he attains the age of discretion, he is entitled to adopt, but under the present Act, no person under the age of 18 can adopt. Also, earlier there was no legal prohibition for a married man to adopt (a boy only, since boys only could be adopted) without consent of his wife but now the law requires a wife's consent. Further, under the old law, a married woman or a widow could never adopt during the life-time of the husband or after his death, as the case may be, except with authority given to her by the husband or consent of the *sapindas* and it would be an adoption to the husband.

Coming to the facts of the present case, the court held that it is clear that the plaintiff was given in adoption by his natural parents to late Ramulu, husband of the first defendant, under the old Hindu law. Prior to the Hindu Adoptions and Maintenance Act there was no such requirement that consent of the wife is necessary; also there was no prohibition to adopt the plaintiff on ground of the alleged *sapinda* relationship. The adoption-deed was reduced to writing, duly attested and registered. "Merely because the mother of late Ramulu settled certain property in 1956 itself immediately after adoption when the plaintiff was just two years old, in favour of the first defendant, it cannot be said that the adoption-deed is itself not a genuine one. The self-acquired property can be settled in favour of anybody, and there is no compulsion to settle the property in favour of a minor child who was just then adopted", the court said.

Order: The judgment of the lower appellate court was held to be 'perverse and without any basis whatsoever' and hence the appeal admitted. The Trial Court order was restored and confirmed.

Comment: The Hindu Adoptions and Maintenance Act has revolutionised the adoption law amongst the Hindus. It has given almost equal rights to females also. However, it is but logical and fair and also statutorily provided, that pre-1956 adoptions would not be affected by the provisions of the Hindu Adoptions and Maintenance Act.

AGE OF ADOPTEE

Adoptee over 15 when Adopted: Custom Proved

Atluri Brahmanandan (dead) through L.R's v. Anne Sai Bapuji, AIR 2011 SC 545

Issue: The issue involved was as to the validity of an adoption of a boy over the age of 15 years.

Facts: The case was a property dispute in which the main issue was whether the petitioner, respondent in appeal, was validly adopted by the deceased who had died intestate. He had filed a suit for recovery of possession of properties left behind by his adoptive father without making a Will in favour of anyone else. The same was challenged primarily on the ground that the alleged adoption was not valid since the respondent was a boy above the age of 15 years at the time when the adoption was alleged to have taken place. Reference may be made to the provision of section 10(iv) of the Hindu Adoptions and Maintenance Act, 1956 (HAMA) which says, "No person shall be capable of being taken in adoption unless the following conditions are fulfilled, namely, [*inter alia*]

(i) XXX

(ii) XXX

(iii) XXX

(iv) he or she has not completed the age of fifteen years, unless there is a custom or usage applicable to the parties which permits persons who have completed the age of fifteen years being taken in adoption (emphasis added).

Another pertinent section in the context of this case is section 16 of the Hindu Adoptions and Maintenance Act under which, in case of a registered adoption deed there is a presumption that the provisions of the Act have been complied with; such presumption however can be disproved.

The respondent contended that the adoption of a child over the age of 15 years was permissible and valid in the "Kamma" community of Andhra Pradesh. He also relied on the provision contained in section 16 of the Act regarding presumption of validity of the adoption registered under adoption deed. The respondent in this case succeeded in proving the custom in the "Kamma" community recognizing adoption of a boy over the age of 15 and this custom and the fact adoption was also recorded in the registered deed of adoption which was not disproved by the appellant. The court referred to a case (unnamed) decided by the Andhra Pradesh High Court reported in 1964 *Andhra Weekly Reporter*, page 156 where the Division Bench has recognised the custom recognising adoption of a boy over 15 by the "Kamma" community. The court further observed relying on *Ujagar Singh* v. *Mst. Jeo*, AIR 1959 SC 1041: ILR 1959 Punj 1735: (1959) Supp 2 SCR 781 that when a custom has been repeatedly recognised by courts, it is blended into the law of land and proof of the same would become unnecessary under section 57 of the Evidence Act, 1872.

Order: The adoption of the son, the original petitioner and respondent in appeal was held to be valid and the appeal challenging the adoption was dismissed.

Comments: Customs have played, and still play, a significant role in our society amongst some communities and some parts of the country, specially. Customs which have stood the test of time and are reasonable and fulfil other requirements of a valid custom have been explicitly saved under Hindu personal laws. Thus, in the case in hand, the issue involved was as to adoption of a child over the age of 15 years. As a matter of general rule, as laid down in section 10(iv) of the Hindu Adoptions and Maintenance Act a child to be adopted needs to be below the age of 15; however, an exception has been made where custom recognises adoption of a child over 15. Practically speaking, a child to be adopted should be of very tender age so that he/she can emotionally integrate into the new family. A grown up child cannot be expected to be emotionally one with the new adoptive family. Such adoptions are made, probably, in view of property matters or the need to have someone to take care in old age. Since adoption changes the entire course of inheritance and property rights, the validity of the same needs to be properly established when challenged.

Adoptee over 15 when Adopted: Custom not Proved

Amit Chandubhai Chauhan v. Ahmedabad, Municipal Corporation
AIR 2011 Guj 145

Issue: The issue of adoption of a son above the age of 15 years without cogent evidence of existence of custom permitting adoption of child above 15, was involved in this case.

Facts: One 'H', an employee in Ahmedabad Municipal Corporation, had adopted the appellant and an adopted deed was executed. The appellant was aged 23 years at the time of adoption. After one year of the adoption, the adoptee mother died and thereupon, the appellant applied for compassionate appointment. His claim for appointment on compassionate ground was rejected in view of section 10(iv) of the Hindu Adoptions and Maintenance Act, 1956 under which a child over the age of 15 years cannot be adopted. It was therefore held that the appellant was not eligible to claim the appointment as he was not the legally adopted son of late 'H'; and further, the husband of 'H' was still alive [thereby perhaps indicating that he had a prior right to such appointment].

Order: The son filed an appeal against this order. His argument was that his case of adoption comes under section 10(iv) where, even though normally only a child who has not completed the age of 15 years may be adopted but an exception has been made where custom or usage applicable to the parties permits adoption of a person over the age of 15 years; and in this case, the appellant claimed that he belongs to the Valmiki caste and community where such custom exists. In supporting this, he annexed an undated certificate issued by the Managing Trustee of Jay Jagdamba Yuvak Mandal Trust (Valmiki Samaj), Sabarmati. However, though this certificate stated that a Valmiki community member may adopt a person who is a major and over 15 and this custom has been prevailing since long, the certificate contained no date nor any seal. The court therefore held that this certificate could not be treated as proof of customary usage prevailing in the Valmiki community permitting such adoption. It observed (at p. 147):

> "This certificate does not inspire confidence as it is undated and it is without any seal and without any affidavit of the person issuing it. Apart from the aforesaid certificate, no evidence has been filed to prove the custom in Valmiki caste or community with regard to adoption."

The appeal was consequently dismissed.

Comment: The idea behind the maximum age limit of the child to be adopted is perhaps to make his/her assimilation in the family easier. In fact, ideally, the child should be an infant of very small age at the time of adoption as that would make adjustment and acceptance of the child in the new family easy for both – the child as well as the adopting family. In many societies and families adoption (of a son particularly) is made to ensure that properties remain inside the family and also for purposes of security in old age and religious reasons. Hence, some communities permit adoption of major child also and though the Act saves such customs, there has to be enough and clear proof of such custom to recognise and confer legal status on such adoptions.

Note: *See* also, inter alia *Nemichand Shantilal Patni* v. *Basantabai,* AIR 1994 Bom 235: 1996 (1) CCC 259: 1994 (2) Hindu LR 55 where alleged custom was not proved, the adoption was held to be not valid; in *Hanmant Laxman Salunke* v. *Shrirang Narayan Kanse,* AIR 2006 Bom 123: 2006 (42) All Ind Cas 158: 2006 (2) Hindu LR 331, while custom permitting adoption of child over 15 was established but the requirement of age difference between the adopter and adoptee was not complied with and hence the adoption was held to be not valid. In *Uma Prasad* v. *Padmavati,* (1999) AIHC 3494 (MP) and *Khagembam Sadhu* v. *Khangembam Ibohal Singh,* AIR 2001 Gau 95, however, custom permitting adoption of person above the age of 15 was proved and hence adoption held to be valid.

Adoption of Muslim Child by Hindu
Kumar Sursen v. State of Bihar,
AIR 2008 Pat 24: 2008 (2) AIR JharR 6: 2008 (4) CCC 569

Issue: Can a Muslim child be legally adopted by a Hindu couple?

Facts: Amongst the personal laws in India, the Hindu law is the only law which provides for adoption statutorily, *viz.*, the Hindu Adoptions and Maintenance Act, 1956. Under section 10(i) of this Act only a Hindu child can be adopted. In the instant case a minor child named Sahadat was born to Muslim parents. He filed an application before the concerned authorities for issue of a caste certificate and also a resident certificate contending that he was adopted by Kamal Prasad Roy, a Hindu by religion and so was entitled to be admitted to the caste of his adopted father and also to a residence certificate. He further wanted to change his name from Sahadat to Kumar Sen. The application and the request was turned down on the ground that the applicant child being a Muslim could not have been adopted by Hindu parents; the claim of adoption was thus rejected. Even though the alleged adoptive father himself stated that the child was brought up by him since very tender age as his own son and therefore wanted that his caste and residence should be legally given to the child but, in view of the specific requirement of section 10(i) of the Act the court declined to do that. It held that the child cannot be given the legal status of an adopted child. As to change of name, the court held that it is permissible and if the name has been changed and the natural parents have no objection, it can continue; further, residence address can be changed but it has to be shown as residence of the adoptive father but not as son of adoptive father but as son of natural parents.

Order: While status of adopted son and request for caste certificate of the alleged adoptive father was refused, the court allowed the child to change his name and residence, but only as son of natural parents.

Comment: Under the provisions of the Hindu Adoptions and Maintenance Act only a Hindu can adopt a Hindu child only. It is time that serious thought be given to enact an all-India uniform law with no barriers of religion.

ADOPTION BY FEMALE

Adoption by Married Female

Brajendra Singh v. State of Madhya Pradesh,
AIR 2008 SC 1056: 2008 AIR SCW 652: (2008) 1 SCALE 372

Issue: The issue involved in this case was as to the validity of an adoption made by a married female.

Facts: The case involved dispute in respect of property and agricultural holdings in the following circumstances. 'M', a disabled lady was married to one 'P'; it appears that she was got married because under the village custom it was imperative for a virgin to get married. 'P' left soon after even without the marriage being consummated. All through 'M' lived with her parents. Twenty-two years later she adopted 'B', the appellant in this case. In view of some disputes under the agricultural land ceiling laws (M.P. Ceiling on Agricultural Holdings Act, 1960) 'M' filed an application seeking a declaration that 'B' is her adopted son. The same was decreed by the Trial Court and affirmed by the first Appellate Court. Against this the State went in appeal before the Jabalpur Bench of the Madhya Pradesh High Court. The court analysed the provisions of the Hindu Adoptions and Maintenance Act, 1956 and held that *vide* section 8(c) thereof, a married female can adopt only after divorce, or death of the husband, or if he has renounced the world or has been declared by a court to be of unsound mind. In this case 'M' did not qualify under the above said conditions and hence her adoption of 'B' was held to be not valid. It was argued on her behalf that her husband never lived with her, the marriage was not even consummated and she was leading a life like a divorced woman. These arguments, however, did not find favour with the court hence the appeal before the Supreme Court where following contentions were made:

(i) the undisputed factual position was that there was no consummation of the marriage as the parties were living separately practically from the date of marriage and it is on the basis of these facts that the Trial Court drew an inference that 'M' ceased to be a married woman;

(ii) the issue of invalidity of the adoption was specifically urged and taken note of by the Trial Court and it was only after taking note of and analyzing the material and evidence on record that it came to the conclusion that 'M' was living like a divorced woman.

The court, however, was not convinced with these arguments and observed (p. 1085):

".... there is a great deal of difference between a female who is divorced and one who is leading life like a divorced woman."

Order: While the court conceded that the case, "projects some highly emotional and sensitive aspects of human life", the declaration sought was refused as 'M' (now deceased) was held to be not legally competent to adopt.

Comment: This case reflects a very unfortunate situation where a helpless, disabled woman, legally married but practically 'divorced' has no right to adopt. While the Personal Laws (Amendment) Act, 2010 seeks to confer gender quality in matters of adoption yet the above like situation (*Brijender Singh's* case) is not addressed. A woman (or even a man) who is married cannot adopt without husband's consent if he is alive unless he suffers from the above mentioned disabilities like ceasing to be Hindu, mentally unsound, etc; but what if the husband deserts and abandons her for ever immediately after marriage? She is neither in married state nor a divorcee nor a widow!

Adoption by Divorced Female before Re-marriage and Proxy Adoption

Narinderjit Kaur v. *Union of India,*
AIR 1997 P&H 280: 1997 (1) Hindu LR 442: 1997 Marri LJ 331

Issue: Is an adoption by a divorced female before re-marriage valid?

Facts: A divorced Hindu woman adopted a female child through her attorney and brother-in-law in whose favour she had executed a special power-of-attorney. All the formalities of physically handing over the child by the natural parents and the taking of the child by the mother's attorney for being handed over to her, and the necessary ceremonies, were performed. A registered deed of adoption was also executed. The plaintiff applied for a new passport. The defendant, passport officer, however, refused to issue a new passport to the child with the adoptive mother's name on the ground that an adoption by proxy was not valid in Indian law. Later on, in the written statement the defendant agreed that the Law Ministry had clarified that the child could be given or taken in adoption by the parents or guardian, 'under their authority'. Section 11(vi) of the Hindu Adoptions and Maintenance Act says:

> "The child to be adopted must be actually given and taken in adoption by the parents or guardian concerned or under their authority with the intent to transfer the child from the family of its birth......to the family of its adoption."

However, a fresh objection was raised by the defendant *viz.*, that the adoptive mother having re-married, she could not adopt and so a passport for the child with the adoptive mother's name could not be issued. The mother came to the court against this.

Order: After going through the facts, the court came to the conclusion that the respondent's plea was untenable as the adoptive mother had re-married in 1994 whereas the adoption took place in 1990. Thus, on the date of the adoption, she had the capacity to take the child in adoption under the provisions of section 8 of the Hindu Adoptions and Maintenance Act. It was accordingly held that the adopted daughter was entitled to a new passport with the name of the adoptive mother in it.

Comment: While there were constraints imposed on a married woman who wished to adopt (*viz*: that the husband should have renounced the world or ceased to be a Hindu or should have been declared by court to be of unsound mind) there were no restrictions on a female whose marriage has been dissolved, to adopt a child in view of section 8 of the Hindu Adoptions and Maintenance Act.

Note: After the amendment of the Hindu Adoptions and Maintenance Act, 2010, even a married woman may adopt a child but consent of the husband is necessary.

CONSENT OF WIFE/WIVES

Wife's Consent Necessary for Adoption

Siddaramappa v. *Gouravva*,
AIR 2004 Kant 230: 2004 (2) Hindu LR 438:
ILR (2004) 3 Kant 3611

Issue: Can a male adopt a child without his wife's consent on the plea that their relations were strained, and therefore, her consent could not be obtained?

Facts: This was a property dispute where the validity of an alleged adoption formed a core issue. An adoption was alleged to have taken place but without the consent of the wife which is mandatory under section 7 of the Hindu Adoptions and Maintenance Act. A plea was taken that the relations between the husband and wife were strained, and therefore, her consent could not be taken.

Order: The court did not accept his argument; in fact this plea was negatived by documentary evidence which established that they were living together at the time when the alleged adoption was made. There was nothing to show that it was impossible to have the wife's consent. Besides, the conditions under which a wife's consent to adoption may be dispensed with are clearly specified in section 7 of the Act *viz.*, (i) that the wife has completely and finally renounced the world, (ii) she has ceased to be a Hindu, or (iii) she has been declared by a court of competent jurisdiction to be of unsound mind. Taking any other plea, according to the court, would be adding words in the statute. Moreover, the words in the proviso "he shall not adopt except with the consent of the wife" are emphatic and render the provision mandatory. Pointing out the logic behind such mandatory requirement, the court remarked (at p. 238):

"Adoption is admission of a stranger by birth to privileges of a child as if born to adoptive parents. With the adoption, the child acquires interest in property belonging to adoptive parents. Thus, the adoption affects the rights of a Hindu wife in the property of her husband. She cannot be compelled to recognise a stranger by birth as her child and be as the mother of the said child. More so when such adoption affects her absolute right to the property of her husband. Therefore, having regard to the object sought to be achieved by the Act and the underlying principle of equality sought to be achieved.......... any other interpretation would be contrary to the letter and spirit of the enactment."

The adoption was, thus, held to be not valid.

Comment: The Hindu Adoptions and Maintenance Act, 1956, has given extensive rights to females in the matter of adoption, though still not equal rights with males. A significant right is the duty of the husband to seek her consent. In this case, the court constructively construed and applied the provision of section 7 of the Hindu Adoptions and Maintenance Act, to invalidate an alleged adoption by a male without seeking his wife's consent.

Note: Adoption made with the consent of one wife only was held to be invalid in *Bhoolaram* v. *Ramlal*, AIR 1989 MP 198; *see* also *Kashibai* v. *Parwatibai*, 1995 AIR SCW 4631: (1995) 6 SCC 213: JT 1995 (7) SC 48. It may be pointed out here that in the matter of giving a child in adoption also, the natural father cannot do so without consent of the mother *Deen Dayal* v. *Sanjeev Kumar*, AIR 2009 Raj 122.

Wife's Consent to be Explicit
Ghisalal v. *Dhapubai*,
AIR 2011 SC 644 (MP)

Issue: The issue of validity of an adoption without the wife's explicit consent was involved in this very significant judgment. Section 7 of the Hindu Adoptions and Maintenance Act specifically requires wife's consent for a valid adoption.

Facts: This was a property dispute where the focal issue revolved around the validity of the adoption of the petitioner 'G'. According to 'G', his biological father gave him in adoption to Gopalji with proper ceremonies and a registered adoption deed. He filed a suit in the court claiming share in properties alleged to be ancestral properties and challenging certain alienations made by Gopalji in favour of his wife 'D'. Both Gopalji and D in their statements denied the adoption. According to Gopalji there was no adoption, no ceremony and the alleged adoption deed was obtained by playing fraud; he further contended that the suit properties were not ancestral and he was entitled to execute gift deeds in favour of his wife. 'D' also denied the factum of adoption and claimed that she had not given any consent for it, that if by taking advantage of the simplicity of Gopalji 'G' obtained some deed, the same is not binding on them and further that the gift deeds executed by her husband Gopalji were valid and 'G' has no right to challenge the alienations. Since the determination of the entire suit depended mainly on the question of validity of the adoption, it may be mentioned that the Trial Court, the lower appellate court and the Madhya Pradesh High Court were all of the opinion that the adoption was valid and consent of the wife can be inferred from the circumstances *viz.*, that she was present in the ceremonies of adoption and did not question the adoption till the stage of filing the written statement in the suit filed by 'G' and further that in the adoption deed Gopalji is said have recorded "that it was his and his wife's esteemed desire to take 'G' in adoption. According to the High Court since the adoption deed was registered a presumption can be raised *vide* section 16 of the Hindu Adoptions and Maintenance Act that the same had been made after complying with all the provisions and requirements for a valid adoption; and further, that *'D's* failure to challenge the adoption deed is a strong circumstance which goes to show that she had consented to the adoption of *'G'* by her husband, Gopalji. On appeal against it to the Supreme Court it was held that the courts below had misdirected themselves in deciding the issue on *D's* consent to the adoption. It observed (at p. 656):

> "Unfortunately, all the courts completely ignored that presence of Dhapubai in the ceremonies of adoption was only as a mute spectator and not as an active participant. [None of the witnesses] stated that before taking *'G'* in adoption, Gopalji had consulted Dhapubai or taken her in confidence and the latter had given her consent or agreed to the adoption....or that she had taken prominent part in the adoption ceremonies. All of them made a parrot like statement that Dhapubai was sitting with other women below the platform (*chabutra*). By no stretch of imagination, this could be equated with her active participation in the adoption ceremonies so as to enable the courts to draw an inference that she had given consent for the adoption of *'G'*. Also, according to the Court, the contents of the adoption deed could not be made basis for assuming Dhapubai's consent as there was nothing to prove that she was a signatory to it or was present at the time of execution/registration of the same."

Further, her alleged failure to challenge it cannot be used against her as there was nothing to show that she was even made aware of the same and deliberately omitted to challenge it. Apart from all the above, there were other discrepancies also to defeat the claim of *'G'*.

After analysing the provisions of the Hindu Adoptions and Maintenance Act, section 7 in particular, and the case-law *inter alia, Kashibai* v. *Parwatibai,* 1995 AIR SCW 4631: (1995) 6 SCC 213: JT 1995 (7) SC 48; *Brajendra Singh* v. *State of Madhya Pradesh,* AIR 2008 SC 1056: 2008 AIR SCW 652: (2008) 1 SCALE 372 the Court held that in the absence of explicit consent of the wife, there was no valid adoption.

Order: The claim of *'G'* that he was the adopted son of *'D'* and Gopalji was negatived in the absence of proof of explicit consent to the adoption by the wife. A wife's mere presence as a spectator in the assembly of people gathered at the place where ceremonies were performed was held to be no proof of her consent.

Comment: The wife's consent envisaged in the proviso to section 7 of the Hindu Adoptions and Maintenance Act needs to be either in writing or should be reflected by an affirmative/positive act voluntarily and willingly done by her. It is significant to point out that prior to the Personal Laws (Amendment) Act, 2010 whilst a husband could adopt after seeking wife's consent, a wife could not adopt even after husband's consent; she could adopt only if the husband suffered certain disabilities provided in section 8(c) of the Act. After the 2010 amendment, the position and right of the husband and wife in this respect, has been brought at par. There would still, however, be hard cases where the parties are not divorced but separated for very long but they would not be entitled to adopt unless the other spouse consents. *Brijendra Singh* v. *State of Madhya Pradesh*, (2008) 1 MLJ 1083 is a vivid example. There should be some mechanism/provision to enable a party to adopt in cases where a marriage is admittedly in a state of limbo with no hopes ever for rapprochement and yet parties for whatever reasons do not want legal divorce.

ADOPTION BY WIDOW

Adoption by Widow under Act: Would the Child be Deemed to be Child of Deceased Husband

Sawan Ram v. Kalawanti,
AIR 1967 SC 1761: (1967) 3 SCR 687: 1968 (2) SCJ 316

Issue: In case of adoption by a widow under the provisions of the Hindu Adoptions and Maintenance Act, 1956, would the adopted child be deemed to be child of the deceased husband also?

Facts: Under section 12 of the Hindu Adoptions and Maintenance Act an adopted child shall be deemed to be the child of his or her adoptive father or mother with effect from the date of adoption and from such date all ties of the child in the family of his or her birth shall be deemed to be severed and replaced by those created by the adoption in the new family; there are however certain restrictions and exceptions also imposed.

In this case, the issue involved was whether on the death of the widow, the son adopted by her would be the heir of her deceased husband. The husband R died leaving behind his widow B. He owned some land and a house. She mortgaged a portion of the land in favour of M. She also made a gift of her house and land in favour of K who was her grand niece. The reversioner, Sawan Ram, challenged these alienations and contended that these were not binding on him. His suit was decreed. Against this, B filed an appeal to the High Court. Pending appeal, she adopted Deepchand as her son. A deed of adoption was executed in 1959; B died within two months of the adoption. Sawan Ram then filed a suit for possession of the house and land. The Trial Court dismissed the suit on the ground that Deepchand, the adopted son, had a preferential claim to the properties as against the reversioner, since he was not merely the adopted son of the widow but also of her deceased husband. The High Court confirmed the decision of the Trial Court. Hence, the present appeal to the Supreme Court, by the reversioner.

Order: His argument was that B having only a life-interest in the properties of her deceased husband, she could not claim the benefit of section 14 of the Hindu Succession Act, 1956, *viz.*, absolute ownership rights, and hence could not alienate the properties. Further, it was argued that the adopted son could not succeed to the property of B's husband because he was not the son of B's deceased husband. The Hindu Adoptions and Maintenance Act having conferred an independent right of adoption on a female Hindu, if a widow adopts a son he becomes the adopted son of the widow only and cannot be deemed to be the son of the deceased husband as the doctrine of relation back has been abrogated by the Hindu Adoptions and Maintenance Act. Further, that under the Act, even an unmarried female Hindu may adopt and the adopted child would be related to her only, likewise, a child adopted by a widow would be her child only. The court, however, did not accept these contentions. It held that under section 5(1) of the Act, the words used are adoption "by or to a Hindu". Adoption to a Hindu was intended, according to the court to cover cases where an adoption is made by one person while the adopted child becomes the child of another person also. In a case where a widow adopts a son, the actual adoption is by the female but the adoption would not only be to herself but also to her deceased husband. Referring to section 12 of the Act, it pointed out that from the date of adoption, all ties of the child in the family of birth are severed and new ties are created in the adoptive family; and it is well recognised that a married female belongs to the family of her husband and accordingly, the adopted child must also belong to the same family. Thus, it was held (at p. 1764):

> "On adoption by a widow..........the adopted son is deemed to be a member of the family of the deceased husband of the widow..........the rights which the child had, to succeed to the property by virtue of being the son of natural father, in the family of his birth, is thus, clearly to be replaced by similar rights in the adoptive family and consequently, he would certainly obtain those rights in the capacity of a member of that family as an adopted son of the deceased of the widow."

Comment: It is significant to note that section 14 of the Hindu Adoptions and Maintenance Act deals with four situations in which a child adopted by one person may become the adopted or step-child of another. There is no mention of whether a child adopted by a widow would also become the child of the deceased husband; and conversely, if the court's interpretation were to be accepted, would on widowers' adopting a child, the child become the child of the deceased mother as well? This needs to be clarified to avoid anomalous interpretations.

Widowed Mother-in-law's Right to Adopt in Presence of Widowed Daughter-in-law

Ashabai Kate v. *Vithal Bhika Nade,*
AIR 1990 SC 670 (Bom): JT 1989 (4) SC 163: 1989 Mat LR 449

Issue: Can a widowed mother-in-law adopt, under the Hindu law, a child in the presence of a daughter-in-law, even though she has remarried?

Facts: This was a property dispute in respect of joint Hindu family governed by Mitakshara law of which a father and son were coparceners. Unfortunately, both died in quick succession in 1942 leaving behind their widows. The widowed daughter-in-law delivered a posthumous female child, Ashabai and after sometime remarried. The widowed mother-in-law adopted a son, Vithal, in 1949, Ashabai, the appellant on attaining majority, filed a suit for possession of properties with *mesne profits* and a decree for money and challenged the power of the grandmother to adopt. The Trial Court upheld the adoption as valid and dismissed the suit of Ashabai; on appeal the lower appellate court granted a decree in her favour. Thereupon the defendants filed an appeal before the Bombay High Court. The High Court held that a Hindu widow's power to adopt is revived the moment there is nobody to continue the line and hence the adoption of the respondent by the widowed mother-in-law was found to be legal. Hence the present appeal by special leave by the plaintiff, Ashabai.

Order: On the issue of validity of the adoption, the court referred to various cases. *Referring to Gurunath* v. *Kamalabai*, (1955) 1 SCR 1135: AIR 1955 SC 206: 1955 SCJ 178 it observed that the rule "that the interposition of a grandson, or the son's widow, competent to continue the line by adoption brings the mother's power of adoption to an end" was being followed for a very long time and has become a part of Hindu law.

The Supreme Court in *Ashabai* also approvingly referred to Justice Chandrarkar's observations in the Full Bench Bombay High Court order in *Ram Krishna Ramchandra* v. *Shamrao*, ILR (1902) 26 Bom 526: 4 Bom LR 315 to the effect that "where a Hindu dies leaving a widow and a son and that son dies leaving a natural born or adopted son or leaving no son but his own widow to continue the line by means of adoption, the power of the former widow is extinguished and can never afterwards be revived", and further that, "when a son dies before attaining full legal competence and does not leave either a widow or a son or an adopted son, then the power of the mother which was in abeyance during his life-time revives but the moment he hands over the torch to another, the mother can no longer take it.

Thus, it was held in *Ashabai* that the widowed mother-in-law had no power to adopt and her power to adopt was extinguished permanently and did not revive even on the daughter-in-law's remarriage. Consequently the adoption of Vithal was held to be invalid in the eye of law and he did not get any interest in the suit properties.

Comment: Even though the adoption was a pre-1956 adoption (*i.e.,* prior to the Hindu Adoptions and Maintenance Act, 1956) yet it is an unfair interpretation of the adoption law. If a widowed daughter-in-law remarries and goes into another family a widowed-mother-in-law has no one left to continue the line except her ownself. It would not be fair to deny her the right to adopt. In view of the Hindu Adoptions and Maintenance Act however now both the widows have an independent right to adopt.

Adoption by Widow when Widowed Daughter-in-law Alive
Ningappa v. Shivappa,
1994 AlHC 2068 (Kant)

Issue: Is a widow whose widowed daughter-in-law is alive, competent to adopt?

Facts: This was a property dispute where the validity of an adoption was a crucial issue for determining the rights of the parties. The main issue involved was as to the right of a widow to adopt when her widowed daughter-in-law is alive. The court analysed the Supreme Court's judgment in *Gurunath* v. *Kamalabai*, (1955) 1 SCR 1135: AIR 1955 SC 206: 1955 SCJ 178, and some other High Court cases.

Order: After analysing the cases and the law on the subject, the court came to the conclusion that the widow has no right to adopt when the daughter-in-law is alive. The claim of a share in the joint family property by the son adopted by a widow during her widowed daughter-in-law's life-time was, accordingly, held to be not tenable. The following *dictum* of the Supreme Court in *Gurunath* was relied upon (at p. 2069 of *Ningappa*):

> "The interposition of a grandson or the son's widow, competent to continue the line by adoption brings the mother's power of adoption to an end."

In *Gurunath*, reference was made to several cases in support of, as well as against the petitioners, including the significant judgment in *Amarendra Mansingh* v. *Sanatan Singh*, AIR 1933 PC 155: ILR 12 Pat 642: 60 Ind App 242. In this case, a widow whose unmarried son died at the age of 20 years and six months, took a son in adoption soon after the son's death. This was held to be valid. The Court reviewed earlier decisions on the point and made the following significant observations (at p. 158):

> "Having regard to this well-established doctrine as to the religious efficacy of sonship, their Lordships feel that great caution should be observed in shutting the door upon any authorised adoption by the widow of a sonless man.......... . The Hindu law itself sets no limits to the exercise of the power during the life-time of the widow.... but there must be some limit to its exercise, or, at all events, some conditions in which it would be either contrary to the spirit of the Hindu doctrine to admit its continuance or inequitable in the face of other rights to allow it to take effect...... ."

Referring to the limits or conditions, the court further observed, "the interposition of a grandson or a son's widow, brings the mother's power of adoption to an end......... But if the son dies himself sonless and unmarried, the duty will still be upon the mother and the power in her which was necessarily suspended during the son's life-time will revive".

These arguments in *Amarendra Mansingh* were however, found to be "not well founded" by the Supreme Court in *Gurunath*: It held that the rule is that "where the duty of providing for the continuance of the line for spiritual purposes which was upon the father and was laid by him conditionally upon the mother, has been assumed by the son and by him passed on to the grandson or to the son's widow, the mother's power is gone". (*Gurunath* at 211). This power, according to the Court, cannot be revived.

Surprisingly, in *Ningappa's* case, *Amarendra Mansingh* was not even referred to and more surprisingly even *Ashabai Kate* v. *Vithal Bhika Nade*, AIR 1990 SC 670 (Bom): JT 1989 (4) SC 163: 1989 Mat LR 449, wherein the arguments were in conformity with the arguments of the respondent in *Ningappa*, was not mentioned.

Comment: It is significant to note that the *Gurunath* case was decided before the Hindu Adoptions and Maintenance Act came in 1956 (though *Ashabai's* case was decided in 1990 but no mention was made in *Ningappa*). The position has since changed and the Hindu Adoptions and Maintenance Act has given almost equal rights to females, including a widow, to adopt. The Act does not restrict a widow's right to adopt if she has a widowed daughter-in-law. Ironically, *Ningappa* judgment in fact, went further still and held that the widowed mother-in-law cannot adopt even if the daughter-in-law re-marries. This ruling appears to be not only against the statutory provision in section 8 of the Hindu Adoptions and Maintenance Act, but also harsh and unreasonable.

Co-widow's Consent not Required

Vijayalakshmamma v. *B.T. Shankar*, AIR 2001 SC 1424: 2001 AIR SCW 1347: (2001) 4 SCC 558

Issue: The requirement of consent of co-wives stipulated in section 7 of the Hindu Adoptions and Maintenance Act, 1956, does not apply in case of widows. A widow may adopt without the consent of her co-widow.

Facts: The husband died leaving behind two widows in 1968. The senior widow took a male child in adoption without consulting the junior widow. The adoption was challenged as being invalid. It was contended that the stipulation in the proviso to section 7 of the Hindu Adoptions and Maintenance Act with the explanation requiring consent of all wives should be read into section 8 as well, which refers to the capacity of female Hindu to take in adoption.

Order: The court did not accept this plea and held that the deliberate omission as regards requirement of consent from co-widow or junior widow, was an indication of Parliament's intention to confer an independent right to a female in this matter. This is in keeping with the changed social set-up recognising equal rights and status for women. The court observed:

> "To subject the exercise of power by senior widow to adopt conditional upon the consent of the junior widow where the Hindu male died leaving behind two widows with no progeny of his own, would render the exercise of power more cumbersome and paradoxical, leaving at times, such exercise of power to adopt only next to impossibility."

That apart, according to the court no injustice would be caused to a co-widow whose consent is not obtained nor required to be obtained by the law since the adopted child would not divest any person of any estate vested in her or him before the adoption. In this case, the husband having died in 1968, all the widows inherited his properties in equal share under the provisions of the Hindu Succession Act, 1956. The adoption by one widow in no way affected the share of the other widow. The court made a reference to *Narayanaswami Naick v. Mangammal*, (1905) ILR 28 Mad 315: 15 Mad LJ 143, decided by a division bench of the Madras High Court where it was held that in the interest of family peace and good relationship, a co-widow would do well to consult the other before adopting but there is nothing in law which compels her to do so and the adoption would be valid.

Thus, the adoption by the senior widow Vijaylakshmamma, without the consent of other widow was held to be valid.

Comment: While the provision for consent of a co-wife has been specifically laid down in section 7 of the Hindu Adoptions and Maintenance Act, there is no such condition laid down in section 8 where a right to adopt has been given independently, *inter alia*, to a widow also. If the Legislature had intended that, it would have explicitly said so.

Merely Bringing up Step-child – No Proof of Adoption
Ram Das v. *Gandiabai,*
AIR 1997 SC 1563: 1997 AIR SCW 317: (1997) 1 SCC 74

Issue: Mere fact that a child has been brought up by his step father is no proof that he has been adopted by the step father.

Facts: This was a property dispute and adoption formed a core issue. The petitioner filed a suit for partition against his deceased father's brother. The latter contested the same and his plea was that the petitioner was no longer a member of the family because he had been given away in adoption to a man whom his mother later re-married; that he was being maintained and brought up by that man and therefore, he had no rights in the properties of his biological father.

Order: The court held that simply because the step father spent money on the maintenance of the petitioner and brought him up because he was the son of his wife's first husband, does not by itself imply that he had been adopted by the step-father. According to the court, even though he was brought up by the step father, he continued to be the member of his deceased father's family and as such, had all the rights of a son of that family.

Comment: Where a woman or widow re-marries, her children do not automatically become the adopted children of the step father and the new family by the mere fact that the step father maintains or brings them up. Some cogent evidence of adoption has to be there to prove that the child no longer has links with the biological family.

Mere Fact of Living in Same House is No Proof of Adoption

Prafulla Bala Mukherjee v. Satish Chandra Mukherjee,
AIR 1998 Cal 86

Issue: Does the mere fact of living in the same house lead to presumption, or establish, a relationship through adoption?

Facts: This was a property dispute where right was claimed on the basis of being an adoptive mother of the deceased. The 'mother' sought a decree for declaration of absolute right, title and interest in respect of property built by the 'adopted son' and also a decree for perpetual injunction restraining his relatives, the defendants, from interfering with occupation and possession of the property. Amongst the facts in support of the alleged adoption, it was contended that the 'adoptive mother' and her family lived in the house of the adopted son and treated him as such.

Order: The court disbelieved the fact of adoption. On the contrary, there were several facts to disprove adoption, like—the adopted son treating his natural mother as his mother and addressing her as such till his own death; making her his nominee in the insurance policy, provident fund, etc., performing the *shradha* ceremony of his biological father, and on his own death, his *shradha* ceremony being performed by his brother. On the basis of these facts and situations the court held that the mere fact that an allegedly adopted son allowed his 'adoptive' mother and her family to live in his house was no proof of adoption.

Comment: While no formal ceremonies are required to prove adoption yet there has to be sufficient evidence of the adoptee being given and taken in adoption by the biological parents and adoptive parents respectively, and also other circumstances which establish the fact of adoption. Simply because a person, out of compassion or generosity, or some other consideration, allows somebody to live in his house does not indicate or prove relationship through adoption.

Holding of Joint Accounts – No Presumption of Adoption

Nilima Mukherjee v. Kanta Bhusan Ghosh,
AIR 2001 SC 2725: 2001 AIR SCW 3062: (2001) 6 SCC 660

Issue: Can holding of joint bank accounts by a person with the deceased lead to an inference that the person was adopted by the deceased?

Facts: A landlord filed a suit for eviction against the appellant who was a relative of the tenant. This relative used to stay in the suit premises along with the tenant. After the death of the tenant, the landlord sought eviction; his case was that after the death of the tenant, the tenancy had become extinct and the appellant was a trespasser and had no right to continue staying in the premises. The appellant raised a plea that she was adopted by the deceased and so in that capacity, she had the right to continue staying in that house. The Trial Court dismissed her case; she lost before a single judge of the High Court as well as in second appeal. Hence, her appeal in the Supreme Court.

Order: The court went through the facts and evidence of the case. The deceased tenant had left no Will, no gift, nor any document in support of adoption; nor was there any evidence of any ceremony or the fact of giving by the biological father and taking by the deceased of the appellant in adoption. The appellant contended that she had a joint bank account with the deceased which was indicative of the fact that she was the adopted daughter of the deceased. The Court, however, dismissed her appeal. It held that the mere fact of having a joint account was no proof of adoption and so she could not be considered to be the adopted child of the deceased tenant.

Comment: The mere fact that a relative was staying with the deceased or had joint bank accounts, without any other documentary or factual evidence of adoption, cannot be proof of adoption.

PRESUMPTION IN CASE OF REGISTERED ADOPTION DEED

Presumption not Irrebutable

Jai Singh v. Shakuntala,
AIR 2002 SC 1428: 2002 AIR SCW 1280: (2002) 3 SCC 634

Issue: Is the presumption regarding authenticity or validity of a registered adoption deed under section 16 of the Hindu Adoptions and Maintenance Act, 1956, irrebutable?

Facts: This was a property dispute between the biological daughter Shakuntala and the alleged adopted son Jai Singh of the deceased Sunda Ram. The plaintiff daugher filed a suit for declaration that she was the owner and in possession of the suit properties and a decree passed in a civil suit and the registered Will and adoption deed recording that Jai Singh had been adopted by Sunda Ram were illegal and result of misrepresentation and thus not binding on her. The Trial Court decreed her suit and two appeals against this including to the High Court were also dismissed. Hence the present appeal. It is significant to note that under section 16 of the Hindu Adoptions and Maintenance Act there is a statutory presumption that in the event of there being a registered document pertaining to adoption there would be a presumption that adoption has been made in accordance with law. The word used in the section is "shall". However, the inclusion of the words "unless and until it is disproved", appearing at the and of the section is indicative of the fact that the situation is not that rigid but flexible enough and it would all depend on the evidence available on record in support of adoption and the genuineness of the deed. In this case, there was enough documentary evidence to dislodge the presumption of genuine adoption, *inter alia*, there was no reference to any ceremonies nor any evidence pertaining to adoption. The property suit in his favour was decreed within less than 10 days and on the same day as the father died. He some how wanted to usurp the properties, so apart from the court decree and the adoption deed, he also propounded a Will which was shrouded with suspicion.

Order: The appeal was dismissed. The court held that while it is true that the registered instrument of adoption presumably stands out to be taken to be correct but the court is not precluded from looking into it upon production of some evidence contra the adoption. It found that the order of the High Court did not call for any interference in the contextual facts.

Comment: A registered deed of adoption raises a strong presumption that all the requirements for a valid adoption have been complied with; this presumption, however, can be negated and rebutted on strong evidence against the authenticity of the adoption and genuineness of the deed, the burden to rebut though is high. When facts and evidence are strong enough to disprove adoption despite a registered Will, the courts will go by these facts and not the presumption.

Registered Adoption Deed: Minor Discrepancies Immaterial

Ranjit Singh Dhillon v. *Punjab School Education Board,* AIR 2004 P&H 382: 2004 (24) All Ind Cas 920: 2005 (1) Marri LJ 314

Issue: Can school authorities refuse to substitute name of parents of adopted child in the school register merely because of minor discrepancies in adoption papers even though the adoption is duly registered?

Facts: A child was adopted by her maternal uncle and all formalities were completed and the adoption-deed was duly registered as well. The parents applied to the school for change of name of the parents of the child in the school register. The District Education Board, however, refused to change the parents' name in the school records on the ground that the name of the biological mother of the child in the admission register was different from the name mentioned in the adoption deed. The parents appealed against this.

Order: The court held that once adoption-deed is registered, the respondent Education Board has no jurisdiction to doubt the authority of the same. The difference in the name of the mother was convincingly explained *viz.,* that after marriage, her name was changed by her in-laws as per the custom in the *Jat* families, and the adoptive father who was the real brother of the biological mother of the child, by mistake, mentioned the original maiden name of the child's mother in the adoption papers. The court observed (at p. 383) "we are of the considered opinion that a *bona fide* mistake cannot be permitted to stand in the way of substantial justice".

Comment: Where an adoption is registered, there is a strong presumption under section 16 of the Hindu Adoptions and Maintenance Act that the adoption has been made in compliance with the provisions of the Act unless and until it is disproved.

Note: Where all rituals of adoption as per provisions of Hindu law were followed, the adoption deed was registered and photographs and negatives of photographs which had been taken at time of adoption formed part of the record, in such circumstances, the Supreme Court held in *Saroja* v. *Santhi Kumar,* AIR 2011 SC 642 adoption cannot be disbelieved.

Change of Caste after Adoption
Khazan Singh v. Union of India,
AIR 1980 Del 60

Issue: Vide section 12 of the Hindu Adoptions and Maintenance Act, 1956 (HAMA) upon adoption an adopted child is deemed to be the child of the adoptive father or mother for all (with few exceptions) purposes. In this context, the issue involved in this case was as to whether a person could change his caste by a valid adoption.

Facts: The petitioner, K.S., was a jat by birth and his father was a milk vendor. K.L., who was a Julaha by caste, was a partner in the petitioner's father's milk vending business. He was old, had no issue and his wife was not in good health so K.S. was given in adoption to him. In 1970 K.S. obtained a Scheduled Caste certificate on the basis that he belonged to Kabirpanthi Julaha caste and it was on the strength of this certificate that he got the job of sub-inspector of police in 1971. In 1975, however, his services were terminated and a notice was also issued to him stating that he was not a *julaha* by birth and hence not entitled to get Scheduled Caste certificate; he was asked to show cause as to why his certificate should not be cancelled and other action against him be not taken for giving false information as to his caste status. In 1976 the Deputy Commissioner of Police *vide* an order, cancelled the schedule caste certificate on the ground that "it was found that the adoption was not valid under the provisions of the Hindu Adoptions and Maintenance Act."

On a petition filed against it, it was contended, *inter alia*, that a person could not change his caste even by a valid adoption. After analysing a few cases *C.M. Arumugam* v. *S. Rajgopal*, AIR 1976 SC 939: (1976) 1 SCC 863: (1976) 3 SCR 82; *N.E. Horo* v. *Jahan Ara Jaipal Singh*, AIR 1972 SC 1840: 1972 (1) SCA 524: (1972) 3 SCR 361; *Urmila Ginda* v. *Union of India*, AIR 1975 Del 115: (1975) 1 Serv LR 419: 1975 Lab IC 1044; *Durgaprasada Rao* v. *Sudarsanaswamy*, AIR 1940 Mad 513: ILR 1940 Mad 653). Justice Ranganathan observed that when considering the legal effect of adoption, motive is immaterial. If it is legal, all the consequences of a valid adoption ensue irrespective of the motive behind the adoption. The following observations are significant (at p. 66):

> "The worst that can be said is that, borrowing a leaf from the "tax-planners" notebook in regard to the permissible, if not exactly laudable, practice of taking advantage of a loophole in the law, the petitioner has done a bit "career-planning." Since it is lawful if it has the legal effect for which he contends it has to be given effect to and it is not permissible to refuse to give the legal effect because the course was adopted by the petitioner in order to obtain a post in Government Service."

Holding that the certificate of scheduled caste issued to the petitioner on the basis of adoption could not be cancelled, the court held (at p. 67):

> "There could be adoptions in the other direction as well and also adoptions with more laudable object of promoting social harmony. I therefore think that the formula "once a scheduled caste, always a "scheduled caste,"

contended for by the learned counsel for the respondent should not receive acceptance. In the long run it may be found that the principle contended for by the petitioner in the present case may not be really opposed to the object and scheme of the Constitution in regard to reservations for Scheduled Castes and Scheduled Tribes. On the other hand if genuine adoptions both ways, become frequent, they may eventually lead to the development of that social equality at which the Constitution aims. I, therefore, hold that the certificate granted to the petitioner was not liable to be cancelled on the ground that the petitioner's claim to be a Scheduled Caste by adoption was unsustainable."

Order: The court held that section 12 of the Hindu Adoptions and Maintenance Act makes the position very clear on this aspect. The adopted child is deemed to be the child of the adoptive father (or mother, as the case may be) for all purposes; and all ties of the child in the natural family shall be deemed to be severed and replaced by those of the adoptive family. The emphatic repetition of the word "all" in relation to "purposes and ties" was held to be significant. The word "ties" is a very wide and comprehensive word and would include all types of bonds, social, religious, cultural or any other, that bound the adoptee with his natural family. Consequently, the court held that "the adoptee is to be treated from the date of his adoption as if he were born in the adoptive family for all practical purposes. From this date we have to forget that he belonged to another family except for the three purposes mentioned in the section [section 12] itself".

It further stated,

"Just as it is not open to a caste to refuse to recognise a new born in the family of one of its members as belonging to the caste, it is not open to the caste to sit in judgment over the statutory status enjoyed by the adoptee."

Since the certificate was given to the petitioner on the basis of adoption and the only point pressed to challenge the certificate was the objection that a person can belong to a caste only by birth and not upon adoption, the issue of validity of the adoption was not discussed and the certificate was held to be valid.

Comment: As per the provisions of the Hindu Adoptions and Maintenance Act adoptions affects the severance of all ties in the family of birth. The motive behind the adoption is immaterial. As observed by the court, adoptions both ways may help the cause of development of social equality and inter-caste harmony.

Multiple Adoption not Permissible

Sandhya v. *Union of India,*
AIR 1998 Bom 228: I (1999) DMC 143: 1998 (1) Hindu LR 653

Issue: Should the adoption law permit adoption of more than one child of the same gender? Is the provision prohibiting this *ultra vires* articles 14 and 21 of the Constitution?

Facts: The petitioners, who had already adopted a daughter, were prevented from taking another female child in view of the provision of sections 11(i) and (ii) of the Hindu Adoptions and Maintenance Act, 1956. Under this provision if the adopters already have a son (biological or adopted) they cannot adopt a son; and if they have a daughter (biological or adopted) they cannot adopt another daughter. The validity of this provision was challenged on the ground that it violated articles 14 and 21 of the Constitution since it discriminated between—(i) parents with unlimited number of children and parents without children; and (ii) parents with any number of children of the same sex and parents prevented from taking any child of the same gender, in adoption.

Order: The court dismissed this argument and observed that "the classification as carved out has not been created by the impugned provisions". As to the challenge under article 21, it was argued that the right to have a family size according to one's choice is a component of the concept of human dignity and the courts having recognised the right to live with human dignity as a fundamental right, there should be no restriction as to the number of children one could adopt. The court conceded that while the right to life does have many facets, and numerous dimensions have been added by judicial interpretation during the last few years, but that could not be stretched to accommodate every personal desire, howsoever laudable. "Doing so", according to the court would be "seriously wrong and totally inappropriate". It observed:

> "Article 21, even by stretching it to its farthest end, cannot embrace such right of having size of family according to one's own choice. A person could have any number of biological children, by Grace of God. That does not certainly render support to claim to have any number of children by adoption."

Consequently, the court held:

> "The Act with its mythological and secular mission has stood the test of time for around four decades and has conveniently withstood the assault as attempted from time to time. We, therefore, refrain from examining the validity of the impugned provisions on the touchstone of articles 14 and 21.

Comment: While it is a laudable idea to provide a home and family to abandoned children who are awaiting adoption but, in view of rising pernicious social activities of child abuse and commercialisation of children, and exploitation of both boys and girls, the law makers might have felt that giving an unbridled right to take any number of children under the garb of adoption, would not be without risk. Also, when there is more than one child of the same gender, not one's own but adopted, there are more chances of discrimination which would have an adverse effect on the child's development and psychology.

No Divesting on Adoption

Kisan Baburao Memane v. Suresh Sadu Memane,
AIR 1996 Bom 50: 1996 (1) Civ LJ 794: 1996 (1) ICC 625

Issue: Can an adopted child divest a pre-adoption donee? Would an adoption by a widow date back to the time of her husband's death or would it take effect from the date she adopts?

Facts: The original property owner died in 1919, and his widow gifted some properties to the defendants in 1948. Several years after this gift, in 1973 the plaintiff was adopted by the widow. The plaintiff filed a suit for possession of these properties on the ground that the right to these properties vested in him since his adoption in 1973, dated back to 1919, when the original owner died. The Trial Court did not accept this argument. On appeal by the adopted son, the lower appellate court reversed the findings and directed the appellants to handover the suit properties to the plaintiff, hence the appeal by the defendants.

Order: The High Court held that under section 12 of the Hindu Adoptions and Maintenance Act an adopted child takes the position of a child of the family only with effect from the date of adoption and section (c) thereof clearly provides that an adopted child shall not divest any person of any estate which vested in him or her before the adoption. Hence, the adopted son was held to have no right to divest suit property vested in the defendants before the adoption.

Comment: Under the pre-Act law, *i.e.*, prior to 1956, a widow adopted to her deceased husband and so the adoption dated back to the time when the husband died but under the Act now, a widow can adopt in her own right; hence the adoption takes effect only from the date when the widow adopts the child. It does not date back to the husband's death.

Validity of Pre-adoption Agreements

Jupudi Venkata Vijaya Bhartiar v. Jupudi Kesava Rao,
AIR 2003 SC 3314: 2003 AIR SCW 4706: (2003) 8 SCC 282

Issue: Is an ante-adoption agreement which provided that the adopted son will not claim any right in certain properties belonging to adoptive family, legal?

Facts: In order to check trafficking in children, the Hindu Adoptions and Maintenance Act, 1956, *vide* section 17 prohibits taking or giving of any payments or rewards in consideration of adoption. In this case, the validity of an ante-adoption agreement between the plaintiff adopted son and the adoptive parents was sought to be challenged. The terms of the agreement provided that the adopted son will not set up any claim with regard to certain properties belonging to the adoptive family. Prior to the adoption, the adopted son had no right whatsoever in these properties. In fact, the plaintiff was being fostered by the adoptive father and his wife for five years prior to the adoption. By an agreement prior to adoption, the plaintiff agreed not to claim any interest in some properties of his adoptive father. However, subsequently, the plaintiff filed a suit for partition in respect of properties mentioned in the ante-adoption agreement. The validity of the agreement was challenged on the ground that it was hit by section 17 of the Hindu Adoptions and Maintenance Act. It was argued that giving up of a right in property to which the plaintiff would have otherwise been entitled to after adoption, would amount to payment or reward, or plaintiff agreeing to make payment or reward to his prospective adoptive father. The court did not accept this argument.

Order: The court held that the plaintiff had no right in those properties at the time of the agreement so there was no question of any payment or agreement to make any payment by the plaintiff to his prospective adoptive father. Such question would have arisen only if the plaintiff had any pre-existing right in the property-which he did not have in this case. There was, thus, no question of any trafficking and the ante-adoption agreement was held to be valid.

Comment: In order to safeguard against any commercial transaction which could motivate the adoption, section 17 has made special provision against it. However, an agreement made long before the adoption, as in this case, is not hit by the section.

Adopted Child cannot take away Right of Parents to Dispose of Property

Ugre Gowda v. *Nagegowda*,
AIR 2004 SC 3974: 2004 AIR SCW 4308: (2004) 12 SCC 48

Issue: Can a mother, after adopting a child, gift away some of her properties which vested in her by succession after the death of her husband?

Facts: A widow adopted a son. She transferred some of her properties which vested in her by succession on the death of her husband, in favour of the plaintiff by way of gift. The son challenged this gift. His plea was that the deed on record was a deed of adoption-cum-settlement and so he challenged the gift of the property to the plaintiff, as being invalid. The Trial Court held that the adoption was not proved; the lower appellate court held that the adoption was proved but the adoptee could not divest the mother of suit properties which vested in her by succession after the demise of her husband. So far as the settlement-deed was concerned, the same was held to be not valid. The High Court, however, gave the verdict in favour of the adopted son and held that the gift deed made by the mother was null and void. Hence the appeal to the Apex Court.

Order: The court analysed the statutory provisions and the facts of the case and restored the lower appellate court's order. It held that the transfer of title by way of gift, in favour of the plaintiff had no relevance with adoption as mere adoption does not deprive the mother of her right to dispose of her own property. As regards the adoption-cum-settlement deed, the court held that it was of no significance—it was not stamped; it did not identify the suit property, nor did it contain valuation. In these circumstances, no right, title or interest was conveyed in favour of the son. The gift made by the mother was consequently held to be valid.

Comment: An adopted child, cannot, *ipso facto*, take away the right of the adoptive parents to alienate their property by way of Will, gift or sale unless there is an agreement to the contrary, in terms of section 13 of the Hindu Adoptions and Maintenance Act.

Note: In *Chiranjilal Srilal Goenka* v. *Jasjit Singh*, AIR 2001 SC 266: 2000 AIR SCW 4323: (2001) 1 SCC 486 also the facts were more or less same. The deceased who had adopted her elder daughter's son made a Will in favour of the younger daughter. The Will was challenged by the adopted son on the ground that there was an oral agreement by the adoptive father under which after the death of the father and mother, the adopted son alone will be the owner of properties. There was nothing in the alleged unsigned letter restraining the father to execute a Will or alienate the property in his life-time. While the arbitrator ruled in favour of the son, on reference to the High Court it was held that even assuming that the alleged letter was an adoption deed, it could at the most state that the son would succeed as an heir to whatever property is left after transfer during father's lifetime or bequest made by him. An adopted child does not automatically become absolute owner of properties of adoptive parents who do not lose the right to alienate their properties during their life-time.

Son Adopted 45 Years after Death of Freedom-Fighter: No Right to his Pension

Abhishek Sharma v. *State of Uttar Pradesh*, AIR 2009 All 77: 2009 (2) ALJ 435: 2009 AIHC 1745

Issue: Right of an adopted child to the family pension of his freedom-fighter father who had died long before the adoption, was the issue involved in this case.

Facts: The freedom fighter died in the year 1952 leaving behind his widow and a minor daughter. Under the freedom fighter's pension rules the widow became entitled to his pension which she received until her death in 1998. The widow had adopted her daughter's son in October, 1997. The child was about seven years old at that time and the adoption was made through a registered adoption deed. After the widow's death this son applied for grant of the family pension as under the pension rules family pension of the freedom-fighter could be granted to his widow and then to the minor son. The claim of the son was however rejected, primarily on the ground that the child was adopted 45 years after the death of the freedom fighter and in view of section 12 of the Hindu Adoptions and Maintenance Act, 1956 the adopted child is deemed to be the child of his adoptive father or mother only with effect from the date of adoption. The court also observed how this case was a glaring example of an effort to defeat the very object of the freedom fighters family pension rules.

Order: The adoptive son's application for grant of freedom-fighter's pension was rejected.

Comment: The case is a pointer as to how benevolent provisions are sought to be misused by manipulations. The authorities saw through it and rightly rejected the claim.

Compassionate Appointment of Child of Unmarried Male

State Bank of India v. Shweta Sahu, (2010) 3 SCALE 44

Issue: The issue involved was in respect to compassionate appointment of a daughter adopted by an unmarried male. The adopter employee, Satish Sahu, died in harness. After his death the respondent, the adopted daughter, claimed compassionate appointment which was allowed, by the Madhya Pradesh High Court. On appeal against this it was held that the adopted daughter was not entitled to such appointment. The Supreme Court referred to clause 3(f) of the Scheme of Compassionate appointment which reads:

"dependent means in case of a married employee a son (including adopted son) or daughter or if deceased has left behind no children of his/her own eligible for appointment, any other relative nominated by the spouse on which she/he will be wholly dependent. *In case of an unmarried employee, dependent means a brother or a sister.*" (Emphasis added)

Order: The court held that an adopted child of an unmarried employee cannot be said to be a dependent under the scheme and hence not eligible for compassionate appointment.

Comment: The judgment seems to be anomalous and not in consonance with the law. The Hindu Adoptions and Maintenance Act, 1956, permits adoption even by an unmarried male (or female) and such adoption is legal for all purposes. There appears to be no justification to deny to such child the legal status of the deceased employee's child for purposes of compassionate appointment. It is time that compassionate appointment rules be amended to conform to the law of adoption.

Adoption *vis-à-vis* Juvenile Justice Act

In the matter of adoption of *Payal @ Sharinee Vinay Pathak*

High Court of Judicature at Bombay, Petition No. 31 of 2009 Order No. 298 of 2009.

Issue: The issue involved was in respect of adoption of abandoned children and the interpretation of the provisions of the Hindu Adoptions and Maintenance

Act, 1956 *vis-à-vis* the Juvenile Justice (Care and Protection of Children) Act, 2000 (JJA) as amended in 2006 in this context. The Juvenile Justice Act was enacted to provide for rehabilitation of orphaned, abandoned and surrendered children. Adoption has been recognised as one of the ways to rehabilitate these children.

Facts: In this case the petitioner, a Hindu couple who already had a daughter, obtained guardianship rights in respect of a surrendered female child. The child lived with them for over four years and thereafter they sought declaration that they are the adoptive parents of the child with consequential rights, privileges and responsibilities under the law. The court referred to various provisions in the Hindu Adoptions and Maintenance Act, 1956, the Constitution of India, the Juvenile Justice Act and the Convention on the Rights of the Child which was ratified by India in 1992. These were analysed in great detail. Under the Hindu Adoptions and Maintenance Act a person or couple who have a child of a particular gender cannot adopt another of the same gender; the Constitution, the Juvenile Justice Act and the Conventions have various protective provisions for children. In fact the court observed *inter alia*, that the right to life under article 21 of the Constitution would include in its ambit the right to adopt and be adopted; in other words, that adoption is a facet of the right to life under article 21. In this case the court held that the right to life that is asserted is, on one hand the right of parents and individuals, men and women who seek to adopt to give meaning to their lives, equally significant in the context of Juvenile Justice Act the right to life that is specifically protected is the right of children who are in need of special care and protection. As to the embargo that is imposed on adoption of same gender child by the Hindu Adoptions and Maintenance Act the court held that this must give way to the statutory provisions in the Juvenile Justice Act. If the two pieces of legislation, both of which are enacted by Parliament are harmoniously construed, there is no conflict of interpretation, the court observed; and alternatively, even if there is, it is the later Act which will prevail – the Hindu Adoptions and Maintenance Act came in 1956 and the Juvenile Justice Act was enacted in 2000. This is on the well-settled principle that where there are two special Acts dealing with the same subject-matter, legislation which is enacted subsequently will prevail. The court however clarified that the general prohibition contained in the Hindu Adoptions and Maintenance Act on same gender adoption will remain in force; the exception created under the Juvenile Justice Act is only in respect of abandoned children. In this case the child sought to be adopted fits the description of a child in need of care and protection *vide* section 2(d)(v) of the Juvenile Justice Act and of a surrendered child under section 41(2) of the same Act and hence eligible for adoption.

Order: The petitioners were declared adoptive parents of the child with all rights and consequences under law.

Comment: The court has harmoniously construed the different provisions in the Hindu Adoptions and Maintenance Act and the Juvenile Justice Act in the background of the object and purpose of the Juvenile Justice Act and the provisions in the Constitution and the International Conventions. There are innumerable children in need of home and family. Orders such as these will help their cause and facilitate the process of adoption for those who wish to adopt.

Right to Adopt: Component of Right to Life

Philips Alfred Malsvin v. V.J. Gonsalves, AIR 1999 Ker 187: ILR (1999) 2 Ker 43: 1999 (1) Ker LJ 247

Issue: (i) Does right to adopt flow from right to life under the Constitution, (ii) can a Christian couple adopt notwithstanding absence of any statute or custom permitting adoption?

Facts: A couple 'adopted' a child with the help of the Church. The child filed a suit for partition and his share in the property left by the deceased 'father', who died intestate. The petitioner's plea was that he was adopted by the deceased and brought up as his son. The petition was resisted by the natural born children of the deceased on the ground that there could be no adoption under the Christian law, and therefore, the petitioner had no right to claim any share in the property of their father. The issues before the court were: (a) whether there could be an adoption under the Christian law, and if so (b) what are the rights of the child over the property of the deceased?

Order: The court upheld the adoption by a queer interpretation of article 21 of the Constitution. It remarked (at p. 189):

> "The right of a couple to adopt a son is a constitutional right guaranteed under article 21. The right to life includes these things, which make life meaningful. The Hindu law, Mohammedan law and Canon law recognise adoption."

And further (at p. 189):

> "Simply because there is no separate statute providing for adoption, it cannot be said that the adoption made by the Correa couple is invalid. Since the adopted son gets all the rights of a natural born child, he is entitled to inherit the assets of Geroge Correa couple".

Thus, the court held that Christian law recognises adoption and the adopted child has the same rights as a natural born child. The petitioner was, accordingly, held to have a right to seek his share in the properties left behind by the deceased.

Comment: If the right to adopt were to flow from article 21 of the Constitution then it implies that everybody, irrespective of religion or community can adopt. In that case there is no need for an all India adoption law, or for any adoption law, for that matter. In this case, the absence of any adoption statute amongst Christians was explicitly recognised, and there was no reference to any custom either, under which the couple 'adopted' the child. The right to adopt was construed as a component of right to life.

Guidelines for Foreign Adoptions

Lakshmi Kant Pandey v. Union of India,
AIR 1984 SC 469: (1984) 2 SCC 244: (1984) 2 SCR 795: 1984 Marri LJ 249

Issue: This is a set of cases where the Apex Court has laid down detailed directives for adoption of children by foreigners. Pursuant to these directives, elaborate guidelines have been issued by the Ministry of Welfare, Government of India in respect of adoption of Indian children by foreigners.

Facts: The case arose out of a letter written by a lawyer to the Supreme Court which was treated as a petition. The letter that set the ball rolling was based on a report published by *The Mail* (from London) which revealed that hundreds of unwanted babies were being transported from the slums of Calcutta to the U.S.A. The paper also reported the death of Nathan, a two-month old baby who died of dehydration on arriving in New York. Taking note of this, the Apex Court laid down various guidelines in the matter of foreign or inter-country adoptions.

Order: Amongst the guidelines laid down by the court, the following may be stated:

(i) Only government recognised agencies should be entrusted with the task of scrutinising applications by foreign parents wishing to adopt Indian children.

(ii) The antecedents of the applicants should be verified, *viz.*, their family background, financial status, health, etc.

(iii) Preferably, the child should be given for adoption before he or she completes the age of three, though there can be no hard and fast rule on this.

(iv) A progress report of the child alongwith a recent photograph, quarterly during the first two years, and half-yearly during the next three years, should be provided.

(v) The parents should either deposit or enter into a bond for a certain amount, to enable the child to be repatriated, if needed.

(vi) The entire proceedings on the application should be confidential and as soon as the order is made on the application, the papers and documents should be sealed.

In view of difficulties faced by some agencies in implementing these measures, the Supreme Court (*Lakshmi Kant Pandey* v. *Union of India*, AIR 1984 SC 469: (1984) 2 SCC 244: (1984) 2 SCR 795: 1984 Marriage LJ 249, again made certain clarifications and modifications, such as:

(i) The scrutinising agency appointed by the court is to be an expert body having experience in the area of child welfare. It should not in any manner be involved with placement of children for adoption.

(ii) The agency engaged in placement of children for adoption should not readily assume that children, including cradle babies who are found abandoned, are legally free for adoption. Such children must be produced before the Juvenile Court so that further enquiries can be made. In States where there are no Children Acts in force, children should be referred to the Social Welfare Department for making further inquiries and tracing their parents and guardians. The procedure should be completed at the latest within three months. Until the report of the Juvenile Court or the Social Welfare Department declaring such children as destitute or abandoned, these children cannot be given in adoption.

(iii) No court in a State shall entertain an application for the appointment of a foreigner as a guardian of a child who has been brought from another State, if there is a Social or Child Welfare agency in that other State which has been recognised for inter-country adoption by the Government of India.

(iv) Representatives of Foreign Social or Child Welfare agencies should be:

(a) Indian citizens with a degree or diploma in social work, coupled with experience in child welfare.

(b) Acting only for one Social or Child Welfare agency and desirably, the geographical area of operation should be limited so that he is able to attend to his functions diligently.

(c) Having a general power-of-attorney to act in India on behalf of the Social or Child Welfare agency, and should also have the authority to operate bank accounts in the name of the foreign agency with the permission of Reserve Bank of India.

(d) Not permitted to receive children directly from the parents.

(e) A person recognised as such by the Central Government. Such recognition should be given by the Government only on the condition that the various requirements laid down are complied with.

(v) Where the child is a handicapped one, the court dealing with an application for appointment of foreign parents as guardians, should not insist on the foreign parents or even one of the them coming down to India for approving the child.

(vi) Every effort must be made to give a child in adoption to Indian parents before considering the possibility of placing it in adoption with foreign parents.

The practical implementation of these amended guidelines also posed difficulties. Hence, the Supreme Court again (AIR 1987 SC 232) issued some new directions in the matter of the procedure to be followed for adoption of children by Foreign and Indian parents. These directives, to some extent modified the earlier ones. These are, *inter alia*:

(i) payment of some amount to the scrutinising agencies for their services;

(ii) formulation of some procedure for prevention of illegal trade of babies;

(iii) maintenance of a consolidated list of prospective Indian parents wishing to adopt;

(iv) no notice to be published in regard to any adoption application whether it is for foreign adoption or adoption under the Hindu Adoptions and Maintenance Act, 1956;

(v) the time required for processing of the adoption application to be reduced;

(vi) the limit of reimbursement of expenses incurred by recognised placement agencies to be raised to ₹ 6,000; and so on.

Comments: Even while elaborate guidelines have been evolved by the Government in 1995, for regulating adoption of children by parents out of the country, yet the procedural wrangles, including delays and technicalities, could dissuade and discourage even genuine couples from adopting abandoned, destitute children. It is unfortunate that the Adoption of Children Bills, which had provisions enabling foreigners to adopt a child in India and take it to their country, had to be abandoned because of opposition from certain quarters. There are innumerable couples who wish to adopt and an unlimited number of children who need a home and family but the absence of uniform adoption laws and simple, swift procedures only encourages short-cuts, commercialisation and risk of exploitation.

Note: In a recent application *Lakshmi Kant Pandey* v. *Union of India*, 2010 (6) SCALE 23 filed by the Missionaries of Charity, a society established by the Late Mother Teresa, the various difficulties being faced by adoptive parents have been pointed out. It has been highlighted that many Indian courts were not accepting documents executed and authenticated abroad as a result of which adoption of children by foreign parents are being delayed. A plea has been made to simplify the procedure to prevent unnecessary delay, expenditure and harassment to foreign couples who wish to adopt. Allowing the appeal, the Supreme Court has directed the courts dealing with adoption/guardianship cases to accept documents authenticated by officers competent to issue certification by "Apostille" in the country of their execution as provided in the Hague Apostille Convention. A direction has also been given to dispose of these cases within the time frame.

Guidelines do not Apply when Child given in Adoption to Foreign Couple by Biological Parent

Anokha v. State of Rajasthan,
AIR 2004 SC 2820: 2004 AIR SCW 1363: (2004) 1 SCC 382

Issue: Do the guidelines in case of foreign adoptions apply even to children living with biological parents, where such parents wish to give the child in adoption to known foreign couple?

Facts: This was an appeal by special leave under article 136 of the Constitution. Baby Alka was the daughter of Anokha and Sumer Singh Yadav who was a taxi driver. The respondents 2 and 3 were a couple of Italian nationality. They used to visit India frequently since about 20 years and used Sumer Singh's taxi to tour the country. Sumer Singh died in an accident which took place after he had dropped the Italian couple at their destination. Sumer Singh and Anokha had six children, five of whom were girls. After Sumer's death, the respondents 2 and 3, who at that time had no child of their own, wanted to adopt one of the daughters, *viz.* Baby Alka to which Anokha agreed. Thereupon, the respondents filed a petition under the Guardians and Wards Act, 1890 stating, *inter alia*, that they had no child of their own, were financially sound, and would love and look after the child and provide her with best education and everything in Italy. They filed the relevant documents also in support of their application. The District Judge issued notices to the welfare department of the State and also to Anokha, the appellant. The notices were also published in the local newspapers. Anokha filed an affidavit stating that she had known the couple for the last twenty years and had no objection if they were appointed guardian of her daughter. A report was also filed on behalf of the Deputy Collector, State Social Welfare Department, recommending that the child could be given in adoption. The respondent couple also appeared personally before the district judge and reiterated on oath that they were financially, physically and emotionally competent to look after the child and would do so. The district judge, however, declined the couple's request on the ground that the child was not sponsored by a social or child welfare agency, recognised or licensed by the country in which the foreign couple resided. This, according to the district judge, was a mandatory requirement as per the *Guidelines* laid down by the Ministry of Welfare in case of adoption of Indian children by foreigners. Anokha filed an appeal against this. The decision of the district judge was affirmed by the High Court. The High Court also directed the couple to make a fresh application after the same was sponsored by a duly recognised agency of their own country. Hence, the present appeal.

Order: The appeal was granted. The court held that the *Guidelines* formulated by the government in the light of the directives issued by the Supreme Court in *Lakshmi Kant Pandey* v. *Union of India*, AIR 1984 SC 469: (1984) 2 SCC 244: (1984) 2 SCR 795: 1984 Marri LJ 249; *Lakshmikant Pandey* v. *Union of India*, AIR 1992 SC 118: 1991 AIR SCW 2806: (1991) 4 SCC 33, and *Lakshmikant Pandey* v. *Union of India*, (2001) 9 SCC 379: (2003) 10 SCALE 536, do not apply to adoption in respect of children living with their biological parents who are sought to be given in adoption to a known couple. In such case, according to the Supreme Court, the court has to deal with the application under section 7 of the Guardians and Wards Act, 1890, and dispose of the same after being satisfied that the child is being given in adoption voluntarily and would be legally adopted, without any inducement or consideration. The court would also satisfy itself on the basis of evidence and documents that the arrangement would be in the best interest of the child. The application of the Italian couple was thus allowed and they were appointed guardians with liberty to take the child to Italy for being adopted under their law. The court, however, required the couple to comply with certain conditions before they remove the child out of the country *e.g.*, affidavits and undertakings to adopt the child within two years, deposits etc., just to ensure the interests of the child until it is legally adopted.

Comment: The *Guidelines* were proposed to ensure that the interests of children who are sought to be given in adoption to foreigners, are well protected and there is no commercialisation or exploitation at both ends – the givers and the takers. However, when a child is with its biological parents, then these *Guidelines* need not be insisted upon. The guardian court has just to satisfy itself that it is a genuine case and the child's interests are well protected.

HINDU SUCCESSION ACT

The Hindu Succession Act, 1956 revolutionised the law of succession amongst the Hindus. It lays down a uniform and comprehensive system of inheritance and applies to those governed both by the *Mitakshara* and the *Dayabhaga* schools. It also applies to those in South India governed by the *Marumakkattayam, Aliya santana, Nambudri* and other systems of Hindu law. The disparity between the property rights of females and males has been considerably narrowed down, Specially after the 2005 amendment though not completely done away with. The cases discussed and analysed in this section are indicative of the improved legal status of females in matters of succession and property rights; there are also cases which point out to the need for further reform in the area.

APPLICABILITY OF THE ACT

Act not Applicable to Scheduled Tribes

Kailash Singh v. Mewalal Singh Gond,
AIR 2002 MP 112: 2002 (1) MPHT 526: 2002 (2) MPLJ 163

Issue: In view of section 2(2) of the Hindu Succession Act, parties belonging to a Scheduled Tribe are outside the purview of the Hindu Succession Act?

Facts: Under section 2(2) of the Hindu Succession Act, 1956, the application of the Act to members of the Scheduled Tribe is excluded unless the same is made applicable by notification by the Central Government. In this case, the parties belonged to the *Gond* tribe of Madhya Pradesh. After the death of one *B*, his lands came into possession of his widow who bequeathed the same to her nephew, who was the plaintiff in the suit, by Will. After her death, the plaintiff came into possession of the properties. This was challenged by the defendants who were the reversioners of the husband of the deceased widow. Their contention was that she being only a limited owner, after the husband's death could not alienate the property. The Trial Court, on the basis of mutation entry in favour of the plaintiff, held that he was in possession and accordingly, issued an order of temporary injunction in his favour. Hence, the present revision.

Order: The crucial issue was whether it is the traditional Hindu law which was in force prior to 1956 which gave a widow a limited estate, or whether it is the Hindu Succession Act which gave her full ownership rights which would apply. After going through the law, facts and evidence, the court held that the widow, *prima facie*, was only a limited owner and the provisions of this Act do not *pro tanto* apply to the member of the tribe as customary law is saved by the provision. As observed by the court (at p. 113):

> "This Act by its own force would not apply to the Scheduled Tribe because of the *non-obstante* clause in section 2(2), but if it is proved that according to customary law of a particular Scheduled Tribe a widow is entitled to inherit as full owner, she may get absolute right."

In this case, there was no pleading or proof that under the customary of the *Gond* tribe a widow was entitled to inherit as full owner. Hence, the revision was dismissed.

Comment: While the Hindu Succession Act has, by and large, enlarged the females' rights in property, Scheduled Tribes have been exempted from its application. Thus, if it is established that parties belonged to a Scheduled Tribe, then the provisions of the Act would not apply.

Enlargement of Widow's Pre-Existing Limited Right
C. Masilmani Muddaliar v. *Idol of Swaminathaswami,* AIR 1996 SC 1697: 1996 AIR SCW 1780: (1996) 8 SCC 525

Issue: A wife's limited right in the properties of her husband in recognition of her pre-existing right of maintenance enlarges into absolute right on the coming into force of the Hindu Succession Act, in view of section 14.

Facts: A male Hindu executed a Will in 1950, bequeathing some properties to his wife and some to the wife of a cousin who was also residing with his family. In the Will, it was clearly indicated that the testator was under an obligation to maintain his wife and also had a moral obligation to maintain his cousin's wife. The Will, however, imposed some conditions in respect of the properties, *viz.*, that there will be no right to alienate the properties and that some charities will be performed from out of the proceeds of these properties. The Will further stated that after the life-time of both the beneficiaries, the properties would be managed by a named trustee who would perform certain *poojas* and charities from the income derived form the properties. On the death of the executor, the legatees came into possession of the property. After the death of the cousin's wife, the widow of the testator sold the properties by a registered sale-deed. The other heirs filed a suit for declaration that the sale was illegal as the widow succeeded only to a limited estate under the Will. The Trial Court held that the widow had only a limited right in terms of the Will in view of section 14(2) of the Hindu Succession Act. The single judge allowed the appeal; the division bench of the Madras High Court set aside the order of the single judge holding that the legatees had only a restricted right as section 14(2) of the Hindu Succession Act was attracted. Hence, the appeal to the Supreme Court.

Order: The court referred to its own earlier judgments on the point and discussed the issue at length [*e.g., Thota Sesharathamma* v. *Thota Manikyamma,* (1991) 4 SCC 312: JT 1991 (3) SC 506: (1991) 3 SCR 717; *Mangat Mal* v. *Punni Devi,* (1995) 6 SCC 88: 1995 AIR SCW 3885: AIR 1996 SC 172; *Gumpha* v. *Jaibai,* (1994) 2 SCC 511; *Seth Badri Prasad* v. *Kanso Devi,* (1969) 2 SCC 586; *Mangal Singh* v. *Rattno,* AIR 1967 SC 1786: (1967) 3 SCR 454: 1968 (1) SCA 191]. The following observations made in *Thota Sesharathamma* (at p. 331-32) were, *inter alia,* relied upon:

> "Devolution of property under the Will would take effect after the demise of the testator and the legatee would be bound by the terms of gift over etc. The stranger legatee cannot take shelter under subsequent change of law to enlarge the operation of restrictive covenant to claim absolute ownership in the property bequeathed to her. But socio-economic amelioration under the Act engulfs an instrument under the sweep of section 14(1) thereof [Hindu Succession Act] it extinguishes the pre-existing limited estate or restrictive condition and confers absolute and full ownership of the property possessed by a Hindu female as on the date when the Act came into force......"

In the instant case (*C. Masilmani Mudaliar*), it was held that the legatee had a right to maintenance under the Hindu Adoptions and Maintenance Act when the property was given to her for her maintenance. Had the property been acquired for the first time without any vestige or pre-existing right under any instrument, document or device, etc., then section 14(2) of the Hindu Succession Act would have applied and she would have had only a restricted right. However, in this case, what was given to her under the Will was *in lieu* of her pre-existing right to maintenance and that being the basis of her right in the property, her limited right blossomed into absolute right. Hence, it was held that when she alienated the property, she was well within her right to do so.

Comment: Section 14 of the Hindu Succession Act is the most revolutionary provision of the Act. It not only concedes equality but also enlarges a female's limited estate into full ownership rights, within the framework of the law. As pointed out by the court, the basic structure of the Constitution permits equality of status and opportunity. Personal laws conferring inferior status to women is anathema to equality, according to the court. Personal laws are derived not from the Constitution but from religious scriptures. The laws thus derived must be consistent with the Constitution lest they become void under Article 13 if they violated fundamental rights. The right of equality is a fundamental right. The Parliament, therefore, has enacted section 14 to remove pre-existing disabilities fastened on the Hindu female limiting her right to property without full ownership thereof. The discrimination is sought to be remedied by section 14(1) enlarging the scope of acquisition of property by a Hindu female appending an *Explanation* with it.

Note: See also *Mangat Mal* v. *Punni Devi*, (1995) 6 SCC 88: 1995 AIR SCW 3885: AIR 1996 SC 172 where it was held that restrictions imposed on property given to female in recognition of her pre-existing right of maintenance have no meaning and she becomes an absolute owner of those properties *vide* section 14(1) of the Hindu Succession Act.

Widow's Pre-existing Right but Acknowledgement that it was Limited

Vankamamidi Venkata Subba Rao v. *Chatlapalli Seetharamaratna Ranganayakamma,*
AIR 1997 SC 3082: 1997 AIR SCW 3122: (1997) 5 SCC 460

Issue: Does a right which pre-existed at the time of coming of the Hindu Succession Act get defeated simply on the basis of widow's acknowledgment that her right was limited?

Facts: A widow got properties from her husband prior to 1956 *in lieu of* her pre-existing right to maintenance. In a compromise decree in 1955, she acknowledged that she had only a limited right for her life-time and after her, the property would revert to her son. In 1959, she again acknowledged this fact.

Bequest of these properties in favour of her daughter was challenged, and set aside; hence, the appeal.

Order: It was argued on behalf of the appellants that the compromise decree was made in 1955, before the Hindu Succession Act came and it was based on a pre-existing right of maintenance but the court did not accept this plea and held that section 14(2) and not section 14(1) of the Hindu Succession Act would apply and the widow's right could not get enlarged into absolute ownership. According to the court, even after the Hindu Succession Act in 1956, in 1959 when widow executed some gift deeds, she had acknowledged that what she had obtained under the decree was only a limited right acquired for the first time under the compromise decree. Bequest of the properties in favour of the daughter was consequently held to be invalid.

Comment: The court seems to have adopted a very literal approach. The fact was that the widow's right was based on her pre-existing right of maintenance; the subsequent compromise decree of 1955, and her acknowledgment of her limited interest in 1959 should not have defeated her right. Her own acknowledgment that she had a limited right should not have had the effect of defeating her legal right. As aptly stated by the Rajasthan High Court in *Revti* v. *Board of Revenue*, 1998 AlHC 4507 Raj, which was a case on adoption though, "An admission made.......which is against the provision of law, will not take away his right title and interest in the property which he is entitled to under the law".

Widow's Pre-Exsisting Right not Effected by any Subsequent Document etc.

Raghubar Singh v. *Gulab Singh*, AIR 1998 SC 2401: 1998 AIR SCW 2393: (1998) 6 SCC 314

Issue: When a widow already has a pre-existing right, any subsequent document or compromise decree recognising that right cannot be said to have been created in favour of the widow, for the first time.

Facts: A Hindu male executed a Will in favour of the grandchild. Under the terms of the Will, the Hindu male and his wife were to have full control over the property during their life-time and only after their death would the property devolve on the legatee, the grandchild. The will also made it clear that after the testator, his widow would have full control over the property. The husband died in 1946. In exercise of her absolute right, she transferred some properties. The validity of the sale was challenged by the reversioners but a compromise decree was passed which recognised the ownership rights of the widow. The Trial Court held that the widow had a life-interest in the property and that was a right which pre-existed at the time of the coming of the Hindu Succession Act, and therefore, upon the coming of the Act, that right ripened into her absolute ownership right in terms of section 14 of the Hindu Succession Act. On appeal, the District Judge reversed the order and the defendants were directed to deliver vacant possession of certain disputed properties. On second appeal, the Madhya Pradesh High Court partly allowed the appeal but held that the widow enjoyed only a limited right to stay in possession and so had no right to transfer the same. It held that though the Hindu Women's Right to Property Act, 1937, was already in existence when the husband died but since that Act was not in force in that particular State so the widow could not be said to have had any pre-existing right which could mature into full ownership after the Hindu Succession Act, 1956. Hence, the appeal.

Order: It was argued against the appellants that the right of the widow was created in her favour under the compromise-deed and so section 14(2) of the Hindu Succession Act would be applicable. The Supreme Court, however, after detailed arguments, held that the terms of the Will and the compromise decree indicate that she had ownership and possession of suit property at the time when Hindu Succession Act came and the same ripened to absolute ownership by virtue of section 14(1) of the Act. Section 14(2) was not applicable according to the court, since the compromise decree did not for the first time, create any independent right in her favour. The court further emphasised that the right of maintenance of a widow is a right which existed under the *Shastric* law even long before the enactment of the Hindu Women's Right to Property Act, 1937, or the Hindu Married Women's Right to Separate Maintenance and Residence Act, 1946. Thus, the right was a pre-existing right and not created by the Act; the Acts only gave the right a "statutory backing", the court observed. The judgment of the High Court was, consequently, set aside.

Comment: A widow's limited pre-existing right transforms into her absolute right on the coming into force of the Hindu Succession Act unless the right is conferred for the first time under any Will or instrument which specifically prescribes a restricted estate in such property.

Widow's Pre-Act Void Marriage – Affect on her Right

Velamuri Venkata Sivaprasad v. *Kothuri Venkateswarlu*,
AIR 2000 SC 434: 1999 AIR SCW 4583: (2000) 2 SCC 139

Issue: Can a widow's re-marriage in 1953, which is void being bigamous, divest her of her limited right to her deceased husband's estate?

Facts: The husband died in 1937. Since the Hindu Succession Act, 1956, was not in existence at that time, whatever the widow got under the terms of the Will or compromise was by way of limited estate only. In 1953, the widow remarried her sister's husband during the subsistence of his marriage (with the widow's sister). Under the Hindu Widow's Re-marriage Act, 1856, there was no bar to a widow's re-marriage; however, *vide* section 2 of the Act all the rights in the properties of her deceased husband which she may have got, would cease on her re-marriage "as if she had then died". In this case, she had married an already married man whose wife was living, so the marriage was void in terms of the Madras Hindu (Bigamy Prevention and Divorce) Act, 1949. (Under section 2 of this Act a bigamous marriage was void.) The issue, *inter alia*, which came up for determination was whether her re-marriage, void though, could divest her of her limited rights to her deceased husband's property? If so, the question of any limited right transforming into an absolute right does not arise because she would have been already divested of any rights in 1953, *i.e.*, prior to the Hindu Succession Act in 1956.

Order: After analyising the case law and general principles of ethics, estoppel and morals, the court came to the conclusion that the widow was barred in view of her re-marriage. Even though the marriage was void, that would not obliterate the disqualification from inheritance by reason of re-marriage. "Voidness of marriage cannot be termed to be an absolute nullity", the court remarked (at p. 442). In support of this proposition, the court referred to section 16 of the Hindu Marriage Act, whereunder even if a marriage is void under section 11 of the Act, a status of legitimacy is conferred on the children. This according to the Court "is a statutory recognition of limited voidness and not a nullity".

The court also emphasised on the doctrine of sincerity, clean hands and 'moral estoppel'. It referred to section 23(1)(a) of the Hindu Marriage Act, under which one who takes advantage of his own wrong or disability cannot be entitled to relief. It also referred to the Latin maxim of *qui approbat non reprobat* (one who approbates cannot reprobate) as a basic principle of law.

Further, according to the court, the Madras Hindu (Bigamy Prevention and Divorce) Act, 1949, is penal in nature. A literal application of the Act according to the court, would lead to incongruity as well as absurdity since it would mean that if she had married someone without a living spouse, she would be divested of property rights by reason of section 2 of the Act but if she married a person with a spouse living, the same tantamounts to no marriage and so she would be entitled to rights in the property of her deceased husband.

In support of the widow's case for the proposition that a void (bigamous) marriage is no marriage in the eyes of the law, *Bhaurao Shankar Lokhande* v. *State of Maharashtra*, AIR 1965 SC 1564: 1966 (1) SCJ 298: (1965) 2 SCR 837, was relied upon. In this case, the Court held that since the solemnization of second marriage of the husband within the meaning of section 17 of the Hindu Marriage Act was not proved, the case did not come within the mischief of section 494 of the I.P.C, even though the first wife of the appellant husband was living when he married again. The husband was, accordingly, held not guilty of the offence of bigamy. Justifying the court's stand in *Bhau Rao*, the court, in *Valamuri Venkata Sivaprasada*, held that these observations were made in the context of a prosecution wherein punishment would be seven years' imprisonment and fine.

Thus, the court held that since the Widow's Re-marriage Act, 1856, was repealed only in 1983 [Hindu Widow's Re-marriage (Repeal) Act], the disqualification laid down in section 2 of the 1856 Act had its full play on the date of widow's re-marriage in 1953, and she became disentitled to inherit the properties of her deceased husband.

Comment: This judgment is an example of how the fact of voidness of a marriage is used to the disadvantage of a female and to the advantage of a male. If a marriage is void, it is deemed to be no marriage and so the "wife" is not entitled to maintenance [*Bakulbai* v. *Gangaram,* 1988 (1) SCALE 188; *Yamunabai Anantrao Adhav* v. *Anantrao Shivaram Adhav,* AIR 1988 SC 644: JT 1988 (1) SC 193: 1988 Cr LJ 793]. On the other hand, if the second marriage is void, the husband who enters into bigamous marriage is held not guilty of bigamy because the second marriage is no marriage. In the instant case however, being bigamous the marriage was void, nonetheless the court construed it as re-marriage to deprive the widow of property rights.

Widow's Right – Entire Ancestral Property cannot be given

Gulabrao Balwant Rao Shinde v. *Chhabubai Balwant Rao Shinde,*
AIR 2003 SC 16

Issue: Can entire ancestral property be given to a widow *in lieu of* her maintenance so as to make her its absolute owner, thereby defeating the claims of other legal heirs of the deceased?

Facts: This was a property dispute between the children of two widows. After the death of the first wife, the deceased had re-married. Children of the first wife filed a suit for recovery of half share of property left by their father. Children of the second wife claimed ownership of entire property on the plea that their mother was the absolute owner of these properties and hence they alone were entitled to these properties. The High Court held that the second wife possessed properties left by the deceased husband *in lieu of* her maintenance and after the coming into force of the Hindu Succession Act, her right enlarged into full ownership in terms of the provision under section 14. Hence, the appeal by the petitioners—children of the first wife.

Order: It was held that in the absence of any pleadings and evidence to the effect that the deceased had given the property to the widow *in lieu of* maintenance, the High Court was wrong in holding that the property in her possession became her absolute property. Apart from that, according to the court, the property in the hands was ancestral in character, and so he had no right to give away the entire property to the second wife by way of maintenance. Accordingly, the children of the first wife were held to be entitled to a share in the properties left by their father.

Comment: Property possessed by a widow *in lieu of* her maintenance becomes her absolute property *vide* section 14 of the Hindu Succession Act; however property which is ancestral cannot be entirely given to a widow for her maintenance so as to make her an absolute owner thereof, thereby defeating the claims of other legitimate heirs.

DWELLING HOUSE AND FEMALE HEIRS

Riders on Female Heirs (Pre – 2005 Amendment)

Narashimaha Murthy v. *Susheelabai,*
AIR 1996 SC 1826: 1996 AIR SCW 2120: (1996) 3 SCC 644

Issue: Can a female class I heir seek her share in the dwelling-house left by her father if there is only one male heir, or does the rider contained in section 23 of the Hindu Succession Act apply even in case of a single male heir?

Facts: A Hindu died intestate leaving behind a son and three daughters. The daughters filed a suit for partition of the properties, which included a dwelling-house. The Trial Court granted preliminary decree for partition in equal shares. The appellant brother challenged the same on the ground that, in terms of section 23 of the Hindu Succession Act the sisters were not entitled to seek a partition unless and until he decided to take his share. The appeal was, however, dismissed *in limine* by the High Court. Hence, the present special leave appeal by the appellant. The court went through various cases and other authorities on the point of, *inter alia*, the right of female heirs to seek partition when there is only one male heir. It also examined various hypothetical situations to indicate the hardship to the sons and their families if female heirs, specially married daughters, were to seek their share in the dwelling-house by partition. The Court also gave illustrations of situations where after working out the equities, the need for postponement of female heirs' right may not arise *e.g.*, in case of a mansion which may not be wholly in use as a dwelling unit by the male heir. In such case, the extent necessary for use as dwelling-house could be preserved by the male members and the rest made partible. In this case, the dwelling-house was let out to a stranger and was, consequently, not in possession of the son so the claim of the daughters was upheld. However, as to the general principle on whether the restriction on female heirs applies even when there is one male heir, the court observed (at p. 1834 *per* Ramaswami J.):

> "Section 23 applies and prohibits partition of dwelling-house of the deceased Hindu male or female........heir/heirs and the right to claim partition by female heirs is kept in abeyance and deferred during the life of the male heir or till he partitions, or ceases to occupy and enjoy it or lets it out or till at partition action, equities are worked out."

And further (at pp. 1833-34):

> "The right of residence to the male members in the dwelling-house of the Hindu intestate should be respected and the dwelling-house may be

kept impartible during the life-time of the sole male heir of the Hindu intestate, until he chooses to divide and give a share to his sister or sisters or alienates his share to a stranger or lets it out to others."

The following observations of Justice Punchhi echoes the same principle (at p. 1837):

"It cannot be forgotten that in the Hindu male-oriented society where begetting of a son was a religious obligation for the fulfilment of which Hindus have even been resorting to adoptions, it could not be visualised that it was intended that the single heir should be worse off, unless he had a supportive second male heir as class I heir."

And likewise (at p. 1837):

"It looks nebulous that if there are two males, partition at the instance of female heirs could be resisted, but if there is one male, it would not. The emphasis on the section is to preserve a dwelling-house as long as it is wholly occupied by some or all members of the intestate's family which includes male or males."

Order: Since the house in question was let out to a stranger, the bar laid down in section 23 was not attracted as the house was not wholly in occupation by the male heirs. The appeal by the brother or appellant against the High Court order allowing the claim of daughters was, thus, dismissed.

Comment: It is at very disconcerting judgment. The rider in section 23 is (now, was) as it is unfair, but to have held that even if there is one male heir, the female heirs, who own a share in the property cannot ask for it until the male heir chooses to do so was nothing but negating the very right of female heirs. In view of the amendment in the Hindu Succession (Amendment) Act, 2005, giving equal property rights to female heirs, judgment such as this would have only academic value to indicate the traditional ethos of male superiority. [Also see *S. Narayanan* v. *Meenakshi*, AIR 2006 Ker 143] where it was held that the right of the male heir to resist sister's partition suit is taken away even in litigation pending at the time of amendment.

Female Heirs Right to Dwelling House Partly Rented out

Kamal Basu Mazumdar v. *Usha Bhadra Chowdhury*, AIR 2004 Cal 185: 2004 (2) Cal HN 383: 2005 (1) Hindu LR 294

Issue: Under section 23 of the Hindu Succession Act, 1956, is a daughter entitled to her share by partition in the dwelling-house when the house is partly rented out and not wholly in occupation by the male heirs?

Facts: Under section 23 of the Hindu Succession Act "where a Hindu intestate has left surviving him or her both male and female heirs specified in class I of the schedule and his or her property includes a dwelling-house wholly occupied by members of his or her family, then, notwithstanding anything contained in this Act the right of any such female heir to claim partition of the dwelling-house shall not arise until the male heirs choose to divide their respective shares therein...... ."

In this case, the house was partly occupied by a tenant when the intestate died. In other words, it was not wholly occupied by members of the deceased so as to attract the bar under section 23 when the petitioner daughter (*i.e.*, sister of the appellant) filed a suit for her share. A preliminary decree was passed in her favour on December 21, 1979. On July 4, 1982, the tenant vacated the house. Thereafter, nearly nine years later, on April 4, 1991, the appellant moved an application in the court for taking into account subsequent fact of tenants' departure and so making a prayer that the final decree in favour of the sister should not be made, as by that time the property had become a wholly occupied dwelling-house by the male heirs. The court below refused the prayer; revision before the District Court was also dismissed and final decree of partition was made. The appellant thereupon moved an application under article 227 of the Constitution which too was dismissed.

For the appellant, it was argued that subsequent facts which might well have a crucial bearing on adjudication of rights of parties must be considered; and further, that even if a preliminary decree was not appealed against but "nonetheless the final decree is challengeable, as the preliminary decree does not even tie up finally the hands of the court before the suit is finally disposed of by the passing of the final decree." For the respondent, on the other hand, it was argued that the females' right had already accrued as per the wording of section 23. The ancestor having died and the house in question being for a considerable time of about nine years, not wholly occupied by members of the family (June 10, 1973 to July 4, 1982) the right to claim partition in favour of the female heirs had doubtlessly arisen at that time and remained so arisen for all that period. And if the court should now opine that on the vacating of the tenant, the right which had arisen had collapsed, then such interpretation would introduce most undesirable uncertainty in the working of section 23. The Court agreed in this and remarked: "The tenants might vacate after the passing of the preliminary decree, after passing of final decree, while the first appeal is pending, or may be when the second appeal is pending; the story almost never ends.......... uncertainty of this nature is more appropriate on a children's playground rather in courts of law".

Order: The court delved on a few hypothetical situations to indicate the hardships if the respondent's arguments were to be accepted. Conceding the claim of the female heir, it observed:

"A look at section 23 shows that this section carves out a very odd legal-estate. Generally speaking, property with serious curtailment of right of enjoyment keeps the transfer valid but curtailment void........ The modern law is not in favour of locked up property or property hedged in by complicated personal restrictions. In section 23, female heir gets her undivided share as much as any male heir but cannot claim partition of family dwelling-house. This is a restriction upon her ownership of the undivided share. This restriction only Parliament can enact. By enacting this, Parliament has created a special type of estate the exact like of which was unknown to law before 1956, although women's limited enjoyment was well-known.

In this case, the subsequent vacation of the house by the tenant was held to be meaningless when the right had already accrued to the female heir at the time of the death of her father.

Comment: While in the facts of the present case, the court conceded the female heir's right, it expressed disconcert at the provision and the potential it has to negate the right of the females. It remarked:

"If the right of the female heirs could arise and collapse, if it could wax and wave, then it would be a question of the estate itself changing from one type into another by operation of statute."

The vagueness, uncertainty and inequality of the provision has now, however, been removed by the enactment of the Hindu Succession (Amendment) Act, 2005, which seeks to give equal property rights to daughters including the right to seek partition of the dwelling-house.

Pending Cases under Section 23 *vis-à-vis* 2005 Amendment

M. Revathi v. R. Alamelu,
AIR 2009 Mad 86: 2009 (77) All Ind Cas 812:
2009 (5) Mad LJ 376

Issue: Prior to the Hindu Succession (Amendment) Act, 2005, *vide* section 23 of the Hindu Succession Act, 1956 a female could not seek partition of the dwelling house in occupation of the male heirs, even though she had an equal share therein. In 2005, after the above mentioned Amendment Act section 23 was deleted. Thus, there is no embargo on a female seeking her share by a partition. The issue in this case was whether the amendment would apply to pending cases.

Facts: This was a partition suit in respect of a dwelling house, filed by a female heir prior to 2005. The same was dismissed on the sole ground that the plaintiff being a female member cannot ask for partition of a dwelling house in occupation of a male heir as per section 23 of the Act. The court however ordered accounts to be furnished to the plaintiff relating to income derived from the house as portion of the house was rented out. On appeal against this, it was argued that since the dwelling house was not in the exclusive possession of the male heirs as part of it was already rented out, so the Trial Court ought to have conceded the petitioner right to partition. During the course of the appeal the amendment came through in 2005, deleting section 23 of the Act.

Order: It was held that even though the amendment Act shall have prospective effect but viewed practically, it is clear that the plaintiff is entitled to the partition in view of the amendment. "The appeal is deemed to be in continuation of the suit proceedings. It would be a mere hyper technicality if the appellant/plaintiff is driven to the extent of filing a fresh suit invoking the said recent Hindu Succession (Amendment) Act, 2005 and in such a case, I am having no hesitation in construing that in this case the erstwhile section 23 is having no application and accordingly partition could be ordered in respect of the 1/8th share of the plaintiff", the court held (at p. 87).

Comment: Section 23 of the Hindu Succession Act was indeed a very unfair and discriminatory provision and the discrimination was compounded by the illogical application/interpretation of the provision in some cases, notably, *Narashimaha Murthy* v. *Susheelabai*, AIR 1996 SC 1826: 1996 AIR SCW 2120: (1996) 3 SCC 644 wherein it was held that even if there is one male heir, the female heirs who have a share in the property cannot ask for it until the male heir choses to do so. This was nothing but negating the very right of the female. However, the section has now been deleted and such cases have only academic value now.

WIDOWED DAUGHTER-IN-LAW

Widowed Daughter-in-law's Right only in Coparcenary Property of Husband

Daljit Singh v. Dara Singh,
AIR 2000 Del 292: 2000 (85) DLT 794: II (2000) DMC 134

Issue: Can a widowed daughter-in-law claim maintenance and share in property from the father-in-law who is not in possession of any coparcenary or joint family property?

Facts: Under section 19 of the Hindu Adoptions and Maintenance Act a daughter-in-law is entitled to be maintained by the father-in-law if she is unable to maintain herself out of her own earning or property or from the estate of her husband or her father or mother or her son or daughter. The liability of the father-in-law, however, arises only if he has the means to maintain her from any coparcenary property in his possession out of which the daughter-in-law has not obtained any share. In this case, the daughter-in-law filed an application for maintenance under section 19 and also a suit for partition of immovable and movable properties alleged to be joint, against her father-in-law, mother-in-law, brother-in-law and his wife.

Order: The court went into the details of the facts and properties and found that there was no evidence that the father-in-law had inherited any ancestral property. As regards partition of properties, it was established that the father, brother and the deceased (husband of the applicant) had started business in partnership in 1990, but the same was dissolved in 1992 due to bad habits, including excessive drinking habit, of the deceased who died in 1995. Thus, he died three years after the business partnership was dissolved. In these circumstances, the court ruled, it could not be said that there was any coparcenary or joint family property in the hands of the father-in-law out of which the daughter-in-law could claim maintenance or share.

Comment: A father-in-law's liability to maintain the daughter-in-law is not absolute. It is conditional on his possessing joint family properties out of which the daughter-in-law has not obtained any share.

Note: See however, *Balbir Kaur* v. *Harinder Kaur*, AIR 2003 P&H 174: 2003 (2) CCC 80: 2003 (2) Marri LJ 499 where the court held that a widowed daughter-in-law is entitled to maintenance under section 19 of the Hindu Adoptions and Maintenance Act, 1956 from out of the self-acquired property of the father-in-law.

Widowed Daughter-in-law: Properties of Deceesed Husband in Possession of Father-in-law

V. Muthusami v. Angammal,
AIR 2002 SC 1279: 2002 AIR SCW 1083: (2002) 3 SCC 316

Issue: A daughter-in-law has a pre-existing right to be maintained from the properties of her deceased husband in possession of the father-in-law. Her limited right blossoms into absolute ownership on the coming of the Hindu Succession Act.

Facts: The father-in-law of a widow received property of her deceased husband and subsequently he made a settlement-deed in 1946, providing for maintenance to her during her life-time. In 1974, she executed an agreement for sale of the property in favour of the plaintiff. This was challenged on the ground that she being only a limited owner, could not alienate the same. The settlement-deed in 1946, it is pertinent to note, was made on the intervention of the *panchayat*. On this basis, a plea was taken that she had only a contractual right of maintenance over the properties of her father-in-law. The High Court, accordingly, held that the sale agreement could not be enforced. Hence, the appeal to the Supreme Court.

Order: The Supreme Court held that the settlement-deed made in 1946 on the intervention of the *panchayat*, was in recognition of her pre-existing right of maintenance against the properties of her husband which came in the hands of the father-in-law. The case was held to be covered by section 14(1) of the Hindu Succession Act and the sale of suit properties possessed by virtue of pre-existing right as full owner, is valid. The argument that the widow claimed maintenance over the properties of her father-in-law was held to be not tenable as she claimed maintenance as of right against the properties left behind by her deceased husband. According to the court, even though she was not in actual physical possession of the land, she could enforce such a right in law. The role of the panchayat was only as an intermediary to help parties to come to a settlement in recognition of her pre-existing right to be maintained from the property of her husband. Hence, after the coming into force of the Hindu Succession Act she became full owner over the suit land with power to execute the sale agreement, the court ruled.

Comment: The Hindu Succession Act has considerably enlarged the rights of females in property not only by conceding equality but also by giving them absolute ownership rights in properties which were held by them as limited owners at the time of the commencement of the Act.

RIGHTS OF STEP CHILDREN

Step-Son's Right

Rattan Prakash v. Bela Sihare,
AIR 1996 Del 356: 1997 (1) Hindu LR 204: 1997 Marri LJ 46

Issue: Is a step-son included in the term 'son' as referred to in section 15(1)(a) of the Hindu Succession Act, 1956?

Facts: The term 'sons' as referred to in section 15(1)(a) of the HSA, which sets out the rules of devolution of property in the case of a Hindu female dying intestate, does not include a step-son. The petitioner in this case had a real brother, a step-widowed mother and a step-sister. After the death of the father in 1952, his property was partitioned and the widow was awarded a life-interest in one-third share under an award made in 1952. The widow challenged the award. The High Court declared her as the absolute owner of the share by an order in 1964. While the partition suit was pending, she died and her daughter filed an application under Order 22, Rule 3 of the Civil Procedure Code, 1908, claiming that the right to suit survived in her favour after the mother's death. The petitioner step-son, on the other hand, claimed that all the children became co-owners as the step-mother died intestate and so they were also entitled to their claim. Hence, the present revision.

Order: The court held, that under section 15(1)(a) read with section 16, the daughter alone was entitled to the share of the mother's property, as the term 'son' mentioned in that clause does not include a step-son. Such step-son would be covered by clause (b) of section 15(1) which refers to the heirs of the husband, but such heirs as mentioned in clause (b) of section 15(1) would be entitled only when there are no heirs specified in clause (a) of section 15(1). In other words, heirs in clause (a) take precedence over heirs mentioned in clause (b). A reference was also made to the following observations of the Supreme Court in *Lachman Singh* v. *Kirpa Singh*, AIR 1987 SC 1616 (1619): 1987 2 SCC 547: JT 1987 (3) SC 175:

> "The words son and step-son are not defined in the Act. According to Collins English Dictionary, a 'son' means a male offspring and 'step-son' means a son of one's husband or wife by a former union. Under the Act, a son of a female by her first marriage will not succeed to the estate of her 'second husband' on his dying *intestate*. In the case of a woman, it is natural that a step-son, that is, the son of her husband by his other wife is a step away from the son who has come out of her own womb."

In this case, the daughter was covered under clause (a) so she took precedence over her step-brother, the petitioner, who fell under clause (b). The revision was accordingly dismissed.

Comment: A step-son (or daughter) cannot be equated with a son or daughter for purposes of inheritance under the Hindu Succession Act. Section 3(h) specifically states that 'son' includes a son adopted in accordance with the law for the time being in force relating to adoption among Hindus. There is no reference to a step-son at all.

Bhagwan Dass v. Prabhati Ram,
AIR 2004 Del 137: 2004 (14) All Ind Cas 807: 2003 (108) DLT 25

Issue: Does a step-son have any right in the properties of a female?

Facts: Under section 15 of the Hindu Succession Act, the property of a female dying intestate devolves, *inter alia*, first upon the sons and daughters (including children of any pre-deceased son or daughter) and the husband. A step-son is not a preferential heir. In this case, the second wife of a man had allowed the son and daughter-in-law of his first wife to reside in one room with kitchen and verandah of a house belonging to her, out of consideration that they were the children of the first wife of her husband. However, after her death, the son started misbehaving with the father. Fed up by this, the father disowned the son and asked him to vacate the house; he filed notices to terminate licence and suit for mandatory injunction and prayed for decree directing the son to handover possession. The son contested this on the ground that he had a right to the property. The Trial Court ruled in his favour; hence the father's appeal. The first appellate court, however, reversed the order. Against this the son filed the present appeal.

Order: The son's appeal was dismissed. The court held that the appellant was not a preferential heir under sections 15 and 16 of the Hindu Succession Act and the husband *i.e.*, the father of the appellant who was alive, inherited the entire property by virtue of the provisions of the Hindu Succession Act. He was, therefore, within his right to terminate the licence of the appellant son and upon such termination of the licence, the right to occupy suit premises by the son would cease.

Comment: A licence given to a step-son and his wife to reside in an independent room of the house belonging to a female out of moral considerations, does not give to the step-son, a right to claim that property after the death of the female.

Debabrata Mondal v. State of West Bengal, AIR 2008 Cal 13: 2008 (2) AIR BomR 222: 2007 (60) All Ind Cas 523

Issue: The issues involved in the case were as to:
(i) succession right of as step-son as heir of deceased husband
(ii) whether a representation can have the effect of a Will
(iii) would the law of escheat apply when there is an heir qualified to succeed to property?

Facts: J married a widower in 1972 who died in 1991. J died issueless in 2002. On her death, her stepsons, the petitioners in the case, claiming to be heir of J applied for mutation of properties leased out to J in 1970 by the State Government, in their name. The authorities turned down their application on the ground that as stepsons, they were not to be treated as heirs of J entitling them to inherit her property. Hence the present writ petition. While the petitioner's counsel relied on the provisions of section 15(i)(b) of the Hindu Succession Act, 1956 under which, in the absence of any sons, daughters or husband, the property of a female Hindu dying intestate would devolve on heirs of her husband, the counsel for the State Government referred to a Supreme Court decision in *Lachman Singh v. Kirpa Singh,* AIR 1987 SC 1616: 1987 2 SCC 547: JT 1987 (3) SC 175 where it was held that the word 'sons' used in section 15(i)(a) of the Hindu Succession Act does not include a stepson of a female Hindu dying intestate.

According to the court, the case is different here. Here the petitioners are J's stepsons and J died issueless and intestate and they inherit as heirs of J's pre-deceased husband.

Another argument advanced by the respondent was that by a representation in 1991, J had expressed her last desire to the Government that on her death, her stepsons should not get the property. This representation according to the court has no effect in the eye of law and as per provision of section 15(i)(b) since J did not have any son or daughter of her own, the petitioners as heirs of the husband would succeed.

Another feeble argument made by the counsel for the State was that in view of J's desire expressed in her representation in 1991, the property would devolve on government by the operation of section 29 of the Hindu Succession Act. However, this argument could not hold ground as the question of escheat *vide* provision is section 29 would arise only when there is no heir left by the female Hindu dying intestate. In this case, the petitioners are qualified to succeed to J's property hence section 29 of the Act cannot be invoked.

Order: The petition was allowed and it was held that the petitioners were entitled to succeed to J's property as heirs of her pre-deceased husband in view of clause (b) of section 15(i) of the Hindu Succession Act, 1956.

Comment: The provision in section 15(i)(b) of the Act appears to be unfair; the Apex Court judgment in *Om Prakash v. Radhacharan,* (2009) 7 SCALE 51, *supra,* clearly demonstrates this and needs a relook.

Step-Daughter's Right
Raj Rani v. Bimla Rani,
AIR 2011 Del 170

Issue: Does the word "daughter" include "step-daughter" for purposes of claiming share in the absolute property of the step-mother?

Facts: The case involved property rights of a step daughter to the absolute property of the step mother. The plaintiff was the step-daughter who sought her one-third share, alongwith the two biological daughters of the deceased. The Trial Court dismissed her suit holding that a step-daughter has no right *vide* the provisions of the Hindu Succession Act, 1956. On appeal by her, the Trial Court finding was reversed and a preliminary decree for partition had been passed apportioning one-third share to each of the parties *i.e.*, the original plaintiff-step-daughter and two biological daughters of the deceased. Hence the present appeal against the order by the two defendants – the biological daughters.

Order: The plaintiff argued that she also being the daughter of step-mother's husband, was entitled to a share in the suit property whereas, according to the defendants their mother being the absolute owner of the parties, they alone could have inherited her property and the plaintiff being not her (deceased's) daughter, *vide* section 15 of the Hindu Succession Act had no right or interest therein. The question before the court was whether the expression 'daughter' as defined in section 15(i)(a) of the Hindu Succession Act includes a step-daughter *i.e.*, daughter of the husband by another wife. After analysing the provision, it was held that the expression "daughter" in the above said section includes daughter borne out of the female's womb by the same husband or by different husbands and includes an illegitimate daughter [in view of section 3(i) of the Hindu Succession Act] it would also include an adopted daughter who is deemed to be a daughter for the purpose of inheritance. Children of pre-deceased daughter/adopted daughter are also covered under the expression "daughter". The court observed (at p. 173):

> "If the Legislature had felt that the word 'daughter' should include the word 'step-daughter', it should have said so in express words. Thus, the word 'daughter' appearing in section 15(i)(a) would not include 'step-daughter' and such step-daughter...would fall in the category of an heir of her husband as referred to in clause 15(i)(b) [and not an heir of the deceased female]"

In support of its view, the court referred to various judgments, *inter alia*, *Mallappa Fakirappa Sanna Nagashetti* v. *Shivappa*, AIR 1962 Mys 140: ILR 1962 Mys 196; *Rama Ananda Patil* v. *Appa Bhima Redekar*, AIR 1969 Bom 205: 70 Bom LR 773: ILR (1969) Bom 252; *Lachman Singh* v. *Kirpa Singh*, AIR 1987 SC 1616 (1619): 1987 2 SCC 547: JT 1987 (3) SC 175. The appeals of the biological daughter was thus allowed and the court held that the property of their deceased mother would devolve only on them.

Comment: Section 15 of the Hindu Succession Act refers to devolution of property of a female Hindu dying intestate. The husband and her sons/

daughters are the primary heirs and others come only in the absence of husband, sons/daughters. Step-sons or step-daughters do not fall in the category of son or daughter. See also *Santosh Kumar Diwan* v. *Sitabai*, AIR 2011 MP 161 – Hindu female dying intestate – her share shall devolve on her daughter as prescribed under section 15(i) and not to her daughter-in-law.

Devolution of Property of Female
Bhagat Ram v. Teja Singh,
AIR 2002 SC 1: 2001 AIR SCW 4507: (2002) 1 SCC 210

Issue: Can a property which is inherited by a female Hindu from her mother, devolve on the female's death, on the heirs of her husband?

Facts: Under section 15(2)(a) of the HSA, any property inherited by a female Hindu from her father or mother devolves in the absence of any son, or daughter of the deceased, upon the heirs of the father. In this case, two sisters S and I inherited property from their widowed mother in 1951, and their estate blossomed into absolute ownership on the coming of the Hindu Succession Act, 1956. On the death of S in 1961, without any issue, the property left by her was mutated in the name of I. The appellant Bhagat Singh, who had entered into agreement of sale with I in 1963, filed a suit for specific performance which was decreed. This was challenged by Teja Singh, the brother of pre-deceased husband of S on the ground that on her (S's) death, the property devolved on him by virtue of clause (b) of section 15(1) of the Hindu Succession Act as heir of S's husband. The Trial Court decreed his suit. On appeal, the High Court also held that on the death of husband of S, property devolved on him (Teja Singh). Hence, Bhagat Singh's appeal to the Apex Court.

Order: The court held that the property held by S was property inherited by her from her mother so clause (a) of section 15(2) applied and Teja Sigh, who was the brother of S's husband had no right in the property left by S. Her property would devolve in the absence of any issue left by her, only on her sister, according to the court. It held:

> "The source from which she (the female) inherits the property is always important and that would govern the situation. Otherwise persons who are not even remotely related to the person who originally held the property would acquire rights to inherit that property. That would defeat the intent and purpose of sub-section (2) of section 15 which gives a special pattern of succession."

Bhagat Singh's appeal was, accordingly, allowed, as according to the Court, the property devolved on the surviving sister I as heir of the mother and not on the heirs of the pre-deceased husband of the deceased sister.

Comment: It would be pertinent to note that this case was first decided in 1999, (*Bhagat Singh* v. *Teja Singh*, AIR 1999 SC 1944: 1999 AIR SCW 1626: (1999) 4 SCC 86). However, since Teja Singh died in 1986, and neither his legal heirs were brought on record nor was the fact of his death brought to the notice of the court at the time of order, on application being filed by the heirs of Teja Singh after the order, the court allowed them to be impleaded. The court gave an opportunity to both the parties to be heard but found no reason to deviate from the order given in 1999, and the same was upheld in the present case.

It may also be pointed out here that the constitutional validity of section 15(2) of the Hindu Succession Act was challenged before the Bombay High Court in *Somu Bai Yashwant Jadav* v. *Balagovind Yadav*, AIR 1983 Bom 156: (1983) 1 Bom CR 632: (1983) 2 Civ LJ 58, on the ground that it was violative of the provisions of articles 14 and 15 of the Constitution on the ground of gender discrimination. This argument was rejected and the court held that if the property has come from the father or the mother of a Hindu woman by inheritance, the law, in furtherance of the clear objective to continue the family unity, directs that such property should go to the heirs of the father and the mother and not to the heirs of the husband. According to the court, upon an analysis of the entire section, it was hard to find any discrimination which lays hostile discrimination, much less hostile discrimination only on the ground of sex, in provisions of section 15(2)(b) of the Hindu Succession Act.

Om Prakash v. *Radhacharan*, (2009) 7 SCALE 51

Issue: The issue involved was as to devolution of property of a female – A widow in this case – dying intestate.

Facts: This was a tragic case where a young girl Narayani, became a widow just within three months of her marriage. She was driven out of her matrimonial home immediately after the husband's death and thereafter never returned there. Her parents supported her, gave her education and she got a job. After four decades of widowhood she died without making a will. She left behind various bank accounts and a huge sum in her provident fund account also. Everything was her self-acquired; there was nothing at all that she got from her husband's/in-laws' side. Upon her death, her mother Ramkishori, filed an application for grant of succession certificate under section 372 of the Indian Succession Act. The respondents, who were sons of sister of Narayani's deceased husband also filed an application for succession certificate. After the death of Ramkishori, her sons *i.e.*, brothers of Narayani, were brought on record. Thus the claim was now between the heirs of Narayani (her brothers) and the heirs of her deceased husband (his sister's sons). The counsel for the appellant *i.e.*, Narayani's brothers, argued that in a case of this nature where the husband of the deceased or her in-laws had not made any contribution towards her nor ever gave her any support during her life-time, sub-section 2 of section 15 of the Hindu Succession Act would apply. Clause (a) section 15(2) says:

> "any property inherited by a female Hindu from her father or mother shall devolve, in the absence of any son or daughter of the deceased – upon the heirs of her father."

The counsel for the respondents, however, relied on section 15(i)(b) *viz.*: "The property of a female Hindu dying intestate shall devolve according to the rules set out in section 16

(a) ....

(b) *secondly, upon the heirs of the husband.*

While section 15 provides that in case of property inherited from the parents side, the same would, on the female's death, devolve on her parents family and if the property is inherited from her husband or in-laws, it shall devolve upon heirs of husband, there is no mention of property which is her self-acquired. The court took the view that the provision contained in section 15(1)(b) would apply and not the one in section 15(2)(a) and consequently dismissed the appeal of Narayani's brothers.

Order: It was held that the heirs of the husband *i.e.*, his sister's son and not the heirs of the deceased's father *i.e.*, her brothers, would be entitled to Narayani's assets as per the provision of clause (b) of section 15(1) of the Hindu Succession Act.

Comment: It is a very unfortunate case. In fact the court itself conceded:

"It is a hard case. Narayani during her life-time did not visit her in-laws' place. We will presume that the contentions raised....that she had not been lent any support from her husband's family is correct and all support had come from her parents but then only because a case appears to be hard would not lead us to invoke different interpretation of a statutory provision which is otherwise impermissible. It is now a well-settled principle of law that sentiment or sympathy alone would not be a guiding factor in determining the rights of the parties which are otherwise clear and unambiguous."

It is submitted that sub-section (2) of section 15 provides only for properties *inherited* by a female from her parents or from her husband/in-laws. There is no reference to her *self-acquired* property. No statutory provision prevented the court from making an equitable and fair order which would have met the ends of justice.

Time for Ascertaining Heirship

Seethalakshmi Ammal v. Muthuvenkatarama Iyengar, AIR 1998 SC 1692: 1998 AIR SCW 1462: (1998) 5 SCC 368

Issue: At what point of time is heirship to be ascertained?

Facts: On the death of the widowed mother-in-law G, the childless widowed daughter-in-law filed a suit for declaration and possession of properties left by her against the defendant who, claiming to be a nephew of G set up a Will by G in his favour. The Will was not accepted by any of the courts, including the High Court. The High Court, however, allowed the second appeal of the defendant on the plea that the appellant *i.e.*, the daughter-in-law was not the heir of G. Hence, the appeal.

Order: Under section 15 of the Hindu Succession Act the property of a female Hindu dying intestate devolves under clause (1) among others, *firstly* upon sons and daughters (including children of any pre-deceased son or daughter) and husband; and *secondly*, upon heirs of the husband. Under the schedule, widow of a pre-deceased son is a Class I heir. According to the High Court, when the husband of G died, their son was alive so the appellant (the son's wife) could not be considered as an heir as widow of the pre-deceased son. The Supreme Court, however, held that heirs under clause 15(1)(b), *i.e.*, heir of the husband, have to be ascertained not at the time of the death of the husband but at the time of the female's death, *i.e.*, the widow mother-in-law's death. It was accordingly held, that succession opened at the time of G's death and since when G died the appellant was indeed the widow of the pre-deceased son so she was an heir of the husband in terms of section 15(1)(b) and the schedule. She was, therefore, held to be entitled to succeed.

Comment: Under the schedule annexed to section 8 of the Hindu Succession Act, widow of a pre-deceased son is a Class I heir, and under clause (b) of section 15(1) the property of a female dying intestate devolves, *inter alia*, "upon the heirs of the husband". Succession opens at the time of death of the female therefore, heirship also should be ascertained at that point of time. If, when the female dies there is a widow of the pre-deceased son who is an heir of her (widow's) husband, then she would succeed to the properties; the fact that when the husband (of the intestate) died the son was alive and the daughter-in-law was not a widow, is not material.

Wife of Murderer Son is Disqualified

Vallikannu v. *R. Singaperumal,*
AIR 2005 SC 2587: 2005 AIR SCW 2820: (2005) 6 SCC 622

Issue: Is the wife of a son who murders his father, entitled to inherit as a widow of the son; as a sole surviving female member of the coparcenary?

Facts: Under section 25 of the Hindu Succession Act, 1956, "a person who commits murder or abets the commission of murder shall be disqualified from inheriting the property of the person murdered, or any other property in furtherance of the succession to which he or she committed or abetted the commission of the murder". And section 27 says, "If any person is disqualified from inheriting any property under this Act it shall devolve as if such person had died before the intestate".

In this case, the son murdered his father R.K. and was convicted under section 302 of the Indian Penal Code, for life imprisonment. The conviction was confirmed by the High Court but the court recommended the Government to reduce the sentence to the period already undergone and so he was released in

July, 1975. Since he was debarred under section 25 of the Hindu Succession Act to succeed to his father's estate, the plaintiff-wife of the son (first defendant) claimed that she alone was entitled to succeed to the properties left behind by R.K. According to her, the first defendant (her husband) must be deemed to have pre-deceased as provided under section 25 read with section 27 of the Hindu Succession Act. She also claimed to be the widow of the first defendant and claimed to be the owner of all the properties left by R.K. as coparcener. The first defendant, on the other hand, contended that the plaintiff's suit was not maintainable as she is not the legal heir of R.K. It was alleged that all the properties acquired by R.K. were joint family properties and he has acquired the same by survivorship. The Trial Court held that all the properties were joint family properties of R.K. and the son (first defendant) and the latter having murdered the former (his father) was not entitled to claim any right under section 6 read with sections 25 and 27 of the Hindu Succession Act. It, however, held that as per proviso to section 6, the plaintiff was entitled to a decree for half share and accordingly it was granted to the plaintiff. The first respondent's appeal against the order was dismissed; he filed a second appeal before the High Court. The High Court held that the plaintiff could not claim as a widow of the son of R.K. She cannot claim one-half share in the property being coparcenary property under proviso to section 6 either. It was also observed that she would have been entitled to half share so long as the deceased-father and son had not partitioned. The first defendant cannot be said to have inherited any share from the victim (R.K.) and the plaintiff can claim as a widow only if there is a succession to the estate of the victim. If there is no succession, the deeming provision that the first defendant shall be deemed to have died before the victim (his father) also will not apply and she cannot claim as a widow of R.K.'s pre-deceased son. It was also held that section 6 of the Hindu Succession Act will also not apply. The principle of justice, equity and public policy will apply and the plaintiff cannot be treated as a fresh stock of descent and the first respondent shall be treated as non-existent as if he never existed. Therefore, the plaintiff also cannot claim as a widow. Since plaintiff claims as a widow of the first respondent and he is disqualified, same disqualification equally applies to her, for, she cannot claim through a murderer husband. Hence, the present appeal.

Order: It was argued for the plaintiff that she being the sole female survivor of the joint Hindu property and as her husband stands disqualified, she is entitled to the entire estate as a sole survivor member of the coparcenary property under the proviso to section 6 read with section 8, as Class I heir. On the other hand, for the first respondent it was contended that the disqualification which was attached to the son equally applies in the case of the wife as she is claiming the estate because of her marriage with the respondent and if he is disqualified, then she is also equally disqualified to claim any property being a coparcener from the estate of her deceased father-in-law. After referring to several judgments, the Court held that: "The effect of section 25 read with section 27 of the Hindu Succession Act, is that a murderer is totally disqualified to succeed to the estate of the deceased. The framers of the Act in the Objects and Reasons, have made a reference to the decision of the Privy Council [*Kenchaya Kom Sanyallappa Hosmani*

v. *Girimalappa Channappa Samasagar*, AIR 1924 PC 209: 51 Ind App 368: 48 Bom 569] that the murderer is not to be regarded as the stock of a fresh line of descent but should be regarded as non-existent. That means that a person who is guilty of committing the murder cannot be treated to have any relationship whatsoever with the deceased's estate."

Thus, it was held that once the son is totally disinherited, then his whole stock stands disentitled. The wife can have no better claim in the property of the deceased than the disqualified son. The appeal of the murderer son's wife was accordingly dismissed.

Comment: Once it is established that a murderer stands disqualified in view of the sections 25 and 27 of the HSA, to inherit properties of his victim, his wife also stands automatically disqualified. Her claim is in no case better than her husband's who is the murderer.

No Disinheritance of Statutory heir
Raman Khanna v. Sham Kishore Khanna,
AIR 2009 HP 42

Issue: Can a statutory heir be disinherited by publishing a notice or disclaimer to that affect?

Facts: The case involved a property dispute seeking partition, share and damages. Pending litigation two defendants along with their only male child died in an accident. The issue of bringing on record their legal representative was raised since under section 21 of the Hindu Succession Act in cases of simultaneous deaths there is a presumption that the younger survived the elder, the representatives would be reckoned in reference to the son who died in the accident along with his mother and father. Since the son left behind no class I heir, his maternal grandmother being Class II heir, was held to be the legal representative as opposed to the claim of the sisters of defendant I, the father who died in the accident, who claimed to be heirs of their brother, defendant I.

An argument that the grandmother had already snapped her ties with the defendants by publishing a notice in the newspaper was held to be of no significance. "... mere issuance of the notice or disclaimer as alleged cannot disinherit statutory heir" the court held (at p. 44).

Right of Pre-emption

Ganeshappa v. Krishnamma,
AIR 2005 Kant 160: ILR 2005 Kant 358: 2005 (2) Kant LJ 262

Issue: Can the right of pre-emption under section 22 of the Hindu Succession Act be invoked against the widow of the class I heir who had succeeded to the properties only after the death of her husband?

Facts: One V died intestate. He had three sons who, being Class I heirs inherited his property. After the death of one of the sons, his widow filed a suit against the plaintiff (one of the other sons of the intestate) seeking partition of the share of her husband. The suit was decreed. The widow, thereafter, sold the properties allotted to her share. Thereupon, the plaintiff made an application under section 22 of the Hindu Succession Act claiming right of pre-emption to purchase the properties allotted to the share of the widow and a declaration that the sale deeds executed by the widow is void and in contravention of section 22 of the Act. The Trial Court held that the plaintiff has a right of pre-emption. In revision the order of the Trial Court was set aside. Hence, the appeal.

Order: It was held, that under section 22, the provision is that if the interest in the immovable property devolved by intestate succession upon two or more heirs specified in Class I of the schedule, then it is between the Class I heirs *inter se* that there is a right of pre-emption. In the present case, the succession for the first time opened after the death of the father and his three sons succeeded as Class I heirs to his property. The widow did not succeed to the property as Class I heir, it is her husband who along with his two other brothers who succeeded. The widow succeeded to the property only after the death of her husband, who is the brother of the plaintiff. The plaintiff could have invoked his right of pre-emption only if his brother during his life-time had sold the property; but in this case it is the widow who inherited the property after her husband's death who has sold the property. Therefore, between the plaintiff and the widow, the question of right of pre-emption would not arise.

Comment: The purpose of section 22 is to give a preferential right to class I heirs to seek transfer of property in his or her name when the other co-heirs propose to sell it so that the property remains in the hands of co-heirs rather than going to strangers. This right, however, is confined only to Class I heirs specified in the schedule.

Karnataka Amendment and Married Daughter's Right

Nanjamma v. State of Karnataka,
1999 AlHC 3003 (Kant): ILR 1999 Kant 1094

Issue: Is section 6A(d) of the Karnataka amendment of the Hindu Succession Act, denying equal rights to daughters married prior to the amendment, violative of article 14 of the Constitution?

Facts: Under section 6A of the Hindu Succession (Karnataka Amendment) Act, 1994, a daughter becomes a coparcener by birth in a joint Hindu family governed by *Mitakshara* law, in the same manner as the son, and has the same rights in the coparcenary property as she would have had if she had been a son, inclusive of the right to claim by survivorship, and is subject to the same liabilities and disabilities in respect thereto as the son. Further, upon partition of the joint Hindu family, the daughter gets an equal share in the property as the son. However, by virtue of clause (d) of section 6A, daughters married prior to the commencement of the Act have been excluded; thus such daughters have been denied the right to claim the share in the coparcenary property as was available to unmarried daughters or to a daughter married after the amendment. Thus, while daughters married after the amendment have a right to claim share in the property, those married prior to the amendment have been deprived. This provision was challenged as being *ultra vires* article 14 of the Constitution which confers the right of equality.

Order: It was argued that married daughters, irrespective of the date of marriage, are a class in themselves and so there should be no discrimination based on the date of marriage. This argument was not accepted and the court remarked (at p. 3005):

> "The principle of equality as guaranteed by article 14 of the Constitution does not mean that every law must have universal application for all persons who are not by nature, attainment or circumstances in the same position, as the varying needs of different classes of persons are found to be requiring separate treatment. Classification is permissible for legitimate purposes."

Consequently, it was held that the impugned clause was neither irrational nor unfair. Before the amendment Act, when daughters had no legal right in the coparcenary properties, the married daughters used to get some share in the property by way of gift, or dowry, etc. It was, therefore, a reasonable classification intended to avoid reopening of the partitions which had been made earlier. Extending the benefit of the Act to a daughter married prior to the Act would unsettle things settled long back in the family. It could be chaotic, affecting not only the rights of the brothers and sisters already settled, but also affect third parties who might have acquired valid rights and title in the property on the basis of the existing law.

Comment: It is significant that realising the discrimination against females by excluding them from coparcenary, some States, by amendment in the Hindu Succession Act, 1956, extended the right by birth to daughters as well (Andhra Pradesh, Tamil Nadu, Maharashtra and Karnataka). The Kerala law entirely abolished the joint Hindu family system by an amendment in 1975. In the context of section 6A(d) of the Karnataka Act (the provision is the same under the Tamil Nadu, Andhra Pradesh and Maharashtra amendments also), which was challenged, the interpretation of the court is expedient and logical. While it might cause hardship or loss to daughters already married at the time of the amendment, yet, viewed practically, if their rights were to be conceded, it would have given rise to insurmountable problems and flood of litigations.

Note: The amendment of the Hindu Succession Act – The Hindu Succession (Amendment) Act, 2005 – provides for equal eights to females in the properties so all discussions prior to this have only academic value now.

Married Daughter's Right to Claim Compensation in Case of Parent's Death

Naraini Bai v. State of Haryana,
AIR 2004 P&H 206: 2004 (17) All Ind Cas 367:
2004 (1) Hindu LR 478

Issue: Can the Government deny payment of compensation in relation to parents who were killed during the 1984 riots, to their married daughter?

Facts: The Government of Haryana took a policy decision to pay *ex gratia* compensation to the heirs of those killed in the 1984 riots. The petitioner brother (son of the deceased) was given fifty per cent. compensation of ₹ 1,65,000 for each of the deceased parents (mother and father who were killed in the riots) but payment of balance fifty percent. compensation was denied to the daughter. Succession certificate was furnished by her as well as by her brother, which showed her as heir of the deceased parents. She was denied the compensation on two counts *viz;* that she was married and in fact, that she was already married before the 1984 riots, and *secondly,* that she did not furnish the succession certificate along with her application.

Order: It was argued on her behalf that the denial was arbitrary, as under section 8 and section 15 of the Hindu Succession Act she was a class I heir as mentioned in the schedule attached to section 8, and also an heir as mentioned in section 15(1)(a) of the Act. It was further contended, that she had attached a copy of the order granting succession certificate and her brother too had furnished succession certificate showing her to be an heir, so there was no justification for refiling the succession certificate by her separately. The arguments of the Senior Deputy Advocate General, Haryana Government were that despite opportunity being granted to her, she never filed succession certificate, and moreover, she was already married before the 1984 riots. These arguments were rejected by the court and it was held that the brother's succession certificate showed her as one of the legal heirs and that was sufficient; *secondly,* under section 8 of the Hindu Succession Act, the Parliament has not made any distinction between an unmarried daughter and a married daughter. Thus, a married daughter is also a class I heir entitled to succeed to the property of her deceased father who died intestate in terms of section 8. Also, section 15(1)(a) of the Hindu Succession Act, categorically states that property of a female Hindu dying intestate would devolve, firstly upon sons and daughters and husband.......... . Thus, the petitioner, though married, is entitled to succeed to properties of the deceased mother.

The court further clarified that 'compensation' stands covered within the meaning of property in sections 8 and 15 of the Hindu Succession Act.

The State was accordingly ordered to pay to the daughter, the amount of compensation due to her within one month, with interest.

Comment: A daughter, upon marriage, does not cease to be a daughter for purposes of entitlement to the compensation in respect of the unfortunate death of her parents in the 1984 riots. The provision of the Hindu Succession Act make no distinction between a married daughter and an unmarried daughter.

Married Daughter's Parents Right to Claim Compensation in Case of Daughter's Death

Ganny Kaur v. *State,*
AIR 2007 Del 273: 2008 (1) AKant (NOC) 44: 2007 (142) DLT 35

Issue: The pertinent issues involved in the case were (i) would the parents of a married girl be eligible to claim compensation for her death? And

(ii) would the law of succession or inheritance apply to determine heirship for claim of compensation amount?

Facts: It was a goose bumps raising case where a family of four, wife, husband and two kids aged 4 and 2, were burnt alive by the mob in the notorious 1984 riots. The only relatives who survived were the mother of the deceased wife and the father of the deceased husband. The Government of NCT Delhi announced an *ex gratia* payment for the next-of-kin of the dead, initially ₹ 10,000 but later raised to ₹ 20,000. This was claimed and taken by the father of the deceased husband, respondent 3 in the case. After some time, the government directed the NCT to pay ₹ 3-5 lakhs to family members of the deceased. The petitioner mother then filed a claim but the authorities were not inclined to pay anything to her with respect to death of her daughter and two grand children. She thereupon filed a writ petition. The father of the deceased husband approached her and the matter was compromised so the writ petition was withdrawn. On 16-1-2006 the Government of India, through the Ministry of Home Affairs, informed, *inter alia,* the Chief Secretary of the NCT of Delhi that payment of *ex gratia* amount of ₹ 3-5 lakhs in each case of death, would be granted in addition to amounts already paid by respective State Governments; however, only those who had earlier received the *ex gratia* were eligible for the enhanced amount. The petitioner was accordingly informed that she was not entitled. Respondent 3 claimed the entire amount. The petitioner contended that she and the respondent were on equal footing, both having lost their child and grand-children; further that section 15 of the Hindu Succession Act, 1956 which mentions the rules of succession to the property of a female Hindu dying intestate whereunder the heirs of the husband are placed on a higher footing than the parents of the girl makes no mention of compensation on account of death of a female. After detailed analysis of legal provisions and case-law, the court came to the conclusion that compensation awarded in respect of the 1984 riots cannot be equated with estate of the intestate which devolves as per principles of succession and inheritance under law. Compensation in question was never a part of property held by the deceased and therefore there is no question of any succession or inheritance of the same.

Order: It was held that both the mother of the wife and the father of the son were equally entitled to the *ex gratia* compensation, *viz.*, 7 lakhs each. If compensation were to be granted only to respondent 3 then it would run counter to all principles of fairness and equity and would mean that State as well as courts give recognition to rights of parents of husband but non to parents of wife. The following observations are pertinent:

> "The *ex gratia* compensation that is provided by the State is not under any personal law but under secular laws of the State governed by the principles enshrined in the Constitution of India and in particular, article 21 thereof because there has been loss of life which it was duty of the State to have protected. When the compensation is provided by the State, the State is blind to the religion of the parties as also their personal laws that may be followed by them based on their religion. The State has to provide compensation so as to assuage the hurt, both financial as well as mental which the surviving members of the family feel every day of their lives..."

In this case the pain and loss suffered by both the parties was in no way different and hence eligibility for claim of *ex gratia* compensation too was equal.

Comment: A very unfortunate case but fair interpretation! Since amount by way of compensation in a tragic death cannot be equated with part of estate of the deceased who dies intestate the principles under the law of inheritance/succession cannot be invoked. Death of a daughter – even married daughter – causes equal pain and misery as that of a son; the deprivation is no different either, whether or not the parents are dependent on her. Upon marriage of daughter, parents do not divest themselves of their responsibility to look after her well being nor *vice versa*. A daughter is as caring as she possibly can be under her circumstances. The traditional view of giving away daughter at time of marriage for all times to come does not hold good any more, as rightly contended in the case. However, the blatant discrimination that exists in section 15(1) of the Hindu Succession Act whereunder heirs of the husband are placed on a higher footing than even the deceased female's own mother and father needs serious thought. It is unfortunate that in a recent case, in *Om Prakash* v. *Radhacharan*, (2009) 7 SCALE 51 where the case concededly was unfortunate and hard specially in view of its peculiar facts, the Apex Court made a strong plea for amendment of the provisions. In fact the law even as it exists could have been construed in a manner so as to be fair, equitable and logical but the court missed this opportunity.

INDIAN SUCCESSION ACT

Repeal of Travancore Christian Succession Act

Mary Roy v. State of Kerala,
AIR 1986 SC 1011: (1986) 2 SCC 209: 1986 (2) Supreme 296

Issue: The issue involved was the repeal of the Travancore Christian Succession Act, 1916, by the Indian Succession Act, 1925, in view of the Part B States (Laws) Act, 1951.

Facts: It was a writ petition under article 32 of the Constitution, challenging the discriminatory provisions of the Travancore Christian Succession Act, 1916. This Act was promulgated by the Maharaja of Travancore and had provisions which were discriminatory against women. Under sections 16, 17, 21 and 22, a widow was entitled to have only a life-interest in the properties of an intestate and this interest was limited as it terminated at death or re-marriage. A daughter was entitled to one-fourth of the value of the share of the sons or ₹ 5,000 whichever was less. Even to this amount the daughter was not entitled, if *stridhanam* was paid or promised to her by the intestate. However, *stridhanam* promised but not paid by the intestate became a charge on his property.

Apart from challenging the constitutional validity of the Travancore Christian Succession Act it was also contended on behalf of the petitioners that in view of the Part B States (Laws) Act, 1951, the Indian Succession Act, 1925, has been extended to these areas and the impugned Act stood repealed. Under the Indian Succession Act, a widow is entitled to one-third share in the property of the intestate and sons and daughters share equally in the remainder.

The Parliament had passed the Part B States (Laws) Act with a view to provide for uniformity of legislation in the country. It provided for extension of some statutes to Part B states and the Indian Succession Act, 1925, was one of those Acts. This Act consolidated the laws applicable to intestate and testamentary succession and repealed many statutes dealing with the subject which were in force at that time.

The Supreme Court did not go into the issue of violation of the right of equality in the matter of succession and inheritance but held that the Travancore Succession Act stood repealed by the Indian Succession Act in, 1951 when, under section 3 of the Part B States (Laws) Act the same was extended to Part B States. The issues considered by the court were:

(i) Whether after the coming into force of the Part B States (Laws) Act the Travancore Christian Succession Act continued to govern intestate succession to the property of a member of the Indian Christian Community in the territories originally forming part of the erstwhile State of Travancore or is such intestate succession governed by the Indian Succession Act; and if it continues to be governed by the Travancore Christian Succession Act whether sections 24, 28 and 29 of the Act were unconstitutional and void as being violative of article 14 of the Constitution.

(ii) Whether the Travancore Christian Succession Act comes within the ambit of "such other law" in section 29(2) of the Indian Succession Act (which is the saving clause), and is saved.

It was contended on behalf of the respondents that section 29(2) of the Indian Succession Act saved the provisions of the Travancore Act and therefore, despite the extension of the former Act to Part B State of Travancore-Cochin, the Travancore Act continued to apply to the Christians in those territories.

Order: After referring to several cases, the court held that the Travancore Act was not saved by section 29(2) of the Indian Succession Act, and hence stood repealed. Thus, the Indian Succession Act is applicable throughout the State of Kerala and in Kanyakumari District of Tamil Nadu. This is so with effect from April 1, 1951.

Comment: The judgment in the case is retrospective as the Travancore Act has been held to be repealed from April, 1951. A review petition by the Kerala Government in the Supreme Court for setting aside the retrospective effect of the judgment was dismissed (on July 18, 1986).

Testamentary Dispositions – Discriminatory Provisions are *ultra vires* Constitution

John Vallamattom v. Union of India,
AIR 2003 SC 2902: 2003 AIR SCW 3536: (2003) 6 SCC 611

Issue: Section 118 of the Indian Succession Act which restricts the manner of testamentary dispositions of property amongst Christians is violative of article 14 of the Constitution.

Facts: Under section 118 of the Indian Succession Act, 1925, "No man having a nephew or niece or a nearer relative shall have power to bequeath any property to religious or charitable uses except by a Will executed not less than twelve months before his death and deposited within six months from its execution, in some place provided by law for the safe custody of the Wills of living persons". This section does not apply to a Parsi *vide* an amendment in 1991. In this case, the constitutional validity of the section was challenged as being violative of articles 14 and 15 of the Constitution on the following grounds, *viz.*, it discriminates (i) against Christians and non-Christians, (ii) against testamentary dispositions by a Christian *versus* non-testamentary dispositions, (iii) against religious and charitable use of property as against all other uses including undesirable uses or purposes, (iv) against a Christian who has a nephew, niece or a near relative and a Christian having no relative, (v) against a Christian dying within 12 months of executing the Will.

It was also contended that citizens in India are entitled to live with basic human dignity that includes a freedom to dispose of their property; freedom to choose a legatee; and also freedom to choose the purpose for which the property can be utilised under a Will and section 118 obstructs that. And further, that it is an integral part of the Christian faith to contribute for religious and charitable purposes as prescribed in Canon law of the Code of Canons of the Eastern Churches and the teachings of the Holy Bible. Section 118 of the Succession Act, violates articles 25 and 26 of the Constitution.

For the *Union of India*, it was contended that—(i) section 118 is a pre-Constitution enactment and remains in force, (ii) Christians are a separate and distinct class and cannot be treated on equal footing with Muslims and Hindus with respect to bequests for religious and charitable purposes; and (iii) marriage, divorce and succession are secular matters and cannot be treated as part of articles 25 or 26 of the Constitution.

Order: After considering the law, facts and arguments of the parties, the Court came to the following conclusions:

(i) As per article 372 of the Constitution, all laws in force in the territory of India immediately before the commencement of the Constitution shall continue in force; this however, is not an absolute rule. Under article 13(1) laws inconsistent with or in derogation of the fundamental rights, shall, to the extent of such inconsistency, be void.

(ii) As per the majority judgment, section 118 of the Succession Act was held to be unconstitutional for being in violation of article 14 of the Constitution, because:

(a) The restrictions therein are peculiar to Christians; there is no such restriction for persons belonging to other religions.

(b) The argument that Christians formed a class by themselves was not accepted as there was no justifiable reason for holding that the classification made was either based on the *intelligible differentia* or the same had any nexus with the object sought to be achieved.

(c) If the purpose of the provision was to protect the interests of near relations against death-bed gifts, restricting death-bed gifts only for religious or charitable purpose was discriminatory.

(d) Even if the purpose behind the impugned provision was to prevent bequest of property under religious influence, there was no justification in restricting testamentary disposition for charitable purposes.

(e) There was no rationale in the classification between a testator who survives beyond twelve months and a testator who does not. The testators constitute a homogenous class and they cannot be divided arbitrarily on the basis of duration of their survival which is unrelated to the purpose of executing a Will. Thus, the period of 12 months had no nexus with the object of performing a philanthropic act.

 (iii) As to article 15, the court held that there was no violation of article 15(1) since the discrimination forbidden by article 15(1), confers a right which is individual in nature. A statute and the impugned provision restricts the right of a class of citizens who may belong to a particular religion, and therefore, not attract the wrath of article 15(1).

 (iv) In the context of article 25 of the Constitution, the court held that this article confers a right to profess, propagate and practice one's religion and that means the freedom of conscience be supplemented by freedom of unhampered expression of spiritual conviction. A disposition towards making gifts for charitable or religious purpose may be a pious act of a person but not an integral part of a religion (at p. 2912).

    J., Lakshmanan, however, dissented. According to him (at p. 2912), the contribution for religious and charitable purpose is a philanthropic act intended to serve humanity at large and is also recognised as a religious obligation. Therefore, bequeathing property for religious and charitable purpose cannot be controlled or restricted by the Legislature as it would offend the fundamental rights of the testator under articles 25 and 26 of the Constitution.

 (v) The court also commented on article 44 of the Constitution and the desirability of having a uniform civil code. It expressed regret that article 44 of the Constitution which states that the State shall endeavour to secure for the citizens a uniform civil code throughout the territory of India, has not been given effect to.

In view of all the above, the impugned provision was declared unconstitutional. As remarked by Justice S.B. Sinha (at p. 2916): "The whole case is based upon undue, harsh and special burden on Christian institutions alone and a substantive restriction is based on uncertain events over which the testator has no control."

Comment: A provision which imposes irrational restrictions on people belonging to a particular religion, in respect of testamentary disposition of their property, is discriminatory and so *ultra vires* article 14 of the Constitution.

SUSPICIOUS CIRCUMSTANCE

Unequal Distribution in a Will *per se* is not Suspicious Circumstance

Sridevi v. *Jayaraja Shetty,*
AIR 2005 SC 780: 2005 AIR SCW 605: (2005) 2 SCC 784

Issue: Would an unequal distribution of properties in a Will, *per se*, be a suspicious circumstance so as to invalidate the Will?

Facts: This was a case under section 63 of the Succession Act, 1925, challenging a Will on the ground of suspicious circumstances surrounding the same.

The testator had three daughters and four sons. Property was bequeathed in favour of two sons, and daughters were excluded. Reasons were given for making the unequal distribution in the Will, *viz.*, that the daughters and other two sons were earlier given their share during partition of the property.

The scribe had categorically stated in his testimony that the Will was scribed by him at the dictation of the testator; the two attesting witnesses had deposed that the testator had signed the Will in their presence while in sound disposing state of mind, after understanding the nature and effect of dispositions made by him. The Will was written in six pages and the testator had signed each of the six pages. Handwriting expert compared the signatures of the testator with his admitted signatures. Thus, it could be said that the Will had been duly executed. The mere fact that the testator was aged 80 years and died 15 days after the execution of the Will could not be taken as a suspicious circumstance.

Order: The appeal filed by the plaintiffs challenging the Will was dismissed. The fact that there was unequal distribution of the properties under the Will was duly explained and justified *viz.*, the heirs who were left out in the Will had already been given share at the time of partition.

Comment: A Will is a sacred document; a Will which is surrounded by suspicious circumstances is not a valid Will. The burden of proving genuineness is on the propounder. Unequal distribution, *per se*, is not a suspicious circumstance.

CUSTOMARY LAW

Custom is an important source of law and under the Hindu law specially, it has played a significant role. The Hindu Marriage Act, 1955 specifically saves customs regarding marriage and divorce from the operation of the Act (section 29 of the Act). Apart from this specific provision, there are references to saving of customs in various other sections also *e.g.*, customs permitting marriage within *sapinda* relationship which is otherwise barred under the provisions of the Hindu Marriage Act. The Hindu Adoptions and Maintenance Act, 1956 also saves customs in respect of adoptions. The essentials of a valid custom are:

(i) It should be ancient or of long standing;

(ii) It should be in continual use; once it is discontinued, it comes to an end;

(iii) It should be clear and unambiguous;

(iv) It should be reasonable;

(v) It should not be opposed to public policy;

(vi) It should not be expressly forbidden by any law.

This section refers to select significant cases where customary law has been invoked.

Marriage under Customary Law: No Religious Rites Required

Sumitra Devi v. Bhikan Choudhary,
AIR 1985 SC 765: 1985 Cr LJ 528: (1985) 1 SCC 637

Issue: The issue involved in the case was whether performance of religious rites is mandatory where a marriage is performed under customary law where there is no such requirement and the marriage is legally acceptable notwithstanding absence of any religious rites.

Facts: This was a wife's application for maintenance under the provisions of section 125 Cr. P.C. for herself and a minor daughter. Her allegations were that the fact that husband was already married and his spouse was living, was not known to her at the time of marriage and after discovery of this fact the relations between her and her husband became strained; he neglected her and the child and refused to maintain them. The husband on the other hand pleaded that the marriage was void; he alleged that his wife was three months pregnant by some other man, at the time of marriage with him and this fact was suppressed by the father of the wife; that after discovery of this fact he did not want to live with her; he also doubted whether the daughter was his. The Sub-Divisional Judicial Magistrate, after examining the evidence produced held that the parties were spouses and the child was born to them; accordingly he ordered separate maintenance for both. On husband's appeal the Additional Sessions Judge reversed the order holding that she had failed to establish the factum of marriage. Her revision against this order, to the High Court was also dismissed. Hence her present appeal by special leave, before the Apex Court.

Order: The husband's defence was that the marriage was void on two accounts, *viz.*, suppression of fact of the wife's pre-marriage pregnancy and further, due to non-performance of religious rites. The Supreme Court acceded that a valid traditional Hindu marriage requires performance of certain religious rites and ceremonies but observed that it is equally true that there can be a marriage acceptable in law according to customs which do not insist on performance of such rites. The Additional Sessions Judge and the High Court adopted a very technical approach, the court observed. Also, these courts did not refer to the fact that the parties lived together for about a decade and all public records are indicative of their relationship as husband and wife. Since there was no mention or reference to the form of marriage in the orders of the lower courts, the Supreme Court remitted the case to the Trial Court for fresh inquiry to lead further evidence in support of the respective stands of the parties in relation to factum of the marriage. The Court also pointed out that under section 125 Cr. P.C. even an illegitimate child is entitled to maintenance so even if the marriage is not recognised the child would still be entitled to maintenance. The court, however, clarified that "our saying so may not be construed as a conclusion against the factum of marriage or as a suggestion that the child is illegitimate. We have no intention to say either way".

Comment: Insistence on strict technicalities in performance of marriage at times leads to undue delay and injustice. When customary law permit marriage without observance of religious rites and ceremonies and there are ample other circumstances indicative of factum of marriage, justice demands a liberal and expeditious approach. In any case, proceedings under section 125 Cr. P.C are summary in nature so strict compliance of technicalities could probably be dispensed with.

Children of Marriage which is Valid under Customary Law are Legitimate

M. Govindaraju v. *K. Munisami Gounder,* AIR 1997 SC 10: 1996 AIR SCW 4157: (1996) 5 SCC 467

Issue: Is a child born out of a relationship which is recognised as marriage under a caste custom, legitimate in the eye of the law?

Facts: The parties belonged to the *Shudra* caste who are governed by their customs in matters of marriage and divorce. The wife walked out of the marriage which was irreversible, as neither of them approached each other for reconciliation. The wife then started living with another man and a child was born from that relationship. Paternity of the child was acknowledged and he was treated as the son of his father. The son filed a suit for share in the joint Hindu family property owned by his father but the same was rejected on the ground that when he was begotten, there was no valid marriage between his mother and father. The High Court branded the child as illegitimate of his parents with no right to claim partition in joint family property. On appeal, the Supreme Court pointed out that the High Court had overlooked the caste factor which was very significant in the case. Under the custom of the caste to which the parties belonged, if a woman is turned out or leaves the house and is not brought back as wife, it is treated as divorce and the spouses are free to rearrange their lives with another partner. In this case, since there was no reconciliation and the woman entered into a relationship with another man, the divorce was held to be complete and the subsequent marriage valid.

Order: The High Court order holding that the child was illegitimate of the other man since there was no legal marriage between him and the mother, and therefore not entitled to joint family properties, was set aside. The parties, according to the Supreme Court had a valid marriage relationship as the earlier marriage of the wife (child's mother) stood dissolved under a caste custom.

Comment: While caste customs need to be given due respect, it is important to ensure that they do not become a tool for bypassing statutory laws.

Tribal Parties, no Custom Established to Prove Second Marriage as Void: Husband not Liable to be Prosecuted for Bigamy

Dr. Surajmani Stella Kujur v. Durga Charan Hansdah, (2001) I Femi – Juris CC 96 (SC): AIR 2001 SC 938: 2001 AIR SCW 711

Issue: The issue involved in the case was whether under the customary law which governed the parties to the marriage, bigamy was an offence or not.

Facts: The parties were, admittedly, tribals professing Hinduism – the wife an Oraon and husband a Santhal. However, their marriage was out of the purview of the Hindu Marriage Act in view of section 2(2) of the Act which says:

> "Notwithstanding anything contained in sub-section (1) nothing contained in this Act shall apply to the members of any Scheduled Tribe within the meaning of clause (25) of article 366 of the Constitution, unless the Central Government, by notification in the Official Gazette otherwise directs."

The parties in this case were governed by their *Santhal* customs and usage. The appellant wife's case was that the husband had solemnised a second marriage during the subsistence of the first marriage with her, and the second marriage being void, he is liable to be prosecuted for the offence of bigamy punishable under section 494 of the Indian Penal Code. The wife relied upon an alleged custom of the tribe which mandates monogamy as a rule. However, nowhere in the complaint did she refer to any alleged custom having the force of law, which prohibits the solemnization of the second marriage. It is significant to note that for a custom or usage to have the force of law, it is necessary that the party relying on it must prove that such custom is ancient, certain and reasonable, and not opposed to public policy.

The wife's complaint before the Chief Metropolitan Magistrate was dismissed and so also her appeal to the High Court. Hence the present appeal before the Supreme Court.

Order: Dismissing her appeal, the court held that mere pleading of a custom enjoining monogamy is not enough unless it is further established that the second marriage is void by reason of its having taken place during the subsistence of an earlier marriage. In order to prove that the second marriage was void, the complainant is under an obligation to show the existence of a custom which made such marriage *null*, ineffectual, having no force of law or binding effect, incapable of being enforced in law or *non est*. The fact of second marriage being void is *sine qua non* for the applicability of section 494 of the I.P.C. The complainant could not prove any such custom which renders the second marriage void.

It was accordingly held that in the absence of notification in terms of sub-section (2) of section 2 of the Hindu Marriage Act, no case for prosecution for the offence of bigamy was made out by the respondent because the alleged second marriage cannot be termed to be void under the Act or under any alleged custom having the force of law.

Comment: While section 29 of the Hindu Marriage Act protects customs, it is necessary to prove the alleged custom.

Absence of Material on Record: Case Remanded to Ascertain Prevalence of Custom

Yamanaji H. Jadhav v. *Nirmala,*
AIR 2002 SC 971: 2002 AIR SCW 674: (2002) 2 SCC 637

Issue: Can a document purported to be a divorce deed obtained by wife's consent and with her signatures as per customary law, be recognised as legal divorce in the absence of material on record or any pleading establishing such custom?

Facts: A husband allegedly, obtained a customary divorce; according to him the divorce deed had her signatures and she had consented to the divorce. The wife filed a suit for declaration that the divorce deed was obtained by the husband by coercion; she therefore sought cancellation of the same. The husband denied allegation of fraud and coercion and stated that she had willingly signed the deed. The Trial Court and the lower appellate court ruled in favour of the husband; however the High Court reversed the order and held that there was no divorce. Hence the husbands present appeal before the Supreme Court.

Order: Dismissing the appeal, the Supreme Court held that Hindu law does not recognise divorce except when the same is allowed by custom (or under the statutory law). In this case there was neither material on record nor pleading of parties showing prevalence of any such customary divorce in the community based on which the divorce document was obtained. The Court observed (p. 972):

> Public policy, good morals and the interests of society require and ensure that, if at all, severance should be allowed only in the manner and for reasons or cause specified in law. Thus, such a custom being an exception to the general law of divorce ought to have been specifically pleaded and established by the party propounding such custom. Since such custom is contrary to the law of land, and which if not proved will be a practice opposed to the public policy.

The case was consequently remanded to Trial Court to ascertain the existence of alleged custom.

Comment: Since divorce is a serious matter, courts require that the existence of a custom which is relied upon, should be cogently established. *See* also *Savitri Devi* v. *Manorama Bai,* AIR 1998 MP 114: 1998 (1) Hindu LR 544: 1998 (1) MPLJ 254; *Jatina Samir Shah* v. *Samir Mohit Shah,* AIR 2009 (NOC) 2149 (Bom).

"Arrangement to Live Separately" is not Divorce Unless such Custom Pleaded or Established

Bauramma v. *Siddappa Jeevappa Patarad,* AIR 2003 Kant 342: ILR 2003 (1) Kant 579: 2003 (1) Kant LJ 581

Issue: Can "an arrangement to live separately" be treated as a "divorce deed"?

Facts: A wife filed an application for maintenance under section 18 of Hindu Adoptions and Maintenance Act. The parties were married in 1966 and the claim was made by the wife in 1995. She claimed past maintenance also. She pleaded desertion and alleged that the husband had another wife and they both ill-treated her and threw her out of the house. The husband resisted the application on the ground that their marriage had been dissolved by consent as per "an arrangement to live separately", and in terms of the provision of section 18 of the Hindu Adoptions and Maintenance Act a claim for maintenance can be made only when there is a subsisting marriage. The Trial Court held that there was no desertion by the husband and *secondly,* she being divorced was not entitled to maintenance under the provisions of the Hindu Adoptions and Maintenance Act. Hence the wife's appeal.

Order: It was held that second marriage by itself is desertion of the first wife and that fact having been proved, no further proof of desertion was required. Besides, "an arrangement to live separately", even assuming that it is proved, could not have the effect of bringing the marriage to an end. Such agreement was, allegedly, entered into long after the enactment of the Hindu Marriage Act. According to the court (at p. 344) "a marriage in law can be dissolved only by a method recognised in law and not otherwise". The so-called arrangement sought to be passed off as a "divorce-deed" could not, *firstly*, be treated as a divorce, and *secondly*, after the coming into force of the Hindu Marriage Act, a marriage could be dissolved only under the provisions of the Act or exceptionally, under custom permitting divorce. In this case there was no assertion by the husband that there was a divorce under a custom prevalent in the community to which they belonged. The marriage was thus held to be subsisting and the wife's claim tenable and *bona fide*. She was, however, not entitled to past maintenance but only to maintenance with effect from the date of her application.

Comment: While maintenance under the provisions of the Hindu Marriage Act can be claimed only when there are or have been proceedings under that Act under the Hindu Adoptions and Maintenance Act a wife can seek maintenance only when the relationship of husband and wife is legally subsisting. A marriage cannot be said to have been dissolved unless it is dissolved under the provisions of the Hindu Marriage Act or by a custom pleaded and recognised in the community to which the parties belong. Also, when second marriage of a husband is established, no further proof of desertion is required. See also *Vishnu Kumar* v. *State of Uttar Pradesh*, 2006 (65) ALR 888 (All): AIR 2007 All 31: 2007 (1) ALJ 152 where it was held that a settlement deed between the parties cannot be accepted as a decree of divorce.

Divorce under Custom – No need to go to Court when Custom Proved

Jasbir Singh v. *Inderjit Kaur*, AIR 2003 P&H 317: 2003 (2) Hindu LR 654: 2004 (1) Marri LJ 175

Issue: When a divorce has been obtained by a legally recognised custom applicable to the parties, do the parties need to go to court for obtaining a divorce? Whether re-marriage after customary divorce is legal and valid?

Facts: Section 29 of the Hindu Marriage Act, 1955 explicitly saves customs regarding marriage and divorce from the operation of the Act and these customs are legally recognised. In this case, a husband sought annulment of his marriage on the ground that at the time of marriage, his wife was already married. The wife's contention was that she had obtained a customary divorce from her previous husband and the petitioner was aware of this as he had seen the written deed of customary divorce; he was therefore estopped from taking the plea that the wife was already married. The wife was a Jat Sikh from district Sangrur in Punjab.

Order: After going through the evidence, the court held that it was established that there is a custom among the Jat Sikhs of Sangrur district which permits divorce and the wife had, indeed obtained the divorce according to the custom. The validity of the custom being saved, it was not necessary for the parties to go to court to obtain divorce on grounds of recognised custom; it is open to the parties to dissolve the marriage out of court, in accordance with the custom. The court relied, *inter alia*, on *Gurdit Singh* v. *Angrez Kaur*, AIR 1968 SC 142: (1967) 2 SCR 789, where the Supreme Court held that there can be valid divorce where custom allows dissolution and on dissolution of a marriage by custom, the party can enter into second marriage in the life-time of the first divorced spouse. The husband's petition for annulment was consequently dismissed as the wife having obtained customary divorce form her previous husband, the marriage with the petitioner was held to be legal and valid.

Comment: When a divorce has been effected under a recognised custom, the parties can remarry and such marriage would be legal and valid.

Note: *See* also *Rita Rani* v. *Ramesh Kumar*, (1995) 2 HLR 338 (P&H): (1995) 2 Punj LR 434: AIR 1995 P&H 337; *Balwinder Singh* v. *Gurpal Kaur*, AIR 1985 Del 14: I (1985) DMC 35: (1985) 1 Hindu LR 369.

Mizo Customary Law
Germanthangi v. *F. Rokunga*,
AIR 2004 Gau 42: 2005 (1) Gau LR 338:
2004 (2) Marri LJ 145 (Aizawl Bench)

Issue: Customary laws have a legal sanction and this was a case for distribution of properties between the spouses, under the Mizo customary law.

Facts: A wife filed a petition for distribution of properties on the ground of desertion by the husband by way of 'abandonment' as per Mizo customary law. According to this law, there is the custom of a husband 'abandoning' his wife which is known as *'Nupui Tlansan'* in Mizo language. 'Abandonment' is defined by N.E. Passy in his monograph on *Lushai Customs and Ceremonies*, as follows:

> "If a man abandons his wife and family and goes away, the house, field and all the property belonging to him becomes his wife's property. His children also go to his wife and she will get marriage price of their daughter. If after a year he tries to return to his wife, his wife can take him back or not as she likes. If she refuses to take him back she is entitled to keep the house, property and the children."

Another compilation of Mizo customary law by Mizo District Council (Mizo Hnam Dan) was also referred to, which says:

> "Section 59—*Abandonment of family*: If a man abandons his wife and family and if that has been accepted as such by a court, his house,

property and children shall go to his wife who will receive marriage price of female children performing all the duties of father when they marry. If the husband returns after three years, the wife can refuse to take him back and in such cases she is entitled to have the house, property and the children of her husband. Abandonment implies to turn away from and also to stop taking care of the wife."

In this case the husband contested the wife's suit and contended that he had not married the other lady but had accepted her only as his mistress without divorcing his wife. There was no cause of action seeking distribution of property, according to him.

The Trial Court held that a case of 'abandonment' had been established and passed a decree distributing the property. On appeal by the husband, the first appellate court held that there was no abandonment. Hence the wife's appeal to the High Court.

Order: The court found that there was 'abandonment' of the wife by the husband since almost five years. During the pendency of the appeal, the husband took the plea of gift and sale of properties in favour of the son. The court held that any gift or sale during pendency of suit has no legal validity. The wife is entitled to the properties from the date of abandonment and her right cannot be defeated by subsequent transfer if customary law of 'abandonment' is to be enforced in its letter and spirit, the court ruled.

Comment: When there is a clear recognised custom in the community to which the parties belong, then those customs will prevail and the parties will be governed by them. Under the Mizo customary law, as discussed in this case, an 'abandonment' is not divorce as is understood in common parlance but just running away and leaving the family to their fate. In such case, the custom is explicit that the properties, house, field and children go to the wife.

Alleged Divorce by Registered Document "*chhor chithi*" – Custom not Proved

Ramesh Chandra Ram Pratap Daga v. *Rameshwari Ramesh Chandra Daga*,
(2005) 2 SCC 33: AIR 2005 SC 422: 2004 AIR SCW 6990

Issues: (i) Can there be a legal divorce on the basis of a registered document of "*chhor chithi*" when such customary divorce is not established?

(ii) Is a wife whose marriage has been declared null and void, entitled to maintenance under the provision of section 25, Hindu Marriage Act?

Facts: The husband was an income-tax practitioner. He was first married in 1963 and had three children. After the death of his wife, he remarried. The dispute involved the issue of validity of the second marriage which the husband denied. The second wife was previously married but no divorce decree was obtained from any court. However, according to the wife, in accordance with the prevalent custom in the Maheshwari Community to which the parties belonged, a *'chhor chithi'* or a document of dissolution of marriage was executed between her previous husband which document was also later got registered. This document was shown to the husband before marriage. The parties lived together for nine years after marriage and also had a daughter. The wife alleged that she was ill-treated due to non-fulfilment of his demands by her father and driven out of the house. She thereafter filed proceedings in the Family Court at Bombay for a grant of decree of judicial separation and maintenance. The husband filed a counter-petition seeking declaration of his second marriage with the present wife as nullity under section 11 coupled with section 5(i) of the Hindu Marriage Act, on the ground that on the date of the second marriage, her previous marriage had not been dissolved by any court in accordance with the provisions of the Hindu Marriage Act. He also disputed the paternity of the daughter. The Family Court granted the wife's petition for judicial separation as also maintenance for the wife and child, and dismissed the counter-petition of the husband seeking declaration that the marriage was null and void.

On appeal against this by the husband, the High Court held that the first marriage of the present wife with her previous husband having not been dissolved by any decree of the court, her second marriage was in contravention of section 5(i) of the Act and had to be declared as nullity under section 11 of the Act. The decree of judicial separation granted by the Family Court was, consequently, set aside. The order granting maintenance was, however, upheld.

The following observations of the court in *Krishnakant* v. *Reena,* 1999 (1) Mah LJ 388: AIR 1999 Bom 127: 1999 (2) Hindu LR 479 were referred to:

> "The Hindu Marriage Act is a piece of social welfare legislation regulating the marital relations of Hindus consistently with their customary law *i.e.,* Hindu law. The object behind section 24 of the Act providing for maintenance *pendente lite* to a party in matrimonial proceedings is obviously to provide financial assistance to the indigent spouse to maintain herself or himself during the pendency of the proceedings and also have sufficient funds to carry on the litigation so that the spouse does not unduly suffer in the conduct of the case for want of funds. The words 'wife' or 'husband' used in section 24 of the Act include a man and a woman who have gone through the ceremony of Hindu marriage which would have been valid but for the provisions of section 11 read with clause (i) of section 5 of the Hindu Marriage Act. These words have been used as convenient terms to refer to the parties who have gone though a ceremony of marriage whether or not that marriage is valid or subsisting just as word marriage has been used in the Act to include a purported marriage which is void *ab initio*.

Both appealed against the order of High Court—the wife against declaration of the marriage as null and void and the husband against the order granting maintenance. For the husband there were lengthy arguments in support of his contention that where a marriage is declared to be null and void by grant of a decree, no maintenance order under section 25 can be made in favour of the unsuccessful party. Reliance was placed on *Nazir Ahmad* v. *Emperor*, AIR 1936 PC 253: (1936) 37 Cr LJ 897: 63 Ind App 372; *Md. Ikram Hussain* v. *State of Uttar Pradesh*, AIR 1964 SC 1625: (1964) 2 Cr LJ 590: ILR (1964) 2 All 423; *Yamunabai Anantrao Adhav* v. *Anantrao Shivaram Adhav*, AIR 1988 SC 644: JT 1988 (1) SC 193: 1988 Cr LJ 793; *Raj Kumar Karwal* v. *Union of India*, AIR 1991 SC 45: 1991 Cr LJ 97: (1990) 2 SCC 409; *K. Vimla* v. *K. Veeraswamy*, JT 1991 (2) SC 182: 1991 AIR SCW 754: (1991) 2 SCC 375; and *Abbayolla M. Subba Reddy* v. *Padmamma*, AIR 1999 AP 19: 1998 (3) CCC 426: I (2000) DMC 266.

As to wife's appeal, the Court on reconsideration of the evidence on record found no reason to reverse the High Court order declaring the marriage as *null and void*. It held (at p. 425):

"A Hindu marriage can be dissolved only in accordance with the provisions of the Act by obtaining a decree of divorce from the court. In the absence of any decree of dissolution of marriage from the court, it has to be held that in law that the first marriage of the wife subsisted when she went through the second marriage..........with the present husband."

Also, the existence of such customary divorce by '*chhor chithi*' as alleged by the wife, was not established.

Regarding the issue of maintenance, the court held that an order for alimony and maintenance can be passed at the time of passing *any decree* or at any time subsequent thereto. Relying on *Chand Dhawan* v. *Jawaharlal Dhawan*, (1993) 3 SCC 406: 1993 AIR SCW 2548: 1993 Cr LJ 2930, it was held that the expression "at the time of passing any decree" as used in section 25 of the Hindu Marriage Act, includes a decree of nullity. 'Any decree', according to the court, cannot be restricted only to, as contended by the husband's counsel, a decree of judicial separation or divorce. "It encompasses within the expression all kinds of decrees such as restitution of conjugal rights under section 9, judicial separation under section 10, declaring marriage as null and void under section 11, annulment of marriage as voidable under section 12 and divorce under section 13, the court stated (at p. 427).

Order: The Supreme Court dismissed the wife's appeal against the High Court order declaring the marriage as null and void; it also dismissed the husband's appeal against the order of maintenance to the wife. Since the custom under which the contesting wife had allegedly obtained divorce from her previous husband had not been established, and no divorce decree had been obtained from any court either, her previous marriage was held to be subsisting at the time of the present marriage and so declared as void. As to maintenance for her after annulment, the court remarked (at p. 427):

"Keeping into consideration the present state of statutory Hindu Law a bigamous marriage may be declared illegal being in contravention of the provision of the Act but it cannot be said to be immoral so as to deny even the right of alimony or maintenance to a spouse financially weak and economically dependent."

Comment: The case is indicative of how a man who wishes to wriggle out of a relationship, can play hide and seek. He had remarried the contesting party knowing well that the only document of alleged previous divorce which she had was the *'chhor chitthi'* and only after satisfying himself did he marry her. As remarked by the court (at p. 427) "this falsehood went to the extent of denying his second marriage and calling his wife only to be a governess of his children from the first marriage". But the court had to go by the law and in the absence of proof of legal/valid divorce from first husband, had to declare the present marriage void. It however, conceded her right to maintenance.

Alleged Divorce by Customary Dissolution deed: Custom not Proved

Subramani v. M. Chandralekha,
AIR 2005 SC 485: 2004 AIR SCW 7099: (2005) 9 SCC 407

Issue: Can a marriage be deemed to have been dissolved by executing a marriage dissolution deed without proof of any custom which permits dissolution in this manner?

Facts: This was a property dispute where the issue of validity of alleged divorce was crucial to deny the claim of property to the plaintiff. The plaintiff was married in 1981; they separated in 1983 and the husband died in 1986. Thereafter she claimed a share in the properties left by the deceased husband. When the parties were separated a registered maintenance release deed was executed in which, on receipt of ₹ 14,000, she released her claim towards maintenance. She later came to know that while writing that deed a recital had been introduced therein that the marriage between her and her husband stood dissolved under customary law prevalent in the community. The plea of the other party was that the deceased had not left any properties as the same were sold to discharge his debts; that the marriage had been dissolved as per dissolution deed; and further that the deceased had committed suicide due to differences with the respondent and therefore she had no right to claim partition nor ask the court to overlook the marriage dissolution deed. The wife averred that parties belonged to Vellala Gounder community and no custom was prevalent in their community to dissolve the marriage under custom, and that even if such a recital was there in the document, the same did not have legal effect and the relationship between her and the deceased continued to subsist.

The Trial Court, after considering the oral and documentary evidence, came to the conclusion that the respondent was entitled to a share in the properties but dismissed the suit on the ground that in the community to which the parties belong, the marriage could be dissolved under custom and the marriage between the respondent and deceased indeed stood dissolved by the marriage dissolution deed. The first appellate court concurred with the findings recorded by the Trial Court. Hence the respondent's second appeal in the High Court. After going through the provisions of section 29 of the Hindu Marriage Act which saves customs and the authorities which laid down that prevalence of customary divorce in the community to which parties belong, contrary to general law of divorce, must be specifically pleaded and established by the person propounding such custom, the court came to the conclusion that the appellants failed either to plead the existence of a custom or prove the same by cogent evidence. In the present appeal to the Supreme Court, *Yamanaji H. Jadhav* v. *Nirmala*, AIR 2002 SC 971: 2002 AIR SCW 674: (2002) 2 SCC 637, was relied upon. The court in that case pointed out that if custom were to be pleaded to prove divorce, it needs to be established and proved by the party propounding such custom.

Order: In the absence of specific plea and proof of custom which allows divorce in the manner alleged in the present case, the court refused to accept that the respondent and the deceased were divorced. The appeal against the High Court order was accordingly dismissed.

Comment: The existence or non-existence of a custom has often been an issue in several cases. In some cases such customs, even if proved, are not fair and equitable. With all respect to the wisdom of the traditions, one wonders whether such customs should continue to subvert the statutory provisions, more so in the wake of strong pleas for enactment of a uniform law.

Married Woman Remarrying without Establishing Customary Divorce: Second Marriage Void – Husband has no Right to Compassionate Appointment after Wife's Death

Vishnu Kumar v. *State of Uttar Pradesh*, 2006 (65) ALR 888 (All): AIR 2007 All 31: 2007 (1) ALJ 152

Issue: Would a husband whose marriage is void since his wife was already married and could not prove the alleged customary divorce from first husband, be entitled to compassionate appointment under the Dying and Harness Rules, after the death of his wife, was the issue involved in the case.

Facts: The petitioner's case in this writ petition was that he was married to the deceased, Geetha. After her death he sought appointment on compassionate ground, under the Dying and Harness Rules. The concerned authority, *viz.*, the District Basic Shiksha Adhikari, Etawah, rejected his application on the ground that he was unable to establish that he was the lawfully wedded husband of Geetha. The petitioner husband had disclosed that Geetha was earlier married to one Ashok Kumar but by a settlement deed they had agreed to separate and further that in the agreement itself there was a stipulation that after this separation both were free to enter into fresh marriage. Hence, according to the petitioner, he was legally wedded to the deceased, Geetha and consequently entitled to the compassionate appointment. The same being rejected, the husband filed the present writ petition.

Order: The court held that there was no infirmity in the order of the authorities which rejected his claim. They had thoroughly examined his claim and came to the conclusion correctly that the husband could not claim the status of the deceased's husband because as per admitted facts there was no legal divorce of the deceased from her first husband and "by no stretch of imagination can a valid Hindu marriage be brought to an end by way of a settlement or compromise". The husband's petition was consequently, dismissed.

Comment: After the coming into force of the Hindu Marriage Act a valid Hindu marriage can be dissolved only under the law, *viz.*, the grounds provided for the divorce, or by a custom which has the force or sanction of the law. An agreement or deed of settlement wherein parties agree to separate cannot have the affect of legal divorce. Hence second marriage without proper legal divorce of the earlier marriage is void and parties have no legal status, rights or obligations *qua* each other.

Document Purporting to be Dissolution deed under Custom not Proved: First Marriage held Subsisting

Mohan Lal Sharma v. Parveen,
AIR 2010 P&H 65: 2010 (1) CCC 418: 2010 (1) ICC 212

Issue: Issue involved in this case was as to the validity of a document of dissolution of marriage by mutual consent, under alleged custom.

Facts: This was a husband's petition under section 11 of the Hindu Marriage Act seeking nullity of marriage alleging that the wife was already married and the marriage was subsisting at the time of their (petitioner's and respondent's) marriage and further, that this fact was concealed from him. The wife's contention was that her earlier marriage had been dissolved by a deed of dissolution by mutual consent; she further took the plea that her earlier marriage was void as the first "husband was an already married man when he married her. Besides, according to her, the husband was in the know of all these facts. While the Additional District Judge dismissed the husband's petition seeking annulment the same was set aside on appeal. The plea that the first husband of the respondent being an already married man could not have legally married her (respondent) was dismissed as she could not establish his earlier marriage. Hence her first marriage was held to be a legal marriage. As regards the plea that this marriage had already been dissolved under a customary deed of dissolution, the court observed:

> "It is well-settled law that in order to succeed on custom the person claiming custom has to plead and prove the custom. Except for the pleading in the petition, there is absolutely no evidence to show prevalent custom in the community of the parties by which the divorce could be granted with intervention of the respectables. (p. 69)

It also remarked:

> "Learned matrimonial court could not have held the marriage between the parties to be valid merely by placing reliance on the document...as the document could not be said to be a document of dissolution of the marriage, as the respondent failed to prove custom. The marriage which was *null* and *void* could not be held to be valid, even if the appellant was in know of previous marriage of the respondent."

Order: The husband's appeal against dismissal of his petition for annulment of the marriage on ground of wife's earlier subsisting marriage was allowed and the marriage between the parties was declared to be dissolved by decree of nullity.

Comment: Section 29(2) of the Hindu Marriage Act saves customs and does not disturb the position which a customary divorce occupied before the enactment of the Hindu Marriage Act; however in order to rely and recognise such customary divorce it is essential to prove the existence and incidents of the alleged custom which must measure up to the essentials of a valid custom and be ancient, certain and reasonable; further, the fact of divorce under such custom also needs to be established.

Customary Divorce: No Ground for Decree under Hindu Marriage Act
Mahendra Nath Yadav v. Sheela Devi,
II (2010) DMC 487 (SC)

Issue: Can a dissolution of marriage through panchayat under custom be a ground for granting decree of divorce under section 13 of Hindu Marriage Act?

Facts: The parties were married in 1990 and in 1991 the *gauna* ceremony was performed. The husband was in the army and the wife a teacher; they hardly got an opportunity to lead a normal family life and soon there were differences between them. The wife obtained a maintenance order under section 125 of the Cr. P.C. and also filed criminal complaints against the husband and his family members. Ultimately in 1997 a panchayat was convened and as per an alleged custom, an amount of ₹ 30,000 was given to the wife's family and a document of divorce prepared. In order to give legal effect to the divorce thus obtained the husband tried to persuade the wife to get divorce from the Family Court, by a mutual consent under section 13B of the Hindu Marriage Act. On her declining to agree to that, the husband filed a petition for divorce under section 13 of the Act on the grounds of desertion and cruelty; the wife thereupon filed a counter-petition for restitution of conjugal rights under section 9. The Family Court granted the divorce decree to the husband and dismissed the wife's petition for restitution on the ground that the marriage had stood dissolved through the panchayat in 1997. On wife's appeal against this, the Allahabad High Court reversed the Trial Court order and held that dissolution of marriage by panchayat as per custom prevailing in that area cannot be a ground for divorce under section 13 of the Hindu Marriage Act; and further, if the husband wanted decree on the basis of customary dissolution of the marriage by panchayat in 1997, he would not have filed the petition under section 13 of the Act. Filing this petition itself means that none of the parties were of the view that the divorce granted by the panchayat was legal. The husband's appeal against this was dismissed.

Order: A divorce obtained under a customary law cannot be a ground for seeking judicial divorce under section 13 of the Hindu Marriage Act on grounds of cruelty and desertion.

Comment: Under section 29(2) of the Hindu Marriage Act dissolution of marriage through recognised customs is legal and if a divorce has been obtained by a legally recognised custom it is not necessary for the parties to go to court to obtain decree of divorce on grounds of recognised custom (*Gurdit Singh* v. *Angrez Kaur,* AIR 1968 SC 142: (1967) 2 SCR 789; *Jasbir Singh* v. *Inderjit Kaur,* AIR 2003 P&H 317: 2003 (2) Hindu LR 654: 2004 (1) Marri LJ 175.) However, such divorce cannot form the basis for seeking divorce on the ground of desertion and cruelty under section 13 of the Hindu Marriage Act.

Marriage Dissolved by *"fahrkhati nama"*: Wife not Entitled to Restitution

Kewal Kumar v. *Pawna Devi,*
AIR 2011 HP 58

Issue: The issue involved in the case was as to the recognition of customary divorce.

Facts: The wife, it seems had filed a petition for restitution of conjugal rights and also for litigation expenses under section 24 of the Hindu Marriage Act. The husband's defence was that the marriage had been dissolved, by a *'fahrkati nama'* under customary law. The Trial Court however granted interim maintenance at the rate of ₹ 500 p.m. and also directed the husband to pay litigation expenses of ₹ 1,000. It is against this that the husband filed the present appeal.

Order: It was argued in the appeal that the wife was pregnant at the time of marriage and therefore the parties agreed to dissolve the marriage by a customary divorce or *fahrkhati nama;* to substantiate this fact, the husband stated that the wife's petition for maintenance under section 125 of the Cr. P.C. had been dismissed on the ground that the marriage stood dissolved by mutual consent, and that the wife was living in adultery; the husband also placed on record a judgment of the civil judge where-by the wife's application seeking declaration that there was a subsisting marriage between them, was dismissed on the ground that the marriage had already been dissolved by customary divorce. The husband's petition was thus allowed and the wife's petition for restitution as also the grant of maintenance *pendente lite* were held to be not maintainable.

Comment: Section 29(2) of the Hindu Marriage Act specifically protects customs provided they satisfy all the ingredients of a valid custom. When marriage is dissolved by 'fahrkhati nama,' the parties cannot seek any relief by way of restitution or litigation expenses for the same.

Note. See also *Chain Singh Verma* v. *Kavita*, (2006) 3 Shimla LC 206 where it was established that the wife had obtained a divorce from her previous husband under a custom and the present husband was present when papers for the customary divorce were prepared, it was held that the present husband's petition for annulment of marriage on ground of wife's first marriage was not sustainable.

SELECT CASES UNDER MUSLIM LAW

Validity of Marriage

Ghulam Kubra Bibi v. Md. Shafi Mohammad Din, AIR 1940 Peshawar 2

Issue: Can a 'marriage' be upheld as valid on the vague statement of two persons that they were witnesses to the *Nikah* without any further details?

Facts: Mohammad Shafi, the 'petitioner' sued Ghulam Kubra, the defandant for restitution of conjugal rights. He also impleaded her parents and sought an injunction, that they be restrained from 'interfering' in his married life. The defendant's defence was that she was never married to Mohammad Shafi. There was also the question whether the girl was of age at the time of her marriage. The *Mullah* appeared and stated that he read the *Nikah* at the instance of the grandfather of the girl. He, however, categorically denied that anyone was sent to the girl to enquire from her whether she agreed to the marriage. One *A* vaguely deposed that there were two witnesses of the *Nikah*, without giving their names. Two 'witnesses' were produced whose statement was vague, incomplete and not reliable. The trial judge held that the girl was of age at the time of marriage and that the marriage was proved. Hence, he passed the decree in favour of the petitioner. On appeal by the defendant and her parents, it was admitted before the district court that the girl was of age. The court consequently, maintained the decree of restitution of conjugal rights but did not think it necessary to issue an injunction to the parents of the girl. Both parties appealed—the girl against the restitution decree, and the plaintiff against the refusal to issue injunction to the parents of the girl.

Order: The court described the entire process of a Muslim *Nikah viz.*, the girl's explicit consent through a relation within the hearing of the witness, the details of the dower, conveying of the consent to the husband in the presence of the *Mullah* and the husband's consent. When both parties say "yes" to the marriage then the *Mullah* reads the scriptures and the marriage is complete.

In the instant case, the court held that the vague allegation by the petitioner that there were two witnesses of the *Nikah* had no value and that it should have been proved that the whole procedure of *Nikah* had been gone through. The man who read the *Nikah* was positive that no one was sent to the girl to enquire from her whether she was a willing party. Also, it was pointed out by the court that the girl was aged 17 at the time of the alleged marriage. The parties were probably unaware of the fact that according to the Mohammedan law, a girl becomes major for purpose of marriage when she reaches age of puberty which is presumed to be 15 years. The parties seemed to be under the impression that she would become major only at the age of 18, as is the general law, and therefore, was given away in marriage by the grandfather and not consulted personally. However, the court held, that in any case two witnesses are required for the Nikah. In this case the credibility of the witnesses was suspect and so it could not be held that there was a valid marriage; which follows that the plaintiff had no right to sue for restitution of conjugal rights. The appeal of the girl against restitution was accepted and that of Mohammad Shafi against non-issue of injunction to the girl's parents was dismissed.

Comment: Since 'purdah' is observed amongst Muslim women, it is required that the girl's consent is properly obtained for the marriage. The requirement of two witnesses in the presence of whom the consent and the other processes of marriage are gone through seeks to further ensure that the girl is a willing party. In the absence of proper proposal, consent and acceptance of the parties, the courts are not inclined to uphold the marriage as valid, as has been done in this case.

Legal Status of Marriage with a Pregnant Woman

Amina v. Hassan Koya,
AIR 2004 SC 1227: 2003 Cr LJ 2540: 2003 AIR SCW 2496

Issue: Is a marriage under Muslim Law with a pregnant woman void or valid?

Facts: A wife filed a petition for maintenance under section 125, Cr. P.C., for herself and for the child. The trial Magistrate granted maintenance for the wife-appellant, but not for the child because the court came to the conclusion that the non-applicant was not the father of the child. On revision petition, the order of maintenance in favour of the wife was reversed by Additional Sessions Judge on the ground that the husband was not aware that the wife was already pregnant at the time of marriage and this fact was concealed from him. On appeal by the wife, the High Court affirmed the reversal on the ground that the marriage was invalid because the wife had concealed the fact that she was already pregnant at the time of marriage, by a person other than the respondent. Hence, the wife's appeal to the Supreme Court.

Order: The High Court decision was reversed. The Supreme Court found a, "basic fallacy" in the husband's plea that he was unaware of the wife's pregnancy which led to the finding by the lower appellate courts that the marriage was invalid. The Supreme Court's view was based on the following factual grounds; *viz.*, the wife delivered the fully-grown baby within four months of the marriage and it is improbable that the husband could not see the five months pregnancy at the time of marriage; his conduct immediately after marriage and at the time of delivery also demolishes his plea of 'not knowing' the fact of wife's pre-marriage pregnancy; he was present at the time of delivery; he gave his name as the father of the child for the official record; thereafter for four years he continued with the marriage and brought up the child. In view of all this according to the court, it could not be believed that the husband was unaware of the fact. Reference was also made to *Kulsumbai Kom Abdul Kadir* v. *Abdul Kadir Walad Saikh Ahmad*, ILR 1921 Vol. XLV Bom 157, in support of legal precedent that concealment of pregnancy at the time of marriage does not render a marriage invalid. In this case, the husband turned out his wife when he came to know about her pre-marriage pregnancy. Consummation of the marriage was also disputed. The wife sued for dower. The husband denied the validity of marriage. It was held that concealment of pregnancy by the wife at the time of marriage does not render the marriage invalid, and therefore, the husband was liable to pay her the dower.

Thus, the wife's appeal was allowed and the trial magistrate's order was restored.

Comment: On the facts of the present case it is clear that the husband could not have been allowed to take the plea that he was unaware of the fact of wife's pregnancy and the judgment of the Supreme Court is also based on the "basic fallacy" of the husband's contention. The husband, according to the court, was "fully aware of the pregnancy of the appellant at the time of marriage and, therefore, he cannot be heard to say that the marriage was invalid or void for that reason."

Marriage – "Assurance" is not "Acceptance" to Marry

Rashida Khatun v. *SK. Islam*,
AIR 2005 Ori 56: 2005 (1) CLR 162: 2005 Mat LR 296

Issue: Can an 'assurance to marry' be equated to an 'acceptance' to marry so as to confer status of legal marriage?

Facts: Parties to the proceedings are Mohammedans belonging to the Islamic faith and are governed by their personal law. Petitioner No. 1 filed an application under section 7(1)(b) and (e) of the Family Courts Act, 1984, for a declaration of status of legally married wife of the respondent and the status of child born to them as the legitimate child of the respondent. According to her version, the respondent is her cousin and intimacy developed between the two, and further, that on the assurance of marriage given by the respondent, she cohabited with him and begot the child. When the respondent declined to treat her as the wife and the child as their son, and also declined to provide maintenance, she filed the civil proceedings. The respondent denied any assurance of marriage, cohabitation and paternity of the child. He also pleaded that in the community *panchayat* which was approached on the issue of petitioner's pregnancy, it was resolved that the author of the child was one S.K. Hardia, and accordingly, a fine of Rs. 5,000 was imposed on him by the *bhadraloks*.

On going through the evidence on record, the Family Court held that she had not acquired the status of a legally married wife but the child was born out of cohabitation between the petitioner and the respondent. Both parties appealed against the order.

Order: As to the validity of the marriage, it was argued that in a Muslim marriage no rituals and functions are necessary and the Muslim marriage being a civil contract, consent of respondent to marry the petitioner and thereafter cohabitation with her was sufficient to prove her status as his wife. Reference was made to the following Annotation, No. 252, in Chapter XIV of Mulla's *Principles of Mohammedan Law*:

> "*Essentials of a marriage.*—It is essential to the validity of a marriage that there should be proposal made by or on behalf of one of the parties to the marriage, and an acceptance of the proposal by or on behalf of the other, in the presence and hearing of two male or one male and two female witnesses, who must be sane and adult Mohammedans. The proposal and acceptance must both be expressed at one meeting; a proposal made at one meeting and an acceptance made at another meeting does not constitute a valid marriage. Neither writing nor any religious ceremony is essential."

In this case, however, the above essentials were not observed. As pointed out by the court (at p. 57) not only the pleadings of the petitioners but also the evidence on record indicated that there was no acceptance of the offer to marry, but there was only an assurance to marry in future and therefore mere cohabitation with such on assurance does not constitute the *factum* of marriage. However, as regards the child's paternity, the court held that the evidence of the respondent does not disprove the contention of the petitioner that the child was born out of physical relationship between them. Thus, both the appeals were dismissed. The marriage was held to be not valid but the child was born to the petitioner and the respondent; in other words, the respondent was the father of the child.

Comment: The court has rightly distinguished between an assurance to marry and an acceptance to marry. In this case there was no acceptance to marry following a proposal—both of which have to be expressed at one meeting—with an action to remain as husband and wife.

DIVORCE

Impotency

Mt. Altafan v. Ibrahim,
AIR 1924 All 116: 21 All LJ 811: 75 Ind Cas 502

Issue: Can a wife be asked to submit to her husband to enable him to prove his potency within a year?

Facts: A husband sought restitution of conjugal rights and the wife filed a petition for annulment of the marriage on the ground of husband's impotency. The court referred to various authorities on the point and the different dimensions of impotency. Under the Muslim law, where a woman brings her husband before a court demanding separation on grounds of impotency, and the fact whether the husband was impotent and the wife was a virgin is disputed, the case is to be adjourned for a year and if after the expiry of the year the woman should still allege that she is a virgin, an inspection by a woman to ascertain the truth can be ordered. The idea is to give an opportunity to the husband to show that the charge against him is unfounded, or that the alleged incapacity is curable and the woman should be required to appear again after a year before the judge in order to establish her claim for the relief.

After medical examination of both the parties, the wife was found to be a virgin but at the same time no abnormality was detected in the husband either. The Trial Court, however, relied on the medical evidence in favour of the husband and decreed restitution and dismissed the wife's application for annulment. On appeal by the wife, the court found that a *prima facie* case was made out in favour of the wife and so a *decree nisi* was passed in favour of the wife. This, however, was kept in suspension for a year to give an opportunity to the husband to prove his competence to perform his marital obligation during the period. The court also directed that the wife "must allow full access to her husband at all reasonable times to exercise his marital rights as her husband".

Against this, the husband filed a Letters Patent Appeal on the ground that the findings of the Trial Court are findings of fact which the High Court should not have reconsidered in appeal. The court, however, held that it was open to the judge to consider this finding afresh and arrive at his own conclusion. The only point for consideration, according to the court, was whether this rule of Hanafi law, as discussed by the various authorities, namely, *Hidaya, Fatwa Kazi-Khan, Durrul Mukhtar, Badul Mukhtar, Fatwa-Alamgiri*, as well as by the English commentators, is a rule of mere procedure which would be taken to have been superseded by the British law of procedure, or whether it contains any part of substantive law, which, in matters of divorce, is enforceable.

Order: The court came to the conclusion that the right of the husband to have an opportunity of demonstrating that he is not impotent is a substantive right recognised by Muslim law. Under the Muslim law a wife has no absolute right to obtain a divorce. She has a right only under certain specific contingencies and conditions. The mere fact that since the marriage the husband has had no intercourse with her and therefore she is still a virgin, would not *per se*, entitle her to a divorce unless it is proved that he is incapable of cohabitation with her. It, therefore, recognises that the husband should have full opportunity after he has been challenged to prove that he is not impotent. This, according to the court is a substantive right and not a mere rule of procedure and hence is enforceable. Accordingly, the *decree nisi* of annulment in favour of the wife was upheld. It would not become absolute till one year during which period the wife was to allow him opportunity and access to exercise his marital rights. If after the expiry of one year, she satisfies the court that the husband continues to be impotent and physically unable to perform his marital obligations, she would be entitled to have the decree made absolute, otherwise the *decree nisi* would be cancelled and her suit dismissed.

Comment: A judgment passed over 80 years ago is obviously unimaginable today: A virgin wife being ordered to submit to her husband for a year so that he can prove his capacity is utterly humiliating!

Wife cannot be Compelled to Submit to Husband to Prove that he Ceased to be Impotent

Abdul Azeem v. Fahimunnisa,
AIR 1969 Mys 226: (1967) 1 Mys LJ 675: 10 Law Rep 412

Issue: Can a wife be compelled to submit to the husband to prove that he has ceased to be impotent after a finding by the court, on wife's petition for dissolution of marriage, that he was impotent?

Facts: This was a wife's petition for dissolution of marriage under section 2(v) of the Dissolution of Muslim Marriages Act, 1939, on the ground that the husband was impotent at the time of the marriage and continues to be so. The same was established and the District Judge recorded a finding to that effect; however, on application made by the husband, he adjourned the proceedings for a year to enable the husband to prove that he had ceased to be impotent. After a year, the wife again made an application for dissolution, and the same was decreed. Against this, the husband filed the present appeal alleging that during that one year he was refused opportunity to which he was in law entitled to demonstrate that he had acquired the ability to consummate the marriage. Relying on *Altafan v. Ibrahim*, AIR 1924 All 116, the husband's argument was that "under the Mohammedan law by which the parties were governed, the husband had an indisputable right to the company of the wife during the period of one year to which proviso (c) to section 2 of the Dissolution of Muslim Marriages Act refers and that the District Judge should have directed the wife to live with the husband during that period in order to consummate the marriage". (at p. 229)

Order: The court dismissed the appeal and held that the opportunity contemplated under proviso (c) does not make it the duty of the wife to allow access to the husband during the period of one year referred, either in her parental house or elsewhere. An interpretation which subjects the wife to this queer predicament cannot be sound, according to the court. The court also clarified that the earlier Allahabad cases, (*e.g.*, *Altafan*) were decided before the Dissolution of Muslim Marriages Act came and that after the Act the rule under Mohammedan law which formed the foundation of the decision in these cases, has been codified. Under the Dissolution of Muslim Marriages Act, a decree of dissolution on the ground of husband's impotency can be postponed only when the husband seeks opportunity to prove his capacity. This shows that such opportunity no longer rests on the rule of Mohammedan law but is derived from the provisions of the Act. The opportunity, as contemplated by proviso (c) to section 2 of the Act, does not make it the duty of the wife to submit herself to him to prove his virility. The court held (at p. 230):

> "It is not necessary to enumerate the processes by which cessation could be established, although it is plain that production of medical evidence is one. There may be others equally efficacious. But we hesitate to recognise the right of the husband to demand the company of his wife to be able to establish the disappearance of his impotence. That right does not flow from anything contained in the Dissolution of Muslim Marriages Act and in the absence of clear provision creating it, we feel reluctant to say that the wife could be compelled to submit herself to the experiments of a humiliated husband whose exacerbation can provoke dangerous reprisals. The duty to involve herself in such great peril does not either expressly or by necessary implication emanate from proviso (c) to section 2 or any other part of the Act which is a complete and exhaustive code on dissolution."

Comment: A very fair judgment where judges have shown sensitivity to the issue by saving the wife from the utterly humiliating process whereunder she was expected to submit herself to the husband's experimentation to prove that he had ceased to be impotent.

Husband's Failure to Maintain – Wife's Ground for Divorce
A. Yousuf Rawther v. *Sowramma*,
AIR 1971 Ker 261: 1970 Ker LJ 544: ILR (1971) 1 Ker 154

Issue: Can a wife seek dissolution of her marriage under clause (ii) of section 2 of the Dissolution of Muslim Marriages Act even if the husband has good reason for not having supported her for a period of two years?

Facts: S, a Hanafi girl around 15, married in 1962 Y, nearly twice her age. The plaintiff had attained puberty even before her marriage and soon after the wedding, they moved to the husband's house. The very next day, the husband left for Coimbatore where he was running a radio dealer's business. After a month, the wife went back to her parents, the reason for her return being blamed by each on the other. The separation lasted for over two years during which span the defendant admittedly failed to maintain the wife. His ground was that he was willing, and indeed anxious, to keep her with him but she wrongfully refused to return to the conjugal home. There were efforts for rapproachment which failed and hence the litigation for dissolution of marriage commenced. The Trial Court dismissed the wife's suit but the subordinate judge's court granted a decree for dissolution in favour of the wife, under section 2 of the Dissolution of Muslim Marriage Act. Hence, the husband's appeal.

Order: The main issue raised by the husband's counsel was as to the right of the wife wrongfully leaving the matrimonial home to claim dissolution through court for mere failure of the husband to maintain the erring wife. Under clause (ii) of section 2 of the Dissolution of Muslim Marriages Act one of the grounds on which a Muslim wife can seek dissolution of her marriage is the "failure of the husband to provide for the maintenance of the wife for a period of two years". Several cases were referred to and cited, both in support of the argument that a husband is not bound to support a wife who is responsible for this or in other words where there is justification for not supporting owing to the wife's own conduct, as well as in support of the contrary argument that irrespective of the wife's failure of duty or wrongful conduct, the husband is duty bound to support her and failing to support for a period of two years or above would give her a ground to seek dissolution of the marriage. Justice Krishna Iyer relied on Tyabji, C.J.'s ratio in *Noor Bibi* v. *Pir Bux*, AIR 1950 Sind 8: 1950 Pak Cas Sind 18, that section 2(ii) of the Dissolution of Muslim Marriages Act does not speak of the wife's right of maintenance but only of the fact of her being provided with maintenance:

> "Muslim morals and ideas undoubtedly expect every husband to maintain his wife as long as the marriage subsists, even when the wife does not deserve to be maintained, and may not in law be able to enforce any claim for maintenance. It is, therefore, no less correct to speak of a man's failure to maintain his wife even when she is not entitled to claim maintenance, than it is to speak of a man's failure to pay his debts of honour or bets or his debts which have become time-barred."

It was held, that under clause (iv) of section 2 of the Act, *i.e.*, where the husband has failed to perform his marital obligations for a period of three years, there is specific reference to "without reasonable cause" while in clause (ii) the words "without reasonable cause" do not occur. This would mean that whatever the cause may be, the wife is entitled to a decree for dissolution of her marriage if her husband fails to maintain her for a period of two years, even though she might have contributed towards the failure of the maintenance by her husband (Beckett, J. in *Khatijan* v. *Abdulla*, AIR 1943 Sind 65: ILR 1942 Kant 535, relied upon by Tyabji, C.J., and in the instant case by Justice Krishna Iyer.) Thus, the husband's appeal was dismissed and the wife was held to be entitled to a decree of dissolution of marriage under clause (ii) of section 2 of the Dissolution of Muslim Marriages Act.

Comment: The mere fact that the wife has not been maintained for a period of two years, irrespective of the circumstances or conduct of the wife leading to the non-maintenance, is enough to give to the wife the ground to seek dissolution of marriage. Thus, the Act imposes an absolute duty on the husband in this respect, failing which the wife may claim dissolution.

Dissolution of Marriage in Terms of a Compromise

Md. Abdul Zalil Ahmed v. *Marina Begum,*
AIR 1999 Gau 28: 1999 (2) Gau LR 369: 1999 (2) Hindu LR 576

Issue: Can a marriage be dissolved in terms of a compromise arrived at by the parties after the filing of the petition by the wife under the provisions of the Dissolution of Muslim Marriages Act?

Facts: A wife filed an application for divorce under the Dissolution of Muslim Marriages Act, 1939 (DMMA). The main grounds for the relief were: husband's failure to perform without reasonable cause, his marital obligation, and cruelty, *i.e.*, physical torture and ill-treatment, making her life miserable.

The Dissolution of Muslim Marriages Act was passed to give certain rights to married women and is not against the tenets of the Quran. The grounds for dissolution of the marriage under section 2 are, *inter alia*, the husband has failed to perform without reasonable cause, his marital obligation for a period of three years, the husband treats her with cruelty, that is to say, habitually assaults her or makes her life miserable by cruelty of conduct even if such conduct does not amount to physical ill-treatment.

After the wife's petition, both the parties filed a joint petition for a decree 'in terms of the application filed by the wife'. The Family Court, however, did not allow this on the ground that mutual consent is not a ground available under the Act. Against this, the husband went in appeal. The Gauhati High Court allowed the petition.

Order: It was held that even though there is no provision for divorce by mutual consent under the Dissolution of Muslim Marriages Act "it should be borne in mind that the parties can compromise such a matter and a decree may be passed in terms of the compromise if otherwise it does not militate against the grounds as reinforced in section 2 of the Dissolution of Muslim Marriage Act, 1939". (at p. 29)

The husband in this case had already remarried and the wife's marriage was fixed up, too. Without a divorce she could not have married again. In view of this, the court held that "it will not be just and proper to keep her hanging in air". A decree dissolving the marriage was accordingly passed.

Comment: This is a very practical judgment where the court, instead of insisting on the strict letter of the statute, adopted an approach which was both realistic and in consonance with the spirit of the law.

Dissolution of Muslim Marriages Act *vis-a-vis* Theory of Break-down of Marriage

Amma Khatoon v. Kashim Ansari,
AIR 2001 Jhar 28: 2001 AIR Jhar HCR 1: 2001 (2) BLJR 1228

Issue: Can a Muslim marriage be dissolved on the ground of irretrievable breakdown by invoking section 2(ix) of the Dissolution of Muslim Marriages Act, 1939?

Facts: A husband used to pressurise and threaten his wife with a view to persuade her to convey her property to him. There was, however, no evidence that the husband had disposed of her property or had prevented her from exercising her right over it. The wife sought divorce under the provisions of the Dissolution of Muslim Marriages Act, 1939. The following provisions of the Act are relevant to the present case. Section 2 says: "A woman married under Muslim law shall be entitled to obtain a decree for the dissolution of her marriage on any one or more of the following grounds..............

(viii) that the husband treats her with cruelty, that is to say,

....

....

(d) disposes of her property or prevents her from exercising her legal right over it........

(ix) any other ground which is recognised as valid for dissolution of marriage under Muslim Law."

It was contended on behalf of the husband that mere pressurising the wife to transfer the landed property would not, by itself, constitute cruelty as defined in section 2(viii)(d) of the Dissolution of Muslim Marriages Act. It could be construed only as a motive for treating her with cruelty.

Order: After analysing the facts, the court rejected the husband's contention and found that there was clear, cogent and convincing evidence of the wife being assaulted and treated with cruelty. It remarked, "it is not necessary that in all cases, the husband would habitually ill-treat his wife in presence of other persons". Her statement before a *panchayat* that "she was fed up with her husband and she had decided no more to visit her matrimonial home and would stay with her parents", was held to be admissible to prove cruelty. On the husband's offer to keep the wife with him and treat her with honour, the court observed that "such a plea cannot be treated as guarantee that in future the husband would treat her with affection and perhaps this plea had been taken by him to defeat the suit".

The marriage was dissolved on the ground of irretrievable breakdown by invoking section 2(ix) of the Dissolution of Muslim Marriages Act *viz.*, "any other ground which is recognised as valid for the dissolution of marriage under Muslim Law". On the basis of the facts, the court observed:

"When an intolerable situation has been reached and the partners are living with hostility for a considerable number of years, it is legitimate to draw an inference that the marriage has broken down in reality and law should recognise it and try to end the relationship. Islam concedes the grounds of dissolution of marriage at the instance of the wife and the statute itself recognises it and preserves it as a saving provision under section 2(ix) of the Act when it enacted "any other ground which is recognised as valid for dissolution of marriage under the Muslim Law".

In this view, the court found support from a well-known *Hadith* in which marriage was allowed to be dissolved on the ground of irretrievable breakdown. Jameela, wife of Sabit Bin Kais, hated her husband though he was very fond of her. It is said that she requested the Holy Prophet to get her husband to divorce her on giving him a garden. Sabit was very ugly and Jameela is reported to have said, 'If I had no fear of God, I should have struck him on the face whenever he approached me'. Thereupon, the Prophet asked Sabit to take back the garden and divorce Jameela. The illustration shows the recognition by the Prophet of the rights of a Muslim wife to ask for divorce when it is shown that the parties could not live within the limits of God.

The court also drew support from one of the decisions of the Pakistan Supreme Court [1986 (1) Cur CC 240 (1) Pakistan (SC)], wherein it is stated to have been observed: "In case of dislike by the wife of her husband, Islam concedes this right to the wife in circumstances of extreme discord and where life becomes torture for both on account of the fixed aversion on the part of the spouses, to seek dissolution of marriage on the ground of *Khula*. This right, however, is not an absolute right by which the wife can herself dissolve the marriage but is a controlled right. The success of the right depends upon the Quazi's reaching the conclusion that the spouses cannot live within the limits of God." Admitting the appeal, the court held that it is manifest that the marriage has irretrievably broken down and on this score too, the wife is entitled to dissolution of marriage which is covered by residuary ground as envisaged in section 2(ix) of the Act. Reference was also made to *Md. Usman* v. *Sainaba Umma*, AIR 1988 Ker 138: (1987) 1 Ker LJ 712: ILR (1988) 1 Ker 28.

Comment: This case is a clear recognition of the principle of breakdown of the marriage as a ground for divorce. Indeed, it serves no useful purpose to withhold divorce when the parties have been living separately for long and there are no prospects of their ever living happily together, for whatever reasons.

'Talaq' to be Effective, has to be Explicitly *'Pronounced'*

Shamim Ara v. *State of Uttar Pradesh,*
(2002) 7 SCALE 183

Issue: Can a plea taken by the husband in his written statement (in response to maintenance petition of the wife under section 125, Cr. P.C.) that he had pronounced *talaq* at some earlier date, be treated as effectuating *talaq* on the date of delivery of the copy of the written statement to the wife?

Facts: The parties were married according to the Muslim Shariat law. The wife filed a petition for maintenance under section 125 of the Cr. P.C. The same was dismissed by the Family Court on the ground that she was already divorced. According to the husband, he had given a triple *talaq*. He made a bald statement saying that he had divorced her on July 11, 1987, at 11 a.m. by a triple *talaq*. No particulars were pleaded. He only made a certain vague generalised accusation against her that ever since marriage he found his wife to be sharp, shrewd and mischievous. The particulars of the alleged *talaq* were not pleaded nor the circumstances under which and the persons,.if any, in whose presence, the *talaq* was pronounced. The Family Court relied on some affidavit filed by him in 1988, in some civil suit, to which the wife was not even a party, wherein he had stated that he had divorced his wife 15 months earlier on July 11, 1987. He further admitted that he had not paid anything towards her maintenance since 1988. The Family Court judge took this as a corroboration of his having divorced his wife. The wife filed a revision before the High Court. The High Court held that the alleged divorce was not given in the presence of the wife and the same was not communicated to her either; however according to the court, it would be taken to have been communicated on December 5, 1990, which is the date of the written statement filed by the husband in response to the wife's maintenance application wherein he stated that he had divorced her. It was accordingly held that the wife would be entitled to claim maintenance from January 1, 1988, to December 5, 1990. After this date, the wife would not be entitled to maintenance from her husband, the High Court held. Against this, the wife filed special leave appeal before the Supreme Court. The single issue was whether the wife can be said to have been divorced and the said divorce communicated to her so as to be effective from December 5, 1990? After referring to various authorities, the court held that the *talaq* to be effective has to be. pronounced. The term pronounce was elucidated to mean "to proclaim, to utter formally, to utter rhetorically, to declare, to utter, to articulate". There is no proof of *talaq* having taken place on July 11, 1987. What the High Court has upheld as *talaq* is the plea taken in the written statement and communication to the wife by delivering a copy of the written statement on December 5, 1990.

Order: The court held that there was no divorce. "A mere plea taken in the written statement of a divorce having been pronounced sometimes in the past cannot, by itself, be treated as effectuating *talaq* on the date of the delivery of the copy of the written statement..........the husband ought to have adduced evidence and proved the pronouncement of *talaq* on July 11, 1987, and if he failed in proving the plea raised in the written statement, the plea ought to have been treated as failed," the court said. The husband was held to be liable to maintain his wife until the obligation comes to an end in accordance with law.

Comment: The judgment seeks to provide some norms and parameters within which the husband can pronounce a *talaq*. The very concept and right of unilateral triple *talaq* has however, being assailed.

Husband's Second Marriage: Ground for Divorce
Abdurahiman v. Khairunneesa,
I (2010) DMC 707 (Ker DB): 2010 (1) KLT 891

Issue: Can a Muslim wife seek divorce on the ground of her husband's polygamous marriage even through polygamy is not illegal under Islamic law?

Facts: A Muslim wife sought dissolution of her marriage under the provisions of section 2(viii)(f) of the Dissolution of Muslim Marriage Act, 1939 on the grounds *inter alia* that '"he has more wives than one and does not treat her equitably in accordance with the injunctions of the Quran". Significantly the provision refers to the wife being treated equitably "in accordance with the injunctions of the Quran" and not "in accordance with the tenets of Islam." In this case the husband discriminated with her in several ways; he also usurped all her property, jewellery and cash, treated her with cruelty and married another woman after having four children from her and also did not treat her equitably in accordance with the injunction of the Quran. Allowing the wife's petition for divorce the court observed (at p. 717):

> "Section 2(viii)(f) of the Act provides an escape route for a married woman who finds a third person intruding into the space of matrimony which has place only for two. Marriage according to the well-accepted modern concept is a space which can accommodate only two and not three or more.... The right of a Muslim husband to have more than one (upto four) wives must be considered in the light of the axiomatic assumption that in matrimony there is sufficient space only for two. If a third one barges in and one within the matrimony is unwilling to accommodate the third, the unwilling spouse must have the option to walk out......"

Invoking the provision of article 21 of the Constitution, the court further remarked:

> "Right to life under article 21 of the Constitution must definitely include the right to a healthy and harmonious matrimonial life. Marriage as an institution becomes meaningless if it were to be endured and not enjoyed. The right to opt out of an emotionally dead marriage will have to, subject to the concerns of public order and morality, be essentially accepted – tomorrow, if not today, as an incident of the right to life. It will of course have to be secured that the economically fragile divorced spouse is adequately protected....."

Order: Notwithstanding the fact that polygamous marriage is permissible under the Islamic law, the wife got a decree of dissolution of her marriage since the husband who entered into another marriage did not, *inter alia*, "treat her equitably in accordance with the injunctions of the Quran."

Comment: A very welcome dimension has been added by invoking article 21 of the Constitution and including happy, healthy and harmonious marriage with respect and dignity, as a component of right to life.

Parakkattil Abu v. Pachiyath Beekkutty,
AIR 2011 Ker 88

Issue: The issue involved in this case was whether under the provisions of the Dissolution of Muslim Marriage Act, 1939 (DMMA) a Muslim wife would be entitled to divorce on the husband's remarriage simply on her assertion regarding inequitable treatment by him.

Facts: This was an appeal by the husband against the order of the Trial Court granting dissolution of marriage under section 2(viii)(f) of the Dissolution of Muslim Marriage Act in favour of the wife. The husband had remarried after 25 years of marriage and having two children from her, without her consent (Though consent would appear to be irrelevant in such cases). The respondent wife had filed a suit for dissolution on the ground that subsequent to his second marriage, he has been treating her cruelly and inequitably. The husband did not appear on the posted date; on the adjourned date he entered appearance through counsel but no counter-statement was filed. He sought time which was not allowed. On wife's affidavit in support of her claim for divorce on ground of cruelty, specifically on ground of inequitable treatment when there is plurality of wives, the Trial Court decreed dissolution. This was challenged by the husband in the present appeal; his contentions were, *inter alia*, that the wife's assertion of inequitable treatment is not correct or acceptable and further, that he did not get an opportunity to raise his contentions. The appeal was dismissed. The Trial Court as well as the High Court relied on the decision in *Abdurahiman* v. *Khairunnesa*, I (2010) DMC 707 (Ker DB): 2010 (1) KLT 891. Reference may be made to the very pertinent and logical remarks of the court:

> "....in a claim for divorce under section 2(viii)(f) of the Act it is the assertion of the woman that matters. She is the best judge to decide whether she has been treated equitably or not when it is admitted or proved that there has been a second marriage and when the wife asserts that she has been treated inequitably and she would like to walk out of such marriage, no court can fetter her rights to quit such marriage. Whether there is cross-examination or not on such assertion of hers, her assertion will have to be accepted. She is the best judge of the situation. Quran mandates that she must be dealt with fairly and justly. Quran declares that it will be impossible for a husband to treat his wife fairly and justly where there is plurality of wives. Her assertion of inequitable treatment is consistent with the Lord's declaration in *Ayat* 129 of *sura* iv. It would be unreasonable for the rational, and blasphemous for the faithful, to question the Lord's declaration.... Hence if she perceives the treatment to be unjust and inequitable, her assertion will have to be totally accepted."

The court in *Abdurahiman* also invoked the constitutional mandate of equality. "The husband has right to unilaterally walk out of marriage – even a monogamous marriage. At least when faced with ignominy of polygamy, the wife must on her assertion be able to secure an order through court to quit such marriage". And further "when the husband unlocks the wicket (or is it the wicked) gate to admit another wife in matrimony he passes on the password to open the main exit gate to the wife in matrimony as also the wife walking in. Either can, thereafter, sooner or later, if she so chooses go to the main exit gate and utter the words "inequitable treatment" and the gate shall open for her to go out leaving her husband behind with all obligations of a divorced husband to his divorced wife." (at para 36 of *Abdurahiman*, referred at p. 40 of *Parakkattil Abu*). The court reiterated that the wife's right is not effected even if she consents to the second marriage or the second wife enters into marriage being well aware of the first marriage.

As to husband's grievance (in *Parakkattil Abu*) that he was not granted further time to file his objections the court held that the same was without any merit. "....the court below had only imbibed the sense of expedition which the circumstances warranted", the court observed (at p. 41). As held by the Division Bench in *Abdurahiman*, "at least the claims under section 2(viii)(f) of the Act deserve to be disposed of quickly and expeditiously – nay instantly – by the courts." (at para 47 thereof).

Order: The husband's appeal against the grant of divorce to the wife on ground of "inequitable treatment" of the petitioner wife after taking a second wife, was dismissed *in limine*.

Comment: Relying heavily and quoting in good detail the observations of the Division Bench in *Abdurahiman v. Khairunnesa*, 2010 (1) KLT 891 (supra), this is a very pragmatic judgment. Even though polygamous marriage, *per se*, is no ground for divorce under the provisions of the Dissolution of Muslim Marriage Act yet, it concedes to the wife the right to walk out of the marriage if she feels that she has been treated inequitably. She is the best judge to feel the inequitable treatment; it is for no one else to sit in judgment over her perception or assertion. As very aptly remarked in *Abdurahiman* if a Muslim husband can unilaterally walk out of even a monogamous marriage why can't the wife in a polygamous marriage seek such relief through the court when faced with the ignominy of polygamy, on assertion of inequitable treatment? An eye-opener indeed for husbands who enter into polygamous marriages thinking or hoping that they can enjoy the luxury of having more than one wife.

Option of Puberty

Ghulam Sakina v. Falak Sher Allah Baksh,
AIR 1950 Lah 45: Pak Cas 1949 Lah 104

Issue: Does a girl given in marriage before the age of 15 years, lose her right to exercise her option of repudiating the same if the marriage has been consummated before she attains the age of 15 years?

Facts: The plaintiff wife filed a suit for dissolution of her marriage. It was her case that she was never given in marriage to the defendant as he proclaimed and if at all it had taken place during her infancy, when she was hardly a year old, she had repudiated the same. According to the defendant, the marriage was performed by the plaintiff's father when she was five years old and that it was an exchange marriage *in lieu of* the marriage of his own sister with the uncle of the plaintiff; he further contended that they lived together and the marriage was consummated. The trial judge found that the plaintiff was married by her father during her infancy but there was no credible proof of the consumation. The plaintiff was thus awarded a decree. On appeal by the defendant, the District Judge came to the conclusion that the marriage was consummated and therefore, the appeal was accepted. Hence, the wife's second appeal.

Order: The sole question for determination in this case was whether the plaintiff had repudiated her marriage in accordance with the provisions of section 2 of the Dissolution of Muslim Marriages Act, 1939. Section 2 provides that a woman married under the Muslim law shall be entitled to obtain a decree for dissolution of her marriage on the ground, *inter alia*, that "she having been given in marriage by her father or other guardian before she attained the age of 15 years, repudiated the marriage before attaining the age of eighteen years provided that the marriage has not been consummated".

In this case, it was not disputed that the plaintiff was married by her father long before she was 15 years old and the suit for dissolution of marriage was instituted when she was 14 years old, according to medical testimony. In any case it was filed before she attained the age of 18 years. The evidence as to consummation was found to be very unsatisfactory. The defendant argued that the plaintiff's refusal to submit to medical examination should be treated as an evidence against her. The court, however, held that such refusal could not be taken to be proof of consummation of marriage which should have been proved as a fact on the consideration of the entire evidence of the case. In any case, the plaintiff, at the time of the alleged consummation was still below the age of 15 years and assuming consummation to be a fact, the court held, "it could not destroy her right to repudiate the marriage after she had attained the age of 15. She had three years within which to proclaim the exercise of that right and the institution of a suit was one mode of proclaiming it". Thus, the plaintiff's appeal was admitted as she had not lost her right to repudiate her marriage.

Comment: Prior to the Dissolution of Muslim Marriages Act, 1939, a minor's marriage contracted by the father or grandfather could not be repudiated unless the father or grandfather acted negligently or wickedly, or the marriage was to the manifest disadvantage of the minor. The Act has removed these conditions and a minor Muslim girl whose marriage has been contracted by the father or grandfather can also exercise her option of repudiation provided (a) the marriage took place before she was 15 years old; (b) she seeks repudiation before attaining the age of 18 years and (c) the marriage has not been consummated. If, however, the marriage is consummated before she attains the age of 15, she does not lose her right.

RESTITUTION OF CONJUGAL RIGHTS

First Wife may Refuse Restitution where Husband Marries Another Woman

Itwari v. *Asghari*,
AIR 1960 All 684: 1960 All LJ 523: 1960 All WR (HC) 397

Issue: Can a Muslim husband who enters into another marriage seek restitution of conjugal rights against the first wife? Is the plea of second marriage available to the wife as her defence?

Facts: A Muslim husband filed a suit for restitution of conjugal rights against his wife who refused to return to him after he took a second wife and accused him of cruelty.

The parties were married in 1950. After some time relations strained and the wife left him and returned to her parents; the husband took no steps to bring her back; contrarily, he married another woman. The first wife filed an application for maintenance under section 488 of the Cr. P.C., and thereupon, the husband filed for restitution impleading her father and brothers as well, as co-respondents. The wife contested. Her defence was that the husband turned her out of the house, had illicit relations with a woman who he later married, and also took her ornaments; in short that he caused her immense physical and mental pain. He had not paid her dower as well. The Trial Court Munsif held that the wife could not establish cruelty. According to him, the mere fact of husband's second marriage does not raise presumption of cruelty. The husband's explanation that "he had not taken his second wife to live in her house with Asghari" found favour with Munsif. Besides, he felt that if she was really aggrieved by the husband's second marriage, she should have obtained a decree of dissolution of marriage. The husband's suit for restitution was accordingly, decreed along with an order directing the co-respondents not to prevent her from going back to the husband. On wife's appeal, the District Judge reversed the finding of the Trial Court. According to him, the husband had filed his suit for restitution only as a counterblast to wife's application for maintenance. Prior to that, he had never made any attempts to bring her back. He was "now putting up a show to get her back only to escape from the liability to pay maintenance allowance", he said. Hence, the husband's second appeal.

Order: On behalf of the appellant, it was argued that the mere fact of the husband taking a second wife was no proof of cruelty as every Muslim has a right to take upto four wives, and if the first wife is permitted to leave the husband merely on that ground, it would be a virtual denial of his right; further, that to defeat a husband's suit for restitution there must be proof of cruelty of such character as to render it unsafe for the wife to return to her husband's dominion. The court observed that it is not the right of the husband to take a second wife which is in dispute but whether "as a court of equity, the court should lend assistance to the husband by compelling the first wife, on pain of severe penalties, to live with him after he has taken a second wife in the circumstances in which he did". Further, according to the court, in a suit for restitution by a Muslim husband against the first wife if the court feels that the circumstances reveal that in taking a second wife, the husband has been guilty of such conduct as to make it inequitable for the court to compel the first wife to live with him, it will refuse relief. The court also pointed out towards the changing social conditions. The most convincing proof of this change is the Dissolution of Muslim Marriages Act 1939, which gives to a wife a right to sue for dissolution of her marriage on several grounds which were previously not available. One of the them is the failure of the husband who has more than one wife to treat all of them equitably in accordance with the injunctions of the Quran. [section 2(f)] "By this Act, the Legislature has made a distinct endeavour to ameliorate the lot of the wife and we (the courts) must apply the law in consonance with the spirit of the legislation", the court observed relying on Sinha J.'s remarks in *Sofia Begum* v. *Zaheer Hasan*, AIR 1947 All 16: 230 Ind Cas 239.

Reiterating the fact that social conditions and habits among Indian Mussalmans have changed considerably the court stated: "Today the importing of a second wife into the household ordinarily means a stinging insult to the first. It leads to the asking of awkward questions, the raising of unsympathetic eyebrows and the pointing of derisive fingers at the first wife who is automatically degraded by society. All this is likely to prey upon her mind and health if she is compelled to live with her husband under altered circumstances." The court also pointed out that in these changed times, a husband who takes a second wife will not be permitted to pretend that he did not realise the effect of his action on the feelings and health of the first wife. Under the law, the husband will be presumed to intend the natural consequences of his own conduct [relying on *Simpson* v. *Simpson*, (1951) 1 All ER 955: (1951) 1 TLR 1019: 1951 P 320. "Under the prevailing conditions, the very act of taking a second wife, in the absence of a weighty and convincing explanation raises a presumption of cruelty to the first."

After analysing the case law and entire circumstances of the case, the court held that the wife had been deserted and neglected by the husband for so many years. In the circumstances, it will be inequitable to compel her to join the husband. The husband's appeal was, accordingly, dismissed.

Comment: The court in this case emphasised the fact that even though polygamy is permissible amongst Muslims, the Muslim Law as enforced in India has considered it as an institution to be tolerated but not encouraged, and has not conferred upon the husband any fundamental right to compel the first wife to share his consortium with another woman in all circumstances. While the court has all through the judgment disapproved of the husband's second marriage, it seems to have kept some leeway when it refers to "circumstances" and "weighty and convincing explanation" for the act which means that second marriage *per se* is not an act of cruelty. The judgment, however, is about half-a-century old and much water has flown down the river since. In the changed scenario today, few would disagree that second marriage, without anything more, is an act of cruelty.

MAINTENANCE

Muslim Husband's Liability under Section 125

Mohd. Ahmad Khan v. Shah Bano Begum,
AIR 1985 SC 945: 1985 Cr LJ 875: (1985) 2 SCC 556

Issue: What is the extent of Muslim husband's liability to maintain his divorced wife under section 125 of the Cr. P.C., 1973?

Facts: Ahmad Khan, an advocate, was married to Shah Bano Begum in 1932, and had five children. They lived together till 1975, when she was driven out of the house by her husband. In 1978, she filed a petition for maintenance under section 125 of the Cr. P.C. As soon as she filed this petition, the husband divorced her 'by an irrevocable *talaq*'. He contended that after the divorce, he had no obligation to maintain her. The judicial Magistrate at Indore ordered him to pay her "a princely sum" of ₹ 25 per month even though the wife had alleged that he was earning ₹ 60,000 per year. On appeal, the Madhya Pradesh High Court raised this amount to ₹ 179.20. Dissatisfied with this order, the husband came in appeal to the Supreme Court. He challenged the maintainability of the petition as also his liability to maintain her after the period of *iddat* and after returning her *mahr*.

Order: The court went into the details of various authorities and translations of the verses of the Holy Quran in support of the view that a Muslim woman who has been divorced by her husband has a right to be maintained even after the period of *iddat*. The husband's plea that since he had returned to her the whole sum of ₹ 30,000 which, under the personal law applicable to them was payable after divorce in terms of the provisions of section 127 of the Cr. P.C., he had no further liability towards her maintenance, was not accepted. According to the court, *mahr* was an obligation imposed on the husband as a mark of respect for the wife. It is not an amount in consideration of divorce. It held:

> "There can be no greater authority on this question than the Holy Quran, "the Quran, the sacred book of Islam, comprises in its 114 *suras* or chapters, the total of revelations believed to have been communicated to Prophet Mohammed, as a final expression of God's Will" ....Verses (*Aiyats*) 241 and 242 of the Quran shows that there is an obligation on Muslim husbands to provide for their divorced wives."

The court, thus, upheld the wife's right to be maintained and imposed costs of ₹ 10,000 on the husband who divorced his wife and threw her out of the house after 43 years of marriage and after having five children. It held, that the provision for maintenance under section 125 of the Cr. P.C., is not dependent on the religion of the spouses. It is a secular law applicable to all irrespective of religion. It observed:

> "The liability imposed by section 125 to maintain close relatives who are indigent is founded upon the individual's obligation to society to prevent vagrancy and destitution. That is the moral edict of the law and morality cannot be dubbed with religion."

Comment: The judgment evoked unprecedented debate and controversy on the Muslim woman's right to claim maintenance from the husband after divorce. It ultimately led to the enactment of the Muslim Women (Protection of Rights on Divorce) Act, 1986.

Muslim Women (Protection of Rights on Divorce) Act does not Affect Right of Minor Children of Divorced Muslim Parents to Claim Maintenance under the Code

Noor Saba Khatoon v. *Mohd Quasim*,
AIR 1997 SC 3280: 1997 Cr LJ 3972: 1997 AIR SCW 3343

Issue: Do the provisions of the Muslim Women (Protection of Rights on Divorce) Act, 1986 (MWA), in any way affect the right of minor children of divorced Muslim parents to claim maintenance under section 125 of the Cr. P.C.?

Facts: The parties were married in 1980, and had two daughters and one son. Disputes cropped up between them and the respondent-husband allegedly turned the appellant wife out of the matrimonial home along with the three children aged 6, 3 and 1½ years at that time. He also refused and neglected to maintain her as well as the children. The wife filed an application for maintenance under section 125 of the Cr. P.C. The husband was directed to pay maintenance to her at the rate of ₹ 200 per month, and to each of the children a monthly allowance of ₹ 150. This order by the Trial Court was made on January 19, 1993. Thereafter, the husband divorced the wife and filed an application in the Trial Court for modification of the earlier maintenance order in view of the provisions of the MWA. The order was modified and under the new order, the wife was awarded maintenance only for the period of *iddat*. The order pertaining to children was not altered as according to the court, the MWA did not affect the rights of the children. The husband challenged this order through a revision petition which was dismissed. He, thereupon, filed a criminal miscellaneous petition under section 482 of the Cr. P.C. in the High Court, challenging the correctness of that part of the order which upheld the right of maintenance of the three minor children, under section 125, Cr. P.C. A single judge of the High Court took the view that after the coming into force of MWA in 1986, the minor children of Muslims are not entitled to claim maintenance under sections 125-127 of the Cr. P.C., and that, under section 3(i)(b) of the MWA, a divorced Muslim woman is entitled to claim maintenance for her minor children only for a period of two years from the date of birth of the child. In view of this, the court held, only the third child who was 1½ years old was entitled to maintenance till she attained the age of two. It is against this order that the wife came in appeal to the Supreme Court.

Order: The question was whether section 3(i)(b) of the MWA, in any way affects the rights of minor children of divorced Muslim parents to claim maintenance under section 125 of the Cr. P.C.

The court held that the MWA was enacted as a sequel to the judgment in *Shah Bano*, AIR 1985 SC 945. The Act was not enacted to regulate the obligations of a Muslim father to maintain his minor children unable to maintain themselves. Children continue to be governed by the provisions under sections 125-127 of the Cr. P.C., the court ruled.

Referring to the language of section 3(i)(b) of the MWA, the court observed that it provides for additional maintenance to the wife for the fosterage period of two years from the date of birth of the child, which is presumably aimed at providing some extra amount to the mother for her nourishment for nursing or taking care of the infants upto a period of two years. It has nothing to do with the right to claim maintenance under the provision of section 125 of the Cr. P.C. Reversing the order of the High Court, the Supreme Court held:

> "These provisions (Section 125 of the Cr. P.C.) are not affected by clause 3(i)(b) of the Act and indeed it would be unreasonable, unfair and inequitable and even preposterous to deny the benefit of section 125 of the Code of Criminal Procedure to the children on the ground that they are born of Muslim parents. The effect of a beneficial legislation like section 125 cannot be allowed to be defeated except through clear provisions of a statute. We do not find manifestation of any such intention in the 1986 Act to take away the independent rights of children to claim maintenance under section 125 of the Cr. P.C."

Comment: The MWA does not preclude the right of minor children born to divorced Muslim parents, to seek maintenance under the provisions of the Cr. P.C. Thus, while a divorced Muslim wife is (allegedly) out of the purview of section 125, Cr. P.C., Muslim children are at par with children belonging to other faiths, in the matter of claiming maintenance under the provisions of the secular statute, *viz.*, the Code of Criminal Procedure, 1973.

Note: See also *Naseem v. State of Uttar Pradesh*, 1999 Cr LJ 301: 1998 All LJ 2270: 1998 (37) All CriC 867 (All) wherein the court held that the Muslim Women (Protection of Rights on Divorce) Act does not take away the jurisdiction or power of a Magistrate to award maintenance to minor children under the provision of section 125 of the Cr. P.C.

Constitutional Validity of Muslim Women (Protection of Rights on Divorce) Act

Danial Latifi v. *Union of India,*
(2001) 6 SCALE 537: AIR 2001 SC 3958: 2001 Cr LJ 4660

Issue: The constitutional validity of the Muslim Women (Protection of Rights on Divorce) Act, 1986 (MWA), was challenged on the ground that it infringed articles 14, 15 and 21 of the Constitution. The five-judge Bench upheld its validity.

Facts: The Muslim Women (Protection of Rights on Divorce) Act was passed after the decision in the *Mohd. Ahmad Khan* v. *Shah Bano Begum*, AIR 1985 SC 945: 1985 Cr LJ 875: (1985) 2 SCC 556, which held that if the divorced woman is able to maintain herself, the husband's liability ceases with the expiration of the *iddat* period, but if she is unable to maintain herself after the period of *iddat*, she is entitled to have recourse to provisions in section 125 of the Cr. P.C. The Muslim Women (Protection of Rights on Divorce) Act was passed with the intention to make the decision in *Shah Bano* ineffective. The Act, *inter alia*, provides for the following:

(a) A Muslim divorced woman shall be entitled to a reasonable and fair provision and maintenance within the period of *iddat*, by her former husband and in case she maintains the children born to her before or after her divorce, such reasonable provision and maintenance would be extended to a period of two years from the dates of birth of the children. She will also be entitled to *mehr* or dower and all the properties given to her by her relatives, friends, husband and the husband's relatives. If the above benefits are not given to her at the time of divorce, she is entitled to apply to the Magistrate for an order directing her former husband to provide for such maintenance, the payment of *mehr* or dower or the delivery of the properties.

(b) Where a Muslim divorced woman is unable to maintain herself after the period of *iddat*, the Magistrate is empowered to make an order for the payment of maintenance by her relatives who would be entitled to inherit her property on her death, according to the Muslim law, in the proportions which they would inherit her property. If any one of such relatives is unable to pay his or her share on the ground of his or her not having the means to pay, the Magistrate would direct the other relatives who have sufficient means to pay the shares of these relatives also. But where a divorced woman has no relatives or such relatives or any one of them has not enough means to pay the maintenance, or the other relatives who have been asked to pay the share of the defaulting relatives also do not have means to pay the shares of defaulting relatives, the Magistrate would order the State Wakf Board to pay the maintenance ordered by him or the shares of the relatives who are unable to pay.

These provisions are contained in sections 3 and 4 of the Muslim Women (Protection of Rights on Divorce) Act which were challenged in the present writ petition. The main grounds for challenge were:

(i) Section 125 of the Cr. P.C. is a provision made in respect of women belonging to all religions and exclusion of Muslim women from its benefits would be discrimination between women and women.

(ii) Apart from gender injustice caused in the country, this discrimination further leads to a monstrous proposition of nullifying a law declared by this Court in *Shah Bano*. Thus, there is a violation of not only equality before law, but also equal protection of laws and inherent infringement of article 21 of the Constitution as well as basic human values.

(iii) If the object of section 125, Cr. P.C., is to avoid vagrancy, the remedy thereunder cannot be denied to Muslim women.

(iv) The Act is un-Islamic, unconstitutional and it has the potential of suffocating the Muslim women, and it undermines the secular character which is the basic feature of the courts.

(v) There is no rhyme or reason to deprive the Muslim women from the applicability of the provisions of section 125, Cr.P.C., and consequently, the present Act must be held to be discriminatory and violative of article 14 of the Constitution.

(vi) The conferment of power on the Magistrate under sub-section (2) of section 3 and section 4 of the Act is different from the right of a Muslim woman like any other woman in the country, to avail of the remedies under section 125, Cr. P.C., and such deprivation would make the Act unconstitutional as there is no nexus to deprive a Muslim woman from availing the remedies under section 125, Cr. P.C., notwithstanding the fact that the conditions precedent for availing of the said remedies are satisfied.

In support of the constitutional validity of the impugned Act, the following arguments were given:

(i) Where a question of maintenance arises which forms part of the personal law of a community, what is fair and reasonable is a question of fact in that context. Under section 3 of the Act it is provided that a reasonable and fair provision and maintenance to be made and paid by her former husband within the period of *iddat*, would make it clear that it cannot be for life, but would only be for the period of *iddat* and when that fact has clearly been stated in the provision, the question of interpretation as to whether it is for life or for the period of *iddat* would not arise.

(ii) Challenge raised in this petition is *de hors* the personal law. Personal law is a legitimate basis for discrimination, if at all and therefore, does not offend article 14 of the Constitution.

(iii) If the Legislature, as a matter of policy, wants to apply section 125, Cr. P.C., to Muslims, it could also be stated that the same Legislature can, by implication, withdraw such application and make some other provision in that regard. Parliament can amend section 125, Cr. P.C., so as to exclude them and apply the personal law, and the policy of section 125 is not to create a right of maintenance *de hors* the personal law.

(iv) In *Shah Bano*, it has been held that a divorced woman is entitled to maintenance even after the *iddat* period from the husband and that is how the Parliament also understood the ratio of that decision. To overcome the ratio of the said decision, the present Act has been enacted and section 3(1)(a) is not in discord with the personal law.

(v) The aim of the Act is not to penalise the husband but to avoid vagrancy and in this context, section 4 of the Act is good enough to take care of such a situation; and infact, the social ethos of Muslim society spreads a wider net to take care of a Muslim divorced wife and not at all dependent on the husband.

(vi) The interpretation to be placed on the enactment should be in consonance with the Muslim personal law and also meet a situation of vagrancy of a Muslim divorced wife, even when there is a denial of the remedy provided under section 125, Cr. P.C., and such a course would not lead to vagrancy since provision has been made in the Act. This court will have to bear in mind the social ethos of Muslims which are different, and the enactment is consistent with law and justice.

(vii) The Parliament enacted the impugned Act respecting the personal law of Muslims, and that itself is a legitimate basis for making a differentiation; that a separate law for a community on the basis of personal law applicable to such community, cannot be held to be discriminatory.

(viii) The personal law is now being continued by a legislative enactment and the entire policy behind the Act is not to confer a right of maintenance, unrelated to the personal law.

(ix) The Act resolves all issues , bearing in mind the personal law of the Muslim community and the fact that the benefits of section 125, Cr. P.C., have not been extended to Muslim women would not necessarily lead to a conclusion that there is no provision to protect the Muslim women from vagaries and from being a destitute.

In view of all the above, it was argued that the Act is not invalid or unconstitutional.

Order: The court analysed the *Shah Bano* judgment and the provisions of the Muslim Women (Protection of Rights on Divorce) Act in detail. It conceded that the Act appears to be, *prima facie*, violative of article 14 of the Constitution which mandates equality and equal protection of law to all persons, and also article 15, which prohibits discrimination on grounds, *inter alia*, of religion. It, however, observed that the validity or otherwise of a statute would depend on the interpretation of the same; and the court decided to interpret it in a manner so as to uphold the validity of the Act on the ground that "the Legislature does not intend to enact unconstitutional laws".

According to the court, section 3 of the Muslim Women (Protection of Rights on Divorce) Act, lays down two separate and distinct obligations on the part of the husband, *viz.*, (i) to make a reasonable and fair provision for his divorced wife, and (ii) to provide maintenance for her. The emphasis is not on the nature of duration of any such provision or maintenance, but on the time by which an arrangement for payment of provision and maintenance should be concluded, namely, 'within the *iddat* period'. Such interpretation, according to the court, would have the effect of excluding from liability for *post-iddat* period, maintenance by a husband who had already discharged his obligations of both 'reasonable and fair provision' and 'maintenance', by paying these amounts in *lump-sum* to his wife in addition to having paid her *mehr* and restored her dower as per section 3(1)(c) and 3(1)(d) of the Act. According to the court, the Muslim Women (Protection of Rights on Divorce) Act actually and in reality codifies what was stated in *Shah Bano* while upholding the validity of the Act. The court summed up its conclusions as follows:

(i) A Muslim husband is liable to make reasonable and fair provision for the future of the divorced wife, which obviously includes her maintenance as well. Such a reasonable and fair provision extending beyond the *iddat* period must be made by the husband within the *iddat* period in terms of section 3(1)(a) of the Act.

(ii) The liability of a Muslim husband towards his wife arising under section 3(1)(a) of the Act to pay maintenance is not confined to the *iddat* period.

(iii) A divorced Muslim woman, who has not remarried, and who is not able to maintain herself after the *iddat* period can proceed as provided under section 4 of the Act against her relatives who are liable to maintain her in proportion to the properties which they inherit on her death according to Muslim law, from such divorced woman, including her children and parents. In case of any of the relatives being unable to pay maintenance, the Magistrate may direct the State Wakf Board established under the Act to pay such maintenance.

(iv) The provisions of the Act do not offend articles 14, 15 and 21 of the Constitution of India.

Comment: The Muslim Women (Protection of Rights on Divorce) Act is on the very face of it discriminatory and against the constitutional mandate of gender equality, as well as non-discrimination based on religion. Even the Court has conceded that the provisions of the Act appear to be *prima facie* violative of article 14. The Court remarked that the "Legislature does not intend to enact unconstitutional laws". But that *per se* is no ground for upholding an Act as constitutional. If it were to be so construed then never would have any law been struck down as *ultra vires*. In this case the court has, through its unconvincing interpretation, imposed a seal of constitutional validity on a statute.

Maintenance – Earlier under Section 125, Cr. P.C. – Later under Section 3 of Muslim Women Act, 1986 – Held Abuse of the Process of Court

Sayeed Khan Faujdar Khan v. Zaheba Begum,
AIR 2006 Bom 39: II (2006) DMC 294: 2006 Mat LR 261

Issue: Can a divorced Muslim wife who withdraws an earlier application for maintenance under section 125, Cr. P.C. on the basis of settlement, subsequently claim maintenance under section 3 of the Muslim Women (Protection of Rights on Divorce) Act, 1986?

Facts: The husband had divorced the respondent wife in 1996. She filed an application for grant of maintenance which was not passed as the parties arrived at a settlement whereby the articles of dowry and *Meher* amount of Rs. 15,000 was given to the wife and as such, the wife informed the court that she was not interested in prosecution of the application under section 125, Cr. P.C. Later she filed an application under the Muslim Women Act for reasonable and fair provision of ₹ 25,000 and maintenance of ₹ 15,000 for *iddat* period and return of remaining articles of *dahej* worth ₹ 50,000. The wife's claim for reasonable and fair provision to the extent of ₹ 10,000 was decreed. This was challenged.

Order: The court held that the earlier settlement made by the parties was binding on the parties. The wife's application under section 3 of the Muslim Women's Act "is nothing but an abuse of the process of the court", the court observed. The husband's petition was, thus, allowed.

Comment: A consent order or settlement arrived between the parties in proceedings under section 125 of the Cr. P.C. operates as estoppel and no party can be allowed to misuse or abuse the process of the court by filing subsequent application under a different Act for the same relief on the same set of facts or circumstances.

Maintenance under Section 125 even after Iddat

Shabana Bano v. Imran Khan,
AIR 2010 SC 305 (MP): 2009 AIR SCW 7490: 2010 Cr LJ 521

Issue: The issue involved was as to a divorced Muslim woman's right to maintenance under section 125 of the Cr. P.C. even after the *iddat* period and secondly whether Family Court established under the Family Court Act has exclusive jurisdiction to adjudicate upon applications filed under section 125 of Cr. P.C.

Facts: Parties were married according to Muslim rites. The husband treated the wife with cruelty with continuing demands for dowry. She went to her parents house for delivery and even after that he refused to bring her back if his demands for dowry were not met. Consequently, the wife filed a petition for maintenance under section 125 of the Cr. P.C.

The husband raised a preliminary objection that he had already divorced her on 20-8-2004 in accordance with Muslim law and hence, under the provisions of the Muslim Women (Protection of Rights on Divorce) Act, 1986 she is not entitled to any maintenance after the divorce and after the expiry of the *iddat* period. This further contention was that she was herself earning and so not entitled to receive maintenance from him. The Family Court awarded a sum of Rs. 2,000 per month as maintenance from 26-4-2004, *i.e.,* date of filing of the petition, to 20-8-2004 *i.e.,* date of divorce and further from 20-8-2004 till the expiry of *iddat* period. No maintenance was held to be payable after that period. Against this the wife filed a revision petition before the Gwalior Bench of the Madhya Pradesh High Court which substantially upheld the Family Court order. Hence the wife's appeal before the Supreme Court. The basic issue for consideration was whether a Muslim divorced wife would be entitled to receive maintenance from her ex-husband under section 125 of the Cr. P.C. and if so, through which forum. As to the forum, the court analysed the provisions of the Muslim Women's Act, the Cr. P.C. and the Family Courts Act and arrived at a finding that the Family Court established under the Family Court Act shall exclusively have jurisdiction to adjudicate upon the applications filed under section 125 of the Cr. P.C. "A bare perusal of section 20 of the Family Court Act makes it crystal clear that the provisions of this Act shall have overriding effect on all other enactments in force dealing with the issue", the court added. As to entitlement of the appellant to maintenance after divorce and post-*iddat* period, the court referred to the provisions of the Cr. P.C., the Muslim Act as also to the judicial pronouncements, notably Shah Bano (*Mohd. Ahmad Khan* v. *Shah Bano Begum,* AIR 1985 SC 945: 1985 Cr LJ 875: (1985) 2 SCC 556) and *Danial Latifi* v. *Union of India,* (2001) 6 SCALE 537: AIR 2001 SC 3958: 2001 Cr LJ 4660 and allowing wife's appeal, held (at p. 309):

> "Cumulative reading of the relevant portions of the judgments of this Court....would make it crystal clear that even a divorced Muslim woman would be entitled to claim maintenance from her divorced husband as long as she does not remarry. This being a beneficial piece of legislation, the benefit thereof must accrue to the divorced Muslim women".

Order: The court held that a divorced Muslim wife is entitled to be maintained under section 125 of the Cr. P.C. even after divorce and the post-*Iddat* period until she remarries.

Comment: The judgment has cleared all doubts and vagueness surrounding the issue post-enactment of the Muslim Women (Protection of Rights on Divorce) Act, 1986. All judgments which held that her right under section 125 Cr. P.C. ceases on divorce or is limited to the period of *Iddat,* are no good law. Her right shall continue as long as she does not remarry.

Kunhimohammed v. Ayishakutty,
AIR 2010 (NOC) 992 (Ker)

Issue: The rights of a divorced Muslim woman to claim maintenance under section 125 of the Cr. P.C. *vis-à-vis* section 3 of the Muslim Women (Protection of Rights on Divorce) Act, 1986, (MWA) was the issue involved in this case. Another issue involved was as to the validity of a divorce by unilateral pronouncement of 'Talaq' without any attempt of reconciliation.

Facts: This was a case where a Muslim wife, after divorce claimed maintenance under the provisions of section 125 of the Cr. P.C. which was resisted by the husband on the plea that after the coming into force of the Muslim Women (Protection of Rights on Divorce) Act, 1986 (MWA) her rights under section 125, Cr. P.C. stand extinguished. The Kerala High Court dealt with this issue in good detail. It stated that when the MWA was enacted, the right of maintenance under section 125 Cr. P.C. was already there and the Parliament was fully conscious of the existence of such right. There is no indication in the MWA that the right under section 125 Cr. P.C. shall stand extinguished. Had this been the intention the Parliament would have stated so. Both rights under section 125 of the Cr. P.C. and section 3 of the MWA were conferred on the divorced Muslim woman and she has a right to choose between them. The Court further pointed out that even other personal laws, the Hindu Marriage Act, Parsi Marriage and Divorce Act and the Divorce Act (Christian personal law) provide for maintenance and permanent alimony and this does not, admittedly, take away the rights of the wives under section 125, Cr. P.C.

As pointed out by the court:

> "The mere fact that the personal law provides for certain claims on divorce cannot *ipso facto* lead to the conclusion that to such persons provisions of section 125 of the Code providing for maintenance to the divorced wives will not apply. The stipulation in the personal law has a totally different purpose and object to be achieved. The motivations under section 125 of the Code are totally different from the stipulations in the personal law applicable to different religious groups. Preventing vagrancy is the primary and dominant rationale of section 125 of the Code. That stipulation is in the domain/zone of secular universal law applicable to all Indians. Inability to maintain oneself is the *mantra* that unlocks the lock to the secular section 125 whereas section 3 of the Act [MWA] has no reference to ability or inability to maintain oneself. The domain of the two statutes....are thus entirely different. Thus it would be improper to reckon the Act as special, as to exclude the general Code. Inasmuch as they belong to two totally different zones/domains, the theory that special excludes the general cannot certainly apply...."

The court further clarified that when payment under section 3 of the MWA is actually made and absolution is granted by the court under section 127(3)(b) of the Code then her right under section 125 of the Cr. P.C. stands extinguished; until then, her right subsists.

Order: In an order of great significance the court has held that section 3 of the MWA does not debar a divorced Muslim woman to claim maintenance under the provisions of the Cr. P.C.; and also that there must be a reasonable cause for *talaq* which must be preceded by attempts of reconciliation.

Comment: Confusion and uncertainty over divorced Muslim woman's right to claim maintenance under the provisions of the Cr. P.C. *vis-à-vis* the MWA has been cleared specially in view of the Apex Court judgment in *Shabana Bano* v. *Imran Khan,* AIR 2010 SC 305 (MP): 2009 AIR SCW 7490: 2010 Cr LJ 521.

Payment of Customary Amounts

Thilothama v. *Kunjappan,*
1983 Cr LJ 273 (Ker): I (1983) DMC 241: 1983 Ker LT 90

Issue: The provision under section 127(3) of the Cr. P.C. would be attracted only when the payments made by the husband under customary or personal law are sufficient to meet the divorced wife's future needs.

Facts: A wife filed an application for maintenance under section 125 of the Cr. P.C. The husband was ordered to pay ₹ 50 per month. He also paid her Rs. 2,000 as compensation for divorce under section 14 of the Cochin Marumakkathayam Thiyya Act, 1115 (Malayalam era). The husband sought cancellation of the maintenance order on the ground that he had paid the compensation which was payable to the wife on divorce under the personal law.

Order: The court held, that the maintenance order could be cancelled only if the sum paid was a reasonable substitute for provision for future maintenance. The amount of ₹ 2,000 paid in this case, "cannot be regarded as the capitalised substitute for continued payment of maintenance at the rate of rupees fifty per month" (at p. 278). The husband's application for cancellation was thus rejected.

Comment: When the amount paid by the husband under customary or personal law is only illusory and not realistic or meaningful provision for a divorced wife's needs, the court would not accept such amount as substitute or settlement of her right of maintenance under the provisions of section 125 of the Cr. P.C.

Can Payment under Customary Law Absolve Husband of his Liability under the Code of Criminal Procedure

Bai Tahira v. Ali Hussain Fissalli Chothia,
AIR 1979 SC 362: 1979 Cr LJ 151: (1979) 2 SCC 316

Issue: Would payment under section 127(3) of the Cr. P.C., howsoever inadequate, absolve a Muslim husband from his liability to maintain his divorced wife under the provisions of section 125 of the Cr. P.C.?

Facts: Ali Hussain had married Bai Tahira as his second wife in 1956. In 1962, he divorced her. Under a compromise entered into between them, the flat in which they were living was transferred to her; apart from that, *mahr* and *iddat* amount of ₹ 5,000 and ₹ 180, respectively, were also stated to have been adjusted under the terms of compromise. However, some years later, the wife filed an application for maintenance under section 125 of the Cr. P.C. The Magistrate awarded a monthly allowance of ₹ 400 for her and ₹ 300 for the child. On appeal, this order was set aside by the Bombay High Court. Hence, the wife's appeal to the Supreme Court which was allowed.

Order: In terms of section 127(3)(b) of the Cr. P.C., if a woman has received upon divorce, the whole of the sum payable to her under the customary or personal law, then the Magistrate shall cancel any maintenance order made in her favour under the provisions of section 125 of the Cr. P.C. This provision raised two questions: *Firstly*, whether the "sum" received by the divorced woman under the personal law included *dower* or *mahr*, and *secondly*, was the wife debarred from claiming further maintenance even if the aforementioned amount paid to her was just nominal? There were conflicting interpretations by the High Courts, for example, in *Rukhsana Parvin* v. *Shaikh Mohd. Hussein*, 1977 Cr LJ 1041: 1977 Mad LJ 231: 79 Bom LR 123 (Bom), *Hamid Khan* v. *Jammi Bai*, ILR 1978 MP 595 and *Qayyum Khan* v. *Noorunisa*, 1978 Cr LJ 1476 (AP): 1978 Mat LR 343, the courts construed the provision as including *dower* or *mahr* and consequently denied maintenance to the claimant wife's. On the other hand, in *Kunhi Moyin* v. *Pathumma*, 1976 KLT 87 and *Muhammed* v. *Sainabi*, 1976 KLT 711, a liberal interpretation was given and the argument that the payment of the amount payable *in lieu of mahr* and other household articles which belonged to her would absolve the husband of any further liability to maintain the wife, was rejected. The present case *Bai Tahira* resolved that controversy. Justice Krishna Iyer held:

> "The payment of illusory amounts by way of customary or personal law requirement will be considered in the reduction of maintenance rate, but cannot annihilate that rate unless it is a reasonable substitute. The legal sanctity of the payment is certified by the fulfilment of the social obligation, not by a ritual exercise rooted in custom."

Though the husband had discharged his obligation in respect of the *mahr* amount of ₹ 5,000 and *iddat* allowance of ₹ 180, he could not be absolved of his obligation under section 125 of the Code "except on proof of payment of a sum stipulated by customary or personal law whose quantum is more or less sufficient to do duty for maintenance allowance".

According to the court:

> "The scheme of the complex provisions in chapter IX has a social purpose. Ill-used wives and desperate divorcees shall not be driven to material and moral dereliction to seek sanctuary in the streets.........where the husband by customary payment at the time of divorce, has adequately provided for divorce, a subsequent series of recurrent doles is contra-indicated and the husband liberated.........The key-note though is adequacy of payment which will take reasonable care of her maintenance."

Comment: The court has given a very pragmatic judgment and made it clear that payment of illusory amounts in the name of payments under customary or personal law would not defeat the wife's right to seek maintenance under section 125 of the Cr. P.C. It may be mentioned that *Bai Tahira's* approach was sought to be nullified by a Member of Parliament (G.M. Banatwalla) by introducing a Bill by providing that any sum payable on divorce to a woman under the personal law would disentitle her from claiming maintenance under the provision of section 125. It was, however, a private member's Bill. In fact, soon after *Bai Tahira* came *Fuzlunbi* v. *K. Khader Vali*, AIR 1980 SC 1730: 1980 Cr LJ 1249: (1980) 4 SCC 125, which reaffirmed with greater force the *Bai Tahira* ruling.

Note: See also *Mohd. Ahmad Khan* v. *Shah Bano Begum*, AIR 1985 SC 945: 1985 Cr LJ 875: (1985) 2 SCC 556.

GUARDIANSHIP AND CUSTODY

Welfare of Child and not Legal Right of the Parties to be Considered

Farjanabai v. S.K. Ayub Dadamiya,
AIR 1989 Bom 357: 1989 Mah LJ 373: (1989) 1 Hindu LR 717

Issue: Can the welfare of a child be subordinated to the legal right of the party to custody of a minor child? Can mother be denied custody on trivialities simply because under the law, a father enjoys a dominant position?

Facts: A father filed an application under the Guardians and Wards Act, 1890, for being appointed guardian of his two minor sons aged seven and nine. Under the Muslim law, the *Shia* law recognises a mother's right to the custody of her children, *hizanat*, until a son is two years old and the daughter, seven. Under the *Hanafi* law, a mother is entitled to the custody of her son till he reaches the age of seven and in case of daughter, till she attains puberty. In this case, the court granted custody to the father. The mother filed an appeal challenging this order.

Order: The mother's appeal was dismissed. The court held that both the children were above seven and that under the Muslim law a mother is entitled to the custody of male children only upto the age of seven. Even though the children in this case expressed a desire to be with the mother, the court held that they were not yet of age when they could make an intelligent choice and that their welfare did not lie with the mother. Some of the reasons for refusing custody to the mother were: (a) her evidence did not support her case that the husband had re-married or contracted illicit liaison; (b) that her evidence indicated that she has difficulty in maintaining the children within the amount of ₹ 100 per month awarded to her by way of maintenance; and (c) that there was, on the record, some doubt to the fixed residence of the mother.

In view of these factors, the court held there was "no good reason why the ordinary rule of Mohammedan law should not be adhered to in the present case and it must, in the circumstances, prevail over the desire of the children".

Comment: One wonders whether in this case the welfare of the minor children would really lie with the father; denying custody to the mother because of such trivial reasons as financial constraints of the mother or doubts as to her fixed residence do not sound to reason; the financial responsibility for the children in any case lies with the father and the amount of maintenance awarded to the mother can be raised for enabling her to bring up the children. The considerations which weighed with the court against denying custody to the mother surely do not make her less competent as a mother. The real reason for the order seems to be the right of the father under the personal law of the parties.

Welfare of Child to have Precedence over Personal Law

Irfan Ahmad Shaikh v. *Mumtaz,*
AIR 1999 Bom 25: 1998 (2) Hindu LR 485: 1998 (3) Mah LJ 583

Issue: Can custody of a minor daughter be given to the mother notwithstanding the fact that she has re-married a stranger, a fact which disqualifies her to have custody under the general rule of Islamic law?

Facts: Custody of a female child was given to the mother after dissolution of the marriage. While the father did not re-marry, the mother married a man who was not within the prohibited degrees of relationship to the child. The father applied for the child's custody and sought disqualification of the mother on the ground that under the general rule of Islamic law, a mother who re-marries a stranger is disqualified to have custody of her child. (Mulla, *Principles of Mohammedan Law,* 7th Edn., 1972, pp. 332-33, para 352)

Order: The court granted custody of the minor daughter to the mother. According to the judge (R.J. Kochar, J.) the desire of the child through a "very close and natural talk with her in her own language" was assessed and the court found that the child wanted to stay with the mother. Earlier, the child had been given in custody to the father with a view to assess his behaviour but he was found not to have given proper attention to her during that period. The court, therefore, gave custody to the mother, notwithstanding her re-marriage with a stranger. The father contended that the mother loses her right to the custody of a daughter if she re-marries a person who is not within the prohibited degrees of relationship. Elucidating this general rule of Islamic law, the court remarked that the Muslim law is not taking "any pedantic view of the matter. The law does not lay down that in any circumstance and at any cost the mother would be disqualified for the custody the moment she gets re-married.... There is no dogmatic insistence that the child must remain with the father even against the wishes of the child the moment the mother gets re-married to a stranger. That is to happen "in normal condition" (at p. 27). In the opinion of the court, the Muslim law has not only laid down a general rule but has also in different matters, "provided for exceptional circumstances" (at p. 27) to be met with. In the matter of custody, it has never ignored the wishes of a minor child who is of the age of discretion", the court remarked.

Comment: The judgment reiterates that consideration of child's welfare supersedes all principles and rules of personal law.

Mother not Earning is Immaterial
Wazid Ali v. Rehana Anjum,
AIR 2005 MP 141: 2005 (2) Hindu LR 562: 2005 (3) MPLJ 319

Issue: Fact that mother is not earning cannot be a logic to disentitle her to minor's custody; paramount consideration is the welfare of the child but preferential right of any person under the personal law cannot be completely ignored.

Facts: The dispute related to the custody of a four-year-old female child, under the Muslim Law. According to the father-appellant, after their relations became strained, the wife left his company along with the child and went to her parents house. After about six months, her (wife's) brother brought the child to the father and left her there saying that he should take care of his daughter. The child was then seven months and 15 days old. The appellant, apprehending mischief, lodged a report in police and also filed application under section 7 of the Guardians and Wards Act, 1890, for being declared as the guardian of the child. In reply, the wife alleged that the father had taken away the child on the occasion of *Eid* festival under a false pretext and since then the child was with him. She thereupon filed a police report and also application under section 97 of the Criminal Procedure Code. Thereafter, the husband filed the application. The wife prayed that the husband's application be dismissed and she be given custody of the child. The Trial Court dismissed the husband's application but at the same time, it did not direct that the child be delivered to the mother. The reason for this was that the respondent wife had not filed a separate application under the Act. Hence, the husband's appeal.

Order: For the husband, it was argued that the child was residing with the father and till he filed the application under section 7 of the Guardians and Wards Act, the mother did not care to get the child; that the child could be better looked after by the father as he was serving as a teacher whereas the respondent-mother was not doing anything and her father had also retired. For the mother, on the other hand, it was contended that the child was only four years old and under the Muslim Law, she was entitled to her custody till the child attained puberty; besides, even if no application was moved by the respondent under section 7 of the Guardians and Wards Act, the custody of the child could still be given to the mother. It was, therefore, prayed that the husband's appeal should be dismissed.

The court held that the welfare of the minor must be the paramount consideration and not the wishes of the parties. It emphasised that the word "welfare of the child" admits of no strait-jacket yardstick. It has many facets, such as "financial, educational, physical, moral and religious welfare". The fact that the mother was not earning is no reason to disentitle her from taking custody of the minor child, the court held. Also, it held that a prayer seeking custody of the minor child made in reply to husband's application, was enough and would amount to an application with the prayer to give the minor child in her custody. In other words, "merely because the prayer has been made in the reply would not in itself be a ground to deny the delivery of the minor child to the mother. Besides, the mother had not kept silent after the child was taken by the father. She was pursuing the matter to get the child's custody though she approached a wrong forum by filing application under section 97 of the Cr. P.C., which was rejected".

The court also pointed out that while the paramount consideration in awarding custody is the welfare of the minor but, it must be "as far as possible consistent with the personal law relating to the parties. The preferential right of any person to the guardianship under the personal law cannot be ignored unless he or she is totally unfair to be appointed as guardian and court must necessarily consider his or her claim in preference to any other".

The custody of the child was accordingly directed to be handed over to the mother under certain terms and conditions, including visitation rights and meetings for the father and paternal grand-parents.

Comment: The fact that a mother makes a prayer for custody of the child in response to the father's application for guardianship, and not by an independent application, is no ground to reject her claim; nor is the fact that she is not earning.

Welfare of Child and not Personal Law nor Re-marriage to Determine Custody

Poolakkal Ayisakutty v. *Parat Abdul Samad*, AIR 2005 Ker 68: ILR (2005) 1 Ker 14: 2005 (1) Ker LJ 7

Issue: (i) Would personal law have precedence over the provisions of the Guardians and Wards Act, in the matter of child custody?

(ii) Would father's re-marriage disentitle him to the custody of his minor son.

Facts: Mother of the child aged 4, committed suicide and after her death he was brought up by the maternal grandparents. Father had filed an application for the child's custody which was allowed by the Family Court. The maternal parents filed an appeal and the earlier order was modified and the father was given only visitation rights. According to the court, the child was living with the grand parents since the death of his mother and his transplantation at this age would adversely affect the child especially when the father had re-married and a child is born to him of the new marriage.

After the death of the grandfather, the father again filed an application before the Family Court for child's custody. It was contended that on the death of the maternal grandfather, the grandmother alone would not be able to look after the child and his welfare demands that he be put in the custody of the father. The petition was allowed and custody of the child was given to the father; hence the appeal by the grandmother. The principles of Mohammedan Law as laid down in sections 352 and 353 of Mulla's *Principles of Mohammedan Law* were referred to. Section 353 is specially relevant. Under it, "failing the mother, the custody of a boy under the age of seven years and of a girl who has not attained puberty belongs to the following female relatives in the order given below.........." And in the given order, the top relative is the mother's mother. Father is not included in the section.

Order: The court held that when the question of the custody of a child is involved, the primary consideration which weighs with the court is the welfare of the child. Reference was made in this context to, *inter alia*, *Jai Prakash Khadria v. Shyam Sunder Agarwalla*, AIR 2000 SC 2172: 2000 AIR SCW 2341: (2000) 6 SCC 598 and *R.V. Srinath Prasad v. Nandamuri Jayakrishna*, AIR 2001 SC 1056: 2001 AIR SCW 1033: (2001) 4 SCC 71. It held:

"A balance has to be struck between the attachment and sentiments of the parties towards the minor children and the welfare of the minors which is of paramount importance. Principles exported by personal law.......cannot be read in isolation and be divorced from the provisions of the Guardians and Wards Act. The overriding consideration is welfare of the child and the personal law would yield to the provisions of the Guardians and Wards Act."

Several decisions were quoted in support of this opinion [*Rafiq v. Bashiran*, AIR 1963 Raj 239: 1963 Raj LW 954: ILR (1963) 13 Raj 558; *Salamat Ali v. Majjo Begum*, AIR 1985 All 29; *Md. Yunus v. Shamshad Bano*, AIR 1985 All 217: 1985 All WC 386: (1985) 11 All LR 313; *Zynab Bi alias Bibijan v. Md. Ghouse Mohideen*, AIR 1952 Mad 284; *Baby Sarojam v. S. Vijayakrishnan Nair*, AIR 1992 Ker 277: ILR (1992) 2 Ker 449: 1992 (2) Ker LJ 257; *Yusuf v. Sakkeena*, 1998 (2) KLT 573: AIR 1999 Ker 54: ILR (1999) 1 Ker 277; *Merlin Thomas v. C.S. Thomas*, AIR 2003 Ker 232: 2003 (6) Ind LD 545: 2003 (1) Ker LJ 633 and *Chakki v. Ayyappan*, 1988 (1) KLT 556].

In the instant case, the grandmother of the child with whom the child was residing was diabetic and was dependent on her other daughter so it was felt that the welfare of the child lies in giving custody to the father. Conduct of remarriage by the father of the child itself was held to be no ground to reject his prayer for custody. Rather, it was held that a child born of the second marriage who is aged 1½ years would be a good company for the child. In view of all the above, the grandmother's appeal was dismissed.

Comment: Cases where human emotions and sentiments are involved, are difficult to decide. The child in this case always lived with the grandmother who had lost her daughter (the child's mother). She had to face two shocks, one, death of her husband (child's grandfather), and second, removal of the child from her custody at the fag end of her life. But, as aptly remarked by the courts, sentiments have to give way to consideration of the child's welfare.

SELECT CASES UNDER CHRISTIAN LAW

Incompatibility or Absence of Prospects of Happy Life: No decree on ground of Mental Illness/Abnormality

C. Solomon v. Josephine*,
AIR 1959 Mad 151: (1959) 1 Mad LJ 171: ILR (1959) Mad 278

Issue: Where allegations of mental illness or abnormality are made, can the court take into account the mere fact of incompatibility and absence of prospects of happy married life and grant relief?

Facts: This was a husband's petition under section 18 of the Indian Divorce Act, 1869 seeking declaration that the marriage was *null* and *void* since the respondent wife was a lunatic and idiot even prior to the marriage; he alleged that at the time of marriage he was told that she was suffering from hysteria but would be alright after marriage. According to the wife, the husband ill-treated her so she ran away and feared for her life. The district judge, decreeing the suit held that 'in a case like this where the circumstances disclosed do not lead to an inference of the possibility of a happy married life, the court has to take a reasonable and generous, and not a rigid view of the evidence.

Order: In confirmation proceedings before the High Court, the order was reversed as the husband failed to establish that the wife was a lunatic or idiot at the time of marriage. According to the court, the basis of the several provisions of the Indian Divorce Act, 1869, is that mere incompatibility between the spouses, or the prospect of an unhappy married life cannot be a valid ground either for divorce nor for declaration of marriage as *null* and *void*. Further the petition is not for dissolution but for declaration that the marriage is void *ab initio*. The result would be to bastardise the two children born when the parties were together for six years. The court observed (at p. 152):

> "If extraneous circumstances ought to have any bearing on the decision of the petition under any of the provisions of the Indian Divorce Act we think that the prospect of rendering two children...illegitimate is far more serious than the possibility of an unhappy married life."

Comment: When a ground is not established no relief can be granted on ground of incompatibility. Moreover, prospect of rendering children as bastard is a serious matter which the court took due note of.

---

* See *K. Kumar* v. *Leena*, II (2010) DMC 519 (Ker): AIR 2010 Kant 75: ILR 2010 Kant 1221 for case on maintenance in section on "Maintenance".

No Mutual Consent Divorce (Pre-2001 Amendment)

Reynold Rajamani v. Union of India,
AIR 1982 SC 1261: (1982) 2 SCC 474: II (1982) DMC 268

Issue: Whether the provision of the English Matrimonial Causes Act, 1973, can be applied to petitions under the Indian Divorce Act, 1869, by virtue of section 7 (prior to the amendment) of the Indian Divorce Act. (In view of the amendment of the Act in 2001, this issue has only a theoretical value).

Facts: A marriage was solemnized under section 27 of the Indian Christian Marriage Act, 1872. After about 12 years of the marriage, the couple presented a joint petition for divorce by mutual consent under section 28 of the Special Marriage Act, 1954 (SMA). The application was dismissed by the Trial Court on the ground that the provision of the SMA could not be invoked in case of a divorce petition under the Indian Divorce Act (IDA) as the IDA did not provide for divorce by mutual consent. A writ petition in the Delhi High Court against this order was dismissed. In appeal to the Supreme Court, the couple applied for permission to amend their joint petition to enable them to rely on section 7 of the IDA, read with section 1(2)(d) of the Matrimonial Causes Act, 1973. The amendment was allowed and they filed an amended petition in the Trial Court seeking divorce on the ground that they had been living separately for over two years, and the marriage had irretrievably broken. Having failed in the Trial Court and the High Court, the parties approached the Supreme Court. It was argued that section 1(2)(d) of the Matrimonial Causes Act, 1973 of England, must be deemed to have been incorporated in the IDA by virtue of section 7 of the IDA. Rejecting the plea, the Supreme Court held that the expression "principles and rules" in section 7 of the IDA, does not refer to grounds on which a suit may be instituted but the manner in which the court could exercise jurisdiction in deciding a case. Were it to be interpreted otherwise, there would be a conflict with section 10 of the IDA which contains the limited grounds for divorce, the court said. The counsel's plea that the court should adopt a policy of "social engineering" and import into section 7 the content of section 28 of the Special Marriage Act, and section 13B of the Hindu Marriage Act (which provides for divorce by mutual consent), was also turned down. "This is a matter of legislative policy. Courts cannot extend or enlarge legislative policy by adding a provision which was never enacted there," the court remarked. (p. 1264)

Order: The parties failed to get a decree of dissolution on the ground of mutual consent since such ground was not available under the IDA (prior to the amendment in 2001).

Comment: The case has only an academic value. This and many other similar cases caused great hardship to parties whose marriage had utterly broken and they mutually wanted to end it, but in the absence of any provision permitting them to do so, they just had to be legally tied down with each other. The position, however, has changed and under section 10A of the Divorce Act as amended in 2001, mutual consent of the parties has been incorporated as a ground for divorce.

Strong Plea for Uniform Marriage Laws

Jorden Diengdeh v. *S.S. Chopra*,
AIR 1985 SC 935: (1985) 3 SCC 62: II (1985) DMC 42

Issue: A strong plea for uniform matrimonial laws was made. Legislative intervention was sought to liberalise divorce laws where the marriage had irretrievably broken down.

Facts: The wife was a Christian belonging to the Khasi tribe of Meghalaya and an officer in the Indian Foreign Service. The husband was a Sikh. They were married under the Indian Christian Marriage Act, 1872. The wife filed a petition for declaration of nullity of the marriage on the ground of impotency of the husband. The same was turned down and instead judicial separation was granted on the ground of cruelty, by a Single Judge of the Delhi High Court. On appeal, the Division Bench affirmed the single judge's order. The wife then filed special leave appeal to the Supreme Court seeking nullity on the ground of husband's impotency.

Order: The court, after reviewing the personal laws of the communities, made a strong plea for a Uniform Civil Code. Justice Chinnappa Reddy observed:

> "It is thus seen that the law relating to judicial separation, divorce and nullity of marriage is far from uniform. Surely, the time has come now for a complete reform of the law of marriage and make a uniform law applicable to all people irrespective of religion and caste."

The court was convinced that the marriage in this case had been irretrievably broken but lamented that there was no way out for the couple since neither irretrievable breakdown nor mutual consent were grounds for divorce under the Indian Divorce Act. It sought legislative intervention to provide for a uniform divorce law and a way out of unhappy situations where couples cannot live happily together. A copy of the order was also sent to the Ministry of Law and Justice for proper action.

Comment: This judgment is of academic value now since the Indian Divorce Act has been thoroughly amended. Mutual consent has now been made a ground for divorce, *vide* section 10A of the amended Divorce Act [Indian Divorce (Amendment) Act, 2001]. Irretrievable breakdown, however, is not a ground under any of the matrimonial laws though the courts do give a lot of weightage to that factor at the time of granting a decree of dissolution. It is however, expected that soon this will be incorporated as a ground for divorce under the matrimonial law statutes.

Annulment of Marriage: Concealment of Vasectomy before Marriage is Fraud

Best Morning v. Nirmalendu,
AIR 1987 Gau 63: II (1987) DMC 214: (1987) 2 Gau LR 324

Issue: The issue involved was, *inter alia*, whether a husband who conceals the fact that he had undergone vasectomy before marriage was guilty of the matrimonial offence of fraud/cheating.

Facts: The wife filed a petition for annulment of the marriage under section 19 of the Indian Divorce Act alleging that the husband had undergone vasectomy operation which fact he had concealed from her and thus committed fraud. She also took the plea of impotency.

Order: The court held that while no case for impotency can be made out since impotency and disability to have children because of the vasectomy are two different things, yet concealing that fact did amout to fraud. It observed:

> "..... Not that every barren marriage is to break down but ....there should be no deception or fraud perpetuated on the wife by the husband in this regard."

The decree of nullity was confirmed on the ground of fraud.

Comments: Concealment of vasectomy by the husband is indeed a serious matter which has the effect of depriving a woman of motherhood. It is a mental cruelty on her and she can seek dissolution of the marriage or have the marriage annulled on ground of fraud.

Note: In *Benjamin Cardoza v. Gladys Benjamin Cardoza*, AIR 1997 Bom 175P: II (1997) DMC 460: 1997 (2) Hindu LR 677 a husband got a decree of annulment where the wife concealed the fact that she had got her fallopian tubes surgically removed and was incapable of having child; see also *Urmilla Devi v. Narinder Singh*, AIR 2007 HP 19 where concealment of fact by the wife that she never had menses was held to constitute fraud entitling a husband to a decree.

Constitutional Vires of Pre-amendment Act (Divorce Law)

Ammini E.J. v. Union of India,
AIR 1995 Ker 252: 1995 (1) Ker LJ 624

Issue: Is section 10 of the Indian Divorce Act, 1869 (unamended), *ultra vires* articles 14, 15 and 21 of the Constitution?

Facts: Two Christian wives filed separate petitions challenging constitutional validity of section 10 of the Indian Divorce Act, 1869. One petitioner wife was deserted by her husband for several years. He neither cohabited with her nor cared to maintain her and their daughter. She also alleged that she was not even aware of his whereabouts. On these facts, she filed a petition for divorce under section 10 of the Act on the ground of cruelty and desertion and by another petition, she challenged the constitutional validity of this section. The court refused to grant divorce on these grounds but directed the Union of India to take note of the recommendations of the Law Commission contained in its 90th Report and take a decision to amend the section within six months [*Mary Soniz Zacharia* v. *Union of India*, 1990 (1) KLT 131]. However, nothing came out of these recommendations. The other petitioner, Ammini E.J., also alleged desertion and cruelty by the husband. She obtained a decree of judicial separation on these grounds, under section 22 of the Act. She, however, filed the present petition challenging section 10 of the Act under which, inspite of her husband's extreme cruelty, desertion and there being "not even an iota of chance of reconciliation", she was held not to be entitled to a divorce unless she alleged and proved adultery as well. Both these above mentioned petitions were discussed in great detail by the special bench in *Ammini E.J.*

The contentions raised by the petitioners were that section 10 of the Act was *ultra vires* articles 14, 15 and 21 of the Constitution of India. There was gender based discrimination inasmuch as the husband needed to prove adultery simpliciter, whereas the wife had to prove adultery with one or other aggravating ground in order to get a divorce. Discrimination on the ground of religion was alleged as women who professed Christianity and were married under the IDA were denied relief on grounds which could entitle wives belonging to other religions or communities, to the relief. Infringement of article 21, *viz.*, protection of life and personal liberty was also alleged as section 10 of the Act compelled a Christian wife to live without dignity with a man who had deserted her and treated her with cruelty. It was accordingly prayed that the words "incestuous" and "adultery coupled with", as used in section 10, be struck down and the remaining part of the section be retained. These arguments were opposed on the ground that despite repeated recommendations of the Law Commission, the Government had not been able to amend the Act because of the strong opposition from the community itself; further, it was contended that allowing the prayer made by the petitioners would amount to judicial legislation or rewriting of a provision which might not be justifiable in law. An interesting argument against the amendment was that if the plea was accepted, the rewritten provision would be discriminatory against husbands who would continue to be entitled to seek divorce only on the ground of adultery while the wife would get additional grounds apart from adultery. This would disturb the very scheme of the legislation which had made divorce provisions more stringent for the wife as against the husband, it was argued.

Order: After considering the contentions of both the parties, the court held that section 10 was violative of constitutional provisions. It observed (at p. 268):

> "We are of the view that the life of a Christian wife who is compelled to live against her will..........as the wife of a man who hates her, has cruelly treated her and deserted her putting an end to the marital relationship irreversibly will be a sub-human life without dignity and personal liberty.......... It can only be treated as a depressed or oppressed

life without the full liberty and freedom to enjoy life as we would desire to lead in the way Constitution has ensured."

It consequently held (at p. 270):

"Whatever may be the conditions which existed in 1869, when the Act was enacted and which might have justified the incorporation of such provisions in the Act it will be difficult to find any justifiable reason in support of the impugned provisions in the light of the provision in Chapter III of the Constitution guaranteeing various fundamental rights especially articles 14, 15 and 21............."

The court, accordingly, found that the words and phrases "incestuous" and "adultery coupled with" used in the impugned provision in section 10 being severable and not inextricable from the rest of the provision could be struck down; and it did that by declaring these words as *ultra vires* while retaining the rest of the provision.

Comment: The judgment has only an academic value now because the IDA has been thoroughly amended and now the grounds for matrimonial relief are almost at par with the Hindu Marriage Act and the Special Marriage Act; the gender based and religion based discrimination has been removed.

Jurisdiction of Ecclesiastical Courts
George Sebastian v. *Molly Joseph*,
I (2000) DMC 716 (Ker)

Issue: Do the Ecclesiastical court have jurisdiction to decide on matters which are governed by the Indian Divorce Act?

Facts: This was a reference under section 20 of the Indian Divorce Act for confirmation of decree for dissolution of marriage. The husband had filed a petition under section 19(4) of the Indian Divorce Act for nullity of marriage on the ground that his wife's earlier marriage was subsisting when he married her and *secondly*, on the ground of her insanity. The wife's defence was that her previous marriage was already declared void by an Ecclesiastical Tribunal and the respondent husband knew about this. The District Judge, simply on the basis of pleadings and admission of the first marriage, passed a decree of nullity in favour of the husband. It held that since there was no decree in regard to the earlier marriage by any civil court under the Indian Divorce Act that marriage would be considered to be subsisting. In confirmation proceedings under section 20 (prior to the amendment of the Indian Divorce Act in 2001) the special Bench of the Kerala High Court observed (see *Molly Joseph* v. *George Sebastian*, AIR 1997 SC 109 (110): 1996 AIR SCW 4267: (1996) 6 SCC 337:

> Canon law (or personal law of Christians) can have theological or ecclesiastical implications to the parties. But after the Divorce Act came into force, a dissolution or annulment granted under such personal law

cannot have any legal impact as statute has provided a different procedure and different code for divorce or annulment."

The District Court was, however, directed to conduct an enquiry and ascertain the subsistence of the first marriage as alleged by the husband. Against this, the husband filed an appeal before the Supreme Court (see *Molly Joseph* supra).

Order: It was observed that since the District Judge had disposed of the application for divorce without any enquiry into the allegation relating to subsistence of the earlier marriage, the High Court was justified in remitting the matter to the District Court for fresh decision. When the matter was taken up afresh the respondent wife did not participate and the only document brought on record was a certificate issued by St. Thomas Cathedral stating that there was a marriage between the respondent and one K. Thomas which was dissolved by Ecclesiastical court. It was held that when a legislature enacts a law even in respect of the personal law of a group of people following a particular religion, then provisions of such statutorily enacted law shall prevail and override any personal law, usage or custom prevailing prior to the Act. Thus after the enactment of the Indian Divorce Act the forum which can dissolve or annul a marriage is the District Court or the High Court. "There is no scope for any other authority, including the Ecclesiastical Tribunal (Church Court) to exercise of power in connection with matrimonial matters which are covered by the provisions of the Divorce Act" the court said (p. 111 *Molly Joseph* supra). Thus even in cases where the Ecclesiastical court purports to grant annulment or divorce, the Church authorities will still be under disability to perform or solemnise a second marriage for any of the parties until the marriage is dissolved in accordance with a statutory law in force.

It may be mentioned that during the course of confirmation proceedings before the High Court, it was brought to court's notice that the husband had died. However, in view of the significance of the issue involved, the High Court delved into the issue. The decree of divorce was accordingly confirmed.

Comment: Statutory law overrides Ecclesiastical law. All matrimonial matters are to be governed by the statute and not by any custom or Ecclesiastical provisions.

Amendment of Divorce Act – Operation to be Prospective

Deepa Raj Kumar Singh v. *Deepak Kumar,* AIR 2005 Pat 71 (FB): II (2005) DMC 352: 2005 (2) Hindu LR 193

Issue: Are decrees of dissolution of marriage passed prior to amendment of the Divorce Act in 2001, deleting requirement of confirmation, subject to confirmation?

Facts: A wife filed a suit for dissolution of marriage under the Indian Divorce Act, 1869, in 1993 when section 17 of the Act pertaining to confirmation by the High Court of dissolution decree was in force. The divorce decree was also passed in 1998, when the said provision was in force. However, in 2001 the IDA was thoroughly amended and as one of the amendments, section 17 in the original form was deleted thereby dispensing with the requirement of confirmation. The question was whether the requirement of confirmation needs to be complied with in view of the deletion of section 17. (This section has been completely recast now.)

Order: It was held that the case would be governed by section 17 of the IDA, since at the time of the decree, this section was still in force, and any amendment which takes place subsequently is prospective in operation and not retrospective. Reference was made in this context to *Larley* v. *John alias Johny*, AIR 2004 Pat 53: 2004 (2) Hindu LR 339: 2005 (30) All Ind Cas 770 (FB), where it was held that unless expressly or by implication made retrospective, every statute is *prima facie* prospective. In this case, none of the parties to the decree entered appearance despite publication of notice in the newspapers. The court, thus, had no option but to confirm the decree of dissolution under section 17 of the unamended Divorce Act.

Comment: Section 17, as it stood prior to the amendment, only resulted in protracting and prolonging the litigation. The requirement of confirmation has now been dropped by the Divorce Act, 2001.

Waiting Period of Two Years for Petition for Mutual Consent Divorce Arbitrary: Reduced to One Year

Saumya Ann Thomas v. *Union of India*,
II (2010) DMC 526 (Ker)

Issue: An extremely pertinent issue was involved in this case, *viz.*, whether the period of two years as the minimum mandatory period of separate living as stipulated in section 10A of the Divorce Act, 2001 (Divorce by mutual consent) is right, just and fair or is it arbitrary, oppressive or discriminatory.

Facts: Parties to the marriage fell out soon after the marriage and a divorce petition was filed by the petitioners. During the course of the proceedings parties agreed to settle their differences and filed a petition for divorce by mutual consent under section 10A of the Divorce Act. They also sought waiver of the six months waiting period as provided under section 10A(2). The Trial Court dismissed the petition as the stipulated period of two years of separate living had not elapsed. Against this, the parties filed a writ petition. While the request for waiver of the six-month waiting period was rejected straight away a very significant order was made in the context of the requirement of two years of separate living for filing the petition for divorce by mutual consent. The court analysed in great detail, the concept of marriage and its indissolubility and the process of liberalisation of the divorce laws. It observed:

"Many a battle had to be fought socially and legally before the concept of divorce by mutual consent was accepted by the polity and approved by the Legislature".

In fact, the Special Marriage Act, 1954 was the first statute to recognise divorce by mutual consent; much later in 1976 the provision was added in the Hindu Marriage Act. Even later, in 1988, the Parsi Marriage and Divorce Act introduced this ground. The Christian personal law, *viz.*, the Divorce Act, was the last to incorporate the provision of divorce by mutual consent by inserting section 10A. Though provision for mutual consent has been made but the period provided for separate living before parties can apply for divorce on this ground is two years as against one year in all other personal laws.

It was argued, *inter alia*, that "the right to marry and the right to secure divorce must be reckoned as basic and essential incidents of the right to life [article 21 of the Constitution]". The prolonged waiting period only brings agony and unhappiness in the life of the spouses who are unable to live happily together. After having considered all the relevant circumstances the, provisions in the other Acts and also provisions contained in articles 13, 14, 21 and 44, the court came to the conclusion that the stipulation of higher period of two years of mandatory minimum separate living for those to whom Divorce Act applies in contra-distinction to those similarly placed to whom section 13B of the Hindu Marriage Act, section 32B of the Parsi Marriage and Divorce Act and section 28 of the Special Marriage Act would apply, offends the mandate of equality and right to life under articles 14 and 21 of the Constitution. In order to "avoid the vice of unconstitutionality" the court resorted to the principle of severability and held that the stipulation of two years can be read down to one year. (*See* also *Ammini E.J.* v. *Union of India*, AIR 1995 Ker 252 for similar approach). It further stated that "the stipulation in section 10A(1) of the Divorce Act that the parties must have been living separately for a period of two years or more is declared to be unconstitutional as the stipulation of the period of two years therein violates the fundamental rights to equality and the right to life under articles 14 and 21 of the Constitution." A plea for uniform civil code was also made.

Order: To save the provision, it severed the stipulation of two years' period under section 10A(1) and read it down as one year. Since the separate living for over a year and the waiting period of six months had already elapsed, a decree of divorce by mutual consent under article 10A of the Divorce Act was granted.

Comment: The two-year separate living period under the Divorce Act as against one year in the Hindu Marriage Act the Parsi Marriage and Divorce Act and the Special Marriage Act is indeed discrimination based only on religion of the parties which has been effectively addressed. A welcome dimension has also been added by invoking right to life under article 21 of the Constitution in matrimonial relationships. In this context the following remarks of Justice G.S. Saraf in *Anita Jain* v. *Rajendra Jain*, AIR 2010 Raj 56 (58) are pertinent:

> "To live with a man [or woman] you hate is a slavery but to be compelled to submit to his [or her] embraces is a misfortune too great even for slavery itself."

It is thus in the fitness of things that disharmony, unhappiness and agony in matrimonial relationships should not be unduly prolonged.

Child Custody and Visitation: Father Flouting Court Order

Elizabeth Denshaw v. *Arvind M. Denshaw,* AIR 1987 SC 3: (1987) 1 SCC 42: 1986 (4) Supreme 487

Issue: A father who flouts a court's order on custody (American court in this case) is guilty of contempt of court and may lose his visitation rights as well. A mother in whose favour the custody order was made and inspite of the order, the father removed the child from her custody, was restored custody of the child.

Facts: The father, an Indian and the mother, an American, divorced each other. Custody of the child was given to the mother with visitation rights to the father. During one of the week-end visitation, the father picked up the child from school and secretly left the country (USA), for India. The mother moved the court in Michigan and arrest warrants were issued against the father; these warrants, however, could not be executed. The mother then came to India and filed a writ of *habeas corpus* directing the father to produce the child in the court and hand over his custody to her.

Order: The court strongly denounced the father's act. Referring to another similar case [*In re: H (infants)*, (1966) 1 All ER 886: (1966) 1 WLR 381] the court observed:

> "The sudden and unauthorised removal of children from one country to another is far too frequent now-a-days, and as it seems to me, it is the duty of all courts in all countries to do all they can to ensure that the wrongdoer does not gain an advantage by this wrongdoing...... The courts in all countries ought..... to be careful not to do anything to encourage this tendency. This substitution of self-help for due process of law in this field can only harm the interests of wards generally and a judge should...... pay regard to the orders of the proper foreign court unless he is satisfied beyond reasonable doubt that to do so would inflict serious harm to the child."

Accordingly, it held that it would not be in the interest of the minor to uproot him from the place of his birth and where he is brought up. Custody was, therefore, granted to the mother.

Comment: The husband-father in this case was held to be guilty of contempt of court by the American court and his visitation rights were also withdrawn. He, however, tendered a written apology. The Supreme Court of India while handing over the custody to the mother made an observation that complete withdrawal of visitation rights to the father, may not be in the interest of the child either. That issue, however, has been left to the American court to decide.

FAMILY COURTS

Constitutional Validity of Family Courts Act, 1984

Lata Pimple v. Union of India,
AIR 1993 Bom 255: 1994 (1) Bom CR 668: 1993 (2) Civ LJ 208

Issue: Are sections 3, 10, 13, 14, 15 and 16 of the Family Courts Act violative of articles 14 and 22 of the Constitution of India.

Facts: This was a batch of writ petitions challenging the constitutional validity of some sections of the Family Courts Act. It was alleged that section 3 which enjoins the State Government to set up Family Courts in metropolitan cities having population of one million and above, is arbitrary and violative of article 14 and the procedure prescribed under sections 10, 14, 15 and 16 is drastic, discriminatory and violative of article 14 (of the Constitution) too. Besides, section 13, which restricts the presence of lawyers in the court as a matter of rule, was also challenged as being violative of a litigant's right to be represented by a lawyer.

Order: The court referred to various cases and came to the conclusion that the impugned sections were not *ultra vires* the Constitution. The provision in section 3, according to the court, is based on a rational and intelligible differentia made to secure the object of the Act. The Legislature provided for setting up of the Family Courts in areas with vast population because of the long delay in the disposal of matrimonial cases.

As regards the procedure prescribed under sections 10, 14, 15 and 16, the idea here is also to facilitate and expedite proceedings without technicalities with emphasis on reconciliation wherever possible. So far as legal representation was concerned, it was held that section 13 of the Family Courts Act does not put an absolute bar. Wherever the court feels that it is necessary in the interest of justice to have legal assistance, it may appoint a lawyer. Litigants too may ask for legal assistance. However, so far as the fundamental right under the Constitution to be represented by a lawyer is concerned, the court clarified that under article 22(1) of the Constitution, it is only where an accused is arrested and detained in custody that he is entitled as a matter of right to be defended by a legal practitioner of his choice. In no other matter is there a fundamental right to have legal representation. Also, as regards the contention that the section is violative of the equality clause since it discriminates between litigants outside the jurisdiction of this court and those falling within this court, it was held that once the classification made by section 3 of the Family Courts Act is held to be reasonable classification, the same argument would hold good in respect of this clause as well. Moreover, there is no absolute bar to seek legal representation, the court held. In the facts of the present case, the Family Court had rejected the petitioner's application to be represented by a lawyer without giving reasons; the High Court, however, found that the petitioner had made out sufficient cause for being permitted legal representation and hence such permission was granted.

Comments: The whole idea of setting up the Family Courts is to expedite disposal of matrimonial cases without much of harassment and expense to the parties as also without much of technicalities and formalities in the procedure. That is the reason why, as a matter of right, the presence of lawyers is not permitted. However, when justice demands that legal assistance be allowed, the courts do grant such permission as has been done in this very case as well.

Plea for Providing Legal Assistance

Leela Mahadeo Joshi v. *Mahadeo Sitaram Joshi,* AIR 1991 Bom 105: II (1991) DMC 125: 1991 (1) Hindu LR 313

Issue: The need and desirability of permitting legal practitioners in Family Courts was discussed. Presently, under section 13 of the Family Courts Act, 1984, no party is, as of right, entitled to be represented by a legal practitioner.

Facts: The parties had sought divorce before the Family Court, on the ground of mutual consent. All the requirements of section 13B of the Hindu Marriage Act, were satisfied and yet the court refused to grant the decree. Hence, the appeal by the parties to the High Court.

Order: The High Court set aside the Family Court order and granted a decree of divorce by mutual consent. The court pointed out that various appeals came up from Family Courts in Pune and Bombay wherein the parties have strongly expressed that in the absence of legal representation they face problems. The cases have either gone by default or had to be either remanded by the High Court or entertained in appeal. The uneducated and poor are totally ignorant and are handicapped in the conduct of their cases in the absence of professional help. Even the educated litigants are not competent to draft pleadings nor have the ability to conduct examination-in-chief or cross-examination. This results in delays and miscarriage of justice. An appeal from the Family Court lies to the High Court, and therefore, pleadings and examination have to be in order. Lay litigants are not expected to know all the intricacies of law and procedure. The court suggested:

> "It would, therefore, be a healthy practice for the Family Court at the scrutiny stage itself to ascertain as to whether the parties desire to be represented by their lawyers, and if such a desire is expressed at this or any subsequent stage of the proceedings, then the permission be granted if the court is satisfied that the litigant requires such assistance and would be handicapped if the case is not permitted."

Comment: The idea of not allowing parties to be represented by a lawyer as a matter of right, was to discourage delays, legal technicalities and formal proceedings in the Family Courts. However, the working of the Act shows that legal wrangles and technicalities are inevitable in any litigation or court proceedings, and the common man does not understand these. Therefore, in the absence of professional assistance, he faces handicap. Hence, the need to provide legal assistance was suggested in this case.

Legal Representation not Allowed
Kailash Bhansali v. *Surender Kumar,*
AIR 2000 Raj 390: 2001 (1) Marri LJ 601: 2000 (2) Raj LR 697

Issue: Can a Family Court without application of any party, grant permission for legal assistance? Can an application for legal assistance be granted when such permission would only result in delay, and harassment to the non-applicant?

Facts: This was a case of protracted litigation between the spouses in the Family Court. A husband sought divorce but his petition was dismissed. Thereafter, the wife filed a petition for restitution of conjugal rights which was decreed. The decree was not complied with and the husband filed a divorce petition again on the ground that the wife failed to comply with the restitution decree. There were adjournments on several dates. The husband, after six months, filed an application before the court seeking legal representation by a counsel of his choice. The wife not only, did not ask for legal assistance herself but objected to the husband's application for such permission. The Family Court however, granted permission to the husband as well as to the wife. Against this order, the wife filed an appeal.

Order: The court, in appeal, held that the Family Court had committed an error and ought not to have granted the husband's application. The very purpose of the Family Courts is to give speedy justice but in this case, the husband used delaying and harassing tactics and even after 12 long years, no amicable solution could be reached. According to the High Court, the Family Court only facilitated the delay at the cost of harassing the wife.

Besides, under section 13, a court is empowered to seek the assistance of a legal expert as *amicus curiae* if it considers it necessary in the interest of justice. Thus, the need has to be felt by the court and not by the parties, otherwise there would be no difference between an ordinary litigation and proceedings under the Family Court. Critcising the order of the Family Court, the High Court observed:

> "The judge passed the impugned order...which is not only against the law but against the human conscience. Family Courts are established for the purpose of speedy justice to the deserted wife and not for this type of harassment. If the Family Courts pass such orders then it will shake the confidence of the litigating public and they will not come to the courts for justice and that will be the saddest day for this institution."

The Family Court order was, accordingly, set aside and it was directed to proceed and decide the case on merits. It is significant to note that the court not only allowed the wife's appeal but also directed the husband to pay a special cost of ₹ 10,000 to the wife within a month, for the harassment and suffering he caused to her.

Comment: The Family Courts have been set up to impart speedy justice. The whole purpose of such courts would be defeated if the courts allowed any party to adopt delaying tactics to harass the other.

Note: See *C.P. Saji v. Union of India*, AIR 2012 Ker 23, is an extremely significant judgment in this context. Under section 30 of the Advocates Act, 1961, every advocate whose name is entered in the (State roll) shall be entitled as of right to practice before all courts/tribunals and such other forums of India. Though the Act was passed in 1961, section 30 thereof was not notified and given effect to for five decades. However, the same has now been notified in the Gazette of India dated 9-6-2011 declaring that the Government appointed 15-6-2011 as the date for giving effect to section 30 of the Advocates Act, 1961. Thus, in view of this, now all lawyers have acquired a right to practice before all courts/tribunals etc. of India as a matter of right thereby overriding the restrictive covenants as contained in section 13 of the Act. This being the position, the stipulation contained in section 13 of the Family Courts Act, 1984 necessitating prior sanction of the said court has virtually become redundant. Consequently, in the facts and circumstances of this case, the court ruled that it is open for a litigant to pursue the cause of action before the Family Court engaging any lawyer of his choice and such lawyer is entitled to present the matter, on filing the Vakalatnama as a matter of right.

Appearance of Recognised Agent not Barred

Cyprian D'Souza v. Rene D'Souza,
AIR 2003 Kant 64: ILR (2002) 4 Kant 5145: 2003 (1) Kant LJ 401

Issue: Though representation by a legal counsel is not as a matter of right allowed under the Family Court Act there is no bar to filing of the petition by an agent.

Facts: A husband sought partition and separate possession of his undivided share in some properties. At the time of filing the suit in the Family Court, he was in the Middle East and so the plaint was presented through a duly appointed agent. The wife's objection was that since the petition was filed through an agent and not personally, it should be dismissed. The Family Court agreed with this objection and dismissed the petition. Hence, the appeal.

Order: The court in appeal held that there is no bar to the filing of a petition by an agent. The purpose of the Family Courts is primarily to ensure reconciliation and amicable settlement of disputes between the parties. This purpose is not adversely affected if a petition is presented by an agent. A dispute can be presented before the court only when parties file their respective pleas or claims. It is only after the initial filing that the stage is set for the Family Court to make requisite endeavours keeping in view the object of the Act. Whenever the court desires that it is essential that parties be present personally so that reconciliation or settlement can be tried and discussed, the court may direct their presence. Initiation of case by filing is just the first step, other procedures follow the filing and that is the time when personal presence is significant. The court referred to its earlier single bench judgment in *Komal S. Padukone* v. *Principal Judge*, AIR 1999 Kant 427: ILR 1999 Kant 1866: 1999 (5) Kant LJ 667, where it was held that a petition can be presented before the Family Court either in person or through an authorised agent. The order of the Family Court was, accordingly, set aside.

Comment: A suit can be filed in the Family Court through an agent. That is not a stage when personal appearance is mandatory. It is only at subsequent stages that the presence of the parties is essential so that the court can personally interact with the parties and make an endeavour to affect reconciliation or settlement of the dispute.

Pavithra v. *Rahul Raj*,
AIR 2003 Mad 138: 2003 (4) All Ind Cas 283:
2003 (2) Hindu LR 680

Issue: Does the embargo on the appearance of the legal practitioner in the Family Court extend to a recognised agent also?

Facts: A husband filed a petition for divorce at the Family Court at Coimbatore. The wife was at that time in the United States. She executed a registered power of attorney in favour of her father. On receipt of summons, the father filed an application seeking permission to defend her daughter but the same was not only rejected by the court, but also an *ex parte* decree of divorce was granted in favour of the husband on the ground that he was entitled to the decree since the wife did not appear personally. Hence, the father's appeal to the High Court.

Order: Explaining the difference between the right of representation through a counsel and representation through an agent the court held that the recognised agent under Order 3, rule 2 of the Civil Procedure Code stands on a different footing from a lawyer. Under Order 3, rule 2, CPC "person holding powers of attorney, authorising them to make and do such appearances, applications and acts on behalf of such parties" are, *inter alia*, the recognised agents of parties by whom such appearances, applications and acts may be made or done. A recognised agent can prosecute, defend or represent till the court requires and accordingly directs the parties to appear in person. Thus, the *ex parte* order of the Family Court was hasty and not on merits, according to the High Court. In the facts and circumstances of the case, the court held that reasonable opportunity should be given to the petitioner by ordering fresh notice by the Family Court.

Comment: Initial stages of a case may not require the personal attendance of the parties. However, when the crucial time comes, presence of parties is mandatory; at that stage no agent can act on behalf of the parties.

Jurisdiction

K.A. Abdul Jaleel v. T.A. Shahida,
AIR 2003 SC 2525: 2003 AIR SCW 2710: (2003) 4 SCC 166

Issue: Does the Family Court have jurisdiction to decide a dispute between parties to a former marriage as against subsisting marriage?

Facts: Under section 7(1)(c) of the Family Courts Act, 1984, a Family Court has jurisdiction in respect of "a suit or proceeding between the parties to a marriage with respect to the property of the parties or of either of them". In this case the dispute was in respect of property claimed by a divorced wife. The parties were married in 1988, and had two children. Some properties were purchased by the husband from the cash which he got from the wife's parents at the time of marriage plus amounts received from the sale of wife's gold ornaments. These properties were to be transferred in her name as per agreement by the parties. The husband, however, failed to do that, hence the wife's suit claiming property as well as maintenance. The husband raised an objection as to the maintainability of the wife's suit on the ground that he had divorced her and the Family Court had no jurisdiction to decide a dispute between former spouses; it could decide disputes only "between parties to the marriage". On divorce, they do not remain parties to the marriage, it was contended.

It was also argued that since the respondent wife had already filed an application under section 3 of the Muslim Women's (Protection of Rights on Divorce) Act, 1986, she could not proceed under the Family Courts Act. The Family Court decreed the suit, hence the husband's appeal to the Kerala High Court which was dismissed. The husband than filed the present appeal.

Order: The court negatived both the contentions. It held that if the expression "suit or proceedings between parties to a marriage" were to be construed as "suit or proceedings between parties to a subsisting marriage", it would "lead to miscarriage of justice and would frustrate the object, wherefore the Family Courts were set up". (at p. 2527)

The court held that the wordings, "disputes relating to marriage and family affairs and for matters connected therewith" in the Preamble, must be liberally construed. The Family Court, thus, was held to have jurisdiction to decide a dispute relating to properties claimed by the parties irrespective of whether the marriage is subsisting or not.

Also, the fact that the wife had already filed an application under section 3 of the Muslim Women's (Protection of Rights on Divorce) Act was held to be no bar for the Family Court to decide the matter.

Comment: In view of the basic purpose and object, and the spirit behind the enactment of the Family Courts Act it is important that the provisions should be liberally construed so as to provide speedy settlements and promote reconciliation wherever possible.

Leby Issac v. Leena M. Ninan,
AIR 2005 Ker 285: ILR 2005 (3) Ker 597: 2005 (2) Ker LJ 652

Issue: Does a Family Court have jurisdiction to entertain a suit filed by a husband for recovery of money as compensation and damages from his wife and father-in-law? What is meant by the expression "in circumstances arising out of a marital relationship" used is *Explanation (d)* to section 7(1) of the Family Court Act.

Facts: The parties were married is 1997. After marriage, the husband discovered that the wife was having illicit relationship prior to the marriage and even thereafter. This fact was in the knowledge of the wife's parents but they suppressed the same and thereby committed fraud on him. Further, the husband contended that all his efforts to persuade the wife to mend her ways were futile. He, thereupon, filed a divorce petition on ground of adultery which was pending before the Family Court.

The husband also filed a suit for decree allowing him compensation and damages for the pain and suffering caused to him and his family which was unascertainable in terms of money. He claimed ₹ 10 lakhs by way of damages.

Order: The Family Court held that it had no jurisdiction to entertain the suit for damages as a suit of this nature is not covered by the provision of the Act. The cause of action set forth in the suit was the alleged misrepresentation on the part of the respondents, the default and wayward attitude of the wife in the discharge of her matrimonial obligations thereby causing mental agony and hence the suit cannot be treated as a suit or proceeding for an order or injunction in circumstances arising out of marital relationship. The husband's plaint was, thus, returned for presentation before proper court; hence the appeal. Under section 7(1), *Explanation (d)* a Family Court has jurisdiction to entertain, *inter alia*, 'a suit or proceeding for an order or injunction in circumstances arising out of a marital relationship'. The High Court analysed the meaning of the words "in circumstances arising out of marital relationship" and held that the above expression means not only those occurrences which transpired during marital life but also includes such circumstances which led to the marriage, which developed thereafter, which place during marital life, which resulted in breaking down of marriage and all those which 'closely' followed as a consequence of all these. The court further observed that "if the intention of Legislature was to take in only those occurrences which take place during a 'marital relationship' there was no necessity to use the word 'circumstances' in *Explanation (d)* to section 7(1) of the Act. The same purpose could have been achieved if *Explanation (d)* is worded in that the term 'circumstances' also. So, the inclusion of word 'circumstances' in the relevant provision is quite significant and it must have been done to include all such circumstances surrounding proceeding and closely following a marital relationship *i.e.*, the principal event of marriage and the eventualities surrounding the same". (at p. 288)

The court held that a divorce petition was pending before the Family Court, between the parties and the present proceeding for dowager also arose more or less from the same set of facts and circumstances, hence the lower court ought to have entertained the case in the same court instead of driving the parties to ordinary Civil Court. The whole issue could be settled in the Family Court itself. "The couple cannot be deprived of the facilities available in the Family Court to arrive at a quicker settlement of their issues." (at p. 290).

The husband's appeal was, thus, allowed and the Family Court was directed to dispose of the matter accordingly.

Comment: A suit for damages by one spouse against the other which arises out of circumstance in relation to marital relationship falls in the jurisdiction of the Family Courts.

Note: See also *Nagaraj* v. *Ammayamma,* I (2002) DMC 439 (DB Kant) wife's suit for injunction restraining husband or anyone claiming through him from interfering with possession of property assigned to her by husband for her exclusive use/occupation allowed; *Muhammed Davood* v. *Hafsath,* AIR 2010 Ker 21 suit by wife for return of her money and jewellery from husband and mother-in-law, allowed; *Madhubala* v. *Pushpa Devi,* AIR 2010 (NOC) 980 (Utr) suit for declaration as to validity of marriage or marital status, allowed; *Neelam Dadasaheb Shewale* v. *Dadasaheb Bandu Shewale,* I (2010) DMC 344 (Bom) suit by husband for *inter alia,* for injunction restraining divorced wife from using his surname allowed; *Thoombath Haris* v. *K. Sherbin,* AIR 2010 (NOC) 230 (Ker) claim for past maintenance due prior to divorce, allowed. On other hand, see *Bharat Kumar* v. *Selma Mini,* II (2007) DMC 538: AIR 2007 Ker 197: ILR (2007) 1 Ker 696 proceeding for declaration of legitimacy of child without any matrimonial cause, not allowed; *Devaki* v. *Narayan,* 2006 (3) HLR 505 (Ker) suit for partition of properties where apart from parties to marriage other sharers also parties, not allowed.

K.B. Anil Kumar v. N.S. Sheela,
AIR 2012 Ker 1

Issue: The issue involved in the case was whether the Family Court had jurisdiction to decide a claim filed by a wife against her husband's brother for return of money and would such suit or proceeding be one arising out of "circumstances arising out of matrimonial relationship", an expression used in section 7(1), *Explanation (d)* of the Family Courts Act?

Facts: The simple facts of the case were thus. The respondent wife stood surety for her husband's brother for certain amounts in chitty transaction. She did so under compulsion and pressure by the husband to maintain conjugal peace while she was staying in the matrimonial home. Since the husband's brother, the appellant, defaulted payment, a sum of ₹ 28,500 was recovered from respondents salary and further, she also remitted the remaining amount of ₹ 92,200 to close the loan transaction so as to avoid further recoveries from her salary which was attached for recovery of the amount due from the appellant. The respondents suit for recovery of the amount of ₹ 1,20,700 was decreed. Hence the appeal against this.

Order: The main argument in the appeal was that the Family Court had no jurisdiction to try the suit as the appellant was not a party to the marriage; it was contended that the Family Court has jurisdiction only in respect of suits and proceedings between parties to a marriage, with respect to the property of the parties or of either of them. After analyzing and referring to a few cases on the issue (*e.g. Abdul Jaleel* v. *Shahida,* AIR 2003 SC 2525; *Leby Issac* v. *Leena M. Ninan,* AIR 2005 Ker 285: ILR 2005 (3) Ker 597: 2005 (2) Ker LJ 652) the court held that the case arose during the subsistence of the marital relationship and the circumstances projected in this case have a direct bearing on the marriage. It observed (at p. 4):

> "... there can be no doubt that the first respondent happened to stand as surety for the appellant....when the marital relationship between her and her husband was subsisting and also when she was staying in her matrimonial home. She happened to stand as a surety only because of the influence or compulsion of her husband. Therefore the amount due from the appellant arose" in circumstances arising out of a marital relationship. It is a 'dispute' coming under *Explanation* (d) to section 7(1) of the Act. As such the suit/petition before the Family Court is perfectly maintainable.

Comment: But for the marital status of the respondent, she would not have stood surety for the appellant. It is therefore, obvious that the dispute in this case arose out of a situation or circumstance directly related to the marital relationship and so within the jurisdiction of the Family Court.

FOREIGN DIVORCE DECREE

Forum Hunting to Invoke Jurisdiction
Satya v. Teja Singh,
AIR 1975 SC 105: 1975 Cr LJ 52: (1975) 1 SCC 120

Issue: Issue of extreme significance, *viz.*, recognition of a foreign divorce decree obtained by a spouse by forum hunting in a foreign jurisdiction was involved in the case.

Facts: The parties, who were Indian Citizens domiciled in India, were married in 1955 according to Hindu rites and had two children. The husband left for U.S.A. in 1959. From 1960 to 1964 he was living in Utah for sometime as a student and then in employment. Since 1965 he had been in Canada. In November 1964 he obtained a divorce decree from a court in Nevada. The wife did not appear in Nevada Court, she was unrepresented and did not submit to its jurisdiction. In 1965 she moved an application for maintenance for herself and her children under section 488 of the Cr. P.C. (now section 125 Cr. P.C.). The husband was represented by his counsel who stated that the marriage had been dissolved by a decree of divorce by a Nevada Court and since she ceased to be a wife by virtue of the divorce decree, the husband was not liable to maintain her (prior to the 1973 amendment, a divorced wife was not entitled to maintenance under the provision of section 488 of the Cr. P.C.)

The Trial Court, however, decreed in favour of the wife and its order was confirmed in revision; in further revision before the High Court it was held that the wife being divorced was not entitled to the maintenance. According to the court, at the crucial time of commencement of proceedings for divorce the petitioner was domiciled in Nevada, that during marriage the domicile of the wife follows domicile of husband and as held in *Le Mesurier* v. *Le Mesurier* [1895] AC 517 "according to international law, the domicile for the time being of the marriage pair affords the only test of jurisdiction to dissolve their marriage...."

On appeal by the wife, the Apex Court held that the decree of divorce granted by the Nevada Court in USA could not be recognised in India. Question as regards recognition to be accorded to Nevada court depends on rules of Indian private International Law. Our notions of genuine divorce and substantial justice and the distinctive principles of our public policy must determine the rules of our private International law. The respondent husband, in this case, went to Nevada as a bird of passage, resorted to the court there solely to found jurisdiction and procured a decree of divorce on misrepresentation that he was domiciled in Nevada. In fact, he had never lived there and after having secured the divorce decree left Nevada soon thereafter. Residence, in order to give jurisdiction must answer a qualitative as well as quantitative test, that is, the two elements of *factum et animus* must concur. The court observed.

"The respondent went to Nevada forum hunting, found a convenient jurisdiction which would easily purvey a divorce to him and left it even before the ink of his domiciliary assertion was dry. Thus the decree of the Nevada court lacks jurisdiction.

Order: The wife's appeal was allowed. The court analysed the provision of section 13 of the C.P.C on recognition of foreign decrees and also discussed the legal position in this regard in the U.K. and U.S.A. It made it clear that the validity of a decree passed in a foreign court must be determined on the terms of section 13 of the Civil Procedure Code. In this case the husband had misrepresented and played a fraud within the meaning of section 13(e) of the CPC for invoking jurisdiction of the foreign court, hence the decree cannot be recognised, the court held.

Comment: The judgment gives rise to an enigmatic situation which the Court conceded thus (at pp. 117-118):

"Unhappily, the marriage between the appellant and the respondent has to limp. They will be treated as divorced in Nevada but their bond of matrimony will remain unsnapped in India, the country of the domicile."

When argued that it would lead to difficulties, the Court remarked (at p. 118):

"It may. But these rules of private international law are made for men and women – not the other way round – and a nice tidy logical perfection can never be achieved" [per Denovan L.J. *Formosa* v. *Formosa*, (1962) 3 All ER 419 (424)]".

Divorce Decree Passed by a Foreign Court, Having Neither Jurisdiction nor Ground—Such Decree cannot be Recognised in India

Narasimha Rao v. *Y. Venkatalakshmi**, (1991) 2 SCALE 1: (1991) 3 SCC 451

Issue: Can a divorce decree passed by a Foreign Court which has neither jurisdiction nor the legal ground to dissolve a marriage under the Hindu Marriage Act, be recognised in India?

Facts: The parties were married in Tirupati, in 1975. They were separated in 1978. The appellant husband had obtained a decree for dissolution of marriage

---

* See also *Neeraja Saraph* v. *Jayant Saraph*, (1994) 6 SCC 461 *supra* at p (119).

from the Circuit Court of St. Louis County, Missouri, U.S.A., in 1980. The wife's participation in the proceedings before the American Court seem to be confined to her replies that she was not submitting to its jurisdiction. Throughout the proceedings, she remained *ex parte* and the American court passed a decree of divorce in her absence.

Thereafter, the husband remarried in India. The wife (first wife) filed a criminal complaint charging him of bigamy. The Trial Court dismissed her case in view of the divorce he had obtained. She then filed a criminal revision petition to the High Court which set aside the Magistrate's order on the ground that he had acted on the photostat copy of the divorce order. The Magistrate was directed to dispose of the petition filed by the appellant (non-complainant) for their discharge afresh, in accordance with law. An appeal to the Apex Court was filed against this order. The appeal raised important issues—if the Indian courts recognise the foreign decree, the second marriage of the appellant would be valid in India; if not the husband would be liable for bigamy under the I.P.C. Besides, non-recognition of the decree would mean that the appellant and the respondent would continue to have the legal status of husband and wife in India whilst under the Missouri laws in the U.S.A., they would be divorced.

The court surveyed the development of rules of private international law which are not codified but are scattered in different statutes and judicial pronouncements. It lamented that the labours of the Law Commission which made significant recommendations on the issue in its 65th Report in 1976, have not fructified. It emphasised the need for guidelines and certainty on the issue of recognition of foreign divorces. It said (at p. 5):

> "We cannot......... lose sight of the fact that today more than ever in the past, the need for definitive rules for recognition of foreign judgments in personal and family matters, and particularly in matrimonial disputes has surged to the surface...... A time has, therefore, come to ensure certainty in the recognition of foreign judgments in these matters. The minimum rules of guidance for securing the certainty need not wait legislative action."

Making a beginning in this direction, the court held that the relevant provisions of section 13 of the Civil Procedure Code, 1908*, are capable of being interpreted in a manner which will secure certainty in conformity with public policy, justice, equity and good conscience. 'The rules so evolved will protect

---

* **13. When foreign judgment not conclusive.**—A foreign judgment shall be conclusive as to any matter thereby directly adjudicated upon between the same parties or between parties under whom they or any of them claim litigating under the same title except—
  (a) where it has not been pronounced by a Court of competent jurisdiction;
  (b) where it has not been given on the merits of the case;
  (c) where it appears on the face of the proceedings to be founded on an incorrect view of international law or a refusal to recognise the law of India in cases in which such law is applicable;
  (d) where the proceedings in which the judgment was obtained are opposed to natural justice;
  (e) where it has been obtained by fraud;
  (f) where it sustains a claim founded on a breach of any law in force in India.

the sanctity of the institution of marriage and unity of family which are the cornerstones of our societal life,' the court remarked (at p. 5). It analysed each clause of the section to substantiate its view. Thus, clause (a), which refers to a court of competent jurisdiction, should be interpreted to mean only the court which the law under which the parties were married so recognises unless both parties voluntarily and unconditionally concede to the jurisdiction of any other court. As regards clause (b), merits of the case should mean that the decision should be based on a ground available under the law in which the parties were married; besides, the decision should be the result of proper contest.

On clause (c), the court opined that a judgment founded on a ground not recognised by the law applicable, the Hindu Marriage Act in this case, is a judgment in defiance of the law and will therefore not be enforceable under clause (f). As regards the requirement of compliance of principles of natural justice laid down in clause (d), the court held that this principle has to be extended beyond mere compliance with technical rules of procedure. The court must ensure an effective contest by requiring the petitioner to make all necessary provisions for the respondent to defend, including costs of travel, residence and litigation.

Order: The court held that the Missouri court had no jurisdiction to award the decree since the ground on which the decree was made, *viz.*, irretrievable breakdown of the marriage, is not a ground recognised under the law governing the parties, *viz.*, the Hindu Marriage Act. Also the decree had been obtained by misrepresenting that he (the husband) was a resident of Missouri whereas the record showed that he was only a bird of passage and was ordinarily a resident of Louisiana. He had, if at all, only technically satisfied the requirement of ninety days residence for purposes of invoking jurisdiction. Thus jurisdiction of forum as well as ground on which the decree was passed not being in accordance with the law under which the parties were married, the decree of the foreign court could not be recognised.

Comment: The guidelines laid down by the Apex Court and the directions for strict observance of the principles of natural justice by foreign courts exercising jurisdiction in matrimonial courts, will surely provide protection to wives whose husbands abandon them and manipulate divorce decree under foreign jurisdictions.

Non Contest of Petition does not Imply Submission to Jurisdiction

Veena Kalia v. *Jatinder Nath Kalia,* AIR 1996 Del 54: 1995 (59) DLT 635: 1996 Marri LJ 423

Issue: Does non-contest by the wife of a divorce petition filed by the husband in a foreign court imply that she had conceded to the jurisdiction of the Foreign Court?

Facts: The husband obtained an *ex parte* divorce decree under section 13 of the Hindu Marriage Act from a court in Nova Scotia (Canada) on the ground of irretrievable breakdown of the marriage. Subsequently, the wife filed for divorce in India on the ground of adultery, cruelty and desertion of the husband. She alleged that the husband left her and two minor daughters aged one and two years to study abroad and deserted her. She also alleged that since over 23 years they have not lived together and that he got married there and had children out of the second marriage. She also claimed maintenance under section 23 of the Hindu Adoptions and Maintenance Act, 1956, for herself and daughters, as also their marriage expenses.

The Trial Court dismissed her petition on the ground that since she had accepted the judgment of the Foreign Court dissolving her marriage, the bar of *res judicata* under section 11 of the Civil Procedure Code, 1908, applied and further, that her petition was *mala fide* attempt to harass the husband and was nothing but misuse of the court process. Against this the wife filed an appeal. It was argued on her behalf that simply because she did not contest the divorce application filed by the husband in Canada, does not imply that she had conceded to its jurisdiction. She further contended that the divorce was obtained on a ground that is not even available under the Hindu Marriage Act and that the husband was neither domiciled nor habitually or permanently resided within the jurisdiction of that foreign court and hence the decree granted by the Supreme Court of Nova Scotia was a nullity.

Order: The court referred to some cases decided by the Supreme Court on the issue of foreign divorce decrees *e.g., Satya* v. *Teja Singh*, AIR 1975 SC 105: 1975 Cr LJ 52: (1975) 1 SCC 120; *Surinder Kaur Sandhu* v. *Harbax Singh Sandhu*, AIR 1984 SC 1224: (1984) 3 SCC 698: (1984) 2 SCWR 116; *Narasimha Rao* v. *Y. Venkatalakshmi*, (1991) 2 SCALE 1: (1991) 3 SCC 451. It held that the rules of natural justice were violated as the foreign court did not care to check up whether the wife had enough means and the necessary documents to defend her case in Canada. Consequently, a decree of divorce in her favour, on grounds of adultery, cruelty, and desertion was passed. A maintenance allowance of ₹ 10,000 per month and ₹ 10 lakh by way of marriage expenses for the daughters was also awarded.

Comment: Cases where husbands desert their wives in India and obtain divorce decrees in foreign courts is not uncommon. Our courts seek to ensure that principles of natural justice are adhered to and the wives are not exploited.

MISCELLANCEOUS

Parsi Law – Presence of Delegates in Matrimonial Trials

Pistonji Kekobund Bharucha v. *Aloo,*
AIR 1984 Bom 75: I (1983) DMC 468: (1983) 2 Bom CR 312

Issue: In proceedings under the Parsi Marriage and Divorce Act, 1936, is the presence of all the delegates mandatory at the time of the verdict?

Facts: Under section 20 of the Parsi Marriage and Divorce Act, 1936 (as amended in 1988), in the trial of matrimonial cases the judge of the matrimonial court is to be aided by five delegates. Prior to the amendment in 1988, the number of delegates was seven. In this case, the plaintiff challenged the verdict of the matrimonial judge on the ground that all the seven delegates were not present during the trial. His argument was that though the trial cannot be said to be vitiated on account of the absence of one or two delegates during the course of trial but that the presence of all the seven delegates at the time of the verdict was necessary.

Order: According to the court, the section is silent as to whether all the delegates are required to be present right through the proceedings and until the time of the verdict. It, therefore, held that all the seven delegates need not be present at the time of the verdict. Hence, there was no illegality in the verdict given by the matrimonial judge.

Comment: The Parsi Marriage and Divorce Act provides for the constitution of special matrimonial courts for hearing petitions under the Act. The judge of the matrimonial court is to be aided by five delegates (prior to 1988, it was seven judges). The requirement of delegates has been dispensed with after the amendment in 1988, in the following cases:

(a) interlocutory applications and proceedings;

(b) alimony and maintenance;

(c) custody, maintenance and education of children;

(d) all matters and proceedings other than the regular hearing of cases.

Stridhana & Criminal Breach of Trust and Misappropriation

Pratibha Rani v. Suraj Kumar,
AIR 1985 SC 628: 1985 Cr LJ 817: (1985) 2 SCC 370

Issue: Can a wife file a case of criminal breach of trust and misappropriation of her *stridhan* under sections 405 and 406 of the IPC?

Facts: The parties were married in 1972. At the time of marriage the father, brother and uncles of the husband had demanded and got dowry worth ₹ 60,000 which was entrusted to the husband and in-laws. Soon after marriage, they started harassing her for more dowry and in 1977, she along with her children, was turned out of the matrimonial home. On the intervention of the *panchas* of the community, Pratibha Rani, the wife, returned to the matrimonial home. Things, however, did not improve and maltreatment continued and once again she was driven out of the house. She made several demands for the return of her clothes, jewellery and other articles but they turned a deaf ear. Consequently, she filed a case for criminal breach of trust and misappropriation of her *stridhan* under sections 405 and 406 of the Penal Code. She also filed proceedings under section 125 of the Cr. P.C., for maintenance. The husband and in-laws sought the quashing of criminal proceeding under the inherent powers of the High Court under section 482 of the Cr. P.C. The High Court (Punjab and Haryana) quashed her complaint and held that section 406 of the IPC does not apply to such cases as after marriage, the wife's *stridhan* becomes joint property of both the spouses and no question of entrustment to his or her property by one spouse to the other, arises. The wife was, accordingly asked to approach the civil courts for return of her *stridhan*.

The wife went in appeal against this order. Allowing the same, the Supreme Court, by a majority judgment, held that simply because the parties are married and living jointly, it does not mean that any one of the spouses can commit acts of criminal breach of trust. The court observed:

> "Criminal law and matrimonial home are not strangers........crimes committed in matrimonial home are as much punishable as anywhere else.

Criticising the interpretation of the High Court, Justice Fazal Ali (for himself and Justice Sabyasachi Mukherji) remarked:

> "It is an extreme travesty of justice for a Court to say that whenever a married woman demands her *stridhan* property from her husband, she would be driven to the dilatory process of a civil court and her husband would be debarred from being prosecuted by a criminal court ..... We are indeed surprised how could the High Court, functioning in a civilised and socialistic society such as ours, play havoc with judicial interpretation of an important branch of law."

Justice Varadarajan in his dissenting order held, that in the absence of any agreement or specific entrustment by a spouse of his or her property to the other, the penal provisions cannot be attracted. According to him:

"The bonds of matrimony........ bar the spectre of the criminal breach of trust *qua* the property of the spouses at the very threshold of the matrimonial home. It cannot enter its hallowed precincts except through the back door of a special written contract to the contrary with regard to such property."

And further, according to him:

"Entertaining complaints of the irate wife or husband against the husband or wife without even an allegation of a specific and separate agreement constituting entrustment of the property.... would have disastrous effects and consequences on the peace and harmony which ought to prevail in matrimonial homes."

Order: By a majority of two to one, the Supreme Court set aside the High Court order and allowed the wife's appeal. Justice Fazal Ali lamented that sometimes the law which is meant to impart justice and fair play to the citizens or people of the country are so torn and twisted by a morbid interpretative process that instead of giving haven to the disappointed and dejected litigants, it negates their well-established rights in law.

According to him, the High Court "seems to have shed all norms of justice and fair play".

Comment: It is a landmark judgment upholding a wife's right to claim back her *stridhan* through criminal process where she is being harassed and the other party refuses to return her belongings. The argument of complete and absolute jointness and partnership of properties after marriage has rightly been rejected by upholding a woman's absolute right on her *stridhan*. The court has very aptly ridiculed the idea that whenever a married woman demands her *stridhan* from her husband she should go to a civil court with its dilatory process.

Accident Claims Compensation to Wife Living Separately
Sachdeva Rice Mills v. *Raj Anand,*
AIR 1988 P&H 136: (1986) 90 Punj LR 576: 1987 ACJ 821

Issue: The issue involved in the case was whether a wife, who is living separately from her husband, would be entitled to claim compensation along with other claimants, in case of death of the husband in an accident? This was a case for compensation for death in accident under the Motor Vehicles Act.

Facts: The husband, Mohinder Pratap Gupta, died in an accident while travelling in a Punjab Roadways bus, in 1981. The claims tribunal awarded a sum of ₹ 1,93,000 as compensation to the claimants *viz.*, mother, widow, son and daughter of the deceased. The mother and son of the deceased argued that since the widow and the daughter had been living separately from the deceased during his life-time and no maintenance was being paid to them they suffered no financial loss on account of his death and therefore not entitled to any compensation. The widow and the daughter, on the other hand, sought to assert an equal right to the compensation.

Order: It was held that even though the deceased was not giving any financial help to his wife and daughter, they did have a subsisting right to claim maintenance from him both under the Hindu Adoptions and Maintenance Act, 1956 as also under section 125 of the Code of Criminal Procedure. "It is well-settled that the father is under a legal obligation to maintain his child and the husband to maintain his wife and that the onus lies on him to allege and prove that his wife and the child are not entitled to the maintenance claimed" the court observed.

Apart from that, as pointed out by the court, section 22 of the Hindu Adoptions and Maintenance Act, 1956 specifically provides that liability to maintenance can be enforced against the estate of the deceased in the hands of his heirs. This being so, it must be held that there was a subsisting right in the wife and daughter to claim maintenance from the deceased during his life-time and further, by virtue of being his heirs they were entitled to succeed to his estate in their own right. Further, there was nothing on record to suggest that the wife and daughter had in any manner disentitled themselves to maintenance or to succeed to the property left behind by the deceased. Hence they had an equal right along with the mother and son of the deceased, to claim an equal share of compensation.

Comment: The mere fact that the wife was living separately from the husband and was not getting any financial help from him is no bar for her claiming share in the compensation payable to his (the husband's) heirs on his death in an accident. She had a subsisting right to claim maintenance during his life-time and after his death, she being an heir is entitled to compensation in equal share along with other heirs.

Note: The Delhi High Court in an order in February 2010 held that remarriage will not deprive a person from claiming compensation for the death of a former spouse; it awarded ₹ 3 lakhs to a woman whose husband died in a bomb explosion in a DTC bus. Justice J.R. Midha rejected the DTC counsel's argument that three years after the death of the man, his widow married and was therefore not entitled to compensation. ("H.C.: Remarriage can't stop compensation", Hindustan Times dated 26-2-2010).

Ex-parte Decree – Whether Abates on Death of Decree-holder

Yallawwa v. *Shantavva,*
AIR 1997 SC 35: 1996 AIR SCW 4185: 1997 (11) SCC 159

Issue: Does the right to challenge an *ex parte* order abate or survive after the death of the decree-holder?

Facts: An *ex parte* divorce decree was obtained by a husband against the wife on the ground of her desertion. The mother-in-law filed a suit against the "wife"(*i.e.* her daughter-in-law) alleging that despite the divorce obtained by her son, she was interfering with the possession and enjoyment of suit properties of her son. The Trial Court granted temporary injunction against the wife. Thereafter, the husband died and the wife filed an application for setting aside the *ex parte* divorce decree on the ground that she had no notice about the proceedings. The Trial Court dismissed the same as being time-barred, but on appeal the High Court condoned the delay and restored the case. The mother-in-law thereupon filed the present appeal. Her primary objection was as to the maintainability of the application after the husband's (*i.e.*, her son) death. It was argued that divorce proceedings represented a personal cause of action and the right to challenge the *ex parte* order does not survive after the death of the decree-holder.

The court analysed the issue in detail and agreed that a divorce petition is a personal cause of action but clarified that if pending trial and before any decree is passed, a party dies, then the personal cause of action would abate indeed, but once a decree is passed whether *ex parte* or bipartite then the question whether the right to sue would survive would depend on the legal affects of the decree. The Court observed (at p. 40):

> "It is obvious that so long as decree is not passed and proceedings are at any stage prior to decree, no rights or obligations of either spouse get crystallised. The marital status of both the parties remains intact as it was prior to the filing of the suit. But once a decree gets passed in such proceedings, the rights and obligations of the respective spouses who are parties to such proceedings get crystallised under the orders of the court. The marriage gets dissolved, the status of the spouses gets changed and they become ex-husband and ex-wife. As a result of such a decree the marriage tie is snapped......the mutual rights of inheritance in each other's property on the death of either of them get extinguished. Therefore, apart from the divorce decree destroying the erstwhile status of husband and wife, it has a direct impact on the property rights of the concerned spouses."

The court also analysed the issues in the context of other statutory provisions, *e.g.*, section 19 of the Hindu Adoptions and Maintenance Act, 1956, entitles a Hindu widow to be maintained out of the property of her deceased husband and failing which she may have to be maintained by her father-in-law under certain conditions. However, if instead of being a widow she has the status of a divorcee, then, as pointed out by the court, she will be denied these rights.

Apart from this, is the aspect of social stigma which is attached to divorce. A decree of divorce is, ostensibly, based on fault or misconduct of the non-applicant. According to the court, such party should not be denied the right to get such finding vacated by filing an appeal or in case of an *ex parte*, by having it set aside.

An objection was raised that joinder of non-spouse in such cases would be against the provisions of section 13 of the Hindu Marriage Act, whereunder only spouses can file a petition. The court, however, did not accept this and held that while initially at the filing stage, the parties must be either the husband or the wife, but once a decree is passed, the stage of launching any petition does not survive. If pending trial a spouse dies, the personal cause of action dies too since no rights are as yet crystallised by then against or in favour of either spouse. After a decree, however, several pernicious legal consequences follow: The court held (at p. 41):

> "Under these circumstances, if the aggrieved spouse who suffers from such legal effects of the adverse decree against him or her is tolled off the gates of the appellate proceedings or proceedings for setting aside such *ex parte* decree, the concerned spouse would suffer serious legal damage and injury without getting any opportunity to get such decree set aside on legally permissible grounds............"

Order: It was held that the High court had already set aside the *ex parte* divorce decree which means that the husband-wife relation subsisted. Now that the husband was dead there was no tie that needed to be snapped by any legal order as it would be like "trying to slay the slain". The original petition of the husband which was restored by setting aside the *ex parte* order, was held to have abated after the husband's death and hence infructuous.

Comment: The Court recognised that divorce is followed by several legal consequences and if one of the parties dies after a decree, the surviving spouse should not be debarred from challenging the decree within the parameters of the law.

Right of Children of Void Marriage

Rameshwari Devi v. *State of Bihar*,
AIR 2000 SC 735: 2000 AIR SCW 273: (2000) 2 SCC 431

Issue: The case concerned payment of family pension and death-cum-retirement gratuity to two wives and their sons. In view of section 16 of the Hindu Marriage Act the children of second bigamous wife were held to be entitled to family pension of the deceased.

Facts: The deceased had entered into a second marriage while his first marriage was subsisting. He had one son from the first marriage, and four sons from the second bigamous marriage which was a void marriage. All claimed a share in the deceased's pension and gratuity amounts. The High Court held that sons of both wives were equally entitled to a share in the family pension and death-cum-retirement gratuity but the second wife would not be entitled to anything. The first wife challenged the order and filed an appeal in the Supreme Court.

Order: It was argued in the appeal that the second marriage being void and no marriage in the eyes of the law, the children born of the relationship would have no rights. The court, however, held that though the second wife could not be termed as the widow of the deceased, the fact that she lived with him for 24 years as his wife and had four sons from him was established. While she (second wife) would not be entitled to any share, her sons would get equal rights alongwith the first widow and her son, the court held.

Comment: While the law does not recognise the status of a second wife, children born to her from the marriage are considered to be legitimate for certain purposes, in view of the provisions of section 16 of the Hindu Marriage Act.

Husband's Property Forfeited under SAFEMA: Wife no Right to Appeal

Shobha Suresh Jumani v. Appellate Tribunal, Forfeited Property,
AIR 2001 SC 2288: 2001 Cr LJ 2583: 2001 AIR SCW 2051

Issue: The issue involved in this case was as to whether a wife whose husband's property has been ordered to be forfeited under the Smugglers and Foreign Exchange Manipulators (Forfeiture of Property) Act, 1976 (SAFEMA) is entitled to file an appeal against such order as a person aggrieved within the meaning of section 12(4) of the Act?

Facts: Detention orders were issued against one Suresh Manohar Jumani under the SAFEMA but this could not be enforced as he absconded. Consequently, his property was ordered to be forfeited and notice thereof sent to the wife because some of the properties stood in her name also. She filed a petition under section 12(4) of the Act which provides that a person aggrieved by an order of the forfeiture of the property is competent to file an appeal against such order. The wife's plea was that she being the wife of the smuggler whose property is forfeited has a vested right to maintenance from her husband and his properties and as such, she is an "aggrieved" person within the meaning of the provision contained in section 12(4) of the SAFEMA. Her plea was dismissed by the Appellate Tribunal as well as by the Bombay High Court. Hence her appeal before the Apex Court.

Order: It was held that a relative or associate who has no interest or right in such (forfeited) property cannot be held to be a person aggrieved. It is true that a wife may be aggrieved because her husband's properties are forfeited but that would not confer a right to file an appeal against such order. There is no infringement of her legal right. For the purpose of the Act, husband and wife are different entities, the court observed. If the properties standing in the name of relative or associate are forfeited on the ground that smugglers of foreign exchange manipulations were holding the said properties in their names or that such properties are legally acquired then to that extent, for challenging the order the relative or associate can be held to be a person aggrieved by the order of the competent authority; but a relative or associate cannot be considered to be aggrieved if the property belonging to the smuggler of foreign exchange manipulator are forfeited under the Act.

As to her right of maintenance under the provisions of the Hindu Adoptions and Maintenance Act, 1956, it was held that section 18 of the Act provides for maintenance of a wife who is living separately as provided under sub-section (2) of section 18; under section 27, dependents claim for maintenance under the Act shall not be a charge on the estate of the deceased unless one has been created in accordance with law *i.e.*, by Will, court order or agreement; under section 21, dependent is defined as a relative of the deceased who is father, mother or widow who has not remarried. It does not include a wife whose husband is surviving. In any case, there was no charge for maintenance created in favour of the appellant wife on the properties which were forfeited. Thus, according to the Court, "she has not suffered any legal grievance and has no legal peg for a justiciable claim to hang on." The appeal was consequently dismissed.

Settlement deed *per se* does not Confer Absolute Right in Properties

Kokilambal v. *N. Raman,*
AIR 2005 SC 2468: 2005 AIR SCW 2435: (2005) 11 SCC 234

Issue: A settlement-deed giving some right to the settlee, and providing that he would become absolute owner of deed properties after the death of the settlor, does not confer absolute ownership rights on the settlee who dies before the settlor.

Facts: M died in 1963, without an issue, leaving behind his widow, K as the sole heir. Since M had no issue, he showered all his love and affection on his elder sister's son V who he was planning to adopt but before he could do so, M died. Keeping in view the wishes of her husband, K got all the last rites performed through V. She also made two settlements on June 2, 1963, and June 27, 1964, and executed a deed of settlement in favour of V. Under this settlement, the income derived from the house properties would be enjoyed by herself and V till her life-time and after her death, it shall be enjoyed by V absolutely. She further authorised V to collect the rental income of the house and pay the taxes and maintenance or repair expenses, and after meeting out these expenses whatever is left will be enjoyed by them both. It was also agreed under the terms of settlement that K would not alienate the property but both of them can jointly do so if they wish. V, who was a bachelor, executed a Will on May 22, 1978, in respect of his other properties except those which were received by him from K. He died as a bachelor on February 1, 1979. On March 27, 1979, K revoked both the settlement deeds made in favour of V and executed a fresh settlement deed in favour of her brother's daughter and her husband. Thereupon, V's brother N.R sought a declaration that the revocation of the settlement made by K in favour of V was null and void and therefore the fresh settlement be declared void. The suit was dismissed by the Trial Court; an appeal before the first appellate court was decreed; against that the appellant filed an appeal in the High Court which was also dismissed by the High Court; hence the present petition by special leave.

Order: The core issue before the court was:

(i) what is the effect of earlier two settlements made by K in favour of V, and

(ii) whether by virtue of these settlements V became the absolute owner, and

(iii) whether after the death of V, K reserved her right to revoke the settlement or not.

The court referred to several cases and after analysing the facts, held that on the death of V during the life-time of K the property could not be inherited by N.R the brother of V. The mere fact that K had divested her right to alienate the property unilaterally, is not enough to show that the entire property stood vested in V. In fact, K had not completely divested her right in favour of V, it was contingent on her death, *i.e.*, absolute right of V would arise only after K's death. It was thus very clear that the part of the settlement providing absolute right on V would come into effect only after the death of K. In this case, V predeceased K, so he was not vested with any absolute right. Another significant factor was that in the Will executed by V in favour of his brother N.R. he made mention of other properties inherited by his parents but not of properties under the settlement-deed made by K. This indicates that these properties had not come to be vested in him at the time when he made the Will, otherwise he would have included them also in the Will. Since V died before K, the contingency under which he would have become the owner did not arise at all and hence K remained the sole owner. The settlement-deed came to an end on V's death and K as absolute owner had full right to execute a fresh settlement deed, the court held.

Comment: A settlement deed under which a settlee has been given certain rights in respect of properties mentioned in the deed, do not make him the absolute owner of such properties.

Petition for Annulment: Death of Mother whether Child can Continue Litigation

Balwinder Kaur v. Gurmukh Singh,
AIR 2007 P&H 74: 2007 (56) All Ind Cas 466: 2007 (2) CCC 587

Issue: After the death of one of the spouses to the litigation involving legality of the marriage, can daughter continue the litigation? The issue involved was as to her *locus* to continue the appeal.

Facts: This was a husband's petition for having the marriage declared void alleging that the respondent was already married and she had concealed this fact from him. The Trial Court accepted his plea and granted a decree annulling the marriage. Against this the wife filed an appeal. However, pending appeal she died. The daughter then sought permission to continue the appeal. Under section 11 of the Hindu Marriage Act a petition for having a marriage declared *null* and *void* can be "presented by *either* party thereto against the *other*". Thus, the courts were confronted with the issue of *locus standi* of the daughter to pursue the appeal after the death of her mother. It was argued on her behalf that even though not a direct party but the outcome of the litigation is bound to impact her in a big way with far-reaching implications. It is obvious that if the marriage between the parents stands annulled *vide* the Trial Court decree and the suit is allowed to abate, it would greatly affect the daughter's legal and social status and rights; her legitimacy will be effected, social stigma will be attached and prospects of marriage affected too. Besides her property rights too would be affected. The court therefore allowed her to continue the proceedings.

The next question involved in this case was as to the validity of the wife's alleged first marriage. If the first marriage is legally proved then obviously the disputed marriage in this case would be a nullity. After going through the evidence on record the court came to the conclusion that in respect of the first marriage there was no proof of performance of the essential ceremonies for a valid Hindu marriage and therefore the alleged first marriage was no marriage; in other words the marriage sought to be annulled on the plea of it being bigamous was held to be legal and not void. The Trial Court decree annulling the marriage was consequently set aside.

Comment: While it is fair that generally it is only the parties to the marriage who should have the *locus standi* to challenge its validity, yet, as aptly held by the Madras High Court in *Ponnuthayee Ammal* v. *Kamakshi Ammal,* AIR 1978 Mad 226 (Mad): 1978 Mad LR 241: 1978 Hindu LR 222 following *Thulasi Ammal* v. *Gowri,* 1964 (1) MLJ 228: AIR 1964 Mad 118: ILR (1964) 1 Mad 65, since an application for nullity is filed by a spouse for the invalidity of the marriage for to own sake or for the collateral purpose of deciding the legitimacy of the issue, the real purpose of such a proceeding is only to establish the petitioner's own status and for establishing that question, it is not necessary that the other spouse is living.

It is necessary however to distinguish between two situations *viz.,* where the proceedings are initiated and contested by the spouses during life-time, and pending final outcome one of them dies and the suit sought to be abated and the other situation where the marriage is sought to be annulled after the death of one (or both) party. In former cases and the likes of *Balwinder Kaur* where several collateral issues involving status of children of the marriage are involved the issue of *locus standi* after death of one of the party should be liberally interpreted. It may be mentioned that in *Parasami Pilai* v. *Sornathammal* where the issue of validity of a marriage contracted between a man and a sexless person arose after the death of a party, it was held that no person other than "parties to the marriage" can obtain such relief.

Court's Inherent Powers to Quash Proceedings under Section 498A etc., IPC

B.S. Joshi v. State of Haryana,
(2003) 4 SCC 675: AIR 2003 SC 1386: 2003 Cr LJ 2028

Issue: Can a High Court exercise its inherent powers under section 482, Cr. P.C., to quash criminal proceedings under sections 498A and 406 of the I.P.C, even though they are non-compoundable under section 320, Cr. P.C.?

Facts: The parties were married in 1999, and stayed together for just a year and then separated. The wife filed complaints against her husband, her mother and younger brother under sections 323, 498A and 406 of the Indian Penal Code. After sometime, the parties, wife and husband, filed an affidavit stating that they had settled their disputes and had agreed for divorce by mutual consent. They, accordingly, made a prayer to the High Court that the criminal proceedings filed against the husband and his relatives, be quashed. This application was opposed by the State on the ground that offences involved were non-compoundable under section 320 of the Code of Criminal Procedure, and the inherent powers of the High Court under section 482 of the Cr. P.C. cannot be invoked to bypass a provision which is mandatory. The High Court declined to quash the criminal proceedings on the above mentioned grounds as contended by the State. Hence, the appeal.

Order: The Supreme Court referred to *Madhu Limaye* v. *State of Maharashtra*, (1977) 4 SCC 551: AIR 1978 SC 47: 1978 Cr LJ 165, and *State of Haryana* v. *Bhajan Lal*, AIR 1992 SC 604 : 1992 Cr LJ 527 : (1992) Supp 1 SCC 335. It pointed out that the categories and grounds on which the power under section 482 could be exercised to quash criminal proceedings, as enumerated in *Bhajan Lal* were illustrative and not exhaustive. The same yardstick cannot be invoked in matrimonial disputes. It held (at p. 680):

> "If for the purpose of securing the ends of justice, quashing of FIR becomes necessary, section 320 would not be a bar to the power of quashing. It is, however, a different matter depending upon the facts and circumstances of each case whether or not to exercise such power."

Further, according to the court, in view of the fact that the parties had resolved their differences, there was no reasonable likelihood of the accused being convicted of the offences. Showing concern for the increasing number of criminal complaints arising out of matrimonial discord, the court suggested that matrimonial litigation should not be encouraged and their disputes should be amicably sorted out rather than fighting in the courts where it takes "years and years to conclude and in that process the parties lose their 'young' days in chasing their cases in different courts". (at p. 682)

The protective provisions like section 498A, I.P.C, were intended to safeguard the interests of a woman and protect them against torture by the husband and his relatives. However, a "hyper-technical view would be counter-productive and there is every likelihood that non-exercise of inherent power to quash the proceedings to meet the ends of justice could prevent woman from settling earlier". (at p. 682)

Comment: Quite often, a woman may resort to criminal complaints and cases out of impulse, or ignorance or advise of friends and relatives unaware of its implications. If at any point of time the parties decide to resolve their problems or settle them amicably, the technicalities of the law should not come in the way, though the court must ensure that it is a *bona fide* case and the complainant is not being coerced or pressuerised to agree to compounding the criminal proceedings. Prior to the present Apex Court judgment also, some High Courts in exercise of their powers under section 482 of the Cr. P.C., allowed the parties to withdraw their cases [*e.g., Daggupati Jayalakshmi* v. *State*, 1993 Cr LJ 3162 (AP): 1993 (3) Crimes 1117: II (1993) DMC 581; *Gursharan Kaur* v. *State of Rajasthan*, 1993 Cr LJ 2076 (Raj): 1993 Cr LR Raj 96: 1993 (1) Raj LW 103] but now with the Apex Court order, the issue has been settled.

Wife of void Marriage: Whether 'relative' under Section 498A, IPC

Ranjana Gopalrao Thorat v. *State of Maharashtra*, 2007 Cr LJ 3866 (Bom): 2007 (5) AIR BomR 271: 2007 All MR (Cri) 2298

Issue: Is a wife of a void marriage a 'relative' for purposes of being implicated in complaint under section 498A of the I.P.C?

Facts: This was a revision application by accused 'R' against rejection of her application for discharge in complaint filed by the brother of deceased under section 498 I.P.C. To state the facts in brief, one Padma was married to accused Baburao. They had two children. She was allegedly ill-treated by the husband and his parents so she filed a complaint against them in the police station. Due to intervention of relatives and for the sake of children she started living with them again. Meanwhile, the husband developed physical relations with the accused 'R' and started living with her and also had two children. After sometime they all, *i.e.*, Padma, 'R', Baburao and his parents, started living together. However, allegedly, she was ill-treated by them and committed suicide. Her brother lodged a report with Magistrate who committed the case to court of sessions. 'R's name was also included amongst the relatives who were allegedly guilty under section 498, I.P.C. Her application for discharge was dismissed, hence the present revision.

Order: It was argued that Padma, the deceased, was the legal wife and R was only a keep and even assuming that Baburao had married her, the marriage was void under the Hindu Marriage Act having been performed during the subsistence of the earlier marriage. Such marriage being *non est*, 'R' cannot assume character of wife. She was not a relative either, which, as defined in the Chambers Dictionary is "a person who is related by blood or marriage" 'R' not being a relative either by blood or marriage could not fall within the scope of section 498A I.P.C and hence discharged for the offence under that section.

Comment: A second marriage during the subsistence of an earlier marriage is void and has no existence in law. The parties to such marriage enjoy no status, rights or obligations *qua* each other nor in their families. They cannot be treated as "relative" either.

Allegations of Dowry Harassment where Marriage not Valid
Reema Aggarwal v. *Anupam,*
AIR 2004 SC 1418: 2004 Cr LJ 892: 2004 AIR SCW 344

Issue: Can a person who enters into a marital arrangement be allowed to take shelter behind a smokescreen to contend that since there was no valid marriage the question of dowry does not arise?

Facts: The parties were married in 1998. The wife was allegedly harassed by the husband and the in-laws for not bringing sufficient and more dowry. In order to kill her, some acidic substance was forcibly put in her mouth; she started vomiting and was taken to the hospital in unconscious state. (All these statements were made by her to the Investigating Officer.) An FIR was registered and on completion of investigation the charge-sheet was placed and charges were framed for offences punishable under sections 307 and 498A of the Indian Penal Code. The accused pleaded innocence. Their plea before the Trial Court was that the victim woman was not his legally married wife since he already had a wife when she married him. In view of this fact, it was contended, that the charge under section 498A was thoroughly misconceived as both sections 304B and 498A pre-suppose a valid marriage of the alleged victim woman with the offender-husband. Since the prosecution had failed to establish that the respondent husband's first marriage had been legally dissolved when he married the victim, the marriage was illegal and section 498A had no application. The accusations under section 307 were, according to the Trial Court, not established. The accused were, accordingly, acquitted. Appeal against this before the High Court was dismissed. Hence, the present appeal.

Order: There were arguments from both the sides which were supported by judgments by the respective counsels. After analysing the arguments and the case law, the court came to the following conclusion:

> "The concept of "dowry" is intermittently linked with a marriage and the provisions of the Dowry Act apply in relation to marriages. If the legality of the marriage itself is an issue, further legalistic problems do arise. If the validity of the marriage itself is under legal scrutiny, the demand of dowry in respect of an invalid marriage would be legally not recognisable. Even then, the purpose for which sections 498A and 304B, IPC and section 113B of the Indian Evidence Act, 1872, were introduced cannot be lost sight of. Legislations enacted with some policy to curb and alleviate some public evil rampant in society and effectuate a definite public purpose or benefit, positively requires to be interpreted with certain element of realism too and not merely pedantically or hyper-technically. The obvious objective was to prevent harassment to a woman who enters into a marital relationship with a person and later on becomes a victim of the greed for money. Can a person who enters into a marital arrangement

be allowed to take a shelter behind a smokescreen to contend that since there was no valid marriage the question of dowry does not arise? Such legalistic niceties would destroy the purpose of these provisions. Such hair-splitting legalistic approach would encourage harassment to a woman over demand of money. The nomenclature "dowry" does not have any magic charm written over it. It is just a label given to demand of money in relation to marital relationship. The legislative intent is clear from the fact that it is not only the husband but also his relations who are covered by section 498A. Legislature has taken care of children born from invalid marriages. Section 16 of the Hindu Marriage Act deals with legitimacy of children of void and voidable marriages. Can it be said that the Legislature which was conscious of the social stigma attached to children of void and voidable marriages closed eyes to plight of a woman who unknowingly or unconscious of the legal consequences, entered into the marital relationship. If such restricted meaning is given, it would not further the legislative intent. On the contrary, it would be against the concern shown by the Legislature for avoiding harassment to a woman over demand of money in relation to marriages. The first exception to section 494, IPC has some relevance. According to it, the offence of bigamy will not apply to "any person whose marriage with such husband or wife has been declared void by a court of competent jurisdiction." It would be appropriate to construe the expression "husband" to cover a person who enters into marital relationship and under the colour of such proclaimed or feigned status of husband subjects the woman concerned to cruelty or coerce her in any manner or for any of the purpose enumerated in the relevant provisions – Sections 304B or 498A, whatever be the legitimacy of the marriage itself for the limited purpose of sections 498A and 304B, I.P.C. Such an interpretation known and recognised as purposive construction has to come into play in a case of this nature. The absence of a definition of 'husband' to specifically include such persons who contract marriages ostensibly and cohabit with such woman, in the purported exercise of his role and status as 'husband', is no ground to exclude them from the purview of section 304B or 498A, I.P.C viewed in the context of the very object and aim of the legislations introducing those provisions."

The following observations are specially pertinent in the context:

"The concept of marriage to constitute the relationship of 'husband' and 'wife' may require strict interpretation where claims for civil rights, right to property etc., may follow or flow and liberal approach and different perception cannot be an anathema when the question of curbing a social evil is concerned."

Comment: It is indeed a landmark judgment. Husbands of a marriage which suffers from a legal flaw will not be allowed to take advantage of that flaw to wriggle out of liability for offences committed under sections 498A and 304B, simply on the plea that these offences pre-suppose a valid or legal marriage between the victim and the accused.

•••